Constructivist Theories
of Ethnic Politics

Although theories of the *formation* of ethnic groups are driven by the constructivist assumption that ethnic identities can change over time, theories of the *effect* of ethnicity on economic and political outcomes are driven by the primordialist assumption that these identities are fixed. This book is a first cut at building—and rebuilding—our theories of politics and economics on a fortified constructivist foundation. It proposes a new conceptual framework for thinking about ethnic identity. It uses this framework to synthesize constructivist arguments into a set of testable propositions about how and why ethnic identities change. It translates this framework—and the propositions derived from it—into a new, combinatorial language. And it employs these conceptual, constructivist, and combinatorial tools to theorize about the relationship between ethnicity, politics, and economics using a variety of methods.

The conceptual tools provided here open new avenues for theory building by representing the complexity of a world of fluid, multiple, and endogenous ethnic identities in an analytically tractable way. The theoretical arguments challenge the bad name that ethnic diversity appears to have acquired in social scientific literature. According to this literature, ethnic diversity and its analogs typically produce regimes that are less stable, less democratic, less well-governed, less peaceful, poorer, and marked by slower rates of economic growth than regimes in which the population is ethnically homogeneous. Ethnic diversity has a bad name in policy prescriptions too, which typically frame it as a "problem" to be solved, mitigated, or eliminated.

Taking the possibility of change in ethnic identity into account, this book shows the theoretical logics linking ethnic diversity to such negative outcomes. When ethnic diversity is associated with malign outcomes, it shows that the cause lies not in the intrinsic nature of ethnic identities, but in environmental factors that interact with them. Ethnic diversity, furthermore, can sometimes serve as a benign force, strengthening rather than threatening democracy, preventing rather than producing violence, and inhibiting rather than accelerating state collapse or secession. This book identifies some of the conditions that associate ethnic diversity with malign or benign outcomes. Even more importantly, it changes the questions we might ask about the relationship between ethnicity, politics, and economics.

Constructivist Theories
of Ethnic Politics

EDITED BY KANCHAN CHANDRA

OXFORD
UNIVERSITY PRESS

OXFORD
UNIVERSITY PRESS

Oxford University Press is a department of the University of Oxford.
It furthers the University's objective of excellence in research, scholarship,
and education by publishing worldwide.

Oxford   New York
Auckland   Cape Town   Dar es Salaam   Hong Kong   Karachi
Kuala Lumpur   Madrid   Melbourne   Mexico City   Nairobi
New Delhi   Shanghai   Taipei   Toronto

With offices in
Argentina   Austria   Brazil   Chile   Czech Republic   France   Greece
Guatemala   Hungary   Italy   Japan   Poland   Portugal   Singapore
South Korea   Switzerland   Thailand   Turkey   Ukraine   Vietnam

Oxford is a registered trademark of Oxford University Press
in the UK and certain other countries.

Published in the United States of America by
Oxford University Press
198 Madison Avenue, New York, NY 10016

© Oxford University Press 2012

Library of Congress Cataloging-in-Publication Data
Constructivist theories of ethnic politics / edited by Kanchan Chandra.
p. cm.
Includes bibliographical references and index.
ISBN 978-0-19-989315-7 (hardback : alk. paper) — ISBN 978-0-19-989317-1
(pbk. : alk. paper)   1. Ethnicity—Political aspects.   2. Ethnic relations—
Political aspects.   3. Ethnic groups—Political activity.   4. Identity politics.
5. Ethnicity—Philosophy. I. Chandra, Kanchan, 1971-
JC312.C69 2012
305.8—dc23
2012006989

ISBN 978-0-19-989315-7
ISBN 978-0-19-989317-1

Printed in the United States of America
on acid-free paper

CONTENTS

Acknowledgments   vii
List of Contributors   ix
List of Tables and Figures   xi

1. Introduction   1
   KANCHAN CHANDRA

PART ONE CONCEPTS

2. What Is Ethnic Identity? A Minimalist Definition   51
   KANCHAN CHANDRA

3. Attributes and Categories: A New Conceptual Vocabulary for
   Thinking about Ethnic Identity   97
   KANCHAN CHANDRA

4. How Ethnic Identities Change   132
   KANCHAN CHANDRA

5. A Combinatorial Language for Thinking about Ethnic
   Identity Change   179
   KANCHAN CHANDRA AND CILANNE BOULET

<h1>PART TWO MODELS</h1>

6. A Baseline Model of Change in an Activated
   Ethnic Demography   229
   KANCHAN CHANDRA AND CILANNE BOULET

7. Modeling the Evolution of Ethnic Demography   277
   A. MAURITS VAN DER VEEN AND DAVID D. LAITIN

8. How Fluid Is Fluid? The Mutability of Ethnic Identities
   and Electoral Volatility in Africa   312
   KAREN FERREE

9. Ethnicity and Pork: A Virtual Test of Causal Mechanisms   341
   DAVID D. LAITIN AND A. MAURITS VAN DER VEEN

10. A Constructivist Model of Ethnic Riots   359
    STEVEN I. WILKINSON

11. Identity, Rationality, and Emotion in the Processes
    of State Disintegration and Reconstruction   387
    ROGER PETERSEN

12. Deploying Constructivism for the Analysis of Rare Events:
    How Possible Is the Emergence of "Punjabistan"?   422
    IAN S. LUSTICK

Bibliography   453

Author Index   469

Name Index   479

Concept Index   489

ACKNOWLEDGMENTS

It is a pleasure to thank the many people who, while not responsible for the arguments we make here, have helped make the book better than it would otherwise be. Thanks are due first of all to Richard Stanley of the Department of Mathematics at MIT, for a short conversation that helped to set this book on its way. Several scholars provided written comments or discussed draft chapters at the conference on "Constructivist Approaches to Ethnic Identity" at the Center for International Studies at MIT, at panels at the American Political Science Association, the Association for the Study of Nationalities, the Laboratory of Comparative Ethnic Processes and the Joint Mathematics Meetings, and at seminars at Columbia University, Harvard University, the Massachusetts Institute of Technology, New York University, and the University of Washington. These include Dominique Arel, Robert Boyd, Tone Bringa, Rogers Brubaker, Bruce Bueno de Mesquita, Lars Erik Cederman, Michael Chwe, Alberto Diaz-Cayeros, Eric Dickson, David Epstein, Jonathan Farley, Robert Haydon, Michael Hechter, Jennifer Hochschild, Orit Kedar, Asim Khwaja, Janet Landa, Margaret Levi, Beatriz Magaloni, Saba Mahmood, Edward Miguel, Shaheen Mozaffar, James Scaritt, Suzanne Shanahan, Katherine Stovel, Steve Van Evera, Leonard Wantchekon, Jason Wittenberg and three anonymous reviewers. Many other scholars, too numerous to name here, have responded to sections of this manuscript, and we thank all of them. Dierdre Siddalls provided excellent support in the initial stages of planning. I am grateful to the Center for Advanced Studies in the Behavioural Sciences (CASBS) at Stanford University, the Harvard Academy of Area Studies, the MIT Center for International Studies, the Russell Sage Foundation, the Department of Political Science at MIT, and the Department of Politics at NYU for institutional and financial support. Finally, I would like to thank Oxford University Press for their painstaking work during the production process, and especially our editor, David McBride, for his sound advice and judgment.

Kanchan Chandra

CONTRIBUTORS

Cilanne Boulet holds a Ph.D in Mathematics from the Massachusetts Institute of Technology where she studied combinatorics.

Kanchan Chandra is Professor of Politics at New York University.

Karen Ferree is Associate Professor of Political Science at University of California, San Diego.

David Laitin is Professor of Political Science at Stanford University.

Ian S. Lustick is Professor of Political Science at the University of Pennsylvania.

Roger Petersen is Professor of Political Science at the Massachusetts Institute of Technology.

A. Maurits van der Veen is Assistant Professor of Government at William and Mary College.

Steven Wilkinson is Professor of Political Science at Yale University.

LIST OF TABLES AND FIGURES

Tables

1.1	Population Repertoire of Attributes (2*2 Case)	25
2.1	Properties Attributed to Ethnic Identity in Our Causal Claims	55
2.2	(Mismatch) Between Other Definitions and Classification	74
2.3	Different Ways of Thinking About "Group" Membership (with Hypothetical Examples)	82
4.1	Change in Membership and Ethnic Identity Change	166
4.2	Change in Content and Ethnic Identity Change	167
4.3	Change in Name and Ethnic Identity Change	168
4.4	Constructivist Variables and Mechanisms	176
5.1	Translating Constructivist Mechanisms into Combinatorics	181
5.2	Population Repertoire of Attributes (Two-Dimensional Case) (Two Values on Each Dimension)	186
5.3	Population Repertoire of Attributes (Two-Dimensional Case) (Three Values on One Dimension, Four Values on Second Dimension)	187
5.4	Population Repertoire of Attributes (Three-Dimensional Case) Two Values on Each Dimension	188
5.5	Full Repertoire of Nominal Categories for Population (2*2 Case)	192
5.6	"Operative" Repertoire of Nominal Categories for Population (2*2 Case)	194
5.7	Full Repertoire of Nominal Categories for Individual (2*2 Case)	195
5.8	Example of Population Repertoire of Attributes	198

5.9a	Initial Population Repertoire of Attributes 201
5.9b	Change in Population Repertoire of Attributes Through Replacement 201
5.10	Example of Initial Population Repertoire of Attributes 202
5.11	Example of Initial Population Repertoire of Attributes 203
5.12	Change in Initial Population Repertoire of Attributes Through Addition of Attribute-Value 204
5.13	Initial Population Repertoire of Attributes 205
5.14	Change in Initial Population Repertoire of Attributes Through Addition of an Attribute-Dimension 205
5.15a	Coinciding Structure 207
5.15b	Cross-Cutting Structure 207
5.15c	Nested Structure 208
5.16	"Operative" Population Repertoire of Categories Defined by Overlap Restriction 211
5.17	"Operative" Population Repertoire of Categories Defined by Restriction on the Number of Attribute-Dimensions 212
6.1	Population Repertoire of Attributes (2*2 case) 236
6.2	Changeland (k = .51): Possibility of Change Exists 242
6.3	Full Repertoire of Nominal Identity Categories in Changeland 243
6.4	Nochangeland (k = .51): Possibility of Change Does Not Exist 245
6.5	Full Repertoire of Nominal Identity Categories in Nochangeland 245
6.6	Limitedchangeland (k = .51): Some Fixity 247
6.7	Full Repertoire of Nominal Identity Categories in Limitedchangeland 247
6.8	Nochangeland (k = .51): Possibility of Change Does Not Exist 260
6.9	Limitedchangeland (k = .51): Some Fixity 260
6.10	Changeland (k = .51): Possibility of Change Exists 260
6.11a	Coinciding Structure 1 (k = .51) 261
6.11b	Coinciding Structure 2 (k = .51) 262
6.11c	Coinciding Structure 3 (k = .51) 262
6.12a	Multipolar Structure 1 (k = .51) 263
6.12b	Multipolar Structure 2 (k = .51) 263
6.13	Bipolar Structure 1 (k = .51) 264
7.A1	Example of Dimensional Weighting Calculation 302
7.A2	Example of Attribute Weighting Calculation for a Given Dimension 303

7.A3   General System Parameters   310
7.A4   Bias Definition Parameters   310
7.A5   Agent-Type Definition Parameters   311
7.A6   Dimension Stickiness Parameters   311
8.1   Population Repertoire of Attributes (2*2 Case)   313
8.2   Raw Data on Ethnic Structure   327
8.3   Summary of Ethnicity Models   332
8.4   Volatility Levels for Different Cases   334
8.5   Estimates of Legislative Volatility in Africa
            (standard errors in parentheses)   336
9.1   Stickiness of Winning Coalition by Size of
            Optimal Winning Coalition   346
9.2   Number of Victors by Stickiness of Coalition
            Specification   352
9.3   Correlation Between Number of Attributes
            Accepted and Leadership Tenure   355
9.4   Comparison of Average Tenure Overall and
            Average Tenure for Complex Coalitions   356
10.1   Distribution of Attribute-Repertoires Across the
            Population in a Typical Ulster Constituency,
            Mid-Nineteenth Century   376
10.2   Minimum Winning Coalitions When k = 0.5   376
11.1   Soviet Nationality vs. Ethnic Self-Awareness   393
11.2   National and Linguistic Breakdown in Moldova
            (percent)   394
11.3   National and Linguistic Breakdown on the
            Right Bank (percent)   395
11.4   National and Linguistic Breakdown on the Left
            Bank (PMR) (percent)   396
11.5   Three Hypothetical Scenarios with Two Minimum
            Winning Coalitions   405
11.6   Hypothetical Distribution of Language and Religion   414

Figures

1.1   Disaggregating "Ethnicity"   12
1.2   Disaggregating "Activated" Ethnic Categories   12
1.3a and 1.3b Hypothetical Distributions of Descent and
               Non-Descent Based Attributes by (a) Stickiness
               and (b) Visibility   15

1.4   Interaction Between Short-Term and
               Long-Term Change   18
1.5   Variants of Constructivism: A Range of Views over
               the Speed and Frequency of Ethnic
               Identity Change   20
3.1   Chosen and Assigned Identities   101
3.2   First-Level Attributes for the Category "Gaysian"   107
3.3   Second-Level Attributes for the Category "Gaysian"   108
3.4a and 3.4b Hypothetical Distributions of Descent-Based
               and Non-Descent-Based Attributes by
               (a) Stickiness and (b) Visibility   118
4.1   Variants of Constructivism: A Range of Views
               over the Speed and Frequency of Ethnic
               Identity Change   140
4.2   Interaction Between Short-Term and
               Long-Term Change   165
5.1   Activated Ethnic Demography #1 in Oneland   196
5.2   Activated Ethnic Demography #2 in Oneland   197
5.3   Nested Structure   208
5.4   Nested Structure   214
5A.1   Our Basic Example   216
5A.2   The Poset of Identity Categories under the Linear Order
               Restriction   221
5A.3   An Example of a Nested Structure of
               Attribute-Repertoires   223
5A.4   The Poset of Identity Categories Corresponding
               to the Nested Structure in Figure 5A.2   223
6.1   Rwanda's Ethnic Demography (1978 Census)   230
6.2   Rwanda's Ethnic Demography (1991 Census)   230
6.3   Brazil's Ethnic Demography (1940 Census)   231
6.4   Brazil's Ethnic Demography (1991 Census)   231
6.5   Sri Lanka's Ethnic Demography (1953 Census)   232
6.6   Sri Lanka's Ethnic Demography (1981 Census)   232
6.7   Possible Activated Ethnic Demographies in
               Changeland   244
6.8   Possible Activated Ethnic Demographies in
               Nochangeland   246
6.9   Possible Activated Ethnic Demographies in
               Limitedchangeland   248
6.10   Index of Permanent Exclusion in Minority-Dominant
               Populations: Percentage of Population with Fixed
               Identities in Minority-Dominant Distributions   258

6.11a   Nested Structure 1 (k = .51)   264
6.11b   Nested Structure 2 (k = .51)   265
6.11c   Nested Structure 3 (k = .51)   265
6A.1   Our Basic Example   274
7.1   Russians in Estonia: The Payoffs of Assimilation   280
7.2   Posner's Model of Dimensional Salience   282
7.3   Optimal Coalition Size and Leadership Tenure   294
7.4   Optimal Coalition Size and Demography   297
8.1   Average Legislative Seat Volatility in Africa   317
8.2   Nesting Structure of Benin   325
8.3   Nesting Structure of South Africa   329
8.4   Nesting Structure of Mauritania   331
9.1   OWC, Stickiness, and Ethnic Coalition Formation   347
9.2   Most Salient Identity Dimension at End of Run   350
9.3   Leadership Tenure by Stickiness   351
10.1   The Constituency and State-Level Incentives
             for Ethnic Riots   363
10.2   Catholic, Episcopalian, and Presbyterian Issue Positions
             Along the Dimensions of Redistribution and Religious
             Equality   377
11.1   Action Cycle with No Reference to Emotion   398
11.2   Action Cycle Illustrating Three Possible
             Effects of Emotion   398
11.3a   Anger Curve (Linear)   406
11.3b   Anger Curve (Inverse Exponential)   406
11.3c   Anger Curve (Exponential Decay)   407
11.3d   Anger Curve (Mixed Exponential)   407
11.4   (a) The Effect of Anger on Identity Shift as a Function
             of Time between Birth and Event and (b) MWC
             Differential and Predicted Identity Shift   410
11.5   The Trade-off Between Differences in Size of Minimum
             Winning Coalitions and Percentages of Inclusion
             of a Stigmatized Group   413
11.6   The Trade-off Between Differences in Size of
             Minimum Winning Coalitions and Percentages
             of Inclusion of a Stigmatized Group with Reference
             to Table 11.5   414
11.7   The Trade-off Between Differences in Size of Minimum
             Winning Coalitions and Percentages of Inclusion of a
             Stigmatized Group with Reference to Table 11.6   416

(See color plates for all figures in Chapter 12, located between pages 448 and 449)

12.1   The Patternof Identity Activation by Agents in VirPak

12.2   One Example of Virtual Pakistan, Baseline Condition

12.3   List of Identities Present in the Spectrum of
                Identities Available in VirPak

12.4   Cross-tabulation Showing Numbers of Agents in
                VirPak, Baseline Condition

12.5   A Portion of VirPak (t = 8) Focused on the
                Northern Punjab

12.6   Average Activation Prevalence of Leading Identities
                in VirPak

12.7   Plurality Rates Across 100 Baseline VirPak Futures
                of Selected Identities

12.8   Three Examples of Punjabi Secessionism

12.9   Patterns of Punjabi Prevalence, Plurality,
                and Secessionism

12.10   Prevalence of Selected Identities: Sorted by Punjabi
                Secessionism

12.11   Punjabistan Secession in Two VirPak Futures

12.12   Trajectories of Activation by Competing Identities and
                Bias Assignment Histories—Future 46 of VirPak

12.13   Trajectories of Activation by Competing Identities and
                Bias Assignment Histories—Future 24 of VirPak

12.14   Trajectories of Activation by Competing Identities and
                Bias Assignment Histories—Future 63 of VirPak

Constructivist Theories
of Ethnic Politics

1

Introduction

KANCHAN CHANDRA

"If you are born poor, you may die rich. But your ethnic group is fixed" (*Economist*, May 14–21, 2005, 80). So goes the "primordialist" way of thinking about ethnic identity. According to it, each of us belongs to one and only one ethnic group, that group membership remains fixed over a lifetime, and it is passed down intact across generations. Wars begin and end, states grow and die, economies boom and crash, but through it all, ethnic groups stay the same.

This way of thinking about ethnic identity drives theorizing in the social sciences on the relationship between ethnicity and political and economic outcomes and processes.[1] Like many influential ideas, its power lies in its invisibility. It is rarely stated explicitly and almost never defended. But it is pervasive in the commonsense assumptions that inform statements about other things. When political scientists and economists build and test theories of the relationship between ethnicity and democratic stability, party systems, voting behavior,

---

[1] In general, while constructivist assumptions dominate studies of ethnogenesis and ethnic identity change (indeed, even asking the question of how ethnic identities are created and change presumes a constructivist perspective), primordialist assumptions dominate theories that are concerned with the effect of ethnic identity on some political or economic outcome. For a survey of primordialist assumptions in theories of ethnicity, politics and economics in general, see Chandra 2001a, 2006a, and 2008a. For a survey of these assumptions in theories of democracy, see Chandra 2001b, Chandra 2005, and Chandra 2008b, and Chandra and Boulet, Chapter 6 in this volume. For a survey of these assumptions in empirical work, see Laitin and Posner 2001, Posner 2004a, Chandra and Wilkinson 2008, and Chandra 2009a, 2009b. For a discussion of these assumptions in theories and arguments about empirical works on specific subjects such as theories of violence, see individual chapters in this volume. For a representative sample of these works on democratic stability, see Rustow 1970, Dahl 1971, Rabushka and Shepsle 1972, Geertz 1973, Rothschild 1981, Horowitz 1985, Mill [1861]1991, Guinier 1994, Snyder 2000, Chua 2003, and Mann 2005; on party systems and voting behavior, see Ordeshook and Shvetsova 1994 and Cox 1997; on economic growth, see Easterly and Levine 1997; on violence, see Posen 1993, Van Evera

economic growth, civil war, riots, state formation, state collapse, welfare spending, public goods provision, and just about everything else, we assume, almost without exception, that the ethnic identities that describe individuals and populations are singular, timeless and fixed for all time.

Public policies and media analyses often make the same assumption. It informs most policy responses to the "problem" of ethnic diversity such as power-sharing executives, federalism, affirmative action, proportionality in the distribution of public goods, quotas in legislative, electoral, or party institutions, and cultural and educational rights. Indeed, the very characterization of ethnic diversity as a "problem" rests on this assumption (Chandra 2001a and 2001b, 2005, 2006b, 2008a and 2008b). And one only has to glance at newspaper accounts of ethnic conflicts in countries across the world—Shias, Sunnis and Kurds in Iraq, Serbs and Croats in the former Yugoslavia, Hutus and Tutsis in Rwanda, Tamils and Sinhalas in Sri Lanka, Malay and Chinese in Malaysia—to see that they are written as if the groups in question have always existed and will live on unchanged, no matter what happens to the countries themselves.

But ethnic identities are not singular, nor are they fixed. "Constructivism"—the principal theoretical revolution in the study of ethnic identities in anthropology, literature, history, political science, and sociology—has shown us that. They can change, sometimes on a very large scale. Consider some examples:

The Native American population in the United States grew by 50% in 1970, by more than 80% in 1980, and over 30% in 1990 (Hitt, August 21, 2005).

The number of Muslims in Bosnia increased by over 75% between 1961 and 1971. During the same period, the number of "Yugoslavs" in Bosnia decreased by 84% (Bringa 1995, 28).

Thirty-one percent of the population of Britain thought of themselves as English in 1992. Less than ten years later, the number had increased to 41%. The same shift in identity was taking place among Welsh and Scots who might have called themselves "British" earlier (*Economist*, April 2, 2005, 51).

In Puerto Rico, the majority of the population changed from "Negro" or "Mulatto" to "White" over fifty years (Dominguez 1997, 267).

In Brazil, the opposite happened—many of those who identified themselves as "White" or "Black" switched to calling themselves "brown." The result was

1994, Snyder 2000, Hegre et al. 2001, Elbadwi and Sambanis 2002, Reynal-Querol 2002, Fearon and Laitin 2003, Collier and Hoeffler 2004, Montalvo and Reynal-Querol 2005, Blimes 2006, Mishali-Ram 2006, Cederman, Girardin and Gleditsch 2009, Wimmer, Cederman and Min 2009, and Cederman, Wimmer and Min 2010 ; on secession and state collapse, see Geertz 1973; and on public goods provision and welfare spending see Easterly and Levine 1997 and Alesina, Baqir and Easterly 1999. Perhaps the best way to establish this rule is to search for the exceptions. Only a handful of recent exceptions theorize about the effect of ethnic diversity on some outcome while allowing for some aspect of change in ethnic identity. These include Appadurai 1996, Laitin 1999, Beissinger 2002, and Chandra 2005.

the transformation of Brazil from a White to a non-White majority nation in thirty years (Nobles 2000, 85).

In Sri Lanka, many of those who had hitherto called themselves "Kandyan" and "Low Country" abandoned these regional identities to unite in a cohesive "Sinhala" identity. The result was the transformation of Sri Lanka's multipolar ethnic demography into a bipolar one (Tambiah 1986, 101–102, Rajasingham-Senanayeke 1999b, 112–114).

In the Russian republic of Bashkoristan, the percentage of the population which identified itself as Bashkir fell by one-half in the first three decades of the twentieth century, while the Tatar population more than tripled in number. A period of relative stability followed, but forty years later, a similar pattern occurred once more, as the Bashkir population fell and the Tatar population increased again. In both cases, large numbers of those who once identified as Bashkir reclassified themselves as Tatar (Gorenburg 1999, 557–558).

These astonishing changes are a consequence of identity shifts among individuals, not of exceptional rates of fertility or migration. Individuals often redefine the ethnic identity categories that describe them. When large numbers do this, the result can be large-scale changes in the distribution of identities in the population as a whole. Ethnic categories activated earlier seem to disappear—a phenomenon, to paraphrase Myron Weiner, of "genocide by redefinition" (Weiner n.d., cited in Geertz 1973, 275). And newly activated ethnic categories sometimes appear to have been created out of nowhere—a phenomenon that Weiner might call "ethnogenesis" by redefinition.

What is more, constructivism tells us, these changes _can be a product of the very political and economic phenomena that they are used to explain_. The processes associated with a stable democracy—elections, parties, cycles of political competition—can create or change the ethnic divisions that are presumed to threaten stable democracy. The processes associated with economic growth—industrialization, urbanization, print capitalism, differential modernization, changes in employment opportunities—can create or change the ethnic divisions presumed to threaten economic growth. The processes associated with the modern state—administrative centralization, the collection of statistics, taxation, language standardization, the creation of centralized educational systems and military and security apparatuses—can create or change the ethnic divisions presumed to cause their collapse. Welfare spending and public goods provision can create or change the ethnic identities presumed to affect patterns of welfare spending and public goods provision. And violence in its many forms can create or change the ethnic differences presumed to cause violence.[2]

---

[2] The arguments about the "reverse causal effects" on ethnic identity of these outcomes and processes are reviewed in some detail in Chapter 5 and then in individual chapters concerned with each of these subjects. For a sample of constructivist arguments that show that elections and competitive politics more broadly can transform ethnic identities, see Weiner 1967, Brass 1970,

Constructivism has undermined the foundation of our previous knowledge about the relationship between ethnicity, politics, and economics. Since our theories about this relationship are based on the unreasonable premises that ethnic identities are fixed and exogenous to politics and economics, their conclusions cannot be reasonable. They are either wrong for the right reasons or right for the wrong reasons. Constructivism also poses a fundamental challenge for new theorizing about the relationship between ethnicity, politics, and economics: how to incorporate the possibility of fluidity and endogeneity of ethnic identity. This possibility may not always be realized. Ethnic identities may in some cases indeed be fixed and exogenous to the phenomenon in question. But the process by which these properties come to be associated with ethnic identity must be incorporated into a theory explaining that phenomenon. Otherwise our theories omit an important explanatory variable, and their conclusions are driven more by that omission than by the intrinsic properties of ethnic identity.

Constructivist arguments are themselves so amorphous, however, that incorporating them into our theories of politics and economics is a difficult task. The term "constructivism" is a post-facto label imposed, not on a unified theory but on a disparate collection of critical insights that shoot down primordialist assumptions. Constructivists agree on the basic idea that individuals have multiple ethnic identities that can change endogenously to political and economic processes. But there are important and implicit disagreements on other key questions: How fast do ethnic identities change? What are the variables that drive these changes? What are the motivations of individuals who change identities? What is the scale of ethnic identity change? Do all individuals have equally fluid identities, or are some more likely to switch identities than others? Constructivism cannot serve as the basis for new theories unless these disagreements are made explicit and synthesized into a coherent set of propositions.

This book is a first cut at building—and rebuilding—our theories of politics and economics on a fortified constructivist foundation. It proposes a new conceptual framework for thinking about ethnic identity. It uses this framework to

Young 1976, 1982, Wood 1984, Giliomee 1989, Thapar 1989, Rajasingham-Senanayeke 1999b, Jung 2000, Chandra 2004, 2005, and Posner 2005). For arguments that link the trappings of economic growth with ethnic identity change, see Deutsch 1953, Andersen 1983, Gellner 1983. There is a vast literature linking various aspects of state formation and consolidation with ethnic identity change. For a sample, see Brass 1974, 1997, Weber 1976, Young 1976, Foucault 1977, Said 1978, Jones 1981, Fox 1985, Laitin 1986, Cohn 1987, Gramsci 1992, Laitin 1992, Pandey 1992, Lustick 1993, Appadurai 1996, Dominguez 1997, Laitin 1998, Scott 1998, Gorenburg 1999, Nobles 2000, Luong 2004, Herrera 2005, Posner 2005. On public goods provision and welfare spending, see, in addition to the works on state formation and consolidation, Bates 1974, Nagel 1982, Fearon 1999, Caselli and Coleman 2001, Chandra 2004. On violence, see Pandey 1992, Tambiah 1992, Brass 1997, Brubaker and Laitin 1998, Jeganathan 1998, Laitin 1999, Beissinger 2002, and Appadurai 2006.

synthesize constructivist arguments into a set of testable and logically connected propositions. It translates this framework—and the propositions derived from it—into a new, combinatorial language. And it employs these conceptual, constructivist, and combinatorial tools to theorize about the relationship between ethnicity, politics, and economics using a variety of methods. Our primary focus is on theorizing about the relationship between ethnicity, politics, and economics from a constructivist foundation. A separate volume, *Measuring Ethnicity*, shows how the concepts and theories advanced in this book can be translated into data collection and the design of measures for empirical studies (for some of its themes, see Chandra and Wilkinson 2008 and Chandra 2009a, 2009b).

The impetus for this project comes from a symposium in APSA-CP on "Cumulative Findings in the Study of Ethnic Politics," in which several of the contributors to this volume participated (Chandra 2001b). That symposium noted that a major impediment to the incorporation of constructivist findings into new research agendas was the absence of a single work that synthesized the constructivist insights of the last thirty years. This book is an attempt to fill that gap. Our intent in doing so is to propose one of the first rather than last words on constructivism (alternative efforts at reformulating constructivism from different premises include Cederman 2001, Hale 2008, and Wimmer 2008). For too many years, the central debate in the study of ethnic identities has been between constructivism and primordialism. This is by now a stale debate that no longer generates theoretically productive insights (Brubaker 2004). This book is an attempt to shift the debate to the more interesting and theoretically fertile disagreements, often implicit, between variants of constructivism and the stakes of these disagreements for our theories. Providing one synthesis of constructivist arguments and inviting readers to disagree with, modify, replace, or transcend this formulation should create the foundation for better formulations to emerge.

The non-incorporation of constructivist arguments in research on ethnicity, politics, and economics, in turn, is a symptom of a much deeper problem to which constructivism is itself not immune: the absence of a conceptual foundation for thinking about ethnic identity (Chandra 2008b). Most comparative political scientists and economists do not define the term "ethnicity" before theorizing about it. Those of us who do often ignore these definitions in our theoretical formulations. As a result, our theorizing has an ad hoc quality to it, with scholars attributing to ethnic identity any property that their conclusions require. Our empirical work has the same feature: We somehow collect data on ethnic identities across the world, specify statistical models, and interpret the associations that result, all without first defining what it is we are looking at (Chandra and Wilkinson 2008). Although the association of the properties of "fixedness" and "exogeneity" with ethnicity has come in for the greatest criticism so far, they are only two of the many properties arbitrarily associated with ethnic identity.

Incorporating constructivism into the study of ethnic politics, then, requires the incorporation of a conceptual foundation into the study of ethnic politics. Accordingly, this book starts at the beginning, with the development of concepts for thinking about ethnic identity, and builds upward from these concepts. It grounds these concepts in an analytical and synthetic review of previous usage, paying as much attention to eliminating those concepts that do not conform to this previous usage as to introducing new ones. Capturing the link with previous usage may be even more important, paradoxically, if we want to discard that usage. Otherwise we will not know what we have discarded or what to replace it with, and are likely to go around in circles, repeating the same mistakes in new waves of research.

The new conceptual vocabulary proposed in this book allows us to represent the complexity of a world of fluid, multiple, and endogenous ethnic identities in an analytically tractable way. This vocabulary can be used to ask and answer questions about ethnic identity from a variety of theoretical and methodological perspectives. Its advantage is that it allows us to express long recognized constructivist processes in a logically connected set of propositions and to move between the individual, the population, and the identity category as units of analysis while recognizing the interactions between them. But it does not presuppose any particular set of assumptions about human nature, or any particular set of models or methodologies. Indeed, the combinatorial expression of constructivism in this book may well give rise to other approaches to constructivism, including some explored in this volume that eventually supersede it.

The approach to theorizing in this volume is to generalize about the "mechanisms" rather than the variables and outcomes associated with ethnic identity change and then incorporate these mechanisms in theories of politics and economics (Elster 1989, Petersen 2001, Tilly 2001). The mechanisms by which ethnic identities change are general and interconnected. But the variables that trigger these mechanisms, the order of these mechanisms in a sequence, and the outcomes they are associated with, may vary (Chandra 2006a). Indeed, each chapter in this volume shows that, and how, the same general processes of ethnic identity change can be associated with particular results in particular contexts.

The theoretical arguments we make challenge the bad name that ethnic diversity appears to have acquired in social scientific literature on its effects (Geertz 1973). According to previous theories of "ethnicity," politics, and economics, ethnic diversity and its analogs typically produce regimes that are less stable, less democratic, less well-governed, less peaceful, poorer, and marked by slower rates of economic growth than regimes in which the population is ethnically homogeneous.[3]

---

[3] For arguments linking ethnic diversity to a negative effect on democracy individually or conditional upon other variables, see Rustow 1970, Dahl 1971, Geertz 1973, Rabushka and Shepsle 1972, Rothschild 1981, Horowitz 1985, Mill [1861]1991, Guinier 1994, Snyder 2000, Chua 2003,

Ethnic diversity has a bad name in policy prescriptions too, which typically frame it as a "problem" to be solved either by inducing homogeneity through partition (Kaufman 1996, 1998, Johnson 2008), or eliminating the basis for ethnic mobilization or restricting ethnic majoritarianism where mobilization cannot be eliminated (Chandra 2008a). But taking into account the possibility of change in ethnic identity, this book shows, dismantles the theoretical logics linking ethnic diversity to such negative outcomes. When ethnic diversity is associated with malign outcomes, the cause lies not in the intrinsic nature of ethnic identities but in environmental factors that interact with them. Ethnic diversity, furthermore, can sometimes serve as a benign force, producing fluid election results that stabilize democracies rather than the fixed results that destroy them, preventing rather than producing violence, and inhibiting rather than accelerating state collapse or secession. "Ethnicity" may well have a bad name, but at least according to the arguments made in this book it does not appear to deserve it. The policy prescriptions that flow from these arguments, as we will see, are also different.

Just as important, the arguments in this book change the questions that we can ask about the relationship between ethnicity, politics, and economics. As long as we believe that ethnic identities are fixed and exogenous to political and economic processes, we can only ask questions about the *effects* of concepts related to ethnic identity—we can hardly theorize about the *causes* of what is presumed to be primordial. But because the models here are based on a constructivist premise, they also raise new questions about the political and economic causes of which ethnic "diversity" is an effect, and about dynamic and mutually constitutive relationships between ethnicity, politics, and economics.

and Mann 2005. For arguments that address institutional designs that can "mitigate" a threat that they all acknowledge, see Lijphart 1977, Horowitz 1985, 1991, Cohen 1997, Gagnon and Tully 2001, Saideman 2002, and Fraenkel and Grofman 2004. Some recent exceptions to this general rule are Gagnon et al. 2003, Chandra 2005, and Birnir 2007, which take a more optimistic view. For theories predicting a negative relationship between ethnic diversity and some form of violence, individually or in conjunction with other variables, see Posen 1993, Fearon 1998, Van Evera 1994, and Snyder 2000. While these theories predict a negative link, the empirical evidence here is mixed. Works that find a positive link between ethnic diversity to war, crises or other forms of violence include Blimes 2006, Mishali-Ram 2006, Hegre et al. 2001, Elbadawi and Sambanis 2002, Reynal-Querol 2002, Montalvo and Reynal-Querol 2005, Cederman et al. 2009, Wimmer et al. 2009, and Cederman et al. 2010. Empirical work that does not find such a link includes Fearon and Laitin 2003 and Collier and Hoeffler 2004. For arguments predicting that ethnic diversity destabilizes states, see Geertz 1973, Smith 1976, and Przeworski 2000. There is now an extensive literature predicting a negative relationship between ethnic diversity and economic growth. For the seminal article in this field, see Easterly and Levine 1997. Alesina and La Ferrara (2005) describe the consensus around this finding, along with exceptions to it. On a negative relationship between ethnic diversity and public goods provision, see Alesina, Baqir and Easterly 1999 and Lieberman 2007. Miguel (2004) accepts this negative relationship and examines the success of nation-building policies in overcoming it.

In some cases, the same questions have been raised from other premises, but the concepts introduced in this book allow us to answer them within an integrated framework, identifying interdependence between processes which we would otherwise miss. In others, the concepts employed in this book generate entirely new questions that we could not have raised before.

Among the new questions that this book raises are questions about primordialism. Constructivist approaches do not, as is often assumed, dismiss primordialist interpretations of ethnic identities—they problematize them. If ethnic identities are in fact constructed, then under what conditions do primordial interpretations of these identities arise and take root (Suny 1999b, 2001)? Why are primordialist beliefs more closely associated with some ethnic categories rather than others? For example, the category Yoruba in Nigeria is more often associated with primordialist myths than the category Hausa-Fulani, where the very name indicates the constructed origins of the category in an amalgamation between Hausas and Fulanis. What are the consequences of such primordial associations? When individuals act "as if" ethnic identity categories are primordial, does this produce different patterns of behavior from when they acknowledge that these categories are constructed? Paradoxically, then, starting from a constructivist foundation allows us to take the roots of primordialism seriously.

1. Plan of the Book

Part 1 of this volume lays out the conceptual framework for thinking about ethnic identity and distilling from it a set of constructivist propositions. Part 2 incorporates these concepts and propositions into theories of ethnicity, politics and economics. This introduction provides a complete sketch of the key concepts and arguments introduced in this book as well as the stakes attached to each.

Readers who specialize in, or would like to specialize in, the field of ethnic politics may wish to begin with Part 1 and read in progression. Readers interested less in ethnic identity for its own sake and more in one or more of the political and economic outcomes and processes associated with it may wish to go directly from the introduction to the relevant chapter in Part 2, and refer to Part 1 as necessary.

The concepts and theories we introduce here apply to one of four units of analysis—a *category*, an *attribute*, an *individual*, and a *population*. The claims we make can differ based on which unit of analysis we are discussing. Readers may find it helpful, therefore, to distinguish between these four units of analysis throughout the book.

2. What Is an Ethnic Identity?

Most social scientists would agree that identities such as "Serb" and "Croat" in the former Yugoslavia, "Aymara" and "Quechua" in Bolivia, "Baluchi, Pathan, Sindhi, Punjabi, and Mohajir" in Pakistan, "Black and White" in the United States, "Yoruba, Hausa-Fulani, and Ibo" in Nigeria and "Zulu, Xhosa and Coloured" in South Africa are all examples of "ethnic" identities. But we diverge on *why* we classify these identities as ethnic—that is, on the definition that justifies placing identities belonging to these types, and only some identities belonging to these types—in a separate analytical family.

This book defines ethnic identities as a *subset of categories in which descent-based attributes are necessary for membership*. All ethnic categories require descent-based attributes, by this definition, although all descent-based categories are not ethnic categories. The precise restrictions that wall off this subset from the larger set of descent-based identities are laid out in Chapter 2. But here it is sufficient to note that this subset includes, subject to those restrictions, identity categories based on the race, region, religion, sect, language family, language, dialect, caste, clan, tribe or nationality of one's parents or ancestors, or one's own physical features.

Nominal ethnic identities are those ethnic identity categories in which an individual's descent-based attributes make her eligible for membership. *Activated* ethnic identities are those ethnic categories in which she actually professes membership or to which she is assigned membership by others. All individuals have a repertoire of nominal ethnic identities from which one or more may be activated.

The key feature of this definition is the distinction it draws between "attribute" and "category." In previous work, the term "ethnic identity" has been used vaguely to mean many different things—a "category" of membership (e.g., African American), an "attribute" that usually signifies membership in a category but does not constitute it (e.g., dark skin), a category-dimension that indicates the class, if any, to which a category belongs (e.g., race), and an attribute-dimension that indicates the class to which an attribute belongs (e.g., skin color). In this book, we use the term ethnic "identity" to refer only to ethnic "categories," distinguishing categories throughout from the attributes on which they are based. This distinction is fundamental to the arguments we make. Throughout, furthermore, we use the words ethnic "group" and ethnic "category" interchangeably to mean simply a cluster of individuals who share a descriptive label, and not necessarily a cluster of individuals who share common interests or think of themselves as a collective (for a critique of the way the terms "group" and "category" have been used in previous literature on the subject, see Brubaker 2004).

Consider the example of Helen, a fictionalized character constructed from Mary Waters's study of West Indian immigrants in New York (Waters 1999),

10 INTRODUCTION

whom we rely on in a running example throughout this book. Helen, as we construct her, is a woman living in New York with attributes such as dark skin, birth in Trinidad, and descent from parents of African (Ghanian) origin. Her repertoire of nominal ethnic identities includes at least the categories West Indian, in which membership requires the descent-based attribute of descent from parents born in the West Indies, Black, in which membership requires the descent-based attribute of descent from parents of African origin, as well as the skin color and physical features believed to signal such origin, and Trinidadian, in which membership requires the descent-based attribute of origin from parents born in Trinidad. Helen sometimes activates, by choice or assignation, the category "West Indian" from this repertoire. At other times, she might call herself or be called "Black." In either case, she need not develop a sense of common interests with others eligible for membership in the categories "West Indian" or "Black."

The notion that descent matters in defining ethnic identity is hardly surprising. Virtually all social science definitions of an ethnic identity emphasize the role of descent in some way. But they specify it differently, to mean a common ancestry, or a myth of common ancestry, or a common region of origin, or a myth of a common region of origin, or a "group" descent rule—and they typically combine descent with other features such as a common culture, a common language, a common history and a common territory. The innovation in this definition is in a subtle but consequential change in the specification of the role of descent, contained in the distinction between "attribute" and "category." It is also a minimalist definition in its stipulation that ethnic identities are defined *only* by the descent-based attributes required for membership. Features such as a common culture, common territory, common history, or a common language are variables that sometimes distinguish ethnic identities rather than the constants that define them.

The main justification for this definition is that it captures the conventional classification of ethnic identities within comparative political science and economics to a greater degree than the alternatives. That is, it captures the underlying commonalities that justify treating otherwise diverse identities such "Serb" and "Croat" in the former Yugoslavia, "Aymara," and "Quechua" in Bolivia; "Baluchi, Pathan, Sindhi, Punjabi, and Mohajir" in Pakistan; "Black and White" in the United States, "Yoruba, Hausa-Fulani, and Ibo" in Nigeria, and "Zulu, Xhosa, and Coloured" in South Africa in a common conceptual category. None of our previous definitions captures these classifications to the same degree. They do not, in other words, describe the identities that we actually count as ethnic in our own work.

Small changes in the specification of the role of descent or other features can produce large differences in whether and how we theorize about ethnic identity change. If we define ethnic identity as an identity based on a common ancestry, for instance, we would expect it to remain fixed over generations, since the fact of a common ancestor will remain fixed over generations. If we define ethnic identity as an identity based on a *myth* of common ancestry or region of origin, we would expect it to change only as these myths change—and theorize about ethnic identity change by theorizing about the processes by which myths are constructed and maintained. If we define ethnic identity as an identity defined by the possession of a common language, we would expect it to change either as people learn new languages or as the structures of languages themselves change—and approach the study of ethnic identity in part through the study of linguistics. If we define ethnic identity as an identity based on a common culture, we would expect it to change only as such shared cultures change, and theorize about ethnic identity change by theorizing about how cultures change.

The definition of an ethnic identity as a category in which descent-based attributes, and *only* descent-based attributes, are necessary for membership is the foundation on which we build arguments about whether and how ethnic identities change. It is this definition, as we shall see, that allows us to think of ethnic identity change in the short term simply as a process of reclassification of elements from a fixed set, translated here as recombination. It is also this definition that drives the methods though which we theorize about such change—in particular, the use of combinatorics.

3. "Ethnicity" Is Not One but Many Concepts

Our theories of the relationship between ethnicity, politics, and economics have typically employed a handful of concepts, each big and blunt, to think about "ethnicity." According to the definition of ethnic identity proposed here, however, "ethnicity" is not one big concept or three, but many tens of narrow ones, each logically connected to the others. These concepts can be grouped into two logically connected families, represented in Figure 1.1, one describing ethnic "structure" and the other describing ethnic "practice." Each family can be disaggregated further in many ways

Ethnic "structure" refers to any concept that describes *nominal* descent-based attributes that characterize individuals or populations or the nominal categories generated from these attributes. These include, in no particular order, an individual's repertoire of attributes, the repertoire of nominal ethnic identity categories generated from these attributes, the distribution of attribute and category repertoires in a population, the characteristics of attribute-dimensions (e.g., their degree of stickiness or visibility), the relationship between attribute-dimensions (e.g., cross-cutting, nested, or ranked), and so on.

Ethnic "practice" refers to any concept related to the attributes and ethnic identity categories *activated* by individuals and populations in different contexts. The set of "activated" categories and attributes for any given country is derived

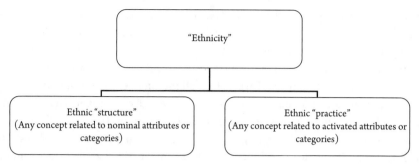

Figure 1.1 Disaggregating "Ethnicity"

from the attributes contained in the ethnic "structure." Since different ethnic identity categories can be activated in different contexts, ethnic practice can refer to as many categories as there are contexts. Figure 1.2 illustrates.

Consider first the distinction between ethnic identities activated in private and public life. There appear to be many examples in the case of ethnic identities in which public and private identities do not coincide. Roosens (1994, 88) notes how migrants to Belgium from Catalunya assume "Spanish" as their public identity when interacting with Belgians or the state, while retaining "Catalan" as their identity when interacting among themselves and with migrants from other regions of Spain. Gorenburg similarly identifies a lack of such congruence in the case of Tatars and Bashkirs in Bashkortostan (Gorenburg 1999, 556). In Sri Lanka, caste identity is more likely to inform private actions such as the choice of marriage partner, but religious or linguistic identities are more likely to be politically activated (Tambiah 1986, Rajasingham-Senanayeke 1999a and 1999b).

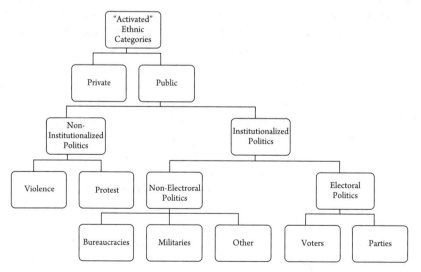

Figure 1.2 Disaggregating "Activated" Ethnic Identity Categories

Among the set of identities that are publicly activated, we can distinguish again between identities that are activated in institutionalized politics, parliament, party politics, the legal system, and so on, and identities that are activated in non-institutionalized contexts, such as civil wars, riots, and social movements.

In many countries, the set of identities activated in both contexts may be identical. But in others, especially in states that outlaw certain types of political participation, they can diverge. In Indonesia, for instance, institutionalized participation by political parties activates religious identities (Muslim and Christian), while regional identities are more likely to be found in the arena of non-institutionalized politics. And in the Belgian Congo, until shortly before independence in 1960, the Belgians had banned colony-wide political parties— but not tribal and regional associations—which led to the structuring of identities in formal politics along quite different lines from those in associational life (Willame 1972, 26).

Among identities that are activated in institutionalized politics, we can distinguish further between identities activated in electoral contexts, party politics, and voting behavior, and in non-electoral contexts, in the corridors of parliament, the military, the judiciary, and the bureaucracy. In Uganda, for instance, the identity of "Nubian" was an identity activated principally in the military and the corridors of the bureaucracy of Idi Amin's regime, while the identities Baganda or Catholic have frequently been activated in the course of electoral politics (Kasfir 1976, 1979).

Among the identities activated in electoral politics, we can distinguish between identities that drive voter behavior and those that drive party strategy. In South Africa, for instance, the African National Congress activates voters based on multi-ethnic appeals targeted to all South Africans, and, in some contexts, on appeals based on the racial category "Black." But voters often vote for it, not as "South Africans" or "Blacks" but on the basis of their particular tribal identities (Xhosa, or Zulu, and so on).

These distinctions represent just one way of representing how different ethnic identity categories can be activated in different contexts. There are many other ways of illustrating and organizing these contexts—and a vast amount of disaggregation is possible. But to the extent that "ethnicity" is not one blunt concept but many narrowly defined ones, causal claims about "ethnicity," should trace not a handful of blunt causal paths from "ethnicity" to the outcome of interest but many precise ones, each corresponding to one of many narrow concepts. These narrow concepts do not exist in isolation, but separating them analytically makes it possible to identify precise relationships between them. Because these concepts are logically interconnected, furthermore, our theories should also be able to model interdependent causal effects.

4. The "Stickiness" and "Visibility" of Descent-Based *Attributes*

The term "descent-based attributes" refers to the sum total of the attributes of our parents and ancestors (which we acquire as an inheritance through descent), our own genetic features (which we acquire through descent, even though they include features which may not have characterized our parents), and all those attributes which we can credibly portray as having been acquired through descent.

Whether acquired honestly or through deception, these attributes acquire meaning only within an externally imposed framework of interpretation. Take, for example, the descent-based attribute of skin color. Helen has a particular shade of skin color, a shade that she was born with. But how do observers interpret that skin color? Is it dark or light? Is it black or brown or white? The answer requires a socially agreed on rule of interpretation, which can vary across different societies. The same shade of skin might be called dark in the present-day United States and light in present-day Brazil.

Descent-based attributes have the intrinsic properties of being "sticky" and "visible," on average, in the short term. "Stickiness" is the property of being difficult to change credibly in the short term, either because objective changes are hard to effect or because it is hard to pass off an objective change as representing descent. "Visibility" refers to the availability of raw data even in superficial observation, regardless of how those data are interpreted and whether the interpretations are "correct." Although most attributes, descent-based and non-descent-based, are not very visible, those that are, are disproportionately likely to be descent-based.

The property of stickiness characterizes descent-based attributes by virtue of their association with the body. Changing aspects of our genetic and physical make-up is intrinsically difficult, although it is becoming easier with advances in medical technology. But even if it were easy, successful deception is hard. In order for one new attribute to be credibly presented as descent-based, it must be consistent with other attributes displayed on the body (what we call the "consistency" requirement) and any evidence that the individual possessed a different attribute in the past must be erased (what we call the "erasure" requirement). In this sense, the property of visibility affects the property of stickiness because it makes consistency and erasure that much more difficult.

To illustrate, consider the attribute of skin color. A change in skin color is difficult—but even if it were easy, portraying a newly acquired skin color as descent-based is not. If Helen changed her skin color from dark to light, for instance, she would also have to change her eye color, hair type, and some of her physical features in order to portray herself as having been born light-skinned. She would also have to erase all evidence of having possessed her previous attributes—for how could she pass off white skin as being a descent-based attribute if it were known that she had once had brown skin? This would entail creating a new social world in which no one was familiar with her old self, and inventing a new history.

By contrast, there are fewer intrinsic barriers, on average, to changing non-descent-based attributes. Consider the attribute of educational qualification. Helen can change this attribute simply by returning to school. There is certainly some difficulty associated with doing so: It requires investments of time and money and both may be hard to come by. But these costs are imposed by the environment, not by the intrinsic properties of the attributes themselves. The properties of descent-based attributes impose the burdens of erasure and consistency: Helen can get a master's degree without having to hide the fact that she had a high school diploma previously, or she can change other aspects of her person or behavior to match her new degree.

Imagine, then, a scale that orders all attributes in the world, in all countries, over time, according to the degree of difficulty associated with changing them (Figure 1.3a) or their degree of visibility (Figure 1.3b). Descent-based attributes (e.g., skin

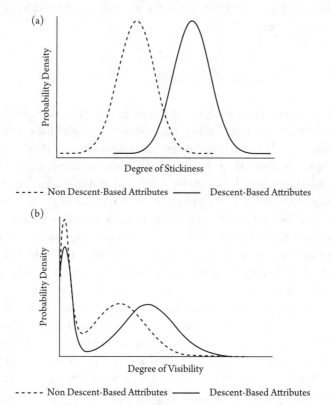

Figure 1.3a and b Hypothetical Distributions of Descent and Non-Descent Based Attributes by (a) Stickiness and (b) Visibility

color) are distributed in the upper half of this scale while non-descent-based attributes (e.g., income) are distributed in the lower half, with an area of overlap in between. The precise shape of these distributions may well be different over time and across space, but the difference in central tendency is likely to persist.

The property of stickiness distinguishes descent-based attributes only in the short term. These attributes can change over the long term, either through a change in the frameworks that govern the interpretation of these attributes or through an objective change in the attributes themselves. Suppose, holding the skin color of the population constant, that the rule of interpretation for skin color at some initial point in time produces a hundred different shades of skin color. At a different point in time, holding the actual skin color of the population constant, a new rule of interpretation is introduced which groups together the first fifty shades as "black" and the last fifty shades as "white." In this instance, the introduction of a new rule of interpretation can produce an entirely new distribution of attributes without any objective change in the skin color of those described. Alternatively, objective processes such as migration or intermarriage, can also change the distribution of shades of skin color in a population. In the long term, then, there may not be any systematic difference in the stickiness of descent-based and non-descent-based attributes.

5. Constrained Change in Ethnic *Categories*

It is a common mistake to assume that the properties of ethnic identity *categories* are the same as the properties of the descent-based *attributes* that constitute them. But they are not. The fact that descent-based attributes are difficult to change, on average, in the short term does not mean that the categories constituted by them are also difficult to change in the short term. It simply means that the set of descent-based attributes acts as an intrinsic constraint on change in ethnic identity categories. Our descent-based attributes generate a repertoire of nominal ethnic identities from which we activate one at any given time. Because the attributes it is generated from are fixed in the short term, this repertoire is also fixed in the short term. But within the constraints of this repertoire, there can be rapid and frequent change in the ethnic identities we activate, even in the short term.

To illustrate, let's return to the example of Helen. She can choose different ethnic identities from within her repertoire to activate, changing from Black to West Indian to Trinidadian, all in the same day, emphasizing her Black identity at work, her West Indian identity in a social setting, and her Trinidadian identity at home. Similarly, observers can assign her to different ethnic identities, from Black to West Indian to Trinidadian, all in the same day.

Note that Helen can activate different ethnic identity categories from within the nominal identity repertoire generated by these attributes, but she cannot in the short term activate ethnic identity categories outside it. Given her descent-based attributes, for instance, she can change her activated categories from "Black," to "Trinidadian," "West Indian," and "Afro-Caribbean," among others. But she cannot activate the ethnic categories German or WASP (White-Anglo-Saxon-Protestant) or Chinese or Malay, because the descent-based attributes for membership in these categories lie outside her nominal repertoire.

The same logic also applies to the ethnic identity categories to which she is assigned. In order to be credibly assigned to some ethnic identity category, she must be seen to possess the descent-based attributes for it—or, at the very least, her visible descent-based attributes must be consistent with the attributes required for the membership in question. Thus, while she may be assigned to categories such as Black, West-Indian and Trinidadian—for which she possesses at least some visible descent-based attributes—she cannot be assigned to categories such as White or German, which, at least in the United States, require the possession of descent-based attributes which not only lie outside Helen's repertoire but are inconsistent with those that lie within.

Descent is but a baseline constraint on ethnic identity change. Other constraints in addition to this baseline may be imposed by the environments in which we live: history, institutional background, economic factors, ideological factors, social norms, and territorial factors may, taken individually or together, eliminate certain categories from the set of feasible choices while privileging others. In Helen's case, for example, social norms in many contexts may well force her to identify as "Black," eliminating other options in her nominal repertoire as viable choices. However, the constraint imposed by descent is intrinsic to ethnic identities and will always exist regardless of the presence of additional environmental constraints.

The existence of this baseline constraint on change in activated ethnic identities is the fundamental distinction between ethnic and non-ethnic identities, on average. The activation of non-ethnic identity categories may well be constrained by environmental factors. But there is nothing intrinsic in the attributes that constitute non-ethnic identities, on average, that imposes such a constraint.

In the long term, however, descent-based attributes can change, and with them, so can the nominal repertoire of ethnic identities available to individuals. Suppose that Helen, for instance, whose parents are English-speaking, marries a Haitian man and learns to speak French in her lifetime. Her own stock of descent-based attributes— and therefore her own ethnic identity repertoire—would remain fixed regardless. But the stock of attributes inherited by her children would change by adding the attribute of "descent from a French-speaker." Thus, the ethnic identity options of these children and their descendants would change. Over the long term, then, we should expect both ethnic and non-ethnic identities to change in open-ended ways.

Sometimes, short-term and long-term changes can be linked. For instance, suppose Helen chooses to activate the category "Black" in the United States, and affiliate herself to a new church associated with African-American history. Her

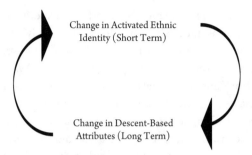

Figure 1.4 Interaction Between Short-Term and Long-Term Change

children then will inherit this church affiliation as part of their stock of descent-based attributes—and this new attribute may reinforce their own decision to activate the identity category "Black" for themselves and acquire still more reinforcing attributes. Thus there will also be a connection between long-term change in the repertoire of descent-based attributes in a population, and short-term change in the activated categories in that population. Figure 1.4 describes this interaction.

From this discussion we can make a general statement about the two families of concepts that describe different aspect of ethnic identities—ethnic "structure" and ethnic "practice." Recall that ethnic "structure" refers to the repertoire of descent-based attributes, and therefore the sets of "nominal" identities, that all individuals in a population possess, whether or not they actually identify with them. Ethnic "practice" refers to the set of "activated" identities that individuals actually employ in any given context.

The ethnic structure of a population, because it is based on the repertoire of descent-based attributes, tends to be fixed in the short term, while ethnic practice, because it is based on activated categories, can change. Over the long term, however, ethnic "structure" can change too. Indeed, there is a relationship between change in ethnic practice in the short term and ethnic structure in the long term, corresponding to the relationship between the change in descent-based attributes and the categories they constitute. Today's "structure," then, can be in part the product of the ethnic practice of a distant yesterday. And today's ethnic practice can affect the ethnic structure of a distant tomorrow.

6. Synthesizing "Constructivism"

At the broadest level, the term "constructivism" refers simply to the position that facts that we take to be "natural" are in fact the product of some human attempt at creation and interpretation. As one author puts it, the main thrust of this position is to argue that "X need not have existed, or need not be at all as it is. X, or X as it is as present, is not determined by the nature of things, it is not inevitable" (Hacking 1999, 6). This position has now taken root in disciplines across the humanities and social sciences. The differences in what constructivism means across these disciplines lie in what X connotes and in which processes produce changes in X.

Within the comparative scholarship on ethnic identities, the term "constructivism" covers a vast collection of works across disciplines that, taken together, refute the primordialist approach to ethnic identities. "Primordialism" is defined by three minimal propositions: (1) Individuals have a single ethnic identity; (2) this ethnic identity is by its nature fixed; and (3) this ethnic identity is exogenous to human processes. The constructivist refutation consists of three counterpropositions: (1) Individuals have multiple not single ethnic identities; (2) these identities are constructed and can change (although often they do not); and (3) such change, when it occurs, is the product of some human process. But those grouped together as "constructivists" in this field agree on little else than these three minimal propositions.

Before going further, it would also be useful to identify what constructivism, at least with respect to ethnic identity, is *not*. It is not, as it is often caricatured, as a body of work which predicts unconstrained change in ethnic identities. Every constructivist text that we are aware of, as well the arguments made in this book, indicate that there are constraints on ethnic identity change (see for instance Young 1976, Kasfir 1979, Suny 1999b, Waters 1999, Mozaffar, Scarritt and Galaich 2003). Even those who go farthest in emphasizing the instability of ethnic identities, describing identity as an "unsettled space" maintain nevertheless that "there are always conditions to identity which the subject cannot construct. Men and women make history but not under conditions of their own making. They are partly made by the histories that they make" (Hall 1996a, 340). The disagreement among those labeled "constructivist" is mainly over what these constraints are, and whether they are themselves the products of some prior process of construction. The position that descent-based attributes are one of the principal constraints on ethnic identity change in the short term would be shared by most works that we term constructivist. But many constructivist authors propose further constraints in addition to descent in the short and the long term.

Figure 1.5 proposes one way of summarizing the range of disagreement among constructivists. It represents the spectrum of views contained within the constructivist label—and their relation to primordialism—in a two-dimensional space, in which the X axis represents the speed of ethnic identity change and the Y axis the frequency. At one end of the spectrum lie arguments according to which ethnic identity change takes the form of a "punctuated equilibrium" with rare and sluggish intervals of change followed by long stretches of stability. These arguments locate the source of ethnic identity change in variables such as "modernization"

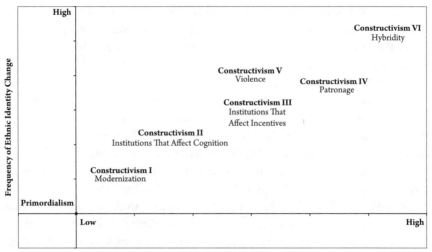

Figure 1.5 Variants of Constructivism: A Range of Views over the Speed and Frequency of Ethnic Identity Change

or institutions that structure cognition such as the modern census. At the other end lie arguments that locate the source of ethnic identity change in the inherent hybridity of ethnic identities. And in the middle lie arguments that locate the source of ethnic identity change in a host of variables including institutions that affect incentives such as party and electoral systems, patronage and violence.

The definition of ethnic identity that we propose here serves as the basis for a synthesis of these disparate views. Constructivist approaches to ethnic identity have typically not made a systematic distinction between the terms "attribute" and "category." Once we do make this distinction, it becomes clear that constructivist arguments that posit that ethnic identities change fast and slow are not contradictory but refer simply to different components of a common process of change. Those variants of constructivism that imply that ethnic identities change slowly and rarely can be read as referring to changes in the underlying repertoire of descent-based *attributes*. The variants that argue that ethnic identities change frequently and rapidly can be read as referring to *activation of new ethnic categories*, or to constraints in addition to descent that restrict such activation, or to the meaning associated with an ethnic identity category.

This book builds on this synthesis to introduce a set of general, logically consistent, mechanisms by which attributes and activated categories—and concepts related to them—change in the short and long term.

• *"Reclassification" of attributes by individuals to activate new identity categories.* When Helen changes her activated ethnic identity category from "Black" to "West Indian" to "Trinidadian," for instance, she simply reclassifies some of her descent-based attributes, while keeping the underlying set of attributes constant.

- *"Switching" by individuals of one or more of their own descent-based attributes.* If Helen changes her skin color from dark to light, and successfully portrays her new skin color as being descent-based, she would have successfully "switched" one of her descent-based attributes. This form of change, for the reasons given earlier, is possible but unlikely in the short term.

- *A change in the "operative" repertoire of nominal ethnic identity categories for a population.* The "operative" or "working" repertoire of ethnic identity categories for a population is the set of categories considered feasible options for activation in any given context. In an electoral context in which candidates are forbidden to appeal to skin color, for example, the category "Black," may not be a feasible option for a candidate with Helen's attributes. In this context, the "operative" repertoire for the population may include the categories "Trinidadian," and "West Indian" but not "Black." If and when the legal framework changes, the "operative" repertoire of the population in the context of elections will also change.

- *A change in the "full" repertoire of nominal ethnic identity categories for a population.* The "full" repertoire of ethnic identity categories for a population is the full set of available identity categories, whether or not they are feasible. Continuing with the example above, this would include the categories "Black," "West Indian," and "Trinidadian" even if the first were not considered feasible for activation during elections.

- *A change in the repertoire of descent-based attributes for a population.* Suppose that over time, the distribution of skin color in a population changed from consisting of predominantly "light" shades to predominantly "dark" shades. This would be an example of a change in the repertoire of descent-based attributes for a population.

The first mechanism—reclassification—is the principal mechanism of change in the short term. The other four mechanisms can occur in the short term in rare cases, but they are more likely to be found in the long term.

These mechanisms are not exhaustive—each can be disaggregated further, and the concepts introduced here can be used to identify still others. However, they capture some of the important ways in which ethnic identities change across contexts and subsume or reformulate others (for instance Laitin 1986, Chandra 2005, Posner 2005).

Each of these mechanisms can be triggered by many different variables, some of which have yet to be identified. Previous constructivist work associates the long-term mechanisms with variables such as modernization and the census, and recombination with variables such as violence, patronage, and party and electoral systems. New constructivist research may well find that these variables affect change in ethnic identity in other ways than previously recognized. Indeed, the chapters in Part 2 of this book highlight some new relationships between these variables and mechanisms. And there are without doubt variables yet to be discovered which may trigger one or more of these mechanisms.

Modeling ethnic identity change, then, requires us to identify the variables and motivations that trigger one or more of these mechanisms. Modeling the *absence* of change in ethnic identity, similarly, requires us to identify the variables and motivations that arrest one or more of these mechanisms. Paradoxically, although we often think of constructivism as a body of theory that explains how ethnic identities change, it is just as appropriate to think of constructivism as a body of theory that explains why ethnic identities *do not* change. From a primordialist perspective, stability in ethnic identities is simply a natural fact. From a constructivist perspective, however, stability becomes a puzzle in search of an explanation. If we see stability in ethnic identities, we need to ask why. Theorizing about why ethnic identities do *not* change is simply the other side of the coin of theorizing about why they do.

7. From Constructivism to Combinatorics

One of the major challenges to theorizing about a constructivist world is describing it. A primordialist world, in which all individuals have one and only one ethnic identity, and the set of ethnic identities for a population is exhaustive and exclusive, is easy to describe. Describing a constructivist world is more complex. It requires us to think in *counterfactuals*, looking beyond the identities that are actually activated in some context, to the entire set of potential identities that might have been activated but were not. It requires us to think in *multiple dimensions*. And it requires us to think about how to represent the *distributions* of these multidimensional sets of identities, actual and counterfactual, across individuals in a population and compare distributions across populations. We have not so far found a means of describing this complex world in an analytically tractable way. And so we have not been able to theorize about it.

Consider, first, the problem of thinking in *counterfactuals*. Each identity category in an individual's "identity repertoire" represents a counterfactual we must rule out in order to explain why they activate any particular one. Previous representations of constructivism assume that identity repertoires contain two or at most three elements—and thus two or at most three counterfactuals (Laitin 1986, Sahlins 1989, Waters 1999, Chandra 2005, Posner 2005). But empirical studies have found the identity repertoires that describe populations to be infinitely larger, with "almost no boundaries" (Laitin 1998, 268, see also Waters 1990, Malouf 2000, and Chandra 2004). They include, at a minimum, all categories that were currently meaningful in each state or elsewhere in the country, categories that had been historically important at some point in the past, and categories that were aggregations or disaggregations of these other categories. The category "White" in the United States, for instance, is an aggregation of previous categories such as Irish American, Italian American, *and* German American. The category "Hispanic" similarly is an aggregation of the categories Dominican, Puerto Rican, Mexican, and so on. The category WASP is an aggregation of the categories White, Anglo-Saxon and Protestant. And each of these categories can, and often is, broken down into its constituent parts. We need a new theoretical language in order to represent this larger, virtually boundless set of counterfactuals for individuals and populations.

Consider, next, the problem of thinking in *multiple dimensions*. We have the conceptual tools now to think about ethnic identity categories made up of one or two attribute-dimensions but not to represent multidimensional sets of both potential and activated identities that belong to more than two dimensions.[4] Yet, many countries have complex structures of ethnic division that include three or more salient dimensions. These include India, in which region, language, caste, religion, and tribe are salient; the United States, in which race, religion, language, region, and nationality are salient; and Malaysia, in which race, language, region, religion, and tribe are salient. We cannot hope to model ethnic identity change in these cases until we have a language that represents such multidimensionality and the possibility of recombination across dimensions.

Consider, finally, the problem of representing distributions of counterfactuals in multiple dimensions within and across *populations*. Representing the distribution of identities in a primordialist world, in which there was no difference between potential and activated identities, all individuals had one and only one ethnic identity, and a population could be represented by a set of mutually exclusive and exhaustive ethnic categories was a simple matter. In a constructivist world, representing the repertoires of potential and actual identities for *individuals* is also relatively simple. But describing sets of activated and potential identities across populations, especially when they are multidimensional and heterogeneous, is difficult. So is comparing populations with different distributions. Faced for example, with a comparison between India, which has at least five commonsensical attribute-dimensions but a small number of attribute-values arrayed on many of them, and Zambia, with two commonsensical attribute-dimensions but a larger number of attribute-values arrayed on

[4] Examples of these descriptions of two-dimensional worlds include Lipset and Rokkan's continuous two-dimensional space representing territorial and functional dimensions of politics (Lipset and Rokkan 1967, 10), Rae and Taylor's index of "cross-cuttingness" (Rae and Taylor 1970), Lijphart's classification of identity structures according to their angles of intersection (Lijphart 1977), basic set theory (Chandra 2005), and Posner's "Ethnic Identity Matrix" (Posner 2005).

them (Posner 2005), how can we tell which country is more diverse? Which country presents individuals with more identity options? We need some metric to represent and compare the distribution of identity repertoires in the two countries.

In response, this book uses the tools of combinatorial mathematics to construct a new language to represent ethnic identity and ethnic identity change for individuals as well as populations. Mathematics is an obvious source of conceptual tools that allows us to represent multidimensional worlds with heterogeneous populations that differ in both activated identities and the repertoires of potential identities. Indeed, political scientists have been experimenting for some time with simple mathematical concepts to capture aspects of constructivism. The more complicated combinatorial language introduced here has the advantage of representing the world we want to analyze in a simple way. Using this language, we can think about a full set of actual and potential identities for any given population, at least in the short term, allowing for any number of dimensions, for combinations across dimensions, and for heterogeneous distributions of these multidimensional identity repertoires across individuals in a population.

The basic idea is simple: If we accept that an ethnic identity is a category of *classification* in which a subset of descent-based attributes are necessary for membership, and those attributes are fixed in the short term, then we can redefine an ethnic identity category as a *combination* of elements from a fixed set. The category "Black" in contemporary New York, for instance, might be defined as the combination {Dark skin *and* descent from parents of African origin}. Similarly, the ethnic category WASP in the contemporary United States might be thought of as the combination {White *and* Anglo Saxon *and* Protestant}.

If, furthermore, activated ethnic identity categories change in the short term through a process of *reclassification* of descent-based attributes, then we can redefine ethnic identity change in the short term as the *recombination* of elements from this fixed set. When an individual in New York changes her activated ethnic identity from "Black" to "West Indian," for instance, she is replacing the combination {Dark skin *and* descent from parents of African origin} with the combination {Birth in Trinidad *or* Guyana *or* Barbados *or* Haiti}, keeping the underlying set of attributes constant.

Moving from an individual to a population, we can represent the distribution of sets of attributes for individuals in a population by replacing the general term "attribute" with a distinction between an "attribute-value" and an "attribute-dimension." An "attribute-dimension," is a class of mutually exclusive attribute-values. For example, one attribute-dimension is "skin color." The *values* on this attribute-dimension might include "Black" and "White." Another is "place of origin," with the values "foreign" and "native." All individuals in a population possess one value on each attribute-dimension (i.e., every person has some skin color and every person has some hair type). We can then represent the distribution of attributes in a population by representing the proportion of individuals who have each value on each dimension.

Imagine, for instance, a population with the two attribute-dimensions of skin color and place of origin and the two attribute-values listed above on each. Imagine, further, that a represents the proportion that has black skin and is of foreign origin (BF), b the proportion that has white skin and is of foreign origin (WF), c the proportion that has black skin and is of native origin (BN), and d the proportion that has white skin and is of native origin (WN). We can represent this population in the 2*2 table (see Table 1.1). We term the generic 2*2 case "Someland."

The full repertoire of nominal ethnic identities for a population consists of all the combinations generated from the descent-based attributes present in that population. For this population, it consists of 2^4 categories—the maximum number of combinations that can be generated from four individual attribute-repertoires (BF, BN, WF, WN). The "operative" repertoire is defined by further constraints, added to the baseline constraint imposed by descent, which determine which categories are viable choices. The operative repertoire, thus, is always a subset of the full repertoire. The ethnic identity categories activated by individuals in this population are chosen from this operative repertoire.

This combinatorial method offers one simple means of representing the distribution of attributes, the repertoires of categories generated from them, and the activated and potential categories, for individuals and populations. We use the 2*2 case in Table 1.1 as a running example throughout this book for the purpose of exposition. But as Chapter 5 shows, combinatorics can easily be used to describe populations with any number of attribute-dimensions and any number of attribute-values. In fact, the advantage of using this combinatorial framework over other methods is most evident when the number of attribute-dimensions and/or the number of attribute-values is larger.

We also use this combinatorial framework to translate the five general mechanisms described above by which ethnic identities change in the short and long term. Each can be disaggregated further where necessary, as well as supplemented with new mechanisms not identified here.

Table 1.1 **Population Repertoire of Attributes (2*2 Case)**

	Black	**White**	
Foreign	a	b	**a + b**
Native	c	d	**c + d**
	a + c	**b + d**	

- The mechanism of change in activated ethnic categories through reclassification, can be translated as the *recombination* of elements from a fixed set.
- Individual switching of descent-based attributes can be translated as the *replacement of an attribute-value* by individuals while keeping the population repertoire constant
- A change in the operative repertoire can be translated as the *addition or subtraction of restrictions* that eliminate attribute-values, attribute-dimensions, or combinations from consideration.
- A change in the full repertoire of nominal identity categories for a population or in the full repertoire of attributes for a population can be translated as
  o *the addition or (subtraction) of an attribute-value* from a population repertoire of attributes, and/or
  o the *addition or subtraction of an attribute-dimension* from a population repertoire of attributes.

The combinatorial form of these mechanisms is new, but the phenomena that it captures are not. What we describe as recombination, for example, has long been recognized in the interdisciplinary literature on constructivism using other terms One such term, to which we have already given a great deal of attention, is "reclassification." Other terms are "fission" and "fusion," or "supertribalization" (Rudolph and Rudolph 1967, Horowitz 1971, van den Berghe 1981). The term "fission" is that form of recombination in which new groups are created by the disaggregation of larger ones. The term "fusion" refers to that form of recombination in which new groups are created through the amalgamation of smaller ones. And the term "supertribalization" describes the construction of large tribal identities by the fusion of smaller ones. What the combinatorial form does allows one to capture previously identified processes with greater precision than before, show that they are part of one general framework, and express the interconnections between them.

8. From Mechanisms to Models of Ethnic Identity Change

The chapters in this book use these mechanisms, and the framework from which they come, as a common point of departure from which to build different models of change in "ethnic demography." The term "ethnic demography" is a placeholder for a more precise concept, introduced in each chapter, that refers to a population-based rather than an individual-based aspect of ethnic identity. Several of the chapters theorize about change in an ethnic demography through the mechanism of recombination (Chandra and Boulet, Chapters 5 and 6, Ferree, Chapter 8, Wilkinson, Chapter 10, Petersen, Chapter 11). Others explore the dynamic interactions between recombination and other mechanisms (Van der Veen and Laitin, Chapter 7, Laitin and van der Veen, Chapter 9, and Lustick, Chapter 12).

Although built on a common foundation, the models use a diverse set of assumptions about human motivations, including the need, conscious or unconscious, to win elections, to obtain material payoffs, to realize policy preferences, to express anger and resentment, to recruit soldiers, and to imitate others in their proximate environment. They also employ a wide range of methods, including ethnography, archival research, game theory, quantitative analysis, and agent-based modeling.

These models address problems that are more complex than those identified in previous models of ethnic identity change. Whereas previous models have focused on a small number of bluntly defined concepts such as "ethnicity" or "ethnic identity," these new models focus on a large number of more precisely specified concepts such as "activated ethnic identity categories," "attribute-dimensions," "nested relationships between attribute-dimensions," "repertoires of nominal ethnic identity categories," the "distributions of identity repertoires," and so on. Whereas previous models have typically focused on a single concept at a time, several of these models focus on the connections between them. Whereas previous models have typically focused on bivariate relationships between a single independent variable and the dependent variable in question, these models address multicausal relationships. Whereas previous models have typically focused on a particular aspect of ethnic identity change at a single point in time, several of these models address dynamic relationships. And whereas previous models have made the task of explanation more tractable by limiting the counterfactuals they consider, these models address a broader range of counterfactuals.

This last point deserves elaboration. A standard approach to explaining the activation of a particular identity category is to consider and eliminate counterfactual identities that could have been activated but were not. The number of counterfactuals previous models consider is just one. Thus, Laitin (1986) explained why identities based on tribe were activated in Yorubaland in Nigeria by explaining why religion was not. Waters (1999) explained why the category "Black" was activated by second-generation immigrants in New York by showing why the alternative category "West Indian" was not. Chandra (2005) explained why political parties that activated identities based on religion in India were stalemated by parties that activated identities based on caste. Posner (2005) explained why identities based on tribe were activated in Zambia by explaining why identities based on language were not. But we know, from the empirical work described in the previous section, that the set of counterfactuals which must be eliminated in explaining any particular choice is very large—"almost without boundaries" (Laitin 1998). The conclusions of these models, therefore, are driven not only by the explanation of why some ethnic identities were not activated but by the implicit assumptions that eliminate consideration of a broader set of counterfactuals.

The formulation of the full repertoire of nominal ethnic identity categories in this chapter transforms the set of the counterfactuals that we consider. By replacing the implicit assumption that ethnic identity repertoires contain two categories or at most three categories with a conceptual statement indicating that it can contain tens, even hundreds or thousands of elements in principle, it places a larger burden on the theorist. In order to explain how ethnic identities are activated, then, the theorist must eliminate, or at least attach probabilities to, hundreds and thousands of counterfactuals, not just one or two. This does not mean that individuals are choosing between hundreds of identities when they decide which one to activate—the "operative" repertoire that they consider may often be more narrowly constructed. But even when we allow for the existence of a smaller "operative" repertoire, the constraints that eliminate many of the categories in the full repertoire from consideration must be part of our theory.

The greater complexity of the problems they confront means that the analytic frameworks and technologies used in these models is also more complex. This makes them more illuminating simplifications of the empirical reality that we seek to understand. These are, furthermore, theoretically productive simplifications: each model not only asks and answers a specific question about ethnic identity change but also develops approaches that generate new questions and new ways in which we can answer them.

Models of Electoral Politics and Change in Ethnic Demography

Primordialist approaches to electoral politics suggest that elections in which ethnic divisions are salient take the form of an "ethnic census" in which fixed ethnic majorities become political winners and fixed ethnic minorities become political losers (Dahl 1971, Rabushka and Shepsle 1972, Horowitz 1985, 1991, Guinier 1994). Previous constructivist work has suggested, by contrast, that electoral politics is an important process affecting ethnic identity change (Weiner 1967, Brass 1970, 1974, Young 1976, 1982, Wood 1984, Giliomee 1989, Thapar 1989, Rajasingham-Senanayeke 1999a and 1999b, Jung 2000, Chandra 2004). Much of this work is devoted to showing *that* elections, and competitive politics more generally, change ethnic identities, not to defining the form of change that occurs or the conditions that make it more or less likely. The handful of theoretical models that do model change in some aspect of ethnic identities in response to electoral politics apply to highly restricted cases, in which change is defined as a switch from one fixed category to another from a repertoire of at most two options (Chandra 2005, Posner 2005). Several chapters in this book take us beyond both primordialism and earlier versions of constructivism by building more general and more fully specified constructivist models of the relationship between electoral politics and ethnic identity change.

Chandra and Boulet propose a general "baseline" model of electoral politics and the possibility of change in a country's activated ethnic demography, by which they mean the set and size of the activated ethnic identity categories for a population. "Are there conditions," they ask, under which majority rule elections can induce the possibility of change in the set and size of ethnic identity categories activated by a country's electorate? Are there conditions under which this activated ethnic demography is certain to remain stable in response to electoral politics? If the possibility of change exists, how *much* change is possible: Is it restricted to only some individuals in a population or to all of them? And is the possibility of change disproportionately associated, as classic democratic theory tells us, with "cross-cutting" or "multipolar" structures of ethnic division as compared to "coinciding" and "bipolar" structures?

The model begins with the observation that "recombination" is a central mechanism of short-term change in electoral politics. An ethnic demography is activated in electoral politics, they argue, by politicians who combine strings of attributes into ethnic identity categories of "minimum winning size," and voters who activate one of these categories in response. The possibility of change, then, exists when the distribution of attribute-repertoires in a population generates multiple combinations of minimum winning size. The certainty of stability exists when it generates only one such combination.

The model generates three main results. (1) Intrinsic fixity in an activated ethnic demography is rare. Even when the attributes that generate ethnic identity categories are fixed in the short term, the possibility of change in activated ethnic categories through elections exists in most cases. (2) In most cases the possibility of change exists for *all* individuals in a population. (3) In contrast to the classic theories, dichotomies such as cross-cutting versus coinciding or multipolar versus bipolar ethnic structures are not informative in predicting the possibility of change. The model proposes them with a single general concept—the "distribution of attribute-repertoires"—which allows us to predict and compare the possibility of change associated with any structure of ethnic division, within or outside these dichotomies.

Chandra and Boulet's model is general in that it identifies the conditions under which the possibility of change or the certainty of stability exists in the general case, in which individuals are permitted to consider all possible combinations, for any number of attribute-dimensions and values on each. But it does not make a general prediction about whether and how this possibility will be realized in specific cases—it simply provides a baseline from which predictions of ethnic identity change can be generated for specific contexts. By identifying all the combinations that individuals might have considered in making their decisions about which category to activate, it identifies the full set of counterfactuals that must be ruled out in explaining any particular choice in any particular context.

Several of the chapters in this book theorize about the additional restrictions that eliminate many of these counterfactuals and define the "operative" choice sets in particular contexts. Van der Veen and Laitin, in Chapter 7, introduce restrictions based on the cognitive capacities of individuals and the information available to them. In Chapter 8, Ferree introduces restrictions based on the possibility of ethnic identity change introduced by the "nested" relationship between attribute-dimensions. In Chapter 10, Wilkinson introduces restrictions based on the ideological proximity between attribute-values on a single dimension. Petersen, in Chapter 11, introduces restrictions based on the emotional costs attached to certain attribute-values and dimensions. Each chapter then models the likelihood and form of change in activated ethnic identities within these restricted choice sets.

In Chapter 6, Chandra and Boulet also open a new line of inquiry about the relationship between ethnic identity change and electoral politics. Some new questions suggested by this chapter include: Who is likely to be the originator of change in an ethnic demography—can we theorize about the identity repertoires of those most likely to initiate change? What is the effect of different electoral rules on change or stability in an activated ethnic demography? Taking the distribution of attributes for a given population as constant, which electoral systems are likely to produce the greatest fluidity? For different electoral rules, what is the proportion of individuals whose identity repertoires prevent them from membership in a minimum winning category? This is a new way of defining the problem of "permanent exclusion" so critical to democratic theory. For any given population, what is the range of electoral rules which will minimize permanent exclusion? What is the relationship between short-term and long-term change in electoral politics: Can the activation of an ethnic identity through recombination in the short term produce a change in the underlying distribution of attributes in the long term? The chapter also has significant implications for data collection on and the measurement of activated ethnic demographies, which are discussed elsewhere.

Van der Veen and Laitin build on this baseline to address the question of how ethnic demographies evolve over time in response to electoral politics. Chandra and Boulet's theory, they note, is one of combinatorial possibilities at some fixed point in time. This chapter, by contrast, theorizes about the dynamics of change, incorporating combinatorial insights into an agent-based model. Van der Veen and Laitin break down the question about the evolution of an ethnic demography into two more specific ones. Their first experiment asks: Do electoral institutions have the same impact on leadership stability and on individual identities in countries where ethnic differences dominate as compared to countries divided on less "sticky" identities? "Leadership stability" is one way of identifying whether the possibility of change is realized in a population: presumably, change in leadership should reflect change in the ethnic categories activated by that leadership to come to power. Their second experiment asks: What is the impact of different electoral systems on the pattern of concentration of attributes in an ethnic demography. By "concentration of attributes," they mean phenomena such as linguistic assimilation, in which some attributes are acquired by large numbers of the population, while others die out.

Both experiments suggest a new theoretical logic linking electoral rules with patterns of evolution in ethnic demographies. The commonsensical expectation in democratic theory is that we should see greater fluidity in winners and losers—and therefore greater turnover in leadership—when the salient attribute-dimensions in a society are less rather than more sticky. But van der Veen and Laitin find, except in a plurality electoral system, stickier demographies are associated with *shorter* tenure in office. With respect to attribute-concentration, common sense might lead us to expect there to be greater attribute-concentration in non-ethnic demographies (i.e., demographies with less sticky attribute-dimensions) than in ethnic demographies, since it is easier for individuals to acquire advantageous attribute-values in the short term. But it is not clear ex ante how different electoral rules would interact with stickiness to affect levels of concentration. Van der Veen and Laitin find that as the winning threshold imposed by an electoral system rises, the concentration of attributes tends to fall in non-ethnic demographies but rise in ethnic demographies. Both results raise several new questions worthy of further theoretical investigation.

One of the key innovations in Chapter 7 is the incorporation of combinatorial framework introduced in this book into an agent-based model. Agent-based modeling makes it easy to model the interactions between multiple, simultaneous processes so critical to constructivist theories. And it is has more potential than perhaps any other technology introduced in this book in its capacity to represent identity repertoires—and therefore the range of counterfactuals—within which identity choices take place. Further, van der Veen and Laitin's model makes it possible to represent the "salience" and "stickiness" of attribute-dimensions as continuous rather than dichotomous concepts, and to introduce a greater degree of variability across the attribute-repertoires of individuals in a population.

Van der Veen and Laitin's ingenious adaptation of agent-based modeling to test constructivist propositions provides the technology to ask fundamental new questions that we would not have been able to answer before: How does "stickiness" of the attribute-dimensions in a demography change over time? What are the conditions under which sticky (and therefore "ethnic") demographies can transform into non-ethnic ones? Does stability in electoral winners require stability in activated ethnic categories—or can stability in leadership coexist despite dynamic transformations of a demography? Do some electoral rules lead to greater instability over time than others? We return to the potential of agent-based modeling as a strategy for theorizing about constructivism in the discussion of the chapters that follow.

In Chapter 8, Ferree proposes and tests an argument about how much fluidity we should expect in activated ethnic identity categories in electoral politics. It has become commonplace, she notes, to assert that ethnic identities are constructed, fluid, and responsive to political, social, and economic contexts including elections. But in the first work to raise this question in the field of electoral politics, she asks exactly how fluid they are. How easily can political entrepreneurs fighting elections construct new ethnic groupings? Not very easily, she argues. The widespread possibility of short-term change identified by Chandra and Boulet in Chapter 6 may be significantly restricted in countries with "nested" ethnic structures—ethnic structures in which attribute-values on one dimension are contained within attribute-values on another. Voters and politicians operating within nested structures, Ferree argues, consider as feasible only those combinations that include all attribute-values on a given node. This finding implies a highly constrained version of constructivism—at least with regard to the short time frame relevant for electoral volatility.

Ferree arrives at this conclusion by devising a novel statistical test of the relationship between ethnic structure and electoral volatility, using a recently developed cross-national dataset on ethnic divisions in Africa (Mozaffar, Scarritt and Galaich 2003). She hypothesizes that in ethnic structures that produce only one winning category, voters should be easily able to coordinate on which category to activate and therefore which party to vote for, and consequently there should be low electoral volatility. However, in ethnic structures with zero or multiple winning categories, voters may not be able to coordinate on which party to vote for and there should thus be high electoral volatility. But the count of the number of winning coalitions in each country varies according to whether we begin from a primordialist or a constructivist position—and according to which model of constructivism we adopt. Accordingly, she creates three different counts of these winning coalitions. The first corresponds to a "primordialist" model. The second corresponds to a highly restricted constructivist model, in which voters are willing to consider only those combinations that include *all* values on a node. The third is a more expansive constructivist model, in which voters are willing to consider all combinations of *some* values within a node. She finds that the statistical model that best fits the data employs the count based on the second variant.

Ferree's chapter introduces two innovations helpful in asking and answering new questions about elections and ethnic identity change. First, it identifies an important link between "nestedness" and electoral outcomes. "Nested" ethnic structures are widespread, but unlike the "cross-cutting" cleavage structures or "multipolar" cleavage structures referred to above, we have no clear intuitions about how they might affect electoral results. Ferree offers a first cut at developing such an intuition, backed by empirical evidence. This should prompt further theoretical investigations: What is it about nestedness that produces this outcome in Africa? Is "nestedness" a proxy for territorial proximity? For cultural distance? Does "nestedness" affect fluidity the same way in other regions? Second, Ferree shows how constructivist hypotheses can be tested using simple statistical tools. One difficulty in incorporating constructivist insights into new research agendas in politics and economics so far is that they are perceived to be difficult to operationalize in econometric models. But not only does Ferree show how this can be done relatively simply, she also generates results that can be combined and compared with the results of other methodological approaches that ask the same question. For example, if "electoral volatility" in Ferree's statistical model can be treated as an approximation of van der Veen and Laitin's "leadership turnover," then we can use their agent-based model to test the robustness of Ferree's findings by incorporating the concept of "nested" ethnic structures in their agent-based model.

In the final chapter on electoral politics, Laitin and van der Veen (Chapter 9) explore the elective affinity between the activation of ethnic identities and the exclusionary distribution of political benefits, also known as "pork." "Is pork-based politics associated with the activation of ethnic identities," they ask, "and if so, why?" Previous constructivist arguments have explained this affinity as the consequence of spatial distribution and network ties between co-ethnics (Bates 1974), the greater visibility of ethnic identities compared to non-ethnic ones in limited information environments (Chandra 2004), and the greater relative stickiness of ethnic identities (Fearon 1999, Caselli and Coleman 2001). Laitin and van der Veen build a constructivist model to explore the last mechanism—the link between pork politics, stickiness, and the activation of "sticky" identities. This is an agent-based model that allows for variation in the "stickiness" of attribute-dimensions. In accordance with the conceptual logic outlined earlier, the more sticky attribute-dimensions represent ethnic attribute-dimensions, while the less sticky ones represent non-ethnic attribute-dimensions. "Pork politics" is operationalized using the size of the "optimal winning coalition:" the value and appeal of exclusionary, distributive politics, Laitin and van der Veen reason, will decrease as the fraction of the population a leader needs to attract increases.

Chapter 9 finds that when political entrepreneurs have incentives to seek small coalitions (due to the goal of distributing a limited amount of pork to supporters), those that win and stay in power are indeed those that attract voters based on their ethnic membership. Further the affinity between ethnicity and pork applies not just to winning coalitions but also to the overall nature of political contestation: If pork is up for grabs, ethnic identities become more politically salient. Moreover, their findings suggest new mechanisms that drive political entrepreneurs to propose and voters to support ethnic coalitions when distribution (i.e., pork) rather than policy drives political competition. Whereas previous works have overwhelmingly suggested that instrumental calculation is the basis of this link, they point instead to an adaptive logic, showing that an affinity between ethnicity and pork emerges even when neither the public nor its leaders consciously take into account differences between ethnic identities and other forms of political identification.

The contribution of this chapter to models of ethnic identity change goes beyond its immediate conclusions. In particular, by allowing the levels of stickiness of attribute-dimensions in an ethnic demography to vary, Laitin and van der Veen make it possible to investigate the dynamics of a "mixed" demography (one in which attribute-repertoires include both ethnic and non-ethnic attribute-dimensions) and non-ethnic demographies.

This opens the way for social scientists to answer a whole host of theoretical questions not restricted only to pork politics. A subset of these includes the following: Under what conditions will political entrepreneurs choose specifications based on ethnic rather than non-ethnic attribute-dimensions? Under what conditions would they prefer mixed to pure ethnic specifications? Under what conditions would they prefer purely non-ethnic specifications? Are there conditions under which ethnic demographies can be transformed into non-ethnic ones and vice versa? Under what conditions might ethnic identities be "softened" by the inclusion of a non-ethnic qualifying attribute in their membership rule? Does this "softening" have a different effect than outright change? And so on.

Models of Violence and Change in Ethnic Demography

Previous constructivist work has suggested that violence, broadly defined, can trigger almost all of the mechanisms of ethnic identity change identified above (see the discussion in Chapter 5 based on Pandey 1992, Tambiah 1992, Brass 1997, Brubaker and Laitin 1998, Jeganathan 1998, Laitin 1999, Snyder 2000, and Appadurai 2006). In Chapter 10, Wilkinson proposes a model linking a specific form of violence—riots—to one mechanism in particular—change in an activated category or attribute-dimension. Wilkinson argues that riots are the means through which political entrepreneurs interested in winning elections either activate new ethnic categories and attribute-dimensions or change those previously activated.

The chapter starts with the baseline model introduced by Chandra and Boulet, conceptualizing elections as a process in which political entrepreneurs string together "minimum winning" combinations of attributes. But rather than treating all combinations of attribute-values in a population's repertoire as equally feasible, it introduces the idea politicians will consider as feasible only "minimum connected winning coalitions," which minimize distance among coalition partners along some issue-dimension that politicians regard as most important, such as economic reforms. Wilkinson then shows how, from a choice of multiple winning coalitions, political entrepreneurs use riots to stabilize an ethnic demography around a minimum winning coalition that consists of attribute-values close to each other on an underlying issue dimension. He illustrates the model with examples from Ireland, India, and the American South.

Both of Wilkinson's innovations to the baseline model of ethnic identity change—the introduction of "issue-dimensions" attached to "attribute-dimensions" and the introduction of a "connectedness" restriction to the combinations voters are willing to consider as feasible—suggest new ways to construct models about ethnic identity change, not necessarily restricted to violence, in the future. The concept of "issue dimension" has typically been used to theorize about party politics in Western democracies and attribute-dimensions (or identities) party politics in the developing world. Both matter, but it is not yet clear how to combine them. Wilkinson shows how the two can be profitably combined, not only in the study of violence but in any scenario in which attribute-dimensions are linked on some underlying dimension. Further, while he himself uses the "minimum connected winning" criterion to denote ideological proximity between attribute-values, it can measure several other concepts including spatial distance, cultural distance, emotional valence (an idea developed by Petersen, Chapter 11, in this volume), income differentials, and so on. Indeed, to the extent that nested structures capture some ordering of values by territorial or cultural proximity, we may be able to use this restriction as an alternate way to represent the nested cleavage structures that Ferree describes in Chapter 8. Wilkinson's use of the Shapley-Shubik index to measure coalitions based on the connectedness restriction furthermore makes a fruitful connection between the combinatorial study of ethnic identities introduced here with an older and better developed literature on coalition theory that may yield further innovations in the future (Shapley and Shubik 1954).

Chapter 11 asks: How does the collapse of the state affect change in an activated ethnic demography? A vast body of previous constructivist work has established that modern states create and maintain ethnic identity categories and the underlying attributes that constitute them (see the discussion in Chapter 4, based on Brass 1974, 1997, Foucault 1977, Said 1978, Jones 1981, Fox 1985, Laitin 1986, Gramsci 1992, Pandey 1992, Lustick 1993, Appadurai 1996, Dominguez 1997, Scott 1998, Nobles 2000, Luong 2002 Herrera 2005, and Posner 2005). Chapter 11 pursues the logical implications of this body of work: If states stabilize existing ethnic demographies, then state collapse should also destabilize them. Petersen describes this collapse formally using the concepts developed in this book. The collapse of state structures, he notes, "loosens" attributes from currently activated categories, thus making them available for new combinations. This creates the conditions for change in an activated ethnic demography.

At the same time, Petersen argues, state collapse simultaneously unleashes emotions such as anger and resentment that restrict the "operative" repertoire of categories individuals are willing to consider feasible. Petersen models this restriction as a trade-off between political and material benefits on the one hand and emotional costs on the other. In the immediate aftermath of state collapse, the emotional costs can be high enough to prevent individuals from activating otherwise beneficial categories identified in the Chandra-Boulet baseline model. However, as survivors die off and the vividness and intensity of the emotional memories among their descendants declines, the overall population becomes less ready to maintain the losses and an identity shift can take place. While state collapse creates the possibility of a change in an ethnic demography, in other words, emotions can play a primary role in determining which categories are activated subsequently, and the extent to which they are stable over time. The argument is illustrated with examples from Moldova and Eastern Europe.

Chapter 11 is a pioneering chapter. In addition to modeling systematically the effect of state collapse on ethnic identity change, it is the first work to integrate the role of emotion in constructivist theory. While many social scientists would surely acknowledge that ethnic identities inspire strong emotions, the role of emotional variables and processes in explaining identity choice and change has not so far been theorized. Horowitz (1985) builds an argument linking emotions such as self-esteem and a sense of belonging to ethnic group behavior. But this argument links emotion to some existing set of ethnic identity categories, not to ethnic identity change. Petersen, by contrast, provides a systematic framework through which the effect of, and their interaction with rationality in influencing identity change, can be modeled. He uses combinatorics to model the range of counterfactuals individuals might consider and their relative weights, economic devices such as indifference curves to model the trade-off between these coun-terfactuals, and then demographic assumptions to show how this trade-off can change over time.

Petersen's analytic framework and technology open a new research agenda on the role of emotions in ethnic identity change. They suggest new questions such as: Do emotions always affect the stabilization of identities or are there condi-tions under which they do not matter? How do emotions attached to ethnic identities compare with those attached with non-ethnic identities? What is the role of properties such as stickiness and visibility in affecting the role of emo-tions: are emotions, for instance, more likely to attach to identities that are vis-ible than invisible? Can emotions play a role in the *construction* of new identity choices as well as the *restriction* of previously constructed choice sets? Can emo-tion be induced forces other than violence? Are there feedback effects between the activation of some ethnic identity categories and the emotional valence of the attributes and dimensions those categories are based on? Such questions about feedback loops, furthermore, can be productively explored by integrating

Petersen's framework with the technology introduced by van der Veen and Laitin in Chapters 7 and 9.

Lustick's model of ethnic identity change reverses Petersen's perspective, theorizing about the effect of change in an activated ethnic demography on "secession of the center," a form of state contraction initiated by elites in the core of the state. In Chapter 12, Lustick proposes a new agent-based model of political competition and change in an ethnic demography. Built to approximate political competition in Pakistan, this model is the most realistic of all the models of political competition and ethnic identity change proposed in this book. The overall framework is the same as in the rest of the chapters: Agents begin with a repertoire of nominal ethnic identity categories, from which they activate one at any given point in time. An activated ethnic demography consists of the aggregation of individual choices. But Lustick's model is distinct in that individuals make decisions about which ethnic identity to activate based not only on the actions of political entrepreneurs, as in the Chandra-Boulet model, but on a variety of influential actors. These include the bureaucracy, the military, religious leaders, landowners, the urban commercial elite, and the media. These actors, furthermore, have varying degrees of influence: There are, for instance, three echelons of bureaucratic authority, and higher-level bureaucrats have more influence than lower-level ones. In a novel conceptual step, "secessionism" too is interpreted as a form of identity change: It occurs when agents initially activated on a regionally concentrated ethnic identity transform into immutable "border cells." "Secession of the center" in Pakistan occurs when the number and distribution of secessionist "Punjabi" agents crosses a given threshold. Based on this model, Lustick argues that while secession of the center is unlikely in Pakistan, it is possible—and identifies the conditions under which it is likely to take place.

One of the principal innovations in Lustick's chapter with respect to theorizing about ethnic identity change is its representation of the *distribution* of identity repertoires in a population. In keeping with the conceptual framework introduced in this book, the population repertoire for Pakistan consists of thirty identity categories rather than just one or two. But this model allows for agent-level variation in both the size and content of identity repertoires. Second, it allows for *regional* variation in both size and content of repertoires—and takes the population density of each region into account. The regional distribution of repertoires of identity categories may well be one of the most significant variables affecting state contraction and other outcomes and processes associated with ethnic differences, but it has not so far been modeled in this book. Third, it allows for correlations between different types of identities in a repertoire: certain identity categories go together in a repertoire while others do not. Such correlations are an intuitive way of representing ethnic structures with "cross-cutting" or "nested" attribute-dimensions. Fourth, in a novel way of conceptualizing "stickiness," identities can vary in whether they are "obtainable" or "unobtainable": Agents can be "born" with unobtainable identities but cannot bring them into their repertoires if they are not already there. Taken together, these innovations produce one of the most realistic, yet analytically tractable, representations of the distributions of identity repertoires that we have in the social sciences.

This model is the first to ask and answer a question about the relationship between the evolution of identities and secession of the center. But it also makes it possible to ask and answer a larger set of questions about the co-evolution of identities and state boundaries. For instance, we could use the same framework to reverse the question, and examine the relationship between change in state boundaries and the evolution of identities theorized about by Petersen in Chapter 11. Indeed, we could use it to theorize about any aspect of the morphology of states addressed in other works (Alesina and Spolare 2003, Lustick 1993), investigating also the dynamic relationships between change in identities, the conditions under which states expand, and the conditions under which peripheries, rather than cores break away.

Further, its sophisticated rendering of the distribution of identity repertoires across populations can be exported to studies of other dependent variables. Thus, for example, this framework could be adapted to explore further the dynamics of the relationship between ethnic structures and electoral volatility highlighted by Ferree in this book, or the role of regionally distributed ethnic identity repertoires on electoral outcomes as suggested by Mozaffar, Scarritt and Galaich (2003), and on civil wars as suggested by Cederman, Girardin and Gleditsch (2009), the relationship between different types of cleavage structures and the pattern and degree of fluidity in activated ethnic identities, or any other study in which we are interested in exploring the effect not only of a currently activated identity but of the distribution of potentially activable identities in a population. This is a significant theoretical advance.

9. Theories of Ethnicity, Politics and Economics

The models of ethnic identity change discussed above are all also models of politics and economics, since they all address the relationship between change in ethnic identity and political and economic processes. Nevertheless, it is worth shifting the emphasis from ethnic identity change to ask: What do we learn from these models about democratic stability, riots, civil war, the distribution of public goods, and state failure and secession? In short, the models in this book both change the conclusions of previous work on this subject and the questions we can ask in the future. The remainder of this section elaborates.

Democracy

Take, for example, the classic argument in empirical democratic theory, as well as a commonsensical presumption, that ethnic diversity threatens democratic stability. The logic of the argument goes as follows: Democracy requires fluid majorities and minorities in order to survive. Ethnically divided societies, however, tend to produce "permanent" majorities and minorities, based on an ethnic census. Consequently, democracy in ethnically divided societies is threatened. The threat, according to these arguments, can be mitigated by "cross-cutting" or "multipolar" structures of ethnic division or by institutions that limit the power of the winning majority. But it cannot be eliminated (Dahl 1971, Lijphart 1977, Horowitz 1985, and Guinier 1994).

The several chapters on electoral politics in this book challenge this argument. Chandra and Boulet show that there is nothing *intrinsic* about ethnic divisions that promotes fixity: Even when we assume that the descent-based attributes that constitute ethnic identity categories are fixed over a lifetime, the possibility of change exists for most populations—and all individuals in most populations. Van der Veen and Laitin's findings go even further in challenging this presumption: They find that except in a plurality electoral system, there is *more* rather than less fluidity in ethnic demographies compared to non-ethnic ones. This is true even when there are restrictions on how politicians and voters choose categories, restricting them to relatively simple combinations. Ferree, who imposes even stricter restrictions on the potential for change, arrives at the same conclusion: Although she argues that voters do not recombine freely, she too finds fluidity (electoral volatility) in those cleavage structures where they recombine. The overall implication is that fixity in electoral results, where it does exist, is not embedded in the nature of ethnic identities. If we see fixed winners and losers in democracies in which ethnic divisions are salient, then, the answer must lie in external factors that combine and interact with ethnic divisions, not in the intrinsic nature of those divisions themselves.

There are also other counterintuitive findings about cleavage structures and majoritarian institutions. Chandra and Boulet argue that there is no relationship between any particular type of cleavage structure and the possibility of change: Most can be associated with either fixity or fluidity. Ferree shows that nested cleavage structures, about which we have had no intuitions so far, are indeed associated with the possibility of change. Further, Laitin and van der Veen suggest that majoritarian institutions—or at least majoritarian electoral systems with a high threshold of winning—produce *more* fluidity (measured as leadership turnover) as well as more assimilation than non-majoritarian systems. They find more fixity, paradoxically, in electoral systems with a low threshold for winning—that is, in non-majoritarian conditions. Just as the problem of fixed results does not appear to be intrinsic to ethnically diverse democracies, then, the conditions that mitigate this problem, where it exists, may also not have to do with preventing ethnic majoritarianism.

Patronage

Previous research on the relationship between ethnic diversity and patronage can be divided into two schools of thought. The first school, represented by a voluminous body of work, argues that ethnic diversity impedes the distribution of public goods, pushing a political system toward patronage goods instead. (e.g., Alesina, Baqir and Easterly 1999). The second school, represented by a handful of more recent work, argues that the causal relationship goes in the opposite direction: patronage-based politics can make ethnic differences more salient (Bates 1974, Fearon 1999, Caselli and Coleman, 2001, Chandra 2004).

Laitin and van der Veen's model supports this second school: They show that patronage politics increases the salience of ethnic attribute-dimensions over non-ethnic ones. This does not eliminate the possibility that the causal relationship may *also* run in the reverse direction. But it suggests at a minimum that there may be a cyclical and dynamic relationship between ethnic divisions and patronage politics, in which patronage politics increases the salience of ethnic attribute-dimensions, and the salience of ethnic attribute-dimensions in turn increases the scope of patronage politics.

Further, this model suggests that patronage politics may be a specific case of a more general class of phenomena: a competitive context in which the threshold for winning is low. Monarchies, military dictatorships, and democratic regimes with proportional electoral rules or restricted suffrage are all cases in which leaders can win control without mobilizing large numerical majorities. Laitin and van der Veen's argument suggests that there may be an underlying commonality driving the salience of ethnic differences in these seemingly disparate regimes that can be represented in a single model. This suggestion provides a foundation on which to integrate studies of ethnic diversity and patronage with broader theoretical models which, while not concerned specifically with ethnic identity, also express regime type as a function of the size of the "selectorate" and the coalition required to win (Bueno de Mesquita et al. 2003).

Riots

Ethnic riots are generally thought to be the result of antipathy or competition between solid ethnic groups. By contrast, Wilkinson argues that ethnic riots are best understood not as the *outcome* of already high degrees of competition, polarization, and hatred between solid ethnic groups but rather as the *means* through which political parties and political entrepreneurs construct solid ethnic categories, however briefly, for a clear political purpose. According to this argument, politicians at a disadvantage in competitive elections use riots to activate previously unactivated or weakly activated ethnic identity categories or dimensions and thus change the situation to their advantage.

Wilkinson's argument generates new predictions compared to previous ones: Whereas previous theories would lead us to look for violence in conditions in which group identities are strong, this one predicts violence in conditions in which group identities are weak (see also Appadurai 2006). It does not, it is worth emphasizing, negate the existence of cases in which there are indeed solid group identities associated with violence—but it suggests a new interpretation of these cases. It directs us to look for incidents of violence in the past that may have produced the solidification of group identities. And it suggests that present-day violence may be not only a product of these previously formed identities but also a means to maintain them in the present and the future. Indeed, it is only when we look at both riots and the activation of ethnic identity as processes rather than single point variables that it becomes possible to model these dynamic interactions. The argument also suggests distinct policy responses to ethnic riots. If riots occur when ethnic identities are weak rather than strong, then one policy measure to prevent ethnic riots, paradoxically, may be institutional measures that strengthen ethnic identities (Chandra 2005, Wilkinson 2004).

State Collapse

The presumption in previous literature on the subject is that state collapse increases the likelihood of conflict between pre-existing ethnic groups who suddenly find themselves without a neutral third party that can enforce an agreement between them (Fearon 1998, Posen 1993). Chapter 11, by Petersen, which shows how state collapse can lead to the activation of new ethnic identities, poses a direct challenge to this presumption. Formalizing and extending the insights of a vast body of previous constructivist work, Petersen argues that states perform a more fundamental function than enforcing contracts between existing groups—they are the force that creates and maintains the groups themselves. When the state collapses, then, the groups in question may well collapse too. And as the state is reconstituted, so are the groups in question.

The precise pattern of group identities that emerge in the wake of state collapse depends on the distribution of attribute-repertoires in a country, the trade-off between the material payoffs and emotional residue attached to them, and the pattern of aging in the population. But the broad point is that groups do not exist independently of states—states and groups co-evolve. This does not mean that conflict may not occur in the wake of state collapse. But if Petersen is right, then such conflict cannot be attributed to firm group identities which are not so firm in the first place. It may be the case, combining Petersen's analysis with

Chapter 10, by Wilkinson, that it is a product of the weakness of group identities. But this would lead us in a different theoretical direction than previous
theories have suggested.

Secession

Secession is normally presumed to be a centrifugal process, driven by minority
ethnic groups concentrated in the geographic periphery of a state. It goes without saying by now that the groups in question are assumed to be fixed entities
that exist prior to and independently of state boundaries. Lustick's Chapter 12
on Pakistan, by contrast, investigates how patterns of identity change, rather than
how a fixed configuration of groups affects secession. Pakistan is the perfect illustration of the standard presumption at work—the often described threat of secession in Pakistan is believed to come from minority groups such as the Baluchis,
Pashtuns, Sindhis, or Seraikis, each of which has a territory associated with it.
Building on a model of identity evolution in Pakistan, Lustick argues, by contrast,
that secession in Pakistan is unlikely—and that if it occurs, secession by the dominant Punjabi group that constitutes the core of the Pakistani state is more likely
than secession by the minority groups that occupy its periphery. More broadly,
this model suggests that allowing for such change may lead to the downgrading
of expectations of secession even in "high risk" cases like Pakistan—and illustrates the mechanisms by which new forms of secession such as "secession of the
center" that have hitherto received little theoretical attention can emerge.

Taken together, the work of Petersen and Lustick also has significant implications for the debates on the effectiveness of partition as a policy to prevent
violence. According to one side of the debate in this literature, partition removes
a significant source of ethnic violence by making the boundaries of states and
ethnic groups congruent (Van Evera 1994). According to the other side of this
debate (Horowitz 1985), congruence between state and group boundaries in the
present is no guarantee against discongruence in the future. New group identities can emerge in territories made "homogeneous" by partition. Petersen and
Lustick's arguments support this second side. Using different frameworks and
assumptions, both show how the initial distribution of identities within state
borders can change through political competition. But these models show how
to model *which* new group identities might emerge within some reconstituted
set of state boundaries, and how fast. Lustick's model, furthermore, does not just
explore a single pattern of identities that might emerge but identifies a range of
counterfactual futures and attaches probabilities to them. These models, thus,
make it possible to make concrete predictions about the nature and distribution
of newly activated ethnic identities in the wake of partition—and to separate
"malign" forms of identity evolution likely to destabilize the boundaries of the
state from within which they emerge from more benign ones.

10. New Questions, New Approaches

In the symposium that motivated this book, Ian Lustick wrote:

> Overwhelmingly, and now even deadeningly, scholars working on prob-
> lems of individual and collective identity have sought to demonstrate
> that the assumptions of the constructivist program, or paradigm, hold,
> and that those who have held or still hold primordialist or essentialist
> expectations and assumptions are wrong, usually laughably wrong. But
> the constructivist research program that has established these assump-
> tions as nearly hegemonic within a large scholarly community has been
> in a slump. It has been too satisfied with its ability to discredit primor-
> dialist approaches, and not sufficiently committed to answering ques-
> tions that primordialists could not ask. (Lustick 2001, 23)

The fortified constructivist arguments made in this book go a long way to bring
us out of this slump. Each one, as we have already seen, raises questions primordialists could not ask, and provides a framework within which to answer them.
The book identifies such questions throughout, in the text or footnotes in each
chapter. Here, I go beyond the particular problems addressed in these chapters
and identify three broad new research agendas opened up by conceptual framework introduced in this book and its combinatorial translation.

One new field of study lies in modeling the interactive relationship between different components of ethnic identity. As long as we think of "ethnicity" as one big broad
concept, as both primordialist and previous constructivist approaches have done, the
questions we can ask about it are typically questions about some external variables
that cause ethnic identity change, and some external variables that change in ethnic
identity affects. Since we cannot ask questions about concepts we do not recognize,
we cannot ask questions about the ways in which change in one component of ethnic
identity can itself cause, or be caused by, changes in others. But if we think of "ethnicity" as an umbrella term for a number of distinct concepts, then it becomes possible
to ask questions about the interdependence between these concepts.

A sample of these questions includes: How does the activation of some ethnic categories affect the underlying distribution of attributes for a population?
To what extent do the ethnic categories we are assigned affect the ethnic identity
categories we can choose for ourselves? Under what conditions are membership
rules standardized—and under what conditions do different membership rules
proliferate? Does the behavior of members of activated categories that are stable
over time or across generations differ from the behavior of members of unstable activated categories? Do individuals with certain attribute-repertoires (e.g.,
repertoires with highly visible attributes) have greater constraints on change in
activated categories than others? What is the relationship between the number

of attribute-dimensions in a population's repertoire and the speed of frequency of change in activated ethnic categories? And so on.

A second area in which this framework may be especially useful in stimulating new research is *the study of elections*. Since Hotelling and Downs, the study of elections has revolved around a spatial representation of "issue-dimensions." This representation has often been unable to incorporate electoral politics based on identities, in which the competition is often over how politicians and voters define the identity categories to which they belong rather than their issue-positions.

The combinatorial representation here is an especially productive way of modeling the manipulation of identities in competitive politics. The simplest approach to modeling such manipulation is to think of attribute-dimensions not as issue dimensions in a continuous space but as discrete partitions in a combinatorial space. Voters here can be represented as a set of attributes instead of preferences. Parties seek to win votes not by defining a correct issue position but by creating coalitions with the right combination of attributes. A more complex approach would be to represent voters and parties as having both a set of attributes and a set of policy preferences and modeling how both are taken into account in electoral choices.

Some questions about the politics of ethnic identities, modeled in this way, and the electoral politics include: Is there a relationship between size and the electoral activation of ethnic identity categories? What restrictions are political entrepreneurs likely to employ in their strategies? Under what conditions might they float expansive rather than restrictive coalitions? Under what conditions might politicians and voters emphasize the primordial aspects of their identity categories, and under what conditions might they want to emphasize its constructed aspects instead? What is the level of complexity in identity construction that voters are able to incorporate in their decisions? Under what conditions might voters activate ethnic categories mutually exclusive rather than overlapping categories? (Mutually exclusive categories may be more likely to be associated with conflict than overlapping categories on the grounds that their members have less in common—or they may be less likely to be associated with conflict on the grounds that there is less to fight over.) Under what conditions do the categories voters and politicians activate converge around a single attribute-dimension? What is the number of attribute-dimensions (dimensions) activated in electoral competition? What are the consequences of having few or many attribute-dimensions activated in electoral politics (or some aspect of politics)? Do we see cycling in dimensions in politics (i.e., the same dimensions become activated on a recurrent basis), or do parties keep moving to new dimensions? Do dimensions appear to get used up as they are activated—or does the activation of some dimensions give them more staying power?

A third area in which this framework generates new questions, and new ways of formulating old questions, is in the study of *ethnicity and genetics*. The relationship between social science approaches to ethnic identity and genetics—and in particular, constructivist approaches to ethnicity and genetics—is a fraught one. Research on ethnic identity in genetics has proceeded largely independently of work on constructivism. Indeed, it has proceeded without reference to conceptual arguments in the social sciences about what "groups" and "ethnic groups" are. To many social scientists in the constructivist camp, on the other hand, the idea of research on the genetic features that distinguish ethnic identities smacks of primordialism.

The conceptualization of an ethnic identity proposed here suggests ways of thinking about the relationship between ethnicity and genetics without assuming at all that there is a primordialist basis to ethnic identity. If all ethnic identities have some combination of descent-based attributes in common, then they must have some combination of genetic material in common. But to the extent that the rules of classification that define ethnic identity categories are not objectively given but constructed by human actions, the combination of genetic materials shared by members of an ethnic identity category should be seen as the genetic *correlate* of the subjectively produced rule of classification, not as an objective *basis* for that identity. Further, the existence of such a genetic correlate also does not mean that we have a single "objective" ethnic identity—*all* of the categories in our nominal repertoire of ethnic identities should have *some* genetic material in common. Consequently, finding a genetic correlate for a particular ethnic identity does not rule out the existence of many other such correlates for many other ethnic identities. Finally, because membership rules for ethnic categories vary in which descent-based attributes they require for membership and how many, the genetic material correlated with particular ethnic categories may vary in its nature and its thickness.

A host of new and interesting questions about the relationship between ethnicity and genetics from a constructivist perspective can be generated from this conceptualization. We might ask, for instance, *which genetic features, if any, are shared by members of any given ethnic identity category?* Much of existing research on genetics and ethnicity is devoted to investigating whether there is genetic evidence for a common ancestor shared by members of some given ethnic category. But a common ancestor is only one of the descent-based attributes that can distinguish ethnic groups, and it does not distinguish very many at that (see Chapter 2). Rather than restricting research only to probing for a common ancestor, it may be more illuminating to probe for a variety of genetic features associated with individual ethnic categories. Neither this question nor others discussed here, it is worth pointing out, assume or require individuals to have a single "objective" ethnic identity—rather, they investigate the variation in the genetic material associated with multiple, subjectively determined ethnic memberships within and across populations.

We might also ask *which categories exhibit more shared genetic material than others—and why*. If ethnic categories are disproportionately descent-based compared to non-ethnic categories, then members of ethnic categories should be more likely, on average, to have shared genetic material than members of non-ethnic categories. This can be treated as a testable hypothesis. Furthermore, we might hypothesize that stable ethnic categories are likely to have a thicker genetic content than others—according to this logic, when ethnic categories are stable over time, members may be more likely to mate with each other than outsiders, thus producing more shared genetic content. Alternatively, shared genetic material may itself become a factor producing stability in constructed ethnic categorizations over time.

We may also wish to explore the relationship between human behavior and the genetic features of ethnic identities. Are *individuals more likely, for instance, to activate categories from their nominal set which have thicker rather than thinner genetic content? Is violence more likely to occur, for instance, across categories that have fewer genetic attributes in common than others?* Hypotheses in response to this question are various: We might expect, for instance, individuals to be less likely to harm those who are genetically proximate than those who are genetically distant. Conversely, genetic distance may produce more anxieties about the cohesiveness of group memberships—and therefore lead to more rather than less interethnic violence. In all these cases, the discovery of a correlation between genetics and ethnic membership, or between genetics and behavior, does not preclude a role for human action—nor does it suggest that genetic features *determine* those actions. Rather, it suggests ways of exploring how the two interact, and how these interactions may vary across ethnic categories within and across populations.

11. Chapter Outline

The chapters in Part 1 proceed cumulatively, each one building on previous ones. Chapter 2 introduces the definition of an ethnic identity employed in this book and defends it against the alternatives. Chapter 3 introduces the distinction between attribute and category and derives from it the properties of "constrained change" and "visibility" that drive the theoretical arguments in this book. Chapter 4 builds on the concepts introduced in the preceding chapters to synthesize constructivist arguments into a set of mechanisms by which ethnic identities change. Chapter 5 then translates these mechanisms into a combinatorial vocabulary.

The chapters in Part 2 use the foundation created in Part 1 to propose theories of ethnicity, politics, and economics. Chapter 6 proposes a general baseline model of electoral politics and change in an activated ethnic demography.

Chapter 7 proposes a model of dynamics of an ethnic demography over time. Chapter 8 examines the link between change in an ethnic demography and electoral volatility. Chapter 9 theorizes about the link between the stickiness of attributes in an ethnic demography and pork politics. Chapter 10 proposes a theory of change in an ethnic demography and ethnic riots. Chapter 11 theorizes about the relationship between state collapse and change in an ethnic demography. And Chapter 12 examines the mutually constitutive relationship between patterns of ethnic identity change and "secession of the center." These chapters all refer to concepts introduced in Part 1, and several to the Chandra-Boulet model introduced in Chapter 6, but they are written independently of each other and can be read accordingly.

PART ONE

CONCEPTS

2

What Is Ethnic Identity?

A Minimalist Definition

KANCHAN CHANDRA

Over the last two decades, comparative political scientists have come to agree that ethnic identities include *some* identity categories associated with one or more of the following types: religion, sect, language, dialect, tribe, clan, race, physical differences, nationality, region, and caste. But we do not have a definition that captures our classification. Many of us who theorize about the effect of ethnic identity, therefore, proceed without a definition. Those definitions that have been proposed do not match the classifications employed by their own authors (Horowitz 1985, Fearon 2003, Chandra 2004).[1]

This chapter proposes a definition that captures the conventional classification of ethnic identities to a greater degree than the alternatives. Ethnic identities, according to this definition, are a *subset of categories in which descent-based attributes are necessary for membership*. All categories based on descent-based attributes, according to this definition, are not ethnic identity categories. But *all* ethnic identities require *some* descent-based attributes for membership. *Nominal* ethnic identities are those ethnic identity categories in which an individual is eligible for membership based on the attributes she possesses. *Activated* ethnic identities are those ethnic categories in which she professes membership, or to which she is assigned by others as a member.

---

[1] Horowitz, for instance, counts Hindus and Muslims in India, Christians and Muslims in Lebanon, and Creoles and Indians in Guyana and Trinidad as ethnic categories even though they do not possess his primary defining characteristic of a myth of common ancestry (Horowitz 1985). Fearon counts "Hindi speakers" as an ethnic group even though individuals who either speak Hindi or have Hindi as their mother tongue do not meet his definitional criterion of having a distinct history as a group or a shared culture valued by the majority of members (Fearon 2003). And Chandra often counts categories based on region as ethnic, even though it is not clear whether these groups meet her definition of ethnic groups as "ascriptive" groups (Chandra 2004, 2005).

Virtually all social science definitions of ethnic identity emphasize the role of descent in some way. Other specifications of the role of descent include (1) a common ancestry; (2) a myth of common ancestry; (3) a common place of origin; (4) a myth of a common place of origin; and (5) a "group" descent rule for membership. Further, they combine descent with one or more of the following characteristics: (6) a common culture or, at a minimum, shared cultural markers; (7) a common language; (8) a common history; (9) a common territory; or (10) conceptual autonomy. But these previous definitions do not capture the standard classification of ethnic identities to the same degree as the one proposed here does.

The innovation in this definition lies in its precise specification of the role of descent—introduced in the distinction between categories and attributes—and in its minimalism. Previous work does not distinguish systematically between descent-based *attributes* and descent-based *categories*, but this distinction is crucial. Ethnic identities are defined by what I will term here the "attribute-descent rule" for membership, as distinct from "group-based" rules or "cultural" membership rules. Ethnic identities, furthermore, are defined *only* by an attribute-based membership rule and not by other features such as a common culture or language or history or territory. These features are best understood as variables that sometimes characterize ethnic identities defined by other means, not as the constants that define them.

Why do we need a definition of ethnic identity if we are approaching a consensus on classification? Because we cannot make reasonable causal claims about the effect of ethnic identity without first defining the concept. By a "reasonable" claim, I mean a claim that gives us some reason to believe that the properties it attributes to ethnic identity are associated uniquely or disproportionately with it. Otherwise, we have no reason to think about it as a claim about the effect of *ethnic* identity at all, rather than as a claim about the effect of any identity, ethnic or otherwise. "Reasonableness" is different from and prior to the question of empirical verification. It refers to presumption rather than proof. Many reasonable claims can turn out to be wrong when subjected to verification. Others may not be verifiable given existing data and methods. But there is little to be gained by setting out to prove or disprove a claim that we have no good reason to believe in the first place.

The reasonableness of causal claims about ethnicity, in turn, depends upon a definition of the term. Every causal claim takes the following form: Ethnic groups are distinguished by property X (such as a common history or a common culture or a common territory, and so on). Property X produces outcome Y (such as patronage or civil war or riots and so on). Therefore, ethnicity produces outcome Y. A definition provides the basis for gauging whether this claim is reasonable by providing a basis for gauging whether some property X (whatever it might be) can be attributed to ethnic identity. We cannot, in other words, talk about what ethnicity *does* unless we first address the question of what ethnic identity *is*.

To illustrate, consider an example from a different field. Suppose I claim that democracy causes economic development by virtue of its ability to provide secure property rights. A commonly accepted definition of democratic government is "government by rule of law." Rule of law implies secure property rights. Consequently, this claim seems on the face of it to be reasonable, although it may well turn out to be false upon verification. Now suppose I claim that democracy causes economic development by virtue of providing territorially based government. There is nothing in the range of definitions of this concept that indicates that the property of territorially based government is uniquely or disproportionately related to democracy. This property appears to be a feature of all modern states. Consequently, this claim is prima facie unreasonable.

Why do we need a definition that captures the previous classifications employed by comparative political scientists, rather than one based on some objective criteria or one that captures the usage of other epistemic or lay communities? So that we can build knowledge about ethnic identity within comparative political science in a cumulative fashion. A self-standing claim about ethnic identity is simply the claim that "Ethnic identity is associated with Y." A cumulative proposition, by contrast, is the claim that "*Consistent with or contrary to previous research*, ethnic identity is associated with Y." For self-standing propositions, one can simply stipulate a definition—"By the term ethnic identity, I mean A"—regardless of its relationship to previous work. But a proposition that builds on or rebuilds the foundation of previous research must either use the term "ethnic identity" in the same way or, when there is a departure, specify the relation between past and present usage. In order to theorize about the effect of ethnic identity in a cumulative fashion, in other words, we must evaluate the previous body of work in comparative political science that argues that ethnicity "matters," retain the insights that survive an evaluation, and discard those that do not. And, in order to evaluate whether and how ethnicity matters in the way these works propose, we need a definition that tells us what the properties of ethnic identities, *as classified by this body of work*, are.

I argue, based on the definition this chapter proposes and the evaluation of the alternatives, that most of our previous causal claims about the effect of ethnic identity are not reasonable *even when evaluated on their own terms*. They associate ethnic identities with properties that cannot be associated with them by definition—at least, with ethnic identities as we classify them. These properties are of three types: (1) the properties identified by definitions that do not capture our classifications; (2) two properties—"fixedness" and "exogeneity"— that contradict the definition that does capture this classification; and (3) several additional properties that are neither associated with ethnic identities in any definition nor justified by a cursory look at the data: networks, norms, and institutions. In the next chapter, I derive two properties—"constrained change" and "visibility"—based on the definition proposed here that might serve as the basis of more reasonable causal claims.

How does this definition, and the properties that are associated with it, apply to classifications of "ethnic" identities in other disciplines or in everyday usage (Fearon and Laitin 2000a)? These other classifications are often narrower than the one employed in comparative politics. Sociologists and philosophers who study the United States, for instance, typically reserve the term "ethnic" for groups defined on the basis of national origin, and less often for groups defined on the basis of race or religion. It is common in this literature to refer to ethnicity *or* race, ethnicity *or* religion, and ethnicity *or* nationality, rather than treating race, religion, and nationality as subsets of the larger category of ethnicity (e.g., Appiah and Gutmann 1996, Waters 1999, Nobles 2000). Everyday usage of the term "ethnic," restricted to those countries in which significant sections of the population speak English or a proximate language, is often also narrower. In everyday usage in Sri Lanka, for instance, the term "ethnic" in English-language conversation refers to identities based on a combination of language and race, but not religion. In English-language conversation in India, it refers to identities based on a combination of language, territory, and sometimes tribe, but not to identities based on caste, religion, or race. And in many cases, references to the word "ethnic"—as in "ethnic" cuisine or "ethnic" fashions"—equate the word either with minorities or with "traditional" culture.

But while the comparative politics convention does not always coincide with classifications of ethnic identities in other communities, it usually encompasses them: All identities classified as ethnic in comparative politics may not be classified as ethnic in other communities, but all identities classified as "ethnic" in these other communities are usually classified as ethnic by comparative political scientists. Consequently, the properties this definition associates with ethnic identities taken together should apply to these identities considered separately. Further, even when the term "ethnic identity" is seen as something that is distinct from race or caste or religion-based identities, it is typically grouped together with these identities as belonging to the same family. In the United States, for example, it is common to talk of "ethnic and racial" identities in the same breath, just as in India it is common to talk of identities based on territory, language, tribe, religion, and caste in the same breath. So a definition that tells us what identities that belong to all of these types have in common should also be useful in evaluating claims about identities classified as ethnic in other communities.

Section 1 of this chapter identifies the properties associated with "ethnicity" by a sample of causal claims in the field of comparative politics and economics. Section 2 outlines the definition proposed here and its relationship to our classification of ethnic identities. Section 3 distinguishes between "ethnic groups" and "nations." Section 4 justifies this definition by evaluating it against a sample of identities that we classify as ethnic in comparative politics. Section 5 compares this definition to the alternatives. Section 6 evaluates these alternative definitions against the same sample of identities. Section 7 uses this evaluation to identify properties that cannot reasonably be associated with ethnic identity. Section 8 uses the properties identified and eliminated to evaluate some of our causal claims about ethnic identity.

Throughout, I use the term ethnic "group" or ethnic "identity" loosely to mean either a cluster of individuals with a common purpose or a cluster of individuals who share only a descriptive label. Both meanings are associated with the word "group" by the Oxford English dictionary and this ambiguity has led to consequential errors in our theorizing (Brubaker 2004, 8–10). Where a precise interpretation of the term "group" is consequential, I address the ambiguity explicitly. But in general, in order to evaluate other work on its own terms, I am also forced in this chapter to use words this previous work employs on its own terms, with the ambiguities intact. In the chapters that follow, I drop the term "group" altogether and employ a more precise distinction between "nominal" and "activated" categories of membership.

1. Properties Assumed by Causal Claims About Ethnic Identity

Table 2.1 summarizes the properties that some of our causal claims ascribe to ethnic identities. This survey of claims is not meant to be exhaustive. I have chosen a handful of examples for illustration.

Consider, first, the claims linking some concept related to ethnic identity with some form of violence.

- According to one such argument, one cause of civil war between ethnic groups is the "security dilemma" introduced by the collapse of the state (Posen

Table 2.1 **Properties Attributed to Ethnic Identity in Our Causal Claims**

Claims	Property Associated with Ethnic Categories
Causal claims linking some concept related to ethnic identity with violence	Fixedness, Common History, Distinct Emotional Responses, Dense Social Networks
Causal claims linking some concept related to ethnic identity with patronage politics	Territorial Concentration, High Cost of Change, Visibility, Networks, Norms, Institutions
Causal claims linking some concept related to ethnic identity with the destabilization of regimes and/or states	Division of Labor, Territorial Concentration, Fixedness

1993). The reasoning underlying this argument is as follows: The collapse of the state governing a multi-ethnic society creates an environment analogous to anarchy in the international environment, with ethnic groups analogous to states. In an anarchic environment, ethnic groups, like states, arm themselves out of fear for their own security. But this makes other groups, like states, more fearful and gives them an incentive to arm themselves also. The result is an increased threat of war, reducing everyone's security in the long run. War is especially likely when the groups in question have a history of rivalry, since this gives each more reason to assume the worst of the other.

- This argument assumes, implicitly, that ethnic identity categories have two properties. First, that, like states, they are fixed entities—for if individuals could change their ethnic identities, then one response to the collapse of the state might be simply to switch to less threatening identities rather than go to war. Second, it implies that ethnic groups are more likely than other types of groups to have a common history. Otherwise, the security dilemma should be an explanation for inter-group conflict in the wake of state collapse in general, rather than ethnic conflict in particular.

- According to a second argument, ethnic violence is motivated by emotions such as fear, hatred, or resentment (Petersen 2002). The initial trigger for such violence, according to this argument, lies also in the collapse of the state. But the target of violence depends upon the specific emotional response aroused among ethnic groups. Groups motivated by fear will choose as their target those ethnic others who are the greatest threat. Groups motivated by resentment will choose as their target those ethnic others who are farthest up the status hierarchy whether or not they are the greatest threat. And groups motivated by hatred will target those ethnic others with whom they have battled in the past, regardless of their threat potential and their position on the status hierarchy. If this argument is to be read, as it is intended, as an argument about *ethnic* violence specifically rather than violence in general, then ethnic groups must have the property of experiencing stronger, or distinct, emotional reactions in the wake of state collapse than other types of groups.

- A third argument attributes the higher frequency of *inter*-ethnic violence in comparison to *intra*-ethnic violence to the assumed property of network ties. The existence of such ties, according to this argument, makes within-group cooperation easier than across-group cooperation (Fearon and Laitin 1996, 730).

Consider now the family of arguments which posits a causal association between some concept related to ethnic identity and patronage politics:

- The reasoning underlying one such argument goes as follows: The goods of modernity are distributed on a spatial basis. It makes sense for individuals desiring access to these goods, therefore, also to organize on a spatial basis. Ethnic groups are territorially concentrated. The struggle for access to these goods, therefore, is organized on a spatial basis. This argument explicitly assumes that ethnic groups have the property of territorial concentration: in the words of one of its principal proponents, "there is no denying that the members of an ethnic group tend to cluster in space; nor can it be questioned but that colonial policy made every attempt to assign ethnic groups to stable and rigidly defined areas" (Bates 1974, 464).

- A second such argument follows a different logic (Fearon 1999, Caselli and Coleman 2001). Patronage politics, according to this argument, requires exclusive coalitions in which entry of new members is costly. Ethnic identities are costly to change and therefore are one basis on which exclusive coalitions can be built. Consequently, patronage politics leads individuals to activate ethnic identities. The property this argument turns on is the relatively higher cost associated with changing ethnic rather than non-ethnic identities.

- Yet another argument highlights the property of visibility (Chandra 2004). Patronage politics, according to this argument, takes place under severe information constraints. The identities most likely to be activated by patronage politics, therefore, are those that are most visible in a limited information environment. Ethnic identities are more visible than other types of identities. Consequently, patronage politics activates ethnic identities. The property this argument turns on is the supposed visibility of ethnic identities.

- A fourth argument explicitly designed to distinguish empirically between different mechanisms that might link ethnicity with co-ethnic favoritism in the distribution of public goods—which we can think of as patronage—assumes the properties of norms, networks, and institutions (Habyarimana et al. 2007). The mechanisms which lead individuals to favor co-ethnics in the distribution of public goods, according to this argument, are based on technology: Co-ethnics are more able to locate and sanction each other than non-ethnics. The ability to locate co-ethnics, the authors argue, is a consequence of network or institutional ties that supposedly bind co-ethnics, while the willingness to sanction co-ethnics is a product of a shared normative framework.

Consider a third family of examples, which links the politicization of ethnic divisions with the destabilization of states or regimes.

- The reasoning underlying one argument linking ethnic identities with the destabilization of states goes as follows: Ethnic groups are "'incipient nations" with a territory and a division of labor, which makes them candidates for creating new nations and states. But classes and economic groups are economically specialized and not associated with territory. Consequently, "economic or class disaffection threatens revolution, but disaffection based on ethnic identities threatens partition, irredentisim, or merger, a redrawing of the very limits of the state" (Geertz 1973, 261). This argument assumes, explicitly, that two properties of ethnic groups are a common territory and functional differentiation. Otherwise, the threat posed by ethnic groups would be no different from the threat posed by class and other economic groups.

- The reasoning underlying another argument, which links ethnic divisions with the destabilization of democracies specifically, goes as follows: Democracies are destabilized by the permanent exclusion of some minority groups from power. Ethnic divisions are fixed. Elections based on ethnic divisions, therefore, produce permanent winners and permanent losers based on ethnic demography. Consequently, the politicization of ethnic divisions threatens democratic stability (Rabushka and Shepsle 1972, Horowitz 1985). The key property of ethnic identity that this argument rests on is fixedness: If ethnic identities are fluid, not fixed, then the other propositions fall through (Chandra 2001a, 2005).

- According to another argument in this family, the introduction of democracy in multi-ethnic societies is likely to lead to conflict for the following reason: Because it is based on the popular vote, democracy empowers economically excluded ethnic majority groups against "market-dominant" minorities, who control a disproportionate share of economic resources (Chua 2003). The conflict between these two groups with opposing interests produces instability, authoritarian backlash, and violence. For this argument to apply to democracy in *multi-ethnic* societies specifically rather than democracy more generally, there must be some property specific to ethnic identities that brings about this conflict. Unequal distribution of economic resources across social groups is a pervasive fact throughout the democratic world, but not all groups are believed to threaten democracy for this reason. The property that Chua's argument implicitly relies on is *fixedness* of both identity and wealth—it is only when individuals from poor ethnic categories cannot move, individually or collectively, to richer ones, that we should see the predicted outcome.

2. What Is an Ethnic Identity?

Ethnic identities, I propose here, are a subset of *categories* in which descent-based *attributes* are necessary to determine eligibility for membership. *Nominal* ethnic identities are those ethnic identity categories in which an individual is eligible for membership based on the attributes she possesses. *Activated* ethnic identities are those ethnic categories in which she professes membership, or to which she is assigned by others as a member. All individuals have a "repertoire" of nominal ethnic identity categories. This consists of all the meaningful membership rules which can be fashioned from an individual's given set of descent-based attributes, with each rule corresponding to a nominal category. The ethnic identity an individual actually activates or to which she is assigned is chosen from this repertoire.

I use this precisely defined distinction between "nominal" and "activated" categories throughout this book and avoid similar sounding distinctions between "latent" and "salient" ethnic identities, "dormant" and "mobilized identities," and "commonsensically real" and "politically relevant" identities. These other distinctions are not always precisely defined. The terms "salient" or "mobilized" or "politically relevant" identities, for instance, are often taken to mean not only shared membership but the sharing of some content, such as common preferences or culture or symbols. But as I use it here, "activating" an ethnic category simply requires an individual to claim membership in it or to be assigned such membership—it does not require her to subscribe to its content, although she may also do that.

By *descent-based attributes*, I mean attributes associated with or believed to be associated with descent. By attributes "associated with descent" I mean attributes that are acquired through genetic inheritance (e.g., skin color, gender, hair type, eye color, height, and physical features), or through cultural and historical inheritance (e.g., the names, languages, places of birth, and origin of one's parents and ancestors), or in the course of one's lifetime as markers of such an inheritance (e.g., last name or tribal markings). By attributes "believed to be associated with descent," I mean attributes around which a credible myth of association with descent has been woven, whether or not such an association exists in fact.

By attributes that are *necessary* to determine eligibility for membership, I mean attributes without which an individual cannot be an eligible member. Consider, for instance the category "Jewish." According to a classic membership rule, "every child of a Jewish mother is automatically considered a Jew" (Gorenberg, March 2, 2008). Because this is a descent-based attribute and describes the religion of one's parents or ancestors, we can say that the category "Jewish" defined in this way is an ethnic category.

Note that according to this definition, descent-based attributes are *necessary*, but need not be *sufficient*, for membership. Compare, for instance, the categories of "Jewish" and "Jewish settler" in Israel. In the first case, a descent-based attribute—birth to a Jewish mother—is both necessary and sufficient for membership. In the second case, this descent-based attribute is necessary but not sufficient—this category also requires the non-descent-based attribute of having settled in the West Bank during one's lifetime. Although the two categories are different, both would be "ethnic" by this definition. Similarly, Hutus and Tutsis in colonial Rwanda would be ethnic categories according to this definition because physical attributes were typically necessary for membership but not sufficient (ownership of herds of cows also mattered) (Mamdani 2001, 49). By the same logic, "White" and "White working class" in the United States, "upper-caste" and "urban upper caste" in India, and Flemish and Flemish socialist in Belgium would all be termed "ethnic" by this definition.

There is an interesting variation among ethnic categories, however, in the extent to which their membership rules require descent-based attributes to be sufficient as well as necessary. In the United States, for instance, one descent-based attribute—descent from parents of African origin—is typically both necessary and sufficient to determine eligibility for membership in the category "Black." But descent is only necessary, not sufficient, for membership in the category "Native American." To be eligible for membership in the category "Native American," individuals must have descended from indigenous inhabitants of North or South America who still maintain community attachment (Yardley 2004). The first is a descent-based attribute. The second is not. The causes and consequences of this variation are subjects worthy of research in themselves. To the extent that membership rules in an ethnic category are constructed, we might well ask why some constructions require only descent-based attributes while others permit non-descent-based ones, and what the implications of mixing descent with non-descent-based attributes are. Here, however, it is sufficient to note simply that both are ethnic categories regardless of these differences.

By attributes that *determine* eligibility for membership I mean either those that are necessary to *qualify* an individual for membership in a category or those that *signal* such membership. Other sources (e.g., Horowitz 1971) draw a distinction between criteria and indicia of membership that may be useful for some analytical purposes. I do not employ it here because it is often difficult to draw in practice and inconsequential for the purposes of definition. Take the example of the category "Black," in the United States. One of the qualifying attributes for membership in the category "Black" is descent from parents of African origin. One of the attributes that signals membership in the category "Black" is dark skin, which conveys information about the origin of one's parents. But these signaling attributes are often taken to be qualifying attributes by individuals and observers alike. Similarly, although the qualifying attribute for membership in the category "Sinhala" in Sri Lanka is descent from parents of Sinhala origin, membership is often claimed and assigned on the basis of diacritica such as name and accent, provided that the name and accent can be credibly interpreted as markers of descent, rather than an actual accounting of ancestors (Daniel 1996, Sivananda 1997, 233–234).

The set of identity categories in which membership is determined by descent-based attributes is large. Ethnic identity categories are a subset of this larger set defined by the restrictions listed below or their equivalents. As with the rest of this definition, I identify these restrictions by working backwards from common usage: Taking categories that social scientists all agree are ethnic, I try to identify the implicit principles that separate them from descent-based categories that social scientists agree are not ethnic.

(1) They are large enough for membership to be impersonal. This restriction rules out categories such as "family," which, although descent-based, would not count as an ethnic category because its members are known and directly related to each other.

(2) They constitute a section of a country's population rather than the whole. This restriction captures our sense of an ethnic identity as a *part* of a whole rather than the whole itself. Thus, "German" would not be an ethnic category in a country that is 100% German, even if membership in the category German met the other defining conditions here. But "Bavarian" would be an ethnic category in Germany if it met the other defining conditions since Bavarians constitute a part of the larger German population—and "German" would be an ethnic category in the United States if it met the other defining conditions, since Germans constitute a part of the larger population in the United States.

(3) If one sibling is eligible for membership in a category at any given place, then all other siblings would also be eligible in that place. This restriction eliminates large numbers of categories, typically based on single attributes distributed arbitrarily across siblings, and retains others, typically based on complex combinations of attributes that characterize all siblings. Categories excluded by this restriction include "women" or "green-eyed people."

(4) The qualifying attributes for membership are restricted only to one's physical features or to the religion, sect, language, dialect, tribe, clan, race, nationality, region, and caste of one's parents and ancestors. I note elsewhere that only some of these attribute-dimensions are analytically distinguishable from each other (Chandra et al. 2006). And even when it is possible to distinguish between these types analytically, an individual attribute might fall across multiple types. But to the extent that an attribute falls within or across one or more dimensions in this family, the categories it constitutes would qualify as ethnic identity categories.

This restriction rules out identity categories such as "English-speaker" when knowledge of English is acquired in the course of one's lifetime, and "Scottish," when the membership rule for that category is "All those who live in Scotland" rather than "All those whose ancestors were born in Scotland." It also rules out a category such as "descendants of Communists" or "descendants of landowners" since the attributes that qualify an individual for membership in that category do not fall in the allowed list.

If some of these restrictions, especially the last, appear arbitrary, they are. Why impose a rule that requires siblings to be equally eligible for membership before a category can be called ethnic? Why allow this particular set of descent-based attributes and not others? I do not offer analytical justifications for these restrictions here, although such a reason may well be identified in the future. It is plausible, for instance, that members of categories that keep siblings together behave differently from those that keep siblings apart.[2] In the absence of such justifications, I do not think that there is so far a good reason to wall off ethnic identities from other types of descent-based identities. But my purpose here is simply to identify those restrictions that are necessary to approximate the conventional classification of ethnic identities. Once we have identified these features, we are in a position also to recognize their arbitrariness and discard them where necessary—or at least modify our interpretations to take such arbitrariness into account.

Let me illustrate this definition using the fictionalized example of Helen, imagined from a mélange of characters in Mary Waters's study of West Indian immigrants in New York (Waters 1999). Born in the English-speaking island of Trinidad to parents of African (Ghanaian) origin, she has dark skin, dark brown eyes, and straight hair. She moved to the United States after obtaining her high school diploma in Trinidad and works there as a food service employee, earning $25,000 a year. She belongs to, and votes for, the Democratic Party there. She married a Haitian man in New York, and learned to speak French, which is now her primary language of communication with her children and husband. Her brother Derek, who has lighter skin, light brown eyes, and otherwise similar features, remained behind in Trinidad. Their parents are well-educated professionals who belong to the People's National Movement (PNM) in Trinidad. They are Presbyterians, but Helen herself converted to Catholicism after meeting her husband.

According to the definition above, Helen's nominal ethnic identity categories include Black (in which the qualifying attribute, according to current norms, is descent from African parents, signaled by attributes such as the color of her skin and physical features) and West Indian (in which the qualifying attribute is descent from parents who lived in Trinidad, signaled by her accent among other attributes). Both these categories are determined by attributes associated, or believed to be associated, with descent, and both of which place Helen and Derek in the same categories. Her ethnic identity categories also include "African American" (in which membership is determined by the attribute of descent from African parents, skin color, and physical features, *in the* United States). Derek, because he stayed behind in Trinidad, cannot call himself "African American." But if he were to move to the United States, he would be eligible for membership in this category just like his sibling.

From these nominal ethnic identities, Helen may activate one or more. She may well begin to call herself "Black" in some contexts, rather than "West-Indian." The activation of this category may or may not be accompanied by an attempt

---

[2] For instance, Will Le Blanc, then a doctoral candidate in political science at MIT, hypothesizes that if individuals care more about the well-being of siblings than more distant connections, we may see a greater degree of within-group altruism among ethnic than non-ethnic categories.

to acquire characteristics that Helen believes are associated with its members. She may begin to dress differently, for instance, or celebrate American festivals in addition to, or in place of West-Indian festivals. But she may just as well make no changes in her way of life and thinking, or invent her own way of living that has nothing to do with imagined commonalities in the additional characteristics associated with Black identity.

An individual's non-ethnic identities, by inference, are all those identities outside the set of nominal ethnic identities. Some of these may also require descent-based attributes for membership. But most of the categories we usually recognize as non-ethnic are typically based on attributes acquired during one's lifetime. Thus, while ethnic and non-ethnic identities do not map directly on to the dichotomy between descent-based and non-descent-based identities, to the extent that all ethnic identities are associated with descent, while many non-ethnic identities are not, we can say that there is an imperfect correlation between descent and ethnicity.

Helen's nominal non-ethnic identity categories according to this definition, for example, include some identity categories also based on descent-based attributes such as "descendant of PNM supporters" (excluded because it is not based on either physical features or the language, religion, race, tribe, caste, sect, clan, dialect, nationality, and place of origin of her parents), "people with dark brown eyes" (excluded because, while it is based on her physical features, it excludes her sibling, Derek), and "female" (also excluded because it excludes Derek). They also include "Catholic" (determined by conversion, openly acknowledged, during her lifetime), "French-speaker," (determined by a language learned during her lifetime rather than her ancestral language), working class (determined by attributes acquired during her lifetime such as her high school diploma and her job as a food service worker), and Democrat (determined by her joining the Democratic party during her lifetime).

3. Ethnic "Groups" and "Nations"

I am concerned here mainly with distinguishing between ethnic and non-ethnic identities—not, as some of the conceptual literature in the field of ethnic politics has been, with distinguishing between ethnic identities and nations. The term "nation" is used within comparative politics to mean many things. Let me here simply indicate the relationship of the different uses of the term "nation" to the term "ethnic identity" as I define it here.

One way the term "nation" or "nationality" is used is to refer to a territorially concentrated subgroup within a larger political unity that is based on descent (e.g., the Kurdish "nation" in Iraq). When used in this way, the term "nation" or "nationality" is simply a subset of the term "ethnic identity" as defined here.

A second use of the term "nation" is as a territorially concentrated group of citizens with their own state. When used in this way, the relationship of the term to the concept of ethnic identity as defined here depends on how the membership criteria for citizens are defined. A nation in which citizenship is based on descent would qualify as a descent-based identity category. But this descent-based category would qualify as "ethnic" only if it described a sub-group of the population of a country but not the whole. A nation in which citizenship is based on civic criteria, such as the United States, would belong to the set of non-ethnic, non-descent-based identities (see Brubaker 1992 for the distinction between blood and birth-based citizenships. On the distinction between "ethnic" and "civic" nationalisms, see Gellner 1983 Verdery 1993, and Brubaker 1996).

4. Justification

In *Ethnic Groups in Conflict*, Donald Horowitz described "ethnicity" as an umbrella classification that "easily embraces groups differentiated by color, language, and religion; it covers 'tribes,' 'races,' 'nationalities,' and castes" (Horowitz 1985, 53). The body of work published in comparative politics has converged on Horowitz's classification, with some quibbles on the margin about whether "castes" should be excluded from the list and whether "clan" "sect" and "region" should be included. Caste is mostly included (e.g., Atlas Narodov Mira 1964, Varshney 2002 Chandra 2004, Htun 2004, Sambanis 2004, Wilkinson 2004, Posner 2005) with some exceptions (e.g., Fearon 2003). Clans are also included (e.g., the inclusion of Somali clans in Horowitz 1985, Alesina et al. 2003, Fearon 2003) with some exceptions (e.g., the explicit dis-cussion of clans as a subunit of ethnic groups rather than ethnic groups them-selves in Collins 2004 and Schatz 2004). "Sects" within larger religious families, although not explicitly named in Horowitz's list, are routinely included by some (e.g., the counting of "Sunnis" in Syria, "Copts" in Egypt, "Ahmadis" in Pakistan by Horowitz 1985, Alesina et al. 2003, Fearon 2003, and Minorities at Risk Database. And so are identities based on region, such as the Scots in the United Kingdom or Northerners and Southerners in the Sudan (e.g., Levi and Hechter 1985, Fearon 2003, Minorities at Risk Database). The broadest possible classification of ethnic identities followed by comparative political sci-entists, then, would comprise of identities belonging to the following types: identities based on color and other physical differences, language, dialect, reli-gion, sect, tribe, clan, race, nationality, caste and region.

These "types," as noted above, are often not themselves analytically distin-guishable from each other. But we typically classify an identity as "ethnic" as long as it is associated with any or all of these types. Consider some examples of identity categories acknowledged as ethnic by all or most of the most influential "counts" of ethnic categories within comparative politics: Horowitz (1985), and the three cross-national datasets on ethnic identities created since—Fearon (2003), Alesina et al. (2003), and Minorities at Risk Database. These counts place the identity "Black" in the United States (associated with color and race), "Serb" in Yugoslavia (associated with religion, language, nationality, and region), "Sunni" in Syria (associated with sectarian differences within Islam), "Yoruba" in Nigeria (associated with tribe, language and region), "Darood" in Somalia (associated with clan), "Tharu" in Nepal, or "Jat" or "Reddi" in India (both associated with caste, language, and region) in a single analytical family.

One indication of the disciplinary convergence lies in the several recently published texts which explicitly follow an umbrella classification similar to Horowitz's. For instance, Varshney (2002) cites Horowitz to group together conflicts based on race, language, religion, tribe, or caste as ethnic (Varshney 2002 4–5). Chandra (2004) uses the term "ethnic group" "to refer to identities based at least on race, language, caste, tribe, or religion" (Chandra 2004, 2). Htun (2004), similarly, uses the term "ethnicity" as an all-encompassing term referring to "social groups differentiated by kinship, tribe, skin color, religion, caste, language, race and other markers of communal identity" (Htun 2004, 453 n.1). Posner (2005) similarly uses the term "ethnic" interchangeably for identities based on race, language, region, religion, tribe, caste, and country of origin.

A second and more important indication lies in the four principal cross-national datasets on ethnic groups that constitute the foundation for cross-national empirical studies of the effect of ethnic identity in comparative political science and economics—the Atlas Narodov Mira 1964), a dataset on ethnic groups in 190 countries published by Alesina (Alesina et al. 2003), a comparable count of ethnic groups in 160 countries published by James Fearon in the same year (Fearon 2003), and the Minorities at Risk (MAR) project. Each of these four datasets also employs this umbrella classification, classifying identity categories based on color, language, religion, nationality, tribe, caste, clan, race, sect, and region as ethnic across countries.

Finally, a third body of works, while not explicitly proposing a classification of ethnic identities, shares in this convergence implicitly, by situating themselves in a literature that does. Even though Yashar's (2005) study of indigenous politics in Latin America, for instance, does not explicitly propose a classification of "ethnic" identities, it describes indigenous politics as one manifestation of a broader class of "ethnic" politics as defined by Horowitz and Varshney, among others. Van Cott (2005) does the same, situating a study of indigenous parties in Latin America within a broader literature on ethnic parties indebted most to Horowitz. Similarly, Wilkinson (2004) studies violence between religious categories within India as an instance of the broader phenomenon of "ethnic" violence, where the term "ethnic" is cited as being consistent with Horowitz (1985), and uses this study to draw inferences about conflict between racially based categories in Malaysia and nationality-based categories in Romania.

In order to evaluate the match between the definition proposed here and this conventional classification, I start with a sample of sets of categories that most comparative political scientists agree to classify as "ethnic"—that is, categories that are classified as "ethnic" by at least three of the five principal comparative sources on ethnic groups: Atlas Narodov Mira 1964, Horowitz 1971, 1985, Alesina et al. 2003, Fearon 2003, the Minorities at Risk Database, and, by implication, the body of work that draws on these sources. This sample includes:

(Black and White) in the United States;
(Serb and Croat) in the former Yugoslavia;
(Mohajir, Punjabi, Pathan, and Baluch) in Pakistan;
(Flemish and Walloon) in Belgium;
(Aymara and Quechua) in Bolivia;
(Yoruba, Ibo, Hausa, and Fulani) in Nigeria; and
(Zulu, Xhosa, and Coloured) in South Africa

Chosen from across continents—North America, Eastern Europe, Western Europe, Asia, Latin America, and Africa—these categories are also widely representative. If we can find a definition that covers all the identities contained in this sample, we can have some confidence that it does not refer to a specific geographic area and should cover the identities contained in the population of "ethnic" identities. Conversely, if a definition does not cover even the identities contained in this sample, on which there is general agreement, then we can be confident that it will not cover other identities contained in the population of "ethnic" identities.

I then ask three questions of each category in the sample: (1) Do descent-based membership rules (subject to the restrictions above) distinguish categories in the same set from each other? (2) Do descent-based membership rules (subject to the restrictions above) distinguish ethnic categories from those that we classify as non-ethnic? (3) Is a descent-based membership rule (subject to the restrictions above) a *defining* characteristic? That is, can it constitute the group or does it simply describe a group that is constituted on some other basis?

I infer the membership rules from descriptions of the groups in the Encyclopedia Britannica and supplement these descriptions with additional sources where cited. Membership criteria are always socially constructed—and there can often be multiple and contested criteria over time. There may well be additional descent-based or non-descent-based attributes required for membership that I do not identify here—and those that I do identify may well fluctuate in their relative importance over time. Rather than defend the substance of any particular membership rule, therefore, I probe only for whether it is reasonable to infer, from the description of the group, that *some* descent-based attributes (subject to the restrictions above) are necessary for membership in these categories, and that different combinations of descent-based attributes (subject to the restrictions above) are necessary for membership in different categories.

In the United States, commonly accepted criteria for membership in the category "Black" require the attribute of descent from even a single ancestor who migrated to the United States from territories in present-day Africa (the so-called one-drop rule), and/or the possession of certain physical features such as dark skin and hair, which may be qualifying criteria in themselves, or simply signals that indicate the presence of the earlier, qualifying criterion (Nobles 2000). Membership criteria for the category "White" by contrast require that all an individual's ancestors have migrated from territories in present-day Europe and/or the possession of some combination of physical features including light skin and hair. Although these criteria do not parallel present-day census criteria, they reflect the weight of previous census and legal classifications.

In the former Yugoslavia, the attribute of descent from one of a number of Slavic tribes that settled in an area inland of the Dalmatian coast and were associated with a state established in 850 A.D. is necessary to be called a Serb. To be called a Croat, in turn, it is necessary to possess the attribute of descent from other Slavic tribes that settled in an adjacent region in northern Dalmatia and were associated with a state established by Tomislav in 950 A.D. These membership rules can also be equivalently expressed through some combination of descent-based attributes including name, physical features, and ancestral language (Cyrillic script for Serbs and Latin script for Croats) and religion (Eastern Christianity for Serbs and Western Christianity for Croats).

In present-day Pakistan, to be eligible for membership in the category "Mohajir," one must have been born in present-day India or be descended from ancestors born in present-day India. This rule can be equivalently expressed using some combination of name, physical features, or ancestral association with Urdu, all of which signal such descent. To be eligible for membership in the category "Pathan," one must possess the attribute of descent from one of a group of tribes that migrated to parts of present-day Pakistan and Afghanistan between the thirteenth and sixteenth centuries. This rule can be equivalently expressed using some combination of name, physical features, or an ancestral association with one of several dialects associated with these tribes, given the common label of Pashto, all of which signal such descent. To be eligible for membership in the category "Baluchi," one must possess the attribute of descent from one of a number of tribes that migrated into present-day Pakistan, Iran, Afghanistan, and Punjab from an original homeland on the Iranian plateau. This rule can be equivalently expressed using some combination of name, physical features, or an ancestral association with the range of dialects given the common label of "Baluchi," all of which signal such descent. And, finally, to be eligible for membership in the category "Punjabi," one must possess the attribute of descent from those who inhabited the territory of undivided Punjab, on either side of the national border, for some unspecified number of generations. This rule can be equivalently expressed using some combination of name, physical features, or ancestral association with the number of dialects spoken in this region, grouped under the common label of "Punjabi," all of which signal such descent.

In twentieth-century Belgium, to be eligible for membership in the category Flemish (Walloon) in Belgium, it is necessary to possess the attribute of descent ancestors who inhabited the northern (southern) region of Belgium or spoke one of the dialects associated with Flemish (Walloon) for some unspecified number of generations before the twentieth century (Zolberg 1974). This membership rule can be equivalently expressed through attributes that signal such descent, including name, physical features, and so on.

In Bolivia, in order to be eligible for membership in the category "Aymara" in the present, it is necessary to possess the attribute of descent from ancestors from some set of tribes who inhabited the northern and central Altiplano from at least the fifteenth century. In order to be eligible for membership in the category "Quechua" in the present, it is necessary to possess the attribute of descent from ancestors from some set of tribes who inhabited the southern part of the Altiplano from at least the fifteenth century. Both rules may be equivalently expressed as combinations of attributes that signal such descent, including name, physical features, and an ancestral association with languages or dialects spoken by the tribes labeled "Aymara" or "Quechua."

In Nigeria, to be eligible for membership in the category Yoruba it is necessary to have the attribute of descent from the inhabitants of a number of city states in southwestern Nigeria, speaking related languages, who came to be associated with the common label of Yoruba in the mid-nineteenth century (Young 1976, Laitin 1986). To be eligible for membership in the category "Ibo" it is necessary to have the attribute of descent from a collection of lineage-based groups that settled in eastern Nigeria and spoke related languages and came to acquire the common label Ibo somewhere between the slave trade and the mid-twentieth century (see also Young 1976). The term "Hausa" refers to the inhabitants of a series of city-states in northern Nigeria which came to acquire the common label "Hausa" sometime during or before the nineteenth century. The term "Fulani" refers to nomadic groups dispersed throughout West Africa, some of which conquered the Hausa city-states in the nineteenth century and settled in them as a ruling class, intermarrying with and adopting the dialects of local inhabitants. The category Hausa-Fulani came about in the twentieth century as an amalgam of the categories Hausa and Fulani. To be eligible for membership in the category "Hausa-Fulani," it is necessary to have the attribute of descent from ancestors who either owned the label Hausa or the label Fulani or both. These membership rules may be equivalently expressed as combinations of attributes that signal such descent, including name, physical features, and an ancestral association with languages or dialects labeled as "Yoruba," "Ibo," or "Hausa."

Finally, in South Africa, to be eligible for membership in the category "Zulu" it is necessary to possess the attribute of descent from a collection of clans associated with the nineteenth-century kingdom led by Shaka, who spoke related dialects that came to be grouped under the common label of a Zulu language. Xhosas share the attribute of descent from other clans settled in a common region, and speaking related languages that came to acquire the common label of Xhosa around the same period. And Coloureds are those who have the attribute of descent from the Khoisan (whose ancestors settled in parts of South Africa by 150 B.C.), slaves imported by the Dutch, Europeans, and later migrants from East Africa belonging to the Bantu language group. The rules for membership in each of these categories may be equivalently expressed as combinations of attributes that signal such descent, including name, physical features, and, in the case of Zulus and Xhosas, an ancestral association with a set of related dialects or languages.

5. Comparison with Other Definitions

The most widely used definitions of ethnic identity proposed in previous literature include the following, in chronological order:

- According to Max Weber, ethnic groups are "those human groups that entertain a subjective belief in their common descent because of similarities of physical type or of customs or both, or because of memories of colonization or migration; this belief must be important for the propagation of group formation; conversely, it does not matter whether or not an objective blood relationship exists" (Weber 1996, 389).
- According to Frederik Barth, an ethnic group is defined by "the cultural features that signal the boundary" (Barth 1969, 15). I refer to this definition through the book as a "cultural" rule for membership as distinguished from the "descent-based attribute" rule for membership introduced here or the "group descent" rule for membership described further below.

  Barth was reacting against an anthropological literature that understood ethnic groups as groups defined by a common culture. For Barth, the defining feature of an ethnic group is the small set of cultural markers that distinguish members from non-members rather than some larger set of cultural values that all members have in common. In his words, the main aspect of an ethnic group is the "boundary that defines the group, not the cultural stuff that it contains" (Barth 1969, 15).

Many current works on ethnic identity, however, including some definitions discussed below, remain untouched by Barth's argument. They continue to conceptualize ethnic groups as groups defined by common "cultural stuff." Gellner (1983), for instance, uses the words "ethnicity," "culture," and "nation" interchangeably, Laitin (1986) presents a theory of ethnic cleavages as "cultural" cleavages, and the large body of work on "multiculturalism" (Taylor 1994, Kymlicka 1995) is premised on the assumption that ethnic groups are self-standing cultural units. Everyday understandings of ethnicity often echo the same idea. This is best be illustrated by the definition of "ethnic groups" offered in Wikipedia: "Ethnic groups are also usually united by certain common cultural, behavioural, linguistic and ritualistic or religious traits. In this sense, an ethnic group is also a cultural community" (http://en.wikipedia. org/wiki/Ethnic_group).

- According to Donald Horowitz: "Ethnicity is based on a myth of collective ancestry, which usually carries with it traits believed to be innate. Some notion of ascription, however diluted, and affinity deriving from it are inseparable from the concept of ethnicity" (Horowitz 1985, 52).
- According to Fearon and Laitin, an ethnic group is "a group larger than a family for which membership is reckoned primarily by descent, is conceptually autonomous, and has a conventionally recognized 'natural history' as a group" (Fearon and Laitin 2000a, 20).
- In a subsequent refinement, Fearon defines a "prototypical" ethnic group as one that has several of the following features as possible: (1) Membership is reckoned primarily by descent [presumably by the descent-rule above] (2) Members are conscious of group membership (3) Members share distinguishing cultural features (4) These cultural features are valued by a majority of members (5) The group has or remembers a homeland (6) The group has a shared history as a group that is "not wholly manufactured but has some basis in fact" (Fearon 2003, 7).
- According to Anthony Smith, an ethnic group is, "a named human population with myths of common ancestry, shared historical memories, one or more elements of a common culture, a link with a homeland and a sense of solidarity" (Hutchinson and Smith 1996, 6).

It is also standard practice in comparative political science, including in my own previous work (Chandra 2004), to use the word "ascriptive" to refer to ethnic categories. But it is not clear what that term means. Those who use the term often associate it with descent. *The Oxford English Dictionary* defines "ascribe" as "to assign, attribute, impute" and "ascriptive" as "attributable, ascribable." *Webster's Third New International Dictionary*, similarly, defines the term "ascribe" as "to refer esp. to a supposed cause, source or author: assign, attribute," and "ascriptive" as "relating to or involving ascription." These definitions indicate that the term "ascriptive" is not associated specifically with birth or descent but with anything that is "given" rather than chosen. But there are many attributes and categories that can be "given" to us that are not descent-based, and many descent-based attributes and categories which, as we will see in subsequent chapters, can be chosen rather than given. Using the word "ascriptive" to define ethnic identities amounts then to defining a term with another term that requires definition. I avoid it altogether therefore in the discussion that follows.

Virtually all definitions in the inventory, with the possible exception of Barth, agree that descent is somehow important in defining an ethnic group. The differences are over how precisely to specify the role of descent, and whether and how other features should be combined with it in defining ethnic groups. The role of descent is specified in five different ways: (1) a common ancestry or (2) a myth of common ancestry or (3) a common region of origin or (4) a myth of a common region of origin and (5) a "group" descent rule for membership. The features combined with descent are (6) a common culture or, at a minimum, common cultural markers, (7) a common language, (8) a common history, (9) a common territory, and (10) conceptual autonomy.

The specifications of the role of descent in these definitions differ from the one I have proposed in subtle but significant ways. The significance of these differences will become apparent when we consider the properties implied by each definition. Each specification of the role of descent leads us to associate very different sets of properties with ethnic identities—and thus is the basis for substantially different research agendas.

According to the definition proposed here, ancestry, or a myth of ancestry, is critical to the definition of an ethnic group, but *common* ancestry, or a myth of *common* ancestry, is not. For instance, the membership rule for classification of individuals as Black or White in the United States separates individuals who have, or are believed to have, some African blood from individuals who do not, or are not believed to, have a drop of African blood (Nobles 2000). This membership rule makes the categories Black and White ethnic categories because it requires the possession of attributes based on ancestry (the proportion of African blood) even though it does not require "common" ancestry. The fact of common ancestry, even if it were verifiable, is irrelevant to this membership rule.

Further, according to my definition, the region in which an individual's ancestors resided, or were believed to reside, can define an ethnic identity, but a *common* region of origin or a myth of a *common* region of origin is not necessary. Thus, the category "immigrant" in Germany is an ethnic category by this definition, even though those who are classified as "immigrants" may be descended from ancestors in many different regions, including Turkey, India, and Afghanistan, and be perceived as such. Further, the region in which one's ancestors resided is simply one of the several descent-based attributes that might define an ethnic identity, not the only one—we can have identities that we count as ethnic which have nothing to do with a region of origin. Thus, the identities Christian and Muslim in Lebanon would be classified as ethnic identities based on attributes such as descent from parents of a particular religious persuasion rather than a common myth of origin.

The attribute-based definition logically encompasses the group descent rule for membership—the group memberships of parents and ancestors variously defined become part of the stock of attributes inherited by their descendants and thus the basis for their own ethnic coding. But there are many identities that we think of as ethnic, which are not captured by the "group descent rule" which the definition proposed here does indeed capture. Thus, I can be a member of "ethnic" categories based on attributes that characterize me but not my parents (e.g., my skin color, or my mixed descent) as well as categories that characterize me but not my parents (e.g., new categories invented in my generation, for which eligibility for membership depends on the attributes they had).

Finally, according to the definition proposed in this chapter, groups can be called ethnic based only on the requirement that descent-based attributes are required for membership. Additional features such as a common culture, a common language, a common history, a common territory, and conceptual autonomy cannot be considered constitutive of ethnic groups, although they are sometimes also associated with ethnic groups defined by other means. I discuss the lack of fit between these "non-descent-based" features and our classification of ethnic groups in some detail in the sections that follow. But given its pervasiveness, let me address here the idea that an ethnic group is defined, even in part, by a "common culture."

A "*common* culture," I will show below, cannot logically be said to be constitutive of ethnic groups as we understand them. But *culture*, conceptualized differently as a framework of interpretation, and *in interaction with descent*, does have a role to play in the "attribute-based" definition introduced in this book in several ways. First, culture matters in determining the "stock" of descent-based attributes we possess. The cultural practices of our parents and ancestors—for instance, the names they adopt—become part of an individual's stock of descent-based attributes. Second, culture also matters in the way we "see" a descent-based attribute. For example, as the next chapter illustrates, the interpretation of a certain shade of skin color as "black" or "white" or something in between, is a product of cultural construction. Third, any given membership rule is a product of cultural construction. For example, for the categories "Black" and "White" in the United States to be considered ethnic categories, society as a whole, or large sections of it, must agree on the membership rules for those categories—or at a minimum agree that membership requires descent-based attributes—and must agree on how to interpret those descent-based attributes. But we cannot see either of these attributes or a membership rule consisting of them, as Barth might, as purely cultural constructions. In each case, what matters is the way in which such this construction interacts with and represents descent. The attribute-based definition proposed in this book points out that this interaction is worth exploring. Indeed, the focus on simplistic concepts such as a "common culture" has kept us from exploring this more complex role of culture in defining an ethnic identity.

6. Matching Alternative Definitions with the Classification of Ethnic Identities

This section evaluates these definitions and their match with our classification of ethnic identities in some detail elsewhere using the same criteria I use for my own definition. For analytical clarity, I consider each characteristic employed in each definition separately. Then, I ask three questions of each defining characteristic: (1) Does this characteristic distinguish ethnic categories included in the sample from others in the same set? (This requires us to ascertain both that each category in each set has this characteristic in common and that different categories in the same set have different values on this characteristic). (2) Does this characteristic distinguish ethnic categories from the categories we classify as non-ethnic? (3) Can this characteristic constitute the group or does it describe a group that is constituted on some other basis?

In each case, I experiment with several ways of interpreting each defining characteristic, choosing the interpretation that has the broadest coverage. Thus, in evaluating the characteristic of "a common region of origin," I interpret the term "region," what a region of origin is, and what having a region of origin in common requires in as expansive a way as possible. The purpose of doing this is less to discern the authors' true intent than to ask: Is there any reasonable interpretation of this definition that captures our classification of ethnic identities?

Table 2.2 summarizes the results of this evaluation. It records whether or not the ethnic category in each row is distinguished from other ethnic categories in a comparable set by the characteristic listed in the column. If this first criterion is met, the table indicates whether the additional criteria are also met. As we see, no characteristic meets this first criterion for all cases. Two characteristics— a myth of common region of origin and a common language—meet this criterion for a majority of cases, but with some important exclusions. However, even when these two characteristics also distinguish between ethnic and non-ethnic categories, they can be taken to be only descriptive but not constitutive of ethnic categories. If no defining characteristic taken singly meets all three criteria, it must also be the case that no combination of these defining characteristics can meet those criteria.

Table 2.2 (Mis)Match Between Other Definitions and Classification

	Common Ancestry	Myth of Common Ancestry	Common Region of Origin	Myth of Common Region of Origin*	Group Descent Rule	Common Culture	Common Language*	Common History	Common Territory	Conceptual Autonomy
Black	No	No	No	Yes	No	No	No	No	No	No
White	No	No	No	Yes	Yes/No	No	No	No	No	No
Serb	No	No	No	Yes	Yes/No	No	Yes	No	No	No
Croat	No	No	No	Yes	Yes/No	No	Yes	No	No	No
Mohajir	No	No	No	Yes	No	No	Yes	No	No	No
Punjabi	No	No	No	No	Yes/No	No	Yes	No	No	No
Pathan	No	Yes	No	Yes	Yes/No	No	Yes	No	No	No
Baluch	No	No	No	Yes	Yes/No	No	Yes	No	No	No
Flemish	No	No	No	Yes	Yes/No	No	Yes	No	No	No
Walloon	No	No	No	Yes	Yes/No	No	Yes	No	No	No
Aymara	No	No	No	Yes	Yes/No	No	Yes	No	No	No
Quechua	No	No	No	Yes	Yes/No	No	Yes	No	No	No
Yoruba	No	Yes	No	Yes	Yes/No	No	Yes	No	No	No
Ibo	No	No	No	Yes	Yes/No	No	Yes	No	No	No
Hausa-Fulani	No	No	No	No	No	No	Yes	No	No	No
Zulu	No	Yes	No	Yes	Yes/No	No	Yes	No	No	No
Xhosa	No	Yes	No	Yes	Yes/No	No	Yes	No	No	No
Coloured	No	No	No	No	No	No	No	No	No	No

* This characteristic also distinguishes many of the groups we classify as ethnic from groups we classify as non-ethnic. But it is not constitutive: it simply describes a group that is constituted by other means.

Common Ancestry

Several ethnic groups, especially in Africa, appear to be defined by common ancestry, broadly defined. In our sample, Yorubas in Yorubaland trace their descent to the ancestor Oduduwa, and Yorubas in different "ancestral cities" trace their descent even more specifically to particular sons of Oduduwa (Laitin 1986, 110). Zulus in South Africa claim direct descent from the patriarch Zulu who was born to a Nguni chief in the Congo basin area. Xhosas, similarly, trace their descent to the common ancestor uXhosa. Outside our sample, Kikuyus in Kenya claim descent from the single ancestor Gikuyu. Indeed, the great influence that scholars who study Africa have had on the study of ethnicity may be one reason why common ancestry is often proposed as a defining characteristic of ethnic groups.

But let's look more closely at what it means to define an ethnic group as a group in which members have common ancestry. Taken at face value to mean simply that two individuals are in the same ethnic group if they share a common ancestor, this definition is meaningless: We can find a point of intersection in the family trees of any two individuals by going back far enough, thus eliminating group differentiation altogether (Cavalli-Sforza 2000). We must, therefore, stipulate the nearness of the ancestral connection on a set of family trees required to call a group an ethnic group. Does common ancestry mean a shared ancestor 1 branch ago, 100 branches ago, or 1 million branches ago? We must also indicate the rule by which ancestry is determined—a patrilineal rule, a matrilineal rule, or some alternative.

Let's stipulate that in order for members of a group to have common ancestry, any two individuals within the group must share a more proximate ancestor than two individuals from different groups. This seems a minimally reasonable elaboration of the common ancestry definition. It avoids making arbitrary decisions about the precise number of branches on a family tree that should be considered in determining common ancestry. And it is also broad enough to encompass a wide range of rules by which ancestry is determined. According to this definition, for instance, we would say that Yorubas are an ethnic group if two Yorubas have a more proximate ancestor, no matter how defined, than a Yoruba and an Ibo, or a Yoruba and a Hausa-Fulani.

Even when elaborated in this minimally reasonable way, common ancestry cannot be taken to be a defining characteristic of the groups we classify as ethnic. Consider the categories "Yoruba" and "Ibo." Let's assume, without searching for verification in the historical record, that two Yorubas can indeed establish closer ties to Oduduwa than a Yoruba and an Ibo. Even when such proximity can be established, it must also be the case that two Yoruba brothers are more closely linked with their father than with Oduduwa, or that two Yoruba cousins are more closely linked with their grandfather than with Oduduwa. Why do we not define the immediate family or an extended kin-network as an ethnic group rather than the category "Yoruba"? The answer can only be that we are using some criterion external and prior to common ancestry to define the Yorubas as an ethnic group. Once Yorubas are defined as an ethnic group by other means, we may well find that they share a more proximate ancestry with those inside rather than outside the group. But we cannot infer the existence of the group from the genealogical history of a given cluster of individuals. The same point refers to all the groups cited above, within, and outside our sample, which are associated with common ancestry.

Even as a secondary defining criterion, furthermore, it does not characterize many of the groups that we classify as ethnic. For most of the categories in our sample, common ancestry appears to be entirely absent as a criterion defining and differentiating categories in the same set. This is true even in Africa: The members of categories such as the Ibo, the Hausa, the Fulani, and the Hausa-Fulani are not characterized by common ancestry. And it is certainly true of categories elsewhere—accounts of the common features and differences between Punjabis, Mohajirs, Baluchis, and Sindhis in Pakistan, Serbs and Croats in the former Yugoslavia, Flemish and Walloon in Belgium, and Aymara and Quechua in Belgium do not even mention the fact of common ancestry. We cannot, thus, take a common ancestry to be a secondary defining feature of an ethnic group.

Indeed, individuals often belong to different ethnic groups *despite* the objective fact of common ancestry, however defined. Consider the categories "Black" and "White," which are often associated with ancestry. We know that many white Americans from former slave-owning families share proximate ancestors with black Americans. Consider the example of E. C. Hart, classified as a Louisiana white, who had several children with Cornelia, a woman of color (Dominguez 1997, 26–27). Hart's children with a white wife would have shared common ancestry at the most proximate level—the same father—as his children with Cornelia. But the two sets of children were not classified in Louisiana as members of the same group—Hart's children with Cornelia were then classified as colored and would now be classified as Black, while his children with a white wife would then and now have been classified as White. At the same time, individuals in the United States whose ties of ancestry that are far more distant, if they exist at all, such as Irish Americans and Lithuanian Americans, or Jamaican and Nigerian immigrants, are classified as members of the same ethnic categories. Whatever rule political scientists are following in classifying these categories as ethnic, it does not rely on common ancestry.

A Myth of Common Ancestry

The objective fact of common ancestry may not serve as either a primary or a secondary defining characteristic for most of the groups we classify as ethnic. But what about a *myth* of common ancestry? Can we plausibly argue that the groups we classify as "ethnic" are defined by a myth of common ancestry, regardless of whether this myth has basis in fact?

In order for a myth of common ancestry to be a primary defining characteristic, we would have to show that the successful propagation or credibility of this myth is not conditional upon other characteristics that also distinguish members. Otherwise, these other characteristics must be taken to be the primary defining characteristic of an ethnic identity, with the myth being only secondary.

A simple example shows that this proposed defining characteristic fails this test. Let's compare the categories of college professors and Yorubas in Nigeria. I doubt that there has been any attempt to propagate the myth that college professors in Nigeria are descended from a common ancestor—and if there were, I doubt that either college professors in Nigeria or others would accept this myth. But there has certainly been an attempt to propagate the myth that Yorubas are descended from a common ancestor and many Yorubas and non-Yorubas accept the myth. Thus, there must some prior characteristic of the category "Yoruba," defined by other means, which makes it possible for a myth of common ancestry to be attached to it, which is missing in the category "college professor." It is this characteristic we should see as a primary characteristic making the Yoruba an ethnic group. A myth of common ancestry appears to be only a secondary defining characteristic dependent on the presence of this more fundamental feature.

Even as a secondary defining characteristic, furthermore, a myth of common ancestry captures only a small subset of those identity categories we classify as ethnic. In our sample, it would capture three categories at best—Yorubas, Zulus, and Xhosas, for all of which the claim of common ancestry may well be a myth rather than fact. But it excludes a good number of groups that we also classify as ethnic, in Africa but also in other regions, which do not claim an ancestor in common and do not differentiate themselves from others in a comparable set on the basis of myths of ancestry. This is the case with Ibos, Hausas, and Fulanis in Nigeria; Coloureds in South Africa; Blacks and Whites in the United States; Mohajirs, Punjabis, Sindhis, and Pathans in Pakistan; Aymara and Quechua in Bolivia; Serbs and Croats in the former Yugoslavia; and Flemish and Walloons in Belgium.

The irrelevance of a myth of common ancestry to membership rules in groups that we commonly think of as ethnic can be illustrated even more clearly when we consider the process by which new ethnic groups form as a result of fissures from old ones. Consider one example of this process of fission from South Asia. By the 1940s, the anti-colonial struggle against the British produced the initial ethnic category of "Pakistan," distinct from the larger category of British India. In 1971, this category generated a new fissure between Bengali Muslims and others, resulting in the separate state of Bangladesh for Bengali Muslims. New fissions within old ethnic categories continue to occur, generating new categories including Punjabis, Sindhis, Pathans, Baluchis, and Seraikis. Each of these new categories contains the capacity for new fissures. If myths of common ancestry define ethnic groups, then the creation of new ethnic groups from old ones should be accompanied by the construction of new myths. But myths of common ancestry were not part of the process by which entrepreneurs and masses within these groups distinguished themselves from each other. Yet these groups are routinely classified by comparative political scientists as ethnic (e.g., Horowitz 1985, 281, Alesina et al. 2003, Fearon 2003). Clearly, something other than the existence of such myths must guide our classifications.

iii. A Common Region of Origin

Perhaps what defines an ethnic category is not the sharing of a common *ancestor* by its members but a common region of origin. Let's stipulate that an ethnic category is associated with a common point of origin if its members can trace descent to individuals who once inhabited a common region. Whether the members of the category migrated from the land of their ancestors or continue to inhabit it is irrelevant.

At first glance, most of the categories in our sample indeed appear to be associated with a common region of origin: Blacks in the United States with origin in Africa, Whites with origin in Europe or Eurasia or the Caucasus, Serbs with an area inland of the Dalmatian coast, Croats with northern Dalmatia, and so on. Only two categories in our sample are not associated with a common region of origin. "Coloureds," descended from European migrants, Africans, and Indians in South Africa, do not appear to have a common region of origin. Nor do Hausa-Fulani, since they are constituted by an aggregation of two groups, each with a distinct point of origin: the Hausa, associated with an area of origin north of the confluence of the Niger and Benue rivers, and the Fulani, associated with a point of origin in lower Senegal.

But there is no logical definition of a "region" that distinguishes categories in the same set from each other. Indeed, the identification of a common region in each case is a consequence of having identified the category first by some other means and then reasoning backward until we also find a common region of origin. We could just as easily associate categories in a comparable set with the same region of origin. When we find that the membership of most of the categories in our sample is associated with a common region of origin, thus, it is not an indication of the power of this definition but its weakness. We could also, by choosing the appropriate definition of region and the appropriate time period, find the same thing among members of categories that we think of as non-ethnic.

To illustrate, let's return to the case of Blacks and Whites in the United States. We associate Blacks in the United States with a common origin in Africa, and Whites with a common origin in Eurasia. But these associations depend on (1) the definition of "region" that we employ and (2) the time period we choose to start at. Some definitions of region and choices of time period would reveal distinct common homelands for both groups, while others would reveal a shared one.

If we categorize "Africa" and "Eurasia" as distinct regions, then we can associate Blacks and Whites with distinct regions of origin and thus as distinct ethnic groups. But there is no analytical reason why we should think of Africa and Eurasia as distinct regions instead of disaggregating further within both categories. If we thought of regions in Africa, including present-day Liberia, Ghana, Cote d'Ivoire, Togo, Benin, and Cameroon, as distinct, then we should have not one but several ethnic groups corresponding to origin in these regions. Similarly, if we thought of regions in Eurasia, including France, Ireland, Germany, Lithuania, Poland, and Italy as distinct, then we would also have several ethnic groups. The identification of Africa and Eurasia as regions of origin requires us first to define Blacks and Whites by some other criteria other than region and then employ that definition of region of origin that captures present-day members of these pre-defined groups and excludes non-members.

Further, even if we take Africa and Eurasia to be distinct regions, arguing that Blacks and Whites originate in these two regions, it makes sense only when based on an arbitrary choice of time period. We can identify distinct points of origin for Blacks, for instance, if we start with the beginning of the slave trade in the sixteenth century. But if we continued going backwards from this point, we would find a point at which both Blacks and Whites originated in present-day Africa (Cavalli-Sforza 2000). And if we went forward, we could just as easily say that both groups share a common homeland—the United States.

The same point applies to all the other groups in our sample. Serbs and Croats and Bosnian Muslims in the former Yugoslavia, for instance, are now associated with distinct homelands in Serbia, Croatia, and Bosnia. But going back in time simply before sixth century A.D., we might have thought of all three groups as possessing a common homeland in the South-central Europe in which the South Slavs settled, or going back even further, to the core in Asia from which the Slavs migrated outwards and so to be one ethnic group, not three. Punjabis, Sindhis, Pathans, Mohajirs, and Baluchs can be seen equally as belonging to distinct territories or as belonging to the same one. The Aymara and Quechua can be seen as having an origin in the same territory (the Andean highlands or the Altiplano or Lake Titicaca) or distinct territories (for instance, the northern and central part of the Altiplano versus the southern part).

The point applies also well beyond the sample. Consider the case of Sinhalas and Tamils in Sri Lanka, who have distinct homelands only if we define northern Sri Lanka as a distinct region and the rest of Sri Lanka as another distinct region—or, going even further back, if we define present-day Tamil Nadu as a distinct region and trace the migration of Tamils from there to Sri Lanka. But there is no a priori reason for us to define the region of origin in this way? If we thought of all of Sri Lanka, or the northern tip of Sri Lanka and the southern tip of India, as a single region, then both the Sinhalese and Tamils would have a common homeland.

Indeed, we can even find a common point of origin for the ancestors of categories not commonly associated with one. Consider "Coloureds" in South Africa, whose ancestors are associated with Europe, Africa and India—on the face of it, different regions of origin. We know that populations who lived in Europe, Africa and India at later times in history migrated from a central core at an earlier time. And that their descendants in this case migrated to South Africa. Thus, we could also argue that the ancestors of the Coloureds had a common point in origin, either by counting the early ancestors who migrated to Europe, Africa and India, or by counting the most recent ancestors, who lived in South Africa.

A *Myth* of a Common Region of Origin

Consider now the characteristic of a *myth* of a common region of origin. Many categories in our sample are indeed associated with a myth of a common region of origin. And this defining characteristic does appear to distinguish ethnic from non-ethnic categories. But this characteristic cannot be considered to be consti-tutive for the reason that its credibility is conditional upon the descent-based attributes that distinguish members.

To illustrate, imagine an attempt to propagate the myth that college profes-sors in Nigeria are descended from those who once shared a region of origin. If all we knew about the individuals described by this myth is that they are college professors, this myth would be difficult to take at face value. But suppose we were also told that these college professors have a patrilineal descent rule, or the same last name, or the same mother tongue, or some shared some other char-acteristic that justifies thinking of them as having ancestors who once inhabited the same region. Given these characteristics, we might be more willing to accept this myth because of the presence of these other characteristics. If this is the case, then these descent-based characteristics that determine the credibility of the myth must be the primary defining characteristics, not the myth itself. The same point applies to other "myths" taken to be defining characteristics, such as a myth of common ancestry.

Even as a secondary feature, furthermore, this defining characteristic excludes three important classes of categories: "hyphenated" categories, created explicitly as the result of an aggregation of smaller ones, "mixed-race" categories, and, for want of a better word, "non-migrant" categories.

The Hausa-Fulani in Nigeria are an example from our sample of the first. As a category transparently formed as an amalgam of two distinct categories, each with a distinct area of origin, this category is not associated with a myth of a common region of origin.

Coloureds in South Africa are an example of the second, along with many "mixed" race categories in many countries outside our sample, including Mestizos in Nicaragua, Bolivia, Venezuela, Uruguay, Peru, Panama, the Honduras, and Mexico; "Pardos" in Brazil; Creoles in Mauritius; and Mulattos in Uruguay and Panama, which we typically do not think of as having a common region of origin but routinely classify as "ethnic" categories. Indeed, these examples have all been chosen from the list of categories classified as ethnic across our datasets. Many of these categories describe the populations of countries in Latin and Central America. Thus this definition would exclude large numbers of categories for at least an entire continent.

As for non-migrant categories, the list is large. It includes categories whose members are regionally concentrated but not distinguished by myths of origin— Punjabis in Pakistan are an example of the type of category, along with Bengalis or Tamils in India—or includes "titular" categories in many countries—Italians in Italy, Lithuanians in Lithuania, Poles in Poland. Although these categories, like any other, could probably be associated with a common region of origin, they are not categories around which such a myth as developed in practice. Non-migrant categories without a myth of origin also include categories whose members are distinguished by descent from those professing different religious beliefs, not by descent from those who have different regions of origin. Consider, for instance, Catholics and Protestants in Northern Ireland. We think of the conflict in Northern Ireland as a prototypical example of "ethnic" conflict. The same is true of Muslims and Serbs in the former Yugoslavia, Hindus and Muslims in India, Muslims, Christians, and Druze in Lebanon, Shias and Sunnis in Iraq, and so on.

The "Group Descent Rule"

According to a different attempt to specify the role of descent, an ethnic group is one in which membership is granted based on the membership of one's parents. In the words of its authors: "In deciding a person's ethnicity, we do not need to know anything about his or her cultural habits, mother tongue, religion or beliefs of any sort. Rather, we simply need to know about parentage. In ordinary usage, to ask 'What is her ethnicity?' is to ask about what ethnic group her parents (or other close ancestors) were assigned to.... *All that is necessary to be counted as a member of an ethnic group is to be able to have accepted the claim to be immediately descended from other members of the group*" (Fearon and Laitin 2000a, 13, emphasis mine). I describe this defining characteristic as the "Group Descent Rule" for membership.

As in the case of most definitions discussed here, we must impose a more precise interpretation on this definition in order to apply it. First, we must interpret what the term "group membership" means. To do this, we must address the following questions: What should we count as a "group"? Do the authors intend us to think of a group as a collection of people who think of themselves, and act, as a collective, or simply as a category of description? What should we count as group "membership?" Does membership mean self-placement in the group, however defined, or does it mean "assignation" by others? Can one be a member in only one group at a time, or is simultaneous membership is possible in multiple groups?

To illustrate the importance of these questions, consider the hypothetical example of a woman whose parents identified as American Jews. Let's also assume that "American Jews" constituted a collective with a shared consciousness during the lifetime of her parents, and both parents shared in this consciousness. Assume, second, that others did not see them as "Jews." They assigned them the label "White." Although this was also a collective with a common consciousness, the parents did not share in it and did not themselves think of themselves as White. Assume, third, that the parents also thought of themselves as Ashkenazi. But for most people in the United States, this was simply a label without a collective consciousness attached to it. Assume, finally, that others also used the label "German-American" to describe them, but that this label had even less of a collective consciousness attached to it than Ashkenazi—and that they did not care for it.

Table 2.3 represents the possible group memberships of the parents given different conceptions of "group" and "membership." If membership in a group means self-placement in an entity with collective consciousness, their group membership would be American Jewish. If membership in a group means self-placement in any category, their group memberships would be both American Jewish and Ashkenazi. If we mean assignation in an entity with collective consciousness, their group membership would be White. If we mean assignation in any category, it would be White and German-American. If by group membership we mean the simultaneous self-placement and assignation in a single category, they would not have any group memberships.

Suppose now that the daughter calls herself "White" and is called "White" by others. Is this an ethnic identity according to the group descent rule? It depends. If we believe that group membership requires self-placement in one or more

Table 2.3 **Different Ways of Thinking About "Group" Membership (With Hypothetical Examples)**

	Self-Placement	Assignation
Collective Consciousness	American Jews	White
No Collective Consciousness	Ashkenazi	German-American

collectives, then this would not be among her ethnic identities, since although she is a member of this "group," we cannot say that her parents were members. If we believe that group membership requires assignation by others in one or more collectives, then this would indeed be her ethnic identity, since this would be among the group memberships of her parents. If we believe that group membership requires a coincidence of self-placement and assignation in one or more collectives, then we could also not say that this was among her ethnic identities, since although she calls herself and others call her White, the same coincidence did not occur with her parents. If we believe that group membership requires assignation in one and only one collective, then the answer would depend on whatever rule we use to select that one group and eliminate others. Note that the answers become even more indeterminate if we consider the possibility of a difference between the "groups" in which she places herself and the "groups" in which others place her, as we did in the case of her parents.

For the remainder of this discussion, I adopt the broadest possible definition of group membership to mean either self-placement or assignation in an entity with or without collective consciousness—and allow for the individual to simultaneously be a member of multiple groups. This broad interpretation may violate some notions of what "group membership means"—it may even violate the authors' intent. But my purpose here is to explore whether there is any interpretation of this definition that would capture all the groups that we (and they) classify as ethnic in our sample—and by implication the population from which it is drawn. The broader the interpretation we adopt, the more identities we make it possible for it to capture. If even this broad definition fails to capture the full set of identities that we classify as "ethnic," we can be sure that a narrower one will also fail to capture this full set.

Let's turn now to a second way in which this definition needs to be more fully specified. Does this definition describe a group as ethnic if the criterion for membership in the group is that the parents of all members were coded as members of the same group *whether or not that group was also considered ethnic*? (hereafter Group Descent Rule 1). Or should we define a group as ethnic if the criterion for membership in the group is that the parents of all members were also coded as members of the same group *and* that group was also considered ethnic? (hereafter Group Descent Rule 2).

To illustrate the difference between the two versions, take the example of American Jews. According to Fearon and Laitin, "many Americans who cannot perform a Jewish ritual and don't speak Hebrew still consider themselves and are considered by others as ethnically Jewish because that is the way their parents and grandparents were coded" (Fearon and Laitin 2000a, 14). For the analyst to code American Jews as an ethnic group, is it sufficient simply that the criterion for membership in the category "American Jew" is that one's parents were coded as Jewish whether or not Jews were considered an ethnic group in the lifetime of one's parents (Group Descent Rule 1)? Or must the criterion for membership in the category "American Jew" be that one's parents were also coded as *ethnically* Jewish, requiring one's grandparents to also be coded as ethnically Jewish, which in turn would require one's great-grandparents to be coded as ethnically Jewish and so on into infinity (Group Descent Rule 2).

Group Descent Rule 2 is circular: For a present-day American Jew to be qualified as ethnic, every preceding generation of his ancestors must also have been descended from *ethnically* American Jews, who themselves should have been descended from ethnically American Jews and so on into infinity. There is no logical way to identify an original set of "ethnic" American Jewish parents. We could apply Group Descent Rule 2 only if we arbitrarily stipulated that some set of identities were ethnic at some starting point, and then coded other identities as ethnic in relation to this initial set. And even then, it would capture a narrower set of identities than Group Descent Rule 1.

Let's stipulate then that Fearon and Laitin's definition refers solely to Group Descent Rule 1—with the very broad definition of group membership given above. This definition can indeed constitute a group rather than simply describe a group defined by other means. But even when most expansively interpreted, it remains too narrow: It does not capture many of the identities that we classify as ethnic, and captures others only some of the time but not others. It also does not distinguish ethnic identities from non-ethnic identities, such as aristocrats, "landowning families," and so on, in which membership can also depend on the group members of one's parents but which is the less important for our purposes than what it includes.

Group Descent Rule 1 excludes the categories "Black" in the United States and "Coloured" in South Africa, which are examples of categories in which membership depends on the racial characteristics—but not the group memberships—of one's parents. The membership rule in the category "Black" in the United States, for instance, does not take the form "You are considered Black if your parents were Black." Rather, it takes the form: "You are considered 'Black' if either of your parents or any of your ancestors had any African ancestry." Thus, you can be "Black" if all your ancestors but one were coded as White. By the same logic, Group Descent Rule 1 would exclude other race-based categories such as "Creoles" or "Mestizos" in parts of Latin and Central America and "Coloureds" in South Africa for most of their history.

It also excludes categories such as "Hausa-Fulani," created as the result of the aggregation of smaller categories—or the disaggregation of larger categories into smaller ones. An individual might be considered Hausa-Fulani not only if both her parents are Hausa-Fulani but if her parents are either Hausa or Fulani. Such a category would not be classified as ethnic by this membership rule.

Indeed, this is the reason that this definition excludes the early generations of many categories in our sample. Many categories are initially created as an aggregation or disaggregation of smaller categories. Consider the category "Yoruba" when it was invented in Nigeria in the nineteenth century. At this time period, the parents of those who were classified as Yoruba were not themselves classified as Yoruba for the reason that this category did not exist during their lifetimes. According to group descent rule, then, the category "Yoruba" in the nineteenth century would not be coded as ethnic. But the category "Yoruba" is universally coded as an ethnic category by all comparative political scientists, without making a distinction between time periods.

Similarly, take the example of the category "Serb," believed to be mentioned for the first time in the sixth century A.D. Those who came to be categorized as Serb at some point after the sixth century A.D. had parents who were not known as Serbs but were members of one or more South Slav tribes that had settled in Southern Europe and had other characteristics in common such as an association with the Orthodox Church and exposure to the Cyrillic alphabet. But according to the group descent rule, the early generations of all those who came to be called Serb would not be counted as having a Serbian ethnic identity because their parents were not called Serbs.

Finally, it excludes categories created as the result of migration or territorial change. The identity category "Mohajir" is an example. This category describes those who migrated to Pakistan from north-India and their descendants. The parents of many of those classified as Mohajir were not classified as Mohajir themselves, since the category did not exist while they were alive—and since they were themselves not migrants as their children were. Applying the group descent rule would lead us to code the first generation of Mohajirs as a non-ethnic group, to the extent that membership in this category did not depend upon being able to code one's parents as Mohajirs. The same would apply to other migrant groups—Irish Americans in the United States, or the Chinese in Malaysia or the Nepalese in Bhutan, for example. Yet, all our datasets count the Mohajirs as an ethnic group independent of time and generation, as they do these other migrant groups.

A Common Culture

As we have seen above, the idea that an ethnic group is constituted by a common culture has been under attack for at least thirty years, starting with the seminal argument of Frederik Barth (1969), but continues to inform current thinking and research on ethnic mobilization or other concepts related to ethnic identity. No matter how we define culture, however, a common culture cannot be taken to be a defining feature of ethnic groups—at least as we classify them. Many of the groups we classify as ethnic do not have a common culture, many "different" ethnic groups do not differ based on culture, and many groups distinguished by a common culture are not classified as ethnic.

A standard definition of a common culture is a shared set of symbols, values, codes, and norms (consistent with Rogowski, cited in Wedeen 2002). Broad definitions of this sort do not specify *which* symbols, values, codes, and norms it is important to share. If we require group members to share all values and codes, it would probably disqualify almost all the groups that we count as ethnic.

Take the category "Yoruba" as an example. Those classified as Yoruba share some aspects of culture so defined—for instance, a common myth of origin, the worship of a common set of deities, and a common language. But there are also many aspects of culture that they do not share. Yorubas who trace their origin to different ancestral cities in Yorubaland, for instance, speak different dialects of the Yoruba language, have localized festivals, and have distinct myths of origin, institutions, and rituals. Christian and Muslim Yorubas not only have different modes of religious practice and observance but different sets of value orientations (Laitin 1986). The symbols, codes, and norms of those classified as "Black" similarly differ a great deal: There are actual or perceived differences between Jamaican Blacks and "American" Blacks based on language, work ethic, and family values (Waters 1999), between Blacks from the north and the south (Lemann 1992), between middle-class and poor Blacks and urban Blacks and rural Blacks (Malcolm X 1964). Without belaboring the point, we could describe similar heterogeneity in symbols, values, and codes within each of the ethnic categories in our sample.

Consider now Barth's more reasonable interpretation: We might say that ethnic groups have a "common culture," not if all members share *all* the same values, symbols, codes, and norms to qualify as members but if they share some *key* symbols, values, codes, and norms that distinguish them from members of other groups. This is a restatement of Barth's claim that ethnic groups are defined by the cultural markers that delineate the boundaries between them, not by the cultural stuff that is contained within these boundaries.

We have already seen that cultural markers such as myths of ancestry, myths of origin, and language distinguish only a subset of the categories we classify as ethnic. The same applies to other cultural features such as religion, dress, food, social customs, and so on. Some ethnic categories, within and outside our sample and outside, are certainly distinguished by the possession of such markers. But others are not. There is no single cultural marker, for instance, that distinguishes Blacks and Whites in the United States.

Where cultural markers do distinguish different ethnic groups, furthermore, they are often not the primary distinguishing criterion—they need to be backed up by descent-based attributes. In Barth's own study of the Pathans, a patrilineal descent rule was a key characteristic distinguishing Pathans from other groups. It is not clear that a Pathan identity could be constituted in their absence, regardless of the presence of any other cultural markers (Barth 1969). The point extends beyond our sample. Sikhs in Punjab can acquire the cultural markers associated with being Hindu, for instance, by cutting off their hair and ceasing to wear a turban. But as long as they can claim descent from a Sikh family, they count themselves, and are counted, as Sikhs rather than Hindus. And, finally, cultural markers do not uniquely distinguish ethnic categories. We might argue that all sorts of non-ethnic groups such as class groups, occupational groups, and gangs are distinguished by cultural markers.

Consider a third interpretation of the "common culture" definition. Suppose that we interpret the common culture definition to mean not that individuals should share all or most of the same values, symbols, codes, and norms to qual-ify as members but that they should share more with each other than they do with outgroup members. In other words, a pair of individuals from the same ethnic group should have more in common than a pair of individuals from dif-ferent ethnic groups. Although it appears initially appealing, this condition is logically unsustainable in a world of cross-cutting ethnic identities.

Let's return, first, to the case of the Yorubas. On one dimension of ethnic identity, we classify the Yorubas, the Ibos, and the Hausa-Fulanis as distinct eth-nic groups. In order to satisfy this condition, we would need to show that a pair of Yorubas might have more in common with each other than a pair consisting of a Yoruba and an Ibo, or a pair consisting of a Yoruba and a Hausa-Fulani. But we know that there is at least one other dimension of identity on the basis of which we can also organize the same population—that of religion—which we also classify as an ethnic identity. On the dimension of religion, we classify the same population as Christian and Muslim, and we also think of Christian and Muslim as ethnic identity categories. If we define ethnic categories by a com-mon culture, this means that any two Christians must have more in common with each other than a Christian and a Muslim. As long as these two dimensions cross-cut to some extent, this second claim contradicts the first. If all Yorubas have more in common with other Yoruba than with Ibos and Hausa-Fulanis, for instance, then all Christians cannot have more in common with each other than with Muslims, because there will be at least some Christians and Muslims who are both Yoruba. The same logic also applies to our other running examples. Individuals in many groups that we classify as ethnic have cross-cutting mem-berships in other ethnic groups. So, if we say that ethnic groups are defined by a common culture as defined above, we would be ruling out an unreasonably large number of cases.

Consider a fourth conceptualization of culture. Suppose when we say that a group has a common culture, we mean simply that its members inhabit the same framework of meaning—they use the same concepts, and can understand each other, whether or not they subscribe to an identical set of symbols, values, codes, and norms, and whether or not they speak the same language. This is akin to Wedeen's conceptualization of culture as "a semiotic practice" (Wedeen 2002). Individuals who share a common culture, then, must, to paraphrase

Geertz, be able to agree that something is a wink rather than a twitch, whether or not they wink at the same time and whether or not they value a wink in the same way (Geertz 1973).

Even with this very reasonable definition, we cannot define ethnic groups as cultural groups. Many ethnic groups are composed of still smaller groups with specialized vocabularies that are not mutually intelligible. In New York in the 1960s, the street vocabulary of sections of Harlem was the equivalent of Sanskrit for many middle-class Blacks (Malcolm X 1964, 317). But both sections would classify themselves, and be classified by others, as members of the same ethnic category—Black. And although a middle-class Black may have been able to comprehend perfectly a White neighbor from her own class and educational background, this shared conceptual vocabulary would hardly lead her, or others, to classify these two individuals as part of the same ethnic group on that basis. Given some prior basis for defining ethnic groups, we can then probe the extent to which they share common frameworks of meaning. But if we were to define ethnic groups as groups that shared such common frameworks, we would lose many of the groups that we routinely classify as ethnic.

While a "common culture" cannot be said to be a defining characteristic, it can certainly be taken to be a variable associated with ethnic groups defined by other means. In the chapter that follows, I note that ethnic groups can vary in the degree to which they share a common "content"—of which culture can be one component. This variation in shared content is a subject worthy of investigation in itself: Under what conditions, we might ask, do ethnic groups develop a shared culture? Variation in shared culture may also be helpful in explaining different patterns of behavior associated with ethnic groups. It is reasonable to hypothesize, for example, that members of ethnic groups that share a common culture be more likely to behave cohesively than members of ethnic groups that do not. But we can explore the causes and consequences of this variation only when we stop treating ethnic groups as associated with a common culture by definition.

A Common Language

According to this criterion, members of the same ethnic category should share a common language, while members of different ethnic categories should share different languages. Let's assume here that sharing a language means either *speaking* that language in the present or having that language as a mother tongue or both. This is a broad interpretation and should capture more categories in our classification than one that employed one or other of the narrower interpretations.

Even broadly interpreted, however, this characteristic captures only a subset of the categories we classify as ethnic. In our sample, the ethnic groups whose members have a common language, which distinguishes them from other groups in the same partition of the population, include Mohajirs, Punjabis, Pathans, and Baluchis in Pakistan associated with the Urdu, Punjabi, Pashtun, and Baluchi languages, respectively; the Flemish and Walloon in Belgium associated with Flemish and Walloon languages, respectively; the Aymara and Quechua in Bolivia associated with Aymara and Quechua languages, respectively; the Yoruba, Ibo, Hausa, and Fulani in Nigeria associated with the Yoruba, Ibo, Hausa, and Fula languages, respectively; and Zulus and Xhosas in South Africa associated with the Zulu and Xhosa languages, respectively.

But consider the important exclusions: Blacks and Whites in the United States speak a common language yet are classified as distinct ethnic groups. At the same time, those classified as Black and White have many different ancestral languages. "Blacks" of Haitian origin, for example, are associated with different ancestral languages than those of Nigerian origin; those "Whites" of Irish origin have a different ancestral language than those of Italian origin. But we classify Blacks and Whites as ethnic groups despite the lack of a common ancestral language shared by members of either. "Coloureds" in South Africa share the Afrikaans language with other groups such as Afrikaaners but are nevertheless regarded as being ethnically distinct.

Even in those cases in which there is an association of the members of an ethnic category with a "common language," we cannot be sure that this association preceded and defined that category. Because I try to err on the side of inclusion rather than exclusion in my evaluation, Table 2.2 takes the existence of a common language at face value and describes a category as being distinguished by a common language if an entry in the *Encyclopedia Britannica* describes it as such. But when looked at closely, the existence of a common language is often a product of ethnic differentiation rather than an indicator of it. Sometimes it occurs as a consequence of a prior process of ethnic differentiation.

Mohajirs in Pakistan, for instance, migrated from many linguistically distinct parts of British India and spoke a variety of languages, including Punjabi and Gujarati. They have come to be associated with Urdu as a consequence of having a distinct ethnic identity, not because of it. Those categorized as Flemish and Walloon in Belgium, for instance, were not initially associated with common languages. The "Flemish" spoke a variety of dialects, and a prominent section of the "Flemish" spoke French. Similarly, the "Walloons" spoke a variety of languages that later began to be seen as dialects of a single one. Similarly, Serbs and Croats in the former Yugoslavia were associated with the common language of Serbo-Croatian even though they were seen as distinct groups. The association of these categories with separate languages—Serbian and Croatian—is a recent development that occurred after a long period of polarization. Zulu and Xhosa, similarly, although now treated as distinct languages with distinct conventions are both part of the same language group and could in principle be seen as belonging to the same language. And although Quechuas and Aymaras are associated with distinct Quechuan and Aymaran language families, both could equivalently be described as belonging to the same, Quechumaran language family. The creation of homogeneous language groups thus can often follow rather than precede ethnic differentiation.

Language then cannot be seen as a defining criterion that captures our classification: It captures only a subset of categories in this classification and even in that subset may often be a secondary rather than a primary defining feature.

A Common History

Consider now another way of defining an ethnic group—an ethnic group is a group that has a common history. Suppose we define history to mean simply a shared past. What does it mean to say that individuals share a past? Does it mean having lived through the same key events in the course of a lifetime? In that case, all individuals of the same age group throughout the world would share a common history, in that they all lived through the same events whether or not they were aware of them.

Suppose we try a definition that is less absurd, defining history to mean events that occurred at least one generation previously, and which were claimed to have been part of the particular experience of some group. For instance, although the potato famine may in some sense be part of the history of the world, it is particularly part of the history of the Irish living at that time, who experienced it most directly. Having a common history then means sharing a connection to events that that marked the lives of the generations that preceded us.

But how would an individual know which generations of people to affiliate herself to when looking for a "common history?" Should someone of Irish descent born in the United States affiliate herself to generations who were born in or lived in the United States? Should she affiliate herself to generations born in Ireland? Should she affiliate herself to subsets of generations born in the United States—for instance, the ancestors of university professors? Or the ancestors of Black men? In order to identify her history, she needs a rule to tell her which group she belongs to.

A common history, then, cannot be the defining characteristic of a group, ethnic or otherwise. To have a common history already presupposes the existence of a group based on other criteria. Anthony Appiah puts it best: "Sharing a common group history cannot be a criterion for being members of the same group, for we would have to be able to identify the group in order to identify *its* history. Someone in the fourteenth century could share a common history with me in a historically extended race only if something accounts for their membership in the race in the fourteenth century and mine in the twentieth. That something cannot, on pain of circularity, be the history of the race" (Appiah 1992, 32).

A Common Territory

Consider now the proposition that an ethnic identity is defined not by a common place or myth of a common place of origin but by current inhabitation of a common territory.

Suppose we take the term "territory" to refer to a subnational administrative unit, such as the Lander in Germany or the states in the United States or the provinces in Iraq. This definition is arbitrary: Since states rarely follow uniform criteria in demarcating administrative regions, what constitutes a territory would vary from country to country. Nevertheless, it is one intuitive understanding of the term "territory." By this definition, the inhabitants of all administrative units within a larger state would constitute distinct ethnic groups. This definition would produce a large nonsensical count of ethnic groups, corresponding to list of all subnational administrative units in the world and their populations.

Consider now a less arbitrary definition—suppose that by the inhabitants of a common territory we mean all those who occupy a contiguous patch of land. If an ethnic identity is defined by inhabitation of a common territory, then it must consist of all those who occupy a contiguous patch of land. This definition too has very little relation to the identities we classify as ethnic. Any given patch of land is contiguous until it encounters discontinuities in terrain such mountains or oceans. This definition, thus, would produce a very small list of ethnic groups, corresponding roughly to the inhabitants of great continental or subcontinental regions. But it goes without saying that these continents and subcontinental regions all encompass many distinct groups that we classify as ethnic.

Suppose we modify this definition to mean that the inhabitants of a common territory are those who belong to a contiguous cluster of people on a contiguous patch of land. The boundaries of a contiguous population might be defined by some minimum threshold of population density. We could think of a rupture in contiguity as a drop in density below this threshold. Even this more sensible conceptualization of a common territory fails to yield a sensible definition of ethnic groups. By this definition, the population of any village and town separated from other villages and towns would be an ethnic group.

Let's try an even more reasonable definition. Suppose we impose a scale requirement, based on area or population: The inhabitants of a common territory are members of a contiguous cluster of people on a contiguous patch of land, with either the population or the area or both meeting some minimum threshold. We need not specify for now what scale requirement might be. Even according to this most reasonable definition, we would exclude many groups that we think of as ethnic—and include groups that we do not think of as ethnic. This definition, for instance, would not only exclude most of the groups in our sample—Blacks and Whites in the United States for instance, or Mohajirs and Punjabis in Pakistan, Serbs and Croats in Croatia, Zulu, Xhosa, and Coloureds in South

Africa, and so on—but force us to count these distinct groups as a single group, since they often coexist as in dense populations on contiguous patches of land.

I have tried to show that no reasonable definition of "territory" and "inhabitation of a common territory" captures our conventional classification of ethnic groups. Thus, this cannot be considered a primary defining characteristic. But can we consider the inhabitation of a common territory a *secondary*, if not a primary, defining characteristic? That is, is an ethnic group, defined by other means, also associated with the inhabitation of a common territory? By the association with a *common* territory, let's say that we mean either or both of two things: (1) the majority of the members of a given ethnic group (defined by other means) live in a given territory and/or (2) the majority of the population of a given territory belongs to a given ethnic group. By *territory*, let's say that we mean a contiguous patch of land that meets some minimal scale requirement. We do not need to specify the precise scale requirement—it may be based on population, or on area, or on the type of settlement found within it (e.g., it should include cities as well as villages).

But a common territory as defined above cannot be taken to be even a secondary defining characteristic for the groups that we classify as ethnic. In our sample only a subset of groups are associated with a common territory as defined above—Serb and Croat in the former Yugoslavia; Punjabis, Baluchis, and Pathans in Pakistan; Flemish and Walloon in Belgium; Yoruba, Ibo, and Hausa-Fulani in Nigeria; and Zulus in South Africa. But several others are not—Blacks and Whites in the United States, Mohajirs in Pakistan, the Aymara and Quechua in Bolivia, and the Xhosa and Coloureds in South Africa are not. And, indeed, there are many examples of groups outside our sample that we call ethnic—the Chinese in Malaysia or Muslims in Sri Lanka or Whites in Brazil for instance, who are not associated with a common territory. Some, such as the Roma, who are classified as ethnic in many countries, are explicitly nomadic.

Conceptual Autonomy

By "conceptual autonomy," Fearon and Laitin mean that "the existence of an ethnic category does not depend conceptually on the existence of any particular ethnic category" (Fearon and Laitin 2000a, 16). But we know from a large literature that the definition of *any* ethnic group presumes and depends upon the existence ethnic "others." Indeed, membership rules exist for the sole purpose of distinguishing insiders from outsiders. This criterion, if applied, would eliminate virtually all ethnic groups from the definition.

A Combination of Characteristics

Although I considered each characteristic individually, most definitions of ethnic identity incorporate several secondary characteristics in addition to the primary characteristic of descent, although the precise combination they employ varies. But any definition that requires a combination of characteristics captures only a subset of most of the identities that comparative political scientists classify as ethnic. This is because, as I have tried to show earlier, each characteristic, taken singly, captures only a subset of these identities at best. Since any single defining characteristic discussed previously captures at best a subset of the classification that we started with, any combination of characteristics will capture a still smaller subset.

7. Properties That Cannot Reasonably Be Associated with Ethnic Identities

In Chapter 3, I identify two properties of ethnic categories—"constrained change" and "visibility"—that can be associated with ethnic identities by definition. These properties are derived from two properties of descent-based attributes. Descent-based attributes, by their nature, are either displayed on the body or must be consistent with the attributes displayed on the body. This association with the body gives these attributes two intrinsic properties: "stickiness" and "visibility." The stickiness and visibility of descent-based *attributes*, in turn, produces the properties of constrained change and visibility in ethnic identity *categories*. But here, I focus on three classes of properties that, given our definition—and the elimination of the alternatives—cannot be taken to be intrinsic properties of ethnic identities.

These properties include the ten properties identified in eliminated definitions such as (1) a common ancestry, (2) a myth of common ancestry, (3) a common place of origin, (4) a myth of a common place of origin, (5) a "group" descent rule for membership, (6) a common culture, (7) a common language, (8) a common history, (9) a common territory, and (10) conceptual autonomy. All these properties, I argue, either do not distinguish the many identity categories that we routinely classify as "ethnic" from each other or from non-ethnic identities or describe an identity category defined by other means. While we may sometimes find ethnic identities characterized by these properties, they are best thought of as variables rather than constants—and variables that themselves require explanation before they can be incorporated in theories of ethnicity and other outcomes.

They also include the properties that contradict the definition that does capture this classification: fixedness and exogeneity. If ethnic identities change within constraints, then they cannot by definition be fixed. And if such change occurs as a product of human action, then they cannot by definition be exogenous to that action.

And, finally, they include those properties neither associated with ethnic identities in any definition nor by even a cursory look at the data. Take, for instance, the property of "networks," routinely used to build theoretical claims about the distinct behavior of those who share an ethnic identity (for instance, in Habyarimana et al. 2007). This property is not implied by any of the definitions I have discussed earlier. And even if we find that members of ethnic groups, however defined, do share network ties, we know, by observation, by anecdote, and by a wealth of literature on this subject, that so do those who go to the same school, those who are in the same profession, those who live in the same neighborhood, those who have the same hobbies, and so on. Networks, then, cannot be taken as properties associated intrinsically with ethnic identity at least on the basis of what we know so far. The same point applies to such properties as "institutional ties" or "norms." "Institutional ties," for instance, characterize some groups that we think of as ethnic (e.g., Shias in Iraq, linked by membership to mosques) but also groups that we think of as non-ethnic (e.g., trade unions that link industrial labor, or party organizations that bring together the party faithful). They also do not characterize some groups that we think of as ethnic (e.g., Hindus in India have not for most of their history been linked through institutional affiliations) and some groups that we do not think of as ethnic (e.g., peasants who have historically had a worse record of organization than the working class or the urban poor).

8. The Weak Presumption That Ethnicity Matters in Our Causal Claims

Only a handful of our causal claims rests on the intrinsic properties of ethnic identity. Among the claims that have a basis in the intrinsic properties associated with ethnic identity are Caselli and Coleman and Fearon's recent work on patronage and ethnic mobilization (Fearon 1999, Caselli and Coleman 2001), Janet Tai Landa's work on trading networks (Landa 1994), and my own work on patronage (Chandra 2004). Caselli and Coleman and Fearon argue that there should be an association between patronage politics and ethnic politics because patronage politics favors coalitions based on identities that are hard to change, and ethnic identities are hard to change.

Although none of these claims were made on the basis of a consistent definition, they are robust to evaluation against the one proposed here. They are all consistent with the property of "constrained change," which, as the next chapter shows, can be treated as being intrinsic to ethnic identities as defined here. By "constrained change," I mean simply the property of being constrained by the set of descent-based attributes individuals possess. Ethnic identities, I suggest, are not quite as hard to change as Caselli and Coleman and Fearon argue—it can be easy for individuals to switch between ethnic identities within the constraint of the underlying set of attributes. But to the extent that change in ethnic identities is more constrained than change in non-ethnic identities, the argument is upheld. Landa (1994) argues that under conditions of uncertainty, the visibility of ethnic cues allows individuals to select trading partners and enforce contracts. Chandra (2004) argues that given the information constrained environment of elections in a patronage-democracy, the visibility of ethnic identities makes them more likely to be activated in voter and party behavior than non-ethnic identities. While these arguments remain to be tested empirically, their reliance on properties that can be taken to be intrinsic to ethnic identities at least makes them logically sustainable.

However, as the next chapter elaborates, the arguments made even in this handful of works should be read as applying to distributions of ethnic and non-ethnic identities rather than each type of identity individually. If we consider individual identity types, we will certainly find some identities that are ethnic that do not have constraints on change or are not visible and thus do not exhibit any particular affinity with patronage. And we will certainly find some identities which are non-ethnic but either have constraints on change or are visible or both—and thus should exhibit an affinity with patronage.

By far the largest number of explanatory claims about ethnicity rests on properties that I have argued earlier are *not* intrinsic to ethnic identities. These include the family of arguments linking ethnic identities with various forms of violence, which rest on claims such as fixedness, a common history, dense social networks, and distinct emotional responses. They also include a subset of the arguments linking ethnicity to patronage, which rely on the properties of networks, institutional ties, and spatial concentration. And they include arguments linking ethnic identity with the destabilization of states and regimes, which employ properties such as territorial concentration, a division of labor, and fixedness.

As such, they cannot be taken as reasonable claims about the effect of ethnic identities in general—they should be reformulated as claims about a specific subset of ethnic identities, or claims about the effect of ethnic identities combined with some additional variable. Rather than reading them to mean that "ethnicity is associated with some dependent variable Y," we should read them as claims meaning either that "some set of identities, which sometimes includes ethnic identities, are associated with dependent variable Y" or that "ethnicity, along with some other variable X, is associated with the dependent variable Y."

As an example of a causal claim that refers to only a subset of identities, consider one that explains the association between modernization and ethnic politics by invoking the property of territorial concentration (Bates 1974, 464). The argument is informed by the study of ethnic politics in Africa, and it certainly appears to be the case that several ethnic categories in Africa are territorially concentrated. But we cannot take either territorial concentration or the memory of a common territorial homeland to be a defining property. Nor does it describe ethnic categories in general. And we can certainly imagine non-ethnic categories that are territorially concentrated. This argument, thus, should be read not as a general argument about ethnic identities but as an argument about "territorially concentrated" identities, a concept that may or may not overlap with ethnic identities.

As an example of a causal claim that probably omits some variable, consider the argument that democracies are destabilized by the permanent exclusion of some minority groups from power. The key property of ethnic identity that this argument rests on is fixedness: If ethnic identities are fluid, not fixed, then the other propositions fall through. But we know, based on the definition proposed in this chapter, that fixedness is not an intrinsic property of ethnic identities—"constrained change" is. If we find that ethnic identities consistently acquire fixedness in a democratic context and that fixedness in turn threatens democratic stability, it must be due to some extrinsic variable that interacts with ethnic identity which has not been theorized.

While we cannot associate several of the properties eliminated here with ethnic identity by definition, we might be able, however, to think of them as variables sometimes associated with ethnic identity—and build theories and raise questions employing this different way of thinking. Rather than explain an outcome associated with ethnic identity through recourse to a common culture, for instance, we can investigate the conditions under which a common culture comes to be associated with ethnic identity. It may well be that the interaction of these non-constitutive properties with constitutive properties such as constrained change and visibility produces distinct causal effects associated with ethnic identity.

Indeed, even the elimination of definitions proposed here should lead us to ask new questions. For instance, I have argued that a common region of origin does not distinguish ethnic identities objectively speaking. But a *belief* in an ancestral region may well affect behavior even when it is not based in fact. Similarly, while properties of fixedness and exogeneity are not constitutive of ethnic identities from an analytical perspective, members of activated ethnic categories may indeed see these categories as fixed and exogenous. Might this belief be associated with distinct effects (Suny 1999b, Gil-White 2001)? We can begin to ask such questions only when we stop thinking of these characteristics as definitions and begin thinking of them as variable beliefs that can come to be associated with ethnic identities defined by some other means.

3

Attributes and Categories

A New Conceptual Vocabulary for Thinking about
Ethnic Identity

KANCHAN CHANDRA

This chapter introduces a new conceptual vocabulary for thinking about ethnic identities as defined previously. The vocabulary is built on a conceptualization of the term "identity" simply as a category, and a distinction between categories and the attributes necessary for membership in them. The conceptualization of "identities" as "categories," is not new. A number of influential works in the study of ethnic identities also employ a categorical approach to identity (see for instance Barth 1969, Tajfel 1981, Laitin 1998, Brubaker 2004). The principal innovation here is the introduction of a systematic distinction between categories and attributes. This distinction is the building block for the arguments about ethnic identity introduced in this book.

In previous work, the term "identity" has often been used interchangeably for an "attribute" that signifies membership in a category but does not constitute it (e.g., dark skin), the "category" itself (e.g., African American), an "attribute-dimension," consisting of a "family" of attribute-values (e.g., the dimension of skin color, on which values might include "dark" and "light"), or a "category-dimension" consisting of a "family" of categories (e.g., the dimension of race in the United States, which has the categories of "Black," "White," and so on arrayed on it). This chapter shows why and how attributes and categories—and therefore attribute-dimensions and category-dimensions— are conceptually distinct, as well as the stakes attached to this distinction.

The reader will encounter many conceptual distinctions in this chapter in addition to this principal one. The value of these distinctions lies in the claims we are able to make, and the questions we are able to ask when we employ them. Blunt concepts for thinking about ethnic identities produce blunt questions and blunt answers. The more precise and complex concepts introduced here produce more precise and complex questions and more illuminating answers. These distinctions, furthermore, are linked in a single, logically connected framework. This framework enables us not only to ask new questions but to trace connections between the answers.[1]

One important set of distinctions is between the "membership rule," "membership," "name," and "content" associated with an identity category. All categories have these four features and could in principle be defined by any or all of them. But, drawing on the arguments developed in the previous chapter, I note that ethnic identity categories are a type of category defined solely by their membership rule. I dub this the "attribute-descent rule" because it is distinguished by the use of descent-based attributes. Other features of ethnic identity categories, such as the membership, name, and content, are supplemental rather than constitutive. They are not, in other words, the basis of a definition of an ethnic identity—they simply describe an ethnic identity defined by other means.

The distinction between the "membership rule" and other features of an identity category has significant implications for theories of ethnic identity change. If we define ethnic identities purely on the basis of the membership rule, then it follows that ethnic identities change only when membership rule changes. But if we define ethnic identities on the basis also of membership, name, or content, then it must follow that ethnic identities change when any of these features change, irrespective of the composition of the membership rule. This latter position is often employed in theories of ethnic identity change, but as we will see, it is inconsistent with the way in which we actually classify ethnic identities in the social sciences. Given these classifications, it is more reasonable to understand a change in features such as membership, name, and content as a change *in* ethnic identities as we classify them but not a change *of* ethnic identities. That said, these features are important and informative in themselves and worthy of study in their own right.

If ethnic identity categories are defined solely by the use of descent-based attributes in their membership rule, furthermore, then their properties should also be determined entirely by the attributes required for membership—and not by the attributes of their membership, name, or content. This chapter identifies two properties derived from descent-based attributes that *can* be intrinsically associated with ethnic identity categories: "constrained change" and "visibility." By "constrained change," I mean the property that ethnic identities can change in the short term

---

[1] Because the membership rules for a category consist of a selection of attributes, for example, we can express those rules as a subset of the full set of attributes for an individual or population. A question about the conditions under which nominal ethnic identity categories are activated, then, can be expressed as a question about the choice of one subset of attributes over others. A change in the underlying set of attributes for a population, furthermore, changes its repertoire of nominal ethnic identity categories, and thus creates a basis for change in the categories chosen or assigned from it. The answers to one question about one set of concepts, then, also affect the answers to questions about others. Subsequent chapters explore these interrelationships in more complex models about ethnic identity change than we have been able to construct before.

only within the constraints of a fixed set of attributes. By "visibility," I mean the property that some information by which an observer can place an individual in an ethnic category is available through superficial information, although there may well be variability and error in how this information is interpreted.

These properties of ethnic identity categories are derived from the properties of descent-based attributes but are distinct from them. Descent-based attributes have the intrinsic properties of being "sticky" or "fixed" on average in the short term. By "stickiness" I mean the property of being difficult to change in the short term, within an existing scheme of classification. Helen's skin color, for instance, would be hard to change in the course of her lifetime. By "visibility" I mean the property of being conspicuous even in superficial observation. Helen's skin color, for instance, would be obviously visible to a casual observer without any further interaction. The greater stickiness and visibility, on average, of descent-based attributes, as this section argues, is a product of their association with the body. This association imposes two requirements: (1) these attributes are either displayed on the body or must be consistent with attributes displayed on the body (what I call the "consistency" requirement) and (2) there must be no evidence of the possession of different descent-based attributes earlier in a person's past (what I call the "erasure" requirement).

The short-term fixedness of descent-based attributes does not mean that descent-based categories are fixed in the short term too. It simply means that descent-based categories can change only within the constraints of the descent-based attributes that constitute them. The greater visibility, on average, of descent-based attributes, in turn, means that descent-based categories are also more visible, on average, than non-descent-based categories. But there is a subtle difference in the nature of the visibility of attributes compared to categories. Descent-based attributes are on average visible within an agreed upon interpretation: In the United States, for instance, Helen's skin color is not only easily observable but would be observed by most observers as "dark." The categories that these descent-based attributes signal, however, while also visible, may not always be interpreted in the same way by all observers. Helen's dark skin, for instance, may be interpreted as placing her in the category "Black" or the category "West Indian." Although the key *attribute* required for membership in either category is visible, there is no single correct correspondence between the attribute and category with which it is associated.

Taken together, the conceptual distinctions introduced in this chapter suggest three guidelines for building reasonable causal claims and asking new questions about the relationship between ethnicity, politics, and economics.

(1) Our claims and questions should disaggregate the concept of "ethnicity." The effect of "ethnicity" on some outcome of interest should be traced, not as one big causal path originating from one big concept but through several causal paths,

possibly interdependent, originating from several narrow concepts such as "attributes," "categories," "attribute-dimensions," "category-dimensions," and so on.

(2) Our claims and questions about the effect of one or more of these concepts should rest on the properties of "constrained change" and "visibility"—and not on properties such as a common culture, network ties, institutional affiliations and so on which cannot be justified by a conceptual argument. While this guideline closes the door on some claims, it opens new doors to new claims and questions.

(3) We should think in distributions, not dichotomies, in making these claims and raising new questions.

Section 1 of this chapter elaborates on the use of the term "identity" to mean a "category." Section 2 then develops the distinction between the terms "attributes" and "categories." Section 3 notes that the definition of an ethnic identity category proposed in this book is based solely on its membership rule—and distinguishes the use of an "attribute-descent rule" for membership from previous definitions that specify membership rules based on group membership or cultural criteria. Section 4 distinguishes between the membership rule that defines ethnic categories from "supplemental" features such as their membership, name, and content. Section 5 elaborates on the process by which nominal ethnic identity categories are "activated." Section 6 identifies the properties of descent-based attributes—fixedness and visibility (with a fixed interpretation), on average. Section 7 uses these discussions to identify the properties of descent-based categories—constrained change and visibility (with variable interpretation) on average. Section 8 draws out the implications of preceding arguments for building theories about the relationship between ethnicity and political and economic processes and outcomes. Section 9, the conclusion, addresses the question of whether the term "ethnic identity" continues to be useful.

1. Identity

An "identity" is a category that can be used to classify or describe an individual—that is, a category for which she possesses the attributes that determine eligibility for membership. For example, a necessary attribute for eligibility for membership in the category "grandmother" is the possession of a grandchild. If I have a grandchild, I am eligible to call myself a grandmother, or others can call me a grandmother. That is among my identities. If I do not possess a grandchild, I am not eligible to call myself a grandmother. That is not among my identities.

All identities, or categories, have a membership rule, membership, content, and name associated with them. By "membership rule" I mean the criteria that distinguish members from nonmembers. This membership rule can be *defined by a single attribute or by several*. The category "grandmother" is an example of a category that requires a single attribute. The category "a Turkish grandmother who is a Republican" is an example of a category that requires several. The "membership" of a category refers to those individuals who are eligible to be included in that category. The content of an ethnic identity category refers to any characteristics shared by all or most of its members in addition to those characteristics necessary to establish eligibility for membership. It is the associations, objective and subjective, that membership in a category carries for insiders and outsiders, whether or not they are true. For instance, we may associate membership in the category "grandmother" with kindliness, cooking, knitting, and rocking chairs, whether or not any particular grandmother actually exhibits these features. The degree to which a category has a content and the content associated with any particular category can vary. The name of a category is self-explanatory.

A key distinction among the identities—categories—that *can* be used to classify an individual is that between nominal and activated identities. *Nominal* identities are those categories that *could be* used for such descriptions—that is, for which an individual possesses the attributes that determine membership. *Activated* identities are those identities from among the nominal set that *are* used to describe an individual, by choice or assignation. Thus, my nominal identities in this situation would include vegetarian, a kind person, a person of Turkish origin, a Republican, a female, and a rich person. If I call myself a vegetarian, or others call me a vegetarian, that would be my activated identity. Unless otherwise specified, the term "identity" always refers to nominal rather than activated identities, and the term "membership" refers to "nominal" membership. The activated membership of an ethnic category refers to those individuals who actually claim membership in that category.

Identity categories can differ according to the context in which they are activated (Figure 1.2 in chapter 1 illustrates this point for ethnic identities). Since different identities can be activated in different contexts, an individual can in principle have as many activated identity categories as there are contexts. We cannot speak of "activated" identities, therefore, without also specifying the context in which they are activated.

Among activated identities, we can distinguish further between *chosen* and *assigned* identities. Figure 3.1 captures this distinction.

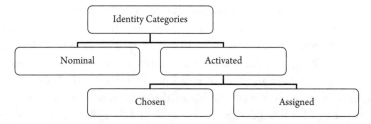

Figure 3.1 Chosen and Assigned Identities

A *chosen* identity is an identity an individual uses to describe herself in any given situation. An *assigned* identity is a category assigned to an individual by others. Chosen and assigned identities may or may not coincide. For instance, the category I use to describe myself at a party might be "artist," while those to whom I am talking might insist on seeing me as a "grandmother." In this case, my activated identity would be that of "artist" while my assigned identity would be that of "grandmother." Thus, when talking about activated identities, we should always be careful to specify whether we mean chosen or assigned identities. Further, choice and assignation are likely to be interdependent: The identities we choose are likely to be affected by those that we are assigned. The difference between choice and assignation of identities—and the connections between the two—opens up a fundamental set of questions about identities in general and ethnic identities in particular. I address these questions later in this chapter.

Two additional distinctions among the many that can be drawn in principle will be helpful as we proceed. The first is a distinction between individual identities—identity categories in which we are sole members—and collective identities—identity categories that have other members. Typically, individual identities are defined by unique conjunctions of attributes. Collective identities are defined by attributes or conjunction of attributes that are not unique. Ethnic identity categories, as we will see, tend to be collective rather than individual. The activation of such categories by either choice or assignation, in other words, is typically an act that asserts not the uniqueness of the individual but some similarity with others who can be described by the same label. This does not mean that an individual who activates an ethnic identity category subscribes to a shared group consciousness. Instead, it underlines only that the use of an ethnic category associates the individual with some minimum descriptive similarities with others classed in the same category.

A second distinction is between identities we activate in a context witnessed by others and private identities (identities we activate in the privacy of our own hearts). The two need not coincide. The following example, chosen from among anthropologist Tone Bringa's respondents in Bosnia, helps make this distinction clear. Bringa notes, of this respondent:

> Atif, a sixty-year-old Muslim and former communist party member, was typical of many of his generation who for most of their lives did not have the choice of calling themselves Muslim for public and administrative purposes, that is, he could not identify with an official Muslim *narod*. Similarly, as a communist party member he was not allowed to practice his religion, and therefore had publicly to deny his Muslim religious identity as well. Atif had been through most of the categories: "Unspecified," "Croat," "Yugoslav," "Serb," and "Muslim." ... This does not mean that the way he perceived and experienced his identity had

changed; indeed, after giving me this list of official categories he added
that in his heart he remained a Muslim throughout. He knew who he
was. (Bringa 1995, 29)

In Atif's case, there was a consistent disjuncture between his publicly and privately held identities. Other individuals, perhaps operating in contexts in which
the costs attached to the public acknowledgement of an identity are lower, may
not experience the same disjuncture.

The arguments made in this book typically concern themselves with collective and publicly held identity categories. We have little to say about how Atif, or
other individuals, might experience their ethnic identities "in their hearts." But
the relationship between individual and collective identities and public and private identities is of interest in itself. Congruence between publicly and privately
held identities may be important both as a psychological concept, indicating
an integrated personality, and as a normative one, indicating some form of personal authenticity. Further, it may also have distinct behavioral consequences:
We might hypothesize, for instance, that individuals whose public and private
identities are congruent behave more predictably than those who are more con-
flicted. The conditions under which publicly and privately held identities are
congruent, and the consequences of such congruence, then, may well form a
subject for exploration in other work.

Wait a minute, you might say. Calling an identity a category seems on the face
of it to trivialize the term. Isn't identity something much more fundamental—an
"essence," *the* essence, that defines us? Note, however, that as defined here, there
is no conceptual distinction between an essence and a classification. Articulating
an essence is only possible through the use of classifications. Consider a person
who thinks of her identity—her essence—as her deep religiosity. Articulating
this essence is simply a way of categorizing herself as follows: "I am a deeply
religious person." She could articulate this essence even more precisely: "I am
a deeply religious person who defines religion as belief in God rather than an
organized religion and uses it to guide my everyday behavior." The more precise
the articulation, the closer it might get to capturing me uniquely. But note that
any such articulation would require the use of categories, simple or complex, to
describe herself. That is exactly what I say that identity is.

This brings us to a second point. An identity may well consist of one or more
categories. But isn't it a *primary* category—one that is more fundamental than
others? Note, in response, that the definition above does not negate the concept
of a "primary" identity—what I call a "chosen" identity is indeed a primary *in
any given situation*. But I treat this primary category as a *subset* of an individual's
identity set, not coterminous with it.

This simply conforms to the rules of grammar. We can certainly distinguish
between identities that individuals see as primary and secondary in any given

context. Simply making this distinction requires us to use the term "identity" for both concepts and qualify it with additional ones. If we reserved the term "identity" only for primary categories in any given context, we would have to eliminate a lot of popular discourse. For instance, we could not use the term "identity repertoire" because it is by definition a term that distinguishes between primary and latent identities. We could not say "Turkish is among her ethnic identities" because if her ethnic categories are not primary, they would by definition not be among her identities.

A third objection to the conceptualization presented previously is that it does not capture the idea of uniqueness. Our identity is often something that we think of the thing that makes us unique. But we know that many categories have many members. Thus, placing ourselves in a category may often be a way of linking ourselves to other individuals and thus *denying* our uniqueness. The category "grandmother" has many members. Thus, when someone calls herself a "grandmother," it is a way of highlighting her sameness with other grandmothers, not highlighting the ways in which she is different.

To this I respond by returning to the distinction I made earlier between categories that require a single attribute or a conjunction of them. The more complex the conjunction, the fewer members the category is likely to include, until we get to get to only one. In that sense, we might say that individuality does indeed consist of an identity category—but one that requires a unique combination of attributes.

Although this conceptualization can capture the idea of uniqueness where it exists, it is worth emphasizing also that asserting an identity is not about asserting the *uniqueness* of individuals—it is about asserting *difference* between groups of individuals who see themselves as alike. Much of the scholarly writing on identity describes identities as social groupings with collective memberships, not statements about individuality. Indeed, if we thought of identity as solely something that captured our uniqueness, we could simply not use terms like "class identities," "ethnic identities," "party identities," and so on, all of which emphasize the similarity of large classes of individuals and their differences from other classes.

A fourth objection to what I have said so far might be the following: Even if we accept that identity is no more than a category, there is something about it that is an *unchanging* categorization? That is, isn't identity something stable, not situational? The definition above does not eliminate the possibility of an unchanging essence—in other words, that the same category is the chosen identity across all situations. But it does not require it. Indeed, it allows us to investigate whether such stable identities exist. For some individuals, the categories we treat as primary may not vary across contexts. Atif's declaration suggests that at least in the context of his privately held identity, there was no variance: He may have thought of himself as Muslim in the workplace, a

Muslim when he decided to marry, and a Muslim when he was walking on the street. But in other cases, there may be variance. If we build the idea of invariance to situation into the very definition of identity, we eliminate by assertion something which should be open to investigation. By defining it as I do here, we do not eliminate the possibility of stability—but we allow ourselves to see where and when it exists.

A fifth objection is that the term "identity" should apply only to categories based on ethnicity, broadly defined, and gender and not other sorts of categories. While I have not seen this argument made explicitly, it is implicit in much of the scholarship to which this book responds. In a recent book titled *Identity and Democracy*, for instance, Gutmann (2003) uses the term "identity" to refer almost exclusively to identities based on race, gender, nationality, and religion. There are occasional references to other things such as disability as a basis for identity—but these are the exception rather than the rule. Note, however, that the very use of phrases like "ethnic identity" or "gender identity" demonstrates the lack of logic in the use of the term "identity" to mean purely ethnicity. Following the rules of grammar, if the adjective "ethnic" qualifies the noun "identity," then the term "identity" must be some broad thing, of which "ethnic identities" represent a subtype.

2. Attribute and Category

In the previous section, I defined "identity" as any category in which an individual is eligible for membership. By an attribute of that category, I mean a characteristic that qualifies an individual for membership in that category, or signals such membership.

Relational Nature of the Distinction

It seems at first that the distinction between "attribute" and "category" is based on the intrinsic nature of the two objects. Take, for instance, the category "Black" in the United States. Membership in this category is typically associated with the attribute of dark skin among others. We might assume, looking at this example, that there are things in the world, such as physical features, which are intrinsically attributes, and other things, such as the social entities created by physical features, which are intrinsically categories.

But this first impression is misleading. The distinction between attribute and category is based on the *relation* between two objects, not their intrinsic properties. In any given domain of analysis, we can distinguish between an object that is a category and an object that is an attribute *in relation to* that category. But objects that are attributes in relation to a category in one domain of analysis can themselves be categories in relation to other attributes in other domains of analysis.

Take, for example, "dark skin" which I describe above as a qualifying attribute for the category "Black." What exactly do we mean by "dark skin"? How do we know it when we see it? In the United States, commonsense conventions tell us that the term "dark skin" applies to shades of skin color that range from light brown to black. Thus, although "dark skin" is an attribute in relation to the category "Black," it is itself a category in relation to attributes describing shades of skin color. Similarly, although, "Black" is category in relation to the attribute "dark skin," it can also be considered an attribute in relation to other categories in other domains of analysis (e.g., "Black Muslim," for which the immediate qualifying attributes include being Black and being Muslim).

Consider other examples. Are "blue eyes" an attribute or a category? Blue eyes can be attributes in relation to a category in one domain of analysis (e.g., White) but categories in relation to attributes in other domains of analysis (grey eyes, light blue eyes, deep blue eyes, greenish blue eyes). And "White" in turn, while it may be a category in relation to the attribute of being blue-eyed, is itself an attribute in relation to a category in a different domain of analysis (e.g., WASP—White Anglo Saxon Protestant).

"Basic" and "Secondary" Attributes

In principle, there may well be no such thing as a "basic" attribute which cannot be broken down further. Let's go back to the example of "dark skin." "Dark skin" can be broken down into attributes such as light brown and dark brown shades of skin. But these shades can also be broken down into other attributes—for example, we could think of the color "dark brown" as being composed of a mix of orange and brown shades. And these shades of orange and brown could themselves be broken down into attributes corresponding to an interval defining the wavelength of light that created these colors. This interval could be broken down still further, so that we never really hit rock bottom.

However, we often treat attributes as "basic" in practice even when they are not in principle. In the United States, for example, people have a commonsensical notion of what constitutes dark skin. This is different from commonsensical notions of what constitutes dark skin in Brazil or India or Nigeria. Nevertheless, we take it as given. While we might match dark skin with categories at higher levels of analysis, we typically do not decompose it into its own constituent attributes.

I define the set of "basic" attributes that characterize individuals as that set of attributes which we take as commonsensically given, even though they can in principle be decomposed further. "Secondary" attributes, by contrast, are transparent constructs of basic attributes which, even though they function as the raw materials for categories at a higher level of analysis, can be disaggregated into their basic components.

In the chapters that follow, I draw upon a body of work in anthropology and history in addition to political science to show how such "commonsense" is typically the result of the institutions introduced by the modern state such as the educational system of a country, the census, the administrative system and the legal system and can itself be transformed over the long term (see, for instance, Weber 1976, Andersen 1983, Gellner 1983, Dirks 2001, Posner 2005). These institutions impose a rule of *selection*—which attributes, among the infinite characteristics that describe individuals should we pay attention to—and a rule of *interpretation*—how should we "see" these attributes. Taken together, I call the rule of selection and the rule of interpretation a classificatory scheme. Here, we can simply assume that in any given country, there is a distribution of "basic" attributes which function as the basis of the creation of categories, without being interpreted as categories themselves. Because institutions change over time, we should expect these commonsensical frameworks, and the basic attributes they create, also to change over time. But in the short term, we can take them as fixed.

At any given time, then, we can break down any identity category into the "basic" attributes that determine membership. But we may have to go through several levels of attributes before getting down to the presumed basics. Take, for instance, the category "Gaysian," in the United States, which, broken down to the most proximate level, is constituted by two attributes: gay and Asian. This first level is represented in Figure 3.2.

We can then break both attributes down further to a second level. According to one standard interpretation, being eligible for membership "gay" consists of the attribute of having a preference for a same-sex sexual partner. And being Asian consists of tracing family origins to one or more of countries including China, Japan, North Korea, Vietnam, South Korea, Malaysia, Indonesia, India, and so on. Note that these definitions of what constitutes being gay or being Asian are contested. I address the implications of such contestation over membership rules below. But here, I simply take them as given for the purpose of illustration. This second level is represented in Figure 3.3.

These attributes can in principle be disaggregated further ad infinitum. We need some rule, for instance, to determine preference for a same-sex sexual

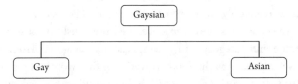

Figure 3.2 First-Level Attributes for the Category "Gaysian"

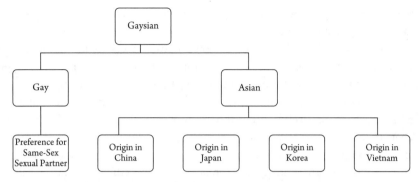

Figure 3.3 Second-Level Attributes for the Category "Gaysian"

partner. And we might want to deconstruct an attribute such as origin in China, identifying the attributes that determine eligibility for inclusion in China and the attributes that determine origin. But we usually don't do that. Most people would arguably be content to take the concepts of "same-sex partner" and "origin in China" as given. We can say thus in the case of the category "Gaysian," we must disaggregate the category to two levels in order to identify its basic attributes.

Attribute-Dimension and Category-Dimension

By the term "attribute-dimension," I mean a set of mutually exclusive and exhaustive *attribute-values*. For instance, the attribute-dimension of skin color in the United States can be defined as a set of two mutually exclusive and exclusive attribute-values: {dark skin and light skin}. Identity categories can vary according to which and how many attribute-dimensions they are based.

By the term "category-dimension," I mean a set of mutually exclusive and exhaustive *categories*. For instance, the category-dimension of race in the United States might be defined as a set of three mutually exclusive categories: {Black, White and Other}.

The distinction between attribute-dimension and category-dimension is relational, just as the distinction between attribute and category is. Given any category, we can determine the attribute-values that define it and therefore the attribute-dimensions to which those values belong. But things that are attribute-dimensions in relation to a category at a higher level of analysis may well be category-dimensions at a lower level of analysis.

Within the literature on identity politics, the term "identity dimension" has so far been used to refer only to "category-dimensions" (Posner 2005). This concept of "attribute-dimension" has not been developed previously because the distinction between attribute and category and its implications has gone systematically unnoticed. But as we will see, it is the more powerful of the two concepts. The attributes on which activated categories are based are, by definition, arrayed on an attribute-dimension. Attribute-dimensions, thus, are relevant in almost any situation in which a category is activated. Nominal or activated categories constructed from these attributes, however, may or may not fall on a common dimension. Consider, for instance, that the categories "White," "WASP," "Jewish," and "Irish" may all be activated in the United States currently. Each category can be said to be generated from attributes on an attribute-dimension, including the dimensions of skin color, religion, and national origin. But the categories do not themselves fall on any common category-dimension. Category-dimensions, therefore, may not exist in many contexts.

3. Defining an "Ethnic" Identity Category by Its Membership Rule

Ethnic identities, as defined previously, refer to a subset of identities in which one family of descent-based attribute dimensions is necessary for membership (i.e., the attribute-dimensions of race, religion, sect, language, dialect, tribe, clan, caste, nationality, and physical differences). It does not matter whether the attributes in question are basic or secondary, since if one of these is descent-based, the other must be too.[2] Non-ethnic categories, by inference, are all those that lie outside this set.

This is the newest of a family of definitions that define an ethnic identity by its membership rule—simply the features that distinguish members from nonmembers, rather than all the features that those members share in common—but differ over how to specify that membership rule. Frederik Barth introduced this approach to definition in his seminal work in 1969, in which he proposed that members of ethnic categories were distinguished from nonmembers by "cultural differentiae" (Barth 1969, 13–16). I call this the "cultural" rule for membership. Writing in 2003, Fearon and Laitin proposed that members of ethnic "groups" were distinguished from nonmembers by the group memberships of their parents and ancestors. I term their rule the "group descent rule" for membership. The membership rule I propose stipulates that members of ethnic categories are distinguished from nonmembers by the descent-based attributes they possess. I term this the "attribute descent rule" for membership.

In principle, an identity could be defined by any or all of four features: its *membership rule*, its membership, its name, or its content. The justification for a minimal definition based solely on a membership rule—and in particular, the

---

[2] We do not need to distinguish between basic and secondary attributes in order to determine *whether* an ethnic identity category is ethnic, but we may need to distinguish between them in order to determine the precise membership rule that defines that ethnic category. This point becomes important in the chapters that follow.

attribute descent rule—was given in Chapter 1. It is only a membership rule–based definition that captures the identities that we actually classify as ethnic. The other features—membership, name, and content—are supplemental features that describe an identity defined by other means.

The membership rules for any category are constructed, are specific to time and place, and can often be contested. In the 2001 race for mayor in Newark, for instance, both leading candidates could be classified as "Black" using the membership rule for this category identified above: dark skin and descent from parents of African origin. But the incumbent, who was darker skinned than his opponent, proposed a different rule. Differentiating between shades of skin color, he associated being Black with "dark brown" rather than "light brown" skin. His campaign slogan, which called him "The Real Deal," underlined this more restrictive rule. This definition takes no position about what the appropriate match between descent-based attributes and categories is, how many generations of descent are required by the match, and who is doing the matching. It stipulates only that when the members of an identity category are classified according to a given set of descent-based attributes, then it becomes an ethnic identity category.

This means that whether or not an identity category is "ethnic" in nature in any given context depends on whether we can identify a consensus on the necessity of descent-based attributes in the membership rules for that category in that context. That is, we can say that a category is "ethnic" if there is one agreed-upon rule according to which descent-based attributes are necessary for membership or, where there is disagreement, we can say that descent-based attributes are necessary for membership regardless of any particular rule. When some of the contested membership rules require descent-based attributes while others do not, we can say that the "ethnic" nature of an identity category is in question. And if none of the membership rules in a given context require the possession of descent-based attributes, we cannot term an identity category an ethnic category.[3]

Recall further that, according to this definition, for an identity to be called ethnic, descent-based attributes should be *necessary* for membership although they need not be sufficient. Further, since membership rules are specific to time and place, whether or not some category is ethnic depends on the time and place. In determining whether or not some category is ethnic, therefore, we

---

[3] Collecting data on ethnic identities using this definition, then, requires us to obtain data on the membership rules which define identity categories. Methodologically, this can be a challenge. Membership rules for identity categories may or may not be explicitly articulated. Even when they are explicit, they may or may not be uniform. The existence of explicit and uniform membership rules, furthermore, is not a random event: It is correlated with political and economic circumstances which attach rewards or punishment to the codification of these rules. I address questions of this nature in *Measuring Ethnicity*, the companion volume to this one.

cannot ask and answer general questions that are independent of a temporal and spatial context—"Is the category 'Black' an ethnic category?" But we can answer questions such as: "Was the category 'Black' in the early part of the century in the United States an 'ethnic' category?" Here the answer is yes, since the 1910 census defined the category "Black" based on features and descent (Nobles 2000, 67). But note that the category of the same name—"Black"—as defined by the U.S. Census of 2000 would not be an ethnic category since it allowed respondents to declare membership in the category "Black" based purely on self-identification, regardless of descent.

4. Distinguishing Between Defining and Supplementary Features

If ethnic identities are defined solely by their membership rule, then their properties should also be determined entirely by the attributes required for membership—not by their membership, name, or content. Making this distinction between defining and supplemental features is important both for its own sake but also for how we theorize about ethnic identity change. If ethnic identities are defined by their membership rule, then they change when that membership rule changes. A change in other features does not change ethnic identity itself although it may change some nonconstitutive feature associated with that identity. As supplemental features, however, they are theoretically important in their own right. This section elaborates.

Membership

Different membership rules will often be accompanied by different memberships. Consider the example of the "Huguenots" and "Jews" in France. These categories have different membership rules—to be a Huguenot, one must be descended from parents who were Huguenots; to be Jewish one must be descended from a Jewish mother—and different memberships, because those who possess the set of attributes selected by the first do not typically possess the attributes selected by the second.

But different membership rules can be accompanied by identical memberships. Consider the categories "Sinhala" and "Buddhist" in Sri Lanka. The membership rules for the two categories are different. For the category "Sinhala" the membership rules include one or more of the following: those whose ancestors are indigenous to the island of Ceylon, or those who parents and ancestors spoke Sinhala or both. For the category "Buddhist," the membership rule is those descended from parents and ancestors who professed Buddhism. However, apart from a tiny minority of those whose ancestors are accepted as indigenous but Christian, most *individuals* who have the attributes of the first category also have the attributes for the second. Consequently, the *memberships* of the categories "Sinhala" and "Buddhist" are virtually the same.

Based on the definition above, categories with different membership rules are different ethnic identities regardless of whether the membership they generate is the same or different. This is simply a logical extension of the definition above, justified on the basis of usage. But it is also commonsensical. It recognizes the fact that those who define themselves or are defined as "Sinhala" may behave differently or be treated differently than those who see themselves as "Buddhist." A government responding to a population that defines itself as Buddhist, for instance, may pay more attention to religious symbols than when the same population defines itself as "Sinhala."

At the same time, we can imagine situations in which what matters most is the membership itself and not the basis for membership. When the Sri Lanka Freedom Party in Sri Lanka attempted to build an electoral majority, for instance, it was indifferent about which of several membership rules it used—Sinhala or Buddhist—since each rule targeted roughly the same membership. In that context, the numbers associated with a category were more important that the basis on which that category was constituted. While this definition describes Sinhala and Buddhist as *different* ethnic identities, it does not prevent us from studying them as examples of a set of ethnic categories that produce the same membership on different bases. Indeed, once we distinguish the membership from the membership rule, we can ask the question: Under what conditions are individuals or entrepreneurs indifferent to the membership rule?

Content

The content of an ethnic identity category refers to any characteristics shared by all or most of its members in addition to those characteristics necessary to establish eligibility for membership. The distinction between "membership rules" and "shared content" echoes Frederik Barth's distinction between the "ethnic boundary that defines the group, not the cultural stuff that it encloses" (Barth 1969, 15). But Barth defined both the membership rules and content of an ethnic category purely on the basis of culture. I define membership rules more narrowly, based purely on descent, and define "shared content" more broadly, to include culture and much else besides.

The content shared by members of an ethnic category may be based on descent. For instance, members of some ethnic categories may have a greater likelihood for certain kinds of illness, based on some shared genetic features. It may be based on cultural features. For instance, the value of egalitarianism is common to many Somalis (Laitin 1977). Shared content can comprise economic attributes such as income—for instance, Mexicans in the United States have lower incomes than Whites—or political affiliation—for instance, the affinity among the majority Blacks in the United States for the Democratic party—or even psychological orientations—for instance, stigmatized minorities such as Scheduled Castes can share in a collective feeling of inferiority in relation to those from more powerful categories.

To the extent that these shared characteristics are not used to determine who is eligible for membership in a category and who is not, they do not *define* an ethnic category. Thus, to the extent that we do not say that egalitarian values were a qualifying or signaling characteristic for membership in the category "Somali," these values cannot be taken to be a defining feature of Somali identity.

Nevertheless, shared content can often be a variable associated with it, and the degree of association is a matter for study in its own right. Members of some ethnic categories may share a great many cultural, economic, and psychological features, while others may share little other than the membership rule that distinguishes them. Further, the degree and type of shared content may produce systematic differences in the behavior associated with members. We can analyze such variation and assess its importance without inferring category membership from content. Indeed, it is only by separating the definition of an ethnic identity category from shared content that we can raise these questions. If we assumed that ethnic categories had a shared content by definition, we would not then be able to ask why some ethnic categories had a greater degree of shared content than others.

Name

According to some approaches to ethnic identities, naming is constitutive of an ethnic identity: It defines the identity and creates its properties (Daniel 1996, Hansen 2001). But this point is belied when we consider how we classify ethnic identities as the same or different in both social science and everyday usage: Ethnic identity categories that we label as the "same" can carry different names, and ethnic identity categories that we routinely label as "different" can carry the same name. While names are not constitutive of ethnic identities as defined here, however, they are of critical information in their own right.

Consider, for instance, the name "Black" in the United States. The membership rule for this category, as discussed above, includes the attributes of dark skin, physical features, and descent from parents of African origin. Another name that has been used for the membership captured by this name includes "African-American." The use of one name rather than another does not denote a change in ethnic identity as defined in this book. Similarly, castes that have historically been treated as "untouchable" in India have variously been termed "Harijan,"

"Scheduled Caste," and "Dalit." These changes in name are important in themselves but do not, by this definition, indicate a change in ethnic identity.

Consider now the membership rules for categories associated with the same name—"Black" in the United Kingdom. In the United Kingdom, the membership rule for the category "Black" is contested. According to one interpretation, the category includes all those with "common experience of racism" who are of "Africa, Afro-Caribbean and Asian origin" (*Economist*, September 20, 2003). This includes Arabs and excludes Jews, Irish, Romany, Aryans, and Caucasians, among others. According to another interpretation, the membership rule is "all ethnic minorities." Here, although the name is the same, we would hardly say that the two rules defined the same ethnic identity.

Nevertheless, the name is often informative in its own right. Names can provide information about either membership rules or content. For instance, the name "Black" as used in the United States signals that membership in the category is defined at least in part on the basis of color. The name "African-American" signals that membership is defined at least in part on the basis of the place of origin of one's ancestors. And the adoption of the names "African-American" and "Black" in place of another name historically used for the same membership—"Negro"—signals a shared pride in color and origin and a shared rejection of the derogatory connotations of the last.

Names can also provide information about genealogy, based on language and meaning. Take the name "Bahujan," employed to describe an ethnic category made up of minorities in India. "Bahujan" is a word in Marathi, Hindi, and other proximate languages, spoken in northern and western India but not in the languages of Dravidian origin largely spoken in southern India. The choice of this word for a name, then, immediately conveyed an origin in northern and western India, not in southern India.

Some names can also provide information about the self-perceptions and strategies of those who name a category. A name that consists of a single word in an indigenous language can often be portrayed as representing a single "people" with a single history—and entrepreneurs who propose such names can often benefit from the myth of such unity or suffer from the burden of providing it. By contrast, hyphenated names and acronyms do not typically come with the same benefits and burdens—their conglomerate origins are more obvious.

Consider, for instance, the contrast between a name such as "Bahujan" and a name such as OBC (Other Backward Caste). The name "Bahujan" was self-consciously used to describe *one* "people" and the party that proposed it carried the burden of manufacturing a credible history for that people. But the name "OBC" made no such claims to history, emphasizing by the cobbling together of the alphabet the cobbling together of disparate peoples. Other acronyms such as Pakistan (composed of letters taken from the names of its constituent regions—**P**unjab, **A**fghania [North-West Frontier Province], **K**ashmir, **I**ran,

Sindh, **T**ukharistan, **A**fghanistan, and Balochistan) and WASP (White + Anglo-Saxon + Protestant), similarly, signal the composite origin of the category, as do hyphenated names, such as Irish-American, French-Arab, and British-Muslim. In all these cases, the ethnic categories in question are all composite in some objective sense. But the choice of the name conveys information about the basis on which whether those entrepreneurs who float seek members, and this can be important in itself.

In the case of hyphenated names, the order of words before and after the hyphen is also nontrivial. Consider the words of a commentator distinguishing between identity politics in America and Europe: "Anyone can be an American. It does not matter where you are from. There are Japanese-Americans, Lithuanian-Americans, Arab-Americans and so on.... In Europe we have British-Asians, German-Turks. Note the difference. In the US the emphasis is the other way around, they are not American Poles but Polish Americans" (Morris, October 22, 2005). To this commentator, the order of words made a substantial difference. The British government appeared to agree. One proposal to respond to ethnic relations in Britain involved giving ethnic minorities new names which resembled the American model (John, August 9, 2005).

Arguing that names are not constitutive of ethnic identity, then, does not preclude identifying and theorizing about the causes and consequences of the names attached to ethnic identity categories.

5. Activating an Ethnic Identity: Choice and Assignation

Activating an ethnic identity, as the previous section noted, is the act of choosing membership in some category or being assigned membership in that category. We can choose membership in an ethnic category in one of two ways: (1) By declaring "I am X." An example of open declaration would be if Helen told her employer that she was "West Indian." (2) By acting as if I am X—that is, by prominently displaying the attributes associated with that category. For example, if Helen were to play up her West Indian accent, she would, in combination with her descent-based attributes, successfully signal membership in that category.

We can be assigned membership in an identity category also in one of two ways: (1) When others declare "You are X." For example, Helen may often be referred to as "Black" by observers in New York even when she thinks of herself as "West Indian." (2) When others treat us as if "You are X." For example, unless Helen signals her West Indian identity, employers in New York assume that Helen is "Black" without actually declaring this perception openly.

There may or may not be convergence between the ethnic identity categories we choose to profess membership in and the ethnic identity categories
to which we are assigned. Barack Obama's experience provides one example.
While he may himself have chosen to classify himself as "mixed race" the category to which he is assigned in the United States is usually "Black." As he
puts it: "If I'm catching a cab right outside this office, the cabdriver doesn't go
by and say, 'Hey, there's this mixed race guy.' They say, 'There's a Black guy'"
(Zahn 2004). Chapter 11 (by Petersen) in this book highlights another example: Individuals in Albania previously classified as "Roma" chose to identify
themselves as "Egyptian," but the local population insisted on assigning them
their old identity as "Roma."

Assignation may often determine choice. As Patricia Williams put it in her
decision to self-classify as "Black": "I was acutely aware that the choice of identifying as black (as opposed to white) was hardly mine; that as long as I am identified as black by the majority of others, my own identifying as black will almost
surely follow as a simple fact of human interdependency" (Williams 1991, 10).
In other cases, assignation may influence choice but not determine it entirely.
For instance, Helen, when assigned membership in the category "Black" may
choose to escape the discrimination associated with it by calling herself "West
Indian." This choice is influenced by assignation—activating membership in the
category "West Indian" is a strategic choice to escape being called "Black." But
it is not entirely determined by it. She may well have utilized other alternatives
such as "Caribbean" or "Trinidadian" that served an equivalent purpose.

Similarly, choice may often determine or influence assignation. Suppose, for
instance, Helen's choice of a "West Indian" identity is accompanied by an overt
insistence that people classify her as such. Helen may object when others classify herself as "Black." In this case, she may be able to determine completely
how she is assigned. Alternatively, if her choice to activate the category "West
Indian" is accompanied by other changes in her dress, accent, and behavior, it
may influence others toward assigning her membership in the category "West
Indian" without determining such an assignation entirely.

The relationship between assignation and choice is an important research subject in itself. Given the greater visibility of the attributes that constitute them,
ethnic identity categories may, on average, be easier to assign, than non-ethnic
identity categories. There may also be systematic distinctions in the degree of
freedom that majorities and minorities have in escaping assignations: In both
the examples above, subordinate social groups such as Blacks in the United
States and Roma in Albania appear to have less freedom in choosing their categories than members of dominant social groups. Alternatively, such freedom
may depend not on position in some power hierarchy but on the visibility of
attributes such as skin color. The patterns of change and stability in assigned
ethnic identity categories, furthermore, may be different from the patterns of

change and stability in chosen ones. Assignation, furthermore, can have important material and normative consequences.

These questions and hypotheses are given greater attention elsewhere. Chapter 11 in this book, for instance, shows how assignation in the category "Roma" produced violence against its members that they might have escaped through the category "Egyptian." Building on a large body of work on racial discrimination economics, Bertrand and Mullainathan (2004) show how assignation in the category "African-American" lowers the employment prospects of those so assigned—indeed, some of those who have the attributes of this category systematically seek to be recognized as West Indian in order to improve these prospects (Waters 1999). In other work, I examine the normative consequences of assignation in restricting liberty in democratic societies (Chandra 2009c). My purpose here, however, is prior: it is to introduce a terminology that allows us to distinguish between chosen and assigned identities and thus theorize about whether and how the two are related to each other.

6. The Properties of Descent-Based Attributes

Descent-based attributes are distinguished, on average, by two intrinsic properties: stickiness and visibility. The greater stickiness and visibility of descent-based attributes, on average, is a product of their association with the body, and the requirements of "consistency" and "erasure" these attributes must meet in order to be credibly associated with descent.

When I say that descent-based attributes are distinguished "on average" by these properties, I refer to the central tendency of *distributions* of descent-based attributes compared to the distributions of non-descent-based attributes, not to the property of an individual attribute compared to another. Individual descent-based attributes in particular contexts may sometimes not be sticky and/or visible. Individual non-descent-based attributes in particular contexts may sometimes be sticky and/or visible. But if we take all descent-based attributes in all contexts and compare them to all non-descent-based attributes in all contexts, there would be a difference in the average proportion of each that is sticky and visible.

Stickiness

Imagine a scale that orders all attributes in the world, in all countries, over time, according to the degree of difficulty associated with replacing them with another in the existing scheme of classification the short term. Descent-based attributes would be distributed in the upper half of this scale while non-descent attributes

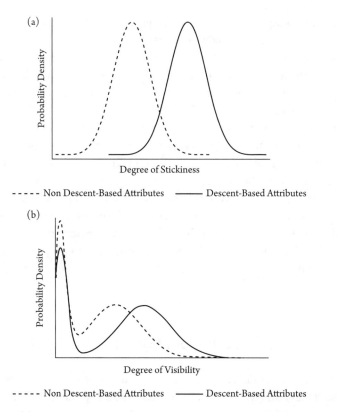

Figure 3.4a and b Hypothetical Distributions of Descent-Based and Non-Descent-Based Attributes by (a) Stickiness and (b) Visibility

would be distributed in the lower half, with an area of overlap in between. Figure 3.4a is one depiction of these imagined distributions.[4]

Many physical attributes are simply impossible to change. And even when changes are possible, which they are beginning to be given advances in medical technology, the new attributes need to be consistent with others visibly displayed on the body in order to pass credibly as "descent-based." Further, for this fiction to assume the status of reality, an individual needs to erase any evidence of having possessed other attributes in her past. The greater stickiness of descent-based attributes, on average, is a product of these requirements of "consistency" and "erasure." The lower stickiness, on average, of non-descent-based attributes is a product of the lower cost of making an objective change and the absence of the need for either consistency or erasure.

---

[4] The precise shape given to each distribution in Figure 3.4 is immaterial, and would be worth investigating empirically. The main point here is that there is a difference in the average tendency of these distributions no matter what their shape.

To illustrate, let's return to Helen's example. Consider a comparison between the difficulty of changing three of her descent-based attributes—skin color, last name, and hair color—and three of her non-descent-based attributes—occupation, party affiliation, and education.

Suppose Helen decides to change her skin color from dark to light, her hair color from black to blonde, and her last name from Brown to Smith. Objectively speaking, the degree of difficulty associated with changing each attribute individually can vary. Skin color can, with medical help, be changed within a single generation, and there are a handful of cases where it has been (Griffin 1996, Larsen 1997). Changes in last name and hair color may, objectively speaking, be easier. Helen could change her last name by applying for court approval in New York and publishing her name in a newspaper. She could change her hair color by spending a few dollars at a hair salon or buying a hair-dye kit at a pharmacy.

But even when technological advances make objective changes possible and easy, credibly portraying her newly acquired attribute as descent-based would either be impossible or costly. Even if she did change her skin color from dark to light, she would have to make changes in a host of other attributes such as hair color and eye color, in order to credibly portray the new skin color as a descent-based attribute. In order to pass her blonde hair off as being a descent-based attribute, she would either have to change some of her other attributes (e.g., skin color) to render them consistent with having been born with blonde hair, or manufacture a myth of ancestry which would account for how she might have been born with these seemingly discrepant features. And in all such cases, she would have to erase all evidence of having possessed her previous attributes—for how could she pass off white skin as being a descent-based attribute if it were known that she had once had brown skin? This would entail creating a new social world in which no one was familiar with her old self, and inventing a new history.

Let's go now to the examples of her non-descent-based attributes—education, income, and party affiliation. Helen could change her educational qualifications simply by returning to school. She could alter her income by asking for a raise—or both her occupation and income by getting a higher-paying job. And she could change her party affiliation by registering with a new party. The credibility of these changes would not require her to change other attributes displayed on the body or require her to erase her previous attributes. While one cannot claim birth in the United States without renouncing birth in Trinidad, for example, getting a master's degree does not require her to disguise the fact that she has a high school diploma.

Here, as well, there can be degrees of difficulty depending upon context. Changing her educational credentials requires an investment of time and money which, in some societies, can be difficult to make. Socio-economic mobility through education in the United States, for instance, is probably easier on average than in India. Social norms or laws may make asking for a raise or changing party membership difficult. But the degree of difficulty here depends upon the external context rather than on some intrinsic property of such attributes. Descent-based attributes, by contrast, are by nature difficult to change, no matter what the context.

Taking the costs of an objective change and a successful deception together, then, we can say that non-descent-based attributes are distributed on the lower half of the scale of stickiness, allowing for some area of overlap in between.

The precise shape, central tendency, and extent of overlap between the distributions of descent-based attributes and non-descent-based attributes are likely to vary across countries. Suppose we compare these distributions for present-day United States and India. In the United States, easy access to advances in medical technology has made changes in some descent-based attributes less costly than before. At the same time, some non-descent-based attributes, such as party affiliation, can be very difficult to change. The result may be distributions which are fairly close together toward the middle of the scale. In India, changes in descent-based attributes remain difficult because of the level of access to new medical technologies. At the same time, with a lower level of economic mobility, changes in non-descent-based attributes such as education or income can also be difficult. As a result, the distributions of descent and non-descent attributes in India might also overlap toward the higher end of the scale. The characteristics of the distributions of attributes in these two countries, further, may well be different from distributions of all attributes across countries taken together.

These distributions are likely to vary also by time period. To the extent that the stickiness of descent-based attributes depends in part on advances in medical technology, we can imagine some point in the future when they will be less sticky than they are in the present, and some point in the past when they were more sticky than they are in the present. At the same time, non-descent-based attributes such as land ownership may also have been likely to be more sticky in the past, given limited mobility opportunities in an agricultural economy than in an industrial one. Indeed, the conditions under which the two distributions can converge or diverge are one interesting area of further research. But the main claim here is simply that regardless of these variations across time and context, there should be a difference in the present in stickiness, on average, associated with both types of distributions.

The greater stickiness of distributions of descent-based attributes, it is worth emphasizing, applies only to the short term. They can change over the long term, either through a change in the frameworks that govern the interpretation of these attributes or through an objective change in the attributes themselves. These changes, for reasons I explain later, are driven by a change in the institutions that determine the objective distribution and subjective distributions of attributes.

Let's return to the example of skin color. Suppose, holding the skin color of the population constant, that the rule of interpretation for skin color at some initial point in time produces 100 different shades of skin color. At a different point in time, holding the actual skin color of the population constant, a new rule of interpretation is introduced which groups together the first fifty shades as "black" and the last fifty shades as "white." In this instance, the introduction of a new rule of interpretation can produce an entirely new distribution of attributes without any objective change in the skin color of those described. Alternatively, objective processes that take place over some long period of time can also change descent-based attributes. Industrialization, for instance, may transform a linguistically diverse society into a linguistically homogeneous one, reducing the number of distinct attribute values on the dimension of language. Similarly, migration may introduce the new attribute-dimension of race in a society in which it was previously not salient. In the long term, then, there is likely to be no systematic difference in the stickiness of descent-based and non-descent-based attributes.

Visibility

Consider, next, the property of visibility. A visible attribute is one about which some data are available through superficial observation: a glimpse of features and dress, a snatch of speech, a glance at a name. The more the data available on an attribute, the more visible it is. When no superficial data sources contain information about an attribute, it is invisible.

Visibility, as defined, refers only to the availability of raw data on an attribute—not to how those data are interpreted. Interpretations of these raw data may well vary and may well be wrong. The difference between a visible and an invisible attribute is simply that there is some data to interpret in the first case, while there are no data to interpret in the second.

Most attributes, whether descent-based or not, are invisible. But descent-based attributes are more likely to be found at higher levels of visibility than non-descent-based ones. And, among highly visible attributes, descent-based attributes are more likely to be found than non-descent-based ones.

Imagine now a scale that orders all attributes in the world, in all countries, over time, distributed according to the degree of visibility associated with them. Figure 3.4b captures imagined distributions of descent-based and non-descent-based attributes on this scale.

Even though both distributions are clustered at the lower end, the central tendency of the distributions of descent and non-descent-based attributes is different—it lies at a higher end of the scale for descent-based attributes than for non-descent-based attributes.

To illustrate, let's return to Helen. Most information about her descent-based and non-descent-based attributes is likely not to be visible. Most of Helen's genetic material, for instance, is not displayed on her features, dress, speech, and name. Nor is a great deal of information about her parents or ancestors. No one could tell by looking at me, for instance, whether her grandparents and their parents came from urban or rural areas.

But among the attributes that are visible, a disproportionate number are descent-based. Some of Helen's descent-based attributes, such as her gender, skin color, hair type, and physical features, are immediately displayed on her person. Others, such as the language of her parents (English), are contained in her name. Less precise information on the religion of her parents is also available in her name, which, even though it does not allow the observer to pinpoint it precisely, allows the observer to rule out religions such as Islam or Hinduism.

There is also some information in superficial data sources about attributes not associated with descent. Speech and features give away the attribute of age, for instance. Language and appearance can sometimes also contain information about education, income, and place of residence (rural or urban). Dress can sometimes convey information about professional or organizational membership (the suits that lawyers and bankers wear, the uniforms of policemen and firemen, badges and rosettes signaling party membership, etc.).

But like stickiness, the visibility of non-descent-based attributes attributes can vary by context. By contrast, there are always some raw data about descent-based attributes and this information is more abundant, For instance, Helen's occupation as a food-service worker is signaled during working hours by her uniform. When she is wearing her uniform, or when she is at work, her income and educational background may be inferred from her occupation. But when she is dressed differently and/or off duty, her non-birth given attributes immediately become less visible. In contrast, some information about her descent-based attributes is always visible, no matter what the context of observation, in her name and features.

Here, as in the case of stickiness, there is an overlap in the degree of visibility associated with both types of attributes, probably larger than the area of overlap associated with the stickiness of both types of attributes. And, as in the case of "stickiness," the shape of the descent-based and non-descent-based distributions and the proportion of descent-based attributes among visible attributes may vary across countries and across time periods. The extent to which speech conveys information about the class background, for instance, depends on the extent to which educational systems transmit different accents. In Russia or France or the United States, for instance, uniform access to public information make the accent less informative about class background. In India or the United Kingdom, a class-segregated educational system makes the accent very informative about class. But the main point is that regardless of these differences across individual countries, if we consider all attributes across all countries and contexts, visible attributes will have a higher proportion of descent-based attributes among them than invisible attributes.

The property of visibility affects the property of stickiness. One reason descent-based attributes are sticky is because it is difficult to change one credibly without also having to change others in order to be consistent. But it is visibility that underlies this difficulty. If descent-based attributes were not visible, then inconsistency between them would have no effect on the credibility of the claim that any one attribute was based on descent.

7. The Properties of Ethnic Identity *Categories*

According to the definition of an ethnic identity category used in this book, all descent-based attributes do not constitute ethnic categories. And ethnic categories need not be constituted *purely* by descent-based attributes. Nevertheless, there is an imperfect correlation between descent and ethnicity—all ethnic identity categories are constituted by descent-based attributes, and descent-based attributes are more likely to be associated with ethnic rather than non-ethnic identities. The properties of ethnic identity categories, then, depend at least in part on the properties of descent-based attributes. Drawing upon these properties, we can make two claims about the properties of ethnic identity categories on average: (1) Ethnic identity categories can and do change in the short term but through a process of constrained choice. By contrast, non-ethnic categories are not systematically subject to the same constraints. (2) Ethnic identity categories are disproportionately visible compared to non-ethnic categories.

Both claims refer to the average tendencies of distributions of the entire set of both types of identities across countries and over time. They may well not apply to some identities of both types across space and time, and they may well not apply to distributions of both types in some countries in some points of time. I discuss each property in turn below.

Constrained Change

It is common to assume that because the *attributes* defining them are fixed in the short term, ethnic identity *categories* are also fixed in the short term. But this is not true. Even when their descent-based attributes remain fixed in the short term, individuals can change between identity categories, often quite rapidly, by combining and recombining elements from their set of attributes differently. But the pattern of change should be constrained by the underlying distribution of attributes. Thus, the property of "constrained change" can be legitimately associated with ethnic identities in the short term, while the property of "fixedness" cannot.

To illustrate, imagine all the meaningful membership rules that can be fashioned from some given set of descent-based attributes. Each membership rule, by definition,

corresponds to a distinct ethnic category. Because a given set of descent-based attributes can generate multiple ethnic identity categories in which an individual is eligible for membership, it follows that it generates a *repertoire* of nominal ethnic identity
categories. The size of this repertoire is likely to vary across countries. But regardless
of this variation, it is likely to contain multiple categories, not just one.

Activating an ethnic identity is the act of claiming membership in one of the
ethnic identity categories from our nominal set—that is, the repertoire of ethnic identities in which we are eligible for membership. It is, in other words, an
act of classification of our descent-based attributes. Changing an activated ethnic identity is simply switching to a different classification of our descent-based
attributes. These attributes act as a baseline constraint on our ability to change
activated ethnic identities in the short term. There may be other constraints
imposed by the context. But within these constraints, there is usually some latitude for change in activated ethnic identities.

Consider Helen again. Helen's stickier attributes consist of her skin color, her
birth in Trinidad, and her descent from African-American parents. While she
cannot change these attributes in the short term, she can, by selecting different
attributes, change the categories in which she activates her membership. If she
emphasizes the attribute of birth in the English-speaking island of Trinidad, she
can activate membership in the category "West Indian." But if she de-emphasizes
her foreign birth and highlights instead the attributes of skin color and descent,
she can activate membership in the category "Black." Her ability to change the
categories that she activates is constrained: While she can change to categories
defined by a different selection of sticky attributes that she possesses, she cannot
change to categories based on sticky attributes that she does not possess (e.g.,
German, if the category German is defined on the basis of birth).[5]

Visibility

The link between the property of attributes and categories is straightforward in
this case. When attributes are visible, membership in the categories based on

[5] The property of constrained change as defined here requires us to accept one important proposition—that the *disaggregation* of "basic" attributes into their component parts requires institutional change while their *aggregation* into larger categories does not. Why should this be the case?
If institutions prevent us from disaggregating the "basic" attribute of "dark skin" by changing the
still deeper attributes that define it, why would they also not prevent us from aggregating the basic
attribute of "dark skin" with other basic attributes to constitute new categories? The reason is simple. Reconstituting the basic attribute of "dark skin" requires us to *alter* a commonsensical presumption, and this requires change in the institutions that impose such a presumption. But using the basic
attribute of "dark skin" to constitute larger categories is *consistent* with this commonsensical presumption. It does not question it—rather, it takes the presumption as given and then builds upon it. Thus,
rather than requiring change in the institutions that impose such a presumption, it reinforces them.

them will also be visible. But note that visibility can co-exist comfortably with multiple identities and with error (Chandra 2004). The information a person displays on her person can make several of her identity categories visible at the same time. There is no reason to expect, furthermore, that there is any agreement in how an individual "sees" herself and how others see her. The same information, furthermore, can be interpreted differently by different observers. And even though information on an individual's declared and potential ethnic memberships is visible, observers can often get it wrong.

Let's return to Helen to illustrate. Two of the ethnic categories in which she is eligible for membership are West Indian, and "Black," made visible by her skin color, hair, and features. She may see herself as "West Indian" in a given context, but given that her attributes simultaneously signal membership in multiple categories, an observer may well see her as "Black." Other observers may interpret the same visible information differently. And still others might simply get it wrong, miscoding her as "Nigerian" or "Brazilian." But the main point is that our ethnic categories are visible enough, on average, to permit such guesses.

Note, further, that the properties of "constrained change" and visibility apply to all descent-based identities rather than ethnic identities specifically—and apply to all descent-based identities only on average. Since ethnic categories are only a subset of categories based on descent-based attributes, we should also see constrained change and visibility in some categories which are based on descent-based attributes but which we do not think of as ethnic (e.g., gender). But because some attributes associated with descent are either not sticky or not visible, those ethnic categories based on such attributes may not exhibit the properties of constrained change and/or visibility. And, finally, since some non-descent-based attributes may also be sticky and/or visible, we might also see the properties of constrained change and visibility associated with some categories that are neither ethnic nor descent-based.

The two properties identified here need not be exhaustive—there may well be others that apply precisely and uniquely to ethnic identities as defined here that have yet to be inferred. Nevertheless, we can identify properties that are *not* intrinsic properties of ethnic identities, either because they cannot be derived from this definition or because they contradict this definition or both.

Among the properties that cannot be derived from this definition—and which the next chapter shows cannot serve as the basis for an independent definition of what constitutes and ethnic identity—are the following: (1) a common ancestry, (2) a myth of common ancestry, (3) a common place of origin, (4) a myth of a common place of origin, (5) a "group" descent rule for membership, (6) a common culture, (7) a common language, (8) a common history, (9) a common territory, and (10) conceptual autonomy. Other such properties

include "norms," "networks," and "institutions" which are neither associated from
any alternative definition nor justified by even a cursory look at the data.

Among the properties that contradict the definition that does capture this
classification are fixedness and exogeneity. If ethnic identities change within constraints, then they cannot by definition be fixed. And if such change occurs as a
product of human action, then they cannot by definition be exogenous to that
action. While we may sometimes find ethnic identities characterized by these
properties, they are best thought of as variables rather than constants—and
variables that themselves require explanation before they can be incorporated in
theories of ethnicity and other outcomes.

8. Implications for Theory Building in Comparative Politics and Economics

The conceptual arguments suggest three guidelines for building reasonable causal
claims and generating new questions about ethnicity.

(1) Our claims and questions should disaggregate the concept of "ethnicity."
The effect of "ethnicity" on some outcome of interest should be traced, not as
one big causal path originating from one big concept but through several causal
paths, possibly interdependent, originating from several narrow concepts.

(2) Our claims and questions about the effect of one or more of these concepts should rest on the properties of "constrained change" and "visibility"—and
not on properties such as a common culture, network ties, institutional affiliations,
and so on which the previous chapter argued are variables that sometimes distinguish ethnic identities, not constants that define them. While this guideline closes
the door on some claims, it opens new doors to new claims and questions.

(3) We should think in distributions, not dichotomies, in making these claims
and raising new questions.

The remainder of this section elaborates.

Disaggregating Ethnicity

Theories of the relationship between ethnicity, politics, and economics typically employ a handful of concepts, each big and blunt, to analyze the effect of
"ethnicity." According to the definition of ethnic identity proposed here, however, "ethnicity" is not one big concept or three, but many tens of narrow ones.
Causal claims about "ethnicity," then, should trace not a handful of blunt causal
paths from ethnicity to the outcome of interest, corresponding to a handful of
blunt concepts, but many tens of precise ones.

If we want to learn how ethnicity is related to patronage, for instance, we should ask at least the following questions: Does the distribution of attributes in a population affect patronage? What about the degree of stickiness of these dimensions? What about the relationship of these dimensions to each other? What about the size of nominal identity repertoires? What about the degree of overlap of attributes between categories in this repertoire? What about the categories activated at the local level in politics? Categories activated at the national level? Network ties across activated categories? The rate of change between activated categories? The degree of inclusion of activated categories in government? And so on.

Different concepts related to ethnic identity may have different relationships with the outcome of interest. It may well be, for instance, that concepts related to ethnic structure have no relation with democratic stability while concepts related to ethnic practice might. And it may well be that concepts related to ethnic practice have different causal relationships; for example, the implicit activation of ethnic identities in political campaigns may well have a different result from the explicit activation of ethnic identities in these campaigns.

What is more, these paths may very well connect, in logical and dynamic relationships, since the concepts to which they are related connect, in logical and dynamic relationships. For example, the effect of the distribution of attribute-repertoires on patronage may well be related to the effect of the size of activated ethnic categories on democratic stability, since the second is a product of the first. And, because a change in activated categories can over time lead to a change in the underlying attribute-dimensions, we should expect there also to be a dynamic relationship between these two concepts and democratic stability over time. Employing the conceptual framework offered here, then, leads us to look for, and enables us to model, interdependent causal effects.

Making Claims Based on Intrinsic Properties

Second, to the extent that ethnic identities are only distinguished by their reliance on descent-based attributes, the only intrinsic properties that can reasonably be associated with them in our theories should be those derived from the properties of these attributes. Here, I have highlighted two such intrinsic properties of ethnic identity categories—constrained change and visibility—derived from two properties of descent-based attributes, although there may well be others that remain to be identified.

At the same time that this imposes a restriction on the range of claims that we can make, it also opens up new areas of inquiry by introducing a new perspective to previous theories about the relationship between ethnicity, politics and economics. Consider the relationship between some concept related to ethnicity and democratic stability. Many of our theories about this relationship rest on the assumptions of fixedness and exogeneity. Given that these properties cannot reasonably be associated with ethnic identity, we have no reason to believe that these theories, as they are specified, are reasonable. But perhaps there is a relationship between the properties we can reasonably associate with ethnic identity and democratic stability. Might ethnic identities produce distinct patterns of politics because they are more visible on average—and therefore have distinct average effects on democratic systems? Might ethnic identities have a distinct effect because they change within constraints? Further, there may also be the possibility that variables that describe all sorts of identities can produce effects unique to ethnic identity by interacting with properties that apply uniquely to ethnic identity.

It also leads us to ask entirely new questions. These include: Does the possibility of change in ethnic identity make violence less likely? Why do some identities *not* change? Do different types of identities (racial, religious, caste, clan, etc.) have distinct degrees of visibility or stickiness? Do particular types of constraints on change have different effects? Might there be a relationship between the degree of visibility of an identity and the degree of constraint on change?

Making Claims About Distributions, Not Dichotomies

Finally, to the extent that the intrinsic properties that distinguish ethnic identities from non-ethnic identities distinguish the average tendencies of distributions of both identities over time and space rather than each identity in each type individually, at any particular point in space and time, our causal claims about the effects of ethnic versus non-ethnic identities should be interpreted and evaluated as claims about the average trends associated with of *distributions* of each type of identity over space and time and not as claims about relationships between individual types of identity at any single point in space and time.

In order to make more precise claims that apply to a dichotomous classification of identities rather than to distributions, and that can be used to generate point predictions rather than trend predictions, we should replace the concept of ethnic identities with the concepts of "sticky" and "visible" identities. Any claims about ethnic identities and descent-based identities are necessarily imprecise because they rely on the underlying property of stickiness and visibility which are only disproportionately related to these identities. But if we theorize about the effects of stickiness and visibility themselves, we should generate more precise results.

9. Should We Continue to Use the Term "Ethnic Identity"?

If we cannot associate unique properties with the identities we think of as ethnic, and if our theories do not rely on properties that can be said to be even non-uniquely associated with ethnic identity, should we then discard the term?

In the short term, the answer is no. Given the extent to which the term "ethnic identity" has guided the construction of theory and data in the past, the threshold of proof we require to discard the term should be high. Thus, the claims of arbitrariness of the term must be investigated and demonstrated thoroughly before the term is abandoned. It may well be that scrutiny by other scholars discovers properties that I have overlooked here. Ultimately, if we are not able to identify any further properties that are unique to ethnic identity, we would be better off substituting the concept of ethnic identity in our theories with concepts such as "descent-based identities" or identities based on "sticky" or "visible" attributes.

One promising direction in which to proceed in identifying others is to explore the fact that offspring of the same parents typically share the same set of ethnic identity options. It may well be that because individuals are more emotionally connected to siblings than non-siblings, membership in ethnic categories should arouse greater emotional attachments, or create a greater tendency to demonize ethnic others, or increase the stakes of conflict, than membership in other types of categories, even those based on descent (e.g., gender). By the same logic, if we assume that individuals care more about the well-being of siblings than more distant connections, we may see a greater degree of within-group altruism among members of ethnic categories than among members of other types of categories.[6] This may be a critical difference between ethnic identity categories such as "Black," other descent-based identities such as "women," and non-descent-based identities such as "Republicans." Even when these other identities are also visible (e.g., women) and sticky (e.g., Republican in the United States), they often cut across siblings, and this may be a consequential fact.[7] Such properties are routinely associated with ethnic groups by comparative political scientists but without justification. Further, even if we cannot find properties that uniquely distinguish ethnic identities, we may well find a package of properties that distinguish them. For instance, although stickiness and visibility do not *individually* distinguish ethnic identities on average from other descent-based identities, it may well be that ethnic identities are more likely to be both sticky and visible than are other types of descent-based identities. The definition proposed here provides an analytical foundation on which to infer such an association, or establish its absence.

While we should not discard the term "ethnic identity" without further work that corroborates the arguments made here, we should continue to use it in our

---

[6] I was introduced to this idea by Will Le Blanc, then a doctoral candidate in the Department of Political Science at MIT.

[7] Indeed, it is surprising, given how important descent has been in the definitions of ethnic identity in comparative political science, how few of our explanatory theories actually explore fields such as sociobiology which can tell us something about the properties of groups which keep offspring together. The work of Pierre van den Berghe is a prominent exception (van den Berghe 1981).

theories only with an awareness of its limitations. Claims about ethnic identity as defined here will be non-unique and imprecise. They will apply to descent-based identities in general—and they will apply to average tendencies across a large number of countries, rather than generating point predictions for specific instances. If it is important to generate point predictions that apply uniquely to some set of identities and not others, the more we should employ the concepts of "sticky" and "visible" identities instead.

Ultimately, if we are not able to identify any further properties that are unique to ethnic identity, we would be better off substituting the concept of ethnic identity in our theories with concepts such as "descent-based identities" or identities based on "sticky" or "visible" attributes. But if we do, does this mean that this attempt at definition was wasted? To the contrary. The negative claim, that ethnicity does not matter, is a discovery of great magnitude. It should have far-reaching consequences for research and data collection, suggesting that we should abandon the large number of theories and datasets that we have on ethnicity and start again on an entirely different foundation. A claim of this magnitude cannot be made lightly. It must be justified perhaps even more strongly than the claim that ethnicity matters on a conceptual basis. And, just as we need to define the concept of ethnic identity to establish that it matters, we need a definition in order to establish that it does *not* matter and why. We also need a definition in order to determine what to replace the concept with—and what not to.

This last point deserves elaboration. Consider three possible replacements for the concept of an "ethnic" identity. Each one requires a definition, at least implicitly—and each one is inconsistent with the definition proposed here.

One option is to discard this umbrella term altogether in favor of the separate "identity dimensions" of religion, sect, language, dialect, tribe, clan, race, physical differences, nationality, region, and caste that are grouped under this term. But this option rests on some implicit conceptualization of ethnic identities according to which identity categories can be organized into neat and mutually exclusive identity dimensions. That understanding is inconsistent with the concepts proposed in this chapter, regardless of whether we understand the term "dimension" as referring to attribute or category. If we analyze attribute-dimensions taken separately, we will overlook the categories constructed from attributes within and across them. As for category-dimensions, these often do not exist: Activated ethnic identity categories in many countries often sprawl across several attribute-dimensions and cannot be neatly organized single mutually exclusive families (Chandra et al. 2006, Chandra 2009b).

An alternative, proposed by Weber (1996), is to replace the term "ethnic" identity with the study of the individual customs, beliefs, language, and religion that constitute these groups. In his words:

> All in all, the notion of "ethnically" determined social action sub-
> sumes phenomena that a rigorous sociological analysis...would have to

distinguish carefully: the actual subjective effect of those customs conditioned by heredity and those determined by tradition; the differential impact of the varying content of custom; the influence of common language, religion and political action, past and present, upon the formation of customs; the extent to which such factors create attraction and repulsion, and especially the belief in affinity or disaffinity of blood; the consequences of this belief for social action in general, and specifically for action on the basis of shared custom or blood relationship, for diverse sexual relations, etc.—all of these would have to be studied in detail. (394–395)

This recommendation rests on a definition of an ethnic group as consisting of those shared customs, beliefs, language, and religion—it is only if we believe that these features constitute the group that we can speak then of considering them separately in place of the group. But according to the definition proposed in this book, such a replacement would not serve its purpose for the simple reason that ethnic groups as we classify them are not constituted in this way.

Brubaker (2004) proposes a third strategy for replacement. In his words:

We need not frame our analyses in terms of ethnic groups ... it may be more productive to focus on practical categories, situated actions, cultural idioms, cognitive schemas, common-sense knowledge, organizational routines and resources, discursive frames, institutionalized forms, political projects, contingent events, and variable groupness ... by framing our inquiry in this way ... we may end up not studying ethnicity at all. (27)

Read closely, Brubaker's argument proposes only that we replace the analysis of *groups* as actors in favor of *categories* and the idioms, practices, and episodic groupness associated with them. But it begs the question of whether and how to replace the concept of *ethnic* categories. If we replace that concept, what should we replace it with? An undifferentiated family of categories with no distinctions? A new taxonomy of categories? If so, what is the appropriate taxonomy? Any such proposal for replacement requires a definition of the term "ethnic."

According to the definition proposed in this book, the appropriate replacement for the concept of an ethnic identity, should we need one, is the concept of sticky and visible identities. Paradoxically, then, a definition of an ethnic identity is just as important if we decide to discard the term than if we choose to retain it. Otherwise, we will go round in circles, creating new terms that either repeat the errors of previous work or create new ones.

4

How Ethnic Identities Change

KANCHAN CHANDRA

Ways of thinking about ethnic identity in the social sciences are normally grouped into two families: "primordialism" and "constructivism." "Primordialism" is a label imposed on many positions that are quite distinct—that ethnic identities are biologically determined, that conflicts take place because of ancient hatreds, that emotions matter in ethnic conflict, and that ethnic attachments are "deeply rooted." But the minimal propositions that unite these positions, and thus justify the use of a common label, is that ethnic identities are *singular, fixed,* and *exogenous* to human processes.

The "constructivist" way of thinking asserts, by contrast, that ethnic identities *can* change, although they need not. "Constructivism," like "primordialism," is a capacious label that covers varied positions. Proponents of constructivist approaches differ over the variables they believe drive change in ethnic identities, the processes according to which they change, the agents of change, the motivations driving these agents, and the speed and frequency of ethnic identity change. The minimal propositions that unite constructivist arguments are three propositions that mirror and refute the primordialist view—that ethnic identities can be *multiple,* can be *fluid,* and can change *endogenously* to human processes.

This book's definition of ethnic identities as a subset of identity categories in which membership depends upon descent-based attributes seems, on the face of it, to belong squarely to the primordialist camp. If ethnic identities are a product of descent, then they are "given" by the past. How can they change in the present and the future? This chapter shows that taking the descent-based nature of ethnic identities seriously is perfectly compatible with a constructivist position. Descent-based identities can and often *do* change. The difference between descent-based identities and non-descent-based identities lies not in whether they change but *how.* Change in descent-based identities—and therefore ethnic identities—is intrinsically constrained in the short term, on average, while change in non-descent-based identities is not. Descent, in other words, constrains but does not eliminate the possibility of change.

The reconciliation of the given-ness of descent with the possibility of change comes from the distinction between attributes and categories—and the particular understanding of "descent-based attributes"—introduced previously. Descent-based attributes are fixed, on average, in the short term—but they are not primordially given. They are constructed by the frameworks of interpretation imposed on the objective characteristics that distinguish a population. Thus, they change over the long term as these interpretations change. Even when descent-based *attributes* are fixed in the short term, furthermore, the activated ethnic categories based on them are not. Within the constraints of the descent-based attributes we possess, activated ethnic identity categories can change even in the short term, often quite frequently and rapidly.

This chapter uses the distinction between attributes and categories to synthesize several variants of constructivism in a common framework. Those variants of constructivism that suggest that ethnic identities change rarely and slowly usually refer to the descent-based *attributes* that characterize individuals and population. Those variants that suggest that ethnic identities change frequently and quickly usually refer to the *categories* that can be activated from within the constraints set by our descent-based attributes—or to supplemental features associated with those categories, such as their name, membership, and content. These different positions, this chapter shows, are complementary parts of a common framework.

I then use this synthesis of constructivist arguments to introduce a general catalog of mechanisms by which attributes and activated categories—and concepts related to them—change. Sketched here in broad, commonsensical terms, these mechanisms will be translated in the next chapter into a combinatorial vocabulary that allows us to incorporate them into models of ethnic identity change. The five mechanisms discussed here are:

(1) Change in the *repertoire* of descent-based *attributes* that characterize a population.
(2) Change in the *"full"* repertoire of nominal ethnic identity *categories* generated by these attributes.
(3) Change in the constraints that define the *"operative"* repertoire of nominal ethnic identity *categories*.
(4) Switching of the descent-based attributes of *individuals* within an existing population repertoire.
(5) Change in the ethnic identity categories activated by individuals through a process of reclassification of attributes from their fixed repertoires.

Of these five mechanisms, the last—reclassification—is the principal mechanism of change in the short term. The first four mechanisms occur mainly over the long term, although they can also take place in rare cases of rupture in the short term.

These mechanisms are not exhaustive. But they capture some of the important ways in which ethnic identities change across contexts, and subsume or
reformulate others suggested by the literature on this subject so far. Consider,
for example, a body of work which theorizes about stability or change in an
"identity dimension" (e.g., Laitin 1986, Chandra 2005, Posner 2005). Change
or stability in "identity dimensions" in this work is typically seen as predicting
perfectly change or stability in activated ethnic *categories* (e.g., Posner 2005).
The framework here suggests that the mechanism of change in "identity dimension" can be more precisely expressed as one of two distinct mechanisms, each
of which operates differently: (1) the addition or subtraction of an attribute-
dimension to the repertoire of attribute-dimensions considered commonsensical
in a population and (2) the activation or deactivation of an attribute-dimension
from the repertoire of dimensions already considered commonsensical. Further,
whether either of these two mechanisms produces a change in the categories
actually activated requires us to theorize about a third mechanism—the process by which individuals reclassify themselves by using these newly available
(or unavailable) attributes. What we have hitherto seen as a single process by
which ethnic identities change, in other words, is actually a composite of three
distinct mechanisms, each of which must be theorized if we are to predict how
a change in dimensional salience affects a change in the category memberships
of individuals and populations (on this, see especially van der Veen and Laitin,
Chapters 7 and 9, in this volume).

These mechanisms refer to change in the defining features of an ethnic identity, not to its supplemental features such as name, membership, and content.
However, I also describe changes in these supplemental features which are
important in their own right. Even as mechanisms describing change in defining
features, furthermore, these are not exhaustive. Each mechanism can be disaggregated further, and the concepts introduced here can be used to identify still
others. However, they capture some of the most important ways in ethnic identities change across contexts and subsume those identified in previous work.

Each of these mechanisms can be triggered by many different variables, some
of which have yet to be identified. Previous constructivist work associates the
long-term mechanisms with variables such as modernization and the census, and
recombination with variables such as violence, patronage, and party and electoral
systems. New constructivist research may well find that these variables affect
change in ethnic identity in other ways than previously recognized. Indeed, several of the chapters in this book highlight some new relationships between these
variables and mechanisms.

Modeling ethnic identity change, then, requires us to identify the variables
and motivations that trigger one or more of these mechanisms. Modeling the
absence of change in ethnic identity, similarly, requires us to identify the variables and motivations that arrest one or more of these mechanisms in particular

contexts. Paradoxically, although we often think of constructivism as a body of theory that explains how ethnic identities change, it is just as appropriate to think of constructivism as a body of theory that explains why ethnic identities *do not* change. From a primordialist perspective, stability in ethnic identities is simply a natural fact. From a constructivist perspective, however, stability becomes a puzzle in search of an explanation. If we see stability in ethnic identities, we need to ask why. Theorizing about why ethnic identities do *not* change is simply the other side of the coin of theorizing about why they do.

Section 1 of this chapter defines the primordialist position. Section 2 defines constructivism and its variants and suggests that they can be synthesized by using the language of attributes and categories. Section 3 defines the limits of constructivist arguments by indicating the views that lie outside this synthesis. Section 4 uses the language of attributes and categories to synthesize these variants into the five mechanisms listed above by which the defining features of ethnic identities change. Section 5 outlines some additional mechanisms by which supplemental features of ethnic identities change. Section 6 shows how the classic constructivist arguments can be productively re-read in light of the mechanisms introduced in Sections 4 and 5. Section 7 discusses how these mechanisms can be used to construct models of ethnic identity change.

1. Primordialism

The *Oxford English Dictionary* defines the word "primordial" as "Of, pertaining to, or existing at or from the beginning; first in time, original, primeval. Also, from which another thing develops or is derived; on which another thing depends; fundamental, radical." To say that ethnic identities are "primordial" according to this definition implies that they are fixed—for if they could change over time, they can hardly be said to have existed from the beginning. It follows that they are singular, since if there were many primordial ethnic identities, we would have to allow for change across them. And—a redundant but important point—it also follows they are also exogenous to human processes, economic, social, and political—for if they could change in response to these processes, then they could hardly be said to have existed from the beginning.

Within comparative politics and economics, the term "primordialism" is a label imposed on many different views—among the others, the view that they are sui generis, with no social source (Eller and Coughlan 1996), the view that they are biologically determined, the view that they involve strong emotional attachment and behavior based on such attachment (Eller and Coughlan 1996, 45, Gil-White 1999), the view that they are historically given (Eller and Coughlan 1996, Motyl 2002, 233), the view that conflicts take place because of

ancient hatreds (Fearon and Laitin 2000b, 849), the view that emotions matter in ethnic conflict (Brubaker 1996, 14), the view that ethnic attachments are
"deeply rooted" (van den Berghe, 1981, 17), and so on.

These several meanings assigned to the term "primordialism" all imply the
dictionary definition of the term—that is, that ethnic identities are fixed, singular, and exogenous. For instance, when Eller and Coughlan speak of "apri-
ority," Motyl of "historically given entities," Fearon and Laitin of "unchanging,
essential characteristics," van den Berghe of "deep roots, Brubaker of "ancient
origins," and Gil-White of "primary groups," they all associate the same proposition with primordialism—that ethnic identities are fixed over time. And if
they are fixed over time, they must also be singular and independent of history.
But the reverse is not true. The proposition that ethnic identities are fixed, singular, and exogenous, in other words, does not imply all of the definitions put
forward by comparative political scientists. It is certainly possible, for existence,
for ethnic identities to evoke strong emotional attachments or have long histories of conflict without being fixed, singular, and exogenous in nature. The
three propositions that unite these many variants and are consistent with the
dictionary definition—that ethnic identities are singular, fixed, and exogenous
to human processes—can be taken thus to be the minimal defining features of
primordialism.

It is hard to find any explicit arguments among social scientists defending
a primordialist view. The three standard names generally associated with primordialism are Clifford Geertz (1973), Edward Shils (1957), and Harold Isaacs
(1975). But none of them explicitly takes the position that ethnic identities are
fixed and exogenous. Geertz describes a "primordial attachment" as one that
stems from the "assumed 'givens' of social existence" (Geertz 1973, 259), allowing from the start for some human process that creates the assumption of given-
ness. Shils describes primordial elements such as "possessing either a common
territory of origin and residence, a common place of work, or ties of blood and
sexual connection" (Shils 1957, 133) A common place of work or sexual connection are manifestly not historically given—and possessing a common territory or origin or residence does not require given-ness. And Isaacs explicitly
allows for the possibility of "group identities bending and shaping themselves
under the pressure of political change" (Isaacs 1975, x).

Indeed, the authors whose definitions of primordialism I referred to above
were describing (and critiquing) someone else's position, not their own. Even
those scholars sympathetic to a primordialist position do not defend it. As
Steven Van Evera notes, in an essay titled "Primordialism Lives!," "The constructivist claim that ethnic identities are socially constructed is clearly correct" (Van
Evera 2001, 20).

It would be wrong to infer from the conspicuous absence of advocates,
however, that a primordialist position does not exist or is weakly supported. It

exists, not in explicit arguments about what ethnic identity is but in the invisible assumptions that inform arguments about other things. It is this invisibility that gives it its extraordinary tenacity. When a point of view is explicitly defended, it can be explicitly challenged. But a position that has assumed the status of common sense, because it is beyond articulation, is above argument. To detect primordialism, then, we must read between the lines of these other arguments.

Consider an example of a press report on the balancing act faced by the United States in introducing democracy in Iraq: "If the Americans bow, once again, to Mr. Sistani's demands, that might enrage Iraq's Kurds and Sunni Arabs. But if they rebuff the ayatollah, they might tip the country's largely pro-invasion Shias, who count for 60% of Iraqis, into opposition" (*Economist*, January 17, 2004, 39). The primordialist bent of this report lies not in what is said but in what is *not* said. It is not said that those who currently identify as Kurds, Shias, and Sunnis have other "ethnic options," based at least on tribe (which splits all three "blocs" into smaller ones) as well as pan-Arabism (which distinguishes Shias and Sunnis from the Kurds). The exercise of these alternative options has different implications for politics in Iraq. If individuals identify on the basis of tribe, for instance, the large number of small groups that result may be less threatening for democratic politics than the currently activated tripolar division of Shias, Sunnis, and Kurds (Dahl 1971). Why might the introduction of democratic politics in Iraq not activate these alternative options as it has in other countries? This is one of the first questions a constructivist would ask, but it does not occur to the author of this article.

Consider as a second example extracts from Robert Kaplan's (1993) book *Balkan Ghosts*. This book is not about identity—instead it is an interpretation of violence in the present-day Balkans. The narrative it offers about that violence, distilled from Part 1 of the book, goes as follows: Once upon a time, there were distinct Slav and Illyrian tribes. The Croats, a Slav tribe, settled in present day Croatia (Kaplan, 1993 23). The Serbs, also a Slav tribe, settled in present day Serbia (Kaplan 1993, 31–33). And the Albanians, descended from the Illyrian tribes, settled in present-day Albania (Kaplan 1993, 43). All this happened a very long time ago, at least a thousand years before the present, if not more. These tribes fought each other over centuries, with intermittent bursts of cooperation. And at the end of the twentieth century, history simply repeated itself, with the same tribes engaged again in the same conflicts.

Kaplan's argument has often been called primordialist because it says that history, in the form of ancient hatreds, matters in explaining conflict. But this position by itself does not make it primordialist. We might argue that history— even ancient history—affects many present-day outcomes while allowing for the fact that that history may be constructed. What makes it primordialist is the assumption that the groups in question are seen as natural. There was never a time, according to Kaplan, when the Croats, Serbs, and Albanians did not exist.

Nor does Kaplan even consider the possibility that there could have been a time when the Croats, Serbs, and Albanians might have become something else. In his view, these tribes have always existed, wandering intact through the mists of time over thousands of years until the present.

A third set of examples come from theories in political science and economics which treat some concept related to ethnicity as an independent variable. The literature on this question is voluminous, most of it published in the last decade. In one of the few explicit articulations of a primordialist position, Ordeshook and Shvetsova's make the remarkable assertion that ethnic heterogeneity "is not a product of individual choice—rather, it is better portrayed as an exogenously determined social state" (Ordeshook and Shvetsova 1994, 108). Although not as baldly stated elsewhere, this is the working assumption in most of this literature.[1]

Take for instance, our classic theories linking ethnic groups to democratic stability: Lijphart's theory of consociationalism, and Horowitz and Rabushka and Shepsle's models of ethnic "outbidding" (Rabushka and Shepsle 1972, Lijphart 1977, Horowitz 1985). These theories identify mechanisms by which mobilized ethnic groups destabilize democratic arrangements and mechanisms by which the tendency toward such destabilization can be constrained. The foundational assumption on which they develop these mechanisms, however, is that the ethnic groups in question are fixed and not themselves subject to redefinition through the political process.[2] The empirical relationship between ethnic diversity and democratic consolidation has been explored most recently by Przeworski et al. (2000) in their influential work on the determinants of democratic consolidation. Przeworski et al. argue that the level of economic development is the most important variable affecting democratic survival irrespective of the level of ethnic diversity. Given our prior expectations about the destabilizing effect of ethnic diversity, this is a significant result. The measures they use for ethnic diversity, however, and the models that they design to explore its effect, retain the assumption that ethnic demography is fixed over time and is exogenous to both political and economic processes.

Consider further examples from one of the most fertile "growth areas" in research on ethnic politics: the application of international relations approaches to ethnic violence, which is generating a voluminous body of books, articles, and dissertations (Posen 1993, Van Evera 1994, Kaufmann, 1996, Fearon, 1998). Posen explains war between ethnic groups in an environment of state collapse as a consequence of a "security dilemma" analogous to that which characterizes

---

[1] For a survey of primordialist assumptions in theories of ethnicity, politics and economics in general, see Chapter 1, n. 1.

[2] For a second look at consociational theory, given constructivist assumptions, see Lijphart 2001.

states in an environment of anarchy. Fearon, using the same analogy with "anarchy," explains ethnic war as the result of a "commitment problem." In Fearon's argument, the majority ethnic group cannot credibly commit to protecting the rights of the minority in the future. Anticipating that its rights will be trampled on in the future, the minority group rebels in the present. Both arguments identify scenarios under which war between groups is more or less likely. But in all scenarios, both assume that the population is divided by one obvious line of cleavage, that all individuals know which side of the cleavage they belong to and which individuals belong to the opposing side, that all individuals agree upon this classification of themselves and others, and that this classification of self and other is exogenous and prior to interethnic violence. These assumptions are consistent only with a primordialist position. Had they taken constructivist approaches seriously, both works would have had to justify, rather than assert, that this particular configuration of ethnic groups was the relevant one for all actors in the conflict. Further, they would have had to establish that violence followed from these "pre-fabricated" group identities instead of itself being a variable affecting the formation of these identities.

A third growth area in research on ethnic politics is works in political economy, which seek to identify the impact of ethnic heterogeneity on a range of political and economic outcomes. The literature on this question is voluminous, most of it published in the last decade. Examples include Ordeshook and Shvetsova (1994) and Cox (1997), who investigate the effect of ethnic heterogeneity on the number of parties; Easterly and Levine (1997) and Collier (1999) who investigate the impact of ethnic heterogeneity on economic growth in Africa; and Alesina, Baqir, and Easterly (1999), who investigate the impact of ethnic heterogeneity on the distribution of public goods in American cities. Ordeshook and Shvetsova's remarkable assertion that ethnic heterogeneity is "an exogenously determined social state" is the working assumption in this literature, most of which treats ethnic demography as an exogenous variable without probing for reverse causation, and employs data collected on the assumption that ethnic identities are somehow self-evident and timeless, "analogous to latitude or distance from the equator" (Laitin and Posner 2001, 14).[3]

2. Constructivism

Constructivist arguments about ethnic identities, taken together, refute the primordialist approach to ethnic identities and thus "denaturalize" the concept of ethnic identity. In response to the position that ethnic identities are fixed,

---

[3] For a review of primordialist assumptions in empirical research on ethnicity, politics, and economics, see Chandra and Wilkinson 2008 and Chandra 2009a, 2009b.

"constructivists" demonstrate that ethnic identities can change. In response to the position that ethnic identities are singular, they demonstrate that individuals can have "repertoires" of multiple ethnic identities. And in response to the position that ethnic identities are exogenous to human history, they demonstrate that ethnic identities can often be endogenous to processes such as modernization, state collapse, institutional design, violence, and political and economic competition. These three propositions—that ethnic identities can be multiple, fluid, and endogenous—are the minimal propositions that scholarship labeled "constructivist" has in common.

But those grouped together as "constructivists" in this field agree on little else than these three minimal propositions. Figure 4.1 summarizes some of these disagreements by organizing a selection of constructivist arguments, identified by the key variable they indicate affects ethnic identity change, on two dimensions: the speed and frequency of ethnic identity change. The arguments discussed here are not mutually exclusive. For example, the modern state is identified by virtually every variant of constructivism as a relevant actor in the processes by which ethnic identity change. They differ mainly in which variable receives central emphasis. Some variants, for instance, describe the state as an intervening variable in a process set in motion by other variables, while others describe the state as the principal force driving such processes. Nor are these arguments an exhaustive compilation of constructivist insights. The variables I address here may well affect change in other aspects of ethnic identity in other ways than I have listed. And there are without doubt variables that I have not addressed here which might affect change in some aspect of ethnic identities. While not exhaus-

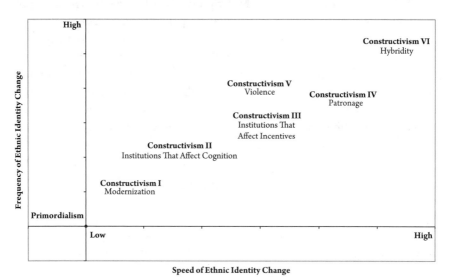

Figure 4.1 Variants of Constructivism: A Range of Views over the Speed and Frequency of Ethnic Identity Change

tive, this selection represents a subset of influential constructivist arguments especially relevant to theorizing about ethnicity, politics and economics.

Primordialism, which takes the position that identities do not change at all, and therefore associates no speed and no frequency with ethnic identity change, lies at the point of origin on this two-dimensional space. Select variants of constructivism cover a wide range of points in this space.

The precise placement of arguments on this chart is not important—the relative placement is. At one end of the spectrum lie arguments according to which ethnic identity change takes the form of a "punctuated equilibrium" with rare and sluggish intervals of change followed by long stretches of stability. These arguments locate the source of ethnic identity change in variables such as "modernization" or "institutions of cognition," a label I use for those institutions associated with the modern state which influence the cognitive frameworks that individuals accept as commonsensical, as distinct from institutions that simply influence the incentives to change identities within some existing framework of interpretation. At the other end lie arguments which locate the source of ethnic identity change in the inherent hybridity of ethnic identities. And in the middle lie arguments which locate the source of ethnic identity change in a host of variables including institutions that affect incentives, patronage, and violence.

These disagreements among constructivist authors over the speed and frequency of ethnic identity change have so far not even been explicitly recognized, let alone resolved. But resolving them is important, since each variant leads us in distinct theoretical directions. Thus, if we believe that ethnic identity change is caused by modernization and therefore occurs rarely and slowly, we should build models of political competition that take ethnic identities as fixed and exogenous in the short term, with the caveat that these models should incorporate the hitherto "omitted variable" of modernization in keeping ethnic identities fixed in the short term. However, if we believe that ethnic identity change is caused by the short-term incentives imposed by political institutions, then our theories of political competition cannot take ethnic identities as fixed and exogeneous even in the short term. These models then should be constructed as models that take the mutually constitutive processes of political competition and ethnic identity change into account.

When looked at closely, these unacknowledged disagreements turn out to be based on unacknowledged disagreements about what ethnic identity is. Those variants of constructivism which imply that ethnic identities change slowly and rarely can be read as referring to changes in the underlying repertoire of descent-based *attributes* that characterize a population and the full *repertoire of nominal ethnic identities* generated from it—but not to the ethnic identity categories which can be activated from them. The variants which argue that ethnic identities change frequently and rapidly can be read as referring to *activation of new ethnic categories*, holding the underlying repertoires of attributes and nominal categories constant—or to constraints imposed on such activation. And the arguments that describe ethnic identities as being in a perpetual process of motion are referring neither to attributes nor to categories but to the content or meaning associated with an ethnic identity category. Once we accept that they are talking about different things, their insights become consistent, and can be logically connected.

Below, I discuss each family of arguments in turn in its own terms, using the word "identity" or related concepts in the sense used by the original authors. Later, I show how these works can be productively re-interpreted and synthesized by using the more precise vocabulary of attributes and categories introduced in this book.

Modernization

The term "modernization" in constructivist work refers to a package of socio-economic processes that define aspects of the transition from agrarian to industrial societies—including "print-capitalism" (Andersen 1983), the emergence of new technologies of communication (Deutsch 1953), and industrialization (Gellner 1983)—as a key variable affecting ethnic identity change. The proponents of these arguments are concerned with explaining the construction of "nations," which they define as the creation of a common culture among individuals who live within the same political borders. But they are sometimes intended to apply, and often read as applying, to cultural, national, and ethnic identities interchangeably as if all three meant the same thing.

Modernization affects ethnic identities, according to these arguments, primarily through its effect on language. Pre-modern populations, according to these arguments, are typically characterized by geographically isolated local communities whose members speak many locally insulated dialects and vernaculars. "Modernization" transforms this linguistic mosaic through several mechanisms. According to Andersen, the advent of "print-capitalism" creates a market incentive to "assemble" spoken vernaculars, within the limits imposed by grammars and syntaxes, into a single print language and therefore a single market (Andersen 1983, 44). According to Deutsch, the advent of new communications technologies such as radio and television creates a "unified field of communication" in which individuals must use the same concepts, if not the same words, in order to speak to and understand each other. And according to Gellner, industrialization, which requires a literate, mobile, labor force, creates a functional imperative for language standardization. States inevitably fulfill this imperative, creating centralized systems of education which educate citizens in one national language and eradicate others. The result is a population that speaks a single standardized language, or a small number of standardized languages. A common language corresponds in this literature to a common ethnicity and a common nationality.

Thus, the result of modernization according to these arguments is the creation of distinct "ethnic groups" or "nations," each with its own language.

Processes such as print-capitalism, the creation of new communications technologies, and industrialization have been introduced periodically into societies at historical turning points after which they assume a more mundane existence. And they have so far occurred gradually. The industrial revolution in England for instance, occurred over the course of two centuries, and, even in accelerated form in subsequent countries and historical periods, over generations. To the extent that it is caused by modernization, then, language standardization should also be introduced at some historical turning point, after which the linguistic map of a society should remain fixed, at least until there is another fundamental transformation of the economy. And to the extent that change in ethnic identity is a product of language standardization, it too should take place at some historical turning point, after which it should remain fixed until the next major transformation.

Institutions of "Cognition"

The arguments linking "institutions of cognition" to an effect on ethnic identities comes from an influential literature in anthropology, history, sociology and political science (Brass 1974, 1997, Foucault 1977, Said 1978, Jones 1981, Fox 1985, Laitin 1986, Cohn 1987, Gramsci 1992, Pandey 1992, Lustick 1993, Appadurai 1996, Dominguez 1997, Scott 1998, Lustick 1999, Nobles 2000, Martin 2001, Luong 2002, Kertzer and Arel 2002, Scott et al 2002, Herrera 2005, Posner 2005) that shows how these institutions create, sometimes unwittingly, "discourses" which acquire the status of objective reality even though they can be contested in principle.

According to these arguments, what we take to be the "fact" of ethnic diversity is itself the result of a discourse: Some countries are thought to be ethnically diverse because of discursive frameworks produced by these institutions that represent them as such, although they could in principle be represented differently. In a comparison of Tanzania and Uganda, for instance, Crawford Young observes that the "fact" that the population of Tanzania is comprised of a large number of small identity groups which compose the population such as the Sukuma and the Nyamwezi, while that of Uganda has a larger plurality group (the Baganda) reflects an accident of classification under colonial rule. Under a different, equally plausible classification, Tanzania and Uganda may well have looked similar in their form and pattern of ethnic diversity (Young 1976, 222).

The arguments associated with the role of institutions of cognition have made a fundamental contribution in establishing the first-order proposition that these institutions shape ethnic identity in rather than simply reflecting it. But they offer vague answers at best to questions aimed at establishing precisely what that effect is. Do these institutions create ethnic identities from scratch where none existed before? Do they transform some ethnic identities that existed previously? Do they simply alter the *salience* of a prior ethnic identity rather than creating or changing that identity itself? And what is the relationship between the objective features of a population and the constructions of knowledge imposed by these institutions? In other words, can these institutions construct Tanzania in any way they please, rendering it like Uganda or the United States or Japan or India? Or, are there objective features that characterize the Tanzanian population that make some constructions more plausible than others?

No matter what their precise role in the construction of ethnic identity, arguments associated with institutions of cognition suggest that these institutions and the identities they construct persist for a long period of time. In one of the most influential studies of the role of the census on the construction of identity, Cohn notes, of the census in British India: "It would not be an exaggeration to say that down until 1950, scholars and scientists views on the nature, structure and functioning of the Indian caste system were shaped mainly by the data and conceptions growing out of the census operations [from the 1880s onwards]" (Cohn 1987 242, see also Jones 1981, 101). Laitin argues that the creation of "tribal" identity as "commonsensically real" and the expunging of religion from the political arena by colonial powers in nineteenth century Nigeria persists well into the present (Laitin 1986). Posner (2005) finds that the repertoire of identities created by the British in nineteenth-century Zambia continues to constrain identity options well into the twentieth century.

Institutions That Structure Incentives

Institutions that structure incentives work differently from institutions that structure cognition. They affect ethnic identity change, not by altering discursive frameworks but by attaching costs and benefits to particular aspects of ethnic identities that are all seen to be real within existing frameworks.

Sometimes, institutions that structure cognition can double as institutions that structure incentives. The census, for instance, in addition to affecting the commonsensical frameworks that individuals operate within, also attaches incentives to the choice of some attributes and categories over others. In other cases, the institutions that structure incentives are different. They include policies governing the allocation of state-controlled jobs and services and entitlements, as well as party and electoral systems. These policies are sometimes consciously designed to produce change in some aspect of ethnic identity, but they can also be the unintended consequences of incentives designed for some other purpose (Yashar 2005).

One example of the way in which institutions affect incentives for ethnic identity change comes from Laitin's (1992, 1998) work on language policy. Rationalizing states, Laitin argues, must win the compliance of their elites, regional, bureaucratic, or otherwise, and also their people, in changing language policy. They try to obtain this compliance by giving these actors incentives to shift their language investments and imposing costs for those who do not shift. Different incentives can result in different choices. Thus, in Estonia, the incentive structures created by the state induced many "Russian-speakers" to encourage their children to learn the titular language of "Estonian" (Laitin 1998). In Bashkortostan, the state's insistence on a literary version of Bashkir drove many Bashkirs to identify themselves instead as "Tatar-speaking" and not to invest in educating their children in the titular language (Gorenburg 1999).

A second example comes from Joanne Nagel's (1982) work on the incentive structure developed by the U.S. Indian policies. These policies induced qualifying individuals to mobilize as Native Americans, even though this was an artificial, externally imposed category. At the same time, they deemphasized other forms of mobilization, on the basis of religion or region or class or ideology.

A third example comes from Posner's (2005) study of Zambia. According to Posner, a single party system, by rewarding coalitions that are larger than the alternatives within a single constituency, created incentives in Zambia for the politicization of tribal identities. A multiparty system, by contrast, by rewarding coalitions that are larger than the alternatives within the entire nation, created incentives for the politicization of linguistic identities.

A broad range of constructivist arguments provide several similar examples. "Indirect rule" in colonial Africa provided incentives for individuals to activate identities based on tribe and region rather than religion (Young 1982, Laitin 1986, Posner 2005). Ignatiev (1995) illustrates how activating a "White" identity race was a strategy to secure an advantage in a competitive society in jobs, political rights and freedom. Chandra (2005) describes the incentives put in place by the Indian constitution's affirmative action clauses for the political mobilization of ethnic identities based on caste, tribe, region, and language—but not religion.

The institutions that structure incentives can (although they need not) change fast—and such change is accompanied by fast and frequent change in activated ethnic identities. Thus, for instance, significant changes in the activated ethnic identity categories of Bashkir and Tatar in Gorenburg's study occurred quite rapidly, following almost immediately on change in institutional polices. Similarly, change in the activated identities in Posner's study of Zambia, occurred at ten-year intervals, as the Zambian political system switched from single-party to multiparty institutions. In other examples, such as Chandra's, such changes occur even more frequently and rapidly, with new identities replacing old ones in every new election.

Patronage

A fourth strain of "constructivist" arguments, which locate the source of ethnic identity change in patronage-driven economies, also implies that ethnic identities can change at moderate levels of frequency and speed. The understanding of patronage and the mechanisms linking patronage-driven economies to the activation of ethnic identity categories are various.

The reasoning underlying one such mechanism goes as follows (Bates 1974): The goods to be distributed through patronage—land, jobs, markets—are distributed on a spatial basis. It makes sense for individuals desiring access to these goods, therefore, to organize spatially. Ethnic groups are territorially concentrated. The struggle for access to these goods, therefore, becomes organized on an ethnic basis. Ethnic groups, according to this argument, are "minimum winning coalitions" constituted for the purpose of extracting patronage benefits. As I argued earlier, we cannot reasonably assume that all ethnic groups are territorially organized or that all territorially organized groups are ethnic in nature. However, that subset of ethnic categories that are territorially organized should, according to this argument, be more likely to be activated in patronage-economies.

According to a second argument (Chandra 2004), a key variable leading to the activation of ethnic categories is not simply the existence of a patronage-driven economy—an economy in which the state controls access to jobs and services and has individualized discretion in the allocation of those jobs and services—but a patronage-*democracy*—a patronage-economy in which control of the state is decided through electoral competition. Electoral arguments about the distribution of patronage, according to this argument, take place in a limited information environment. Given the norms of modern government, political candidates cannot make open promises about whom to favor in the allocation of jobs and services which should in principle be accessible to all citizens. Consequently, they are reduced to sending signals about whom they are likely to favor. The identities most likely to be activated in limited information environments, on average, are ethnic identities, because of their superior visibility. Patronage politics in democratic contexts, therefore, gives both politicians and voters incentives to activate ethnic identity categories.

A third such argument highlights a different logic (Fearon 1999, Caselli and Coleman 2001), locating the relationship in the property of "stickiness" rather than visibility or territorial concentration. Patronage politics, according to this argument, requires exclusive coalitions in which entry of new members is costly. Ethnic identities are costly to change and therefore are one basis on which exclusive coalitions can be built. Consequently, patronage politics leads individuals to activate ethnic identity categories.

Violence

A number of arguments linking violence to construction and change in ethnic identities also imply that such change can occur at moderate levels of speed and frequency. According to one such argument, an act of violence that can in principle be driven by many different motivations, with participants who can in principle be described in many different ways, can, in the presence of some discursive frameworks, acquire an ethnic label after the fact (Pandey 1992, Brass 1997, Brubaker and Laitin 1998, Jeganathan 1998). Ethnic labeling subsequently has a self-fulfilling effect: Individuals who belong to the ethnic categories believed to have been engaged in hostilities in the first act mobilize to retaliate and defend themselves against possible future incidents. Such mobilization can provoke further incidents of violence result that create a sense of ethnic solidarity and bring about ethnic polarization that did not exist before.

Consider an example drawn from the work of the anthropologist Pradeep Jeganathan (1998) in Sri Lanka. Jeganathan describes a single act of violence in the dense urban neighborhood of Patupara in Colombo—the forcible eviction of a family, the Josephs, from their home—during a wave of "ethnic" violence in Sri Lanka in 1983. The family in question was Tamil. The evictions were carried out by Sinhalese "boys." led by a local thug, Gunadas. But there also were also important differences between victims and perpetrators in terms of class (the Josephs were a relatively well-off family, while Gunadas and his gang were from a poorer background), social relations (the Josephs were tenants of a landlord who was the de facto employer of the thug and his "boys"), and personal history (the Josephs had antagonized their poorer neighbors after the "haughty" Mrs. Joseph slapped a neighborhood child). When a wave of violence broke out elsewhere in Sri Lanka in 1983, and prevailing discursive frameworks resulted in the framing of this violence as ethnic, it provided cover for the landlord to incite the boys to evict the tenants and frame the act as a Sinhala-Tamil event. In a different context, and within a different framework, the same act could just as easily have been described as an act of "non-ethnic" violence, driven by class resentment or personal enmity rather than ethnic differences.

A second way in which violence can affect ethnic identity is to induce individuals to switch to an ethnic identity by raising the costs of not doing so. In the Basque region in Spain prior to the emergence of violence, for example, many Basques thought of themselves as Spanish rather than Basque (Laitin 1999). Basque ethnic entrepreneurs raised the cost of maintaining a Spanish rather than a Basque identity by engaging in selective violence against fellow Basques and against the Spanish police. In Laitin's words:

> The sources of harassment and perhaps even terror can be found in a rational calculation by radicals that the movement would stagnate without adding the cost of fear to those who find comfort in the status quo...violence aimed at Spanish police authorities and the kidnappings and "revolutionary taxation" of Basque industrialists were instrumental actions designed at reconfiguring the payoff function of fellow Basques in their assessments of the value of maintaining a "Spanish" life style. (Laitin 1998, 41)

A third way in which violence can affect ethnic identity is by transforming the meaning and practice associated with it (Tambiah 1992). Tambiah's study of violence in Sri Lanka, for instance, shows how the progressive involvement of Buddhist monks and Buddhist revivalism in violence and the politics that leads up to it has transformed the nature of Buddhist doctrine and practice. Some aspects of this transformation included the doctrinal "purification" of Buddhism by a selective emphasis on some doctrinal tenets deemed to be modern and the devaluation of others deemed "superstitious," the replacement of an individualist with a collective ethnic, the "thinning" out of the moral content of Buddhism, reducing it to a marker of political entitlements rather than a moral practice, and the fusion of Buddhism as a religion with a single category of people—Sinhalas—and with the territory of Sri Lanka.

Hybridity

A final set of arguments suggests that ethnic identities change so fast and so frequently that they are perennially "unsettled" (Hall 1996a, 339, Hall 1996b, Bhabha 1990). One of the most influential of this set of arguments is made by Homi Bhabha, who locates the source of change in the inherent "hybridity" of such identities (Bhabha 1990, 1994). Bhabha's primary concern is to make an argument about the hybridity, and therefore fluidity, of "nations." But he applies this argument—and is read as applying this argument—to many sorts of identities, including identities based on gender, age, sexual orientation, and ideology, as well as identities that I have defined here as "ethnic."

Bhabha's argument goes as follows: The nation—and identity categories of other types—is an imagined community created by a shared representation of culture. The cultural representation(s) that are believed to constitute this imagined community are defined through an encounter with those not believed to belong—what Bhabha calls "the writing of cultures articulated in difference" (Bhabha 1990, 312). Others have made a similar point—that the self is defined in relation to the other—that is not the same (Barth 1969, Brass 1974). These previous arguments imply that the "self," once defined, assumes a stable and homogeneous form—and the "other" in relation to which it is defined is a different identity category. For example, the English nation in these arguments is a stable homogeneous entity, formed in opposition to other nations such as the French nation or the German nation. Bhabha's point is more subtle. The "self," according to him, is never stable but constantly in the process of definition—and the relevant "other" which prompts such definition is more often within the boundaries of the imagined community than outside. The definition of "Englishness," for example, is an ongoing process that takes place not in relation to other nations, such as the French, but to Englishmen and women not fully assimilated into that idea. And the relation between the dominant idea of

Englishness and these "internal minorities," through which culture is defined, is one of proximity rather than opposition.

Self-definition through an encounter with internal difference, according to Bhabha, depends on articulation (or enunciation or performance). The self, in other words, does not exist only as a wordless mental construct. It is created when we say to ourselves or others: "This is what it means to be X." However, and herein lies the crux of the argument, no two articulations of the self are the same, even when they employ identical words. They are similar—but each new utterance represents a slightly displaced version of a previous one. As a result, a nation or other identity category is never fully defined, and never defined once and for all: It is constantly in the process of being defined through an attempt at the articulation of the idea to audiences being incorporated. This is what Bhabha means by the "intrinsic hybridity" of identity.

3. What Constructivism Is Not

In the next section, I use the language of attributes and categories to synthesize the range of views contained within constructivism within a single framework, and use that framework to propose five general mechanisms by which ethnic identities change. But before doing that, it is worth highlighting what constructivism—at least as identified through the texts reviewed here—is *not*. Just as the term "ethnicity," has come to be associated with many features which do not capture the identities it is meant to describe, the term "constructivism" has come to be associated with many meanings that do not distinguish the arguments that it actually applies to.

Constructivism Is Not the Argument That "Biology Does Not Matter"

Constructivist arguments are sometimes described as if they are the antithesis of views that take biology and descent seriously. As one anthropologist of race puts it: "In anthropology, we call it [race] a social construct—something that was built, fabricated, constructed in a given society. But more often than not, people claim that race is biological" (Brehm 2004, 5). If race is constructed, the argument implies, it cannot be biological.

If by saying that ethnicity is "biological" in nature, we mean that ethnic identities are determined entirely by objectively given genetic features with no role for human action and interpretation, then constructivism would indeed be the antithesis of biology-based arguments. But we cannot talk of biology without talking of interpretation. Take skin color, for instance. Biology determines the shade of skin we have. But how we "see" that objectively given shade is a product of socially constructed interpretations. The same shade of skin may be taken to be light in India, brown in Brazil, and black in the United States.

Constructivism in the study of ethnic identities consists of arguments about how humans interpret the raw material provided by biology, how they match those interpreted materials to fashion identity categories, and thus how they activate membership the identity categories created out of those interpreted biological materials. The argument that constructivism matters, then, cannot be said to mean that "biology does not matter." Quite the opposite—saying that constructivism matters is saying at the same time that "biology *does* matter." The question is how. Note that the opposite is also true. Taking biology seriously also requires taking constructivism seriously, for there is no biology without interpretation.

Constructivism Is Not the Argument That "Ethnic Identities Are Created out of Thin Air"

Although they are often caricatured as such, I have not encountered any constructivist text that suggests that ethnic identities can be constructed out of thin air—that we are all free to become, anyone and anything we want. Rather, each text identifies constraints on how these identities can be imagined (see for instance Young 1976, Kasfir 1979, Suny 1999b, Waters 1999, Mozaffar, Scarritt and Galaich 2003). Even those who go farthest in emphasizing the fluidity and instability of ethnic identities, describing identity as an "unsettled space," maintain nevertheless that "there are always conditions to identity which the subject cannot construct. Men and women make history but not under conditions of their own making. They are partly made by the histories that they make" (Hall 1996a, 340).

The disagreement among those labeled "constructivist" is mainly over what these constraints are, and whether they are themselves the products of some prior process of construction. The position that descent-based attributes are one of the principal constraints on ethnic identity change in the short term would be shared by most works that we term "constructivist." But many propose further constraints in addition to descent in the short and the long term. Paradoxically, one accurate way of describing constructivism as applied to the study of ethnic identities would be that it is the study of constraints on how ethnic identities change. Any study that meets this description must take as its starting premise the essence of the constructivist position—the fact that ethnic identities *can* change.

Constructivism Is Not an Argument That "Ethnic Identities Are Always Fluid"

To say that ethnic identities are constructed is only to say that they *can* change, not that they always do. As we see from Figure 4.1, constructivist scholarship does not propose that such fluidity always exists or exists to the same degree. But it reminds us that fixity cannot be taken to be an intrinsic feature of ethnic identities but must be explained.

Imagine for instance a continuous scale representing the degree of fluidity of ethnic identities across countries. Countries such as Rwanda, in which Hutu, Tutsi, and Twa identities have remained fixed over a long period, might lie at one end of this scale (Mamdani 2001). Countries such as Sri Lanka and Zambia would probably lie somewhere in the middle. Countries such as India, which has continuously generated new political majorities and minorities, based on language, religion, caste, and tribe, would lie closer to the opposite end of the scale (Chandra 2004, 2005). Finding such a continuum would be entirely consistent with the constructivist approach. But this approach tells us that stability where we find it is not natural, as it is in the primordialist approach, but an artificial fact in search of explanation.

Constructivism Is Not (Only) the Argument That "Ethnic Identity Change Is a Product of Instrumental Calculation"

The idea that ethnic identity change occurs as a result of a process of instrumental calculations at the individual level about the costs and benefits attached to various ethnic identity choices is an important strain within constructivism. Indeed, a surprisingly large body of constructivist work explicitly or implicitly describes such situations (Barth 1969, Melson and Wolpe 1970, Bates 1974, Brass 1974, Young 1976, Kasfir 1979, Nagel 1982, Horowitz 1985, Malkki 1995, Laitin 1998, Waters 1999, Dirks 2001, Posner 2005).

Such calculations, the arguments go, are attached to expectations of material benefits or psychic benefits or both. Thus, Black respondents in Mary Water's study "Black Identities" call themselves West Indian rather than Black at work because the first category carries higher returns on the job market (Waters 1999), Scheduled Caste entrepreneurs in Chandra's study of patronage politics in India adopt the larger ethnic identity category of "Bahujan" because it places them in a winning coalition, Hutu refugees in Malkki's study of politics in the aftermath of conflict call themselves Waha because it permits integration into the local economy (Malkki 1995), and Pathans in Barth's study of ethnic boundary maintenance switch to a Kohistani or a Baluchi identity when the psychological and status returns of doing so are greater than the costs (Barth 1969).

But the idea that ethnic identity change is driven by instrumental calculations at the individual level is a subset of views represented among constructivists rather than the whole. Several other arguments do not attribute instrumental calculations to the agents of ethnic identity change. Waters's study of ethnic identity choices among "Whites," for instance, while it allows for instrumental choice, often describes individuals' self-identifications as expressive rather than instrumental (Waters 1990, 1999). Studies of the far-reaching effect of census on ethnic identity change note that census officials were often driven more by intellectual curiosity and the imperative of good governance than an instrumental calculation about the costs and benefits of employing various categories. And perhaps the most influential constructivist arguments to date describe the processes by which ethnic identities change as role of large-scale historical processes not driven by individual-level instrumental calculation at all (Weber 1976, Andersen 1983, Gellner 1983).

The chapters in this volume reflect the diversity of views about individual behavior within the constructivist label. Several of the chapters assume instrumental individuals who make calculated choices aimed at maximizing their payoffs (e.g., Chandra and Boulet, Chapter 6, in this volume). Others modify the instrumental view to take factors such as emotions into account (e.g., Petersen, Chapter 11, in this volume). Still others model individual behavior as a consequence of adaptation to their environments or networks rather than of instrumental calculation (e.g., Van der Veen and Laitin, Chapter 7, Laitin and van der Veen, Chapter 9, and Lustick, Chapter 12, in this volume). And other models built using the concepts proposed here may well abandon the individual-level focus altogether while still remaining true to basic constructivist intuitions.

4. The Mechanisms by which Ethnic Identities Change

This section introduces a catalog of mechanisms describing how concepts related to descent-based attributes and categories change. The five mechanisms discussed here are (1) change in the repertoire of descent-based attributes that characterize a population; (2) change in the *"full"* repertoire of nominal ethnic identity *categories* generated by these attributes; (3) change in the constraints that define the *"operative"* repertoire of nominal ethnic identity categories; (4) change in individual descent-based attributes within this repertoire; and (5) change in the ethnic identity categories activated from this repertoire. The first four are likely to occur over the long term. The last one is especially likely in the short term.

These mechanisms are not drawn out of thin air. They represent a distillation of the insights of the constructivist work just described, using the language of attributes and categories introduced in this book. As we proceed, therefore, the reader familiar with constructivism will encounter classic constructivist arguments, translated in a new vocabulary. That is, I translate general statements that refer to "ethnic identities" in these texts to refer to either "attributes" or "categories" and to specific concepts related to attributes or categories such as a repertoire of attributes, the full repertoire of nominal categories, constraints on the full repertoire, the operative repertoire of nominal categories, activated ethnic identity categories, the content of ethnic identity categories, and so on. This translation makes it possible to represent constructivism as a single, logically coherent and testable framework. Later in this chapter, I shift the focus back to those classic constructivist texts themselves, showing how this vocabulary can be used to read them with greater precision.

Each mechanism identified here can be linked to several variables. Of those variables identified by previous constructivist arguments, we can say that "institutions of cognition"—and in particular, the modern census—are the most important in determining the creation of and change in the repertoire of descent-based attributes that characterize a population, and the full repertoire of nominal ethnic identities generated by it. But many other variables and processes, including institutions that structure incentives such as party and electoral systems, patronage-driven economies, and violence, can trigger one or more of the other mechanisms.

Change in the Repertoire of Basic Descent-Based Attributes

Change in the repertoire of basic descent-based attributes for a population is the first and most fundamental mechanism by which ethnic identities change. Recall that a "basic" descent-based attribute is a descent-based attribute we take as commonsensically given, even though it can in principle be deconstructed further. The "repertoire" of basic attributes for a population is a small number of attribute-dimensions with values on each which are taken as "commonsense" descriptors of the population as a whole.

The repertoire of basic attributes for a population is a subjective construct. In principle, an infinite number of descent-based attributes characterize the population of any country, most of them nonstandardized and noncomparable. A small sample of these attributes include height, weight, cranium size, ear length, skin color, names, ancestral language, ancestral religion, ancestral occupations, and so on. Different attributes, at different levels of aggregation, may well be treated as important in different local contexts. Knowledge about these local patterns of heterogeneity also may well be localized. But in practice, there is some process that reduces this vast, localized pattern of heterogeneity to a small number of standardized attribute-dimensions and values for the population in any given country.

To illustrate, consider the case of the United States. Although an infinite number of attributes characterize individuals in the United States in principle, we pay attention only to some (e.g., skin color or place of origin) and not to others (e.g., cranium size or ear length or last name). Other populations in other countries may focus on different attributes. For instance, in Rwanda, ear length and in India, last names are considered more important than shades of skin color. And the attributes seen as important are often interpreted in the same way. For example, a range of shades of skin color are commonly interpreted as "dark" in the United States. This is more the result of shared system of interpretation than an objective reality. The same shade of skin might well be interpreted as "brown" in Brazil and "fair" in India.

Constructivist work shows us that "institutions of cognition"—and in particular, the modern census—have historically been key variables responsible for the creation of the repertoire of basic attributes. In the present, there may be other variables, such as the media and economic markets, that have not been sufficiently theorized about but may have an effect comparable to that exerted by the census in earlier historical periods. Although I illustrate the remainder of this argument by referring to the role of the census, then, the reader may substitute other comparable institutions for it.

The census reduces the vast amount of localized heterogeneity objectively present in a population to a small number of standardized, "commonsensically real" attribute-dimensions and values across the country, about which there is common knowledge. The interpretive scheme imposed by the census operates in the following ways:

(1) It imposes a rule of *selection* that tells us which attributes individuals should pay attention to and eliminate others from public consciousness. In the United States, for instance, the census influences the weight that individuals place on skin color relative to other markers such as last name. By contrast, the census in India directs attention to last name rather than skin color by collecting information early in its history on endogamous groups—called "jatis"—often identified by last name rather than skin color.

(2) It imposes a rule of *interpretation* which tells us how to "see" these attributes across local contexts. In the United States, for instance, the census created over time a uniform, dichotomous interpretation of particular shades of skin color, which might in principle be interpreted in many ways, as either "black" or "white" (Dominguez 1997, Nobles 2000). In India, census takers created a standardized, all-India list for the first time of jati memberships, deciding which jati names in each local community were the same or different, and assigning correspondences between different jati names at the local level to be treated as equivalent (Cohn 1987, 244).

(3) It *standardizes* selection and interpretations across local contexts. In both the United States and India, for instance, the census rendered skin color and last name into attributes relevant across local contexts, and imposed uniform rules of interpretation so that these attributes would be seen the same way in each context.

(4) It often *groups these attributes into "attribute-dimensions,"* with each dimension consisting of a number of attributes believed to be mutually exclusive elements in a single family. In some cases, this grouping may be natural. Attributes

related to "skin color," for instance, fall into a natural type. But other attribute-dimensions are the result of interpretation.

In India, for instance, the census created "attribute-dimensions" by labeling some set of endogamous groups and not others "jatis" and then treating these groups as comparable elements in the broader class of "caste" identities, rather than as identities belonging to the dimension of "race" or a "tribe" or a "religion." This grouping was not "objectively" more correct than others. There is no reason in principle why those classified as a jati and therefore a caste in Uttar Pradesh (e.g., Telis) should not think of the endogamous group to which they belong as associated with a "tribe" or a sect or a religion. Indeed, there is no reason at all for members of this jati to see themselves as members of a class comparable to others. The grouping of some of these memberships in a common class is an artifact of an interpretation imposed by census takers trying to make sense of the world in which they found themselves.

(5) It counts the number of individuals who possess each attribute on each dimension. The function *of "enumeration"* is as important as those of selection, interpretation standardization and grouping (Appadurai 1996).

(6) Finally, the census communicates information about these attributes and counts to a nationwide audience—thus creating for the first time a snapshot of these attributes for the population as a whole. In other words, it *creates common knowledge* about them for the first time.

Over time, the snapshot created by the census acquires the status of a commonsensical reality, helped along by country-wide administrative and educational systems that portray the interpretations crystallized in the census as an "objective" description of the population.

Earlier, I noted that constructivist arguments about "institutions of cognition" evade the question of whether there are any objective features that constrain the schemes of interpretation that can be imposed on a population. Can the census, or another authority, interpret the features that describe a population any way it pleases? In answer, I suggest here that any interpretive scheme, including that imposed by the census is undoubtedly constrained by objective factors in "creating" the repertoire of basic attributes for a population. It can amplify or erase objective differences when they exist, but it cannot create them where they do not.

To illustrate, imagine a country in which the entire population consisted of Helen and her identical twins. Helen's skin color, and that of her twins, is an objective feature, produced by objective processes such as intermarriage, generational change, migration, or immigration. The interpretive scheme imposed by the census can determine only whether Helen and her twins notice skin color as opposed to other attributes, and how they see it (whether they call that shade light, dark, or tan). But it cannot create differences in skin color in this population for the simple reason that these differences do not exist objectively.

By contrast, imagine a country in which one half of the population consists of Helen and her identical twins and the other half of Derek and his identical twins. In this population, the census has more latitude for interpretation. It can determine whether these individuals "see" their objectively different shades of skin color as indeed different (much as popular perceptions in Brazil see very fine differences in gradations of skin color as different) or the same (much as we in the U.S. group see distinct shades together as "dark") (Telles 2004).

Understanding the role of interpretation in the creation of our set of basic attributes, therefore, is not a matter of the imposition of reality but a matter of how an objectively present reality is filtered and shaped.

Schemes of interpretation for entire populations are likely to change slowly. Even when the census or another comparable institution alters an aspect of its interpretive scheme, these changes take time to filter down to the commonsensical reality which they create. This means that the basic repertoire of descent-based attributes in a country can be taken as fixed in the short term although it may well change over the long term.

Within some fixed scheme of interpretation, as the previous chapter argued, the descent-based attributes of individuals are fixed, on average, while non-descent-based attributes are not. To illustrate, consider a framework of interpretation that classifies Helen's annual earnings of $25,000 or below as "low" income and annual earnings above $25,000 as high income—and a range of skin colors as "dark" and a range of skin colors as "light." Within this framework of interpretation, she could change her non-descent-based attribute of low income to high income even in the short term by changing jobs or obtaining a promotion or a raise. But she cannot change the descent-based attribute of dark skin to light skin within her lifetime—and even then, it would be difficult to successfully "pass" it off as a descent-based attribute. For this reason, we can take the repertoire of basic attributes for individuals also to be fixed in the short term.

In the long term, however, these schemes of interpretation can change, and thus the repertoire of descent-based attributes that characterizes a population can change as well. A change in these schemes can produce a change in the repertoire of attributes regardless of a change in objective features. To illustrate, suppose there is no change in the objective shades of skin color that characterize the population of the United States, but a new framework of interpretation is introduced, which interprets the same range of skin colors in a new way: Instead of a dichotomous interpretation of a range of shades as either "dark" or "light," suppose we now have a more fine-grained interpretation of shades of skin color as "dark brown" skin, "light brown skin," and "light skin." In this case, we can imagine changes in the descent-based attribute of skin color for large sections of the population without any actual change in the present in skin pigmentation.

Change in objective features is not irrelevant—but they should affect the stock of commonsensical attributes only when they are registered by the census or census-like institutions. Those that do not obtain subjective recognition will remain invisible in the collective imagination, despite their objective existence in the minds of those who possess them.

Change in the "Full" Repertoire of Nominal Ethnic Identity Categories

The descent-based attributes that describe a population are the raw materials from which a nominal ethnic identity category is constructed. Recall that a "nominal ethnic identity" is an identity category for which an individual has the descent-based attributes for membership. Creating such a category requires some entrepreneurship: Someone must string some selection of descent-based attributes together into a membership rule and give these attributes a name. Once this is done, we can say that a nominal identity category has been constructed. Individuals who are eligible for membership may or may not activate it.

Note that this notion of how ethnic identity categories are constructed requires us to accept one important proposition—that the *disaggregation* of "basic" attributes into their component parts requires institutional change while their *aggregation* into larger categories does not. If institutions prevent us from disaggregating the "basic" attribute of "dark skin" by changing the still deeper attributes that define it, why would they also not prevent us from aggregating the basic attribute of "dark skin" with other basic attributes to constitute new categories? The reason is simple. Reconstituting the basic attribute of "dark skin" requires us to *alter* a commonsensical presumption and this requires change in the institutions that impose such a presumption. But using the basic attribute of "dark skin" to constitute larger categories is *consistent* with this commonsensical presumption. It does not question it—rather, it takes the presumption as given and then builds upon it. Thus, rather than requiring change in the institutions that impose such a presumption, it reinforces them.

By a "full" repertoire of nominal ethnic identity categories for a population, I mean all the nominal ethnic identity categories that *can* be generated from of the repertoire of descent-based attributes for a population. The repertoire of nominal ethnic identity categories for an *individual* consists of all the nominal categories in the population repertoire for which she has the attributes of membership.

The concept of an "ethnic identity repertoire" is perhaps the most fundamental of the concepts associated with constructivism. But this formulation differs from previous theoretical work on this subject in the size it attributes to this repertoire. The conceptualizations of an ethnic identity repertoire in previous theoretical models assume that it contains two or at most three elements (Laitin

1986, Sahlins 1989, Waters 1999, Posner 2005). The conceptualization here suggests that it is far larger, with tens, possibly hundreds, of options. The precise size of such a repertoire will vary across populations, since the basic attributes that generate it are likely to vary across countries. But, because even a small number of descent-based attributes can generate a significantly larger repertoire of multiple nominal ethnic identity categories, it should in most instances be large.

The large size associated with an ethnic identity repertoire in this formulation, is a better representation of empirical reality, often captured better in empirical work rather than analytical models. For instance, Laitin found, in trying to operationalize the identity repertoire for the Russian diaspora in the former Soviet Union that it had "almost no boundaries" (Laitin 1998, 268). Waters found a similarly large repertoire even when she ruled out large clusters of identity options by restricting her sample of respondents by race (only White), religion (only Roman Catholic), and place of origin (only European origin) and then asking these respondents only about ancestry rather than other possible descent-based attributes or categories (Waters 1990). And in my own research in trying to operationalize ethnic identity repertoires across Indian states (Chandra 2004), I found the ethnic options to be virtually limitless. They included all categories that were currently meaningful in each state or elsewhere in the country; categories that had been historically important at some point in the past; and categories which were aggregations or disaggregations of these other categories. Indeed, there is no shortage of examples in which individuals expand an existing identity repertoire by aggregating or disaggregating categories already present within it.

To illustrate this new conceptualization, consider first a highly simplified example with Helen, her parents, and her grandparents on both sides, each of whom can be described by a single, identical attribute-value—birth in Trinidad. Assume that we do not know anything about the family prior to the grandparents' birth in Trinidad. Even when all individuals in this population have an identical attribute-repertoire consisting of one element, we can generate a large number of distinct membership rules—and thus ethnic identity categories—in which they would be eligible for membership. These membership rules include "those whose mothers were born in Trinidad," "those whose parents were born in Trinidad," "those whose grandparents were born in Trinidad," and so on. The membership of each of these categories, furthermore, would also be different. The first two categories include Helen, her mother, and her father. The third category includes Helen alone.

Consider now introducing even a little bit of heterogeneity in attributes of Helen's ancestors. Suppose that Helen's paternal grandfather was born in Africa, while the attribute of birth in Trinidad for all other individuals in this population remains the same. This small change can serve as the basis for still more membership rules, including "those who have any ancestors born in Africa," those who can trace patrilineal descent from an ancestor in Africa, and so on. We can see immediately from this example that even small additions to the stock of descent-based attributes that characterize individuals in a population dramatically increases the number of ethnic identity categories that can be fashioned from them.

Note that the ethnic identity categories in which Helen is eligible for membership depend not only on her own descent-based attributes but also on the descent-based attributes of others in the population. Consider for instance the membership rule: "Those whose parents were born in Trinidad or Jamaica." This membership rule, generated by taking into account the attribute-values for others in the population, is different from the rule generated by taking into account Helen's attribute-values only—"Those whose parents were born in Trinidad"— and thus counts as a different ethnic identity category. Thus taking the stock of descent-based attributes in the population into account may produce a still larger repertoire of nominal ethnic identity categories.

The full repertoire of nominal ethnic identities is bounded and fixed in the short term, because the repertoire of attributes it is generated from is also bounded and fixed in the short term. Change in the nominal ethnic identity repertoire parallels the process of change in the descent-based attributes from which it is constructed. Since those attributes change only over the long term, the repertoire of nominal ethnic identity categories is also fixed in the short term and changes only over the long term. Since the variables driving change in those attributes change the scheme of classification imposed by the census or some other equivalent institution for enumerating and categorizing the population, change in the repertoire of nominal ethnic identities is driven by the same variable.

Change in the "Operative" Repertoire of Nominal Identity Categories

The *"full"* repertoire of ethnic identity categories may be reduced, depending on the context, to a smaller *"operative"* repertoire. In some contexts, individuals may systematically fail to consider some categories contained in the nominal repertoire as being available for activation, either because they are not commonsensical, even when the attributes that generate them are, or because they are not feasible, even when they are commonsensical. The variables that affect notions of feasibility include, but are not restricted to, some of those identified by constructivist work above, including institutions that affect cognition and institutions that structure incentives such as party and electoral systems, "violence," and "patronage-democracy."

To illustrate, let's take Helen. Her repertoire of nominal identity categories, defined by their membership rules, includes: "African American," "West Indian," "Trinidadian," and "Ghanian Presbyterian." The first three categories are familiar—they are part of

everyday consciousness in the United States, and became part of Helen's consciousness too once she immigrated to the United States—but the last one is not. And
of the familiar categories, not all are always viable choices. When she is at work,
for instance, calling herself Trinidadian may not really be a viable choice if no one
knows where Trinidad is: The only viable choices in that environment may be West
Indian or African American. The size and contents of Helen's "operative repertoire"
then can fluctuate across the contexts in which she finds herself.

We can think of the "operative" repertoire of nominal ethnic identities as a subset of the full repertoire of nominal ethnic identities, defined by restrictions that
eliminate some nominal categories from consideration in individual contexts. These
restrictions can take several forms: They may apply to individual attributes, or to individual categories, or to entire attribute-dimensions. But even when it is smaller than
the full set, the "operative" repertoire of ethnic identities may well remain large.

To illustrate, consider the case of Hutus and Tutsis in Rwanda. The colonial
state established a fixed definition for these two initially fluid categories and then
sorted the Rwandan population into these two primary categories. The defining attributes which qualified an individual for membership in these categories
included genealogy, physical measurements, and the ownership of large herds
of cows (Mamdani 2001, 99). Once the colonial state had classified every individual according to these attributes, it created a battery of institutions, such as
separate education systems and identity cards, which policed the possession of
these attributes and made it even more difficult for individuals initially classified
in one category to pass into the other (Mamdani 2001, 101). These policies, we
might imagine, impose the tightest form of constraint possible on the full repertoire of ethnic identities: By not acknowledging any other form of ethnic self-
description, it renders all categories but "Hutu" and "Tutsi" virtually invisible.
But the "operative" repertoire for individuals in Rwanda remained sizable nonetheless. It included at least identities based on clan, on region, and on religion,
not to mention non-ethnic categories such as those based on class and political
affiliations, all of which have been activated in post-colonial politics in Rwanda
(Newbury and Newbury 1999, Newbury 2001, Lacey 2004, Walker 2004).

The "operative" repertoire is bounded: Because it is by definition a subset of
the full repertoire, the size of the operative repertoire will never exceed the full
size of the nominal repertoire of identities. Unlike the "full" repertoire, however,
the "operative" repertoire may well change in the short term, depending upon
context and the variables that influence it.

Individual "Passing" or "Switching" Within an
Existing Population Repertoire of Attributes

The term "passing" refers to a process by which individuals "switch" their own
descent-based attributes within some fixed repertoire of descent-based attributes

for a population and thus "pass" into an identity category for which they are not initially eligible. The incentives for passing come from processes and variables such as modernization, electoral politics, and public policy changes, which can make some identity categories more profitable than others. But the ability to pass successfully depends on their being some major social and political discontinuities which allow individuals to replace their descent-based attributes without fear of discovery.

To illustrate, suppose that Helen changes her skin color from dark to light and decides to activate the ethnic identity category "White." She would have to make changes in a host of other attributes, such as her hair, her eye color, and her physical features, in order to credibly portray the new color as a descent-based attribute. And, she would have to erase all evidence of having possessed her previous attributes—for how could she pass off white skin as being a descent-based attribute if it were known that she had once had brown skin? In normal circumstances, this would be close to impossible: Even if she changed all the attributes displayed on her body, she could still be "outed" by family, by friends, by acquaintances, by even minor investigations into her previous life. But suppose that Helen leaves her family behind and moves to a new country— these circumstances make it possible to create a new social world and invent a new history, with a smaller probability of tracking her prior self. It is in such circumstances that she may be able to pass into the category "White."

Examples of such "passing" typically come from cases of migration or state collapse or civil war, each of which can make such total abandonment of a previous life possible. Consider the example of the attempt by Oxchuc Mayas in southern Mexico to change the attributes of language, dress, behavior, and traditional occupation in order to "pass" as Ladinos (Siverts 1969). The acquisition of these new attributes went hand in hand with higher status and greater wealth. For Oxchuc Mayas to obtain the attributes of Ladinos, however, was not easy. It required acquiring fluency in a new language, a new occupation, and, most important, migration to a new area in order to conceal information about origin and genealogy. In Siverts's words, "passing the ethnic barrier...requires a complete transposition, involving the abandonment of home, family and whole way of life" (Siverts 1969, 111). Lisa Malkki's study of Hutu refugees in Tanzania provides a second such example. Malkki shows that these refugees acquired new names, new family connections through intermarriage, new ritual practices, and new histories in order to exit the categories "Hutu" and "Hutu refugee" and claim membership instead in the new categories of "Waha" or "Muslim" (Malkki 1995).

In the absence of such discontinuities in settled life, the replacement of an attribute-value is more likely to take place over generations. As an example, consider the case of Lapps and Norwegians in Norway. The principal attribute distinguishing members of these categories, according to the Norwegian anthropologist Harald Eidheim, is language (Eidheim 1969, 40). Membership in the category "Norwegian" brings greater payoffs than membership in the category "Lapps," and Lapps seek to exit their low-status category through language assimilation. The politically powerful Norwegians, rather than policing the acquisition of attributes that permit entry into their category as in the case above, encouraged the "Norwegianization" of the Lapps. But the ability to portray Norwegian as a descent-based attribute in this case would require at least one generational change if not more.

Reclassification of Activated Ethnic Identity Categories Within an Existing Repertoire of Categories

Activating an ethnic identity, as the previous chapter noted, is the act of choosing membership in some category or being assigned membership in that category. Change in our activated ethnic categories occurs either when we change the categories in which we choose membership or when others change the categories in which they assign us membership or both.

The opportunity for change in an activated ethnic identity comes from the existence of multiple categories within a repertoire: As long as there is more than one category in a repertoire, the opportunity for change exists. An individual can change her activated ethnic identity by choice in the short term simply by emphasizing a new combination of attributes, and thus a new ethnic identity category, from within her fixed repertoire. Her assigned ethnic identity category, similarly, can change if observers use a new combination of attributes from within her fixed repertoire to assign her. Such change *can* occur frequently and rapidly, although it need not.

Helen, for instance, can choose different ethnic identities to activate, from Black to West Indian to Trinidadian, all in the same day, emphasizing her Black identity at work, her West Indian identity in a social setting, and her Trinidadian identity at home. Similarly, observers can assign her to different ethnic identities, from Black to West Indian to Trinidadian, all in the same day, emphasizing her Black identity at work, her West Indian identity in a social setting, and her Trinidadian identity at home.

The possibility of short-term, rapid, and frequent change in activated ethnic identity categories may not always be realized. Many individuals may decide not to change their activated ethnic identities despite the existence of that possibility—many may not even be aware that the possibility exists. The speed and frequency of change in activated ethnic identities, furthermore, may vary across context and individuals. Some may change their ethnic identity rarely, defining themselves in the same way regardless of the setting. But the point is that the descent-based character of ethnic identities does not preclude—indeed it provides—the opportunity for ethnic identity change if individuals so desire. If we see fixedness in activated ethnic identities in the short term, then, this should be treated not as a natural fact associated with ethnic identity but as a fact which needs to be explained.

A common objection to the idea that activated ethnic identities can change in the short term goes as follows: "If I am Black, how can I become 'White'?" How can a person with one identity assume its polar opposite? But the change in activated categories that I describe here does not take place between mutually exclusive categories. Such categories cannot, by definition, co-exist in one person's attribute-repertoire. Consider the examples "Black" and "White." One qualifying attribute for membership in the category "Black" is dark skin. One qualifying attribute for membership in the category "White" is light skin. If one has dark skin, one cannot have light skin. Thus, mutually exclusive categories such as Black and White in the United States cannot both be in a person's repertoire of nominal identities.

Instead, change in activated categories occurs between categories that are consistent with each other. Consider for instance the categories Black and Jewish. The membership rule for the category "Black" in the United States simply requires an ancestor, any ancestor, to be "Black." The membership rule for the category "Jewish" requires descent from a Jewish mother. These rules are perfectly compatible. It is possible for an individual to be simultaneously eligible, therefore, for membership in the categories "Black" and "Jewish." Both of these nominal identities may or may not be activated at the same time—a matter I touch on below—but they can surely co-exist in a nominal set.

This mechanism does not presuppose any particular set of motivations and variables. The motivations and variables that drive change in activated ethnic identity categories are various. These motivations, conscious or unconscious, might include a desire to assimilate (for instance, in a party with Trinidadians, Helen may want to activate the identity category Trinidadian to blend in with other Trinidadians), or a desire to distinguish oneself from others in some context (for instance, in a party with other Trinidadians, Helen may want to activate the identity category Black to distinguish herself), a desire for higher status or higher economic returns (for instance, Helen activates the category West Indian rather than Black at work because this category is associated with greater status and economic returns), psychological considerations (for instance, a desire to live an integrated life might drive Helen to activate the same ethnic category across contexts regardless of the returns associated with it), and other motivations that we have not yet imagined. The variables that previous constructivist arguments have identified include discursive frameworks, public policy, patronage politics, party and electoral systems, violence, and private-sector economic returns, among others. We can well imagine others, not yet theorized about.

While change is made possible by our descent-based attributes, however, it is also constrained by them. The baseline constraint is imposed by the full repertoire of nominal ethnic identities. An individual can activate different ethnic identity categories from within the nominal identity repertoire generated by these attributes, but she cannot in the short term activate ethnic identity categories outside it. Given her descent-based attributes, for instance, Helen can change her activated categories from "Black," to "Trinidadian," "West-Indian," and "Afro-Caribbean," among others. But she cannot activate the ethnic categories German or WASP or Chinese or Malay. These ethnic categories require descent-based attributes for membership that lie outside her nominal repertoire and are not available for activation.

The same logic also applies to the ethnic identity categories to which she is assigned. In order to be credibly assigned to some ethnic identity category, she must be seen to possess the descent-based attributes for it—or, at the very least, her visible descent-based attributes must be consistent with the attributes required for the membership in question. Thus, while she may be assigned to categories such as Black, West Indian, and Trinidadian—for which she possesses at least some visible descent-based attributes—she cannot be assigned to categories such as White or German, which, at least in the United States, require the possession of descent-based attributes which not only lie outside Helen's repertoire but are inconsistent with those that lie within.

In addition to this baseline constraint, there may also be additional constraints, imposed by the environments in which we live: History, institutional background, economic factors, ideological factors, social norms, and territorial factors may, taken individually or together, eliminate certain categories from the set of feasible choices while privileging others. These constraints, which make up the operative repertoire defined above, are the product of contextual factors and may vary by context. But regardless of the number and nature of these additional constraints, there is always a baseline constraint, set by the descent-based attributes we possess, on the ethnic identity categories we can activate in the short term.

The existence of this baseline constraint on change in activated ethnic identities is the fundamental distinction between ethnic and non-ethnic identities, on average. The activation of non-ethnic identity categories may well be constrained by environmental factors. But there is nothing intrinsic in the attributes that constitute non-ethnic identities, on average, that imposes such a constraint.

Interaction Between Long-Term and Short-Term Changes

Of the five mechanisms described above, the first four—change in the repertoire of basic attributes for a population, change in an individual's attributes within a basic repertoire, change in the full repertoire of nominal identity categories for a population, and change in the operative repertoire of nominal ethnic identity categories—are likely to take place mostly over the long term, although they may occur in the short term in rare cases. The last—change in activated ethnic identity categories—is likely to be the principal mode of change in ethnic identities over the short term.

There may also be a mutually reinforcing relationship between changes in a population's stock of descent-based attributes and the nominal identity repertoires

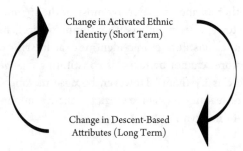

Figure 4.2 Interaction Between Short-Term and Long-Term Change

constructed from them—and the categories activated in the short term. Imagine, for instance, that at some initial point in history, political entrepreneurs work to transform the interpretation of some descent-based attribute—for instance, taking a shade of skin color commonly interpreted as "dark" and arguing that we should see it in a more differentiated way, separating "light brown," "dark brown," and "black." If successful, this enterprise would make a piecemeal change in the stock of descent-based attributes in the future—and therefore the ethnic identities subsequently available for activation. Figure 4.2 summarizes this relationship.

From this discussion we can make a general statement about the two families of concepts that describe different aspect of ethnic identities—ethnic "structure" and ethnic "practice." Recall that ethnic "structure" refers to the repertoire of descent-based attributes, and therefore the sets of "nominal" identities, that all individuals in a population possess, whether or not they actually identify with them. Ethnic "practice" refers to the set of "activated" identities that individuals actually employ in any given context.

The ethnic structure of a population, because it is based on the repertoire of descent-based attributes, tends to be fixed in the short term, while ethnic practice, because it is based on activated categories, can change. Over the long term, however, ethnic "structure" can change too. Indeed, there is a relationship between change in ethnic practice in the short term and ethnic structure in the long term, corresponding to the relationship between the change in descent-based attributes and the categories they constitute. Today's "structure," then, can be in part the product of the ethnic practice of a distant yesterday. And today's ethnic practice can affect the ethnic structure of a distant tomorrow.

5. Change in Supplemental Aspects of Change in Ethnic Identities

An ethnic identity category is defined here by its *membership rule* and not by its membership (the collection of individuals included the category produced by this rule of classification), its "content" (i.e., any cultural or economic or psychological or other attributes shared by most of the membership in addition to those necessary to separate members from nonmembers), and its name. Since these features do not constitute ethnic identities (at least as we classify them), change in these features cannot be taken as constituting change in ethnic identities (at least as we classify them). However, because membership, content, and name are important features in their own right, change in any of these features may be important in its own right.

Membership

A change in the membership rule an individual activates may or may not go together with a change in *membership*. Table 4.1 outlines the different possible scenarios.

Suppose Helen activates the category "Black," replacing her initially activated category of "Trinidadian." The membership of both categories is different. Thus, with a change in the membership rules that she activates, there is also a change in the membership that she affiliates herself with. Described in the top left cell of Table 4.1, this is an easily recognizable case of change in an activated ethnic identity.

But consider now the categories "Sinhala" and "Buddhist" in Sri Lanka. The membership of the two categories is virtually the same. Nevertheless, given the definition used here, if an individual switched from calling herself Sinhala to calling herself Buddhist, this would count as a change in ethnic identity. This scenario is represented in the top right cell of Table 4.1.

Consider now an instance in which the membership rule for a category which Helen activates stays the same but there is a change in membership. Suppose Helen activates the category "Black," and the membership rule for the category "Black" remains the same, but the individuals eligible for membership in that category increase, through the discovery of new ancestral records that demonstrate black ancestry. Such change in membership would not count as a change in ethnic categories by this definition as long as the membership rule stays the same. This is the scenario captured in the bottom left cell of Table 4.1.

While we cannot call a change in membership a change in ethnic identity, we can certainly imagine situations in which change in membership is more

Table 4.1 **Change in Membership and Ethnic Identity Change**

	Membership Changes	*Membership Stays the Same*
Membership Rule Changes	Change in ethnic identity	Change in ethnic identity
Membership Rule Stays the Same	No change in ethnic identity	No change in ethnic identity

important than change in the basis for membership. There are many situations in which numbers are all that matter. Stability in the membership rule may not matter if the size of the coalition changes. For instance, politicians in the United States worried that with an influx of Hispanics, the character of New York politics might change. And change in the membership rule may make no real difference if the size of the coalition does not change. When the Sri Lanka Freedom Party in Sri Lanka attempted to build an electoral majority, for instance, it was indifferent about which of several membership rules it used—Sinhala or Buddhist—since each rule targeted roughly the same membership. These examples all describe change in an aspect of an existing ethnic identity that is worth studying in its own right.

Content

Change in shared content and change in membership may or may not go together. Table 4.2 outlines the different possible scenarios.

Change in the membership rule often goes hand in hand with change in shared content—indeed, one can induce the other. Thus, Barack Obama's activation of the category "Black" rather than other categories in his nominal set (e.g., "mixed race," "Hawaiian," etc.) was accompanied by the acquisition of a different content than that associated with these other categories, such as joining a black fraternity and volunteering in a church community group in a black neighborhood (Obama 2004). Alternatively, we might say that it was through participation in such activities associated with part of the shared content of being "Black" that he made the decision to activate the ethnic identity "Black" and deemphasize others.

But a change in membership rule would, in the framework above, count as a change in ethnic identity even if it were not accompanied by a change in content. Consider the historical changes in the membership rule for the category "Black" in the United States. For much of the nineteenth century, an individual qualified for membership in the category "Black" as defined by the U.S. census if *all* her ancestors were of African origin. Those with "mixed" ancestry were classified

Table 4.2 **Change in Content and Ethnic Identity Change**

	Shared Content Changes	*Shared Content Stays the Same*
Membership Rule Changes	Change in ethnic identity	Change in ethnic identity
Membership Rule Stays the Same	No change in ethnic identity	No change in ethnic identity

separately. By 1930, this rule changed: An individual qualified for membership in the category "Black" if *any* of her ancestors were of African origin (Nobles 2000). This change in membership rule may well not have been accompanied by a change in the economic, cultural, and social practices of those classified as "Black": It is nevertheless a change in ethnic identity as defined above.

Consider now the example of a change in the *content* associated with a category whose membership rule remains constant. The "one-drop" membership rule for the category "Black" remained constant in the U.S. census for much of the twentieth century. We can be certain that the "content" of this category changed over this long time period. Indeed, it would be surprising if the content of any category with a stable membership rule over a long period of time did *not* change. Even "Hutus" and "Tutsis" in Rwanda, categories that are often seen as the prototypical examples of stability in membership rule over a long period of time, exhibit instances of such change in content (Newbury 1988, 10). Such change in content would not count as a change in ethnic identity according to the definition provided here, but it is important in its own right.

Name

Ethnic identities can stay the same even when a name changes, as long as the membership rule associated with that name does not change. And ethnic identities can change even when the name stays the same, as long as the membership rule associated with the name changes. Table 4.3 summarizes this point.

As an instance of a change in name without a change in ethnic identity, consider, for instance, the case of those castes in India that were formerly termed "untouchable." During the nationalist movement, Gandhi popularized the name "Harijan," meaning "Children of God," for these castes. Over time, this name came to be considered patronizing, and it has been replaced by others, including Dalit (meaning "broken to pieces," and associated with greater self-assertion) and Scheduled Caste (a bureaucratic term referring to how these castes are identified in the Constitution). However, the membership rule associated with all three names remained the same: Those who were formerly treated as "untouchable." We would not call this an instance of ethnic identity change, to the extent

Table 4.3 **Change in Name and Ethnic Identity Change**

	Name Changes	Name Stays the Same
Membership Rule Changes	Change in ethnic identity	Change in ethnic identity
Membership Rule Stays the Same	No change in ethnic identity	No change in ethnic identity

that the membership rule did not change. More recently, a fourth name has been floated—"Bahujan"—to describe members of these castes. But this name is also associated with a new membership rule—"all those who do not belong to the 'twice born' Hindu castes." This instance would be called a change in ethnic identity to the extent that the membership rule also changed.

Similarly, in Sri Lanka, those who belong to the category commonly recognized as "Estate Tamil" have experimented with a variety of names: "Tamils of Indian Origin," "Tamils of Recent Indian Origin," "New Tamils," "Indian Tamils," "Hill Country Tamils," and so on (Daniel 1996). But to the extent that these names described the same membership rule, these changes in name do not, according to the definition proposed here, describe a constitutive change in ethnic identity.

As an instance of a change in ethnic identity despite stability in the name, consider now the use of name "Kshatriya" in the Indian state of Gujarat. In the 1950s, the membership rule for those who belonged to the category named Kshatriya was highly restrictive: Descent from a small number of families was necessary, along with additional rules of interdining and intermarriage. By this rule, Kshatriyas constituted 5% of Gujarat's population (1931 Census, cited in Kohli 1990, 241). By the 1980s, the rule changed so that all those who described themselves as being "martial by nature" were eligible to be Kshatriyas (Weiner 1967, 99). By this membership rule, "Kshatriyas" constituted approximately 29% of Gujarat's electorate. Although the same name continued to be used here, the changes in the membership rule should surely lead us to describe this as a change in ethnic identity. Indeed, because the new membership rules did away with the descent-based requirement altogether, an ethnic category was transformed into a non-ethnic one.

Although a change in ethnic identity is not defined by change in name, a change in name is important in its own right. It can convey change in the cultural or psychological, or historical or economic attributes shared by members of a category in addition to those needed for membership, and in the political and social strategies employed by members and leaders. In the United States, for example, the change in name of those of African ancestry from "Negro" to "African American" or "Black" indicated a significant change in the way that members of this category perceived themselves and were perceived by others. A change in the name of those once categorized as "untouchable" to "Harijan" and then to "Dalit" indicated a similar change: The names "Harijan" and "Dalit" both have more positive connotations than the name "untouchable." The term "Dalit," furthermore, has come to be associated with greater self-assertion and signals a more independent political stance than the term "Harijan." Even when we do not treat names as constitutive of ethnic identities as defined here, then, it is important to study the implications of changes in name in their own right.

6. Re-reading Classic Constructivist Arguments

So far, my focus has been on identifying the mechanisms by which concepts related to ethnic identities change and bringing in constructivist insights where necessary. This section now returns the focus to the constructivist arguments discussed previously, showing how they can be re-read using the conceptual vocabulary introduced previously.

Modernization

Modernization-based arguments should be read not as describing the creation of *ethnic identities* per se but as describing the creation of a new *attribute-dimension* that can be an element in the creation of some ethnic identity categories—"ancestral language." The first linguistic shifts brought about by modernization occur during the lifetimes of affected individuals, as they make investments for themselves and their children in learning new languages (Laitin 1998). The language(s) acquired during the lifetimes of this first generation become included among the set of attributes inherited by its successors. The speed and frequency of a change in this attribute may well be low—but this does not mean that the ethnic identity categories generated from this attribute cannot change rapidly and frequently.

Institutions of "Cognition"

In the language of this book, we can think of institutions of cognition as affecting ethnic identities in two distinct ways, each of which can be more finely disaggregated. First, they create the repertoire of descent-based attributes and therefore full repertoire of nominal ethnic identity categories for a population. Second, they impose constraints on this full repertoire in particular contexts.

We can disaggregate the mechanism by which the repertoire of descent-based attributes and nominal ethnic identity categories is constructed into the following submechanisms: the creation of a rule of selection of attribute-values, the creation of a rule of interpretation of attribute-values, the creation of attribute-dimensions, the creation of standardized interpretations about these attribute-values and dimensions, and the enumeration of these selected, interpreted, standardized attribute-values and dimensions.

We can disaggregate the mechanism by which constraints are imposed on the full repertoire of ethnic identity categories generated from these attributes into the following submechanisms: the elimination of individual attribute-values, attribute-dimensions, or categories from consideration.

Following the logic of the argument introduced in the preceding section, institutions of cognition are constrained by the objective features of the population. While they can interpret these objective features in many different ways, they cannot operate outside them. Thus, while they can render the population of Tanzania in many different ways, they cannot render it identical to the population of Uganda, the United States, Japan, or India unless the distribution of key objective features in these populations is identical.

If we understand institutions of cognition as creating the repertoire of attributes and categories, and imposing constraints on this repertoire, we can accept in toto the argument that these aspects of ethnic identity change slowly over long periods of time without precluding the possibility of change in activated ethnic identities in the short term. Note that this still leaves a great deal of room for change. Within the constraints imposed by these institutions, individuals should still be able to use the raw materials provided by the census to change the ethnic identity categories that they activate in the short term.

Institutions That Structure Incentives

One way in which institutions affect incentives for ethnic identity change, the earlier section argued, is by attaching costs and benefits to the languages that individuals choose to learn (Laitin 1998). Read in the language of this book, we can say that institutions that structure incentives by *affecting investments in new attribute-values* such as language in one generation can change the repertoire of descent-based attributes for succeeding generations.

Language is but one of the many attributes that describe individuals and can be passed down through descent. Institutions also attach costs and benefits to the acquisition of other attributes and thus determine the ease with which they can be replaced. As the previous chapter noted, descent-based attributes are "sticky" in part because replacing them requires an individual to successfully manufacture a myth of descent.

In communist Bashkortostan, the administration made such deception easy. In Gorenburg's words:

> Local administrators had a great deal of leeway in enforcing the requirement that newborns' ethnic identity corresponded to that of their parents. In a region like Bashkortostan, where the administration sought to increase the Bashkir proportion of the population, administrators at the birth registry often turned a blind eye towards cases where Tatar parents declared their baby to be of Bashkir ethnicity. Furthermore, Tatars were encouraged to declare themselves Bashkirs when joining the Communist Party. Party leaders were only too glad to modify the necessary identity documents to allow such a change. Despite the formal Soviet Union-wide policy that an individual's ethnic identity match the identity of at least one of his or her parents, republic leaders created conditions where this requirement could be widely ignored by local administrators. (Gorenburg 1999, 571)

In other cases, institutions may well make such passing difficult.

A second way in which institutions affect incentives for ethnic identity change is by *inducing the activation of some previously nominal categories over others* in the operative repertoire. This is the process at work, for example, in Nagel's account of the incentive structure developed by the U.S. Indian policies, which favored the activation of tribal categories at the expense of religious or regional or class or ideological ones.

A third way in which institutions affect incentives for ethnic identity change is by *changing the size and content of the "operative" repertoire of ethnic identities* by eliminating certain attribute-dimensions or categories from consideration. Such eliminations are based on assessments of feasibility rather than common sense: Individuals eliminate some attribute-dimensions or categories from consideration, not because they do not think of them as not being "commonsensically real" but because they think of these categories as being insufficiently rewarding.

Read in the language of this book, this is the mechanism at work in Posner's (2005) study of Zambia. The multiparty system in the Zambian case eliminates consideration of the attribute-dimension of language, favoring instead the attribute-dimension of tribe. The second system has the opposite result: It eliminates consideration of the attribute-dimension of tribe in favor of the attribute-dimension of language. The result is that voters are left with a smaller operative repertoire of categories from which to choose. Posner employs some very restrictive assumptions, according to which the elimination of one attribute-dimension reduces the size of the operative repertoire to a single category. The model considers only two dimensions (tribe and language), with fixed category memberships on each. Further, it assumes that individuals cannot construct new categories by combining attribute-values within and across dimensions. Consequently, all individuals have only one tribal category and only one linguistic category in their "full" repertoire, and when the party system eliminates one dimension from consideration, the only choice left in the "operative" repertoire is the other. This means that the elimination of the tribal dimension from consideration permits a perfect prediction about which linguistic category will be activated, and vice versa. In the more general case, the elimination of some attribute-dimensions need not reduce the operative choice set to a single category. But it can narrow the set of choices significantly, thus narrowing the range of counterfactuals that need to be ruled out in order to explain why any particular category is activated.

Given the distinction between attributes and categories, institutions that structure incentives are often associated with a faster and more frequent pattern of ethnic identity change. This should not be surprising. Rapid change in these institutions can easily be accompanied by rapid changes in the constraints which define individual repertoires, since individuals do not have to alter their commonsensical frameworks in order to respond to such change. And change in the relevant constraints may well lead individuals to activate different ethnic identity categories in the short term.

Patronage

Read in the language of this book, we can think about the patronage-economy as imposing constraints on the full repertoire of nominal ethnic identities created by the census. Bates's argument suggests that this constraint eliminates all categories that are not territorially concentrated from consideration. Chandra's argument suggests that this constraint eliminates all attribute-dimensions that are not visible from consideration. Within these dimensions, it also applies to categories: only categories of a winning size permitted. Fearon's and Caselli and Coleman's argument also applies to feasible attribute-dimensions: It eliminates from consideration all attribute-dimensions that are not sticky.

These constraints are likely to stay in place as long as the variable that creates them—a patronage-driven economy or democracy—also stays in place. However, there is room for change in activated ethnic identity categories within these constraints. Indeed, the arguments imply that politicians will have incentives to activate new identity categories within these constraints, thus leading to more rapid and frequent change in ethnic identity categories than that predicted by previous variables.

Violence

The first argument linking violence with change in ethnic identity at moderate speed and frequency pointed to the role of discursive frameworks in assigning an act of violence an ethnic label after the fact (Pandey 1992, Brass 1997, Brubaker and Laitin 1998, Jeganathan 1998). Read in the language of this book, we can interpret this argument to mean that given some previous set of discursive frameworks, an act of violence can result in the activation of particular ethnic categories over others. If the discursive frameworks of the past do not include ethnic identity categories, violence will not result in the activation of ethnic identities. If there are no previous discursive frameworks, violence will not even be accompanied by a uniform interpretation, let alone an ethnic one. Note that violence in this account does not have an independent causal effect on the activation of ethnic categories. It simply provides the occasion by which past discourse and present-day elite interests interact to produce that outcome.

A second argument suggested that violence induced individuals to switch to an ethnic identity by raising the costs of not doing so. Read in the language of this book, we can take this argument to mean that violence is a cause for the activation of an ethnic identity from within some nominal set (for instance, when those who possess the attributes for "Spanish" activate the category "Basque" instead) or of individual "passing" or "switching" within a population repertoire of attributes (for instance, when those who possess the attribute of Spanish speaker switch to acquiring Basque language instead). Contrary to many theories which indicate that violence is the *product* of prefabricated identities, this argument suggests that it is the *means* by which these identities are fabricated. Similar predictions, although from a different logic and applying to different concepts related to ethnic identity, are made in the work of Horowitz (1985) (here, ethnic outbidding, which can take the form of violence, becomes a means of creating cohesiveness among members of pre-existing ethnic identity categories), Chandra (2005) (here, violence becomes a means for parties to activate formerly nominal ethnic identity categories and police their boundaries), Bates de Figueiredo and Weingast (1998), and Snyder (2000) (here, violence can be a low-cost way to activate an attribute-dimension related to ethnicity rather than the economy), and Appadurai (2006) (here, violence can be a means by which ethnic minority categories are activated by those members of a majority ethnic identity category anxious about defining the boundaries of their own identities).

A third argument suggested that violence affects ethnic identity change by transforming the meaning and practice associated with it (Tambiah 1992). Read in the language of this book, we can take this argument to mean that violence can transform the *content* of an ethnic identity category. The change effected by violence on Buddhism, in Tambiah's account, is not in the membership rules for the category "Buddhist" and Sinhala. These rules appear to have been initially constructed somewhere around the twelfth century and, while they may have undergone revisions since, are treated as stable by the twentieth century. What appears to have changed during this period is what it means to be Buddhist and what it means to be Sinhala. To the extent that violence leads to a change in the activation of an ethnic identity or its content, it is reasonable to associate with moderate levels of speed and frequency. For the reasons articulated earlier, both these forms of change can occur fast and rapidly in the short term, even when the attributes determining membership in these categories remain fixed.

Hybridity

Read in the language of this book, we can think of arguments linking "hybridity" and ethnic identity change as referring to the content of an ethnic category. Like Tambiah, Bhabha is not referring to the process by which descent-based attributes are constructed, or to the stringing together of membership rules based on these attributes or even to the activation of categories defined by these membership rules. Rather, he is concerned with changes in the meaning of some activated ethnic identity category for its adherents. Bhabha's argument places one aspect of change in meaning—itself one aspect of change in content—at the extreme end on both dimensions, while remaining consistent with the possibility that other aspects of content may change at a different pace.

7. From Mechanisms to Models of Ethnic Identity Change

A "model" of ethnic identity change is an abstract statement that outlines the causal logic by which one or more variables causes a change in some aspect of ethnic identity in some context. Such a model should define the precise aspect of ethnic identity change it seeks to explain, the key variable or variables that causes change, the chain of mechanisms through which the two are linked, the agents who realize these mechanism, their motivations, and the background conditions necessary for this argument to work.

There are likely to be *many* models of ethnic identity change rather than a single one. Why? First, because "ethnicity" as defined here is not one but many connected concepts, corresponding to the two families of ethnic structure and ethnic practice. A model explaining one concept, such as the activation of ethnic identities, should be connected to but may be different from a model explaining another concept such as creation of a repertoire of attributes. Second, because the variables, agents, motivations, and background conditions that trigger the same mechanisms can be many. Each of these variables, furthermore, can trigger more than one mechanism in any one context—and may trigger different mechanisms in different contexts. And in different contexts, the same variable can trigger different combinations and sequences of mechanisms.

Table 4.4 summarizes some of these links between variables and processes identified by constructivist work discussed above and these mechanisms. It is not exhaustive, because the subject of constructivism is by no means exhausted. The variables addressed here may well affect change in other aspects of ethnic identity in other ways than I have listed. And variables that I have not addressed here might affect change in some aspect of ethnic identities in ways not listed.

If we want to theorize about the causes of any particular mechanism—for instance, of the activation of ethnic identities—we would want to model the distinct causal paths by which many distinct variables such as violence or electoral politics produce change in activated ethnic identities. Alternatively, if we want to model the effect of a particular variable (e.g., violence) on ethnic identity change, we would want to model several distinct relationships between violence and the activation of individual ethnic identity categories, between violence and the content of those categories, between violence and the activation of individual attribute-dimensions, and so on.

Table 4.4 **Constructivist Variables and Mechanisms**

Variable/Concept	Change in Repertoire of Descent-Based Attributes for Populations and Individuals	Change in Full Repertoire of Nominal Ethnic Identity Categories for Populations and Individuals	Change in "Operative" Repertoire of Nominal Ethnic Identity Categories for Populations and Individuals	Individual "Switching" of Descent-Based Attributes Within a Repertoire	Change in Activated Ethnic Identities	Change in Name, Membership, or Content or ethnic identity category
Modernization	X	X				
Institutions of Cognition (e.g. Census)	X	X	X			
Institutions that Affect Incentives			X	X	X	
Patronage-Democracies			X		X	
Violence			X	X	X	X
Hybridity						X

The challenge in building these models lies in the complexity of the problem they have to solve. Whereas previous models have focused on a small number of blunt dependent variables, new models must focus on a large number of precisely specified dependent variables. Whereas previous models have typically focused on bivariate relationships between a single independent variable and the dependent variable in question, new models must be capable of addressing multicausal relationships, in which many variables trigger the same mechanism. Whereas previous models have typically focused on a particular aspect of ethnic identity change considered separately, new models must address the dynamic connections between different concepts related to ethnic identity change. And whereas previous models have made the task of explanation more tractable by limiting the counterfactuals they consider, new models must address a far broader range of counterfactuals. The result, in all probability, will be greater complexity in our models. But more complex theories may serve as more illuminating simplifications of the empirical world we seek to understand.

What are the implications of this synthesis of constructivist views for theories that approach "ethnicity" as an independent variable explaining political and economic outcomes and processes? It suggests that there are indeed some concepts related to ethnic identity—namely, the family of concepts related to ethnic "structure," including the repertoire of attributes for a population and the full repertoire of nominal ethnic identity categories—which can be taken as fixed and exogenous to most economic and political processes in the short term. However, concepts related to ethnic "practice," including activated ethnic identity categories, or the "operative" repertoire of ethnic identity categories or the content associated with an ethnic identity category, cannot reasonably be taken as fixed and exogenous even in the short term. Nearly every variable identified above has an effect on some aspect of ethnic practice in the short term: Institutions associated with the modern state, patronage-based economies, and violence can all induce changes in the operative repertoire and thus bring about change in activated ethnic identity categories in the short term. Several of these variables can also affect the content of these identity categories in the short term—indeed, Bhabha's argument suggests that the content can never be taken as a fixed independent variable. Further, given that the survey of constructivist work is not exhaustive, in capturing either the arguments that have been made in the past or arguments that could be made in the future, we can well imagine plausible relationships between variables not identified here and concepts related to ethnic practice.

The implication for our theories of "ethnicity" as an independent variable is that they should make a consistent distinction between ethnic structure as defined above and ethnic practice. Models of the relationship between some aspect of ethnic practice and most political and economic processes must either model the possibility of endogeneity explicitly or make a case for why such endogeneity should not be presumed to exist. Indeed, it may be more reasonable to think about ethnic practice, politics, and economics as mutually constitutive processes rather than as independent and dependent variables. Alternatively, we could reasonably retain the assumptions of fixedness and exogeneity by reformulating these theories where possible as theories of the effect of concepts related to ethnic structure. Suppose, for instance, we want to theorize about the relationship between ethnic diversity and economic growth in the short term. Activated ethnic categories and concepts related to them cannot be assumed, based on the arguments above, to be fixed and exogenous to economic growth in the short term. But concepts such as the repertoire of descent-based attributes or the full repertoire of nominal categories for a population can. We should specify the concept of ethnic diversity in these short-term theories, then, to refer to some aspect of ethnic structure. Modeling the relationship between some aspect of ethnic identity and economic growth over the long term, however, would require us to address the possibility of an interaction between growth and the underlying distribution of attributes.

5

A Combinatorial Language for Thinking about Ethnic Identity Change

KANCHAN CHANDRA AND CILANNE BOULET

The previous chapters argued that "ethnic identities"—Black and White, Hindu and Muslim, Serb and Croat, Sinhala and Tamil, Mestizo and Ladino—are categories of classification in which membership requires the possession of descent-based attributes. Ethnic identity change in the short term consists simply of the process of reclassification of fixed descent-based attributes to generate new ethnic categories. In the long term, ethnic identity change also takes the form of change in the underlying set of descent-based attributes themselves.

This chapter shows that an ethnic identity category as defined above can be understood as a *combination* of elements from a fixed set. Based on this simple reformulation, we propose a new combinatorial framework for thinking about ethnic identity and ethnic identity change. This allows us to describe the complexity of a constructivist world, with its large identity repertoires, in multiple dimensions, that differ across individuals and populations, in a way that is amenable to theory building.

This framework turns on one key property intrinsically associated with ethnic identities: the stickiness of the descent-based attributes that constitute them. Descent-based attributes, the previous chapter argued, are disproportionately sticky in the short term compared to non-descent-based attributes. Thus, they can be taken as fixed in the short term. This opens the door to a combinatorial formulation, which requires a choice of elements from a fixed set. Ethnic identities are disproportionately based on such attributes, and so especially amenable to such a formulation. But in principle, this combinatorial framework should apply to *any* identity that is generated from a fixed set of attributes.

Once we express an ethnic identity category as a combination, we can translate each of the concepts introduced in this book in the language of combinatorial mathematics. Our emphasis throughout is on translating rather than justifying these concepts (see Chapters 2, 3, and 4 for a justification). We express the concept of an "attribute" as a "value" on an attribute-dimension. This leads to precise reformulations of several concepts introduced in the previous chapter: the repertoire of *attributes* for a population, the repertoire of *attributes* for an individual, the repertoire of nominal ethnic identity *categories* for a population, the repertoire of nominal ethnic identity *categories* for an individual, the *activated* ethnic identity categories for a population, and the *activated* ethnic identity category for an individual. It also allows us to introduce some fundamental new concepts such as the distribution of individual repertoires of attributes for a population.

Throughout, we illustrate these concepts using a simple 2*2 example, with two attribute-dimensions with two values on each. But since a key advantage of using this combinatorial language is that it provides a general method for representing populations with any number of attribute-dimensions and any number of attribute-values on each, this illustration is always followed with a description of the general case of a population with any number of attribute-dimensions and values on each, and examples of populations that are likely to consist of more than two attribute-dimensions.

Building on the combinatorial translation of basic concepts, we express the five mechanisms of ethnic identity change introduced in the previous chapter in a combinatorial language. Change in activated ethnic identity categories through reclassification can be expressed as a process of *recombination* of elements from a fixed set. "Passing" by individual switching of attributes can be expressed as the individual *replacement* of existing attribute-values within an existing population repertoire. Change in the "operative" repertoire of nominal ethnic identity categories can be expressed as the *imposition of restrictions* on attribute-values, a combination of attribute-values, or entire attribute-dimensions in the full repertoire. Change in the full repertoire of nominal ethnic identity categories or the full repertoire of attributes for a population can be disaggregated further and expressed as one of two distinct mechanisms: the addition of a commonsensical attribute-*value* to an existing repertoire or the subtraction of an old one, and the addition (or subtraction) of a commonsensical attribute-*dimension* to an existing repertoire.[1] Table 5.1 lists these translations and the mechanisms to which they correspond.

Of these five mechanisms, the one most likely to operate in the short term is "recombination." Indeed, this mechanism has long been recognized in the

---

[1] A change in the underlying repertoire of descent-based attributes for individuals or populations will *always* produce a change in the full repertoire of nominal ethnic identity categories for individuals and populations. This is because the full repertoire of nominal ethnic identity categories is simply the set of combinations consisting of elements from the underlying repertoire of attributes. Any change in that repertoire of attributes will change the set of combinations derived from it.

Table 5.1 **Translating Constructivist Mechanisms into Combinatorics**

Mechanism of Ethnic Identity Change	Combinatorial Translation
Change in activated ethnic identity category through reclassification of descent-based attributes.	Recombination of descent-based attributes
Individual "switching" of attributes	Replacement of descent-based attributes within a population repertoire
Change in the "operative" repertoire of nominal ethnic identity categories for individuals and populations	The imposition of new restrictions on attribute-values, combinations of attribute-values or entire attribute-dimensions on the full repertoire
Change in the "full" repertoire of nominal ethnic identity categories for individuals and populations	Addition (or subtraction) of a commonsensical attribute-value or attribute-dimension
Change in the repertoire of descent-based attributes for individuals and populations	Addition (or subtraction) of a commonsensical attribute-value or attribute-dimension

interdisciplinary literature on constructivism, albeit using different terms, as an important process by which ethnic identities change in the short term. One such term, to which we have already given a great deal of attention, is reclassification. Other terms are "fission" and "fusion" or "supertribalization" (Rudolph and Rudolph 1967, Horowitz 1971, van den Berghe 1981). The term "fission" is that form of recombination in which new groups are created by the disaggregation of larger ones. The term "fusion" refers to that form of recombination in which new groups are created through the amalgamation of smaller ones. And the term "supertribalization" describes the construction of large tribal identities by the fusion of smaller ones. The use of a combinatorial language shows that these previously noted phenomena are all particular cases of the same general phenomenon.

These mechanisms apply to ethnic identities in general. But the variables that trigger these mechanisms, the agents who act accordingly, and their motivations may well be particular. Correspondingly, the outcomes that these mechanisms are associated with may vary across contexts. Further, these mechanisms show only that ethnic identity change *can* occur, and *how* it occurs when it does. But they do not show that it *will* occur. Put differently, they are a means of formalizing the potential for change intrinsic to ethnic identities. This potential for change may be realized in different ways, in different patterns, in different contexts—and in some contexts, it may not be realized at all.

Section 1 of this chapter introduces a combinatorial translation of the key concepts introduced in previous chapters. Section 2 introduces a combinatorial translation of the mechanisms by which ethnic identities change. Further sections extend the simple translations offered in this chapter to more complicated situations. Section 3 shows how to extend the translation to scenarios in which attribute-dimensions are not independent of each other. Section 4 extends it to formalize specific forms of restrictions on the operative repertoire of nominal identities.

Throughout this book, the claims we make can differ based on whether the unit of analysis is a *category*, an *attribute*, an *individual*, or a *population*. For example, an ethnic identity category may be defined as a combination of *attributes* using the "and" operator. But if we want to describe the *individuals* eligible for membership in the same category as a combination, we may have to switch to the "or" operator. To illustrate, consider the identity category "Black." Given current membership rules in the United States, this category corresponds to the following combination of *attributes*: {dark skin *and* descent from parents of African origin}. But the equivalent combination of *individuals* could be expressed differently: {dark-skinned individuals descended from parents of African origin who are born in the United States, *or* dark-skinned individuals descended from parents of African origin who are born outside the United States}. Further, the repertoire of either identity categories or attributes for an *individual* depends on, but is not the same as, that for the *population*. The reader may find it helpful to keep the distinctions between these four units of analysis in mind while reading this chapter.

1. A Combinatorial Vocabulary for Thinking About Ethnic Identity

Throughout, we first introduce a term that describes a *population*, which we then use to construct a second term to describe an *individual* in that population. We use a fictional example to illustrate the analytical features of each term where necessary, and actual examples to highlight its empirical applicability.

Attribute and Category

An identity "category," as defined previously is a classification that separates one or more individuals from others. An "attribute" is a characteristic necessary to qualify for membership in a category. Returning to Helen's example, "African American" is one of her identity categories, for which dark skin and descent from parents of African origin are among her qualifying attributes.

Recall that the distinction between attribute and category is relational: An object that is an attribute in relation to a category at some higher level of analysis can itself be a category in relation to other attributes at a lower level of analysis. "Dark skin" for instance, while an attribute in relation to the category "African American" is itself a category constructed from a range of shades of skin color (e.g., dark brown or light brown), each of which is an attribute in relation to it.

Nevertheless, we can make a distinction between "basic attributes"—things which we take as commonsensical givens in the short term even though they can in principle be broken down still further—and "secondary attributes"—constructs of basic attributes, which function as attributes in the creation of categories at higher levels of analysis but are themselves categories in relation to "basic" attributes. In our example, dark skin can be thought of as a basic attribute which we typically do not break down further. "African American," by contrast, can be thought of as a category in relation to this attribute, but an attribute in relation to other categories such as "African-American Muslim."

The term attribute here refers throughout to "basic" attributes. The term "category" refers to any construct of basic attributes, whether or not that category itself serves as an attribute for others at higher levels of analysis.

Attribute-Dimensions and Attribute-Values

By the term "attribute-dimension," we mean a class of attributes with exhaustive and mutually exclusive values. The term "attribute" always refers to a particular attribute-value on a particular attribute-dimension.

For example, one attribute-dimension is "skin color." The *values* on this dimension might include "black" and "white." We depict this dimension and the values on it as follows:

Skin color: {black, white}

Another attribute-dimension might be country of origin. The values on this dimension might include "foreign" and "native," represented as follows:

Origin: {foreign, native}

The attribute-values on a given attribute-dimension are exhaustive (everyone in a population has some skin color, and some place of origin) and mutually exclusive (If you have black skin you cannot have white skin. If you are of foreign origin, you cannot be of native origin).

Throughout, we assume the existence of discrete values on an attribute-dimension. Attribute-dimensions with continuous values are accommodated by expressing ranges of values as discrete intervals.

"Basic" attribute dimensions are a class of "basic" attribute-values. "Secondary" attribute dimensions are a class of "secondary" attribute-values. Unless otherwise specified, we use the term "attribute-dimensions" throughout to refer to "basic" attribute-dimensions.

Category-Dimensions and Categories

By the term "category-dimension," we mean a class of categories with exhaustive and mutually exclusive values. As in the case of attribute-dimensions, we also assume the existence of discrete values on category-dimensions

Just as the distinction between "attribute" and "category" is a relational one, the distinction between attribute-dimension and "category-dimension" is a relational one. Category-dimensions produced by attribute-values on some underlying set of attribute-dimensions can themselves be attribute-dimensions in relation to category-dimensions at another level.

However, just as any population has a set of "basic" attributes, it also has a set of "basic attribute-dimensions" which can be used in the formation of category-dimensions but are not themselves be disaggregated further in the short term.

Repertoire of "Basic" Attributes for a *Population*

By a population, we mean the collection of individuals in a given country. The term "repertoire of attributes" for a population refers to all attribute-dimensions and attribute-values understood to be commonsensical in that population.

In principle, we know individuals within and across populations possess a vast range of characteristics, any of which might potentially be the defining attributes for membership in some category: height, weight, length of nose, eye color, hair type, length of hair, occupation, dress, last name, income, etc. As Chapter 4 argued, however, this very large set of possibilities is filtered by institutions of cognition. These institutions impose a scheme of classification which tells individuals in any given population which of these attributes to pay attention to and how to "see" them. This scheme of classification produces a bounded repertoire of "basic" attributes for that population that is fixed in the short term but can be reconstructed in the long term.

Throughout this chapter, the term "attribute" refers only to this commonsensical repertoire. We assume, furthermore, that all individuals have the same commonsensical perception and have perfect information about the contents of this repertoire.

The list below represents a simple example of a population with two commonsensical attribute-dimensions and two values on each. We will use this as our running example throughout this chapter. Each row describes an attribute-dimension, associated with a set of values.

Skin color: {black, white}

Origin: {foreign, native}

In general, the list of of attributes for a population, with j attribute-dimensions and n_i values for attribute dimension A_j, can be represented in the following way:

$$A_1: \quad \{a_{1,1}, a_{1,2}, \ldots, a_{1,n_1}\}$$
$$A_2: \quad \{a_{2,1}, a_{2,2}, \ldots, a_{2,n_2}\}$$
$$\ldots$$
$$A_j: \quad \{a_{j,1}, a_{j,2}, \ldots, a_{j,n_j}\}$$

We assume for now that these dimensions are independent: that is, having black skin on the dimension of skin color does not affect the probability of being of either foreign or native origin. In practice, attribute-dimensions are often correlated, in structures that have been categorized in previous literature as "cross-cutting," "coinciding," and "nested." We relax the assumption of independence, and consider these relationships between attribute-dimensions in a later section of this chapter.

The basic building block of our theories of ethnic identity change should be this repertoire of attributes and attribute-dimensions (for both individuals and populations) rather than a repertoire of categories and category dimensions. Categories and category- dimensions are derived from this repertoire of attributes.

Repertoire of Attributes for an Individual

Previously, we described the repertoire of attributes for a *population*. The repertoire of attributes for an *individual* in this population consists of one value on each attribute-dimension in the population repertoire.

Consider our running example, with the repertoire of two attribute-dimensions and two values on each.

Skin color: {black, white}
Origin: {foreign, native}

This population repertoire can generate the following four individual repertoires: Black and Foreign (BF); Black and Native (BN); White and Foreign (WF); and White and Native (WN).

Different population repertoires of attributes will produce different sets of individual repertoires. Suppose, for instance, that we have a population with three attribute-dimensions and two values on each.

Skin color: {black, white}
Origin: {foreign, native}
Height: {tall, short}

This population repertoire will generate the following eight individual repertoires: Black and Foreign and Tall (BFT); Black and Foreign and Short (BFS); White and Foreign and Tall (WFT); White and Foreign and Short (WFS); Black and Native and Tall (BNT); Black and Native and Short (BNS); White and Native and Tall (WNT); White and Native and Short (WNS).

In general, the larger the population repertoire, the greater the number of individual repertoires it will generate. Where we have j attribute-dimensions and n_i values for attribute-dimension A_j, the total number of distinct repertoires is $n_1 n_2 \ldots n_j$. This general formulation allows us to model populations such as India and the United States with more multidimensional and complex repertoires of attributes than the simple 2*2 case.

Note that each attribute-dimension in a population repertoire of attributes is represented as one attribute-value in an individual attribute- repertoire. The larger the number of attribute-dimensions in a population repertoire, the larger will be the number of elements in an individual attribute-repertoire. In general, in a population with j attribute-dimensions, an individual repertoire of attributes consists of a j-tuple, with one value from each attribute-dimension.

Distribution of Individual Attribute-Repertoires Within Populations

Populations may differ from each other based on their repertoires of common-sensical attributes. However, populations with an identical population repertoire can also differ from each other based on the *distribution* of individual attribute-repertoires within them.

One population generated from the example above, for instance, might have a very high proportion of individuals with BN repertoires and low proportions of individuals with BF, WN, and WF repertoires; another might have more individuals with a WN repertoire than any other; and so on.

These distinct distributions can be represented as in Table 5.2, in which the proportion of individuals with different repertoires is represented by the values a, b, c, and d. Let's term this generic case "Someland."

Here, a is the proportion of individuals in this population with the repertoire BF; b is the proportion of individuals with the repertoire WF; c is the proportion of individuals with the repertoire BN; and d is the proportion of individuals with

Table 5.2 **Population Repertoire of Attributes (Two-Dimensional Case)**
            (Two Values on Each Dimension)

	Black	**White**	
Foreign	a	b	**a + b**
Native	c	d	**c + d**
	a + c	**b + d**	

the repertoire WN. There can be as many distinct populations are there are non-negative values of a, b, c and d, subject to the restriction that a + b + c + d = 1.

If we have two dimensions with larger numbers of values, we can also represent the distribution of individual attribute-repertoires in a two-dimensional table. Suppose, for instance, that our population has three values on the attribute-dimension of skin color—Black, White, and Brown—and four values on the attribute-dimension of place of origin—African, European, Asian, and Native. We could represent this population repertoire of attributes in the two-dimensional table shown in Table 5.3.

Table 5.3 **Population Repertoire of Attributes (Two-Dimensional Case) (Three Values on One Dimension, Four Values on Second Dimension)**

	Black	**White**	**Brown**	
African	a	b	c	a + b + c
European	d	e	f	d + e + f
Asian	g	h	i	g + h + i
Native	k	l	m	k + l + m
	a + d + g + k	b + e + h + l	c + f + i + m	

Here, there can be as many distinct distributions of individual attribute-repertoires for the same population repertoire of attributes as there are values of a, b, c d, e, f, g, h, i, j, k, l, and m, subject to the restriction that the values are non-negative, and that a + b + c + d + e + f + g + h + i + j + k + l + m = 1.

If we have a population repertoire with more than two attribute-dimensions, representing the distributions of individual attribute-repertoires in the form above will require a multidimensional table, with its number of dimensions corresponding to the number of attribute-dimensions in the repertoire. An alternate way to think about distributions in this case, therefore, is simply to list the distinct individual repertoires that correspond to the population's repertoire of attributes and the proportion of the population associated with each. Table 5.4, for instance, represents the proportion of individuals with each attribute-repertoire for the population described earlier, with three attribute-dimensions and two values on each.

> Skin color: {black(B), white(W)}
> Origin: {foreign(F), native(N)}
> Height: {tall(T), short(S)}

There can be as many distinct populations in this case are there are non-negative values of a, b, c, d, e, f, g, and h, subject to the restriction that a + b + c + d + e + f + g + h = 1. We can similarly represent the range of distributions of individual repertoires that correspond to a population repertoire with any number of attribute-dimensions and any number of values on each dimension.

Table 5.4 **Population Repertoire of Attributes (Three-Dimensional Case) Two Values on Each Dimension**

Repertoire	Proportion
BFT	a
BFS	b
WFT	c
WFS	d
BNT	e
BNS	f
WNT	g
WNS	h

We rely upon the simple 2*2 case throughout for the purpose of exposition. But many of the populations we want to model may have repertoires of multiple attribute-dimensions with different numbers of values on each.

Countries such as India, for example, in which there appear to be several commonsensical attribute-dimensions with large numbers of values on each, are likely to have a distribution with a very large number of individual attribute-repertoires, each of which captures a small proportion of the population. Countries such as the United States, in which there appear to be several commonsensical attribute-dimensions but with a smaller number of values on each, should have a distribution with a smaller number of individual attribute-repertoires, each of which captures a larger proportion of the population. And countries such as Japan, which appear to have fewer commonsensical attribute-dimensions and fewer attribute-values on each should produce a small number of individual attribute-repertoires, each comprising a large proportion of the population. A separate manuscript, *Measuring Ethnicity* (Chandra 2011), discusses how data on the distributions of individual attribute-repertoires might be collected—and shows how the data can be used to generate more meaningful indices for ethnic diversity than those that we have so far that allow us to compare populations with different number of attribute-dimensions.

The *Membership Rule* for an Identity Category Can Be Expressed as a Combination of Attribute-*Values*

The membership rule for a category can now be defined as a combination of attribute-values using the "and" or the "or" operator, or some combination of the two. For example, some of the identity categories that can be constructed from our running example include the combinations {Black}; {Black and Foreign}; {Black or White}; and {Black or (White and Foreign)}.

Ethnic identity categories, we argued previously, are a subset of all categories that can be generated from a set of descent-based attributes. Thus, we can translate them as a subset of all combinations that can be generated from that set of descent-based attributes.

For example, the category "West Indian" in Waters's study (Waters 1999) might be thought of as a combination of values on three attribute-dimensions (skin color, native language, and place of birth), using both the "and" and the "or" operator: {Dark skin *and* English-speaking *and* (Born in Guyana *or* Barbados *or* Jamaica *or* Trinidad…)}.

The category "Russian-speaking population" in Laitin's study of Estonia might be written as a combination of values on two dimensions (language and nationality), using both the "and" and the "or" operator: {Russian-speaker *and* (Russian *or* Ukrainian *or* Belarusian *or* Polish *or* Jewish *or* Finn)} (Laitin 1998).

The category "Nubian" in Idi Amin's Uganda might be thought of as a simpler combination of values on one dimension (tribe), using only the "or" operator: {Baganda *or* Basoga *or* Banyoro *or* Acholi *or* Langi *or* Batoro *or* Kakwa…} (Kasfir 1979).

The category "Other Backward Caste" in India might be thought of a comparably simple combination of values on a single dimension (caste), also using only the "or" operator: {Yadav *or* Kurmi *or* Patel *or* Lodh *or* Nai *or* Saini…}.

The category "White" in the United States is a combination that might be described as {Irish American *or* Italian American *or* German American or…}.

The category "Hispanic" in the United States can be expressed as {Dominican or Puerto Rican or Mexican or…}.

The category WASP, meanwhile, is an "and" combination: {White *and* Anglo Saxon *and* Protestant}.

Identity categories so constructed can be of varying degrees of complexity. They might for instance correspond to only one value on an attribute as the category "Black" does in our example. They might combine several values on one attribute-dimension as the category {Black or White} does. They might combine one or more values across dimensions, as the category {Black and Foreign} does. And, while the examples from the small repertoire above all use either the "and" or the "or" operator, identity categories from a larger repertoire of attributes can be constructed by using a combination of "and" and "or" operators across and within dimensions. In general, the greater the use of the "and" operator, the more restrictive is the definition of a category. The greater the use of the "or" operator, the more permissive is the definition of a category.

The *Membership* of an Identity Category Can Be Expressed as a Combination of Individual Attribute-*Repertoires*

The membership *rule* for a category is expressed as a combination of distinct *attribute-values*. But the *membership* of a category is expressed as a combination of *individual attribute-repertoires* in that population, with each individual attribute-repertoire corresponding to a distinct type of individual. The size of the membership of each combination or category is given by the proportion of individuals in the population belonging to each attribute-repertoire.

To illustrate, the simple 2*2 case we have been discussing has four attribute-values—Black, White, Foreign, and Native—and four distinct individual attribute-repertoires—BF, WF, BN, and WN—which constitute a, b, c, and d proportion of the population, respectively. The *membership rule* for the category "Black" in Someland consists of a single element combination of attribute-values (Black). But its *membership* consists of a more complex combination of individual attribute-repertoires (BF or BN), constituting (a + c) proportion of the population. By the same logic, the membership rule for the category "Black Foreigners" consists of two attribute-values ("Black Skin *and* Foreign Origin)," but we could express its membership as a single-element combination of individual attribute-repertoires (BF), constituting a proportion of the population.

The *Name* of a Category May or May Not Be Expressed as a Combination

The combination which defines the membership rule for a category need not be captured in the name of a category. Consider for example the combination of attributes "Black and Foreign." This combination may be given any one of a number of names—the population in question may quite literally label this category "Black and Foreign." But it may just as well call it something else— "immigrants," for example, or "Otherlanders," or any number of other labels.

Conversely, the name of an identity category need not be informative about the combination which defines its membership rule. Some names do contain such information. The name WASP in the United States embodies a combination of (secondary) attributes that defines the membership rule for the category (White-Anglo-Saxon-Protestant). Others convey at least partial information. The name "Black" for instance conveys the information that skin color may have something to do with the membership rule in this category—but the membership rule for this category requires a combination of attributes including but not restricted to skin color. But many names are entirely uninformative about the membership rule. The name "Bahujan" in India, for instance, conveys no information about the membership rule, which is a combination of values on the attribute-dimensions of caste, religion and tribe: {Backward Castes and Sikh and Christian and Buddhist and Scheduled Tribe…}.

Similarly, the combination of individual attribute-repertoires that defines the membership of a category need not be related to the name of that category. The combination (BF, BN, and WF), for instance, may be named exactly that—"All Black Foreigners, Black Natives, and White Foreigners"—but it is unlikely. This membership may be equivalently described by another name invented for the purpose, such as "People of Color," which need not be an accurate description of the individual attribute-repertoires of members.

The name of an identity category also need not convey information about the individual attribute-repertoires of members of that category. Even the very informative name WASP conveys only the information that members have the secondary attributes of being White, Anglo-Saxon, and Protestant in their repertoire, as well as the basic attributes that constitute them (e.g., light skin is a basic attribute that constitutes the secondary attribute of "White"). But it does not convey information about the attribute-repertoires of eligible members other than the fact that they contain these attribute-values. The same is true of the other examples above.

We are concerned throughout this section with the membership rule and the membership—not with the name of a category. The name, as Chapters 3 and 4 argued, is important in its own right. But naming possibilities cannot be captured in a combinatorial vocabulary. There can be any number of names used to describe a particular membership rule or membership, many of which will have no relation to a combinatorial expression. And any particular combinatorial expression need not be matched by any particular name. Indeed, the question of when the combination that defines a membership or a membership rule is made transparently visible in the name chosen for a category and when it is concealed is a question worthy of research in its own right.

Full Repertoire of Nominal Identity *Categories* for a Population

We conceptualize the full repertoire of nominal identity categories for a population as the full set of combinations of attribute-repertoires that can be generated from its repertoire of commonsensical attributes. In general, the total number of different combinations, with no restrictions, that can be generated from a repertoire of j types of attributes and n_i values for attribute type A_i is $2^{n_1 n_2 \cdots n_j}$.

In the case of our running example, the size of this set is $2^4 = 16$. Table 5.5 provides the list of categories in the identity repertoire, the membership of each category, and its size.[2] (Note that these combinations include the entire population and the empty set.)

Strictly speaking, the full repertoire of nominal ethnic identities is even larger than the full set of combinations of distinct attribute-repertoires. This is because any

---

[2] One common way of thinking about an ethnic category is as a "negative" identity category, defined by the criteria that exclude the "other" rather than the criteria that characterize its members. Thus, we may arguably define "Hindu" as all those who are *not* (Muslim or Christian), or "Black" as all those who are *not* White. Note that this way of thinking about ethnic identity categories is encompassed by the formulation we offer here. Thus, the category "Not White" can be thought of as the combination (WF and WN), which includes all those who have white skin in their repertoire but excludes all those who have dark skin.

Table 5.5 **Full Repertoire of Nominal Categories for Population (2*2 Case)**

Definition of Category	Allowed Individual Repertoires	Size
∅	∅	0
Black and Foreign	BF	a
Black and Native	BN	c
White and Foreign	WF	b
White and Native	WN	d
Black	BF, BN	a + c
White	WF, WN	b + d
Foreign	BF, WF	a + b
Native	BN, WN	c + d
Black or Foreign	BF, BN, WF	a + b + c
White or Foreign	BF, WF, WN	a + b + d
Black or Native	BF, BN, WN	a + c + d
White or Native	BN, WF, WN	b + c + d
(Black and Native) or (White and Foreign)	BN, WF	b + c
(Black and Foreign) or (White and Native)	BF, WN	a + d
Entire Population (Black or White; Foreign or Native)	BN, WN, BF, WF	a + b + c + d = 1

one combination of distinct attribute-repertoires (or membership) can correspond to more than one combination of attribute-values (or membership rule). Consider the combination of the attribute-repertoires BF, BN and WF. The membership rule for this combination listed in the table is simply "Black" or "Foreign." A category which requires the possession of either the attribute-value "Black" or the attribute-value "Foreign" will automatically include those with the attribute-repertoires BF, BN, and WF. But note that a different membership rule that captures the same membership could simply be "Not White and Native." We can take the full repertoire of nominal ethnic identity categories as defined here, then, as to be an underestimate of the true range of identity options that actually describe a population.

The large size of an "ethnic identity repertoire" posited here, to reiterate a point made in the previous chapter, is a fundamental departure from previous theoretical work on this subject. This work, which typically assumes that an identity repertoire contains two or at most three elements (Laitin 1986, Sahlins 1989, Waters 1999, Posner 2005), and does not permit any combinations between them, produces simple models that do not correspond to empirical reality. Empirical work that has tried to operationalize the identity repertoire, in Russia, or the United States or India, found large repertoires with "almost no boundaries" (Laitin 1998, 268, Waters 1990, Chandra 2004). We know, furthermore, that individuals routinely combine and recombine elements in their repertoires to fashion new identity categories. The conceptualization of an ethnic identity repertoire offered here attempts to capture this empirical reality. It produces more complex, but also more illuminating models. In order to explain how ethnic identities are activated, then, the theorist must consider tens or hundreds of counterfactuals.

The "Operative" Repertoire of Nominal Ethnic Identity Categories for a Population

Although the full size of the repertoire of identity categories can be very large, individuals may not actually consider each category in it when they decide which one to activate. The "operative" repertoire that they choose from may be more narrowly constructed. Consider an example from South Africa in the 1950s. The many possible combinations generated by the underlying distribution of attributes in South Africa then included "Zulu," defined as a combination of clans: {Usuthu or Buthelezi or...}, and "Natalian," defined as a combination of races living in Natal: {White + African + Colored}. Among individuals looking for identities to activate in politics, the combination Zulu was accepted without comment. But the combination Natalian was implausible, even to those who might have wished otherwise (Mandela 1994).[3] We can say, then, that the "operative" repertoire of nominal ethnic identity categories in South Africa in the 1950s, at least in the context of political mobilization, did not include the category "Natalian." Although it belonged in the full repertoire, there was some restriction, operating implicitly or explicitly, that eliminated it from consideration.

We can think of the "operative" repertoire of nominal ethnic identity categories, then, as defined by restrictions that separate that subset of ethnic categories that individuals consider feasible from others that they do not. These restrictions must be explicitly identified and incorporated into a theory of ethnic identity change. Identifying the full repertoire of nominal ethnic identities can often serve as a useful heuristic in identifying these restrictions. Once we identify the full range of possible combinations, we can begin asking and answering questions about why some are implausible through a process of elimination.

---

[3] Describing his trial for treason in South Africa, for instance, Nelson Mandela (1994) remarks at a white judge who apparently thought of himself as a "Natalian"and shared a sense of regional pride at the achievements of Blacks from the region. "Natalians," writes Mandela, "are noted for their loyalty to their region, and these peculiar bonds can sometimes even transcend color. Indeed, many Natalians thought of themselves as white Zulus" (235). The very fact that the judge's self-perception was thought to be so remarkable reveals how implausible this combination is in relation to others.

Consider one example of how a restriction can define the "operative" repertoire in a particular context. Suppose that the distribution of patronage goods by politicians to co-ethnic voters requires ethnic memberships to be visible: co-ethnics cannot identify each other in the absence of visible attributes (see Chandra 2004 for elaboration). Assume, in our 2*2 example, that skin color is visible but place of origin is not. In this context, the "operative repertoire of nominal ethnic identity categories" will consist of those categories defined by skin color—"Black" and "White." "Foreign" or "Native" would fall out of the operative repertoire because these categories are not "visible." And categories such as "Black Foreign" or "Black Native" or "White Foreign" or "White Foreign" would also fall out because in the absence of visibility, individuals will not be able to draw distinctions between "Black Foreign" and "Black Native." The "visibility" restriction, in other words, eliminates fourteen of the sixteen categories in the full repertoire from our consideration, producing an "operative" repertoire of two. Table 5.6 describes this "operative repertoire." The shaded cells represent the categories in the repertoire. Those not shaded have been eliminated by this restriction.

Table 5.6 **"Operative" Repertoire of Nominal Categories for Population (2*2 Case)**

Definition of Category	Allowed Individual Repertoires	Size
∅	∅	0
Black and Foreign	BF	a
Black and Native	BN	c
White and Foreign	WF	b
White and Native	WN	d
Black	BF, BN	a + c
White	WF, WN	b + d
Foreign	BF, WF	a + b
Native	BN, WN	c + d
Black or Foreign	BF, BN, WF	a + b + c
White or Foreign	BF, WF, WN	a + b + d
Black or Native	BF, BN, WN	a + c + d
White or Native	BN, WF, WN	b + c + d
(Black and Native) or (White and Foreign)	BN, WF	b + c
(Black and Foreign) or (White and Native)	BF, WN	a + d
Entire Population (Black or White; Foreign or Native)	BN, WN, BF, WF	a + b + c + d = 1

Section 4 of this chapter, and several chapters in this book, introduce several different types of restrictions and shows how they produce an operative identity repertoire in particular contexts. There may well be no single restriction that defines the operative repertoire in all contexts. But no matter what particular restrictions are employed, the size and content of the operative repertoire will always be bounded by the size and content of the full repertoire.

Full Repertoire of Nominal Identity Categories for an Individual

An individual's repertoire of nominal identity categories with distinct memberships consists of all those combinations of individual attribute-repertoires that include her own.

In our 2*2 case, for example, the repertoire of nominal identity categories with distinct memberships possessed by an individual with the attribute-repertoire BF includes the following combinations, listed in Table 5.7.

In general, an individual repertoire of categories with distinct membership, with no restrictions, has size $2^{n_1 n_2 \cdots n_j - 1}$. An individual's operative repertoire of nominal ethnic identity categories is a subset of this larger set, defined by the restrictions that apply to the population repertoire.

Operative Repertoire of Nominal Identity Categories for an Individual

The operative repertoire of nominal identity categories for an individual will be a subset of the full set, defined by the restrictions relevant to that particular context.

Table 5.7 **Full Repertoire of Nominal Categories for Individual (2*2 Case)**

Membership Rule	Membership	Size
Black and Foreign	BF	a
Black	BF, BN	a + c
Foreign	BF, WF	a + b
Black or Foreign	BF, BN, WF	a + b + c
White or Foreign	BF, WF, WN	a + b + d
Black or Native	BF, BN, WN	a + c + d
(Black and Foreign) or (White and Native)	BF, WN	a + d
Black or White	BN, WN, BF, WF	a + b + c + d = 1

If we restrict the "operative" repertoire to only those categories that are combinations of "visible" attribute-dimensions, and if skin color is a visible attribute-dimension while place of origin is not (see example above), then, all individuals will have an "operative repertoire" consisting of one and only one category. Individuals with the attributes BN or BF will only have the category "Black" in their operative repertoire, while individuals with the attributes WF or WN will only have the category "White" in their operative repertoire.

Activated Categories for Populations and Individuals

Of the ethnic identity categories contained in a repertoire, whether defined by membership rule or membership, individuals activate only one at any given time. Consequently, the ethnic identity categories activated for the population as a whole will be a small subset of the categories in the nominal repertoire.

To illustrate, let's take the example of "Oneland," a particular case of our running 2*2 example. Suppose that the sizes of the attribute-repertoires in Oneland are as follows: BF (a =.4), WF = (b = .25) BN (c = .25), and WN (d = .1). Suppose individuals in Oneland activate the categories "Black and Foreign," "Black and Native," and "White." This would produce an activated ethnic demography, which would look like the illustration in Figure 5.1.

Alternatively, suppose that individuals in Oneland activate the categories "Black" and "White." This would produce a different activated ethnic demography, represented in Figure 5.2.

As the example should make clear, Oneland can be characterized by a large number of activated ethnic demographies. At the same time, however, there are activated ethnic demographies that *cannot* be activated on the basis of the distribution of attribute-repertoires in Oneland. For instance, no possible combination of attribute-repertoires in Oneland will produce a bipolar ethnic demography with a population that is 80% Black and 20% White.

Note that there is no reason to expect that activated ethnic categories are mutually exclusive or exhaustive. Activated ethnic identities can in principle overlap, and they can in principle describe less than the entire population. Further,

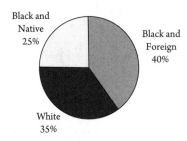

Figure 5.1 Activated Ethnic Demography #1 in Oneland

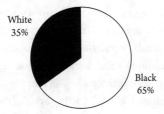

Figure 5.2 Activated Ethnic Demography #2 in Oneland

although they are generated from attributes organized into attribute-dimensions, the ethnic categories activated in a population need not fall neatly along any one category-dimension. In Ethnic Demography #1, for example, the activated categories "Black and Native," "Black and Foreign," and "White" do not fall in a common family. We cannot describe them as belonging to the dimension of skin color, because two out of three categories are based on a combination of attributes of skin color and region. But we cannot describe them as belonging to the dimension of region because one of the three categories is not based on region at all, while in the other two "region" is combined with race. In Ethnic Demography #2, the activated categories "Black" and "White" do fall neatly along a single category-dimension. But there is no reason to expect this to be generally the case. This is a point of fundamental importance for both theoretical and empirical work on activated ethnic identities, to which we return in Chapter 6 (see also Chandra 2009a and 2009b and Chandra and Wilkinson 2008).

2. The Mechanisms by Which Ethnic Identities Change

Using the combinatorial vocabulary developed so far, we can formalize the mechanisms of ethnic identity change introduced in the following ways: (1) recombination, (2) the replacement of an attribute-value by individuals while keeping the population repertoire constant, (3) a change in the restrictions that define operative repertoire of nominal identities, (4) the addition or (subtraction) of an attribute-value from a population repertoire of attributes, and (5) the addition or subtraction of an attribute-dimension from a population repertoire of attributes. The first is the most likely during the short term, while the last four are likely to occur mainly over the long term.

These mechanisms, further, are connected. Changes in the underlying repertoire of attributes alter some aspect of the repertoire of nominal identity categories for individuals and populations and may also affect the categories that are activated. The activation of new categories through recombination, in turn, might trigger attribute-changes of any of the three kinds listed, as individuals who end up in less advantageous categories look for ways to improve their position. Any of these mechanisms might initiate a dynamic sequence of changes in ethnic identities for individuals and populations across generations. A full theory of identity change, therefore, must model the dynamic relationship between these mechanisms. Some of the subsequent chapters in this volume (e.g., Chapter 7, by Maurits van Der Veen and David Laitin, and Chapter 12, by Ian Lustick), attempt to do that.

Recombination

Ethnic identity change through recombination occurs when one or more individuals reclassify themselves by employing a new combination of attributes within their existing repertoires. This change takes place in their activated ethnic identity categories, keeping their nominal identity repertoires constant. When Helen changes her activated ethnic identity from "Black" to "West Indian," for instance, she is activating the combination {Birth in Trinidad *or* Guyana *or* Barbados *or* Haiti} in place of the combination {Dark skin *and* descent from parents of African origin} while keeping her underlying set of attributes constant.

Ethnic identity change through recombination at the individual level can, but need not, require an individual to select different attributes from her own repertoire—it simply requires herself to associate herself with a different combination defined over attribute-values that characterize the population. For example, when Helen chooses to activate the category "West Indian" rather than "Black," she is selecting the attribute of birth in Trinidad over the attributes of skin color and African descent. But suppose that she activates the category "immigrant" instead of the category "West Indian," where the category "immigrant" is defined by the combination of attributes of {"Birth in Mexico or England or Ghana or Trinidad or India or…}." In this case, she changes the combination with which she affiliates without changing the attribute she selects, since the same attribute allows her to choose membership in either combination.

When individuals change their activated ethnic identities through recombination, this results in a change in the pattern of activated ethnic identities in the population as well. To illustrate, consider an example of a population with the following repertoire of attributes (see Table 5.8).

Table 5.8 **Example of Population Repertoire of Attributes**

	Black	**White**
Foreign	.25	.25
Native	.25	.25

If all individuals initially activate, as Helen does, the attribute of skin color, the activated ethnic demography in this population would consist of two categories:

Black, consisting of 50% of the population and White, consisting of 50%. But if all individuals switch, as Helen does, to emphasizing the attribute of place of origin, the activated ethnic demography in this population would consist of two different categories: Foreign, consisting of 50% of the population and Native, consisting of 50%.

Changes in activated ethnic identity categories for a population through recombination are easiest to spot when the change in combination is also accompanied by a change in the *name* of the category. In the example above, for instance, the change in activated combinations was signaled by a change in the name of the category from "Black" to "West Indian." But it is also common for those who initiate such changes to disguise them by retaining the same name despite proposing a new combination as a membership rule (see, for example, the discussions of the names "Kshatriya" in Chapter 4 or "Afrikaaner" in Chapter 6).

Of all the mechanisms by which ethnic identities change, recombination is likely to be the most common in the short term. Two factors, identified in previous chapters but worth recalling here, explain the ease of ethnic identity change in the short term through recombination. First, combining attribute-values differently builds upon what we take to be commonsensical: Unlike other mechanisms discussed here, it does not require us to alter our frameworks about what constitutes common sense. Second, change in activated categories through recombination occurs between categories that are complementary, not mutually exclusive. An individual cannot, within this framework, switch between categories that require mutually exclusive attribute-values for membership because her repertoire cannot, by definition, possess both attribute-values.

There are many examples of changes in activated ethnic identities through recombination in the short term at the individual level. The West Indian immigrants in Mary Waters's study of New York (who are the basis for the fictionalized example of Helen), for instance, routinely switch between combinations in the course of a single day, calling themselves West Indian at work, Trinidadian at a party, and Black in some other context.

There are also several examples of change through recombination at the level of the population. In Brazil, the 1940 census reported a "White" majority of 63% and "Brown" and "Black" minorities of 21% and 15% each. In 1991, the set of color categories the census used to describe Brazil's population remained virtually the same, but the sizes of each had changed dramatically. As individuals with the same set of attributes matched them to different categories, the "Brown" minority doubled, the "Black" minority shrunk by two-thirds, and the category "White" also shrunk, barely making it past the majority threshold (Nobles 2000). An extreme example of change comes from the case of Sri Lanka. In 1953, the first census in post-colonial Sri Lanka reported a multipolar ethnic demography, with five significant categories: the Low Country Sinhalese (42%); the Kandyan Sinhalese (27%); the Indian Tamils (12%); the Ceylon Tamils (11%); and the Ceylon Moors (6%). Thirty years later, Sri Lanka's ethnic demography had been transformed into a majority-dominated demogaphy through the combination of the categories "Low Country Sinhalese" and the "Kandyan Sinhalese" into a Sinhala category (74%), looming large over three minorities: Sri Lankan Tamils (13%); Indian Tamils (6%); and Sri Lankan Moors (7%).

Although change in our activated ethnic identities *can* take place in the short term through recombination, it need not. We are likely to see many cases of stability empirically. A prototypical example of population-level stability is Rwanda. Rwanda's first census, taken in 1978, reported a Hutu majority of 91% and a Tutsi minority of 8%. But unlike Brazil, these figures remained stable. The next census, taken thirteen years later, reported exactly the same set of categories, with the same sizes. But the point is that the descent-based character of ethnic identities does not preclude—indeed it provides—the opportunity for ethnic identity change if individuals so desire. If we see fixedness in activated ethnic identities in the short term, then, this should be treated not as a natural fact associated with ethnic identity but as a fact which needs to be explained.

Replacement of Attribute-Values Within Existing Population Repertoire

Ethnic identity change through the replacement, objective or subjective, of an attribute-value occurs when one or more individuals change their attribute-value to another *existing* attribute-value on the same dimension. Although more precisely defined here, the phenomenon that this mechanism describes has long been recognized in the literature on ethnic identity change as "passing."

To illustrate, suppose that Helen undergoes a chemical procedure to change her skin color from black to white. This is an objective replacement of an attribute-value. Suppose she pretends to be born in New York and erases evidence of her birth in Trinidad. This is a subjective change. In both cases, the old and the new attribute-values already exist in the population. Helen simply switches from one attribute-value to another within an existing population repertoire.

Such replacement produces a change in an individual's underlying repertoire of attributes. This change may be reflected also in a change her activated category. Or it may simply change the nominal set, altering the set of identities that an individual might potentially activate in the future without affecting her activated identity in the present.

When one or more individuals replace an attribute-value in this way, the result is a change in the proportions of attribute-values and therefore nominal categories in a population as a whole. But there is no change in the attribute-values and categories that describe that population. There also need not be a change in its activated categories.

To illustrate, return to our stylized population, which has the following initial repertoire of attributes (see Table 5.9a).

Table 5.9a **Initial Population Repertoire of Attributes**

	Black	White
Foreign	.25	.25
Native	.25	.25

If 10% of the population passes, as Helen does, by replacing the attribute "foreign" with the attribute "native," this would produce the following change in the proportion of the population with each attribute (see Table 5.9b).

Table 5.9b **Change in Population Repertoire of Attributes Through Replacement**

	Black	White
Foreign	.15	.25
Native	.35	.25

This would alter also the proportion of some nominal categories in this population. Note, for instance, that while the proportions of Black and White remain unchanged, such passing would create a majority "Native" category of 60% and a minority "Foreign" category of 40%. These categories may or may not be activated.

There are several examples of such replacement, sometimes on a large scale. However, even when individuals can replace attributes such as a new last name or a language easily, it is difficult to pass the new attributes off as descent based. As previous chapters have argued, doing so either requires a change in or an eradication of all other descent-based attributes that are inconsistent with the new one. When such replacement takes place, therefore, it typically occurs either in instances of large-scale migration or other unsettled circumstances, which renders deception easier, or across generations, which permits attributes replaced voluntarily in one generation the character of being acquired through descent for future generations.

Lisa Malkki's study of Hutu refugees in Tanzania, for instance, shows that these refugees acquired new names, new family connections through intermarriage, new ritual practices, and new histories in order to exit the categories "Hutu" and "Hutu refugee" and claim membership instead in the new category of "Waha" or "Muslim" (Malkki, 1995). As an example of the replacement of an attribute-value over generations, consider the case of Lapps and Norwegians in Norway. The principal attribute distinguishing members of these categories, according to the Norwegian anthropologist Harald Eidheim, is language (Eidheim 1969). Membership in the category "Norwegian" brings greater payoffs than membership in the category "Lapps," and Lapps seek to exit their low-status category through language assimilation. The politically powerful Norwegians, rather than policing the acquisition of attributes that permit entry into their category as in the case above, encouraged the "Norwegianization" of the Lapps. But the ability to portray Norwegian as a descent-based attribute in this case would require at least one generational change if not more.

Change in the Restrictions That Define the "Operative" Repertoire

Restrictions on the full repertoire of nominal ethnic identities can be imposed on attribute-values, attribute-dimensions, or categories to produce the "operative" repertoire. To illustrate, consider the population repertoire shown in Table 5.10.

Table 5.10 **Example of Initial Population Repertoire of Attributes**

	Black	White
Foreign	.25	.25
Native	.25	.25

Suppose that at some initial point, employers in the food industry pay attention only to "visible" attributes when making hiring decisions, and skin color is visible while place of origin is not. The initial operative repertoire of nominal ethnic identity categories, then, includes only the categories Black and White.

Imagine now a new law that imposes penalties on the use of skin color in hiring decisions. Employers may respond by collecting information on place of origin to differentiate between potential employees. This would change the operative repertoire of categories to "Foreign" and "Native."

A change in the restrictions that define the operative repertoire may or may not produce a change in activated ethnic identity categories. In the simple 2*2 example above, a switch from one attribute-dimension to another must necessarily produce a change in activated ethnic identity categories, because each individual has only one category available to her on any given dimension. But in population repertoires with two attribute-dimensions but more than one attribute-value on either of these dimensions, or population repertoires with more than two attribute-dimensions, a change in the operative repertoire need not at the same time drive individuals into new activated categories.

A number of constructivist texts, as the previous chapter noted, describe the imposition of such restrictions: The electoral system in Zambia restricts the categories that individuals consider feasible based on size (Posner 2005), colonial discourse in India restricts the categories available to interpret acts of violence (Pandey 1992, Brass 1997), and colonial discourse in Nigeria restricts the dimensions available for politicization (Laitin 1986).

Addition/Subtraction of a New Attribute-Value on an Existing Attribute-Dimension

A fourth mechanism through which ethnic identities change is the addition of a new attribute-value on an attribute-dimension already treated as commonsensical in a population, or the subtraction of a attribute-value from such a dimension. This change may be reflected also in a change in an individual's activated category in the present. Or it may simply change the nominal set, altering the set of identities that an individual might potentially activate in the future.

Suppose Helen, for instance, decided not to change her skin color to "white"—an attribute-value that already existed on the attribute-dimension of skin color—but to "brown," a new skin color altogther. She might do this objectively, by undergoing a skin lightening procedure and explaining to others how to interpret the new color. Or she might do it subjectively, simply by reinterpreting the same skin color as "brown" rather than "black," and training others to follow suit. To imagine subtraction, imagine the process in reverse, with Helen learning to see, and showing others how to see, different shades of skin color on an existing dimension (Black and White) as the same. This would effectively reduce the number of attribute-values on the dimension of skin color from two to one.

Like replacement, the addition or subtraction of a new commonsensical attribute-value produces a change in an individual's underlying repertoire of attributes. But in contrast to replacement, the result is a change not only in the proportions of attribute-values but also in the composition of the population repertoire of attributes. To illustrate the effect on the population, return to our stylized 2*2 example, which has the following repertoire of attributes (see Table 5.11).

Table 5.11 **Example of Initial Population Repertoire of Attributes**

	Black	White
Foreign	.25	.25
Native	.25	.25

If 10% of the population decides, as Helen does, that they have "brown" skin instead of "black," and all individuals in this 10% are of foreign origin, this would produce a change in the attribute-values in that population, described in Table 5.12, as well as in the proportion of the population with some of these attribute-values.

Table 5.12 **Change in Initial Population Repertoire of Attributes Through Addition of Attribute-Value**

	Black	Brown	White
Foreign	.05	.10	.25
Native	.35	0	.25

This change would be accompanied by a change in the repertoire of nominal identity categories in the population. It introduces new categories to that repertoire and changes the size of some previous ones. These new categories may or may not be activated.

As an actual example of the addition of a new attribute-value on an attribute-dimension that is already commonsensically given, consider the introduction of new ancestral religions into the United States, including Islam, Buddhism, and Hinduism. A second example comes from the recent innovation in the U.S. census to allow individuals to identify themselves as belonging to more than one race. The dimension of race is already commonsensically real in the United States. But this innovation in effect exponentially increases the number of values on the attribute-dimension of race, each corresponding to a distinct combination of races with which an individual chooses to describe herself. A third example comes from the attempt by Hispanics in the United States to see the label "Hispanic" and have others see it as a race rather than an ethnicity. This example describes in effect the subtraction of the attribute-value "Hispanic" from a dimension describing language/region of origin (what the U.S. census terms "ethnicity") and the addition of this value to the dimension of race.

Addition (or Subtraction) of a New Attribute-Dimension

A fifth mechanism by which ethnic identities can change is through the addition (subtraction) of a new attribute-dimension into the commonsensical framework within which individuals in a population function. This might come about through either an objective or a subjective process (we elaborate on both below), but it requires in both cases the transformation of common sense and spread of common knowledge about the addition or subtraction.

The addition or subtraction of a new attribute-dimension changes the repertoire of nominal ethnic identities for populations and individuals, adding new categories into that repertoire or subtracting from them as the case may be. But there is no reason to expect a corresponding change in the ethnic identity category actually activated or deactivated. In some instances, we might see an immediate change in activated categories. In others, there may be stability over a long period of time despite these changes in the underlying attribute-repertoire from which it is generated.

Let us return to the 2*2 example, which is characterized by the two attribute-dimensions of skin color and place of origin. Suppose that an individual in this population begins wondering about her ancestral religion, which she had never thought about previously. She recalls that her parents were Presbyterian and the fact that she is a child of Presbyterians becomes one of the commonsensical attributes that describes her in her own mind. Suppose, finally, that her new awareness is not a private matter: Others hear about it. These would be examples of the addition of a new attribute-dimension—and therefore an attribute-value—at the individual level. When significant numbers of individuals add attributes in this way, the result is a change in the number of attribute-dimensions that describe a population—and therefore in the repertoire of attribute-values for that population. To illustrate, consider the following population repertoire of attributes (see Table 5.13).

Table 5.13 **Initial Population Repertoire of Attributes**

	Black	White
Foreign	a	b
Native	c	d

Suppose now that this population "discovers" ancestral religion, with half describing themselves as the children of Presbyterians (P) and the other half describing themselves as the children of Catholics (C). The result would be the transformation of a two-dimensional repertoire of attributes into a three dimensional one. The individual attribute-repertoires of individuals in this population are summarized in Table 5.14, with P and C standing for Presbyterian and Catholic, respectively.

Table 5.14 **Change in Initial Population Repertoire of Attributes Through Addition of an Attribute-Dimension**

Initial Individual Attribute-Repertoires	Individual Attribute-Repertoires with a New Attribute-Dimension Added
BF	BFP
	BFC
WF	WFP
	WFC
BN	BNP
	BNC
WN	WNP
	WNC

Imagining the process in reverse would give us an example of the subtraction of an attribute-dimension from the commonsense framework of a population.

The example above described the process of addition of a new attribute-dimension that began with individual-level changes, which produced an aggregate change in the population repertoire. But the process may happen in the opposite order as well. Suppose, for instance, that the census in this country determined that collecting data on "ancestral religion" was important for some reason and began to collect information about it, sending citizens who had never paid attention to this searching among their memories and old family records. Suppose that the census then published an account of this new descriptor of the population. Over time, we can imagine this top-down process transforming individual attribute-repertoires. The same process might drive the subtraction of an attribute-dimension from the imagination of the population.

The addition or subtraction of a new attribute-dimension can occur simply through the introduction of a new attribute-value on a new dimension or through the introduction of an entire class of values. For example, the discovery of one ancestral religion—Presbyterianism in the example above—would have introduced the new attribute-dimension of religion to this population, with two values (Presbyterianism and Other). The discovery of several attribute-values simultaneously (Presbyterianism, Catholicism, etc.) produces a more finely differentiated attribute-dimension but is not necessary for this dimension to be added.

One example of the addition of a new commonsensical attribute-dimension comes from the history of migration in the United Kingdom and its corresponding recognition in the census. The migration of colonial subjects, from South Asia, the Caribbean, and Africa, to the United Kingdom over the course of the twentieth century, when recorded by the census introduced the attribute-dimension of "race" into a population in which it had not had a commonsensical reality earlier. An example of the subtraction of a commonsensical attribute-dimension through an objective process comes from the process of language standardization which, by producing a linguistically homogeneous population, can do away altogether with the attribute-dimension of language. An example of the subtraction of an attribute-dimension through a subjective process comes from the removal of the attribute-dimension of race from the commonsensical lexicon in colonial India. Early colonial anthropology is full of references to races in India, and the use of the term "race" is interchangeable with "caste." But "race" was not used in the political sphere, and at some point in the early twentieth century references to race all but disappeared. The Indian census in post-colonial India has never collected data on race. Consequently, race has not been a commonsensical dimension in India for many decades.

3. Extensions: Representing Relationships Between Dimensions

So far, we assumed for the sake of simplicity that attribute-dimensions are independent. But we can now turn to the question of how to represent attribute-dimensions which are correlated in some way. In brief, each of the common patterns of correlation can be represented by reducing it to a distribution of attribute-repertoires.

Suppose we have a "coinciding" cleavage structure, by which we mean that individuals who possess one value on one attribute-dimension possess exactly the same value on another attribute-dimension. This can be represented by Table 5.15a, in which all those who are Black on the attribute-dimension of skin color are Foreign on the attribute-dimension of place of origin; and all those who are White on the attribute-dimension of skin color are Native on the attribute-dimension of place of origin. This structure of division can be reduced to the following two attribute-repertoires of sizes .61 and .39.

Table 5.15a **Coinciding Structure**

	Black	**White**	
Foreign	.61	0	**.61**
Native	.0	.39	**.39**
	.61	**.39**	

No of Repertoires of Attributes: 2
BF, WN
Sizes: .61, .39

Suppose we have a cross-cutting structure, in which individuals who have the same value on one attribute-dimension (e.g., Black) can have different values on the second attribute-dimension (e.g., one can be Foreign and another Native). This structure, captured in Table 5.15b produces four distinct attribute-repertoires of sizes .41, .20, .20, and .19.

Table 5.15b **Cross-Cutting Structure**

	Black	**White**	
Foreign	.41	.20	**.61**
Native	.20	.19	**.39**
	.61	**.39**	

No. of Repertoires of Attributes: 4
BF, BN, WF, WN
Sizes: .41, .20, .20, .19

Finally, suppose we have a nested cleavage structure, in which values on one attribute-dimension are nested within values on another. A simple example of a nested structure is given in Figure 5.3.

An individual in this population can have the attribute-values White (W) or Brown (Br) on the dimension of skin color only if she has the attribute-value Foreign (F) on the attribute-dimension of place of origin. And she can have

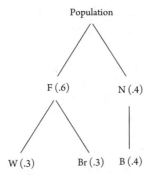

Figure 5.3 Nested Structure

the attribute-value Black (B) on the dimension of skin color only if she has the attribute-value Native (N) on the attribute-dimension of place of origin.

This structure, represented in Table 5.15c, produces three distinct repertoires:

Table 5.15c **Nested Structure**

	Black	**Brown**	**White**	
Foreign	0	.3	.3	**.60**
Native	.4	0	0	**.40**
	.4	**.3**	**.3**	

No. of Repertoires of Attributes: 3
BN, BrF, WF
Sizes: .4, .3, .3

In general, we can reduce any cleavage structure to the numbers and size of distinct individual repertoires of attributes that it produces and thus both identify the potential for identity change (discussed below) associated with them and compare across them.

4. Extensions: Restrictions That Define the "Operative" Repertoire

The restrictions that can eliminate some categories from the operative repertoire in particular contexts are many. They include institutionally created discourses or incentives, the distance between attribute-values on a continuous scale (e.g., people may prefer combinations that include proximate rather than distant languages), the degree of difference in economic interests (e.g., people may prefer combinations that include similar rather than conflicting economic interests), the degree of visibility (e.g., people may prefer combinations that include easily identifiable attributes), the degree of stickiness (e.g., people may prefer combinations that include attributes that are harder to change over attributes that are easier to change), the degree of complexity (e.g., people may prefer simple combinations over complex ones), the degree of heterogeneity (e.g., people may prefer combinations with fewer attribute-repertoires or attribute-dimensions), the availability of information (individuals may not consider as feasible categories defined by attribute-values on which they do not have full information), and so on.

Our guess is that there are very few universal restrictions that define the operative repertoire of ethnic identity categories in all situations. But there may be several that can, separately or together, recur in particular classes of situations. This section identifies and formalizes four such restrictions: (1) the "Overlap" Restriction; (2) the Number of Dimensions Restriction; (3) the Linear Order Restriction; and (4) the Nestedness Restriction. Note that the order in which we impose restrictions matters. Suppose, for instance, we assume that individuals consider feasible only those categories that are of minimum winning size—and of these categories, they consider only those categories that overlap in some attribute-value. The operative repertoire we end up with may well be different from the repertoire that is generated if we reverse this order.

These restrictions are likely to be common but are not exhaustive. Indeed, identifying the restrictions that define our operative choice set of ethnic identity categories is one of the most important research agendas in the study of ethnic identity change. Chapters in this book theorize about and formalize several such restrictions. Chandra and Boulet (Chapter 6) propose that the operative repertoire in electoral politics will be restricted only to coalitions of "minimum winning" size and provide a specific formulation of what "minimum winning" means in a combinatorial context. Van Der Veen and Laitin (Chapter 7) incorporate the restriction that individuals should consider simple over complex combinations. Wilkinson (Chapter 10) incorporates the restriction that individuals should consider "connected" combinations made up of proximate rather than distinct attribute-repertoires. Petersen (Chapter 11) incorporates the idea that there is a threshold below which individuals will not consider combinations with a negative emotional content. Finally, Ferree (Chapter 8) incorporates a restriction that individuals are likely to consider combinations only within the same node of a nested structure rather than across nodes.

These chapters also experiment with different ways of thinking about restrictions than we propose here. The way in which we approach the question of restrictions here is simple: Individuals either consider some attribute-values, attribute-dimensions, or combinations or they do not. Other chapters explore the possibility of formalizing restrictions by assigning preference orderings or weights across values, dimensions, or combinations.

Overlap

Among the possibilities available in principle, individuals may consider as feasible ethnic categories only those in which all members have at least *one* attribute-value in common. We call this the "overlap" restriction, since it requires that the attribute-repertoires of all individuals in a category overlap in at least one attribute-value. This restriction may be the most generally applicable of all the restrictions we introduce here. It captures many examples of feasible ethnic categories that we have considered across contexts.

In the United States, for example, this restriction would rule out "residual" categories such as "Italians, Blacks and Jews," where membership is defined by a combination of commonsensical attributes that its members do *not* posses rather than any one single commonsensical attribute-value that they *do* possess. When there are attempts to propose such categories, this restriction would suggest that these would be considered feasible ethnic categories only if those who attempted to create them first introduced a new "commonsensical attribute-dimension" that produced a "commonsensical value" that all members had in common. But it would retain categories such as "White" as a feasible option, since in order to qualify for membership in the category "White" all individuals must share the attribute of light skin.

The overlap restriction produces a significantly smaller "operative" repertoire of categories. The appendix to this chapter describes the size of this operative repertoire for different numbers of dimensions. In the case of our running 2*2 example, this restriction would permit a category such as Black (with membership BW and BN) since all members have one attribute in common—black skin. But it would eliminate a category such as "Black Native or White Foreigner" (with membership BN and WF) from consideration because members of this category do not have any single attribute in common. Imposing this restriction on the 2*2 example would reduce the full repertoire of sixteen categories to an operative repertoire of eight categories, represented by the shaded categories shown in Table 5.16.

Number of Attribute-Dimensions

Of all the commonsensical attribute-dimensions in their repertoire, individuals may only consider feasible those categories defined by combinations of attribute-values on a small number of dimensions. Such a restriction may be imposed because of cognitive constraints that hold across contexts: We may simply not be able to imagine categories with a very large number of dimensions. It may be imposed because of coordination problems: Individuals may be able to coordinate more easily around categories with a small number of attribute-dimensions than large ones (on this, see Ferree, Chapter 8, in this volume). They may be

Table 5.16 **"Operative" Population Repertoire of Categories Defined by Overlap Restriction**

Membership	Size
∅	0
BF	a
BN	c
WF	b
WN	d
BF, BN	a + c
WF, WN	b + d
BF, WF	a + b
BN, WN	c + d
BF, BN, WF	a + b + c
BF, WF, WN	a + b + d
BF, BN, WN	a + c + d
BN, WF, WN	b + c + d
BN, WF	b + c
BF, WN	a + d
BN, WN, BF, WF	a + b + c + d = 1

imposed by particular incentive structures. Thus, for example, the incentives in the job market in a given country may effectively restrict the attribute-dimensions individuals consider feasible by attaching incentives to them but not to others.

To illustrate, let's go back to Helen. She could in principle be described as a Presbyterian-Trinidadian-English-Speaking-African-American, a category that consists of attribute-values on the dimensions of national origin (Trinidadian), mother-tongue (English), religion of descent (Presbyterian), and the place of origin of her ancestors (African). But individuals appear to rarely use so many dimensions to categorize themselves or others. In the examples we have considered, we typically come across categories consisting of attributes on two dimensions (e.g., Black Muslim) or at most three (White-Anglo-Saxon-Protestant).

Our running 2*2 example illustrates the impact of this restriction on the size of the operative repertoire. The maximum number of dimensions in this population repertoire is two. The only restriction we can impose on the permissible number of dimensions in this example, therefore, is one. Considering categories defined by combinations of attribute-values on one dimension would include the categories such as BF, BN (defined as a combination of the value

"Black" on the dimension of skin color), WF, WN (defined as a combination of the value "White" on the dimension of skin color), BF, WF (defined as a combination of the value "Foreign" on the dimension of place of origin), and BN, WN (defined as a combination of the value "Native" on the dimension of place of origin). All other combinations are eliminated because each requires a combination of attribute-values on two dimensions. For example, the combination "Black and Foreign" with membership BF is a combination of values on both dimensions. So is the combination Black or White and Foreign, with membership (BF, BN, WF). This restriction reduces full repertoire of sixteen categories to an operative repertoire of four categories, represented by the shaded portion in Table 5.17.

In the very simple 2*2 case, this restriction produces only unidimensional ethnic categories, each defined by a single attribute-value. If there were more than two attribute-values on two dimensions, this restriction would produce unidimensional ethnic categories based on combinations of multiple attribute-values. And if the population repertoire consists of more than two dimensions, this restriction will produce categories based on multidimensional combinations of attributes.

Table 5.17 **"Operative" Population Repertoire of Categories Defined by Restriction on the Number of Attribute-Dimensions**

Membership	Size
Ø	0
BF	a
BN	c
WF	b
WN	d
BF, BN	a + c
WF, WN	b + d
BF, WF	a + b
BN, WN	c + d
BF, BN, WF	a + b + c
BF, WF, WN	a + b + d
BF, BN, WN	a + c + d
BN, WF, WN	b + c + d
BN, WF	b + c
BF, WN	a + d
BN, WN, BF, WF	a + b + c + d = 1

Linear Order

Suppose that the attribute-values on some dimension are linearly ordered in relation to each other. According to this restriction, individuals will consider feasible only those categories defined by combinations of attribute-values that are adjacent to each other (in other words, only connected or convex sets are seen as feasible). This restriction captures notions of "distance" between attribute-values on some metric. We can think of adjacent attribute-values as representing cultural or economic or territorial or social or ideological proximity, and nonadjacent attribute-values as representing distance.

The appendix to this chapter illustrates the impact on the size of the linear order restriction on "operative" repertoire of categories in the general case. By way of illustration, suppose our population repertoire of attributes consists of the two dimensions below, with three values on the dimension of skin color:

<blockquote>
Skin color: {black(B), brown(Br), white(W)}
Origin: {foreign(F), native(N)}
</blockquote>

Suppose further that the shades of skin color—black, brown, and white—are ordered in relation to each other, so that Black is adjacent to Brown and Brown is adjacent to White, but Black and White are nonadjacent values. This restriction would render infeasible any category that included the attribute-values "Black" and "White" on skin color but not the value "Brown." Thus, a category such as "Black Foreigners or White Foreigners" would be infeasible since it requires nonadjacent values on the dimension of skin color. But the category "Black Foreigners or Brown Foreigners" would be feasible, since it includes adjacent values on all dimensions. The category "Black Foreigners or Brown Foreigners or White Foreigners" would also be feasible for the same reason.

Nestedness

This restriction takes the relationship between attribute-dimensions into account. According to one version of this restriction, when attribute-dimensions are in a nested relationship to each other, individuals will only consider those categories feasible which include combinations within a node but not across nodes. According to a second version, individuals will only consider those categories feasible which are defined by combinations that include all values on a given node. Sharing a node in a nested structure can often indicate proximity on some common metric. These restrictions, thus, may be seen as another way of formalizing the way in which distance across attribute-values may matter in determining the size of the operative repertoire.

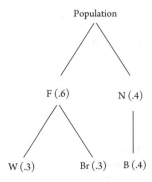

Figure 5.4 Nested Structure

The appendix to this chapter elaborates on the effect of different forms of the "nestedness" restriction on the size of the operative repertoire. To illustrate, let's go back to the simple example of a nested structure represented in Figure 5.4.

The first version of this restriction would eliminate categories such as "White Foreigners or Brown Natives" with membership (WF, BN) because the combination that defines it sprawls across nodes—but it would permit categories such as "White Foreigners" with membership WF or "Brown Foreigners" with membership BF because they are defined by attribute-values that share a common node.

The second, narrower version of this restriction would eliminate not only the category "White Foreigners or Black Natives" but also the category "White Foreigners" because it does not include all those who share the node of foreign origin. This restriction would render feasible only categories such as "Foreigner" with membership (WF, BrF) or "Native" with membership BN because they include all values that share a node.

Many other plausible restrictions do not require additional formalization. Suppose, for example, we believe that in some contexts (e.g., patronage), the "operative" repertoire is likely to consist only of those attribute-dimensions that are visible or sticky or have been privileged for historical or cultural or institutional or ideological or economic or territorial reasons. In all of these cases, we can treat these dimensions as the only relevant ones to constitute the population repertoire and proceed along the lines previously outlined.

Appendix

In this appendix, we prove and expand upon the combinatorial results used in Chapter 5. First, we consider the case where no restriction is placed on the repertoire of nominal identity categories for a population. This gives us the full repertoire. Subsequently, we give sample results for cases in which the operative repertoire of identity categories is subject to a restriction. In particular, we consider the overlap restriction, the linear order restriction, and the nestedness restriction. For each of these cases, we examine the size of the population's repertoire of identity categories, the size of an individual's repertoire of identity categories, and the maximum number of attribute-repertoires in an identity category.

1. Full Repertoire of Nominal Identity Categories

Size of the population's full repertoire of nominal identity categories

Lemma. Given a population with j attribute-dimensions and n_i values along attribute-dimension A_i for $1 \leq i \leq j$, the population has $n = n_1 n_2 \ldots n_j$ repertoires of attributes.

Proof. An attribute-repertoire is defined by choosing one value from each dimension. There are n_i choices on the ith dimension which gives a total of $n_1 n_2 \ldots n_j$ distinct repertoires of attributes.

Proposition. Given a population with n attribute-repertoires, there are 2^n identity categories (including the empty set and the whole population) if we do not impose any restriction on operative combinations.

Proof. Consider every subset of the set of attribute-repertoires. There are 2^n such subsets since, for each of the n attribute-repertoires, the attribute-repertoire is either in the subset or not in the subset. Thus we have $2 \times 2 \times \cdots \times 2 = 2^n$ subsets. This includes both the empty set and the whole population as subsets.

Note that together with the lemma, this implies that for a population with j attribute-dimensions and n_i values along attribute-dimension A_i for $1 \leq i \leq j$, the population has $2^{n_1 n_2 \cdots n_j}$ nominal identity categories (including the empty set and the whole population).

It can be interesting to graphically present these $2^{n_1 n_2 \cdots n_j}$ nominal identity categories. A particularly useful way to do so is to consider the poset structure of the categories ordered by containment and look at its Hasse diagram. This idea is presented and used in the appendix to chapter 6. The poset whose Hasse diagram is shown in figure 5A.1 is the poset of the full repertoire of nominal identity categories used in our basic 2×2 example. Note that it contains $2^{2 \times 2} = 2^4 = 16$ nodes each representing a nominal identity category.

Size of an individual's full repertoire of nominal identity categories

Proposition. Given a population with n attribute-repertoires, there are 2^{n-1} identity categories in that individual's repertoire of identity categories if we do not impose any restriction on operative combinations.

Proof. Any identity category in an individual's repertoire of identity categories must include the attribute-repertoire of that individual. To determine all identity categories to which an individual may belong, it suffices to determine which of the remaining $n - 1$ attribute-repertoires are also included in the identity category. We have 2^{n-1} subsets of the remaining attribute-repertoire and therefore 2^{n-1} identity categories in that individual's repertoire of identity categories (including the whole population as an identity category).

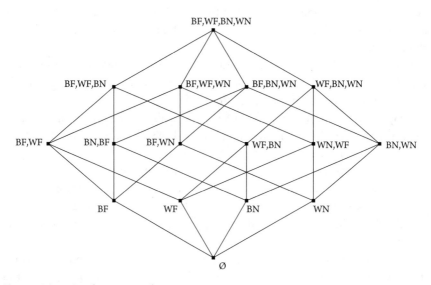

Figure 5A.1 Our basic example

This implies that for a population with j attribute-dimensions and n_i values along attribute-dimension A_i for $1 \le i \le j$, an individual's full repertoire of categories contains $2^{n_1 n_2 \cdots n_j - 1}$ nominal identity categories.

Maximum number of attribute-repertoires in a nominal identity category

Since the entire population is allowed as a category when there is no restriction imposed on nominal identity categories, a population with j attribute-dimensions and n_i values along attribute-dimension A_i for $1 \le i \le j$ has a category consisting of $n_1 n_2 \ldots n_j$ attribute-repertoires.

2. Overlap Restriction

We define the "overlap restriction" to be the following idea: Any operative identity category must have at least one attribute-value (from some dimension) shared between all included attribute-repertoires in that identity category.

Size of the population's repertoire of operative identity categories

Note that the whole population does not have one attribute-value and therefore is not allowed under the overlap condition.

Proposition. Given a population with one attribute-dimension and n_1 attribute-values along this dimension, there are n_1 identity categories (not including the empty set and the whole population) that are operative subject to the condition that one attribute-value must be shared by all members of that identity category.

Proof. There is only one dimension along which the shared attribute may be found. Along that dimension, only one attribute-value may be allowed since otherwise there will not be one value shared by all. Therefore, there are n_1 operative identity categories.

Proposition. Given a population with two attribute-dimensions and n_1 and n_2 attribute-values along these dimension, there are

$$n_1(2^{n_2} - 1) + n_2(2^{n_1} - 1) - n_1 n_2$$

operative identity categories (not including the empty set and the whole population) that are operative subject to the condition that one attribute-value must be shared by all members of that identity category.

Proof. If the shared value lies along dimension 1, then there are n_1 choices for that shared value. Once the shared value is selected, any combination of attribute-repertoires that contain that selected value is allowed. There are n_2 such attribute-repertoires and so we get $2^{n_2} - 1$ non-empty choices giving a total of $n_1(2^{n_2} - 1)$ identity categories that share an attribute-value along dimension 1. Similarly, along dimension 2, we get $n_2(2^{n_1} - 1)$ identity categories that share an attribute-value along that dimension. However, we must be careful to eliminate any over-counting; there are $n_1 n_2$ identity categories that share an attribute-value along both dimensions 1 and 2, the attribute-repertoires themselves. This gives a total of $n_1(2^{n_2} - 1) + n_2(2^{n_1} - 1) - n_1 n_2$ operative identity categories subject to the overlap condition.

Note, this proof shows that $n_1(2^{n_2} - 1) + n_2(2^{n_1} - 1) - n_1 n_2$ identity categories share either one or two attribute-values. Since $n_1 n_2$ identity categories share two values, $n_1(2^{n_2} - 1) + n_2(2^{n_1} - 1) - 2n_1 n_2$ share *exactly* one attribute-value.

Proposition. Given a population with three attribute-dimensions and n_1, n_2, and n_3 attribute-values along these dimensions, there are

$$n_1(2^{n_2 n_3} - 1) + n_2(2^{n_1 n_3} - 1) + n_3(2^{n_1 n_2} - 1) - n_1 n_2(2^{n_3} - 1) - n_1 n_3(2^{n_2} - 1)$$
$$- n_2 n_3(2^{n_1} - 1) + n_1 n_2 n_3$$

operative identity categories (not including the empty set and the whole population) that are operative subject to the condition that one attribute-value must be shared by all members of that identity category.

Proof. For dimension 1, there are n_1 attribute-repertoires. Having chosen one to be between all individuals in an identity category, there are now $n_2 n_3$ attribute-repertoires from which to choose a non-empty identity category. This can be done in $2^{n_2 n_3} - 1$ ways. However, by our previous theorem, $n_2(2^{n_3} - 1) + n_3(2^{n_2} - 1) - n_2 n_3$ of these share one or two more attribute-repertoires. This gives a total of $n_1(2^{n_2 n_3} - 1) - n_2(2^{n_3} - 1) - n_3(2^{n_2} - 1) + n_2 n_3$ identity categories that share *only* one attribute-value if that value is along dimension 1. Similarly, we get $n_2(2^{n_1 n_3} - 1) - n_1(2^{n_3} - 1) - n_3(2^{n_1} - 1) + n_1 n_3$ and $n_3(2^{n_1 n_2} - 1) - n_1(2^{n_2} - 1) - n_2(2^{n_1} - 1) + n_1 n_2$ identity categories that share exactly one value along dimensions 2 and 3.

Now we must add the identity categories that share exactly two values. If the two shared values are along dimensions 1 and 2, we get $n_1 n_2$ choices for the shared values and $2^{n_3} - 1 - n_3$ ways to choose the values along dimension 3 without sharing a value on that dimension as well. Therefore, we have $n_1 n_2(2^{n_3} - 1 - n_3)$ identity categories that share exactly two values (and have two values along dimensions 1 and 2). We get similar terms from shared values coming from dimensions 2 and 3 and from dimensions 1 and 3. This gives us $n_1 n_2(2^{n_3} - 1 - n_3) + n_1 n_3(2^{n_2} - 1 - n_2) + n_2 n_3(2^{n_1} - 1 - n_1)$.

Finally, we have $n_1 n_2 n_3$ identity categories that share three attribute-values. These are the attribute-repertoires themselves.

Taking the sum of these numbers we get $n_1(2^{n_2 n_3-1}) + n_2(2^{n_1 n_3-1}) + n_3(2^{n_1 n_2-1}) - n_1 n_2(2^{n_3-1}) - n_1 n_3(2^{n_2-1}) - n_2 n_3(2^{n_1-1}) + n_1 n_2 n_3$

For situations in which we have more than three attribute-dimensions, this analysis can still be done, though it becomes increasingly messy. However, there is a reasonable way to make a list of all operative identity categories subject to the restriction that at least one attribute-value must be shared by all. We will proceed dimension by dimension. For each value along a dimension, we form *all* subsets of the set of attribute-repertoires, that have that attribute-value. Thus some operative identity categories will be listed twice again. To eliminate this redundancy, we look at how many attribute-values each identity category in our list has in common. If two values are shared, the identity category is listed twice, if three values are shared, the identity category is listed three times, ect.

This method also allows us to give a very coarse upper bound on the number of operative identity categories subject to the overlap condition. Given a population with j attribute-dimensions and $n_1, n_2, ..., n_j$ attribute-values along each dimension, there will always be fewer than

$$\sum_{i=1}^{j} n_i \left(2^{\frac{n_1 n_2 \cdots n_j}{n_i}} - 1 \right)$$

operative identity categories subject to the overlap condition. As noted in chapter 5, this number is significantly smaller than the $2^{n_1 n_2 \cdots n_j}$ categories in the full repertoire.

Size of an individual's repertoire of operative identity categories

This problem is similar to the previous one and the proofs use similar counting methods.

Proposition. Given a population with one attribute-dimension and n_1 attribute-values along this dimension, then there is only one identity category in an individual's repertoire of operative identity categories (not including the whole population) subject to the condition that one attribute-value must be shared by all members of that identity category.

Proof. The only operative identity category that constains a particular individual is that individual's attribute-repertoire.

Proposition. Given a population with two attribute-dimensions and n_1 and n_2 attribute-values along these dimension, then there are $2^{n_1-1} + 2^{n_2-1} - 1$ identity categories in an individual's repertoire of operative identity categories (not including the whole population) subject to the condition that one attribute-value must be shared by all members of that identity category.

Proof. If the individual's attribute-value along dimension 1 is the attribute-value that is shared, there 2^{n_2-1} operative identity categories. Similarly, that number is 2^{n_1-1} if the common value is along dimension 2. However, we have counted twice the case that both dimensions are shared (that is the case that the identity category is the individual's attribute-repertoire). This gives us a total of $2^{n_1-1} + 2^{n_2-1} - 1$ identity categories in an individual's repertoire of operative identity categories.

Proposition. Given a population with three attribute-dimensions and n_1, n_2 and n_3 attribute-values along these dimension, then there are $2^{n_1 n_2-1} + 2^{n_1 n_3-1} + 2^{n_2 n_3-1} - 2^{n_3-1} - 2^{n_2-1} - 2^{n_1-1} + 2$ identity categories in an individual's repertoire of operative identity categories (not including the whole population) subject to the condition that one attribute-value must be shared by all members of that identity category.

Proof. If the individual's attribute-value along dimension 1 is the attribute-value that is shared, there $2^{n_2 n_3-1}$ operative identity categories. Similarly, that number is $2^{n_1 n_3-1}$ if the common value is along dimension 2 and $2^{n_2 n_3-1}$ if the common value is along dimension 3.

However, we have counted twice the case that exactly two dimensions are shared. There are $2^{n_3-1} - 1$ cases in which dimension 1 and 2 are shared but dimension 3 is not. This gives $2^{n_3-1} + 2^{n_2-1} + 2^{n_1-1} - 3$ cases where exactly three dimensions are shared. We also have exactly one case in which three attribute-values are shared.

This gives us a total of $2^{n_1 n_2-1} + 2^{n_1 n_3-1} + 2^{n_2 n_3-1} - 2^{n_3-1} - 2^{n_2-1} - 2^{n_1-1} + 2$ identity categories in an individual's repertoire of operative identity categories.

Maximum number of attribute-repertoires in an operative identity category

Proposition. Given a population with j attribute-dimensions and n_1, n_2,..., n_j attribute-values along these dimension, subject to the condition that one attribute-value must be shared by all members of that identity category, the maximum number of attribute-repertoires in an operative identity category is $\frac{n_1 n_2 \cdots n_j}{n_k}$ where n_k is the smallest of n_1, n_2,..., n_j.

Proof. To form an identity category with as many attribute-repertoires included as possible, subject to the restriction that one attribute-value must be shared , we select one dimension and one value along that dimension and include all attribute-repertoires that have that value in the identity category. This gives a total of $\frac{n_1 n_2 \cdots n_j}{n_k}$ attribute-repertoires in that operative identity category. To maximize this number we let n_k be as small as possible.

3. Linear Order

Given a population with one salient dimension which consists of n linearly ordered attribute-values, we will only allow identity categories that are defined by giving an allowed range of values on that dimension. The poset of operative identity categories for a population with one salient dimension which consists of six linearly ordered attribute-values is shown below.

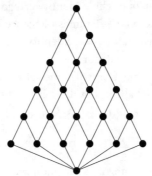

Figure 5A.2 The poset of identity categories under the linear order restriction

Size of the Population's Repertoire of Operative Identity Categories

Proposition. Given a population with one salient dimension which consists of n linearly ordered attribute-values, there are $\dfrac{n(n+1)}{2}$ identity categories in the population's repertoire of operative identity categories. (This does not include the empty set but does include the whole population.)

Note the poset shown above contains $\dfrac{6\times7}{2}=21$ nodes plus one for the empty set.

Proof. Each allowed identity corresponds to a range of acceptable values. Therefore, to determine the category, we must simply choose its lower bound and its upper bound. There are $\binom{n}{2}$ ways to choose two distinct elements from an n element set and n ways to choose an element which is both the upper and lower bound at the same time. This means there are $\binom{n}{2}+n=\dfrac{n(n+1)}{2}$ ways to choose an upper and a lower bound from an n element set. Therefore there are $\dfrac{n(n+1)}{2}$ identity categories in the repertoire of operative identity categories (not including the empty set but including the whole population).

Size of an Individual's Repertoire of Operative Identity Categories

Given a population with one salient attribute-dimension which consists of n linearly ordered attribute-values, the number of identity categories in and individual's repertoire of identity categories will vary depending on whether that individual's attribute-value is extreme or average.

Proposition. Given a population with one salient attribute-dimension which consists of n linearly ordered attribute-values, if an individual has an extreme value (i.e., the lowest or highest) on the attribute, there are $n - 1$ identity categories in that individual's repertoire of operative identity categories (excluding the whole population).

Proof. Since the individual's attribute-value is extreme, one of the bounds which defines that individual's possible identity categories is already determined. The second bound can take on $n - 1$ values (since we want to exclude the whole population). Therefore, there are $n - 1$ identity categories in that individual's repertoire of operative identity categories.

Proposition. Given a population with one salient attribute-dimension which consists of n linearly ordered attribute-values, if an individual has a average value (i.e., the $\frac{n+1}{2}$ th value if n is odd, or the $\frac{n}{2}$ th or $\left(\frac{n}{2}+1\right)$ th value if n is even) on the attribute, there are $\left(\frac{n+1}{2}\right)^2$ identity categories in that individual's repertoire of operative identity categories (including the whole population) if n is odd, and there are $\frac{n(n+2)}{4}$ identity categories in that individual's repertoire of operative identity categories (including the whole population) if n is even.

Proof. We must determine the bounds which define identity categories to which our individual may belong. If n is odd, there are $\frac{n+1}{2}$ choices for the lower bound, since there are $\frac{n+1}{2}$ attribute-values which are lower on the linear order. Similarly, there are $\frac{n+1}{2}$ choices for the upper bound. Discounting the whole population, this gives a total of $\left(\frac{n+1}{2}\right)^2 - 1$ identity categories in the individual's repertoire. If n is even, the same analysis can be carried out. In this case we get $\frac{n}{2}$ choices for one bound and $\frac{n}{2}+1$ choices for the other bound.

Maximum Number of Attribute-Repertoires in an Operative Identity Category

Given a population with one salient attribute-dimension which consists of n linearly ordered attribute-values, the maximum number of attribute-repertoires in an operative identity category is n since the whole population is allowed as an operative identity category.

4. Nestedness

In this section, we consider situations in which the attributes form a nested (tree-like) structure. In particular, we only look at instances in which *every* dimension fits in the nested structure. We give our results in terms of the number of nodes and leaves in the tree and in terms of the degree of the nodes, that is, the number of edges coming out from a node below it.

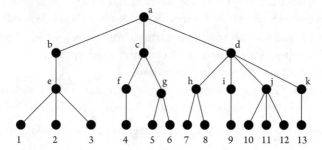

Figure 5A.3 An example of a nested structure of attribute-repertoires

In the pictured tree, there are eleven nodes and thirteen leaves. The number of edges coming out below each node is $n_a = 3$, $n_b = 1$, $n_c = 2$, $n_d = 4$, $n_e = 3$, $n_f = 1$, $n_g = 2$, $n_h = 2$, $n_i = 1$, $n_j = 3$, $n_k = 1$.

We consider two possibilities: first, allowing only combinations that include all branches at a node, and second, allowing any combination at a node. Allowing only combinations that include all branches at a node leaves the tree above as the poset of operative identity categories. Allowing any combination at a node gives the following poset as the poset of operative identity categories.

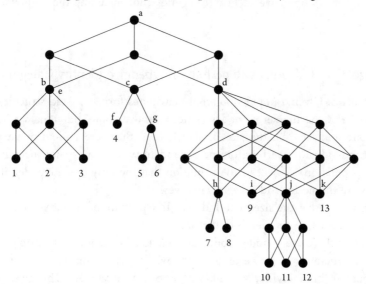

Figure 5A.4 The poset of identity categories corresponding to the nested structure in Figure 5A.3

Size of the Population's Repertoire of Operative Identity Categories

Proposition. Given a population whose attributes form a nested structure with j internal nodes and l leaves, there are $j + l - 1$ identity categories in the population's repertoire of operative identity categories (not including the empty set and the whole population) subject to the condition that the only operative identity categories are the nodes and leaves themselves.

Proof. If the only operative identity categories are the nodes and leaves, we simply have to exclude the whole population. This gives $j + l - 1$ identity categories in the population's repertoire of operative identity categories (not including the empty set and the whole population).

Proposition. Given a population whose attributes form a nested structure with j nodes where n_i denotes the number of edges coming out below the ith node, there are $\left(\sum_{i=1}^{j} 2^{n_i} \right) - 2j$ identity categories in the population's repertoire of operative identity categories (not including the empty set and the whole population) subject to the condition that combinations are allowed at nodes only and any combination is allowed at a node.

Proof. For each node i, consider the identity categories that can form at that node. Node i has n_j children and there are 2^{n_i} possible set composed of those children. We exclude the empty set, since it is not wanted anyway, and the set of all children, which leaves $2^{n_i} - 2$ sets. The set of all children (i.e., the node itself) is excluded from this number because it will be counted as a subset of the set of children of its parent. Summing over all nodes, this gives a total of $\left(\sum_{i=1}^{j} 2^{n_i} \right) - 2j$ operative identity categories (not including the empty set and the whole population).

Size of an Individual's Repertoire of Operative Identity Categories

Proposition. Given a population whose attributes form a nested structure with j nodes, let C be the set of nodes (strictly) above some individual's attribute-repertoire and let c be the size of set C. Then there are c identity categories in that individual's repertoire of operative identity categories (not including the whole population) subject to the condition that the only operative identity categories are the nodes and leaves themselves.

This means that the size of an individual's repertoire of operative identity categories depends on the depth of the tree.

Proof. If there are c nodes above an individual's identity category, $c - 1$ of those are operative since we disallow the whole population. However, we have not counted that individual's identity repertoire as a category. This gives a total of $c - 1 + 1 = c$ identity categories in that individual's repertoire of operative identity categories.

Proposition. Given a population whose attributes form a nested structure with j nodes where n_j denotes the number of edges coming out below the ith node, let A be the set of nodes (strictly) above some individual's attribute-repertoire in the tree of attribute and let a be the size of the set A. Then there are $\left(\sum_{i \in A} 2^{n_i-1}\right) - a$ identity categories in that individual's repertoire of operative identity categories (not including the whole population) subject to the condition that combinations are allowed at nodes only and any combination is allowed at a node.

Proof. An individual can only be in identity categories of nodes above it. This is the reason for considering the set A. As in the previous proof, we consider the set of operative identity categories at each node. We only consider nodes that contain our individual and therefore are considering 2^{n_i-1} operative identity categories at that node. (The sets we are counting are the subsets of the other children at that node.) We also disallow the set of all children at a node. As in the previous proof, this is a operative identity category but is counted at the node above it. Since no subset will be empty (they all contain our individual) we do not need to exclude the empty set. Therefore, each node in A will contribute $2^{n_i-1} - 1$ operative identity categories and in total there will be $\left(\sum_{i \in A} 2^{n_i-1}\right) - a$ identity categories in that individual's repertoire of operative identity categories (not including the whole population).

Maximum Number of Attribute-Repertoires in an Operative Identity Category

Proposition. Given a population whose attributes form a nested structure with j nodes, consider the set B of nodes at the top level just below the whole population. For $b \in B$, let m_b denoted the number of leaves below the node b. Then the maximum number of attribute-repertoires in an operative identity category is the largest m_b subject to the condition that the only operative identity categories are the nodes and leaves themselves.

Proof. In the tree, combinations at nodes further up the tree contain more attribute-repertoires than those further down. Since we do not allow the whole population to form, we are looking for the child of the top node that has the greatest number of leaves below it. This exactly what is described in the proposition.

Proposition. Given a population whose attributes form a nested structure with j nodes where n_i denotes the number of edges coming out below the ith node, consider the set B of nodes at the top level just below the whole population. For $b \in B$, let m_b denoted the number of leaves below the node b. Let m denote the smallest m_b. Then the maximum number of attribute-repertoires in an operative identity category is $\left(\sum_{b \in B} m_b\right) - m$. subject to the condition that combinations are allowed at nodes only and any combination is allowed at a node.

Proof. In the tree, combinations at nodes further up the tree contain more attribute-repertoires than those further down. Therefore, we consider combinations at the top node to find the operative identity category that includes the most attribute-repertoires. Since we do not allow the whole population to form, we are looking for the identity category that will exclude the smallest number of attribute-repertoires. Therefore, we will take the identity category that includes all nodes in B except the node that has the smallest number of leaves below it. That gives an identity category with $\left(\sum_{b \in B} m_b\right) - m$ attribute-repertoires and shows that this is the maximum allowed.

PART TWO

MODELS

6

A Baseline Model of Change in an Activated Ethnic Demography

KANCHAN CHANDRA AND CILANNE BOULET

Most studies of the relationship between ethnicity, politics, and economics assume that a country's "activated ethnic demography"—the set and size of the ethnic categories activated in its population in the aggregate—is fixed. If the possibility of change is acknowledged at all, it is usually as an outcome of migration or intermarriage, and the presumption is that too few individuals have the option of change in the short term to make a difference in the aggregate (Alesina et al. 2003, Gutmann 2003). But an activated ethnic demography *can* indeed change in the short term—and large numbers of people can participate in such change. Such change does not always occur. But there is variation across countries in whether or not their activated ethnic demographies change over time, suggesting that fixity, when it occurs, cannot be treated as natural but is a fact in need of explanation. There is also variation in the magnitude of such change—that is, in the proportion of individuals who change their activated identities—across countries.

Consider the variation in the incidence and magnitude of change in the activated ethnic demography of thee countries, described using census data: Rwanda, Brazil, and Sri Lanka.[1] Rwanda's first census, taken in 1978, reported a Hutu majority of 91% and a Tutsi minority of 8%.[2] The next census, taken thirteen years later, reported exactly the same set of categories, with the same sizes (see Figures 6.1 and 6.2). At least in the context of the census, then, Rwanda's

---

[1] Census data, as Chapter 4 argued, should be read not as an objective snapshot of the population but as a record of categories activated, by choice or assignation, in the context of the census. The ethnic categories—and therefore ethnic demography—activated in this context may or may not coincide with those activated by individuals in other contexts.

[2] We report here only those categories that are 1% of the population or higher, at the highest level of aggregation as reported in the census.

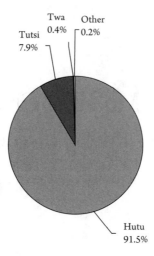

Figure 6.1 Rwanda's Ethnic Demography (1978 Census)

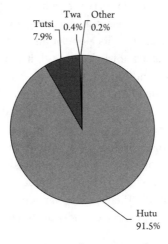

Figure 6.2 Rwanda's Ethnic Demography (1991 Census)

activated ethnic demography has remained fixed during this time. Brazil lies somewhere in the middle. In 1940, the Brazilian census reported that Brazil had a "White" majority of 63%, and "Brown" and "Black" minorities of 21% and 15% each. In 1991, the set of color categories the census used to describe Brazil's population remained virtually the same, but the sizes of each had changed dramatically. The "Brown" minority had doubled. The "Black" minority had shrunk by two-thirds. And the category "White" had also shrunk, barely making it past the majority threshold (see Figures 6.3 and 6.4). Sri Lanka is a more extreme case. In 1953, the first census in post-colonial Sri Lanka reported a multipolar ethnic demography, with five significant categories: the Low Country Sinhalese

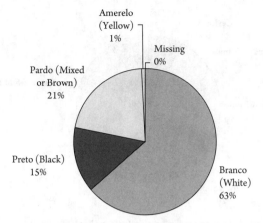

Figure 6.3 Brazil's Ethnic Demography (1940 Census)

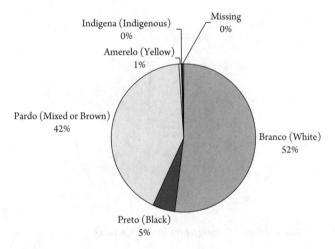

Figure 6.4 Brazil's Ethnic Demography (1991 Census)

(42%); the Kandyan Sinhalese (27%); the Indian Tamils (12%); the Ceylon Tamils (11%); and the Ceylon Moors (6%). Thirty years later, Sri Lanka's ethnic demography had been transformed into a majority-dominated one, with a Sinhala majority (74%) and three minorities: the Sri Lankan Tamils (13%); Indian Tamils (6%); and Sri Lankan Moors (7%) (see Figures 6.5 and 6.6).

Why does the activated ethnic demography of some countries change while that of others remains stable? And what is the magnitude of change in activated ethnic identity categories that is possible? *If* change can occur, in other words, what proportion of individuals in the population has the option to change? This chapter proposes a baseline model of short-term change in activated ethnic demography through electoral politics. By a "baseline" model, we mean a

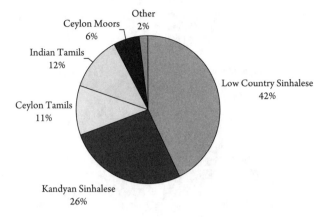

Figure 6.5 Sri Lanka's Ethnic Demography (1953 Census)

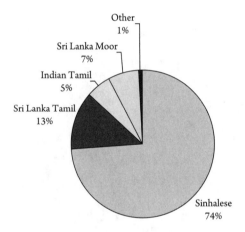

Figure 6.6 Sri Lanka's Ethnic Demography (1981 Census)

model that, rather than generating a universal prediction about the possibility of change in ethnic identity across all contexts, creates a baseline from which specific predictions can be made in particular contexts. Electoral politics is not the only variable which can produce such change. But it is an important one that has been suggested by previous constructivist work and needs to be theorized further.

Previous arguments linking elections to change or stability in some aspect of an activated ethnic demography fall into three broad categories: (1) arguments that link electoral politics with change or stability in individual identity *categories* (Weiner 1967, Brass 1970, Young 1976, 1982, Wood 1984, Giliomee 1989, Thapar 1989, Rajasingham-Senanayeke 1999a and 1999b, Jung 2000, and Chandra 2004); (2) arguments that link electoral politics with change or stability in identity "*dimensions*" where the term dimension may refer either to category-dimensions or attribute-dimensions (Chandra 2005, Posner 2005); and (3) arguments about the possibility of change associated with certain "cleavage structures." Thus, "cross-cutting" structures are believed to be more likely to produce a change in the activated identity *dimension,* where the term "dimension" is similarly ambiguous, than "coinciding" structures, and "multipolar" cleavage structures are more likely to produce a change in activated ethnic identity *categories* than bipolar structures.

The model introduced here is more general in its scope than the arguments alluded to earlier. These previous works typically explain change or stability in *one* of the elements of an activated ethnic demography—one category or one dimension, however defined—but not in the full set of categories and dimensions in an activated demography as a whole. They also apply to highly restricted worlds, where only two commonsensical dimensions of ethnic identity, however defined, exist, and individuals are not permitted to fashion ethnic identity categories by fabricating combinations across dimensions. Yet, these combinatorial fabrications, as we will see, stand at the very heart of electoral politics. The model proposed in this chapter maps the possibility of ethnic identity change for any distribution of attributes, with any number of attribute-dimensions and values, and any set of combinatorial possibilities. It thus incorporates previous arguments as particular cases in a more general framework. Finally, it is also the first model to theorize about and estimate the *magnitude* of possible change.

The intuition informing the model is that politicians seeking to win elections in societies in which descent-based attributes are salient are combinatorial entrepreneurs, who fashion ethnic identity categories by stringing together attributes into combinations most advantageous to them. These politicians cannot, in the short term, create the initial commonsensical repertoire of attributes. That repertoire, constructivist texts tell us, is typically created by institutions of cognition, typically at a historical period that predates the introduction of elections and representative government. But when elections are introduced in an environment in which other institutions have already made these attributes relevant, they attach high stakes to the categories constructed from these attributes and the numbers attached to each. Acting within the constraints of these attributes, politicians fashion ethnic identity categories to propose to voters. Voters activate one of the ethnic identities from the set presented to them by politicians, resulting in an initial activated ethnic demography. Change occurs if either rival politicians or voters or both recombine these attributes into new categories. Such changes can occur in the short period of a single election because they require simply a reclassification of existing attributes, but not a change in the attributes themselves.

The two key independent variables are a population's ethnic structure—that is, the repertoire and distribution of attributes in that population—and the institutionally determined minimum winning threshold (modeled here as the value k). The model's key assumption is that in electoral politics, individuals will be driven to activate those ethnic identity categories in their repertoire that are of "minimum winning size." This is by now a broadly accepted intuition in the work on ethnic politics (Riker 1962, Bates 1974, Chandra 2004, Posner 2005). But we define it here for multidimensional worlds in which new combinations of attributes are possible. We argue that change in an activated ethnic demography is possible when that population's ethnic structure generates multiple nominal ethnic identity categories of minimum winning size, and identify the conditions under which this possibility exists. By contrast, change in an activated ethnic demography is not possible when the ethnic structure of that population generates only one category of minimum winning size.

The model generates three main results: (1) In contrast to predictions that the activated ethnic categories in most populations are fixed during the course of elections (Horowitz 1985, Ordeshook and Shvetsova 1994), we find that most distributions of attribute-repertoires in most populations produce the possibility of some change in the activated ethnic demography. Populations in which at least some individuals do not have the possibility of change in their ethnic identities, in other words, are extremely rare. (2) In contrast to the suggestion that only a handful of individuals have the option to change, we find that most distributions of attribute-repertoires produce the possibility of change for *all* individuals in a population. In those rare cases where some individuals do not have the possibility of change, we indicate precisely their proportion in the population. (3) In contrast to the classic intuitions on the subject, we find that the possibility of change for both populations and individuals is not predicted by dichotomies such as "cross-cutting versus coinciding cleavages" or "bipolar versus multipolar" cleavages. We propose replacing these dichotomies with a single general concept—the "distribution of attribute-repertoires,"—which allows us to predict and compare for the first time the possibility of change associated with any sort of cleavage structure.

These results all apply to the *structural* possibilities for change in an activated ethnic demography. We do not provide a theory of how political agency operates within this set of structural possibilities. In this, we follow previous works on the relationship between "ethnic diversity" and electoral outcomes, all of which model structure rather than agency. The difference, however, is that previous structural models are deterministic: They focus on showing how some set of structures narrows down the effective choice sets politicians face to a single element (Chandra 2005, Posner 2005). Once the choice set is so narrowed, no role remains for agency. This argument shows, by contrast, that even the most restrictive ethnic structures leave political actors with a large set of choices. It is a rare world indeed in which the choice set politicians face is entirely determined by structure. In doing so, it creates a framework within which a theory of political entrepreneurship can be developed while taking the constraints of structure into account. The conclusion sketches an outline of what such a theory might contain.

In this "baseline" model of the possibility of change in an ethnic demography, individuals are permitted to consider the entire set of possible combinations for which their attributes make them eligible. This set, as previous chapters have argued, is very large. It can run into tens, often hundreds, of options. But individual voters and politicians usually do not actually work through each of these many options when activating any one ethnic category in their repertoire. Despite the availability of many choices in principle, they typically consider some restricted set. We do not so far have a theory about the restrictions that separate plausible combinations from implausible ones. This baseline model serves as a heuristic in theorizing about these restrictions. By identifying the full set of counterfactuals that individuals might have considered but did not, it makes it possible to theorize about which ones they find implausible through a process of elimination. A theory of these eliminations is one aspect of a full theory of political agency alluded to above. Several of the remaining chapters in this book build on this baseline model to theorize about the kinds of combinations that are more plausible than others in particular classes of situations.

Section 1 reviews the concepts we use to think about ethnic identity change. Section 2 builds on this review to define an "activated ethnic demography." Section 3 introduces the model and illustrates this model for individual (hypothetical) populations. Section 4 provides real-world examples of such change. Section 5 discusses the general results. Section 6 discusses the implications for research on ethnic demography as an independent variable. Section 7 concludes with a discussion of extensions to, this model, some of which are taken up in the chapters that follow. The appendix to this chapter elaborates on the mathematical concepts introduced in the model.

1. Review of Concepts

An *ethnic identity* is an arbitrary subset of categories in which descent-based attributes are necessary for membership. Since these attributes are fixed in the short term, it can be equivalently defined as a combination of elements from a fixed set.

Nominal ethnic identities are those identity categories for which an individual possesses the attributes of membership. *Activated* ethnic identity categories are those ethnic categories in which they actually profess, or are assigned to, membership.

Nominal ethnic identity categories are embedded in a population's ethnic *structure*. Activated ethnic identity categories are a part of its ethnic *practice*.

By a *population*, we mean the collection of individuals in a given country.

By *basic* attributes, we mean that small number of characteristics of a population which individuals take to be commonsensically real, and which they believe cannot be broken down further, even though in principle there are infinite numbers of characteristics that describe a population, each of which can be disaggregated further (see Chapter 3). Throughout this chapter, the term "attribute" refers to only to these basic attributes.

The *repertoire* of basic attributes for a population consists of all the "commonsensical" attribute-dimensions for that population and the attribute-values on each. In our running example below, the population repertoire consists of two attribute-dimensions with two values on each.

Skin color: {black, white}

Origin: {foreign, native}

This population repertoire can generate the following four *individual repertoires*: Black and Foreign (BF); Black and Native (BN); White and Foreign (WF); and White and Native (WN).

The *distribution of attribute repertoires* for a population—the most important concept on which we rely in this chapter—describes the proportions in which individual attribute repertoires are distributed in a population. The same population repertoire can generate many different distributions. To illustrate, consider the population repertoire of attributes in Table 6.1. The proportion of individuals with different repertoires is represented by the values a, b, c, and d:

Here, a is the proportion of individuals in this population with the repertoire BF; b is the proportion of individuals with the repertoire WF; c is the proportion of individuals with the repertoire BN; and d is the proportion of individuals with the repertoire WN. The proportions a, b, c, and d can take on many different values, subject to the restriction that a + b + c + d = 1. Each combination of values would produce a distinct distribution of attribute-repertoires for a population.

The full repertoire of nominal identity categories for a population consists of all the combinations of attributes that can be generated by its repertoire of

Table 6.1 **Population Repertoire of Attributes (2*2 case)**

	Black	**White**	
Foreign	a	b	**a + b**
Native	c	d	**c + d**
	a + c	**b + d**	

attributes. For this population, this full repertoire consists of sixteen categories. These are: Ø; Black and Foreign; Black and Native; White and Foreign; White and Native; Black; White; Foreign; Native; Black or Foreign; White or Foreign; Black or Native; White or Native; (Black and Native) or (White and Foreign); (Black and Foreign) or (White and Native); the entire population.

The *"operative" repertoire of identity categories for a population* consists of all the combinations in the nominal repertoire that individuals actually consider when making their decisions. It is a subset of the nominal repertoire created by identifying the restrictions which eliminate implausible combinations.

An *individual's full repertoire of nominal identity categories* consists of those categories for which she is eligible for membership based on her individual repertoire of attributes. For example, an individual with the individual repertoire of attributes BF would be eligible for membership in eight categories, namely: Black; Foreign; Black and Foreign; Black or Foreign; White or Foreign; Black or Native; (Black and Foreign) or (White and Native); entire population. In fact, in our example, every individual will be eligible for membership in exactly eight categories.

Activating an ethnic identity category requires individuals to activate some combination of attributes from the full set of nominal identities which they possess—in other words to choose one combination from among the many in which they are eligible. *Change in activated ethnic identity categories* then is simply a matter of recombination of attributes from this fixed set—in other words, it requires individuals to switch to a different combination for which they are eligible.

2. "Activated" and "Structural" Ethnic Demography

The terms "activated" and "structural" ethnic demography are close to but more precise than an older concept in the literature on ethnicity: ethnic "diversity." The term "ethnic diversity" is an ambiguous term that is rarely defined in the literature that uses it. While it refers, obviously, to the existence of ethnic differences in a population, it is not clear whether this means differences in the activated ethnic identity categories that describe that population—what we term "ethnic practice"—or differences in the nominal ethnic identity categories that describe this population, or their underlying attributes—what we term "ethnic structure." In either case, it is not clear which particular concept within the large family of concepts that describe either ethnic structure of practice the term "ethnic diversity" refers to.

In this chapter, we avoid the use of the concept of ethnic diversity altogether in order to avoid importing the ambiguity in that concept. By an "activated ethnic demography," we refer to *the set and size of the activated ethnic identity categories that describe a population*. When referring to the set and size of the *nominal* ethnic identity categories that describe a population—as well as to concepts such as attribute-dimensions, attribute-values, the repertoires of attributes for populations or individuals, or the repertoire of nominal ethnic identity categories for populations and individuals—we use the general term "ethnic structure" or "structural" ethnic demography. That structure, along with an exogenously determined "minimum winning threshold," is one of the key determinants of the possibility of change in the activated ethnic demography in our model.

The normal summary measure for the older concept of "ethnic diversity" is the ELF Index, calculated according to the formula $1 - \Sigma s_i^2$, where s_i is the proportion of the ith activated ethnic category, $i = \{1, 2, \ldots, n\}$. This formula measures the probability that two randomly drawn individuals from a population belong to different ethnic groups. But for it to be meaningful as a probability measure, the ELF index formula requires the ethnic categories to be mutually exclusive (i.e., an individual who is a member of ethnic category 1 cannot be a member of ethnic categories 2 through n) and exhaustive (every individual in the population is a member of some ethnic category).

However, neither the structural or activated ethnic demography as defined here can be meaningfully measured by the ELF index. The nominal ethnic identity categories that make up a population's structural ethnic demography may be exhaustive, but they are not mutually exclusive. The activated ethnic identity categories that make up a population's activated ethnic demography need neither be exhaustive nor mutually exclusive. Nor do they need necessarily belong to a single "category-dimension."

Indeed, the data we do have show that most categories activated in an ethnic demography are not mutually exclusive or exhaustive and belong to more than one dimension. In data that we have collected from an accompanying dataset (Constructivist Dataset on Ethnicity and Institutions (CDEI)) on activated ethnic identity categories (see description in Chandra and Wilkinson 2008 and Chandra 2009b), we occasionally find cases in which activated categories belong to a category-dimension. In Guyana, for instance, the two activated categories—Afro-Guyanese and East Indian—could be said to belong to a dimension based on region of origin. But these are exceptions that prove the rule. In most of the countries that we study, the ethnic *categories* activated do not belong to any commonsensical family. CDEI's count of politically activated ethnic categories in India, for instance, produces the following categories: Hindu, Muslim, Sikh, OBCs, Scheduled Castes, Jharkhandis, Assamese, and Tamils. These activated categories, taken together, do not belong to any commonsensical family. In Belgium, the activated categories are Flemish Speakers, French Speakers, Walloons, Brussels, French-speaking Brussels, Native-Flemish-Belgian, Native-French-Belgian, and German. These do not belong to any common dimension either—the categories Flemish speakers, French speakers, and possibly "German" belong to the dimension of language. The categories Walloons and Brussels belong to the dimension of region. The category French-speaking Brussels cannot itself be ranked on some commonsensical dimension—nor can the categories Native-Flemish-Belgian and Native-French-Belgian.

We cannot, therefore, use the ELF index to summarize an activated ethnic demography, or for that matter a structural one. In other work, we discuss alternatives to the ELF index in empirical work (Chandra and Wilkinson 2008, Chandra 2009a, 2009b). This chapter, however, does not require a precise numerical measure. Thus we simply refer to the relevant concept in words where necessary.

The fact that activated categories need not be exhaustive or mutually exclusive, or belong to a single dimension, changes the question we should ask in explaining change or stability in an activated ethnic demography. A standard approach to explaining change in an activated ethnic demography attempts to explain the conditions under which a particular dimension of ethnic identity (e.g., tribe) is activated rather than *another* (e.g., language) (e.g., Lipset and Rokkan 1967, Laitin 1986, Posner 2005, and, for instances of work on other types of identity dimensions, Rogowski 1990). Implicit in this question is the assumption that activated ethnic categories fall on one ethnic identity dimension or another—and that such dimensions are activated one at a time. The conceptual framework used here suggests, however, that the question we should ask is a different and more difficult one—"Under what conditions are *categories* activated rather than others?"—allowing for the possibility that the activated categories in question may sprawl across multiple dimensions. This is also a point of fundamental import for how we theorize about ethnic identities, how we collect data on them, and how we design measures of concepts related to activated ethnic identities. But we defer questions of data and measurement to a forthcoming second volume *Measuring Ethnicity* (Chandra 2011).

3. Model

At the outset, we assume an electoral context in which the repertoire of basic attributes for an electorate is entirely "ethnic" in nature, in which individuals have perfect information about the distribution of individual attribute-repertoires, and in which the winner is decided by simple majority rule. By "ethnic" attributes, we mean only that subset of descent-based attributes, defined in previous chapters, which determine eligibility for membership in ethnic categories. These attributes, for reasons outlined in Chapters 2, 3, and 4, are visible and fixed in the short term.

The process by which only ethnic attributes come to be the commonsensical descriptors of voters and politicians, and information about their distribution becomes widely available, is exogenous to the model. It has been theorized about elsewhere as an outcome associated with electoral politics in "patronage-democracies." Individuals in such democracies may favor ethnic over non-ethnic attributes from their repertoire of commonsensical attributes either because of their greater visibility (Chandra 2004) or because of their greater "stickiness" which independently or in conjunction with visibility makes it easier to prevent infiltration in the winning category (Fearon 1999, Caselli and Coleman 2001).

We are interested in the possibility of fluidity in countries in which ethnic identities have already become the paramount feature of politics because these are the countries presumed to be most likely to demonstrate fixity in their activated ethnic demography (e.g., Horowitz 1985). Countries of this type, therefore, are an extreme case. If we find that the possibility of fluidity exists even in such countries, then we should also expect to see fluidity in countries in which both ethnic and non-ethnic attributes are commonsensical, or in which politics is dominated entirely by non-ethnic attributes. Other chapters in this volume build on the baseline introduced here by considering populations in which the commonsensical repertoire consists of both ethnic and non-ethnic attributes.

Formally defined, an electoral context includes all of the following information:

- the repertoire of commonsensical "ethnic" attributes for the population,
- the distribution of the individual repertoires of attributes over the population,
- perfect information about the distribution of individual repertoires over the population, and
- a value, k >.5, defined as the minimum winning threshold.

Here, we take the value of k to be exogenously determined. We are concerned then only with examining the potential for change in an activated ethnic demography in a majority rule institutional context—not by explaining the genesis of the majority-rule institutions. One important extension to this model, discussed in the conclusion, is to endogenize these institutional rules. A second, developed in other chapters in this volume, is to examine the effects of non-majoritarian institutions on the possibility of change in an ethnic demography.

We conceptualize elections in these societies as a process in which political entrepreneurs present voters with a choice of ethnic categories. They fashion these categories by stringing together a combination of attributes most likely to attract the support of an optimal coalition, giving that combination a name and imbuing it with meaning. Voters then choose one category from among those presented in which to activate membership. The political choices in this society, in other words, are based on ethnic headcounts rather than on issues (Chandra 2004).

We assume that voters, when presented with a choice of ethnic categories in which they are eligible, will want to belong to the winning side. In a majority rule system, this means that they will choose to belong to a majority ethnic category. Further, given a choice of majority ethnic categories, they will want to belong to one of minimum winning size and be able to coordinate on activating a single category of that size. We do not make any assumptions about the motivations of individual voters, the nature of the payoff, how the payoff will be distributed, or the conditions that produce coordination. We put all these variables into a "black box" to be addressed in a model of political agency. But we do assume that ordinary voters and political entrepreneurs are instrumental actors who make decisions through a process of conscious calculation of the payoffs associated with alternative categories, and that, no matter what their motivations and payoffs, they will prefer to be in a smallest winning majority for which they are eligible. In so doing, we build upon an intuition introduced first by William Riker (Riker 1962) and developed further in subsequent work (Bates 1974, Chandra 2004, Posner 2005).

Although the concept of a minimum winning coalition or category is an old one, it has not so far been clear what it means in a constructivist world. Does it mean a category of minimum winning size among the ethnic categories that *are* activated, or categories of minimum winning size among potential ethnic identity categories that *could be* activated? And how do we identify a minimum winning category when faced with attributes arrayed on several dimensions? Here, we give this concept a precise combinatorial formulation, taking into account currently activated as well as potential identity combinations, for any number of dimensions. Given a competitive context in which some value k, $.5 < k < 1$ is a minimum winning threshold, we can define a category as minimum winning in a context if it does not include the entire population, and fulfils two further conditions:

- its size is $\geq k$, and
- it does not contain any other possible category whose size is also $\geq k$.

The first condition gives us all categories that are larger than the minimum winning threshold. We call this the set of all winning categories. The second condition eliminates "extra-large" majorities which contain smaller majorities within them. It defines minimum winning categories, therefore, as "minimal by containment."

We assume, finally, for the purposes of completeness, that those who are not eligible for membership in any category of minimum winning size will join the largest category that they can of those remaining. This particular assumption is not necessary to the model. These individuals do not affect the possibility of change in the short term regardless of what assumption governs their identity choices. Their only recourse for change lies in the long term, in attempting to alter the population's repertoire of attributes to their advantage.

An activated ethnic demography for a population is the aggregation of individual choices. It is formed when all individuals have made their choice. The *possibility of change* in an activated ethnic demography then depends on the number of minimum winning categories that can be generated from the distribution of individual repertoires of ethnic attributes in a population.

When there is more than one minimum winning category, those who stand to lose when one category is activated have the option of reversing their situation if they can successfully induce potential members of an alternative winning coalition to declare this alternative membership. In this case, then, the possibility of change exists, although whether or not that possibility is actually realized will depend on additional variables.

But if the distribution of individual repertoires of ethnic attributes generates exactly one minimum winning category, then we say that there is no possibility for change in this ethnic demography. When only one minimum winning category exists, those eligible should declare membership in it. Since no other minimum winning category exists to which they can belong, they have no incentive to reclassify themselves. Those who are not eligible will choose the largest of their remaining options, but which one they choose is immaterial. Having made their choice, they will not change, since there are no rewards for switching. As a result, the ethnic demography for that context will be stable.

Illustrating Possibility of Change in an Activated Ethnic Demography

To illustrate, compare the examples of "Changeland," and "Nochangeland." Suppose that the value of k—the winning threshold—in both cases is 51%. This is a case of a simple majority rule system (Table 6.2).

There are three "minimum winning categories" in Changeland: "Foreign," with membership BF and WF and size .55, "White or Native," with membership WN, WF and BN and size .7, and the category "Black Foreigners or White Natives," with membership BF and WN and size .55. To see this, consider the full repertoire of nominal ethnic identity categories in Changeland, listed in Table 6.3.

The six categories of majority size are highlighted in bold. Of these, only three (listed above) are of minimum winning size—that is, they do not contain smaller majorities within them. They are represented in the shaded rows

Table 6.2 **Changeland (k = .51): Possibility of Change Exists**

	Black	**White**	
Foreign	.30	.25	**.55**
Native	.20	.25	**.45**
	.5	**.5**	

Table 6.3 **Full Repertoire of Nominal Identity Categories in Changeland**

Definition of Category	Allowed individual repertoires	Size
∅	∅	0
Black and Foreign	BF	.3
Black and Native	BN	.2
White and Foreign	WF	.25
White and Native	WN	.25
Black	BF, BN	.5
White	WF, WN	.5
Foreign	**BF, WF**	**.55**
Native	BN, WN	.45
Black or Foreign	BF, BN, WF	**.75**
White or Foreign	BF, WF, WN	**.8**
Black or Native	BF, BN, WN	**.75**
White or Native	**BN, WF, WN**	**.7**
(Black and Native) or (White and Foreign)	BN, WF	.45
(Black and Foreign) or (White and Native)	**BF, WN**	**.55**
Entire Population (Black or White; Foreign or Native)	BN, WN, BF, WF	1

of the table. The other three are all extra-large: eliminating at least one repertoire would still produce a minimum winning category. Consider for example the category "Black or Foreign." Since "Foreign" itself is a category of majority size, the category "Black or Foreign" can be winnowed down to the minimum winning category of "Foreign." The same can be said of the categories "White or Foreign," and the category "Black or Native."

Note that when we express the membership rules of categories by referring to the individual repertoires of attributes included in them, they can sound complicated. But in actual electoral practice, political entrepreneurs can make categories with fairly complex membership rules sound rather simple, usually by attaching simple names to them (recall the distinction made in Chapters 3, 4, and 5 between the name and membership rule of a category). For instance, the category defined as "White or Native" might simply be described as an oppositional category that consists of all those who are not Black Foreigners, with a name invented for it. Some examples of this phenomenon include the invention of the name "Bahujan" in India (with the membership rule defined as all those who are not Hindu upper-caste) or the name "People of color" in the United States (with the membership rule defined as all those who are not White). Later in this chapter, we provide several other examples of complex combinations in everyday electoral politics across countries.

In Changeland, and in other simple examples, we can determine the number of "minimum winning categories" simply by working out the composition and size of each category individually. But a more precise way to determine this number is to look at the partially ordered set (poset) generated by each repertoire of attributes for a population. In general, any set of possible categories generated from a repertoire of attributes for a population can be represented as a poset. The appendix describes this poset further. For example, we show it is a lattice. We also determine its structure for any number of types of attributes in the population repertoire and any number of values.

Given that there are three minimum winning majorities in Changeland, there are also three possible activated ethnic demographies, represented in Figure 6.7. In each case, we name the ethnic category of minimum winning majority size and organize the remaining population into the largest possible category that remains, producing only two activated categories—a majority and a minority—for each demography. As noted above, this assumption is not necessary to the model but is adopted for purposes of completeness.

Because we assume that only ethnic attributes are commonsensical in this population and that individuals are able to coordinate on a single minimum winning majority at any given time, the activated ethnic categories that result will be exhaustive and exclusive. But this need not be true of all ethnic demographies. The activated ethnic demographies in Changeland, furthermore, do not always fall along a single category-dimension. In the examples above, the activated categories belong to a single dimension in the first two cases, but not in the third.

Nochangeland is a different story. The possibility of change does not exist here, at least when k = 51% (Table 6.4).

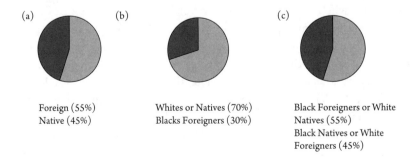

(a) Foreign (55%)
    Native (45%)

(b) Whites or Natives (70%)
    Blacks Foreigners (30%)

(c) Black Foreigners or White Natives (55%)
    Black Natives or White Foreigners (45%)

Figure 6.7 Possible Activated Ethnic Demographies in Changeland

Table 6.4 **Nochangeland (k = .51): Possibility of Change Does Not Exist**

	Black	**White**	
Foreign	.6	.1	.7
Native	.1	.2	.3
	.7	.3	

To see this, consider the full repertoire of nominal ethnic identity categories in Nochangeland land listed in Table 6.5. As above, the majority categories are highlighted in bold and the minimum winning majorities are shaded.

Nochangeland has seven majority ethnic categories, but only one of minimum winning size: "Black Foreigners." All other majority categories contain this one and are thus not of minimum size. This is a population which, given the assumptions above, can produce only one activated ethnic demography, with a 60% Black and Foreign majority, and a minority consisting of those who are White or Native (see Figure 6.8). This minority category will be consolidated

Table 6.5 **Full Repertoire of Nominal Identity Categories in Nochangeland**

Definition of Category	Allowed individual repertoires	Size
Ø	Ø	0
Black and Foreign	**BF**	**.6**
Black and Native	BN	.1
White and Foreign	WF	.1
White and Native	WN	.2
Black	BF, BN	.7
White	WF, WN	.3
Foreign	BF, WF	.7
Native	BN, WN	.3
Black or Foreign	BF, BN, WF	.8
White or Foreign	BF, WF, WN	.9
Black or Native	BF, BN, WN	.9
White or Native	BN, WF, WN	.4
(Black and Native) or (White and Foreign)	BN, WF	.2
(Black and Foreign) or (White and Native)	BF, WN	.8
Entire Population (Black or White; Foreign or Native)	BN, WN, BF, WF	1

Black Foreigners (60%), White Natives (40%)

Figure 6.8 Possible Activated Ethnic Demographies in Nochangeland

given the assumptions above or may be fragmented. But this is a demography in which there is no possibility of change. It is also a population in which 0% of the population has an incentive to reclassify: Those who are in the majority have no incentive to switch, and neither do those who are in a minority.

Measuring the Magnitude of Possible Ethnic Identity Change

For all populations, we are interested not only in whether the option of change exists but also in the proportion of the population that has the option to change. In populations that generate only one minimum winning category, the activated ethnic identities of the entire population are "fixed": those who are eligible for the sole minimum winning category are locked into that ethnic identity category because no alternative exists, and those who are eligible only for categories of smaller size are locked into those categories for the same reason. In Nochangeland, for instance, neither those in the winning nor those in the losing category have other "winning" options. Consequently, no one has the possibility of change.

When there is a possibility of ethnic identity change in the population, it does not follow that 100% of individuals have the option of ethnic identity change. Changeland, above, is indeed a case in which all individuals in Changeland have the possibility of change. Each has at least one alternative winning ethnic option, and some have more: Those with the repertoires BF, WF, and WN each belong to two winning categories, while those with the repertoire BN belong to one. Thus, we can say that 100% of individuals in Changeland have the possibility of a change in their activated ethnic identity categories through electoral politics. But in other cases, some sections of a population can be locked into single ethnic identity categories even when there are multiple winning categories in a population. Consider the case of Limitedchangeland, shown in Table 6.6.

Of the sixteen combinations that can be generated in Limitedchangeland (see Table 6.7), there are three "minimum winning categories": "Black," with

Table 6.6 **Limitedchangeland (k = .51): Some Fixity**

	Black	**White**	
Foreign	.4	.26	**.66**
Native	.26	.08	**.34**
	.66	**.34**	

membership BF and BN and size .66, the category "Foreign" with membership BF and WF and size .66, and the complex category ((White and Foreign) or (Black and Native)) with membership WF and BN and size .52.

Figure 6.9 describes the possible activated ethnic demographies in Limitedchangeland.

Although multiple majorities, and therefore multiple activated ethnic demographies, exist here, there is nevertheless also a permanent minority: individuals with the repertoire WN, who constitute 8% of the population. These individuals do not have any potential identity option which would place them in a winning position. All their identity options are either too small to cross the winning

Table 6.7 **Full Repertoire of Nominal Identity Categories in Limitedchangeland**

Definition of Category	*Allowed Repertoires*	*Size*
∅	∅	0
Black and Foreign	BF	.4
Black and Native	BN	.26
White and Foreign	WF	.26
White and Native	WN	.08
Black	**BF, BN**	**.66**
White	WF, WN	.34
Foreign	**BF, WF**	**.66**
Native	BN, WN	.34
Black or Foreign	BF, BN, WF	**.92**
White or Foreign	BF, WF, WN	**.74**
Black or Native	BF, BN, WN	**.74**
White or Native	BN, WF, WN	**.6**
(Black and Native) or (White and Foreign)	**BN, WF**	**.52**
(Black and Foreign) or (White and Native)	BF, WN	.48
Entire Population (Black or White; Foreign or Native)	BN, WN, BF, WF	1

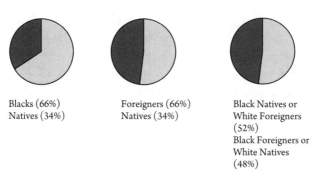

Blacks (66%)
Natives (34%)

Foreigners (66%)
Natives (34%)

Black Natives or
White Foreigners
(52%)
Black Foreigners or
White Natives
(48%)

Figure 6.9 Possible Activated Ethnic Demographies in Limitedchangeland

threshold or too big, containing within themselves a smaller winning category. Limitedchangeland, then, is an example of that class of cases in which some proportion of the population does not have the possibility of change even though this possibility exists at the aggregate level.

Individuals who do not have the option belong to any minimum winning coalition, we suggest, are those who have no possibility of change. To measure the magnitude of the possibility of change in activated ethnic demography across populations, then, we construct an Index of Permanent Exclusion (IPE), a continuous measure that indicates, for any given distribution of attribute-repertoires under a simple majority rule system, the percentage of the population always on the losing side regardless of the number of minimum winning coalitions. Given any distribution of individual repertoires $\{a_1, a_2, a_3, \ldots a_n\}$, where $a_1 \geq a_2 \geq a_3 \ldots \geq a_n$, we can define permanent exclusion formally as follows: We can say that a_i is permanently excluded if, for all winning coalitions which contain a_i, there is a subset of that coalition which is winning and does not contain a_i (see the appendix to this chapter for an elaboration). Thus, we can summarize the magnitude of ethnic identity change as follows: In populations with only one minimum winning coalition, the magnitude of ethnic identity change is zero, since neither those in the majority nor those in the minority have an incentive to change. In populations with multiple winning coalitions, the possibility of ethnic identity change is inversely related to the Index of Permanent Exclusion: the smaller the percentage that is permanently excluded in a population, the greater the proportion of the population that might pursue ethnic identity change.

Varying the Majority Threshold (k)

The only difference in the three examples above was in the distribution of attribute-repertoires: In a simple majority rule system, different distributions generated different possibilities and magnitudes of change. But note that the possibility of change in an activated ethnic demography depends not just on the distribution of attributes but also on the winning threshold.

Suppose, keeping the distribution of attributes constant, we change the winning threshold in the examples above to .60. In other words, suppose that the institutional rule changes here from a simple majority to a supermajority. This can alter the nature of the minimum winning categories, the possibility of ethnic identity change, and the magnitude of ethnic identity change. For instance, with this new rule, Changeland will have only one minimum winning category and therefore will no longer be associated with the possibility of change. Nochangeland would continue not to have the possibility of change for any individuals in the population: Its sole minimum winning category would continue to be (Black and Foreign) or (White and Native). In Limitedchangeland, the minimum winning categories corresponding to the new threshold would become Foreign (with membership BF, WF), Black (with membership BF, BN), and White or Native (with membership BN, WF, WN). This would transform it from an example in which some section of the population does not have the option to belong to a minimum winning category to one in which all do.

An alternative way to measure the possibility of change in an ethnic demography, then, is to take the distribution of attributes as constant and vary the institutional rule. Distributions of attributes which consistently produce fixity across a variety of institutional rules would be more robust to the possibility of change than distributions in which the results are sensitive to changes in these rules.

Predictions for Specific Populations.

We can identify whether or not the distribution of attribute-repertoires in any population produces the possibility of change for the population as a whole and for individuals within that population by going through the steps below. Later in this chapter we shift focus from individual distributions to general patterns across populations.

1. Identify the repertoire of basic attributes for the population of that country.
2. Infer the individual repertoire of attributes for that country.
3. Estimate the proportion of individuals with each repertoire.
4. List all possible categories for this population and their sizes. In large cases, draw the poset of all possible categories.
5. Identify the minimum winning threshold k for a given context.
6. Identify the number of minimum winning categories from the poset.
7. If the number of minimum winning categories is 1, then there is no possibility of change in the ethnic demography across time; if the number of winning coalitions is greater than 1, then there is a possibility of change.

8. Use the Index of Permanent Exclusion to calculate the proportion of individuals who have the possibility of ethnic identity change in populations with multiple minimum winning coalitions.
9. Now vary the value of k. The greater the range of values of k for which the number of minimum winning categories is 1, the more robust this ethnic demography is to change across context.

4. Real-World Examples

The activation of an ethnic identity category during elections—and change in activated categories—can take many different forms. One, perhaps the most familiar, entails activating a category that has already been prefabricated by some previous process—that is, a category that has a string of attributes combined into a membership rule and a name to go with it. One example of such a maneuver comes from Posner's (2005) study of Zambia. Categories based on tribe (such as Bemba) and language (such as Bemba-speaker which included tribes including but not restricted to the Bembas) had been fabricated by colonial rule at the turn of the century. But they were not always politically activated. Multiparty elections in Zambia in the 1990s activated language-based categories, while earlier one-party elections activated prefabricated tribe-based categories.

A second example comes from the north Indian state of Punjab (Chandra 2004). Electoral politics in Punjab during the 1980s was defined by the religious divide separating Hindus from Sikhs. In 1997, however, an alliance between the pro-Sikh Akali Dal and the pro-Hindu BJP, which gave both parties incentives to emphasize commonalities instead of differences, led to their activation of the regional identity as "Punjabi" which included both Hindus and Sikhs as members. The membership rules for the "Punjabi" identity had already been well-established in India since at least the 1960s. But the category "Punjabi" had not been activated in electoral politics until this election pushed it into prominence. Similarly, elections provided the occasion for the activation of categories such as "Luba" in Zaire (Young 1982), "Hindu and Muslim" in India (Brass 1970, Thapar 1989), and "Serb and Croat" in the former Yugoslavia (Gagnon 1994/1995). In each case, the categories themselves were fabricated by some pre-existing set of institutions. But they were available for activation when political entrepreneurs went looking for suitable categories with which to fight elections.

In many cases, however, activation takes the form of simultaneously stringing together attributes into a new category and making the category relevant in the minds of the population. Political party competition in India is replete with such examples. In India in the 1990s, political parties that stood to lose if most of the population identified itself as Hindu, defined as the combination {Yadav or Saini or Gupta or Mishra…}, floated new categories such as "Bahujan" or

"OBC," defined as the combination {Yadav or Saini or Ahirwar or Mohammad or Mathew…}, which eliminated some attributes (e.g., Gupta or Mishra) while adding others (Mohammad or Mathew). These categories were introduced during electoral politics, and crystallized over the process of election campaigns. In the new elections that followed, the same parties that had floated these large aggregates attempted to carve out smaller ones based on caste such the "most backward castes (MBC)," and the "forwards among backwards." Elsewhere, other politicians were also using elections to carve out new categories based on region, such as Uttarakhand, Jharkhand, Chattisgarh, or Bundelkhand. Unlike the examples given above, many of these categories could not be said to exist in fully fabricated form prior to the elections. Instead, the process of activation of these categories during elections went hand in hand with their simultaneous fabrication.

In South Africa, similarly, politicians employed different combinations of attributes to define membership in the category Afrikaaner throughout the twentieth century, driven by electoral considerations (Jung 2000). At the turn of the century, the category was defined by a single attribute: {Descent from Dutch colonizers}. In the 1920s, the National Party defined the category Afrikaaner to include a larger combination: {Descent from ancestors in France *or* Holland *or* Germany *or* England}. In the 1930s, reconstituted sections of the former National Party proposed a more restrictive combination, defining the category Afrikaaner as a combination of attributes on the dimension of language in addition to descent. Thus, Afrikaaner came to mean the combination {(Descent from ancestors in France or Holland or Germany) *and* (Afrikaans language)}. In the 1960s, the need to build a larger coalition led the National Party to propose new combination with a new name. This time, it mobilized the combination {Afrikaaner or English-speaker} under the common label of "White" (Jung 2000).

Categories activated in this way leave open the potential for still new categories to form through a similar mechanism. As Jung (2000) notes,

> if there are more than two ethnic groups and more than two ethnic parties, leaders have incentives merely to enter into coalitional arrangements with one or two other parties. Such arrangements are as likely as not to create a cleavage with equal conflictual potential as that which the alternative vote was meant to attenuate. For example, two or three ethnic parties might enter a coalition against two or three other ethnic parties. Alternatively, two ethnic groups, say from the northern part of the country, might enter into an apparently permanent alliance that in turn fosters an entirely new, and potentially conflictual, regional cleavage. (241)

The Sinhalese majority category in post-independence Sri Lankan politics, for instance, is but a combination initially introduced in electoral politics of the

Low Country Sinhalese and the Kandyan Sinhalese (themselves a combination of attributes at lower levels) (Rajasingham-Senayeke 1999a and 1999b). At the time of independence, Sri Lanka had a multipolar structure of ethnic division, with five significant ethnic categories: the Low Country Sinhalese (42%), the Kandyan Sinhalese (27%), the Indian Tamils (12%), the Ceylon Tamils (11%), and the Ceylon Moors (6%). But over repeated elections, the Low Country and the Kandyan Sinhalese coalesced into a new identity category—an undifferentiated Sinhalese majority corresponding to roughly 70% of the Sri Lankan population—and excluded the Tamil minority. (Tambiah 1986, Rajasingham-Senanayeke 1999a and 1999b).

The case of Uganda in the immediate aftermath of independence offers a third example. Uganda during this period had at least two cross-cutting ethnic attribute-dimensions, based on region and religion. One initially advantageous category—the Baganda—consisted only of an attribute-value on the dimension of region. Competitive politics in Uganda soon produced new combinations in subsequent elections such as the Baganda protestants, which combined attribute-values on the dimension of religion with those on region, as well as corresponding coalescence among those left out, especially the non-Baganda Catholics (Kasfir 1976, Young 1976).

In still other cases, the activation of new categories during elections may involve not the resort to a prefabricated category or the fabrication of an entirely new category but simply a change in the membership rules associated with a category already named previously. Such a change, according to the arguments made in Chapters 3 and 4, is in effect the creation of a new ethnic category. But in these cases, by retaining the same name, political entrepreneurs provide at least the illusion of sameness.

In the west Indian state of Gujarat, for instance, "Rajput" or "Kshatriya" entrepreneurs strung a new set of attributes together into a new category of winning size. The category "Rajput" is generally used interchangeably with the category "Kshatriya" to describe those who belong to the "twice-born" warrior caste. Prior to independence, the membership rules for the category Kshatriya or Rajput included birth, a small number of last names, as well as strict patterns of interdining and intermarriage. By these criteria, Rajputs or Kshatriyas constituted 5% of Gujarat's population (1931 census cited in Kohli 1990, 241). With the onset of competitive elections in post-independence India, "it was clear that voter numbers were going to be crucial for winning elections and thus for state power and patronage" (Kohli 1990, 244). Rajput politicians could hardly hope to emerge as a significant force in Gujarat politics with only 5% of the population. Rather than bowing to the "predetermined" fate of a minority group, however, these politicians engaged in a large-scale attempt to swell the numbers of their "own" ethnic category by relaxing the strict criteria for membership. Although they kept the name "Kshatriya" and thus propagated the illusion of sameness, the attributes relevant for membership in the Kshatriya category were expanded to include Bhils, Ahirs, Bariyas, Dharalas, and "all backward people who are martial by nature" (Weiner 1967, 99). The strategy transformed the nature of politics in Gujarat. By 1984, "Kshatriyas" constituted approximately 29% of Gujarat's electorate (Wood 1984).

Elsewhere in the colonial world, others were similarly involved in "spreading awareness" about categories named previously—or, in other words, creating new membership rules with memberships of a size that permitted political competition. Thus, for instance, the general secretary of the Ibo Federal Union in the years preceding independence attempted to make rural citizens in eastern Nigeria, who "could not even imagine all Ibos" "aware" of their ethnicity as Ibos, and demonstrate that the Ibo of the former Midwest Region were really part of the same group as these of the Eastern Region (Young 1982, 63–64). Others were involved in addressing the questions of whether Kongo and Lari in Congo were one group or two, whether southerners in Uganda were a common group distinct from northerners, or whether other narrower distinctions such as "Ganda," "Soga," "Kiga," or "Gisu" were more relevant (Young 1982, 64). In all these cases, politicians were using the names of previously fabricated categories but constructing new membership rules with which to tailor the memberships to an electorally advantageous size.

Some readers may object to the idea that the activation of different combinations in electoral politics is evidence of a change in their ethnic identities. According to this perspective, what voters and politicians are doing in these cases is simply subscribing to different electoral coalitions. Changing their coalition memberships need not indicate any fundamental change in their sense of self. This objection is based on the implicit assumption that ethnic identity is a deeply held, private belief. We do not challenge the assumption that individuals may well activate some ethnic identity privately, and this may nor may not coincide with the ethnic identity they profess in public life (see Chapter 3). Nor do we argue that the identity they activate in public in electoral politics is congruent with or overrides the identity they profess privately. But, we suggest here, the identities they profess publicly are important in themselves, regardless of their relationship with their private worlds. Publicly declared identities in electoral politics are often taken by all participants as the relevant identities of all concerned, and public policies and political strategies follow these identities. Indeed, it is difficult to see how identities could in fact affect politics unless they were enunciated in some public context.

A second objection could be raised to the idea that the distributions of attributes in a population act as a constraint on the possibility of change in activated ethnic identity categories. If politicians can reconstruct categories in the short term, why can't they reconstruct the attributes on which these categories are based? This question is addressed at length in previous chapters, but the answer is worth summarizing here. The process by which attributes are constructed is not identical to the process by which categories based on those attributes are constructed. The basic map of attributes is constructed by institutions of cognition. These institutions do not, as politicians and voters do, impose a rule of classification on a pre-existing, country-wide distribution of attributes which is already part of the common knowledge of all citizens. Rather, they create that country-wide distribution and then *institutionalize* it as common knowledge. Voters and politicians can then subsequently use attributes *within* this distribution to fashion new categories relatively easily—but they cannot change this distribution without altering the institutional structures. This explains why one process is more rapid than another: A change in classifications within an existing distribution of attributes occurs within an existing institutional framework. But a change in the distribution itself cannot occur without a change in the institutions that give that distribution the status of reality.

Recall that this notion of how ethnic identity categories are constructed requires us to accept one important proposition—that the *disaggregation* of "basic" attributes into their component parts requires institutional change while their *aggregation* into larger categories does not. If institutions prevent us from disaggregating the "basic" attribute of "dark skin" by changing the still deeper attributes that define it, why would they also not prevent us from aggregating the basic attribute of "dark skin" with other basic attributes to constitute new categories? The reason is simple. Reconstituting the basic attribute of "dark skin" requires us to *alter* a commonsensical presumption, and this requires change in the institutions that impose such a presumption. But using the basic attribute of "dark skin" to constitute larger categories is *consistent* with this commonsensical presumption. It does not question it—rather, it takes the presumption as given and then builds upon it. Thus, rather than requiring change in the institutions that impose such a presumption, it reinforces them.

Finally, why is it reasonable to consider, for any distribution of attributes, the entire map of possible combinations? We know that some combinations are usually considered feasible choices in politics while others are not (see discussion in Chapters 4 and 5). Thus, if we measure the potential for identity change in a population by considering all possible combinations instead of simply those that are plausible, we are certainly overestimating the potential for identity change. But we do not have any theory about the principles that separate permissible combinations from those that are not permissible. It may well be that there are no general restrictions that are always employed in all classes of situations in electoral politics. Here, therefore, we consider the full, unrestricted repertoire in this model as a baseline to establish the possibility of change. Once we identify the full range of possible combinations, we can begin, as subsequent chapters do, to ask and answer questions about why some are implausible through a process of elimination. But without knowing what the possibilities are to begin with, we cannot ask why they are not realized.

5. Identifying General Patterns

Can we identify distributions of attribute-repertoires more likely to produce the possibility of change than others? Can we identify distributions in which larger numbers of individuals within these populations have the option to change than others? And if so, how do these distributions map on to the ethnic cleavage structures—bipolar and multipolar, coinciding and cross-cutting—that we believe are associated with fluidity or fixity?

In order to probe for general patterns, we turn to simulations, constructing a "dataset" of imaginary populations. Each observation in the dataset represents a distinct population with a particular distribution of attribute-values. We identify distinct distributions of attribute-values by considering all possible partitions of 100, subject to the restriction that the size of attribute-repertoires differs only in multiples of two. This generated 204,226 distinct partitions, or 204,226 distinct "populations" with up to fifty attribute-repertoires.

There are many possible distributions of attribute-repertoires consistent with this restriction. Thus, a population may have fifty distinct repertoires of size 2% each (2%, 2%, 2%,..................), or five attribute-repertoires of different sizes (for instance, 24%, 22%, 20%, 18%, 16%), or three distinct repertoires of different sizes (for instance, 20%, 40%, 40%), and so on. Using this simulation, we investigate the results for a simple majority rule system, in which k is .51.

We impose the restriction that the size of attribute-repertoires should differ only in multiples of two because of the computational cost of calculating the Index for finer-grained partitions. We do not have reason to believe that the patterns we see in this dataset would differ for finer-grained partitions. But once we have identified these general patterns, we can explore this idea further through proof rather than simulations.

The remainder of this section presents the general patterns that emerge from the dataset above. It makes three points: (1) Distributions of attribute repertoires that do not generate the possibility of short-term change in ethnic identities are rare. Most distributions of attribute-values generate this possibility. (2) When the possibility of change in an ethnic demography exists, it does so for most individuals in a population. (3) The possibility of change *in an ethnic demography* for a population as a whole and for *all individuals* in that ethnic demography is not predicted by dichotomies such as cross-cutting versus coinciding or nested versus non-nested or bipolar versus multipolar cleavages. These dichotomies should be replaced with the general concept of "distribution of attribute-repertoires."

1. *Most* distributions of attribute-repertoires produce the possibility of some change in the activated ethnic demography of the population. The dominant assumption in the literature on ethnic divisions and electoral politics is that ethnic divisions, because of their intrinsic properties, are associated with fixity in ethnic demography and therefore fixity in electoral coalitions. As Horowitz puts it, in elections marked by ethnic divisions, the same majorities and minorities are likely to form and exist forever and ever (Horowitz 1985).

Our model suggests that we are likely to see *some* fixity associated with ethnic divisions because of the intrinsic constraints imposed on them by the fixedness of the attributes that constitute them. But populations whose distributions of attributes do not generate the possibility of change are rare. Only 3.5% of the partitions we examine in our simulation contain no possibility of change in activated ethnic demography because they generate only one category of minimum winning size. Some 96.5% of the possible distributions of attribute-repertoires generate multiple minimum winning majorities.

We term distributions that do not generate the possibility of fluidity "majority dominant," since they are those in which a single attribute-repertoire comprises a majority of the population. Nochangeland, discussed above, is one example. "Minority-dominant" distributions—that is, distributions in which the largest attribute-repertoire constitutes a minority of the population—always generate the possibility of change. Note that "minority dominant" is a multidimensional concept, distinct from the concept of a "multipolar" cleavage structure as defined in previous work (e.g., Dahl 1971) because it refers to multiple dimensions. Both majority-dominant and minority-dominant distributions can be associated with many different types of "cleavage" structures (more on this below).

We do not know how attribute-repertoires are distributed in the real world. But in order to associate "ethnic divisions" with fixity to the degree that the previous literature has led us to expect, we would have to make the unreasonable assumption that only "majority-dominant" distributions are to be found in the real world. It is more reasonable to assume that all types of distributions are to be found in the real world, with "majority dominant" distributions being only one strain among many. And if this were the case, then we would also have to conclude that the possibility of change in an activated ethnic demography exists in most cases.

Note that this does not mean that we will actually see fluidity in activated ethnic demographies in most cases. Notwithstanding the possibility of change contained in the distribution of attribute-repertoires, we may well see fixity. But where we see fixity, the model here suggests that we must look for the answer in restrictions imposed by the external world on the combinations that can be generated from the attributes embedded in this structure—not in the inherent structure of ethnic divisions themselves. Thus, to return to the examples with which we began this chapter, the model suggests that the fixity of the ethnic demography in Rwanda is a likely product not of the ethnic divisions in Rwanda per se but of exogenous restrictions that prevent the emergence of alternative majorities within Rwanda either independently or in conjunction with features of Rwanda's ethnic attribute-dimensions.

How does the possibility of change in activated ethnic demographies as conceptualized here compare with the possibility of change in activated non-ethnic demographies? In earlier chapters, we argued that change in ethnic identities in the short term is constrained by the intrinsic stickiness of their qualifying attributes. Non-ethnic identities, we argued, are constituted by attributes that typically do not have the intrinsic property of stickiness. Based on this distinction, we might reasonably suppose that there is no reason to expect any intrinsic possibility of fixedness in activated demographies comprised of non-ethnic categories (although there may well be environmental constraints that produce such fixity).

Compared to a possibility of unconstrained change in electoral contexts in which non-ethnic divisions are salient, the possibility of change in electoral contexts dominated by ethnic divisions is intrinsically lower. We can conclude then, that while we do not have reason to predict total fixity in activated ethnic demographies as we have been doing so far, we may well be justified in expecting a greater degree of fixity in ethnic rather than non-ethnic demographies.

2. Most distributions of attribute-repertoires produce the possibility of change for *all* individuals in a population. A second general pattern that we are interested in is the proportion of individuals associated with different distributions of attribute-repertoires who have *no* possibility of change. Some 95% of all distributions in our sample generate the possibility of change for *all* individuals in a population. The proportion of distributions in our sample as a whole that do not generate the possibility of change for at least some individuals in a population is only 5%.

Among the 5% of distributions in which fixedness exists for at least some proportion of the population, 3.5% are majority dominant. These distributions, corresponding to the case of Nochangeland above, have only one majority and only one minority. No one in these populations has the possibility of change. But fixedness also exists for a minority-dominant distributions, corresponding to the case of Limitedchangeland above. In such cases, even when there are multiple minimum winning majorities, there remain some individuals who will not have the possibility of change because they are not eligible for any one of them. Only 1.5% of the distributions in our sample are of the sort that resemble Limitedchangeland—they produce fixity for at least some proportion of the population. But interestingly enough, fixedness when it exists in such cases usually affects only a small proportion of the population.

Figure 6.10 shows a frequency distribution of the Index of Permanent Exclusion—that is, the proportion of individuals who do not have the option of change—for this small sample (1.5%) of distributions. The X axis describes the proportion of the population that is permanently excluded. The Y axis describes the frequency.

As we see from the chart, the magnitude of the population that has a fixed ethnic option in minority-dominant distributions is never more than a quarter of the population. In a quarter of the cases, only 2% of the population does not have the possibility of change. And in the majority of cases, less than 6% of the population does not have the option of change.

Numerically speaking, 2–6% of the population is not very large. But conflicts in multi-ethnic democracies often involve minority groups of this tiny size. The conflict in the Chittagong Hill tracts in Bangladesh, for instance, involves the Chakma minority, which constitutes less than 2% of the population. Similarly, violent ethnic conflict in India, in Punjab or the Northeast, has often involved minority groups that are 2% of the population or less. In Angola, the Cabindans who comprise merely 1.5% of the population are engaged in armed struggle against the government. The "imprisonment" of even small numbers of individuals in single ethnic identities can, thus, be politically consequential. Such small minorities may be more vulnerable to majority domination—and some studies argue that small minorities are more likely to arouse majority anxiety than large ones and therefore provoke repression (Appadurai 2006). To the extent that we believe that in populations in which non-ethnic categories are activated, all individuals have some possibility of change, the possibility of imprisonment in an ethnic category may be larger in populations with activated ethnic categories.

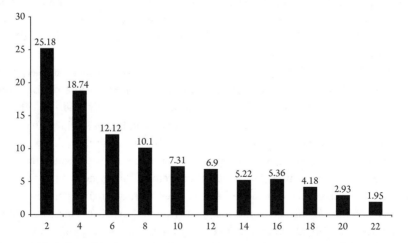

Figure 6.10 Index of Permanent Exclusion in Minority-Dominant Populations: Percentage of Population with Fixed Identities in Minority-Dominant Distributions

3. The possibility of change *in an ethnic demography* for a population as a whole and for *all individuals* in that ethnic demography is not predicted by dichotomies such as cross-cutting versus coinciding or nested versus non-nested or bipolar versus multipolar cleavages. These dichotomies should be replaced with the general concept of "distribution of attribute-repertoires." Previous intuitions propose that the possibility of change can be predicted by two dichotomies describing "cleavage structures": cross-cutting versus coinciding and multipolar versus bipolar. A cross-cutting structure is believed to be associated with the possibility of change while a coinciding structure is associated with fixity. A multipolar structure is associated with the possibility of change while a bipolar structure is associated with fixity (Dahl 1971). Some other dichotomies also describe cleavage structures (e.g., nested vs. non-nested, dispersed vs. centrally focused (Horowitz 1985)) but do not have clear predictions for the possibility of change associated with them.

But according to the model just proposed, there is no direct association in most cases between these typologies of cleavage structures and the possibility of change in an activated ethnic demography. Cross-cutting cleavage structures and coinciding cleavage structures can produce the possibility of both change and fixity. Multipolar cleavage structures also produce the possibility of both change and fixity for at least some individuals in a population. A bipolar structure is the only one always associated with fixity, but it is only a special case of the "majority-dominant" distributions of attribute-repertoires that produce fixity.

There is also no clear relationship between these typologies and the magnitude of change in an activated ethnic demography. Cross-cutting and coinciding cleavage structures can be associated with no change, small-scale change, and large-scale change. Multipolar structures are typically associated with *some* possibility of change, but this change can be associated with either small-scale or large-scale change. Further, they are only one special case of ethnic structure in which change occurs. Bipolar cleavage structures are always associated with fixity for all individuals in the population, but, as we have argued above, they too are only one special case of distributions of attribute-repertoires in which there is no possibility of change.

Rather than talk about the association between different categorical types of cleavage structures on the possibility of fluidity, we should break down the cleavage structure to the distribution of attribute-repertoires and use that to generate predictions of fixity or fluidity. Any "cleavage structure" can be reduced to a number of distinct attribute repertoires in a population and their proportion. And given these numbers and proportions, we can predict the possibility of change for any population. We do not need any additional information about which "cleavage structure" a population fits in. Further, the general concept of distribution of attribute-repertoire has the advantage of

Table 6.8 **Nochangeland (k = .51): Possibility of Change Does Not Exist**

	Black	White	
Foreign	.6	.1	.7
Native	.1	.2	.3
	.7	.3	

Table 6.9 **Limitedchangeland (k = .51): Some Fixity**

	Black	White	
Foreign	.4	.26	**.66**
Native	.26	.08	**.34**
	.66	**.34**	

Table 6.10 **Changeland (k = .51): Possibility of Change Exists**

	Black	White	
Foreign	.3	.25	**.55**
Native	.2	.25	**.45**
	.5	**.5**	

allowing us to make predictions about cleavage structures to which no predictions of the possibility of change have been attached so far (e.g., "nested" structures) as well as allowing us for the first time to compare predictions of the possibility of change across cleavage structures. The remainder of this section elaborates.

Cross-Cutting Cleavage Structures

By a cross-cutting structure, we mean that individuals who have the same value on one attribute-dimension (e.g., Black) can have different values on the second attribute-dimension (e.g., one can be Foreign and another Native). The standard belief is that such a result cannot be produced by a cross-cutting cleavage structure. But indeed, it can.

Nochangeland, cited above, is a classic case of a cross-cutting cleavage structure (see Table 6.8). Yet, as we have already noted, this distribution is associated with fixity for 100% of the population.

Limitedchangeland, also cited above, is another classic example of a cross-cutting cleavage structure (see Table 6.9). As noted above, this distribution is associated with fixity for 8% of the population.

Reconsider, finally, Changeland. This is also a classic case of a cross-cutting cleavage structure (see Table 6.10). But this one is associated with the possibility of change for all individuals in a population.

Simply presented with a cross-cutting cleavage structure, therefore, we cannot say anything about the possibility for change.

To do that we would have to examine a different concept: the distribution of attribute-repertoires. Nochangeland has a distribution of four attribute-repertoires of the following sizes: BF (.6), WF (.1), BN (.1), WN (.2). Limitedchangeland has a distribution of four attribute-repertoires of the following sizes: BF (.4), WF (.26), BN (.26), WN (.08). Changeland has a distribution of four attribute-repertoires of the following sizes: BF (.30), WF (.25), BN (.20), WN (.25). Given this information, we can calculate the percentage of individuals who do not have any possibility of identity change) using the procedure identified earlier and elaborated on in the appendix without reference to cleavage structure.

Coinciding Cleavage Structures

By a "coinciding" cleavage structure, we mean that individuals who possess one value on one attribute-dimension possess exactly the same value on another attribute-dimension. The standard presumption about coinciding cleavage structures is that they always produce fixity. But they do not. They can also be associated with no possibility of change, some possibility of change, and total possibility of change:

Consider, for instance, the case of Coinciding Structure 1 (see Table 6.11a). This is a population with two attribute-dimensions: skin color and place of origin. There are four values on each. On the attribute-dimension of skin color, the four values are: black, gray, yellow, and white. On the attribute-dimension of place of origin, there are also four values: European, Asian, African, and Native. This cleavage structure is "coinciding" in that all those with black skin are of European origin, all those with gray skin are of Asia origin, all those who have

Table 6.11a **Coinciding Structure 1 (k = .51)**

	Black	**Gray**	**Yellow**	**White**
European	.6	0	0	0
Asian	0	.1	0	0
African	0	0	.1	0
Native	0	0	0	.2

No. of Repertoires of Attributes: 4
BE, GAs, YAf, WN
Sizes: .6, .1, .1, .2

Table 6.11b **Coinciding Structure 2 (k = .51)**

	Black	Gray	Yellow	White
European	.4	0	0	0
Asian	0	.26	0	0
African	0	0	.26	0
Native	0	0	0	.08

No. of Repertoires of Attributes: 4
BE, GAs, YAf, WN
Sizes: .4, .26, .26, .08

yellow skin are of African origin, and all those with white skin are of native origin.

Despite this coinciding relationship across attribute-dimensions, and the different number of attribute-values on each dimension, this population generates an identical distribution of attribute-repertoires to Nochangeland above. The result, as in the cross-cutting case above, is no possibility of change for anyone in the population.

Consider now Coinciding Structure 2 (see Table 6.11b). The attribute-dimensions and attribute-values are the same as in Coinciding Structure 1, but the proportions of individuals with each attribute-value are different.

Despite this coinciding relationship across attribute-dimensions, and the different number of attribute-values on each dimension, Coinciding Structure 2 generates an identical distribution of attribute-repertoires to Limitedchangeland above. The result, as in the cross-cutting case above, is that no possibility of change exists for 8% of the population.

Consider, finally, Coinciding Structure 3 (see Table 6.11c). Despite its different cleavage structure, this population generates an identical distribution of attribute-repertoires to Changeland above. The result, as in Changeland, is that the possibility of change exists for all individuals in the population.

Table 6.11c **Coinciding Structure 3 (k = .51)**

	Black	Gray	Yellow	White
European	.30	0	0	0
Asian	0	.25	0	0
African	0	0	25	0
Native	0	0	0	.2

No. of Repertoires of Attributes: 4
BE, GN, YAf, Was
Sizes: .30, .25, .25, .2

Multipolar Cleavage Structures

Recall that a multipolar cleavage structure refers to an ethnic structure in which there is only one attribute-dimension and more than two attribute-values, none held by a majority.

A multipolar cleavage structure is always associated with the possibility of fluidity for *some* individuals in a population. But it need not be associated with the possibility of fluidity for all of them. Compare the two examples of a multipolar distribution in Tables 6.12a and 6.12b.

The first case is associated with the possibility of fluidity for only some individuals in the population: the Ws do not have the possibility of change. The second permits the possibility of change for all individuals in the population.

Further, multipolar distributions are simply a special case of a larger class of distributions of attribute-repertoires associated with the possibility of change for some individuals in a population—"minority-dominant" distributions. Similar distributions can be produced by many other cleavage structures, including cross-cutting, coinciding, and nested ones.

Simply being presented with a multipolar cleavage structure is not very informative about the possibility of change for all individuals in a population. And being presented with the possibility of change for all individuals in a population, we cannot predict whether or not we will see a multipolar structure. For this, we have to look precisely at the number and size of attribute-repertoires. Note that the two multipolar structures above produced distributions of attribute-repertoires exactly identical to Limitedchangeland and Changeland (although these earlier examples were of cross-cutting attribute-dimensions). It is these distributions on which we should focus.

Bipolar Cleavage Structures

Recall that a bipolar cleavage structure refers to an ethnic structure in which there is only one attribute-dimension and two attribute-values, one of which is held by a majority of the population and another by a minority.

Table 6.13 provides a simple example of a bipolar structure. Given that one attribute-value comprises a majority of the population, only one minimum

Table 6.12a **Multipolar Structure 1 (k = .51)**

Black	Gray	Yellow	White
.4	.26	.26	.08

Table 6.12b **Multipolar Structure 2 (k = .51)**

Black	Gray	Yellow	White
.30	.25	.25	.2

Table 6.13 **Bipolar Structure 1 (k = .51)**

Black	White
.6	.4

winning coalition exists in this case, and there will always be fixity. This would be true of any bipolar cleavage structure.

A bipolar cleavage structure, however, is simply a special case of a majority-dominant distribution of attribute-repertoires. Such a distribution can be associated with any number of attribute-dimension and values. A bipolar cleavage structure simply happens to be the special case of a majority-dominant distribution with one attribute-dimension and two values. While all bipolar structures are associated with fixity, all structures associated with fixity are not bipolar.

Moving away from the classic dichotomies of "cleavage structures" toward the general concept of distribution of attribute-repertoires has two further advantages. First, it allows us for the first time to make predictions about the possibility of change for cleavage structures to which no clear prediction has been attached by previous work. Consider the case of a nested cleavage structure is one in which the attribute-values on one dimension are nested within the attribute-values of another.

Nested 1 in Figure 6.11a is one example. There are two attribute-dimensions in this population: skin color, with the attribute-values of black, gray, yellow, and white, and place of origin, with the attribute values of foreign and native. The values of "black" and "gray" on the attribute-dimension of skin color are nested within the attribute-value of "Foreign" on place of origin: Those whose skin color is black or gray are also those who have a foreign place of origin. Similarly, those whose skin color is yellow or white are also those who have a native place of origin. The classic literature on ethnic divisions does not attach any prediction to whether such nested structures will produce the possibility of change or the possibility of fixity. But by reducing this structure to a distribution of attribute-repertoires, we can make such a prediction.

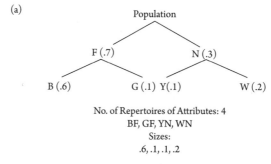

(a)

Population

F (.7)   N (.3)

B (.6)   G (.1) Y(.1)   W (.2)

No. of Repertoires of Attributes: 4
BF, GF, YN, WN
Sizes:
.6, .1, .1, .2

Figure 6.11a Nested Structure 1 (k = .51)

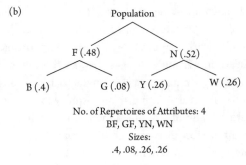

Figure 6.11b Nested Structure 2 (k = .51)

Nested 1, as we see, produces a distribution of attribute-repertoires identical to Nochangeland. Consequently, we can say that this population does not have the possibility of change in its activated ethnic demography.

Nested 2 (see Figure 6.11b), however, can be reduced to a distribution of attribute-repertoires identical to Limitedchangeland. Consequently, we can say that this population does have the possibility of change in its activated ethnic demography for most individuals: Only 8% do not have the possibility of change.

Nested 3, by contrast, generates a distribution of attribute-repertoires identical to that in Changeland (see Figure 6.11c). Consequently, we can say that this population has the possibility of change in its activated ethnic demography for all individuals in its population.

Second, the concept of a distribution of attribute-repertoires allows us for the first time to compare the magnitude of the change that is possible across different types of cleavage structures.

Consider some abstract comparisons first. Does a multipolar structure with many attribute-repertoires of different sizes (e.g., .4, .25, .15, .05, .05, .05, .05) generate more or less change than a multipolar structure with a small attribute-repertoire of equal size (e.g., .25, .25, .25, .25)? Does a cross-cutting cleavage structure with two dimensions and four attribute-values on each generate greater possibilities for change than a cross-cutting cleavage structure with three

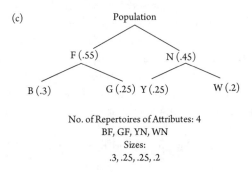

Figure 6.11c Nested Structure 3 (k = .51)

dimensions and two attribute-values on each? How do the possibilities for change in a cross-cutting cleavage structure compare with a nested cleavage structure?

To illustrate the real-world importance of these comparisons, consider a comparison between India and Zambia. At least five attribute-dimensions are salient in India (Chandra 2004)—religion, caste, language, region and tribe—and the attribute values on one a cross-cutting relationship with those on others. Thus, individuals who are all Hindu on the dimension of religion will have different values on the dimension of caste (e.g., backward caste or upper caste.) In Zambia, by contrast, only two dimensions of identity are salient: tribe and language (Posner 2005). The values on these dimensions have a nested relationship with each other: Thus, those who are Bemba by tribe are nested within the attribute-value of Bemba-speaker on the dimension of language. Which country has a greater possibility of change in its activated ethnic demography?

These are important questions, which the traditional dichotomies between cleavage structures cannot help us answer. The concept of distribution of attribute-repertoires, by contrast, makes these comparisons possible. All that is required is that we reduce each example to the distribution of attribute-repertoires—and then, using the Index of Permanent Exclusion, measure the proportion of individuals in each case who have some possibility of ethnic identity change.

6. Implications for Using "Ethnic Demography" as an Independent Variable

Ethnic "diversity" is perhaps the most important country-level independent variable in social scientific work relating ethnicity, politics, and economics. We theorize about what the effect of ethnic "diversity" is on democratic stability, on party and electoral systems, on riots and war, on state collapse, and so on, and we measure this effect in statistical studies using summary measures such as the ELF Index as a measure of ethnic diversity.

The argument made here suggests that we should replace the concept of "ethnic diversity" in our theories with the concept of an activated or a structural ethnic demography or, as the chapters following demonstrate, even more precise concepts related to particular aspects of an activated or structural ethnic demography, such as the number of minimum winning coalitions embedded in an ethnic structure (Ferree, Chapter 8), or the degree of stickiness of attribute-dimensions in a demographic structure (Laitin and van der Veen, Chapter 9). Further, it suggests that we be specific about the time and context when describing any concept related to an activated ethnic demography, since the categories activated at one time and place need not be the same as in another.

It also suggests ways in which we can incorporate the possibility of change in an activated ethnic demography in our independent variables. Consider, for instance, the concept of ethnic "majoritarianism." This concept is for the most part associated with negative effects: Large majorities are hypothesized, among other things, to threaten democratic stability (Dahl 1971, Lijphart 1977, Horowitz 1985), to produce genocide or other forms of violence (Appadurai 2006), and to block the distribution of public goods (Alesina Baqir and Easterly 1999). The common thread running through these arguments is the presumed antipathy that members of an ethnic majority have for those in an ethnic minority. Political systems that are ethnically fragmented, the arguments go, may produce more benign outcomes (Dahl 1971). Of course, the logic can also run in the opposite direction. Systems with large majorities may be more stable, produce less violence, and support the distribution of public goods, since the dominance of a single ethnic majority may defuse fear of ethnic minorities. But we are not wedded here to particular hypotheses about the effects of ethnic majoritarianism or fragmentation. Our concern instead is of how to think about the concepts of majoritarianism or fragmentation if the categories activated by individuals in a country can change.

One way to reconstruct the concept of ethnic "majoritarianism" is calculate the range of variation there is in the size of an ethnic majority, when activated. Ethnic demographies which produce overwhelmingly large ethnic majorities no matter which one is activated may have different effects from ethnic demographies in which the size of the majority fluctuates. Let's return to the examples of Changeland, Nochangeland, and Limitedchangeland from section 4 of this chapter. In Changeland, the size of the majority ranges from 55% to 70%. In Nochangeland the size of the majority does not change. In Limitedchangeland, the size of the majority ranges from 52% to 66% of the population. Notwithstanding the possibility of change in these cases, then, we might code them all as cases of "moderate majoritarianism," distinct from overwhelming majoritarianism, and see if the outcomes associated with each vary.

By the same logic, we may wish to look at ethnic minorities instead of majorities. For instance, populations such as Changeland, in which all individuals have some possibility of change, may be different from those in Limitedchangeland, in which some individuals have no possibility of change. Furthermore, there may also be theoretically relevant distinctions between populations in which all individuals have many options to change compared to populations in which some individuals have more options than others. We explore precisely these distinctions in other work (Chandra and Boulet 2005). Drawing on a body of work on permanent exclusion, for instance, we hypothesize that notwithstanding the possibility of change, demographies in which some proportion of the population has no winning option should produce greater levels of violence than those in which all do. The hypothesis that violence is most likely under those institutional arrangements in which some individuals are likely to be consistent losers comes from previous work. But what this model allows us to do is to determine the space within which violence can be induced, holding the distribution of attributes constant, by determining the range of minimum winning thresholds that will produce permanent losers. Alternatively, it can also be used to explore the ways in which the population can be partitioned to change previous losers into winners. Violence, then, should be most likely for that limited set of cases in which the repertoires of attributes for some set of individuals is such that they are likely to be losers given not only currently activated identities and current institutions but also other imaginable identities and institutional arrangements.

Alternatively, we could shift the focus from theorizing about the *size* of activated ethnic majorities to the attribute-dimensions to which they belong. When the categories activated shift, there may or may not be a shift in those attribute-dimensions. In the case of Changeland, for instance, the majority "Foreign" consists exclusively of attribute-values on the dimension of place of origin. The other two majorities include values on both dimensions. None of these dimensions include those of language or religion or caste. Thus, notwithstanding the possibility of change, we could easily classify this case in a way that allows us to theorize about questions such as whether the activation of majorities constructed using values from a single attribute-dimension are associated with different political consequences from those constructed using values from across dimensions. We could also ask whether the activation of some attribute attribute-dimensions (e.g., religion) is associated with different political consequences than others (e.g., language) (Laitin, 1998, Wilkinson 2001).

We might also theorize about the effect of the emergence of category-dimensions on economic and political outcomes. In both Changeland and Limitedchangeland, for instance, the minimum winning categories sometimes fall into a commonsensical "category dimension" and sometimes do not. Using the framework proposed here, we can investigate the conditions under which category-dimensions emerge in electoral politics, and the consequences of the emergence of such dimensions for outcomes of interest.

The empirical implications of the framework presented here are discussed in *Measuring Ethnicity* (Chandra 2011) but it is worth noting here that we can also reconstruct statistical measures using the logic just described. One common measure in statistical studies, for instance, is the size of the largest ethnic group in a country. This measure is meaningless in the face of change in an activated ethnic demography: In calculating the size of the largest ethnic group, should we refer to all groups contained in the ethnic structure or some activated group and if so, which one? But, we suggest here, we can construct time invariant measures such as the maximum change in the size of the largest group for this population, taking the absolute value of the difference between the largest winning category and the smallest. In the case of Changeland, this would be 15%, and in the case of Limitedchangeland, it would be 14%.

Similarly, in those cases in which the activated ethnic demography meets its assumptions of exclusiveness and exhaustiveness, we could also calculate the range of fluctuation in the value of the ELF index and use and interpret the measure accordingly. Many populations have multiple ethnic demographies that can be activated that meet the conditions of exhaustiveness and exclusiveness. Which ones might the ELF index capture? One solution is to calculate a distinct ELF index for each set of activated ethnic categories that can be activated, and thus to estimate the maximum change in this measure for particular populations. Once we know the maximum change in any of these measures for all countries in a dataset, we can determine the magnitude and direction of bias in an econometric analysis that does not take fluidity into account.

Finally, the framework proposed here allows us to ask questions about endogenous relationships, if any, between ethnic demographies and the institutional context in which they operate. The two principal determinants of an ethnic demography in our model are the minimum winning threshold k and the underlying distribution of individual repertoires of attributes. One way to define electoral systems is to think of them as devices that set a minimum winning threshold in a given context. Holding the distribution of individual repertoires of attributes constant, this model allows us to ask: What electoral system will be optimal given the distribution of identity repertoires in a population? Individuals with the power to determine the choice of electoral system should, other things equal, choose that value of k that maximizes the probability of producing a *unique* minimum winning category in which they are eligible for membership. By comparing the different outcomes that individuals with some given repertoire of attributes might obtain under different values of k, we can predict that value of k that they should find optimal.

Note that the insight that individuals will choose an electoral system that is optimal for them is itself unremarkable. We know for instance that ethnic minority groups are likely to prefer proportional electoral systems, while ethnic majority groups are likely to prefer first past the post-electoral systems. The contribution of this model is making it possible to ask and answer the question of what institutional arrangement is optimal for some set of individuals, given not only their currently activated identities but also their large repertoire of potential identities.

7. Extensions to This Baseline Model

First and most important, instead of treating all permissible identity categories as being equally viable choices, as we have done, extensions of the model might consider restrictions that make some combinations more viable than others. The previous chapter outlined some restrictions that we believe should have some general applicability: Individuals may consider as feasible only those ethnic categories which have at least one attribute-value in common (the overlap restriction), or those categories which are made up of attribute-values on a small number of dimensions (the number of dimensions restriction), or those categories constituted by attribute-values that are "adjacent" to each other on some underlying scale (the linear order restriction, according to which people may, for instance, prefer combinations that include proximate rather than distant languages or combinations that include similar rather than conflicting economic interests), or those categories constituted by attribute-values that share a common node in a nested structure (the nestedness restriction).

Several chapters in this volume develop these restrictions and identify others. Laitin and van der Veen (Chapter 9) introduce the restrictions that individuals are likely to consider only *within*-dimension rather than *across*-dimension combinations, and that individuals have limited information on the distribution of attribute-repertoires across the population. Petersen (Chapter 11) introduces restrictions based on stereotypes and emotional weights attached to individual attribute-dimensions or values. Wilkinson (Chapter 10) introduces a restriction based on the issue positions associated with individuals with different attribute-values: Building on the linear order restriction, he argues that individuals will consider feasible only those categories that consist of attribute-values that are "connected" to each other on the underlying issue dimension. Finally, Ferree (Chapter 8) explores the relevance of the nestedness restriction in electoral politics.

There are many other ways of thinking about restrictions on feasible choice sets that remain open for further work. The plausibility of some combinations relative to others may be affected by institutionally imposed incentives, by historical paths, by the degree of visibility (e.g., people may prefer combinations that include easily identifiable attributes), by the degree of stickiness (e.g., people may prefer combinations that include attributes that are harder to change over attributes that are easier to change), by the degree of complexity (e.g., people may prefer simple combinations over complex ones), and so on.

We can model such restrictions in several ways. We might, for instance, weight *attribute-dimensions* or attribute-values differently, as Petersen does in Chapter 11 to capture the lower value of categories defined by stigmatized types of attributes. We might weight *combinations* of attributes differently. And, finally, we might modify the assumption of perfect information. Less demanding assumptions about information include the following: (1) Individuals have information about the *range* in which individual repertoires of attributes are distributed rather than exact proportions. This is the assumption employed by van der Veen and Laitin (Chapter 7). (2) There may be variation in the *reliability* of information associated with different types of attributes. We could model this by associating different types of attributes with different degrees of error and allotting weights accordingly. (3) Individuals have information about the proportions in which each value on each type of attribute is distributed in the population but not how these values are combined in individual repertoires.

A *second* important extension lies in exploring the effect of different institutional rules on the possibility of change. The general patterns identified here apply only to winner-take-all situations in which the outcome is determined by a simple majority rule. But we do not explore here the general effect of changes in the size of the majority required: What might the effect of larger or smaller values of k be on the possibility of change in an ethnic demography? Are there distributions of attribute-values where the possibility of change or fixity is robust to large changes in the minimum winning threshold? What is the possibility of change associated either with other decision rules in a winner-take-all system (e.g., a plurality rule) or with systems that are not winner-take-all (e.g., in which the payoff is distributed proportionally among groups). Other chapters in this volume extend this model to include these other decision rules. The chapters by van der Veen and Laitin, in particular, explore several aspects of change in an ethnic demography by varying the size of the threshold required to win.

Third, we require a model of political agency that tells us when the possibilities embedded in some cleavage structure will actually be realized in politics and when not. It may well be that in some institutional conditions, politicians do not try to activate multiple majorities even when the potential for such activation exists, or do not succeed when they try. All of the chapters in this book make distinct arguments for how political entrepreneurs utilize the structural possibilities they find embedded in an ethnic demography. Perhaps the most sophisticated model of political competition offered in this volume is that proposed by Ian Lustick (Chapter 12), which combines the role of political entrepreneurs with that of other influential agents such as bureaucrats and the military and is able to represent the effect of several tiers of bureaucratic authority as well as the geographic distribution of these agents on ethnic identity change.

Fourth, in a point already alluded to previously, extensions might model the possibility of endogeneizing k. The institutional rules which affect human choice at one point in time are themselves a product of those choices in the past. Often the choice of institutional rules depends upon expectations of their likely outcome. This is especially true in ethnically divided societies, where representatives of ethnic identity categories are often involved in negotiations over the choice of institutional rules, and often press for that rule which they believe is most likely to place them in a winning position. Indeed, politicians have every incentive to choose institutional thresholds that generate not the possibility of change but the certainty of fixity of an ethnic demography that privileges their own ethnic category. It is important, then, to theorize also about the affects of particular distributions of attribute-repertoires on the choice of minimum winning threshold.

Finally, we require a model of the dynamics as well as the statics of ethnic identity change. As we noted in earlier chapters, short-term change in an ethnic demography can also produce long-term change in a feedback effect. For instance, we know that those political entrepreneurs who end up in a winning position often engage in attempts to change the distribution of attributes in their favor by changing the language of citizenship or state employment (Brass 1974, Laitin 1998), by legislating the use of different last names (Scott 1998), or by using the census to amplify counts of some attributes while depressing others (Jones 1981). Changes in the underlying distribution of attributes, in turn, can have long-term effects on the nature of winning coalitions, and on the institutional rules adopted, some of which may not be fully or correctly foreseen. Indeed, under some conditions, we may well see the evolution of populations defined by an ethnic structure and practice into countries in which non-ethnic attributes become more relevant over time. A full model of the possibility of change in an ethnic demography should model these long-term as well as short-term effects, and the interactions between the two. Chapter 7, by van der Veen and Laitin, explicitly models these interactions.

Appendix

1. Full Repertoire of Nominal Identity Categories

Consider the full repertoire of nominal identity categories. Since some nominal identity categories are contained in others, it is natural to consider their partial order defined by containment. Note that this containment can be thought of in terms of which attribute-repertoires are in the identity category or which individuals belong to an identity category. Either way, we obtain the same containment relationship between nominal identity categories.

Mathematically, this structure is called a partially ordered set (poset) and considering the poset structure of the full repertoire of nominal identity categories can facilitate our analysis of a particular ethnic demography. For basic information about posets we refer the reader to (Birkhoff 1967; Stanley 1997; and Ganter and Wille 1999).

The full repertoire of nominal identity categories is composed of all subset of the set of attribute-repertoires. By definition the Boolean lattice, B_n, is the poset of subsets of a set containing n elements, ordered by containment. Therefore, if n is the number of attribute-repertoires for our populations, then the poset of nominal identity categories is the Boolean lattice, B_n

Posets may be graphically represented by the use of a Hasse diagram. In a Hasse diagram, dots represent the element of the poset and lines represent containment. If $x \subset y$, then y is drawn above x. A line is drawn between x and y if $x \subset y$ and there is no z such that $x \subset z \subset y$. The poset B_4 whose Hasse diagram is shown in figure 1 is the poset of the full repertoire of nominal identity categories used in our basic 2*2 example.

Though in this appendix we consider the full repertoire of nominal identity categories, we should note that to draw the poset of operative identity categories when a restriction is applied we can draw B_n and erase the nodes that are not allowed under the restriction.

2. Finding Minimum Winning Categories

Given a context in which some value k with $0.5 < k < 1$ is a minimum winning threshold, we define a category as minimum winning if it does not contain the

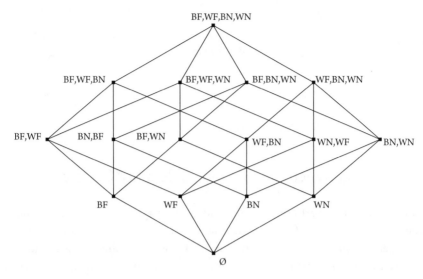

Figure 6A.1 Our basic example

whole population, its size is greater than or equal to k, and it does not contain another category whose size is also greater than or equal to k. So these are the smallest (by containment) categories that are large enough to be winning.

On the Hasse diagram of our poset, we may label each node indicating the proportion of the population eligible for membership in that identity category. The winning categories are those whose proportion of the population is greater than or equal to k. The minimum winning categories are the winning categories that do not have another winning category below it. Applying a restriction to limit the operative identity categories can change the list of minimum winning categories, but the procedure to find them remains the same.

One way to evaluate the possibility for change in an ethnic demography is to look at the number of minimum winning categories. The greater the number of minimum winning categories, the greater the possibilities for change. (It cannot be emphasized enough that we are talking about the possibility of change and not the probability that change will occur.)

It is interesting to note that at no point in our analysis have we needed to consider the content or description of the identity categories. In order to find the number of minimum winning categories we only need to know the number of individual attribute-repertoires and the proportion of the population with each individual attribute-repertoire. As a result, the number of minimum winning categories depends only on the number and size of the attribute-repertoires.

It can also be interesting to look at the composition of the minimum winning categories, in particular to see whether an individual belongs to any minimum winning category. This is done in the next section.

3. Index of Permanent Exclusion

We say that individuals with a particular attribute-repertoire are permanently excluded if they are in no minimum winning categories. In other words, if they are members of a winning category, that category would still be winning without them. The Index of Permanently exclusion of a population is the proportion of the population that is permanently excluded.

We will show that, in the full repertoire of identity categories, whether or not an attribute-repertoire is permanently excluded depends only on the proportion of the population with that attribute-repertoire and not on the content of the attribute repertoire. To do this we show how to calculate whether or not an attribute-repertoire is excluded using only the proportion of the population in each attribute-repertoire.

Suppose we have n attribute-repertoires, $A_1, A_2, \ldots, A_n$, having sizes $a_1 \geq a_2 \geq a_3 \geq \ldots \geq a_n$. (We assume the attribute-repertoires have been ordered so that they are decreasing in size.)

Proposition. If A_i is permanently excluded then A_j is permanently excluded for all $i \leq j$.

Proof. To see that A_j is permanently excluded, let C be a winning category that includes A_j. There are two cases to consider.

First, if A_i is in C, then $C - A_i$ is still winning because A_i is permanently excluded. However, we know that the size of $C - A_j$ is greater than or equal to the size of $C - A_i$ because $a_i \geq a_j$. This implies that $C - A_j$ is winning.

Second, if A_i is not in C, then let $D = (C - A_j) \cup A_i$ be the category obtained by removing A_j from C and adding A_i. Since $a_i \geq a_j$, the size of D is greater than or equal to C, which tells us that D is winning. But A_i is permanently excluded so we conclude that $D - A_i = C - A_j$ is also winning. In both cases, $C - A_j$ is also winning and so we have that A_j is permanently excluded.

It follows that to check if there is any permanent exclusion, we simply need to check whether A_n is permanently excluded.

We want a general criteria to check if A_i is permanently excluded. It follows from the proposition that to be permanently excluded, A_i must not be in any minimum winning category composed of the attribute-repertoires $A_1, A_2, \ldots, A_i$. (We can disregard $A_{i+1}, \ldots, A_n$.) In other words, if C is any category composed of the attribute-repertoires $A_1, A_2, \ldots, A_{i-1}$ and C is not winning, then $C \cup A_i$ is not winning either. To check this for every category composed of the attribute-repertoires $A_1, A_2, \ldots, A_{i-1}$, we must consider every subset of $a_1, a_2, \ldots, a_{i-1}$ and compute if the sum ρ of those numbers. If none of the partial sums is $k - a_i \leq p < k$, then the attribute-repertoire A_i is permanently excluded.

This gives a criteria for checking whether there is any permanent exclusion. If any partial sum, p, of the numbers $a_1, a_2, \ldots a_{n-1}$ is $k - a_n \leq p < k$, then we do not have permanent exclusion. Otherwise, if none of the sums, p, is $k - a_n \leq p < k$, we do have permanent exclusion.

Finally, the index of permanent exclusion is the sum of the size of each permanently excluded attribute-repertoire. That is, $a_i + a_{i+1} + \cdots + a_n$, where A_i is the largest permanently excluded attribute-repertoire. It is worthwhile to note that this procedure depends only on $a_1, a_2, \ldots, a_n$ the size of each attribute-repertoire and not on the content of the attribute repertoires.

7

Modeling the Evolution of Ethnic Demography

A. MAURITS VAN DER VEEN AND DAVID D. LAITIN

1. Introduction

How do ethnic demographies evolve? Chandra and Boulet have demonstrated the incredibly large range of possible activated ethnic demographies given any set of attributes in a population. However, their theory is one of combinatorial possibilities at some fixed point in time, not one of dynamics. They do not investigate the rules and possibilities of change from one activated demography to another within the same society over time. Nor do they investigate the dynamic relationship between activated ethnic demographies and the underlying structure that generates them, or the evolution of structural ethnic demographies within the same society over time.

This chapter builds upon the conceptual framework established by Chandra and Boulet, and from it constructs an agent-based model that provides a method to study the dynamics of change in an ethnic demography, both activated and structural. The term "activated ethnic demography" refers to the set and size of activated ethnic identity categories for a population (Chandra and Boulet, Chapter 6). The term "structural" ethnic demography refers to the attributes and dimensions in a population and the nominal categories that can be generated from them, regardless of whether or not they are, or can be, activated.[1]

Earlier versions of this chapter were presented at a workshop in August 2003 and at the Ninth World Conference of the Association for the Study of Nationalities, Columbia University, April 2004. We thank Ian Lustick for his inspiration for this research project. We thank as well David Epstein for his comments at that workshop, and all members of the Laboratory of Comparative Ethnic Processes (LiCEP) for their criticism and support.

[1] In this chapter as well as in Chapter 9, the term "attribute" refers to an attribute-value and the term "dimension" refers to an attribute-dimension, unless otherwise specified.

Agent-based modeling is an especially promising tool to explore constructivist propositions about ethnic identity change for several reasons. First, it allows us to test the validity of causal mechanisms specified in previous theories. Second, it makes it easy to model the interactions between multiple, simultaneous processes critical to constructivist theories. Third, it allows us to model not only a single empirical outcome but also the distribution of expected outcomes. Thus, it may help us understand whether an observed outcome is an outlier (and perhaps influenced by other factors not in our model) or the modal outcome to be expected from our theoretical framework. Fourth, and along the same lines, it allows us to generate more precise predictions than we would be able to produce otherwise. Finally, it goes further than combinatorics in its ability to describe the complexity of a constructivist world—for instance, we can use it as we do here to represent "salience" and "stickiness" as continuous rather than dichotomous concepts, and to introduce a greater degree of variability across the attribute-repertoires of individuals in a population. In Chapter 9, we apply this methodology to lend support to a theory that illustrates the link between distributive politics and the increased salience of ethnic identities. But our goal in this chapter is to acquaint readers with the method, and to show how one can model ethnic dynamics using computer simulation tools.

As a way of illustrating this approach, we use our technology in this chapter to model several of the processes discussed by Chandra and Boulet in Chapters 5 and 6. In particular, we investigate whether electoral institutions (modeled in Chandra and Boulet by the value of k) have the same impact on leadership stability and on individual identities in countries where ethnic differences dominate as compared to countries divided on less "sticky" identities. The assumption by Chandra and Boulet is that when dimensions are sticky, leaders should stay in power longer. We also ask what the impact of different electoral systems is on the pattern of concentration of attributes in an ethnic demography. By "concentration of attributes," we mean the tendency of some attributes to be acquired by large numbers of the population, and the tendency of others to die out. Linguistic standardization, for instance, in which some languages are acquired by large numbers of a population while others die out, would be an instance of attribute concentration (e.g., Weber 1976, Laitin 1992). This is a question for which there are no clear intuitions. Common sense might lead us to expect there to be greater attribute concentration in non-ethnic demographies (i.e., demographies with less sticky dimensions) than in ethnic demographies, since it is easier for individuals to acquire advantageous attributes in the short term. But it is not clear how different electoral rules would interact with stickiness to affect levels of concentration. Both questions could not have been raised from a primordialist position, but they are opened up by the constructivist foundation developed in this book and by its combinatorial translation.

The findings produced by the agent-based simulations suggest previously untheorized patterns, worthy of future empirical investigation. Contrary to the assumption by Chandra and Boulet, we find that greater stickiness in dimensions is associated with a longer leadership tenure only in a plurality electoral system. This pattern disappears as soon as we introduce a specific vote threshold, whether it is high or low. In all cases in which the winner is decided by a specific vote threshold, stickier demographies are associated with *shorter* tenure in office. Our second simulation experiment also generates a counterintuitive result. We find that as the winning threshold imposed by an electoral system rises, the concentration of attributes tends to fall in non-ethnic demographies but rise in ethnic demographies. Both experiments suggest a new theoretical logic linking electoral rules with patterns of evolution in ethnic demographies. They also illustrate the limitations of partial models of ethnic processes when we know that ethnic processes, as we shall elaborate, operate and interact on several different levels.

The chapter is divided into three parts. The first motivates the approach and discusses the central processes at work in our model of ethnic demography. The second presents an overview of the actual agent-based model. In the third section, we present and discuss the results of our simulation experiments. An appendix to this chapter gives specific details on the model and the parameter settings used.

2. Why Agent-Based Modeling?

Until now, game theory has been the method of choice in accounting for changing ethnic demographies. It has been especially useful in modeling ethnic cascades, for example, in the processes of ethnic assimilation with the goal of social mobility or ethnic separation with the goal of political autonomy (Laitin 1998). Our contention here is that agent-based models can contribute to our understanding of real-world processes in ways complementary to game-theoretic models. As is the case with game theory, computational modeling forces us to be explicit about all the different factors that affect the behavior of actors in the model. Unlike game-theoretic models, however, agent-based models are uniquely able to handle large numbers of purposive actors with different characteristics, interacting both locally and globally, whereas game-theoretic models tend to be limited to small numbers of identical actors (or at best actors drawn from a very small number of fixed types) with limited scope for interaction (cf. Lehtinen and Kuorikoski 2007).

The dynamics of ethnic demographies as postulated by Chandra and Boulet (Chapters 5 and 6 in this volume), are complex. Of the several mechanisms which they theorize about as driving ethnic identity change over time, we adopt three in our agent based model: (1) "replacement" or the attempt by individuals to acquire politically valuable attributes in place of less valuable ones, (2) changes in the political salience of different dimensions, and (3) the process by which particular attributes are combined into single, broader categories. Of these, the second requires further elaboration. Chandra and Boulet propose a blunt, dichotomous notion of the salience of a dimension: The dimensions in a population's repertoire are either "activated" (what we understand as "salient") or they are not. There is no provision for different *degrees* of salience. This dichotomous understanding of "activation" or "salience" is true also of other work on cleavage salience at least in the study of ethnicity (e.g., Posner 2004b). Our model allows us to think of salience as a continuum rather than a dichotomy and to vary the degree of salience of each dimension in individuals. Thus, we can ask and answer questions for the first time about changes in the degree of salience of dimensions in the population as a whole and across individuals in that population.

Each of these three processes, to be sure, can be subjected to game-theoretic analysis individually, holding the other two constant. However, since these processes mutually interact, finding formal (game-theoretic) equilibria for changes in ethnic demographies is not presently possible. Let us now review the three interdependent processes.

The first is that of strategic investment by minorities in the attributes of the majority population. To the extent that they succeed in acquiring these attributes, individuals from the minority population will be able to "pass." The process has been analyzed in the context of game theory by means of what Thomas Schelling (1973) called "tipping" games with two equilibria. Laitin (1998) applied this model to the Russian-speaking minority in the former Soviet Republic of Estonia. After independence was restored to Estonia in 1991, the nearly 40% of the population in the country that spoke Russian had to decide whether to seek assimilation into the new national culture as Estonians or to demand a separate Russian-speaking minority status with regional political autonomy. If all Russian-speakers sent their children only to Russian schools, this would be part of an effort to demand regional autonomy.

As Figure 7.1 models the situation, all Russians are assumed on average to be better off by assimilating. If all Russians remained in the Russian school

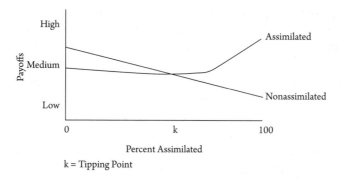

Figure 7.1 Russians in Estonia: The Payoffs of Assimilation

system, the outcome would be close to zero on the x axis, and each member of the non-assimilated population would receive a higher payoff (the value for each non-assimilant on the y axis) for retaining Russian than trying to "pass" as an Estonian. Russians who then sent their children to Estonian-medium schools would be considered sellouts and perhaps get ostracized from their home communities. They would get a lower value for being assimilated when none of the original Russian speakers had assimilated. Since no Russian family at the lower end of the x axis has an incentive to assimilate, the outcome of no Russians assimilating is an equilibrium.

However, if many Russians think that most other Russians are ready to switch to the Estonian-medium schools, they would fear a cascade to the 100% Estonian medium, in which retaining Russian would have a very low payoff. Thus if Russians thought other Russians were ready to switch (and other Russians thought the first set would switch), there would arise a second equilibrium, one that resulted in assimilation. The processes of moving toward the "tipping point" k (i.e., the point at which if one person switches, the average benefit for all would go up in the direction of the switch, setting off a cascade in that direction) is well understood in a game-theoretic context. However, consider how the situation may evolve if assimilation becomes more (or less) politically salient. This will affect the cost-benefit calculation of each agent, and thus shift the tipping point k. Another important variable left implicit in the foregoing story is just how hard it would be to switch—can it be accomplished quickly, or would it take years? The situation gets more complex still if the political salience of assimilation varies based on the rate at which agents are assimilating or on the rates of immigration or emigration of Estonians or Russians. It is thus dangerous to draw conclusions about ethnic demographies by analyzing only incentives to assimilate.

The second process of ethnic demographic change concerns shifts in the political salience of different dimensions, such as race, language, and religion. Every population has some number of commonsensical dimensions—but from this commonsensical set, some dimensions may become activated to serve as the basis of activated categories in some societies, while others may not. Thus, the dimension of religion is activated in northern Ireland, of race in urban politics in many American cities, and of language in other places, like Belgium.

The question of why some dimensions become activated over others has been a long-standing puzzle in political sociology. Lipset and Rokkan (1967) set the agenda in their study of the origins of cleavages in modern democracies. They developed a theory of cleavage freezing: The most salient social differences within a society in the period when electoral politics get going will continue to define politics even under conditions in which the cleavage is no longer socially significant. Thus the French party system became institutionalized in a period in which the church was fighting mightily with the state for the right to monopolize education. The religious cleavage (Catholics vs. seculars) therefore persisted (i.e., became "frozen") as the key to political identifications in France for a century after the battle had been decided (in favor of the seculars).

Numerous other theories have been offered since. Laitin (1986) emphasized the power of colonial states to reward supplicants for political favor if they did so according to their rights as a member of a group on a certain line of cleavage. This form of state power could thereby make some cleavages dominant (the tribal cleavage in Yorubaland) and others recessive (the religious cleavage in Yorubaland). The puzzle of cleavage salience was recently given a game-theoretic foundation by Posner (2005). Posner relies on the theory of minimum winning coalitions (Riker 1962). The intuition here is that there are fewer people to divide the spoils of office the smaller the winning coalition. Using this game theoretic approach, Posner models a world in which there are two "category" dimensions (A and B) along which the population is divided. Each dimension has n categories. The category with the highest population for each dimension gets the first listing (a_1 and b_1).

Posner's idea is that the key pivot group is in section w, shown in Figure 7.2, made up of those people who are in the largest category of both dimensions. They will identify with politicians who aggregate voters through a message that attracts supporters by emphasizing the dimension that has the lowest number of members still large enough to become the leader of any coalition government. In the hypothetical example below, English-speaking Latinos are the pivot, and they will emphasize their "Latino" identity if 40% of the votes would constitute a minimum winning coalition. If not, they would be the pivotal actors in an English-speaking identity group in which language, not ethnicity, was the key cleavage. Through this model, we have a game-theoretic prediction of dimensional salience.

Again, however, this example ignores crucial other processes that will often be at work at the same time. After all, as we discussed above, voters not in either

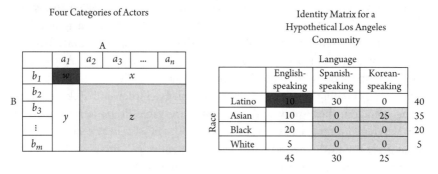

Figure 7.2 Posner's Model of Dimensional Salience. Source: Posner (2005): 133-137.

of the largest groups will be trying to obtain the desired attributes. If the rate at which they are able to do this is noticeably different for the two dimensions considered in the figure, then both the calculations of would-be leaders and the actual political outcomes may well be different. Voter calculations may also be different if it is possible to combine their existing attributes into new categories. Finally, this model does not allow us to investigate the effects of changes in the *degree* of salience of either dimension.

The third process in the changing demography of ethnicity is that of the grouping of attributes on one or more dimensions into categories. Categories that define groups along dimensions are lumpy. On the dimension of race in the United States, there are two categories: White and non-White. However, in the West Indies anthropologists have long noted a large number of race categor- ies on the same dimension (e.g., Jordan 1962). More recently, Chandra (2004) describes changes in the category space over time in a single society, India. For many years there were a plethora of lower caste categories. In reaction to the affirmative action policies aimed at the so-called harijans, and electoral factors as well, these distinct lower castes organized themselves as "other backward castes." While at first this category had a constructed and not-very-real feeling to it, over time people begin to identify themselves in this new and larger (along the dimension of caste) identity category. Similarly Laitin (1998) has documented the emergence of a new ethnic category in several post-Soviet states called "the Russian-speaking population" that combines Russians, Ukrainians, Belarusans, and Jews. The ethnic dimension then had two categories: the titular nationality and Russian-speakers. This process of category reconstruction has not yet been modeled in a game-theoretic way, but because it is discrete and simple, it invites formalization.

To reiterate: Each of these processes—attribute replacement, change in the salience of dimensions, and attribute-recombination into categories to change the size of coalitions—can be profitably subjected to game theoretic analysis. As we have suggested, however, in the real world all three processes are taking place simultaneously, and it would stretch the mathematical imagination to solve for equilibrium outcomes if all three processes are permitted to work themselves out in interaction with each other. It is in complex interactions such as these that agent-based models, while losing some mathematical elegance, have consid- erable heuristic value.

To put it differently, whether a game-theoretic or an agent-based approach is preferable depends both on one's theoretical framework and on the questions one is interested in answering. The greatest strength of game-theoretic models is that certain outcomes can be analytically determined. The associated weakness, of course, is that mathematical tractability tends to require simplification and a relatively small number of moving parts (actors, strategies, etc.). Agent-based models do not suffer from this weakness. In exchange for giving up precise

analytical outcomes—and accepting experimentally determined distributions
of outcomes instead—these models make it possible to examine what happens
when hundreds or thousands of agents interact, with different interaction topol-
ogies, and without any artificial restrictions on the complexity of their decision
strategies.

Given the centrality of multiple, simultaneous processes within constructivist theories, constructivist models are especially likely to benefit from the richness offered by agent-based models. More generally, conjectures and hypotheses
involving interactions between multiple variables are more readily addressed in
a context where all parameters can be systematically varied, as is the case in
agent-based modeling. Indeed, numerous other scholars of ethnic politics have
begun to take advantage of the promise of agent-based modeling in recent years.
Among others, in addition to the work of Lustick (Chapter 12, in this volume;
Lustick, Miodownik, and Eidelson 2004), it is worth noting the agent-based
framework for modeling the interaction between ethnicity and resource availability developed by Bhavnani, Miodownik, and Nart (2008), and a model designed
to understand different rates of ethnic mobilization in the former Yugoslavia
(Srbljinovic et al. 2003).[2]

We believe, then, that an agent-based modeling approach holds promise
for addressing the issues laid out in the Chapter 1 of this volume. Obviously,
agent-based models cannot prove anything about the real world, any more than
game-theoretic models can. They can, however, provide valuable insights in a
number of ways. First, agent-based models make it possible to test the validity of hypothesized causal mechanisms linking different empirical observations,
especially moving from individual-level behavior to polity-level outcomes. The
political science literature is rife with informal hypotheses regarding the causal
mechanisms at work in generating certain outcomes from particular sets of initial conditions. Often these mechanisms cannot easily be empirically verified.
However, if they can be specified (operationalized) with sufficient precision, an
agent-based model can provide one basis for verification. If this model generates
the observed outcome from the known starting conditions, it would raise confidence that the hypothesized causal processes are the ones at work in the real
world. If it fails to produce the known outcomes, this suggests that something
is either lacking or wrong in our ideas about the causal processes at work. Such
information can be crucial in the process of refining our theories.

Second, agent-based models allow us to get a sense of the distribution
of expected outcomes. This may provide valuable insights into the degree
to which observed empirical patterns can be considered "normal." In other

---

[2] Indeed, agent-based modeling has become sufficiently familiar as an approach to merit a
brief discussion in an overview of the recent literature on "Ethnicity, race, and nationalism" in the
Annual Review of Sociology (Brubaker 2009).

words, it may help us understand whether an observed outcome is an outlier (and perhaps influenced by other factors not in our model) or the modal outcome to be expected if our theoretical framework and its operationalization are correct.

Third, but along the same lines, agent-based models allow us to generate more specific predictions than we would be able to produce otherwise. Theoretical formulations often do not allow us to make very precise predictions. They allow us to predict whether particular outcomes are more or less likely, for example, but not whether outcome A is ten times more likely than outcome B, or instead only twice as likely. With agent-based models we can generate as many artificial case studies as we wish, in order to get a more precise sense of the nature and distribution of the possible outcomes we are interested in.[3]

3. An Agent-Based Model of the Evolution of an Ethnic Demography

One of the goals of this book is to set the foundation for the cumulation of knowledge about ethnicity and its construction. It is therefore imperative that we define our central theoretical terms—attribute, dimension, and category—in as consistent a manner as our different methods allow. But we also need to be clear where our formulations differ.

The fundamental unit in our model is the attribute, corresponding to "attribute-value" in Chandra and Boulet's work. This is the narrowest classification possible on a given dimension and in a given context. In our model, attributes cannot exist in the absence of a dimension ("attribute-dimension" in work of Chandra and Boulet). Attributes can be seen as providing the most specific relevant answer to the following question—"What are you like with respect to X?"—where X is the dimension in question. In the real world, the dimension is at times implicit, but it is always there. To give but one example, "color" is not a meaningful identity component until we specify whether we are interested in skin color, hair color, eye color, and so on (perhaps even political color—witness the "purple" cabinet in the Netherlands during the late 1980s, which was a mixture of the "red" Labour party and the "blue" Liberals).

Both dimensions and the attributes on each dimension are context-specific, and a dimension on one level may turn into an attribute at another level. For example, one might be Lutheran on the dimension of Protestantism ("What

---

[3] For a useful recent discussion of the promises and pitfalls of agent-based modeling more generally, see Miller and Page 2007; see also Cioffi-Revilla 2010; Edmonds 2010.

kind of a Protestant are you?"), Protestant on the dimension of Christianity ("What kind of a Christian are you?"), and Christian on the dimension of religion ("What is your religion?"). In our model, we take the politically relevant dimensions as given. However, it is worth noting that these can change over time and will certainly vary across different contexts. For example, in many European countries, the dimension of Christianity has been gradually replaced in political significance by that of religion, as immigrants from Islamic countries become an increasingly visible political group.

This brings us to the third main conceptual variable: the category. In our model, a *simple* category is a grouping of attributes *within* a dimension. To stay with the above example, in European countries, individuals may still distinguish themselves as Protestant versus Catholic but also recognize their membership in the politically relevant category "Christian," which is the union of those two attributes (possibly three, if one includes Orthodox Christianity). The combination (union or, more commonly, intersection) of categories on multiple dimensions by political leaders is termed a *"complex* category" in our model. The American category of WASP is a complex category specifying the intersection of Whites (on the racial dimension), Anglo-Saxons (on the ethnic dimension), and Protestants (on the religious dimension).

Our model aims to study the evolution of ethnic demographies given micro-theories found in the literature about how individuals change their identities over time and how leaders stake out particular politically relevant categories. Attributes are the raw materials for building ethnic coalitions. Entrepreneurs choose a simple category (constructed from a set of attributes on a single dimension) or a compound category across dimensions to win the allegiance of agents in order to build winning coalitions; agents seek to alter their attribute sets to wend their way into winning coalitions, but also to increase their similarity with their social contacts. Our model supplies a range of parameters that can be varied to observe the consequences of purposive behavior by agents and entrepreneurs alike in joining and building winning ethnic coalitions.

Agents

Agents 'live' and interact on a two-dimensional grid on which their interactions are almost exclusively local, with their immediate neighbors.[4] There are two types of agents in our model: "basic" agents and "leaders."

---

[4] To be precise, actors interact with the eight agents directly adjacent to them (their so-called Moore neighborhood) on the grid. In addition, they are self-aware: They know their own attributes. Agents do not move around on the grid, nor do they develop new social contacts over the course of the simulation. Their set of contacts is thus fixed.

The Repertoire of Attributes for the Population and for Individual Agents

The key feature of each agent in our world is her repertoire of attributes. Each agent has a fixed-length repertoire of attributes, one each from those dimensions deemed to be politically salient by that agent. Agents differ not just in terms of their attributes on a given dimension but also in terms of the dimensions that they consider salient to keep within their repertoire. In our model, there are eight dimensions for the population as a whole, with five possible attributes on each. The repertoire of each individual agent consists of five of these eight dimensions, and thus of five attributes. Attribute distributions across dimensions are independent in the current formulation of the model.[5]

Within the repertoire, the different dimensions are ranked by salience. Attributes are sorted within each agent's repertoire in declining order of their political salience to the agent in question. Each agent has a few (usually two or three) attributes it considers particularly important, and a larger number that are rather less crucial to its overall self-identification. The salience of these dimensions can vary across agents—that is, the same dimension may be more salient for some agents than others.

To bring this model more in line with our theoretical understanding of ethnicity, we add a parameter that we call stickiness. "Stickiness" affects the ease with which agents can change their attributes on a particular dimension. Dimension stickiness is set by a parameter. Each dimension has a value on this parameter, representing the degree of difficulty of changing one's attributes. If stickiness is set to zero, agents can change attributes at will. If it is set to higher values, agents must interact with another agent that has this attribute for a number of consecutive rounds before the actual change can take place.[6] It is a key assumption in our model, in line with Ernest Gellner's suggestion that cultural identities are "entropy resistant" (Gellner 1983, 64), that a defining quality of ethnicity is that of high relative stickiness (see also Chandra, Chapter 1, in this volume). It is relatively easier (i.e., less sticky) to change attributes such as ideological affiliation (e.g., from moderate left to moderate right) than it is to change attributes based on your language, your caste, or your race.

Our introduction of degrees of stickiness goes beyond Chandra and Boulet's combinatorial formulation, in which all dimensions in a repertoire are of equal

[5] Of course, these settings are arbitrary. Future work could develop probability rules on the distribution of attributes on any dimension or elective affinities of attributes across dimensions.

[6] The intuition here is that interaction with agents who have another attribute will increase an agent's willingness to invest considerable resources into obtaining the other attribute. An empirical illustration would be the amount of effort required to "pass" as White—and the willingness of some people to invest quite heavily in such an effort—in the United States prior to the civil rights era.

stickiness. It brings us closer to the conceptual understanding of ethnic identity outlined in earlier chapters—where the attributes that constitute ethnic identity categories are distributed on a scale of stickiness. In this chapter, we consider all dimensions to be of equal stickiness. But in Chapter 9, on the politics of pork, we allow stickiness to vary and show that this variation can be an important factor in explaining political outcomes.

The Repertoire of Categories for Agents and the Population

Categories in our model are constructed by leaders. A leader's specification of a category takes the form of a set of attributes within each dimension that satisfy the leader's conditions. For example, on a religion dimension, a leader might indicate that she will accept Catholics as well as Anglicans. Individuals choose between the category specifications offered by leaders and activate an attribute in their repertoire accordingly.

Going beyond Chandra and Boulet's baseline model in which all combinations are equally feasible, we propose two restrictions that define the operative choice set from which leaders choose their specifications. First, leaders will only propose combinations of attributes that are numerically contiguous. In other words, a proposed coalition cannot accept attribute-values "1 or 3" but could accept "1 or 2." The theoretical logic justifying a contiguity restriction was developed by Chandra and Boulet in Chapter 5, and other chapters on electoral politics also make some use of this or a similar restriction (see Chapter 10 for Wilkinson's discussion of "connectedness" and Chapter 8 for Ferree's discussion of "nestedness," which can also be interpreted as contiguity). Second, if a leader specifies attributes on multiple dimensions, agents must have at least one of the acceptable attributes on each dimension in their repertoire. In other words, whereas attributes are connected by a logical OR within a dimension, across dimensions they are connected by an AND. For example, a leader may say she accepts those who are Catholic *and* working-class, but not that she accepts those who satisfy just one of those attributes (Catholic *or* working class). We also impose restrictions on the maximum share of the possible attributes on a dimension a leader is allowed to claim as well as on the information the leader takes into account when proposing these specifications, discussed further below. Even with these restrictions, the size of the operative repertoire of categories is quite large in practice.

Leaders and Coalitions

At every electoral round leaders put forward a specification—a category or a combination of attributes—aimed at attracting a winning coalition of agents. In so doing, they take into account information about their own attribute-repertoires, some information about the population, and their own performance in previous rounds.

The strategy by which leaders develop the coalition specification they offer for agents to select (detailed in the appendix to this chapter) aims to meet the following conditions:

1. They satisfy the membership requirements themselves.
2. Its potential size safely exceeds the sufficient share of the vote.
3. Its potential size is as small as possible while still satisfying items 1 and 2.
4. It is not a superset of a specification already on offer by another leader.[7]

In making their choices, leaders have only limited information about the population they are targeting. Specifically, the size of each attribute's subpopulation is public information (i.e., known to leaders as well as other agents), but intersections across dimensions are not known. In other words, it may be known that 40% of the population is Catholic and 20% is working class, but nobody knows the precise share of the population that is Catholic *and* working class. Leaders guess at such intersections by assuming independence across dimensions, so that in the above example the "guesstimated" share of agents who are Catholic *and* working class would be 40% x 20% = 8%.[8]

Optimal Winning Coalitions

A central parameter in the model is the optimal coalition size for both leaders and their supporters. In discussing Posner's work above, we referred to the minimum winning coalition size as though it was a simple (and fixed) fact of political life. It need not be. In our model, we refer to this value as "optimal winning coalition" (OWC). The notion is very similar to Riker's concept of minimum winning coalition (Riker 1962). However, the use of the term "optimal," rather than "minimum," indicates that leaders also aim not to overshoot this share of the total vote: A coalition of OWC + 1 voter is assumed to be more attractive, to leaders and voters alike, than one of OWC + 1,000 voters. As we will show below, OWC interacts in important ways with the existing ethnic demography in

[7] The reason for this requirement is quite straightforward. A superset of another specification would not be appealing to voters, who would either affiliate with the narrower specification or, if unable to do so themselves because they do not meet the requirements, would realize that those who *could* choose the other specification would do so. It is not, therefore, a useful strategy for a leader to offer such a superset.

[8] Note that the real value could be either well above or well below this estimate (in this example possible values range from 0% to 20%). In fact, as figure 7.2 implies, in the real world political actors often have a fairly good sense of the size of at least some intersections. Future extensions to our model may make such knowledge a parameter that can be set by the user.

a polity. Similarly, in Chapter 9 in this volume, we vary the value of this parameter in order to study the implications of optimal coalition size for the nature of
political competition in a polity. It is important to note that leaders cannot be
sure that they will attract every agent who might satisfy their specification, so
there is always some uncertainty involved, and leaders will aim for a coalition
size that somewhat exceeds their optimal desired level.

Change in Activated Attributes and Categories

At the beginning of each run, agents are "seeded" with an activated attribute for
each dimension in their identity repertoire. This activated attribute is subject to
change at every time step or turn—of which there are 1,500 in each run of an
experiment—through contacts with agents whose identities differ. Based on the
attributes they activate, they will end up subscribing to different coalition specifications. Thus the set and size of the activated categories in the population—
the activated ethnic demography—changes also with each time step.

The identity evolution process is based on that developed in Ian Lustick's
Agent-Based Identity Repertoire (ABIR) model (Lustick 2000; Lustick et al.
2004). Every turn, each agent looks around at its social contacts and decides
whether or not to change its identity. In addition, the agent takes into account
the identity repertoire of the political leader for whom it voted during the last
electoral round, as well as the particular attributes represented in the categories
put forward by political leaders (with a bias toward the category specified by the
winning leader, if there is one), plus an additional system-wide stochastic bias
which reflects unpredictable (or unmodeled) aspects of the polity that affect the
attractiveness of different attributes.

During this "survey" of its environment in each turn, each agent calculates
the weight of all different dimensions and of the attributes on each dimension
based on her social contacts, and determines whether or not one or more of the
relevant thresholds are met. The calculation of this dimension-weight and attribute-weight is somewhat complex, since it involves multiple components. Agents
poll each of their social contacts (including themselves, since they're self-aware)
to get information about the dimensions in the repertoires of those contacts and
the attributes within those dimensions. The dimensions are weighted by their
salience in a particular contact's repertoire. Moreover each contact's contribution is multiplied by her influence level. Agents of different types may have different influence levels, as specified in their type's *Influence* parameter. Typically,
basic agents have an influence of 1 and leaders have an influence of 2. All these
weights are added to arrive at a total weight for each dimension. Agents will
compare the weight of the most salient dimension (or dimensions) to the relevant thresholds to see whether to make a change in the dimensions constituting
their repertoire and their rankings.

In deciding how to update, agents use a process of reasoning similar to that used by the leaders. They too have limited information about the distribution of attributes in the population: They know that the size of each attribute's subpopulation is public information (i.e., known to leaders as well as other agents), but intersections across dimensions are not known. Once each leader has decided its specification, each agent sorts all specifications in declining order of attractiveness. Specifically, agents look for leaders whose conditions they meet and whose expected coalition size safely exceeds the minimum winning coalition by the smallest possible margin. In addition, however, agents are somewhat loyal to the leader whose coalition they joined last round, which introduces a certain threshold to be met before they will switch allegiances, as described in more detail in the appendix to this chapter.

When updating their repertoires, agents can do four things. First, they can add a new dimension to their repertoire, replacing one that was already in the repertoire. Adding a dimension represents a decision that a particular dimension (religion, caste, etc.) is politically relevant. Second, agents can take a dimension already in the repertoire and raise its salience. Third, agents can decide that a new dimension is sufficiently important to warrant not just inclusion but also immediate promotion to a salient rank. Fourth, and finally, an agent can decide to change its attribute within a given dimension. Different types of agents have specific thresholds for each of these actions, as described in the appendix to this chapter.

In the time between electoral rounds, agents (as well as leaders) continue to update their identity repertoires along the lines described above, with the goal of improving their chances to lead or be a member of a winning coalition. As a result, the distribution of attributes across the population can change (sometimes substantially) from one round to the next, and even winning leaders may want to update the categories they specify from time to time, for example, to fend off an oversized coalition if too many agents acquire the relevant attributes to join that leader's coalition.

Choosing a Leader

The final feature of the model to discuss is the process by which agents choose among the coalition specifications put forth by the different leaders in the model in an "election." An election takes place after twenty-five time steps. Since there are 1,500 time steps in each run of an experimental condition, this means that there are sixty elections in each run.

At each electoral round, once each leader has decided her specification, the leaders are sorted in declining order of appeal to agents. Agents look for leaders whose expected coalition size (i.e., taking into account the yield the leader expects) exceeds the OWC. However, they have a certain degree of loyalty to the leader whose coalition they joined last round. First, if their leader's last round ended up with a winning coalition, and they still match her specification, they will continue to ally themselves with this leader. If they no longer match their previous leader's specification, they will simply go with the most appealing leader whose specification they *do* match. If they still match their old leader's specification but they also match the specification of a more appealing leader, they will only go with the latter if her expected coalition size exceeds the optimal coalition size and that of their old leader does not, or if neither or both of the specifications can attract a winning coalition, and the candidate leader's expected coalition size is closer to the OWC level by more than the share of the population specified by the parameter *Agent Loyalty*.

4. Experimental Results

In this section, to illustrate the workings of our model, we present the results of two sets of experiments. The first explores the relationship between *ethnic attachments* (i.e., the stickiness of the dimensions) in a polity and the stability of political leadership under different electoral rules. The second examines rates of assimilation (i.e., the concentration of identities in a set of attributes on a dimension), again with varying electoral rules and levels of ethnic salience. These experiments are intended to be indicative of the type made possible by our model and to stimulate the development of new hypotheses and insights about processes of ethnic demography change. Before we consider our findings definitive it would, of course, be necessary to investigate their robustness rather more thoroughly (cf. Bryson, Ando, and Lehmann 2007; Galán et al. 2009; Wilensky and Rand 2007).

All experiments were run on a square 100 x 100 torus (a grid wrapping around both horizontally and vertically, so there are no edges and each agent has eight Moore neighbors), with 10,000 agents. As noted above, there were eight dimensions in the system, each with five possible attribute-values. Each agent had attributes in its repertoire for five of the eight dimensions. The distribution of identities and attributes in agent repertoires was randomized at the start, with all dimensions equally represented, and with an initial distribution of attributes within each dimension of 40%, 20%, 10%, 20%, and 10% (this was to provide a certain amount of attribute concentration even at the start).

There are five leaders in the polity. Simulation experiments were run for 1,500 time steps, with a vote taking place every twenty-five rounds, giving a total of sixty "elections" in each run. Depending on the electoral rule—here the target vote share (measured as the value of the OWC)—it is not always possible for leaders to achieve a winning coalition in round 1 (except, of course, in a plurality system). However, as agents change their attributes under the influence of information from their neighbors as well as from leaders, eventually certain attributes will be present in sufficiently large subpopulations to allow leaders to put together a winning coalition. Since the initial rounds are thus occupied by somewhat transitory processes of identity consolidation, we present results below starting from time step 501 (i.e., after the first twenty electoral rounds).[9]

Experiment 1: Political Stability in Different Contexts (Varying Stickiness and OWC)

Chapters 5 and 6 by Chandra and Boulet assumed that political entrepreneurs and even voters in patronage-democracies would prefer a political arena in which allegiance is determined on the basis of ethnic attributes, apparently because these are stickier and hence make it easier to contain the size of a winning coalition. The implicit assumption here is that this would make it easier for leaders to hold on to power, and thus make political outcomes more stable. Others have argued, following this logic to its extreme, that pressure from excluded groups might lead to systemic destabilization: medium-term stability leads to long-term instability (Horowitz 1985). However, despite some intuitive appeal, it is not clear that the logic is valid. In our first experiment, we examine how ethnic politics (proxied by stickiness) affects the stability of political outcomes.

We interacted six different OWC values and four different levels of stickiness, for a total of twenty-four different experimental conditions. The OWC values we used were 0.3, 0.4, 0.5, 0.6, and 0.7, as well as a value indicating that leaders simply try to have a plurality of the votes. For stickiness levels we used values of 0, 10, 50, and 100. In the first two cases, stickiness is well below the length of an electoral round, so agents living in proximity to other agents who have a particular attribute can easily acquire that attribute from one electoral round to the next. In other words, the political demography is not ethnic. In the latter two cases, the demography more closely resembles one where ethnicity matters politically, as it takes agents two to four electoral cycles at minimum to acquire a desired attribute.

For each condition, we performed fifty runs. The dependent variable of interest was the number of electoral rounds a particular leader continued to obtain her desired vote share. Figure 7.3 illustrates our central findings. We averaged tenure levels for the two low stickiness conditions and for the two high stickiness conditions. The vertical axis shows the average number of electoral rounds a leader remained victorious under the different conditions. In situations where more than one leader obtained the OWC, we looked only at the top vote-getter. This explains the anomalous height of the low-stickiness bar at OWC 0.3: Multiple winners were far more prevalent in low-stickiness conditions than in

---

[9] It is worth noting, however, that the substantive findings do not change if we calculate results starting at time step 1.

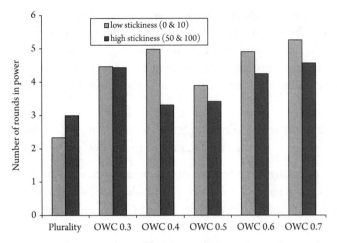

Figure 7.3 Optimal Coalition Size and Leadership Tenure

high-stickiness conditions (they were six times as common when stickiness was 0 as when stickiness was 100). We underestimate these leaders' tenure by considering them no longer "victorious," even when they still obtain their OWC, as soon as another leader obtains more votes.[10]

The left-most pair of bars shows the results for a plurality system, where the leader with the largest number of votes wins. Here the pattern is as that suggested by the logic discussed above: The stickier the politically salient dimensions, the longer the tenure of the political leader. Note, however, that this pattern disappears as soon as we introduce a specific desired vote level, whether it is high or low. In fact, in all of these cases, stickier demographies are associated with *shorter* tenure in office.

The most plausible explanation for this unexpected finding, we believe, is that there are offsetting patterns at work here. It is true, of course, that higher stickiness makes it more difficult to join winning coalitions for those outside them. This, in turn, makes it easier for leaders to fashion durably successful coalitions, which likely explains our findings for a plurality system. However, when the OWC is at a fixed level—and leaders will thus try to avoid ballooning constituencies—difficulties in flexibly adjusting to a changing underlying demography (due to investment in winning attributes) may trip leaders up. In more fluid demographies, for

[10] It would be of interest to examine leadership victory patterns more thoroughly; for example, is one leader dominant throughout a run, failing to "win" only for brief periods at a time, or do we see a regular alternation among all leaders? Investigating such a question would require extensive additional simulation runs: As noted earlier, the results presented here are intended simply to illustrate the promise of our approach. Indeed, one of the strengths of our model is not only that it makes the investigation of such new questions possible but, perhaps more important, that it may point us to heretofore undertheorized implications of models of ethnic demography found in the literature.

example, leaders are likely to fine-tune their offerings through the use of ever-changing complex categories (e.g., left-wing and pro-environment) and thereby retain their winning coalitions without their ballooning. In stickier demographies, this is less likely to be a successful strategy, perhaps because entrepreneurs cannot qualify themselves through the rapid acquisition of the attribute on another dimension that would make for an optimum offering.

A second observation from this experiment is that the trend in leadership tenure is U-shaped as we move from low to high levels of OWC. The lowest (i.e., least stable) point occurs at a lower level of OWC for ethnic (i.e., sticky) demographies than for more flexible demographies, but the basic trend is clear. As one moves away from simple absolute majority (or a value somewhat below it) in either direction, the average tenure of leaders increases, regardless of whether or not the political demography is ethnically based.

One likely explanation for this result is that there are two effects at work. As OWC declines below 0.5, it becomes increasingly possible to have multiple winning leaders. This means, in turn, that leaders are less likely to attempt to poach one another's constituents and, conversely, that there is often not much incentive for voters to jump ship, given that they have a certain amount of loyalty to their existing leader. As a real-world example, if a party such as the Greens in a proportional representation system needs only 5% of the vote to have seats in a parliament, people who vote Green are not likely to change their vote as long as the threshold was met in the previous election. As OWC rises above 0.5, it becomes increasingly difficult for leaders, regardless of the stickiness of the underlying political demography, to put together credible alternative coalitions that might displace the currently victorious one. The implication here is that once a supermajority is reached, it is more difficult to unravel. McGann (2004) makes a similar argument about the stability of supermajorities using game-theoretic analysis.

Experiment 2: OWC Levels and the Evolution of Political Demography

Our second experiment used the same set of experimental conditions and runs to investigate a different variable, which more explicitly highlights the importance of political institutions for the evolution of political demographies. The dependent variable here was the average degree of concentration within a given dimension of population attributes at the end of a run. We wanted to see how far populations had evolved from their initial distribution across attributes of 40%, 20%, 10%, 20%, and 10%. A standard measure of concentration is the Herfindahl index, which is the sum of the squares of the population shares. Initial Herfindahl index levels were thus $0.4^2 + 0.2^2 + 0.1^2 + 0.2^2 + 0.1^2 = 0.26$. A completely even distribution across the five possible attribute-values would give a Herfindahl index of 0.2.

Given the incentive structures of our agents and leaders to build winning coalitions, we expect the concentration to increase over time in every experimental setup. Indeed, in many runs, certain attribute-values disappear from the population entirely by the end of the run. Similarly, in the real world, languages and religions die.[11] It stands to reason that it is easier for particular attributes to disappear the less sticky they are. Hence we would expect concentration to be higher in low-stickiness demographies than in high-stickiness (ethnic) demographies. Figure 7.4 shows that this expectation is borne out in the experiment, as the highest line is that for the lowest stickiness, and every increase in stickiness leads to a lower line.

However, Figure 7.4 also allows us to answer a much more interesting question: What is the impact of different OWC levels on the degree to which this type of concentration takes place? Here the result is much less intuitive. As the figure shows, for non-ethnic demographies, concentration is reduced as OWC levels rise. For ethnic demographies, however, concentration rises along with OWC levels. What explains this pattern? In demographies with non-sticky identities, increasing the desired vote share level encourages leaders to broaden their coalitions, so that they accept multiple attribute-values on a particular dimension. This reduces the number of agents who have an incentive to try to acquire a different attribute on a given dimension.

This same process takes place in ethnically based demographies, of course. However, a countervailing process is stronger here. As OWC levels rise, the number of possible coalition specifications that would secure the desired vote level for a leader falls. This means that more leaders will be forced to provide very similar specifications, which in turn increases the incentives for agents to acquire a few specific attributes. In less ethnically organized polities, agents can react faster to different proposed specifications, and it is thus more plausible for leaders to propose new coalitions based on different dimensions or attribute combinations. This experiment thus suggests that in regard to the homogenizing effects of strategic attribute acquisition, ethnic-like coalitions may well respond differently from non-ethnic-like coalitions as electoral rules change.

5. Conclusion

This chapter and its appendix serve as both a complement to and a supplement for the mathematical models presented by Chandra and Boulet. The ease with which the components of Chandra and Boulet's formulations can be translated into an agent-based model illustrates the promise of agent-based modeling for investigating the types of issues highlighted in the first part of this volume. In addition, our agent-based model makes it possible to vary certain parameters

[11] For examples on language, see Dorian 1989.

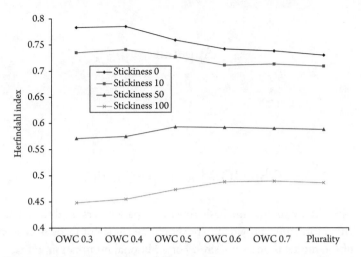

Figure 7.4 Optimal Coalition Size and Demography

held constant in Chandra and Boulet's theoretical discussion—but not in the real world—allowing us to investigate some questions that are difficult, if not impossible, to address in the Chandra-Boulet formulation.

The theoretical motivation for using agent-based models in this context is our recognition of the complexity of the phenomenon under study. While formal modeling may be superior for understanding attribute acquisition, or changes in dimensional salience, or in the recombination of attributes to form ethnic categories along any dimension, it is not a useful tool at present for analyzing the mutual interdependence of these processes in a single super-game (cf. Lehtinen and Kuorikoski, 2007).

The empirical motivation lies in the suggestiveness of the experimental findings presented in the last part of the chapter, as well as those we present in Chapter 9, where we focus attention on a more realistic "world" where different dimensions have different levels of stickiness. As noted above, our findings, as well as the explanations we offer for the patterns that emerge, are intended to be suggestive rather than definitive. In order to be confident both of the patterns we found and of our proffered explanations, additional robustness checks are essential. Nevertheless, we believe these findings convincingly demonstrate the promise of an agent-based modeling tool in helping us refine our theories and generate new and interesting hypotheses to test in the area of ethnic demography.[12]

---

[12] It is testimony to the power of agent-based models to inspire such new theorizing that more than once, upon presenting our model, even respondents critical of the inevitable complexity of our model were sufficiently intrigued by our findings to suggest new model parameters that might be introduced in order to investigate additional questions (while, of course, increasing the model's complexity further).

Appendix

EthnicID Model Specification

In this appendix we discuss the basic functional parameters used to construct the model. The information provided here should be sufficient to recreate a working version of the model if one so desires. For additional information, please contact the first author. A list of the default parameter values follows at the end of the appendix.

System Topology

The "world" in the ethnicID model is a society of "agents" populating a 100 × 100-square grid. The grid format is determined by three system parameters. *GridSize* specifies the length of each side; *WrapHorizontal* and *WrapVertical* specify whether or not the grid wraps around from left to right and from top to bottom, respectively. The grid represents social connections among agents, not geographical ones. The grid-based organization underscores the fact that for most people in a society, most connections are local. The social connections of each agent are set at the start of each run and remain fixed for the duration of the run.

The default format for social connections is for each agent to be in touch with all eight of her immediate neighbors, the so-called Moore neighborhood. In addition, the agent will be self-aware (i.e., she will also take into account her own status when determining her choices). Several additional parameters introduce the possibility of modifying slightly this purely local way of setting up a model society. As we know empirically, although most social connections are local—that is, most of our social "neighbors" will be "neighbors" of each other—in real life most people have social connections across society that are not shared with their neighbors. Consequently, future models could introduce non-local interactions among agents that would reduce the average cultural distance between randomly paired agents within the grid. This insight lies behind the well-known concept of "six degrees of separation."

Mathematically, the commonly accepted way to recreate this feature, also known as the "small world effect" (Watts 1999), is randomly to replace a small fraction of local connections by connections to random agents anywhere in the society. In our model world, two variables govern this process. *SmallWorld* turns it on and *SWreconnectProb* determines the probability by which any given connection to a neighbor is replaced by a connection to a random (possibly far-flung) other agent.[13]

The Attribute Repertoire

The key feature of each agent in our world is her repertoire of "identity components." An identity component is a particular attribute on a particular dimension. Each agent has a fixed-length repertoire of identity components, specified by the *RepertoireSize* parameter for her agent type (*BasicRepertoireSize* for default agents). The number of possible dimensions in the world is specified by the parameter *IDSpectrumSize*, and the number of possible attributes on each dimension is set by *NrAttrs*.

At the start of each run, agents are randomly assigned dimensions up to *RepertoireSize*. On each dimension, they are randomly assigned attributes, with the proviso that the distribution of attributes need not be even. Instead, it is governed by the parameter *Attr1Fraction*. This is the probability that an agent will be assigned the first attribute. In order to get an equal distribution of attributes, *Attr1Fraction* can be set at $1/NrAttrs$. Attribute distributions across dimensions are independent.[14]

Within the repertoire, the different dimensions are ranked. In order to operationalize the value of a particular rank, a salience function is associated with the rankings. This function is hard-coded (and thus changeable only by the programmer) and is currently set to be $1/(1+e^{8x})$. The specific calculation used is to distribute *RepertoireSize* points within the interval $-0.5 \ldots 0.5$, and then applying the function to the resulting values. Thus, for a repertoire size of 3, we would use the values -0.25, 0, 0.25, resulting in salience levels 0.881, 0.5, and 0.119. This function was selected in order to produce a distribution of high-salience and low-salience identity components that seemed intuitively plausible.

---

[13] Note that connections in our model transmit information only and are one-way. In other words, our network graph is directed, so when an agent has her connection to a neighbor replaced by one to a random other agent, that neighbor may retain a connection to our agent.

[14] A special parameter value of -1 for *Attr1Fraction* can be used only if there are five possible attribute values. It results in an initial distribution across attributes of 40%, 20%, 10%, 20%, and 10%, and it has the effect of making larger coalitions possible from the start. This is the setting used in the experiments described in this volume.

Identities change over time through contacts with agents whose identities differ. The identity evolution process is based on that in Lustick's Agent-Based Identity Repertoire (ABIR) model (Lustick 2000). Every turn, each agent looks around at her social contacts and decides whether or not to change her activated attribute. The order in which agents do so is determined by the value of three parameters. For each type of agent, there is a parameter *GoFirst* that specifies whether that agent type is among those who update in a first wave. Leaders have their *GoFirst* parameter set to true; for basic agents it is false.

Within a wave, *AsynchUpdate* determines whether updating takes place asynchronously. If so, agents will observe the new identities of those of their contacts who have already updated in the present round. This makes it possible in theory (albeit highly unlikely) for a particular change to propagate all the way across the society in a single turn. With *AsynchUpdate* set to false, updating happens as though all agents do so at once (i.e., synchronously). This means that every agent bases her decisions on her contacts' repertoires at the end of the preceding turn. Synchronous updating has received a bad reputation in the agent-based modeling literature for generating outcomes that are artifacts of the synchronicity. Although this reputation is somewhat undeserved, we prefer to keep *AsynchUpdate* true. When updating takes place asynchronously, it obviously matters in which order agents update. It would probably not be a good idea to let this order remain the same from one turn to the next, let alone to allow this order to be from the top left agent systematically down to the bottom right (which *would* allow information to spread all the way across the population in one turn). Parameter *RandomUpdateOrder*, when true (the default value), specifies that the order is to be random and changed from one time step to the next.

The Evolution of Attribute Repertoires

When updating their repertoires, agents can do four things. First, they can add a new dimension to their repertoire, replacing one that was already there. Adding a dimension represents a decision that a particular dimension (religion, caste, etc.) is politically relevant. Typically (exceptions being made only for repertoire sizes smaller than three), dimensions are added one rung above the bottom ranking, moving the previous penultimate down to the bottom rank, and dropping the previous bottom-ranked dimension. Second, agents can take a dimension already in the repertoire and upgrade its salience ranking. Third, agents can decide that a new dimension is sufficiently important to warrant not just inclusion but also immediate promotion to a salient rank. In this case, the new dimension is typically (again with exceptions for small repertoires) inserted one rung below the top ranking, with all others shifting down, and the bottom one once again dropped. Fourth, and finally, an agent can decide to change her attribute within a given dimension. Every type of agent has a specific threshold for each of these actions: *TAdd*, *TRaise*, *TAddRaise*, and *TAttr* (the *T* stands for "threshold").

At each turn (the model runs for *MaxRounds* turns), each agent calculates the weight of all different dimensions and attributes on each dimension among her social contacts and determines whether or not one or more of the relevant thresholds are met. The calculation of this dimension-weight and attribute-weight is somewhat complex, since it involves multiple components. Agents poll each of their social contacts (including themselves) to get information about the dimensions in the repertoires of those contacts, and the attribute values within those dimensions. The dimensions are weighted by their salience in a particular contact's repertoire. Moreover each contact's contribution is multiplied by her influence level. Agents of different types may have different influence levels, as specified in their type's *Influence* parameter. Typically, basic agents have an influence of 1 and leaders have an influence of 2. All these weights are added to arrive at a total weight for each dimension. Agents will compare the weight of the most salient dimension (or dimensions) to the relevant thresholds to see whether to make a change in the dimensions constituting their repertoire and their rankings.

The weight of each dimension as calculated from an agent's social contacts is supplemented from three additional sources. First, agents count the leader to whose coalition they belong (if any) as one of their social contacts, so this leader's repertoire is added into the mix. Second, a set of system-wide biases keeps track of the dimensions and attributes currently used by any leaders in the system to compose coalitions. Any dimension or attribute thus in use receives a positive bias, to reflect its society-wide political value. Moreover, the dimensions and attributes in use by a leader who has managed to put together a winning coalition receive a slightly larger bias than those used by the less successful leaders. The size of this bias is set with the parameters *WinningLIDbias* (winning leader's ID (dimension) bias), *NonWinningLIDbias*, *WinningLAttrBias* (for attributes), and *NonWinningLAttrBias*.

Finally, in order to reflect (or attempt to proxy for) unpredictable changes in the political value of particular dimensions and attributes within a society, we include a set of stochastic biases. Biases for the dimensions are chosen from a uniform random distribution between the parameters *MinIDBias* and *MaxIDbias*. Each turn, the probability of any given bias changing is given by the parameter *P_updateIDbias*. Corresponding values for the attributes are *MinAttrBias*, *MaxAttrBias*, and *P_updateAttrBias*. An additional parameter for each set of biases determines whether or not the biases must be integer-valued, or are also allowed to take on fractional values. To get integer-valued biases, *IntIDbias* and *IntAttrBias* must be set to true.

All these different components are summed to determine whether an agent should change her attribute repertoire. Table 7.A1 shows a brief example for a world with five dimensions (with three possible attribute values each) and a repertoire size of 3, where an agent has four social contacts and, as well, belongs to a leader's coalition. Note that the leader's contributions weigh twice as heavily as those of all the other agents. If one of the contacts (or the agent itself) were to be a leader too, her contributions would also be weighted twice as heavily.

The agent's actions depend on the values of her thresholds. The agent will look at the dimensions in order of their descending weight and see whether any of the dimensions meet any of the thresholds, with the limitation that no more than one addition and one ranking upgrade is performed in a given turn. (If the add-raise threshold is met, both actions will be performed on the same dimension.) Let us say the raise threshold is 3, the add threshold 4, and the add-raise threshold 5. Note that no dimension meets the add-raise threshold. One dimension, 3, does meet the add threshold. This dimension is then added, the second-lowest dimension, 2, is dropped to lowest, and the lowest-ranking dimension, 4, is dropped. Note that this dimension would have met the ranking-upgrade threshold, but by the time it is up for consideration, it is no longer in the repertoire, and it does not meet the threshold for being added back in.

When a new dimension is added to the repertoire, agents also need to include an attribute on this dimension. They choose new attribute X with a probability proportional to that attribute's relative weight in the attribute-summing exercise that parallels the dimension summing exercise just discussed. The attribute-summing exercise is very similar to that for dimensions, except that here the ranking of a dimension within a contact's repertoire plays no role (a contact's influence still does, however). Table 7.A2 gives the calculation of attribute-weights for dimension 3 in Table 7.A1. (Note that the agent itself, contact 1, and the leader do not contribute since they did not have dimension 3 in their repertoires.) The sum of all attribute-weights within this dimension is 5. This means that our agent will choose attribute 0 with a probability $1.3/5 =$ 26%, attribute 1 with a probability $1.1/5 =$ 22% and attribute 2 with a probability $2.6/5 =$ 52%.

Table 7.A1. **Example of Dimensional Weighting Calculation**

Dim.	Self	Contact 1	Contact 2	Contact 3	Contact 4	Leader	Leader Biases	Stochastic Biases	Sum
0	0.881			0.119			0	−1	0
1		0.119			0.119	1.762	0.5	0	2.5
2	0.5	0.5	0.119		0.5	1	0	−1	1.619
3			0.5	0.881	0.881		1	1	4.262
4	0.119	0.881	0.881	0.5		0.238	0	1	3.619

Table 7.A2. **Example of Attribute Weighting Calculation for a Given Dimension**

Attr.	Self	Contact 1	Contact 2	Contact 3	Contact 4	Leader	Leader Biases	Stochastic Biases	Sum
0					1			0.3	1.3
1		1						0.1	1.1
2				1			1	0.6	2.6

It is important to realize that adding a dimension (and, conversely, dropping one) does not indicate that the agent loses this attribute—dropping the hair color dimension does not represent baldness (or albinism). Instead, it represents a decision by an agent that that dimension is not *politically* relevant (or salient). This helps explain the procedure followed for adding a new dimension. The idea is that if we know nothing about an agent's attribute on a dimension, we can get a reasonable guess by looking at her social contacts.[15]

These same attribute sums are examined for the dimensions an agent already had in her repertoire, when deciding whether an agent ought to change her attribute on a particular dimension. Rather than consider an attribute's weight in isolation, an agent will consider its weight in comparison to the weight of her own attribute. If the weight of the most-favored attribute exceeds that of the agent's own attribute by more than the attribute-threshold, the agent will shift her own attribute choice to that most-favored value.

One crucial complication affects this process. Dimensions can be more or less sticky, which affects the ease with which agents can change their attribute on a particular dimension. Dimension stickiness is set by the parameters *DimXstickiness* (where X is the dimension's identifying number).[16] The value specified for the stickiness parameter determines how many turns in a row an agent must want to change her own attribute to a specific other attribute before being allowed to do so. If the value is 0, attribute changes take place as just described. If not, the agent will record that she wanted to change to attribute value Y, and she will mark that she has tried to do so once. The next turn, if attribute Y is the most-favored attribute again, and again passes the threshold test, the agent will see if the dimension's stickiness is just 1. If so, she now changes. If not, she increases the marker to 2. This continues until the stickiness value is met. If at any time the most-favored (and threshold-meeting) attribute is not Y, or Y fails to meet the threshold, the record of attempted changes is reset to 0. Thus if we want an agent's attribute on a

---

[15] If this idea is judged problematic, it is always possible to set agent repertoire sizes to equal the number of dimensions in the model, so that no dimensions will be added or dropped at all.

[16] Note that the stickiness of a dimension refers to the difficulty of changing *attributes* on that dimension, not the difficulty of adding or dropping the dimension as part of the repertoire.

dimension to be unchangeable, we can simply set the stickiness to a value greater than the number of turns, or time steps, for which the model will be run.

This covers the repertoire updating process but for one small caveat. In order to prevent agents from getting stuck with repertoires that turn out to be politically unappealing, they will from time to time drop the least salient dimension in their repertoire and replace it by a random dimension not yet in the repertoire. This new dimension is added in the same way as are new dimensions meeting the add threshold: one rung above the lowest salience (with exceptions for small repertoire sizes), with the previous dimension at that location being pushed down to the bottom rung. The parameter that specifies the chance of an agent taking this course of action is *ReplaceProbability*.

Leaders and Their Coalition Specifications

The default agent type is the basic agent. In our experiments, only one other type of agent exists: leaders.[17] Their number is specified by the *LeaderFraction* parameter. In a population of 10,000 agents, a value for this parameter of 0.0005 produces the five-leader setup used in our experiments. The social location of leaders within the grid is randomly determined at the time a run is initialized. As noted above, leaders update before basic agents do. Their influence is twice that of basic agents, and their updating thresholds are a little higher too.[18]

Leaders, taking into account their own repertoire, some information about the population, and their own performance in previous rounds, put forward a specification every round, aiming to attract a sufficient share of the vote to constitute a "winning" coalition of agents. A round lasts a certain number of turns, as specified by the parameter *VoteInterval*. On the time steps between rounds, the repertoires of all agents (including leaders) may change quite a bit, so that leaders may want to update their specification even if they attracted a winning coalition in the previous round.

The desired vote share is specified with the parameter OWC (optimal winning coalition). If this parameter is larger than 0, it is taken to represent the fraction of the population leaders will shoot for. Thus, a value of 0.5 means that half of the population must side with a leader for her to be considered a victor.

---

[17] The model has the capacity to include additional types of agents, such as influential agents that are not political leaders but do have a stronger impact on their neighbors than do basic agents. Another possible agent type would be a kind of broadcaster, or media outlet, which would communicate information to many agents but take inputs from just a few. This would serve further to shrink the social distance across the polity.

[18] Since they are considered public figures, their behavior will be more closely monitored, and therefore it ought to be less easy for them to change their activated attributes and repertoires than it is for other agents.

If the parameter equals 0, however, the system is taken to be one where the largest coalition wins, regardless of its size (i.e., a system of plurality). When formulating a coalition specification, leaders cannot be sure that they will attract every agent who might satisfy their specification. They take this into account by guessing their likely "yield" based on information about previous rounds and the specifications put forward by other leaders.

A leader's specification takes the form of a set of attributes within each dimension that satisfy the leader's conditions. For example, on a religion dimension, a leader might indicate that she will accept Catholics as well as Anglicans. The maximum share of the possible attributes on a dimension a leader is allowed to claim is specified by the parameter *MaxAttrShare*. This is to prevent leaders from simply accepting anyone who has a particular dimension in their repertoire. In addition, the accepted attributes must be numerically contiguous. In other words, a proposed coalition cannot accept attribute values "1 or 3" but could accept "1 or 2." The contiguity criterion allows wraparound, so in a situation with four possible attributes (*NrAttrs* = 4), "3 or 0" would be acceptable. If a leader specifies attributes on multiple dimensions, agents must have at least one of the acceptable attributes on each dimension in their repertoire. In other words, whereas attributes are connected by a logical OR within a dimension, across dimensions they are connected by an AND. For example, a leader may say she accepts those who are Catholic *and* working-class but not that she accepts those who satisfy just one of those attributes (Catholic *or* working class).

The strategy by which leaders develop the coalition specification they offer for agents to select is fairly complex, although most of the components are relatively straightforward. The description below considers many more options than will usually be considered in practice. However, for the sake of completeness it is necessary to spell out exactly what leaders will do in each conceivable situation.

In order to make their choices, leaders must know something about the population they are facing. It is obviously not realistic for leaders to know how many agents meet any particular coalition specification (it would also be prohibitively expensive computationally to keep track of this kind of information). But some basic information about the population composition is usually common knowledge within a society. In our model, the size of each attribute's subpopulation is public information (i.e., known to leaders as well as other agents). Intersections across dimensions are not known, however. In other words, it may be known that 40% of the population is Catholic and 20% is working-class, but nobody knows the share of the population that is Catholic *and* working-class. Of course, leaders have to guess at such intersections. The way they do so is to assume independence across dimensions, so that in the foregoing example the "guess-timated" share of agents who are Catholic *and* working-class would be 40% x 20% = 8%. Note that the real value could be either well above or well below this estimate (in this example, anywhere between 0% and 20%).

There are two parameters that affect how leaders update their condition specification. *AlwaysMaximize* (set to true by default) determines whether a leader always tries to put forward a specification that could in theory be a winning specification. This may require multiple changes to the specification in a single round. When this parameter is set to false, leaders will tend to make just a single change to their specification to see how that turns out, even if they estimate that their coalition will fall short of a winning coalition. *LeaderMeetsAll* (also true by default) determines whether leaders must satisfy every dimension in their own specification. This parameter only enters into force when a leader's repertoire has changed over the course of a round so that she no longer meets her own specification. When leaders make deliberate changes to their specification, in contrast, they *must* always meet each dimension of their new requirements. Leaders are allowed to update their specification in descending order of their success in the previous round. In other words, the leader whose coalition was largest at the previous round goes first, then the leader with the next-largest coalition, and so on. Leaders will at all times attempt to avoid creating a situation where their specification matches that (or represents a superset) of a leader who has already updated the repertoire this round.

The first thing leaders do is check whether they still meet their own specification. If not, they correct that (assuming *LeaderMeetsAll* is true) before doing anything else. On each dimension on which a change needs to be made, the leader examines four possible options:

1. Include her own attribute among those accepted. This is possible only if the leader currently does not accept the maximum number of accepted attributes on a dimension (cf. *MaxAttrShare*) and if the leader's own attribute is contiguous with those already accepted.
2. Include her own attribute while dropping another attribute previously accepted. This is possible only when the attribute is contiguous with those already accepted.
3. Drop all attributes accepted on this dimension and replace them simply by her own attribute. This may be necessary if the latter is not contiguous with any of the attributes currently accepted.
4. Drop the dimension from the specification. This is necessary if the leader has dropped this dimension from her own attribute repertoire, but it is also an option if none of the other options is particularly appealing (because it is likely to exclude most of the leader's potential constituents) and the previous specification included multiple dimensions.

For each of these options, the leader guesstimates the size of the coalition to expect after the change is made, and the most appealing option is chosen.

Options are appealing if they produce a leader's guesstimated coalition size greater than, yet as close as possible to, the OWC size, given expectations about the likely yield.

Once these changes have been made, leaders evaluate whether they need to consider making any additional changes to their specification. If their guesstimated coalition size now exceeds the target coalition size, they will not make further changes if *AlwaysMaximize* is false. If the latter is true, however, they will be thorough and check whether any additional changes might leave them potentially even better off. First, leaders examine whether their current guesstimated coalition size (i.e., given their current specification and their knowledge about the population's current distribution of repertoires) is too large or too small. If it exceeds the target, the leader will try to limit the potential size of her coalition; if not, she will try to increase it. Since repertoires change between rounds, and since agents that did not vote for the leader last round may do so this round (and *vice versa*), it makes sense to go with the current estimate of coalition size rather than the actual coalition the leader received last round. In a plurality-based system, the target coalition size is the coalition of the winning leader last time plus.

When leaders try to reduce the size of their coalition, they have two options. First, they may reduce the number of attributes accepted within each dimension in the specification. Second, they may add an additional dimension in which agents have to match an attribute. The options are considered in that order (i.e., first try to minimize what is accepted on a dimension before adding an additional dimension). To reduce the number of attributes accepted within a dimension, a leader runs down each dimension currently in the specification on which more than one attribute is accepted. On each dimension she sees whether she could drop an attribute other than the leader's own without creating a situation where the accepted attributes are noncontiguous. If so, she records the expected resulting coalition size. If an attribute could be dropped at either end, the one that results in the most appealing expected coalition size is marked. Once this calculation has been performed for every dimension in the specification, the leader will drop the attribute whose elimination will bring the leader closest to (yet still above) the target coalition size. When *AlwaysMaximize* is true, the process will be repeated as long as attributes can be dropped while keeping the expected coalition size over the target size.

The next option (much riskier, and therefore considered only second) is to add an additional dimension to the specification that agents will need to match as well. Here the leader will run down each dimension in the leader's repertoire that is not in the current coalition specification. For each such dimension, the leader calculates whether there is a combination of attributes including her own that, when added to the specification, would result in a better expected coalition size. The most promising dimension (and set of attributes) is then added to the specification. When *AlwaysMaximize* is true, this process may be repeated for additional dimensions, but in practice that is extremely unlikely to happen, as a guesstimated intersection across more than two dimensions will rarely exceed the target coalition size.

If a leader exhausts all these possibilities without having made any changes to her specification and with a coalition during the last round that fell short of the target coalition size, or with a specification that exactly matches that of a leader who changed her specification earlier, then more drastic measures will be necessary. At this point, the only acceptable option is to change the dimension (or dimensions) the leader has in her specification. Doing so is part of the procedure for trying to increase coalition size, which we discuss next.

Options to increase coalition size are essentially the mirror image of those described above. First, a leader will try to increase the number of attributes accepted on any given dimension. Next, a leader will consider reducing the number of dimensions on which any attributes are specified. To increase the number of attributes accepted on a given dimension, the leader runs down all dimensions in the specification. On each dimension, she evaluates whether she can add an attribute without running afoul of the *MaxAttrShare* limit. If so, she marks which attribute (on either end of the currently accepted set of attributes) brings the largest expected gain. If not, she evaluates whether adding an attribute at one end of the set while dropping one at the other end will increase the expected coalition size (as long as the one dropped is not the leader's own attribute, of course). Again, if there are two alternatives, she marks the most appealing one. After doing this for each dimension, the leader makes the most appealing possible change. When *AlwaysMaximize* is true, the process will be repeated until no further improvements are possible.

Next, leaders will see if dropping a dimension from their specification brings a potential improvement. If multiple dimensions are left, the leader will find which dimension to drop to obtain the most appealing coalition size (closest to the target size yet greater than it), and drop it. If *AlwaysMaximize* is true and the number of remaining dimensions exceeds one, this process is repeated. If only one dimension is left, this step is taken only if the leader has not yet been able to make changes to her specification, or if she has only been able to make a change that results in her specification matching that of a leader who updated earlier (this is also the situation discussed above when leaders fail to find ways to change their specification so as to reduce the expected coalition size).[19]

---

[19] Dropping the final dimension is equivalent to restarting from scratch. This is, therefore, also the procedure leaders will follow during the very first round, when they have no past specifications to fall back on, or any information about coalition sizes in previous rounds. (During the first round, the order in which leaders choose their specification is randomly determined.)

At this point, leaders will consider each dimension in their repertoires and see whether it is possible on any single dimension to present a specification with a chance of attracting a winning coalition yet which does not match exactly the specification of another leader. If so, the leader adds the dimension (and set of attributes within it) that results in the most appealing expected coalition size. If not, then leaders add the dimension that will give them the largest expected coalition size, even though they do not expect to win with it—they will try to improve upon this next round. If they fail to find any dimension on which they can stake out an offer that does not clash with that of another leader, they will accept such a clash, and simply add the dimension on which the subpopulation for their attribute is largest (and add *only* their attribute on this dimension—this truly is a fallback option) and expect to work from there next round.[20]

Choosing a Leader

The final feature of the model to discuss is the process by which agents choose among the coalition specifications put forth by the different leaders in the model. Fortunately, this process is rather more straightforward than the process by which leaders determine the specifications they offer. Once each leader has decided her specification, the leaders are sorted in declining order of appeal to agents. Agents look for leaders whose expected coalition size (i.e., taking into account the yield the leader expects) exceeds the OWC. However, they have a certain degree of loyalty to the leader whose coalition they joined last round. First, if their leader last round ended up with a winning coalition, and they still match her specification, they will continue to ally themselves with this leader. If they no longer match their previous leader's specification, they will simply go with the most appealing leader whose specification they *do* match. If they still match their old leader's specification but they also match the specification of a more appealing leader, they will only go with the latter if her expected coalition size exceeds the optimal coalition size and that of their old leader doesn't, or if neither or both of the specifications can attract a winning coalition, and the candidate leader's expected coalition size is closer to the OWC level by more than the share of the population specified by *AgentLoyalty*.

---

[20] Note that this kind of outcome becomes rapidly more likely if the number of leaders exceeds the number of dimensions in the model.

Default Parameter Values

Tables 7.A3 through 7.A6 show all the parameters and their default values, as used in the experiments discussed in Chapters 7 and 9.

Table 7.A3. **General System Parameters**

Parameter	Value	Parameter	Value
GridSize	100		
WrapHorizontal	True	WrapVertical	True
MaxRounds	1500		
VoteInterval	25		
AsynchUpdate	True	RandomUpdateOrder	True
IDSpectrumSize	8	NrAttrs	5
Attr1Fraction	−1		
OWC	0.5 (varied in this chapter)		
AgentLoyalty	0.05		
MaxAttrShare	0.6		
AlwaysMaximize	True	LeaderMeetsAll	True
SmallWorld	True	SwreconnectProb	0.002
ReplaceProbability	0.03		

Table 7.A4. **Bias Definition Parameters**

Parameter	Value	Parameter	Value
MinIDbias	−2	MinAttrBias	0
MaxIDbias	2	MaxAttrBias	1
P_updateIDbias	0.01	P_ updateAttrBias	0
IntIDbias	False	IntAttrBias	False
WinningLIDbias	1.5	WinningLAttrBias	1.5
NonWinningLIDbias	0.75	NonWinningLAttrBias	0.75

Table 7.A5. **Agent-Type Definition Parameters**

Agent-type ->	Basic	Leader
Fraction		0.0005
RepertoireSize	5	5
GoFirst	False	True
Influence	1	2
Traise	8	9
Tadd	8	9
TaddRaise	10	11
Tattr	2	2.25

Table 7.A6. **Dimension Stickiness Parameters**

Parameter	Value	Parameter	Value
Equalstickiness	True		
Dim0stickiness	0 (varied in this chapter)	Dim1stickiness	0
Dim2stickiness	10	Dim3stickiness	10
Dim4stickiness	25	Dim5stickiness	25
Dim6stickiness	50	Dim7stickiness	50

8

How Fluid Is Fluid?

The Mutability of Ethnic Identities and Electoral
Volatility in Africa

KAREN FERREE

1. Introduction

It has become commonplace in studies of ethnic politics to assert that ethnic identities are constructed, fluid, and responsive to political, social, and economic context. Few scholars today would contest this. Yet intriguing questions persist about the mutability of ethnic configurations. Just how fluid are ethnic identities? How quickly and easily can new ethnic groupings be constructed? Is the construction of new groups a process that spans generations and responds only to long-term trends and processes? Or do these creations emerge quickly, at the fingertips of politicians? Furthermore, are all ethnic coalitions equally possible and likely? Can new groups be assembled out of any social and cultural material lying around or are some combinations easier to stitch together than others?

These questions have great relevance to the study of elections. In countries where ethnic differences are highly salient (a large number of the new democracies in existence today), they likely affect the party system in numerous ways. Intuitively, the number of politically relevant ethnic groups probably shapes the nature of the electoral coalitions that form. Furthermore, the fluidity of ethnic groupings may also be important: Where ethnic groups are fluid, electoral coalitions are likely to be less stable. In contrast, fixed ethnic groups may constrain the number of coalitions that are possible.

Existing studies have explored some but not all of these issues. For example, work by Amorim-Neto and Cox (1997), Ordeshook and Shvetsova (1994), and others have looked at the impact of ethnic diversity on the effective number of parties in the party system. By and large, these studies have ignored constructivist intuitions, treating ethnic identities as fixed and frozen in time. In this chapter, I push beyond these studies in two ways. First, I focus on an alternative aspect of party systems—electoral volatility—that is less understood but at least as important as the effective number of parties. Specifically, I consider the hypothesis that ethnic structures that produce a single winning coalition are more likely to produce stable electoral outcomes than ethnic structures that produce multiple or zero winning coalitions. Second, I explore how different ways of operationalizing the possibility of ethnic identity change—from "primordialist" notions that ethnic identities are singular, fixed, and exogenous to "constructivist" notions that ethnic identities are multiple, fluid, and created through political processes—affect the relationship one observes between ethnic structure and volatility.

I explore these questions using data from recent African elections collected by Scarritt and Mozaffar (1999). Africa represents an excellent laboratory for exploring the impact of ethnic divisions on party systems. Over the past two decades, numerous African countries have begun experimenting with elections. Multiple election results are therefore available for a reasonably large set of countries. Furthermore, volatility rates have ranged widely over these elections, with some countries exhibiting very low volatility and others extremely high. Finally, there is general consensus among students of African elections that ethnic identities play a vibrant and significant role in most African elections—and that other factors like policy preferences figure less centrally. Such homogeneity and relative simplicity in the basis for social cleavages facilitate comparisons across cases. This chapter therefore focuses on Africa as its empirical terrain.

Elsewhere in this book, the term "ethnic group" is used interchangeably to refer to any identity category in which membership requires the possession of descent-based attributes. Here, I use it in a narrower sense. By "ethnic group" I mean those who share a basic attribute-value in a population. Consider the running example used in this book, with two dimensions based on skin color and place of origin and two values on each: Black and White on the dimension of skin color, and Foreign and Native on the dimension of place of origin (Table 8.1).

Table 8.1 **Population Repertoire of Attributes (2*2 case)**

	Black	**White**
Foreign	a	b
Native	c	d

In this chapter, I reserve the term "ethnic group" only for "Blacks," "Whites," "Foreigns" and "Natives." These are the "actual" ethnic groups in this society. They come "prefabricated" by institutional and historical processes already discussed in previous chapters. Any categories or groups constructed by combining these attribute-values at lower or higher levels of analysis (e.g., Black and Foreign) would be "potential" ethnic groups.

The results presented here suggest that ethnic structure *does* bear a systematic relationship to electoral volatility: Countries with a single winning coalition of ethnic groups tend to be less volatile than countries with multiple winning coalitions or none at all. However, this relationship is sensitive to how ethnic identity change is modeled. The model that best fits patterns of volatility in Africa is one that takes into account the multidimensional nature of African ethnic groups yet does not allow for the creation of new ones. Thus, in contrast to the baseline model introduced by Chandra and Boulet (Chapter 6, in this volume), I find that while individuals switch between existing groups on existing attribute-dimensions dimensions, they do not create new ones through recombination. This finding implies a more constrained version of constructivism—at least with regard to the short time frame relevant for electoral volatility.

The remainder of the chapter is structured as follows: first, I sketch the current state of the art on the role of ethnic divisions in elections; I then turn to the dependent variable, electoral volatility, and discuss existing explanations for it. Following this, I outline a basic hypothesis about the relationship between ethnic structure and electoral volatility and discuss how different conceptions of the fluidity of ethnic groups affect this hypothesis. Finally, I test these conjectures using data from recent African elections.

2. Ethnic Diversity and Party Systems

Numerous recent studies have fruitfully used the constructivist lens to explore the relationship between ethnic differences and election outcomes in particular countries, Chandra (2004), Posner (2004a, 2004b, 2005), and Wilkinson (2004) being but a few examples. These studies take it as an article of faith that ethnic identity is constructed, fluid, and multidimensional in nature. Indeed, constructivist approaches to ethnic identity have by and large become the norm in political science.

In contrast, cross-national studies of elections and ethnic diversity have generally treated ethnic identities as fixed and exogenous, thus conforming more with primordialist models than constructivist ones. Such studies have justified this assumption by arguing that, although ethnic identities may be fluid over the long run, from the short-term perspective of elections, they can be taken as given. Thus, classic pieces by Ordeshook and Shvetsova (1994), Amorim Neto and Cox (1997), and Cox (1997) use a *static* measure of ethnic identity to demonstrate that the effective number of parties in a country is a joint function of the permissiveness of electoral rules and the ethnic heterogeneity of the society. Restrictive systems (like those with single-member plurality rules) tend to produce only a small number of parties, even in ethnically diverse countries. In contrast, the number of parties in permissive systems (those with proportional representation and low thresholds) depends on the degree of diversity: Heterogeneous countries tend to support large numbers of parties, while homogeneous ones tend to produce relatively few.

Mozaffar, Scarritt, and Galaich (2003) provide a detailed look at these issues for African countries. They utilize a new measure that focuses on "politically relevant" ethnic identities (identities that have been politicized, though not necessarily particized) and captures the "nesting" nature of ethnic groups in Africa (i.e., the tendency of groups to fracture and subdivide into smaller groups). More so than earlier measures, this variable corresponds with constructivist intuitions because it acknowledges the multidimensional nature of ethnic identities and the potential for multiple groups to be salient at once. However, in using this measure, they simply collapse the nesting complexity into a single score. Thus, although they produce intriguing findings—controlling for geographic concentration and district size, ethnic fragmentation on its own *reduces* the number of parties in the party system, rather than increasing it—their operationalization of ethnic identities is as static as earlier ones.

There is thus a *disconnect* between theoretical and case-specific approaches to the role of ethnicity in elections and the treatment of ethnic identities in existing cross-national studies. While the first emphasizes the fluid and constructed nature of ethnic identities, the second assumes ethnic identities are fixed and exogenous to the political process. This is a potentially important contradiction: If you take constructivist theory seriously, there is no single "measure" of ethnic identity for a country but multiple, shifting ones. Which of these do you plug into an equation? How do you capture the fact that they are shifting? And more fundamentally, *does it matter* that they are shifting or is this change slow enough that static assumptions are justified (see also Fearon 2003, Posner 2004b, and Chandra, Chapter 4, in this volume)? These are important questions that have not been satisfactorily addressed by the existing literature. Below, I examine them by considering the relationship between ethnic structure and volatility. Before turning to specific hypotheses, however, it is useful to review existing work on electoral volatility.

3. Electoral Volatility

Volatility is typically measured using Pedersen's index of volatility, which is simply the net change in each party's seat or vote share from election to election. Pedersen's index is calculated by summing the total change in the percentage of seats or votes won or lost by all parties between two elections and dividing by two (Mainwaring and Scully 1995, 6). Intuitively, this measure captures the extent to which seats or votes change hands between elections.

Though less studied than the effective number of parties in the party system, volatility is arguably just as important. The negatives of high volatility are

well-known. Mainwaring and Scully (1995) include volatility as a key component of institutionalization and suggest that, when volatility is high, "democratic
politics is more erratic, establishing legitimacy is more difficult, and governing
more complicated" (22). Parties come and go at the whim of sudden and violent shifts in electoral coalitions. This increases the chances of populists coming
to power and generates uncertainty for voters. Parties in power, unclear if they
will be around tomorrow, have short time horizons and scant patience for policies that bear fruit over the long term.

On the flip side, as detailed by Giliomee and Simkins (1999), low volatility can
also be a problem, especially when it is symptomatic of permanent exclusion of one
portion of the electorate from power. Dominant parties can grow complacent and
less inclined to work hard to deliver positive outcomes. Patronage links and incumbency advantages can become ever more entrenched, multiplying the barriers for
the opposition. And those members of the polity whose experience of elections
involve unbroken strings of failure may become bitter and hardened against the
notion of democracy, viewing it as tyranny of a fixed majority, not a pluralistic wax-
ing and waning of shifting coalitions (see also Lijphart 1999 and other writings). In
short, too much electoral volatility can be a bad thing, but so can too little.

Electoral volatility varies both across regions and within regions over time. In
general, the newer democracies of the developing world have had higher levels of
volatility than the older democracies of Europe and North America. Mainwaring
and Scully (1995) show that legislative volatility in Latin America has been
much higher, on average, than volatility in Europe. Mean legislative volatility for
Latin America for the 1960–1989 period (for some countries, a smaller period)
was 24%. They compare this with Bartolini and Mair's (1990) data for Europe
(1885–1985), which shows that the highest single case for 303 election periods
was 32% in Weimar Germany and the highest mean over all election periods
was France, at 15%. Bielasiak (2002) shows that the new democracies in Eastern
Europe and Former Soviet Union (FSU) also have higher rates of legislative volatility than Western Europe: average volatility during the 1990s for East Central
Europe and Southeast Europe was around 20%, for the Baltic states, around
31%, and for FSU Europe, around 42%. Finally, Kuenzi and Lambright (2001)
show that average legislative volatility in Africa has been quite high, at 28%, with
several countries exceeding 50%.

While variation in volatility levels is well documented, explanations for these
patterns are underdeveloped. Many authors do not go much further than imply-
ing that volatility is simply a function of being a new democracy, one of the
growing pains of consolidation. Parties are weak and have only superficial ties to
populations, coordination problems are common because information regarding
the support levels of parties is lacking (few polls, no history to go on). Voters
meander between parties from election to election, searching for an electoral
coalition that will stick.

Although these broad explanations no doubt have some validity, they do not explain the large variations in volatility levels *among new democracies*. Indeed, although volatility is higher on average in new democracies, mean levels obscure tremendous variation. In Latin America, Mainwaring and Scully's data reveal countries like Peru (with a volatility of 54%) and Brazil (41%) but also countries like Colombia and Uruguay (both around 9%). Variation is also large in Bielasiak's post-communist states: In the Czech Republic, volatility is similar to the higher end of countries in Europe (Italy) at 13%, while in Russia it is around 47%.

Kuenzi and Lambright's African countries perhaps display the largest levels of variation. Figure 8.1 presents an updated version of the data published in their article and reveals that African countries range from the highly volatile (Madagascar, Niger, Benin, and Togo, all above 50%), to the reasonably stable (South Africa and Botswana, between 10 and 20%), to the stuck in the mud (Malawi and Mozambique, below 5%). The age of the democracy cannot account for these patterns (Africa's oldest and most stable democracies like Mauritius and Botswana are found at both the top and bottom ends of the graph). So what does?

In what is perhaps the most comprehensive analysis of volatility in new democracies to date, Roberts and Wibbels (1999) explore three basic hypotheses about volatility. First, as suggested by the economic voting literature, they posit that volatility is a function of economic crisis—because voters either desert incumbents who do not perform or flock to incumbents who do. Second, they contend that volatility should respond to institutional parameters: It should be

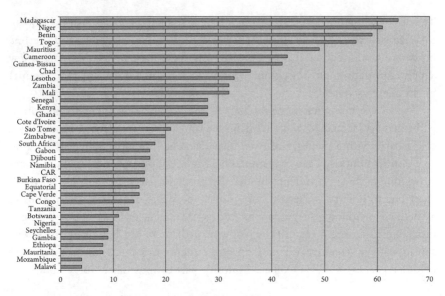

Figure 8.1 Average Legislative Seat Volatility in Africa
Based on Kuenzi and Lambright 2001, with some updates.

higher where constitutions have been rewritten, where new groups have recently been enfranchised, where there are many parties, where the party system is less institutionalized, and where there is ideological polarization. Finally, they look at the nature of cleavage structures, suggesting that volatility is highest where partisan competition is not structured by an organized class cleavage. Their results suggest support for all three hypotheses, especially those relating to economic performance and institutions. Building on Roberts and Wibbels (1999), Tavits (2005) explores how institutional and economic factors play out over time as party systems stabilize, and Mainwaring and Zoco (2007) confirm several findings for a large cross-national sample, particularly those related to economic performance and party number.

In the following analysis, I incorporate some of the variables suggested by Roberts and Wibbels (especially the institutional ones) to examine electoral volatility in Africa, but I focus primarily on a different type of variable all together: the number of winning coalitions embedded in a country's ethnic structure. This builds on their insight that cleavage structure should matter but focuses on ethnicity instead of class. While class is undoubtedly an important variable in the Latin American and European contexts, in other regions (Africa, South and Southeast Asia, parts of Oceania), ethnic divisions supersede it.[1]

4. Cleavage Structures and Electoral Volatility

Two prior literatures are relevant to understanding the relationship between cleavage structures and volatility: the literature on cabinet stability and the one on coordination failure. This section harvests these literatures to produce a few simple conjectures on how group structure (the set size of different groups) might relate to volatility.

One of the most persistent findings in the literature on cabinet duration in parliamentary democracies is that majoritarian governments (those formed by a single party with a majority of seats in parliament) are more stable than either coalition or minority party governments. The intuitions behind this finding are straightforward: Governments unified by a single party are less likely to fall apart due to internal bickering than governments that depend on the parties in a coalition continuing to get along. And governments that can count on party discipline to ensure a majority of votes in parliament are less likely to be dissolved via a no-confidence vote than governments that must court the support of other parties to stay in office. Minority parties must also worry about the

---

[1] The empirical work in the following section builds on the analysis of electoral volatility in Ferree 2010.

majority coming together in spite of its political differences to propose a new government.[2]

This suggests a societal analogy for electoral volatility: Societies characterized by a large group that constitutes a majority of the voting population on its own should produce less volatile party systems than societies that do not have such a group. The logic behind this hypothesis is simple: Parties that capture the support of a single majority group have little reason to court new support: They can rule on their own. Furthermore, voters supporting these parties have little reason to abandon ship for a party that is not likely to win. Thus, the constituency of these parties is likely to be quite stable. In contrast, parties supported by a single minority group have incentives to seek additional voters. This is true even if the minority is the largest group in the country: The party must always worry that the majority, even though divided into multiple groups and supporting multiple parties, will unite to deprive it of power. Indeed, this incentive for the majority to unite under the banner of a single party is a further source for electoral shifts. Consequently, volatility should be higher in these systems. Volatility should also be higher in situations where a party formed from a coalition of groups captures a majority: Groups may squabble over the distribution of benefits and consequently dissolve their partnership, causing support for the party to evaporate.[3] We might expect that systems without a majority group alternate between uneasy minorities winning a plurality and unstable electoral majorities composed of multiple groups. In general, such systems are likely to be volatile. Thus, a straightforward hypothesis about the sources of electoral volatility suggests that societies characterized by a large group that constitutes a winning coalition on its own should produce less volatile party systems than societies that do not have such a group.

Though intuitive, this logic needs to be augmented with an understanding of electoral coordination problems. Coordination failure occurs when voters with common interests split their support among two or more candidates or parties instead of concentrating them (Cox 1997). The logic of winning coalitions outlined above assumes that voters in the majority group will coordinate successfully, focusing all of their support on a single party. Should they prove unable to do this, however, their numerical dominance may fail to translate into electoral stability as voters swing from party to party between elections, trying to isolate a single point for coordination.

---

[2] For a basic review, see Lijphart 1999.

[3] This assumes that there is some magic to having a group with a name and some kind of story about itself that endows greater stability to an electoral coalition than simply a "marriage of convenience" between groups that have no name or story to back them. That is, if reds and blues can call themselves purples and can tell a story about why they are united as a group, this provides their electoral coalition with greater stability than if reds and blues simply agree to vote for the same party but have no story about how they together formed a group with some sort of social meaning.

When might large groups suffer from coordination problems? One can imagine at least two sources, one unrelated to group structure, the other contingent upon it. The first involves political squabbles among elites: Two identical parties emerge to represent the same group, and a war of attrition occurs before one is eliminated. Cox (1997) analyzes these sorts of coordination problems in depth. They are likely to occur frequently early on in the democratization process (Moser 1999, Zielinski 2002) and may occur episodically afterwards, but they are probably worked out over time as voters and parties gain information on which of the competitors is the better one, or at least the one most preferred by a majority of the group. In the long term, averaging over many elections, such failures probably produce "noise" but not systematic patterns.

A second source of coordination failure is more structural: If the large group divides into smaller groups, parties may arise to mobilize these smaller groups, and hence split the vote of the larger one. If none of these smaller groups can rule on its own, this kind of coordination failure is likely to be short-lived: Voters and elites should have a clear focal point for coordination (the larger group), assuming they care most about capturing a majority. But if one of these smaller groups *can* rule on its own (so there are *multiple* winning coalitions in the country), coordination failure may be more endemic. Essentially, the voters and elites of the smaller majority group face a dilemma: Vote with the larger group, capture a majority with a wider margin, or vote with the smaller group, face a close race, but share the spoils with fewer people. While some models of ethnic structure (Posner 2004a, 2005) assume that voters will opt for the smaller group to minimize sharing, this is not obvious. Studies of parliamentary cabinets, for example, have suggested that oversized cabinets arise precisely due to the need to include more parties than necessary (to have some insurance in case something goes wrong). It is likely that voters and elites vary in terms of their risk aversion, so some opt to choose the larger safer group, whereas others choose the smaller riskier one. If this occurs, coordination failure emerges. And it is likely to be a resilient form of coordination failure because the smaller group has a viable claim to being able to rule on its own. Essentially, this is a situation in which there are two reasonable focal points for coordination, and no clear way of distinguishing between them. As a result, coordination failure is both likely and difficult to resolve.

Altogether, the logic of coalition formation, combined with the logic of coordination failure, suggests the following three expectations: If there is a *single* winning coalition for the country (a group larger than 50% that cannot be subdivided into another group larger than 50%), we should expect to see stability. If there is *no* winning coalition for the country (no group exceeds 50%), then we should expect volatility. And if there are *multiple* winning coalitions (the group larger than 50% can be subdivided into at least one smaller group that is also larger than 50%), then we should also expect to see volatility.

A few caveats should be noted about this logic. First, it assumes a certain institutional structure: One that creates incentives for coalescence amongst political competitors (i.e., one that rewards parties that achieve majorities). Two types of institutions are likely to create these kinds of incentives: "strong" electoral institutions (small district size in particular) and presidentialism (especially when executive and legislative elections are concurrent).[4] If these institutions are absent, then the logic above may need to be modified because parties may no longer place as much value on achieving a majority. However, given that most democracies outside Western Europe (especially those in Latin America and Africa) use either strong electoral institutions or presidentialism or both, the conjectures outlined above are likely to hold in many cases.

A second caveat is that voting is based exclusively on group identity—whatever that may be. This does not imply that voters are strictly expressive. They might be voting on the basis of policy, where policy preferences are homogeneous within the group. Or they may be using group based cues to determine how best to vote in their interests (Ferree 2004, 2006). Regardless of the particular microlevel logic, the important point is that voters act on the basis of group identity alone—cross-cutting influences like policy preferences that are not perfectly correlated with group identity must be minimal. Such policy preferences (or preferences based on an alternative identity like class) may split the coherence of groups and make alternative coalitions possible.

Altogether then, we should expect electoral stability when there is a single winning coalition, volatility otherwise, conditional on being in an institutional environment that creates incentives to seek majorities and a social environment in which group identity drives voting behavior to the exclusion of other considerations.

5. A Focus on African Ethnic Groups

Note, nothing in the prior analysis assumes that "groups" need to be ethnic groups. Indeed, assuming that group identity is a strong predictor of voting behavior, many sorts of groups (class, religious, ideological, etc.) might be relevant to explaining volatility. However, the remainder of this chapter focuses on a specific type of group (ethnic) and a particular region of the world (Africa). There are several advantages to limiting the focus in this way, and they all relate to controlling for background factors.

First, there is ample evidence that ethnic identities are highly relevant to elections in Africa—to the exclusion of other kinds of considerations like policy. In

---

[4] On electoral systems, see Cox 1997. On presidentialism, see Shugart and Carey 1992 and Mainwaring and Shugart 1997.

a comprehensive survey of African elections, Nicolas van de Walle notes that "the low salience of ideology for [African] parties is unmistakable … Ideological differences have been minor across parties, and debates about specific policy issues have been virtually non-existent." He also contends that "election campaigns have been conducted almost entirely on the basis of personal and ethno-regional appeals for support" (van de Walle 2003, 304–305). In making these judgments, he builds on a large amount of prior research that documents the high salience of ethnic identities in African politics and the low salience of nearly everything else, particularly policy.[5] African elections can therefore be thought of as a divide-the-dollar game between different ethnic groups, making the logic described above especially applicable to this region. Furthermore, because ethnic identities are uniformly important in Africa, cleavages structures are more comparable than they are in other areas of the world where one country might be divided by region, another by class, another by patron-client ties, and so on. Such heterogeneity of cleavage structure makes comparisons more difficult.

A further benefit of focusing on Africa is that the institutional structures of African countries almost uniformly create incentives for politicians to try to capture majorities. As numerous studies have noted (Bratton and van de Walle 1997, van de Walle 2003, Lindberg 2004), presidentialism is by far the dominant regime type among African democracies. Indeed, as van de Walle (2003) notes, only four multiparty democracies in Africa have parliamentary systems (Botswana, Lesotho, Mauritius, and South Africa). Of these, only South Africa uses proportional representation with large districts. In fact, large district proportional representation is almost as rare in Africa as parliamentarism, being found only in a handful of cases (South Africa, Namibia, and Mozambique being the only ones relevant to this chapter). Thus, with the exception of South Africa, all African cases to date have had a presidential system, low district size, or both, with most having both. As a result, there are strong institutional incentives for coalescence in African systems: Parties and politicians have every reason to seek an electoral majority if they can. This means that the logic outlined earlier is likely to be relevant in Africa—unlike areas of the world where parliamentary structures are combined with weak electoral systems.

One possible drawback to focusing on Africa, however, is the quality of its elections. Some observers (e.g., Bratton 1998) have been pessimistic about the quality of African elections, citing low turnover rates, declining levels of

[5] The literature on the role of ethnicity in African politics is enormous. Classics include Mitchell 1956; Bates 1974; Kasfir 1976; Horowitz 1985; Laitin 1986; and Vail 1989. More recent work includes Scarritt and Mozaffar 1999; Englebert 2000; Norris and Mattes 2003; Wantchekon, 2003; Ferree, 2004, 2006; Posner 2004a, 2004b, 2005; Ferree and Horowitz 2010; Bratton and Kimenyi 2008; Eifert, Miguel, and Posner 2010. Virtually any work that deals with the politics of specific African cases touches on the importance of ethnicity, and most cross-national work on Africa considers ethnicity as a control variable at the very least.

participation, and high levels of fraud as indications that African elections have more to do with making nice to the international community and less to do with what African electorates actually want. While there is certainly some truth to this view, others like Lindberg (2004) have found it too negative: When electoral quality is measured systematically using a wide range of indicators and plotted over time, African elections display enormous variation (some are quite competitive, participatory, and involve little fraud) and average quality appears to be improving over time (countries that have managed to have three elections have reasonably high-quality results). Thus, while quality is certainly something to keep in mind (and to control for where possible), ignoring the African cases because of quality concerns is too drastic.

In sum, Africa's uniformity of cleavage structure, the significance of group identity to politics, the insignificance of policy and ideology, and the nature of its political institutions all create a natural laboratory for exploring the hypotheses laid out earlier—advantages must be weighed against the possibility that some elections may be somewhat less than fully free and fair.

6. Operationalizing Ethnic Structure

Multiple datasets purport to measure the ethnic breakdown of a country. Roeder (2001) and Fearon (2003) have updated the traditional measures collected by Soviet ethnographers in the early 1960s, and Posner (2004b) provides a measure of "politically relevant" ethnic groups in Africa. While these datasets have their positives, this analysis relies on Scarritt and Mozaffar's dataset on African ethnic groups (Scarritt and Mozaffar 1999). There are several benefits to Scarritt and Mozaffar's data. First, like Posner (2004b), they focus on politically relevant ethnic groups—that is, those that have been the basis of political action in the past (though not necessarily party formation). And second, they capture the *nested* (i.e., multidimensional), structure of ethnic groups in Africa. This later quality holds some significance for this chapter, so it is worth examining it in greater depth.

In order to test conjectures about the relationship between ethnic structure and volatility, we need a measure of the number of winning coalitions produced by a country's configuration of ethnic groups. While this might seem like a simple calculation, it turns out to be somewhat more complicated—especially if one wants to take seriously constructivist notions of ethnic identity change. Our count of the number of winning coalitions in each country varies according to whether we begin from a primordialist or a constructivist position—and according to which model of constructivism we adopt. This affects whether or not a country is coded as having multiple winning coalitions or a single one—and consequently has a large impact on predictions about volatility. It is easiest

to demonstrate this point by working through some concrete examples using the
Scarritt and Mozaffar (1999) dataset on African ethnic groups. The remainder of
this section does this, and then proposes three different ways of modeling the
possibility of ethnic identity change, each with different implications for how
different African cases get coded.

These data can be taken as reflecting the distribution of attribute-repertoires
of each country in Africa. Benin, for example, has three attribute-dimensions,
based on region, tribe, and sub-tribe. These dimensions, and the values on each,
are listed below:

Region: {Southerners (70%), Northerners (30%)}
Tribe: {Fon (55.5%), Yoruba-Nagot (13.6%), Bargu, (22.5%), Peul, (2.4%),
other}.
Sub-Tribe: {Fon (25%), Gun (12%), Aizo (4.5%), Yoruba-Nagot (13.6%),
Bariba (12.3%), Otamari/Somba (5.7%), Peul (Fulani) (2.4%), other}

Mozaffar and Scarritt, as I do, take each attribute-value on each attribute-
dimension as an ethnic group. Any combinations of attribute-values across or
within dimensions would be "potential" ethnic groups.

There is a "nested" relationship between these attribute-dimensions. Nesting
simply means that large ethnic groups can be divided into several smaller ethnic
groups, which can in turn be divided into even smaller ethnic groups, and so on.
Furthermore, like Russian dolls, the larger groups perfectly contain the smaller
ones, so identities do not cross-cut. The nesting nature of African ethnic groups
has long been noted by anthropologists studying African societies (e.g., Evans-
Pritchard 1940), though nesting is not unique to Africa (Latinos in America, for
example, are also a nested group). Figure 8.2, from Scarritt and Mozaffar, shows
the nesting structure for Benin.[6] At the highest level of aggregation, the country
can be divided into Southerners (70%) and Northerners (30%). Each of these
groups can then be broken into sub-groups. The Southerners break down into
the Fon (around 56%) and the Yoruba-Nagot (around 14%), and these sub-
groups divide into a third set of groups (the Gun, the Aizo, etc.).[7]

Nesting is important for the analysis here because it affects how many groups
we see and how big those groups are. If Benin is coded on the basis of the highest level of aggregation, it has two groups, one of which is larger than 50%. If it

---

[6] Scarritt and Mozaffar's data show only the three levels of the nesting structure (in some cases,
fewer), but in practice, the smallest groups in the structure also can be broken down into even
finer tribal and sub-tribal distinctions.

[7] These do not add up to 100 because Scarritt and Mozaffar focus only on groups that are
politically salient. Thus, the other sub-groups making up "Southerners" are not salient. Presumably,
these people would instead identify as Southern, not as part of a sub-group.

```
┌──────────────────────────────────────┐
│  SOUTHERNERS  (70%)                    │
│                                        │
│      Fon (55.5)                        │
│                                        │
│           Fon (25)                     │
│                                        │
│           Gun (12)                     │
│                                        │
│           [Aizo (4.5)]                 │
│                                        │
│              [Other smaller groups (14)] │
│                                        │
│      Yoruba-Nagot (13.6)               │
│                                        │
│  NORTHERNERS  (30)                     │
│                                        │
│      Bargu  (22.5)                     │
│                                        │
│           Bariba (12.3)                │
│                                        │
│           Otamari/Somba (5.7)          │
│                                        │
│      Peul (Fulani) (2.4)               │
└──────────────────────────────────────┘
```

Figure 8.2 Nesting Structure of Benin
From Scarritt and Mozaffar 1999.

is coded on the basis of its lowest level of aggregation, it has many groups, and they are all small. Clearly, this affects the number of winning coalitions that one sees for the country. Furthermore, any attempt to code the number of winning coalitions (or, for that matter, to code the size of the largest group, or to create a factionalization index) must first deal with the prior question of *what level to look at.* This issue cannot be resolved simply by appealing to greater or lesser degrees of salience. All of these groups are salient. Thus, nesting creates dilemmas for coding cases—dilemmas that many studies simply ignore by arbitrarily focusing on one "cut" of ethnic identities and ignoring the others. If we are to take constructivist notions of ethnic identity change seriously, however, we must consider all levels of the nested structure, for this is what constructivists have in mind when they speak of multidimensionality.

A further point that emerges from looking at the Benin data involves the possibility of new groups forming out of old ones. Constructivists argue that ethnic groups are *created* rather than given in some primordial way by nature. Thus, there is nothing set in stone about the particular roster of groups for a country. Obviously, if we take this logic to the extreme, then it is useless to list a country's groups, because new groups will be created and added all the time. Taking a less extreme version of the logic, we might posit that a likely source for group formation is the amalgamation of existing groups into new ones—especially where there are advantages to being large. Thus, in the Benin case, what is to stop some of the sub-groups in the "Southerner" category from banding together to create a new group—one that is smaller than "Southerners" but still a majority? Depending on whether or not we allow these sorts of new groupings to count, we get different numbers of winning coalitions—a point that will be further developed below.

This all suggests that before we can test our simple conjectures about ethnic structure and volatility, we must first come up with a "model" of ethnic identity change. In particular, we must resolve whether or not multidimensionality matters and how to deal with it, and we must resolve how we will deal with the possibility of combinations. Most existing cross-national work on ethnic diversity and party systems opts for one set of assumptions on these issues, whereas constructivist theories suggest different ones. Here, I propose three different sets of assumptions or models. The first corresponds to a very "fixed" or primordial notion of ethnic identities. It ignores the multidimensional structure of ethnic groups and takes the existing set of groups on one dimension as fixed, ignoring other dimensions. The second relaxes one of these assumptions but not the other: It acknowledges the multidimensionality of ethnic identities in Africa but still takes existing group boundaries as fixed. And the final one relaxes both assumptions, seeing ethnic identities as multidimensional and allowing for the possibility that new groups might form out of the material of old ones.[8] Each of these different models produces a different coding of the African cases. Below, I discuss each model in greater depth.

The first model is the simplest and conforms most closely with primordialist approaches to ethnic identities. It ignores the nested structure of the groups and the possibility that groups might recombine into larger groups to capture majorities. This is the most common way of dealing with ethnic identity in cross-national studies: Only a single breakdown of the population is considered and all sub-groupings are ignored. These assumptions result in a twofold division of the data: cases with winning coalitions (a group surpassing 50% of the population) and cases without winning coalitions. South Africa, where Africans are 76% of the population, provides one example of a winning coalition case; another is Benin, where Southerners are 70% of the population. Kenya, where the largest group (the Kikuyu/Meru/Embu grouping) is only 28% of the population, provides an example of a case with no winning coalition. In the dataset used in this chapter, fifteen of thirty-five cases do not have a winning coalition (see Table 8.2, column 1, for specifics).

To reiterate the expectations presented earlier, volatility should be low in winning coalition cases like South Africa and Benin because parties need only capture the support of a single group. In contrast, volatility should be high in places like Kenya, as parties seeking a majority must build coalitions that span multiple

[8] An even more radically constructivist notion would be to admit (as mentioned earlier) that *entirely* new groups could form. This notion is impossible to operationalize. Therefore, the focus here is on a more moderate version of constructivism.

Table 8.2 **Raw Data on Ethnic Structure**

Country	No Nesting*	Nesting, no node Combinations		Nesting, node Combinations	
	No WC	Single WC	Multiple WC	Single WC	Multiple WC
Benin			x		x
Botswana		x			x
Burkina Faso		x		x	
Cameroon	x				
Cape Verde		x		x	
CAR	x				
Chad	x				
Congo	x				
Cote d'Ivoire	x				
Djibouti		x		x	
Ethiopia	x				
Equatorial Guinea		x		x	
Gabon	x				
Gambia	x				
Ghana	x				
Guinea-Bissau			x		x
Kenya	x				
Lesotho		x		x	
Madagascar	x				
Malawi		x		x	
Mali	x				
Mauritania		x		x	
Mauritius			x		x
Mozambique	x				
Nigeria		x		x	
Namibia		x		x	
Niger		x		x	
Sao Tome Principe		x		x	
Senegal		x			x
Seychelles		x		x	
South Africa		x			x
Tanzania		x		x	
Togo	x				
Zambia	x				
Zimbabwe		x			x

groups, and coalitions tend to be unstable. What is left out of this coding is the possibility that there might be *multiple* winning coalitions. Because nesting is ignored, divisions within groups are not relevant to the story and therefore cannot generate coordination problems.

The second conceptualization of ethnic identity is more complicated than the first. Like the first, it takes the existing set of groups as fixed (no new creations possible). However, unlike the first, it acknowledges the multidimensional and nested nature of ethnic groups in Africa. Thus, it captures some but not all constructivist insights: It captures the sense that individuals have multiple identities that might matter to them and that they move freely between them, yet it sees the set of identities that individuals have as fixed. This conceptualization opens up the possibility of *multiple* winning coalitions. Returning to Figure 8.2, the mapping of groups in Benin, we find a clear example of this: both the Southerners and the Fon (a subset of Southerners) exceed 50% of the population. This suggests a potential coordination problem in Benin: Voters who are members of both winning coalitions may be uncertain about which way to align. On the one hand, they might prefer to go with the smaller winning coalition (the Fon, with 56% of the population), under the rationale that a smaller coalition means fewer people to share with. On the other hand, the larger winning coalition (Southerners, with 70% of the population) offers more insurance. As voters with different risk acceptance levels make different decisions about how to vote, the group ends up splitting its votes. In the next election, voters attempt to correct, switching their support in an effort to coordinate. This logic suggests that multiple winning coalitions can generate coordination problems and volatility.

Benin can be contrasted to the South African case (Figure 8.3), where none of the sub-groups of the African category exceeds 50% (Zulus are the largest, at 22%). In South Africa, Africans should face little confusion over how to vote and coordination problems should be minimal. Parties might emerge that attempt to divide the African vote along ethnic lines, but they are unlikely to get much support. Hence, volatility should be low in South Africa but high in Benin.

There are therefore three relevant categories for the second model of ethnic identity change: multiple winning coalition cases (like Benin), single winning coalition cases (like South Africa), and zero winning coalition cases (Kenya). The difference between the first and second models is the separation of the multiple winning coalition cases from the single winning coalition cases. In the first model, these are lumped together; in the second, they are differentiated. The zero winning coalition cases stay the same across both models.

Table 8.2 (columns 2 and 3) shows the data for the entire sample. There are three cases where there are multiple winning coalitions, Benin, Mauritius, and Guinea-Bissau. These cases drive the distinction between the first and second models of ethnic identity change: In the first model, they are coded as winning

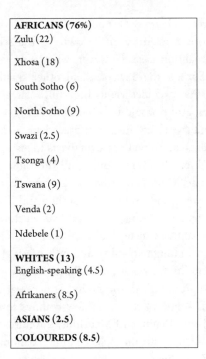

Figure 8.3 Nesting Structure of South Africa
From Scarritt and Mozaffar 1999.

coalition cases and are predicted to have low volatility. In the second model, they are coded as multiple winning coalitions and are predicted to have high volatility. How these cases fall therefore provides clues to whether or not nesting matters.

The third conceptualization relaxes the fluidity of ethnic groups even more, permitting groups within a particular node of the nested structure to combine together to form new groups.[9] This conforms most closely with constructivist notions that identities are both multiple and created. It results in the same set of categories as the second coding (no winning coalition, single winning coalition, and multiple winning coalition), but now there are more cases of multiple winning coalitions because some countries that were previously coded as single winning coalitions are now coded as having multiple ones.

[9] Thus, this conceptualization privileges "nearness" in the nested structure as a criterion for the types of combinations that can form—that is, groups that are "near" each other (in the same node) can combine, but groups that are "far" from each other (in different nodes) cannot. Why might this be true? Generally speaking, we might expect that nearness is indicative of some sort of *affinity*. In Benin, for example, nodes indicate geographic proximity. All of the groups in the "Northern" node are located (unsurprisingly!) in the northern part of the country. We might therefore expect them to have an easier time joining with each other than with groups located far

Thus, in South Africa (Figure 8.2), none of the ethnic groups comprising the "African" category forms a majority on its own, so the second model codes it as a single winning coalition case. However, what is to stop the Xhosas from combining with the Sothos, the Tswanas, and other smaller groups to form a sub-African coalition that excludes Zulus but still is large enough to capture a majority? The resulting group would be a "created" group, stitched together from smaller groups, without significant historical precedent, and would represent precisely the sort of amalgamation that constructivists focus upon. Of course, many such groups are possible: The Zulus could pull the same move to exclude the Xhosas, or the Zulus and Xhosas (together 40% of the population) could pull in one or two smaller groups and exclude the Sothos and Tswana. Given the fact that many constructions are possible, South Africa's electoral picture would now have many winning coalitions instead of just one. We might therefore expect coordination problems and high volatility in South Africa. In contrast, we would continue to predict stability for Mauritania (Figure 8.4), even under this coding, because all of the sub-groupings in the node are necessary to capture a majority. Table 8.2, columns 4 and 5, show the new codings for all the countries. In addition to Guinea-Bissau, Benin, and Mauritius, the third coding generates several new cases of countries with multiple winning coalitions (Botswana, South Africa, Senegal, and Zimbabwe).

We therefore have three different variants of the hypothesis that ethnic configurations producing a single winning coalition will be associated with more electoral stability than configurations that do not (summarized in Table 8.3). The first corresponds to the way ethnic identities are most commonly operationalized in cross-country studies and is closest to primordialism: It ignores the multidimensional nature of groups and codes simply on whether or not there is a group that exceeds 50% of the population. The second acknowledges multidimensionality, coding whether or not groups that exceed 50% of the population contain within them subgroups that also exceed 50% of the population. But it does not allow combinations of existing groups either within or across nodes. The third variant allows combinations. It is more constructivist than the

---

away, in the southern regions of the country. Nearness in the nested structure may also be indicative of cultural affinity. Groups in a node may share a similar language and/or cultural practices, making collective action perhaps easier than it would be between groups that do not share these common reference points. Finally, if a particular node was endowed with economic, political, or social significance by past events in a country, then groups in that node may share common experiences and/or material situations that cause their preferences to converge. For example, in South Africa, apartheid endowed racial differences with material significance. Hence, groups in the same racial node (Africans, for example) might be expected to have similar preferences. For a variety of reasons, then, we might expect that nearness in the nested structure indicates affinity of some sort: Groups "near" each other will have an easier time coming together than groups "far away" from each other. I thank Michael Bratton for suggesting this point.

| **MOOR (84%)** |
| Bidan (White) Moors (43%) |
| Haratin (mainly Black) Moors (41%) |
| |
| **BLACK AFRICANS (KEWRI) (16%)** |
| Fulani (15%) |

Figure 8.4 Nesting Structure of Mauritania
From Scarritt and Mozaffar 1999.

second variant because it acknowledges the possibility that new groups can be constructed out of the material of old ones. Table 8.2 provides the codings for the first three variants of the hypothesis.

By exploring the relationship between these codings and volatility, we can simultaneously explore two questions: First, is there any relationship between ethnic cleavage structure and volatility? And second, do constructivist claims "matter" for explaining party systems? Does one of the codings outperform the others?

7. Data

The dependent variable for this analysis is average legislative volatility levels (calculated as explained before via Pedersen's index) for a cross-section of thirty-five African countries.[10] The data are an updated version of the data presented in Kuenzi and Lambright (2001) and include all countries that have had back-to-back multiparty elections as of Spring 2003 (Nigeria is the last new case added).[11] Although calculating election-to-election volatility levels would increase the size

[10] Why not use vote volatility instead of seat volatility? Vote volatility is certainly a more pure measure of shifts in voting because seat volatility involves the extra step of translating votes into seats and thus can be affected by the nature of the electoral system. However, this is only a problem if the electoral system affects the seat/vote translation in a way that correlates with seat volatility. Otherwise, the translation effect is just random noise. In the African data, this appears to be the case: According to Kuenzi and Lambright (2001), seat volatility is uncorrelated with the size of electoral districts (a good proxy for the translation effect). Therefore, while using seat volatility instead of vote volatility introduces extra noise into the test, it is most likely random noise and should, if anything, make results harder to find. On a practical level, data on vote volatility are harder to get. Most sources on election results provide seat data, not vote data.

[11] Many thanks to Gina Lambright and Michelle Kuenzi for making these available. Thirty-four of the cases come courtesy of them. I added Nigeria after the 2003 elections. I also modified their data in one instance: For Lesotho, I use only the 1998 to 2002 volatility score, dropping the earlier 1993 to 1998 scores. As noted in Kuenzi and Lambright (2001), this earlier score is extremely high (99%), for reasons that were idiosyncratic to that particular period and unlikely to be repeated. Indeed, the later period had a volatility score of around 30%.

Table 8.3 **Summary of Ethnicity Models**

	Acknowledge Nesting?	*Allow Combinations?*
Ethnicity Model 1 (Fixed)	NO	NO
Ethnicity Model 2 (Multidimensional)	YES	NO
Ethnicity Model 3 (Multidimensional and Created)	YES	YES

of the sample by including multiple observations for several cases, average volatility levels are preferable for two reasons. First, the data on ethnic structure are only available for a cross-section. And second, averaging the volatility levels should give a better measure of long-term patterns than election-to-election numbers, which can move around a great deal for idiosyncratic reasons.

The key independent variables are five variables modeling the number of winning coalitions in a country's ethnic structure suggested by the analysis of the previous section. The first is a dummy variable for cases that have zero winning coalitions (*no_WC*). There are fifteen countries in this category. The remaining deal with the cases that have at least one winning coalition. The second set of coding rules (nesting, no combinations) produces one set of single winning coalition cases (*single_WC_2*) and multiple winning coalition cases (*multiple_WC_2*). There are seventeen countries in the first category and three in the second. The third set of coding rules (nesting, combinations) produces the same categories, but the cases in these categories shift. Thus, the third coding produces single winning coalition cases (*single_WC_3*) and multiple winning coalition cases (*multiple_WC_3*), but now there are twelve countries in the first category and eight in the second. In essence, *single_WC_2* and *single_WC_3* are substitutes for one another (as are *multiple_WC_2* and *multiple_WC_3*) and never appear in the same specification.

In addition, I also include a few controls suggested by the literature. Following Roberts and Wibbels (1999), I include Kuenzi and Lambright's measure for the average age of the major parties (those that received at least 10% of the seats) competing in the election (*mean_age*). This operates as a rough proxy for the degree of institutionalization of the party system. Along similar lines, I use a measure of the number of periods contained in the dependent variable (*number_of_periods*). I also include a measure for the average effective number of parties (*ENP*), based on the data in van de Walle (2003) plus some supplements. Roberts and Wibbels (1999) and Mozaffar, Scarritt, and Galaich (2003) both find this variable to have a significant positive relationship to volatility: The more parties there are, the higher the level of volatility. To control for the effects of changes in participation levels (produced, for example, by election boycotts), I exploit the data in Lindberg (2004) to create a variable measuring the average absolute change in turnout levels between elections (*change_turnout*). And finally, to control for the quality of elections, I use two different measures: first, a variable measuring the average "freeness and fairness" of elections (*free_and_ fair*). Elections are coded zero if there were enormous problems with fraud, one if there were serious problems that affected results, and two if fraud did not affect the quality of elections. These codings were based on van de Walle (2003) and Lindberg (2004). To supplement this, I also use a variable that indicates whether or not there was an election boycott (*opposition_participate*), from Lindberg (2004).

8. Results

This section reports basic descriptive statistics for volatility levels for different ethnic configurations as well as the results of some simple statistical tests. Because the data are a cross-section and only a limited number of African countries have had back-to-back multiparty elections, the sample size for these explorations is small (thirty-five when the full sample is used). This makes significant effects difficult to find and magnifies the impact of outliers. All results should be considered with this caveat in mind.

Table 8.4 shows average volatility levels (with standard deviations) for the categories of cases associated with each of the three models. These simple means suggest two points: first, that *ethnic structure* correlates with volatility levels; and second, that how *the possibility of ethnic identity change* is modeled matters. Comparing the first two rows, the average level of volatility for cases without a winning coalition is higher (at twenty-seven) than cases that have at least one winning coalition (twenty-three). Even stronger patterns emerge when the winning coalition category is split into cases with a single winning coalition and cases with multiple winning coalitions. Rows three and four make this split according to the second model of *ethnic identity change* and the results are dramatic. Single winning coalition cases have much lower volatility levels (eighteen) than both multiple winning coalition cases (fifty) and no winning coalition cases. Rows five and six split the winning coalition cases according to the third model of ethnic identity change. Here the pattern mimics the pattern for the second model but is not as strong: Single winning coalition cases have less volatility (nineteen) than either multiple winning coalition cases (thirty) or no winning coalition cases, but the gap is not as wide.

Further evidence for these patterns can be gleaned by re-examining the data in Figure 8.1. The data appear to show a natural break-point between Sao Tome and Principe (with a volatility score of 21) and Cote d'Ivoire (with a volatility score of 27). Above this point there are fifteen higher volatility cases and below it there are twenty lower volatility cases. Of the top fifteen cases of volatility,

Table 8.4 **Volatility Levels for Different Cases**

	Mean	Standard Deviation	Number of Observations
No winning coalition	27	17	15
At least one winning coalition	23	17	20
Single winning coalition (model 2)	18	13	17
Multiple winning coalition (model 2)	50	9	3
Single winning coalition (model 3)	19	15	12
Multiple winning coalition (model 3)	30	18	8
Overall	25	17	35

only two (Niger and Lesotho) are coded as having single winning coalitions by the second coding scheme. In contrast, fourteen of the twenty lowest volatility cases are coded as having a single winning coalition. Furthermore, all of the cases coded as having multiple winning coalitions by the second coding scheme (Benin, Mauritius, and Guinea-Bissau) are in the top six highest levels of volatility for the sample. Finally, the expansion of the multiple winning coalition category produced by the third coding scheme only muddies the patterns. The highest volatility scores are the countries that were originally coded as having multiple coalitions. The new additions (Senegal, Zimbabwe, South Africa, Tanzania, and Botswana) almost all fall among the lower volatility scorers. This provides more evidence that the second breakdown of the data bears the strongest relationship to volatility patterns.

A few outliers emerge from this analysis. First, and most spectacularly, Niger contradicts all expectations. In spite of having a single winning coalition (by all codings), it has the second highest volatility score in the sample (over 60). Niger had four sets of legislative elections during the 1990s: 1993, 1995, 1996, and 1999. Continuity was reasonably high for three of these elections (1993, 1995, and 1999), with the same parties performing in similar ways and low overall volatility levels. The high volatility score for Niger therefore appears to be driven by one election, 1996, which followed on the heels of the early dissolution of the 1995 legislature and a coup. During this election, a party new to the scene (the National Union of Independents for Democratic Renewal) won 71% of the vote. There were boycotts of the election and irregularities that probably affected results (see Lindberg, 2004). After the 1996 election, this party disappeared. Thus, Niger's high volatility score probably represents the idiosyncratic events of 1996 (i.e., the appearance of a party of independents in the context of civil conflict). Should elections persist in Niger, and should the patterns of 1993, 1995, and 1999 continue, Niger's volatility score should decline.

At the other end of the scale, Gambia, Ethiopia, and Mozambique all have extremely low volatility (under ten), yet all are cases without a winning coalition. How these cases avoid volatility without having a dominant ethnic group is not clear. Gambia's elections have almost all been considered highly fraudulent, which might explain its stability, but this is less true for Ethiopia and is not true at all for Mozambique (with very good marks on election quality). In Mozambique, the civil war, which divided people into two partisan camps, may have created a dimension of politics independent of ethnicity—but this insight requires more analysis than can be undertaken here. Ethiopia's result also requires further case work.

Table 8.5 extends this analysis by exploring the relationship between the variables measuring ethnic structure and volatility by using ordinary least squares (OLS).[12] The first three columns test the three different sets of variables measuring ethnic structure (with no controls) on the full sample. The second three columns again look only at the ethnic structure variables, but drop the biggest outlier mentioned above (Niger). The final four columns test only the second and third models of ethnic identity change, drop Niger, and include a wide range of controls. In all specifications, the single winning coalition cases are subsumed by the constant, so the effects of the other ethnic structure variables should be interpreted relative to them. Several noteworthy patterns emerge in these regressions.

First, the ethnic structure variables matter, and they matter more or less as anticipated. The size and significance of the coefficients on these variables vary across different models of ethnic identity change and different specifications (to be discussed below). However, the no winning coalition coefficient is always positive. Similarly, the multiple winning coalition coefficients are also always positive. This suggests that, compared to countries with a single winning coalition, countries with no winning coalition or multiple ones tend to have higher volatility levels.

A second pattern that emerges in the regressions is that, with the exception of the effective number of parties (ENP), none of the control variables seem to matter in explaining African volatility levels. ENP is significant (or borderline significant) in both specifications that included it (9 and 10), and the sign of the coefficient (positive) confirms earlier findings: Fractionalized party systems appear to have higher volatility than concentrated ones. Why this is the case is not entirely clear, but the pattern is robust. In contrast, the coefficients on all of the other control variables are insignificant, making the impact of the ethnic structure variables all the more impressive.

A final pattern that comes out of the regressions is that how ethnic identity change is modeled matters. The second model (which allows for

---

[12] OLS is appropriate because the dependent variable (average legislative seat volatility) is approximately normal in distribution. While it is bounded by 0 and 1, there is no evidence of truncation or bunching near the bounds.

Table 8.5 Estimates of Legislative Volatility in Africa (standard errors in parentheses)

	Full Sample						Minus Niger			
	1	2	3	4	5	6	7	8	9	10
No winning coalition	4.23	8.92*	8.59	6.22	11.58**	12.43**	11.11**	13.11*	8.48	8.24
	(5.81)	(5.25)	(6.48)	(5.47)	(4.62)	(5.97)	(5.32)	(7.17)	(5.63)	(6.54)
Multiple winning coalition (nesting but no combos)		31.30***			33.96***		37.37***		29.17**	
		(9.29)			(8.08)		(9.24)		(11.13)	
Multiple winning coalition (nesting and combos)			10.92			14.76**		17.32*		13.03
			(7.64)			(6.99)		(9.22)		(8.24)
Average age of parties with 10% of seats							-.12	-.13	.01	.12
							(.25)	(.31)	(.27)	(.28)
Free and Fair							-2.70	-1.42	-3.44	-3.30
							(4.33)	(5.29)	(4.31)	(4.70)
Number of Election Periods							-.03	-.68	.72	.75
							(1.92)	(2.49)	(1.98)	(2.25)
Opposition participates							1.56	5.28	-4.48	-9.23
							(11.45)	(13.99)	(12.23)	(13.36)
Absolute change in turnout levels							-30.70	-13.72	-19.92	.39
							(23.12)	(27.78)	(24.29)	(24.94)
Average ENP (seats)									3.68	7.24**
									(2.87)	(2.60)
n	35	35	35	34	34	34	31	31	31	31
Adjusted R²	-.01	.23	.02	.01	.35	.11	.30	-.04	.32	.19

* p ≤ .10; ** p ≤ .05, *** p ≤ .01

multidimensionality but not recombination) appears to fit the data the best. Looking first at the most simple specifications (equations 1–3), we see that the ethnic structure variables that correspond to the second model (equation 2) are more systematically correlated with volatility than the ethnic structure variables that correspond to the first model (equation 1) or the third one (equation 3). In equation 2, both ethnic structure variables are statistically and substantially significant: on average, countries with no winning coalition score about 9 points higher on the volatility rating, while countries with multiple winning coalitions score about 31 points higher. These are medium to large effects. The overall mean volatility score for the entire sample is 25, with a standard deviation of 17 (see Table 8.4). In contrast, in equations 1 and 3, none of the ethnic structure variables are significant. When the troublesome outlier Niger is dropped (equations 4–6), the fit of the model improves in all cases, but the second model (equation 5) still outperforms the others. The third model of ethnic identity change (equation 6) shows up as significant also, but it does not fit the data as well as the second one.

The strength of the second model vis-à-vis the first and third persists when the full range of controls is added. Without ENP, the controls increase the size of the coefficients on the ethnic structure variables while not affecting their significance levels. When ENP is added, all of the ethnic structure coefficients take a hit and only the coefficient on multiple winning coalitions for the second model (equation 9) remains significant.[13] While at first this might seem problematic, it is most likely driven by multicollinearity between the ethnic structure variables and ENP.[14] One possible interpretation of equations 9 and 10 is that ENP is a channel through which the ethnic structure variables affect volatility: Having a single winning coalition dampens both the effective number of parties *and* volatility levels. Given this logic, the diminishment of the coefficients on the ethnic structure variables in these equations should not be taken as an indication that these variables are not important. However, as causality is difficult to sort out in these models with very few observations, this interpretation should be treated as speculative.

Altogether, the data suggest support for two conclusions: first, that ethnic structure bears a systematic relationship with patterns of electoral volatility in Africa; second, that *how the possibility of ethnic identity change is modeled* matters. The model that seems to best fit these data is the one that acknowledges that

[13] When Niger *is* included in the sample, the ethnic structure variables for the second model of ethnicity are robust to the inclusion of a large number of controls, provided ENP is not in the specification. The coefficient on multiple winning coalitions is particularly resilient. It is pushed below standard significance levels only when Niger is included in the data, and *all* the controls (including ENP) are used.

[14] ENP is correlated with single winning coalition (second model) at -.37, with multiple winning coalition (second model) at .42, with single wining coalition (third model) at -.17, and with multiple winning coalition (third model) at .03.

multidimensional nature of ethnic identities yet ignores the possibility that new groups might form from old ones through recombination. Thus, these data suggest that while *switching* between basic attribute-values goes on, the amalgamation of smaller attribute-values into larger groups does not. This finding implies a highly constrained version of constructivism—at least with regard to the short time frame relevant for electoral volatility.

What might account for the limited fluidity of ethnic groups? A brief glimpse at South Africa may provide some clues. In South Africa, in keeping with the results presented here, Africans have consistently coordinated *as Africans*, even though smaller combinations of African ethnic groups are possible. As mentioned earlier, the Xhosas and the Zulus could have attempted to create a majority by banding together and pulling in one of the smaller African tribes (or even one of the non-African groups). The non-Zulu groups could have banded together to exclude the Zulus. And so on. Yet, these new groups have not been constructed. Why?

Constructing a new group and endowing it with meaning is hard and costly work. Furthermore, there is no guarantee that the new group will not face challenges from alternative new groups. There are many stories political entrepreneurs could tell about different sub-groupings of South African ethnicities. For example, the Xhosa and Zulu languages are both Nguni languages and are much closer to each other than they are to the languages of the Tswana, Sotho or Pedi. This is a potential source for unity. The Xhosa and the Zulu are also coast dwellers. Perhaps this is the kernel for a regional identification. But these bases for identification would have to compete with alternatives: Zulus, Sothos Pedi, Swazi, and Ndebele all live in the northern and eastern parts of the country. Perhaps they could use this as a basis for identification. Similarly, Tswana, Xhosa, and coloureds could claim a western and southern orientation. The point is, there are many groups and none is more "natural" than the rest. So any new group could and would be challenged. Given the costs of creating a new group, perhaps the risk that it would simply fall apart to a different grouping outweighs whatever slight benefits would be gained by excluding a few people from the ruling coalition. Understanding this, South African politicians choose to stick with the existing African focal point rather than risk debilitating coordination problems with uncertain benefits for trying to create a competing group.

It is of course important to emphasize that these results are constrained by the nature of the data that generated them. The dataset is small, magnifying the effects of outliers like Niger. In many cases, the number of elections averaged to produce a country's mean level of volatility is low, increasing the impact of odd elections and general noise. Furthermore, a more disturbing issue is that the differences between the three models of ethnic identity change hang on a small number of cases. This is especially true for the first and second models. The distinction between these models rests on the slender shoulders of three cases: Benin, Mauritius, and Guinea-Bissau. These are the only countries where nesting produces multiple groups larger than 50%. They also happen to be cases with very high volatility levels. Consequently, these cases drive the coefficient on multiple winning coalitions for the second model.

One way of looking at Benin, Mauritius, and Guinea-Bissau is to see them as very large outliers to the relationship between ethnic structure and volatility for the first model of ethnic identity change. If they are treated as outliers and dropped from the sample, then the first model (equation 1) does a reasonable job of explaining volatility levels. An alternative way to deal with them is to keep them in the sample but to include a dummy variable for them—the "Benin-Mauritius-GB" effect, so to speak. However, both of these "solutions" are very atheoretical—they see these cases as different but offer no explanation as to why.

This chapter finds a third way: It proposes a story about *why* these cases are different, a story based on their ethnic structure and the assumption that the multidimensionality of ethnic identity should matter for explaining behavior. This is more satisfying because it is more theoretically informed. But it still rests on an interpretation of three cases. Alternative stories are certainly possible, and to know if this particular story is a good one requires further testing—in particular, careful causal tracing through case studies.

In general, case studies would help provide answers to several questions impossible to address here. First, is the volatility driven by new parties entering the scene or by existing parties pulling votes from other existing parties? Second, do ethnic divisions map onto support for parties, as assumed? In other words, is the party system a reflection of ethnic divisions and exactly how does it map? And third, does coordination failure drive volatility for cases where there are multiple groups larger than 50% and is this coordination failure a function of ethnic group structure? For example, in Benin it is clear that Southerners have consistently failed to coordinate as Southerners (Degboe, 1995). However, what is less clear is the role that nested ethnic groups has played (or not played) in this coordination failure and whether this coordination failure drives volatility. For more on these cases, see Ferree (2010).

9. Conclusion

The results presented in this chapter support the notion that nesting may create coordination issues when it generates multiple groups larger than 50%. At the same time, they also suggest that volatility is *not* driven by the presence of many, similarly situated groups (i.e., groups close together in the nesting structure) that can be combined in multiple ways. The presence of multiple *actual* groups larger than 50% may create a coordination problem, but the presence of multiple *potential* groups larger than 50% does not, suggesting that there are limits on the types and nature of ethnic coalitions that can be formed (at least in the short run). Thus, the results presented here—provisional though they may be—offer confirmation of some constructivist notions (multidimensionality) but suggest caution for others (the unlimited short-term fluidity of ethnic coalitions). Of course, it is important to emphasize that I am making no claim that these results are global, that is, that identity construction never matters or that multidimensionality is always important. In other words, these findings about the fluidity of ethnic identities may well be peculiar to the specific outcome studied here—electoral volatility.

These findings also suggest that those doing work in the future on ethnicity and party systems should think carefully about how to model the possibility of change in ethnic identities before simply sticking it in the right-hand side of a statistical equation. This task would be facilitated if cross-national databases of ethnic groups followed the example set in Scarritt and Mozaffar (1999) and coded the multiple dimensionality of ethnic identities. Africa is not the only area of the world with nested ethnic groups. In the United States, the "Latino" group breaks into several smaller groups (Mexican American, Cuban, Puerto Rican, etc.). Furthermore, in other areas of the world—India, for example— ethnic groups may be less nested and more cross-cutting (e.g., caste and linguistic groups cut across religious groups, and so on). It would be useful to capture all this information rather than simply providing a single "snapshot" picture of ethnic groups. Snapshots necessarily distort and make judgments about which cut of the population is more important. They also make it difficult to test more sophisticated models of ethnic identity change.

9

Ethnicity and Pork

A Virtual Test of Causal Mechanisms

DAVID D. LAITIN AND A. MAURITS VAN DER VEEN

1. Introduction

There is a broadly recognized elective affinity between the activation of ethnic identities and the exclusionary distribution of political benefits, also known as "pork."[1] For many decades, Irish machines in U.S. cities provided special benefits or pork, such as easy entry into the city police force, for their Irish constituencies. Indian "Dalits" or former untouchables will form an ethnic party only if it can provide them jobs (Chandra 2004). The Shas party in Israel cultivates an orthodox political identity mostly to get subsidized schools for religious instruction of their children. This affinity has been broadly recognized (and classically portrayed in Shefter 1977) but not adequately explained. Fearon (1999) offers a theoretical reason to explain this empirical pattern of the activation of ethnic identities and pork tending to be found together, highlighting the incentives proffered to both publics and leaders to construct different types of coalition depending on the nature of the political goods to be distributed.

In this chapter, relying on the agent-based model introduced in Chapter 7, we present evidence supporting the basic causal logic in Fearon's account. Our models show that when political entrepreneurs have incentives to seek small coalitions (due to the goal of distributing a limited amount of pork to supporters), those who win and stay in power are those who attract voters based on their ethnic membership. Moreover, our findings elucidate the mechanisms that drive political entrepreneurs to propose and voters to support ethnic coalitions

---

[1] Geertz (1973) identified a type of uncivil politics (though more about status than pork) connected with ethnic or so-called primordial identities. Bates (1983) provided the first rational choice account linking ethnicity and distribution. Chandra (2004) limits her study of ethnic party formation to "distributive" democracies, thereby assuming that the study of ethnicity in democratic systems revolves around the politics of pork.

when distribution (i.e., pork) rather than policy drives political competition. In particular, we show that an affinity between ethnicity and pork emerges even when neither the public nor its leaders consciously take into account differences between ethnic identities and other forms of political identification. Finally, the affinity between ethnicity and pork applies not just to winning coalitions but also to the overall nature of political contestation: If pork is up for grabs, ethnic identities become more politically salient.

Fearon's (1999) basic argument is fairly straightforward:

> For coalitions formed to capture political "pork," there is a strong incentive to limit the size of the winning coalition in order not to dilute each winner's share of the spoils. This means that some criterion is needed to distinguish losers from winners so they can be excluded from entry into the winners' coalition. And for this purpose, the ascriptive mark of ethnicity fits the bill much better than do marks or criteria that can be *chosen* (or easily acquired) by anyone who wants access to the pork. If pork is dispensed on the basis of a criterion that can be chosen, like party affiliation, then the winning coalition will rapidly expand. Thus, *the politics of pork favors coalitions based on features not easily chosen or changed by individuals.* (5) (italics in original)

These features are not only difficult to mimic, but they are also "sticky," in that they are difficult to change. It is this stickiness that will be our central focus in this chapter.

Our argument proceeds in three steps. In the first part of the chapter, we lay out Fearon's argument in more detail and discuss ways to adapt his model to our agent-based modeling framework. We also lay out some basic observable implications as hypotheses that follow from Fearon's model. In the second part, we present the results of several tests designed to investigate the validity of these hypotheses. In the third part, we discuss possible extensions and additional implications of the model.

2. Implementing a Political Identity Game

Fearon proposes a political identity game to illustrate the emergence of ethnicity under conditions of distributive politics. In his game, all members of a population vote simultaneously for any social category they like ("human being," "blue eyed," "professor," etc.). The social category that gets the highest number of votes wins. This results in a reward shared equally by all members who voted for that social category. Since all members of the population have multiple categories in which they are members, this is a game with multiple equilibria. The best strategy to play in this game (to maximize one's share of the pork) is to choose a category in which one is a member[2] that has a chance of being the most popular category yet would count fewer members than other available categories that could also conceivably win.

Fearon offers a set of empirical implications of his political identity game, all of which have some preliminary and informal support. For example, one finding that is consistent with the model is the often observed (but not adequately explained) result that a change in political boundaries changes the ethnic category labels that are politically salient (cf. Bates 1983; Horowitz 1985, 66; Posner, 2004b). Another important empirical finding that lends support to the model is the positive bivariate relationship linking the number of salient ethnic groups in a country and the share of the gross domestic product (GDP) accounted for by government spending, which is a good indicator of pork (Fearon 1999, 20).

Here we offer a different, non-empirical test for the model. Our goal is to investigate whether there is anything distinctive about ethnic politics, as compared to normal everyday coalition politics. Or, specifically, whether Fearon's basic model suffices to produce meaningful differences between these different types of politics. We use an agent-based model in which agents are endowed with a repertoire of attributes on different dimensions. Political entrepreneurs make offers to agents for their support (by naming an attribute or set of attributes for their coalition), and agents align with entrepreneurs (if they qualify as members) seeking to be a member of a winning political coalition.[3]

In our model, we can vary the level of stickiness of particular dimensions. As Chandra points out in Chapter 3 of this volume, one central feature of ethnic identities is commonly held to be the "stickiness" of the attributes on which they are based. The more difficult it is for agents to change their attribute on a particular dimension, the more "ethnic" that dimension can be taken to be. We can also vary the size of the optimum coalition. By standard political reckoning, the smaller the optimal coalition size, the more politics is distributive. Only when the fruits of government are distributed to party faithful—and thus can be excluded from others—would it be rational for party leaders to aim for a coalition representing less than 100% of the voters. Smaller optimal coalition sizes are therefore symptoms of a system in which the distribution of jobs, welfare payments, and other benefits is political (as opposed to based on merit, or other allocation criteria).

There are two key implications of pork rather than policy driving political competition. First, people will want to be part of the winning coalition, because this is necessary to receive private benefits. Second, the receipt of pork may, over time, change the interests and the influence of agents within a system. Receiving

---

[2] Fearon shows why choosing a category in which you are not a member is (weakly) dominated by choosing any category in which you are a member.

[3] For details of the model, see the appendix to Chapter 7.

a public-sector job obviously affects one's interests with respect to public-sector funding, for example. Even more significantly, the prevalence of financial handouts may, in turn, influence political outcomes through new investments in lobbying.

In our model, neither the interests nor the power of agents change over time. In other words, we incorporate only one aspect of the implications of pork, namely, the interest in being part of the winning coalition. We do not model the actual reward the agent receives for winning and ignore strategies of agents beyond the simple vote. On the one hand, this is rather a thin model of pork politics. This might initially appear to subvert or weaken the basic logic of Fearon's model. On the other hand, we add a variable that Fearon's model takes for granted: the share of the vote a leader needs to get access to power. In Fearon's model, it is assumed that this share will be an absolute majority (or, in a few cases, a plurality). However, whether this is the case depends on the structure of the polity (and the size of the politically relevant population, or "selectorate"), as a promising body of recent research has suggested (Bueno de Mesquita et al. 2003).

In our model, a parameter for the optimal winning coalition (OWC) represents the share of the public (or selectorate) that leaders strive to represent. In many systems this will be 0.5 + epsilon, as Fearon assumes. However, one can imagine systems where it is either more or less. If OWC falls below 0.5, leaders have an incentive to restrict their coalition below what most political models assume, which may strengthen the basic logic outlined by Fearon. If, in contrast, OWC is high— at the extreme, leaders simply aim for the largest possible coalition—Fearon's logic is less likely to apply, since leaders will be trying to represent as many constituents as possible. Note that Fearon's logic here has become divorced from assumptions about the implications of the distribution of material benefits, even though his basic reasoning, as summarized in the quotation earlier, still applies.

We thus expect the value and appeal of exclusionary, distributive politics to decrease as the fraction of the population a leader needs to attract increases. As the OWC increases, political entrepreneurs will benefit less from focusing on exclusionary, sticky identities in putting together their coalition specifications. When a relatively small share of the population suffices to give one a share in the division of the spoils, on the other hand (i.e., OWC is small), we would expect leaders to be much more interested in trying to limit the size of the group they represent, and thus to emphasize stickier dimensions in their offerings. The incentives facing individual agents, clearly, are similar. This logic should be reflected in an inverse relationship between the OWC size and the average stickiness of the dimension on which a winning coalition is staked out.

To translate the preceding argument into the terms of our model, we are interested in the relationship between low optimal coalition size (i.e., distributive politics) and the salience of sticky dimensions in the winning offering (i.e., ethnic politics). The following three observables, stated here as hypotheses, summarize our expectations:

H1. Winning coalitions in systems where OWC is low will disproportionately feature sticky (more ethnic) dimensions, whereas winning coalitions where OWC is high will disproportionately emphasize non-sticky dimensions

H2. In systems where OWC is low, the political salience (i.e., the ordering of preferred dimensions for political organization) of sticky (ethnic) dimensions will rise, whereas that of non-sticky identities will fall. The opposite pattern will occur where OWC is high.

H3. The average tenure of a leader will be longer when her coalition is constructed around sticky dimensions in low-OWC systems and when her coalition is based on non-sticky dimensions in high-OWC systems.

The next section presents our results.

3. Experimental Results

Our basic experimental setup is for the most part identical to that described in Chapter 7. This means that each population consists of 5 leaders and 9,995 basic agents located on a square wraparound grid (i.e., a torus), there are eight dimensions in the system, and each dimension has five possible attributes. The attribute-repertoire of each agent has attributes on five of these eight possible dimensions. Each "run" of an experimental condition has 1,500 time steps. An "election" or "electoral round" takes place every twenty-five time steps.

At every electoral round, leaders propose specifications of OWCs to agents. These specifications meet the conditions laid out in Chapter 7. Agents update their own repertoire accordingly, and this updating continues in each time step between electoral rounds. The entire process repeats over several electoral rounds. To test our hypotheses we ran simulations under six different levels of the OWC: 0.3, 0.4, 0.5, 0.6, 0.7, and *Max*, a value indicating that leaders simply sought a plurality of the votes.

In a noticeable departure from the experiments in Chapter 7, however, different dimensions were assigned different stickiness levels. Recall that the term "stickiness" refers in our model to the number of consecutive turns an agent must want to replace her own attribute on any specific dimension before being allowed to do so. It is determined by the parameters *DimXstickiness* (where X is the dimension's identifying number).[4] If the value on this parameter is 0, attribute changes take place as just described. If not, the agent will record that she wanted to change to attribute value Y, and mark that she has tried to do so once. The next turn, if attribute Y is the most-favored attribute again, and again passes

[4] Note that the stickiness of a dimension refers to the difficulty of changing *attributes* on that dimension, not the difficulty of adding or dropping the dimension as part of the repertoire.

the threshold test, the agent will see if the dimension's stickiness is just 1. If so, she now changes. If not, she increases the marker to 2. This continues until the stickiness value is met. If at any time the most-favored (and threshold-meeting) attribute is not Y, or Y fails to meet the threshold, the record of attempted changes is reset to 0. Thus if we want an agent's attribute value on a dimension to be unchangeable, we can simply set the stickiness to a value greater than the number of time steps for which the model will be run.

Two dimensions were assigned a stickiness of 0; two a stickiness of 10; two a stickiness of 25 (equal to one voting interval); and two, finally, a stickiness of 50. As in Chapter 7, each agent had attributes in its repertoire for five of the eight dimensions, randomly but not evenly assigned, to make winning coalitions likely from the start.

As noted above, simulations were run for 1,500 time steps, with a vote taking place every twenty-five rounds, giving a total of sixty "elections" in each run. With initial rounds occupied by somewhat transitory processes of identity consolidation, we present here results starting from time step 501 (i.e., after the first twenty electoral rounds). Each of the six OWC conditions was run 100 times with randomly initialized populations. Data from this experiment that allow us to test our first hypothesis appear in Table 9.1. The first four rows in Table 9.1 show the fraction of the times that the winning coalition used a dimension of a particular stickiness level (these four lines will sum to 100%). The final row represents the average degree of stickiness among the dimensions used in winning coalitions.

Table 9.1 shows, as predicted, a clear pattern as one moves to higher optimal coalition requirements, with reliance on stickier coalitions decreasing. The 0.3 and 0.4 optimal coalition levels show the greatest reliance on very sticky

Table 9.1 **Stickiness of Winning Coalition by Size of Optimal Winning Coalition**

Dimension Stickiness	OWC 0.3	OWC 0.4	OWC 0.5	OWC 0.6	OWC 0.7	Maximize
0	22.51	17.69	55.06	46.81	44.72	62.78
10	19.75	21.35	27.30	41.73	41.35	32.63
25	26.29	25.28	13.82	07.92	10.57	03.98
50	31.44	35.68	03.81	03.55	03.37	00.63
ASWC	24.14	26.18	08.09	07.93	08.46	04.57

The first four rows of each column, reflecting the percentage of winning coalitions constructed from each level of stickiness, sum to 100. The formula used to calculate ASWC (average stickiness of winning coalition) is to sum across all dimensions the product of the number of rounds a dimension is used in a winning coalition and the stickiness of that dimension, and to divide that sum by the total number of winning coalitions over the course of the run.

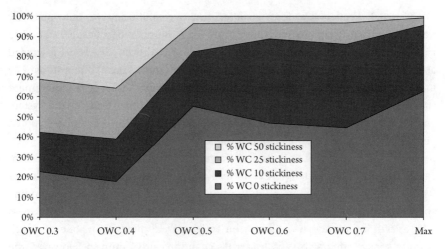

Figure 9.1 OWC, Stickiness, and Ethnic Coalition Formation

dimensions; the other three intermediate optimal coalition levels much less so; and the maximum structure least. Another way of looking at this table is to read down the columns. At an OWC level of 0.3 OWC, we expect leaders to converge on highly sticky dimensions, and the data (22% of the winning coalition at 0.3 optimum are 0-level stickiness, while 31% are at 50-level stickiness) confirm our expectations. Conversely, at maximum OWC, where we predict advantages for inclusiveness, 63% of the winning coalitions are non-sticky (0-level stickiness), whereas less than 1% of the leaders win with dimensions that are at the stickiness level of 50.

Figure 9.1 graphically illustrates the same findings. Here the height of each layer represents the percentage of winning coalitions that feature dimensions with the stickiness level corresponding to that layer, with the total adding up to 100%. This display shows even more clearly how ethnic (highly sticky) coalitions are regularly successful only at low levels of OWC. Figure 9.1 also illustrates the two apparent thresholds where a major shift takes place in the appeal of different types of coalitions: at the transition from a minority to a majority requirement (0.4 to 0.5) and again at the transition from a large majority requirement to a desire for the maximum possible coalition size (0.7 to max).

The causal logic shaping this powerful emergent pattern is illustrated if we look at some randomly chosen runs of the model.[5] First, consider systems where

---

[5] To ensure true randomness, we programmed a random number generator to pick a number between 1 and 100, and the corresponding run of the OWC = 0.3 condition was selected for examination. This process was repeated for the selection of random runs for two other OWC conditions (0.5 and 0.7). The number of each run corresponds to the value of the random number seed used to start that run. This makes it possible easily to recreate a particular run.

OWC is 0.3. Leaders aim for a coalition just over 3,000 in size, but preferably not greater than that.[6] In our sample run (run number 68), leaders choosing higher-stickiness dimensions as the basis for their coalitions clearly get rewarded at a greater rate than those who choose the lower-stickiness dimensions. For example, the longest-ruling leader stakes out a position based on a requirement that agents must satisfy its specification on the two dimensions in the system with the highest stickiness in the system (50). This allows an uninterrupted period of rule of fourteen electoral rounds.

A brief discussion of this leader's fortunes will serve to illustrate the processes at work. This leader (leader 1) displaces another successful leader (leader 0) who has won for several rounds using a coalition specification demanding specific attributes on both dimension 3 (with stickiness 10) and 6 (stickiness 50). Specifying particular attributes on two separate dimensions, one of which is quite sticky, suffices to keep leader 0's coalition fairly compact. However, the number of agents satisfying the conditions on dimension 3 grows steadily, as one might expect. After four successful elections, leader 0 therefore reduces the number of attributes accepted on dimension 3. One round later, she reduces the number again, now accepting just one attribute. At this point, it becomes harder to constrain coalition growth.

Soon after, then, leader 0 is displaced by leader 1, whose tenure will turn out to be the longest during the course of this run. Leader 1 also specifies two separate dimensions, but *both* have a stickiness of 50. Even with this greater stickiness, the new leader drops one of the attributes she accepts on dimension 6 after just one round in power. At this point, the coalition becomes fairly stable and lasts for thirteen more rounds. By the end of this, as agents who can attain the winning attribute begin to acquire it, the coalition size has grown from 3,143 to 3,743, creating a considerable amount of space for competing leaders to attempt to undercut the coalition by staying closer to the minimum level of 3,000. Indeed, a new victor emerges in leader 2, who accepts just a single attribute on the relatively sticky dimension 4 (stickiness 25), which results in a coalition of 3,367. This coalition grows by about thirty members over the course of each of the next two electoral rounds, and the run ends before another leader has managed to arrive at a coalition that could undercut it.

Overall, after the period of initial consolidation (i.e., starting at time step 501), the only time a non-sticky dimension ever appears in the winning coalition is when it is added as a second condition, to help contain the size of the coalition generated by an offer emphasizing a highly sticky dimension. This happens a couple of times over the course of the run. In other words, leaders respond to the small size of the OWC by moving to offer coalitions based on

---

[6] To be exact, they aim at a coalition that is 102.5% of the optimal level, since they expect always to lose some voters. In practice, therefore, they shoot for 3,075 votes, not 3,000.

sticky dimensions and by making specifications even more difficult to meet by demanding matches on two separate dimensions. Or, perhaps better, the system rewards leaders who take such steps—leaders, after all, do not consciously *choose* more ethnic dimensions.

The contrast to a run where both leaders and the public desire to be a part of the largest possible coalition is quite striking, even at the level of an individual run. In our sample run here (run 23), the average stickiness of the winning coalition is 4.57, as compared to the 24.3 for the run just discussed where the OWC was 0.3. In this run, three dimensions alternated for supremacy. In addition, leaders abandoned their winning coalitions more often and, apparently, more recklessly. Still, though the leaders alternated their offerings rather often, the dimensions that were in the winning repertoires alternated much less. The political salience of the three dimensions that had early advantage grew considerably over the course of the run. The final outcome underscores the contingent nature of these runs, with an above-average sticky dimension (stickiness 25) becoming the most politically salient. Despite the relative stickiness of this dimension, leaders offering categories on this dimension maximized their coalition sizes by all accepting multiple attributes on this dimension. It was as though having ended up in a system where sticky dimensions had emerged to be politically salient, leaders attempted to mitigate the problem by being inclusive of different identities (modeled as a range of attributes) within this dimension. A real-world example might be the construction of a "Christian" category in the United States through the combining of Protestants *and* Catholics on the relatively sticky dimension of religion.

This discussion logically brings us to our other two hypotheses. The second hypothesis suggested that political salience, on average—though not in every run, as we just saw—should shift toward more ethnic dimensions in low-OWC conditions, and toward less sticky dimensions in high-OWC conditions. This is so because salience affects the likelihood that agents will keep or drop a particular dimension in their repertoires. High-salience dimensions do not get dropped (only demoted, perhaps, if even more salient dimensions are added). Moreover, if many neighbors have high salience on a dimension, that greatly increases the likelihood that agent will add it, and, in turn, will add an attribute similar to that of its neighbors. This, in turn, of course, has implications for the likely evolution of coalition sizes. Low-salience dimensions are unlikely to see their potential coalition sizes grow very fast.

There is a more indirect way—which we informally call "political climate"— in which salience affects leaders' choices of dimensions when calculating their offers. Political climate here refers to a combination of two features of our simulated political systems. First, our model introduces biases in favor of dimensions used in winning as well as non-winning coalitions. Second, as just noted, the relative salience, at the population level, of different dimensions also affects agent decisions with respect to their own attribute-repertoires.

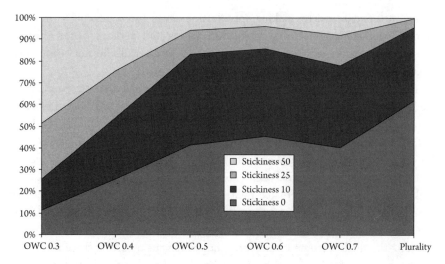

Figure 9.2 Most Salient Identity Dimension at End of Run

To the extent that agents agree on the salience of a particular dimension, that dimension will remain dominant among the dimensions used by leaders in putting forward coalitions. In other words, while the political climate does not directly determine the coalitions proposed by winning and non-winning leaders alike—since leaders are not consciously aware of it—it has serious implications for the longer-term viability of different coalitions. The resulting pattern is, once again, emergent, resulting from mutual causation: The choices of leaders affect the evolution of attribute-repertoires (and salience), and changes in the latter shape the choices leaders make down the line. It therefore follows that the salience of sticky dimensions should increase in low-OWC institutional environments and decrease in high-OWC institutional environments.

Figure 9.2 provides evidence from our experiment clearly supporting this expectation. We see that as OWC rises, the most salient dimension at the end of the run is increasingly likely to be a non-sticky dimension. Conversely, as OWC falls, the most salient dimension at the end of the run is increasingly likely to be the stickiest dimension in the system, just as we expected.

The final hypothesis looks at these overall patterns from the individual leader level. Are leaders in fact rewarded for staking out the preferred dimensions suggested by our analysis here? Figure 9.3 provides the evidence.[7] Here we see that leadership tenure goes up with stickiness when OWC is below 0.5, whereas it falls with stickiness as OWC rises above 0.5. Interestingly, the sharpest drop occurs at a lower stickiness threshold when OWC is 0.5 than when OWC is

[7] We have here omitted the OWC 0.3 condition, since our tracking data make leadership tenure figures problematic in situations in which multiple leaders can simultaneously achieve OWC. This same issue was briefly noted in Chapter 7.

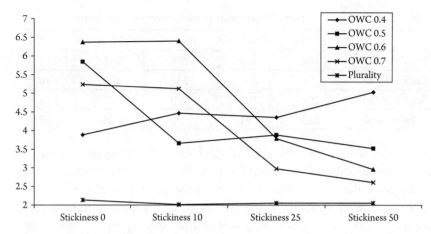

Figure 9.3 Leadership Tenure by Stickiness

higher. This is probably due to an effect discussed in Chapter 7: When OWC is 0.5 there is likely to be a greater number of alternative coalitions that might meet the OWC level. As a result, the penalty for choosing a dimension with even a slightly higher value on stickiness (making it harder for voters to flexibly adjust) is greater.

It is also interesting to note that the penalty for choosing a dimension with higher stickiness is much less in a plurality system than in the fixed-OWC systems. Although there is a slight negative trend to the bottom line in Figure 9.3, compared to the others it is essentially horizontal. On the other hand, it is also obvious that this system results in a far more volatile overall pattern of leadership succession. In fact, it is probably more accurate to say that the benefit of choosing a dimension with lower stickiness is much less (as opposed to the *cost* of choosing *higher* stickiness). In a system where the main goal is to attract more votes than whoever won in the previous round, undercutting another leader is never rewarded. This means that leaders' choice of dimensions to attract constituents will be determined almost entirely by features of the political system that are largely contingent, such as the political salience of a particular dimension in a particular run, and the degree of concentration of agents across the attributes within a dimension.

A slightly different take on our third hypothesis is shown in Table 9.2. Here we show the number of individual victors, not considering their tenure. The same pattern emerges: When OWC is 0.4 (i.e. less than an absolute majority), more victors choose the stickiest dimensions. In contrast, as OWC grows, an ever greater share of the victors chooses low-stickiness dimensions.

In sum, then, the experimental data bear out all three of our hypotheses. In addition, as we emphasized earlier, our hypotheses are borne out even though neither leaders nor agents know anything about the relative stickiness of

Table 9.2 **Number of Victors by Stickiness of Coalition Specification**

	OWC 0.4	OWC 0.5	OWC 0.6	OWC 0.7	Plurality
Stickiness 0	168	338	276	185	1173
Stickiness 10	192	255	252	175	646
Stickiness 25	201	109	79	77	74
Stickiness 50	243	44	45	28	19

different dimensions, *and* there are no tangible material benefits to being a part of a winning coalition that might have implications for the functioning of the polity down the line. In other words, the patterns predicted by Fearon *emerge* as a result of the structure of the system, without conscious reasoning about rewards or any built-in theory as to how best to exclude people from a coalition. The ability to demonstrate such emergent patterns is one of the key strengths of agent-based modeling. Our findings here show that Fearon's basic logic holds even in the absence of some of the auxiliary assumptions about reasoning ability and knowledge he makes in his original paper.

4. Extensions

Fearon's paper raises several issues that are not fully addressed in his political identity game. Yet they lead to conjectures that could be examined in our virtual world. Thinking about ways to investigate such further conjectures helps elaborate the Fearon model further, as we show with respect to two important features of the model.

Ethnic Politics and Choices Among Polarized Policy Goods

In addition to the argument about pork, Fearon (1999) presents a second reason for which ethnically based politics may emerge. He argues that ethnic coalitions form when "preferences over public policies are shared within groups but are polarized across groups" (11). This polarization results, he notes, because often such issues have status as well as material implications. Without the status component, the argument reduces to pork. The difference introduced by the status component, then, is that benefits accrue also to those who *could* have been a member of the winning coalition but were not. Consider the issue of national language, which Fearon highlights as one possible polarized policy good. This is a "pork" issue in the sense that it allocates costs and benefits (of operating successfully in the society) in a way that is not identity-blind, as some form of need-based or merit-based allocation might, ideally, be. But it is not a pork issue in the sense that the benefits cannot be limited to those who voted for the coalition that chooses the language—instead, all those who speak the language obtain the benefits.

However, in any context where votes are secret, it is impossible to tell who voted for a particular leader.[8] The stereotypical example of pork barrel politics is regionally based: A senator works to get a new military base established in her state, for example. However, the economic benefits to the state cannot be limited to those who voted for that senator only. This consideration further reduces the difference between polarized policy goods and pork, and it seems as though it might undermine some of the central logic of Fearon's argument, which is mostly in terms of pork. As our experiments have already suggested, however, "real" pork is not necessary for Fearon's basic predictions to hold. Indeed, in our model the reward is of status only, and not material in nature. Whereas Fearon does not discuss whether his logic would also apply in a situation of polarized policy goods, our results demonstrate that it does. Indeed, our results show that the only necessary feature is some form of exclusivity or excludability. This excludability need not be based on the supporter-nonsupporter distinction, nor must it consist of tangible material rewards. All that is necessary is the ability for members of the political system to distinguish those who meet the conditions of a coalition from those who do not.

One implication that follows from this insight is that if we were to replace our simplistic agents with agents who reason in the ways Fearon assumes, the outcome might actually change in ways unforeseen by Fearon. Consider a situation in which an agent qualifies for two coalitions, each of which could plausibly become a winning coalition. A reasoning agent should consider not just which is the most likely to produce the smallest possible winning coalition but also what the likelihood is that her vote would make a difference. If that likelihood is small for coalition A but larger for coalition B, it makes sense to go with coalition B. If coalition A wins, and our agent meets its specifications, she will still benefit from the distributive benefits, after all. Clearly this might give rise to some unexpected indeterminacy in outcomes, along the lines of the standard rationalist voting paradox.[9]

Fearon (1999) suggests a partial solution to this problem by noting that "Over time, if a population comes to mobilize and vote as (say) Luos, Kikuyus, Luhyias, Kalenjin [four of the major ethno-linguistic communities in Kenya], and so on, this will become 'naturalized' at least in the sense of being overwhelmingly and correctly expected as the basis for political coalitions" (14). It is not clear, however, that this is fully satisfactory. This solution assumes an essentially

---

[8] This point is made by Golden (2003) in regard to Shefter's (1977) work.

[9] The standard paradox is as follows: If everyone votes, the chance that your vote will make a difference is negligible. Therefore, it makes no sense to vote. Yet if everyone were rational in this way nobody would vote. In consequence, the chance that any vote would make a difference is very large. So if everyone is rational in this way, what is the rational choice: to vote or not to vote?

unchanging membership in different categories. However, even when categories are infinitely sticky, differential rates of birth and death will still change relative coalition sizes over time. Imagine a situation where a small fraction of Luos and a large fraction of Kikuyus share an identity feature such as rancher with one another but not with their fellow Luos or Kikuyus. If Kikuyus dominate the political system but the number or fraction of Luos who identify as ranchers grows, it becomes rational at some point for Kikuyu ranchers to hedge their bets and vote for a leader campaigning on behalf of ranchers. Kikuyus will still benefit if things are as "naturalized" as Fearon expects even without voting for a Kikuyu leader, but many of them will also benefit if things are less naturalized and the new rancher coalition wins. Here a change in demography can alter patterns of pork voting despite naturalized voting blocs having earlier emerged.

The Costs of a More Complex Coalition Specification

A concatenation in Fearon's terms is a social category made up of not a single social label (e.g., Kikuyu) but of a combination of labels (e.g., Kikuyu or Luo). If concatenations were permissible, then political entrepreneurs could forget about ethnic categories and build coalitions of named individuals (Joe A. + Sam B. + Sara C.) until the coalition was safely over the minimum winning value. However, as Fearon (1999) observes, a "concatenation raises the costs of forming, advertising, and distributing benefits...A simple way to represent this inefficiency," he reasons, "would be to suppose that the benefits available for distribution to a winning coalition are reduced depending on the number of primary categories that comprise it" (16).

In our model, we permit two forms of concatenation. We allow for an expansion of the acceptable category space within a dimension, allowing for two or three attributes that are relatively similar to one another, to form a category. We also permit leaders to demand that voters meet conditions on two distinct dimensions, such that to be in the winning coalition, an agent must be both Kikuyu and Catholic, for example. This latter case we call a complex concatenation.

In our model, the direct costs of expanding the category space on any dimension for an entrepreneur are no higher than choosing a single attribute on that dimension, since the entrepreneur knows how many agents have each attribute on any dimension. In Fearon's model, too, these costs should be minimal. After all, one can imagine two leaders joining forces, each aiming to attract one-half of the necessary OWC. In a pork situation (but perhaps less so in a polarized policy goods situation), the only real cost here should be that faced by the colluding leaders in reaching a credible agreement to share the spoils.

However, there are potential indirect costs to be faced, arising from the fact that in our model the situation is dynamic. And the more attributes one accepts, the more difficult it becomes to correctly anticipate both how many voters will choose one's coalition and how the coalition size will change over time. Consider, for example, a situation in which the OWC = 0.5, and on the religion dimension we have 40% Catholics, 40% Protestants, and 20% Orthodox. If there are two competing leaders offering {Catholic or Orthodox} and {Protestant or Orthodox}, neither will be certain how many Orthodox voters would actually join the coalition. (This is not a problem that exists when leaders accept just a single attribute and follow a rule stating that they cannot mimic a competitor's offering.)

As a result of this unpredictability, we would expect there to be a small but non-negligible cost associated with accepting a larger number of attributes. Table 9.3 shows that this expectation nicely holds in our experiment: In every single OWC condition, the correlation between the number of attributes accepted in a coalition and a leader's tenure is negative.

Clearly there is a cost to offering a more multifaceted specification. It is important to note that this cost arises from a different source than that considered by Fearon. Instead, it is, as with our other findings, *emergent*: Accepting multiple attributes implies greater unpredictability leading to strategic miscalculation. As a result, we find that leaders who accept more attributes on balance last less long in power than those who accept fewer attributes.

The second type of concatenation should have even stronger effects, again because of predictability issues, now aggravated by incomplete knowledge. Neither leaders nor basic agents in the model have complete information on the size of the intersections of attribute holders across dimensions. All anybody knows is the membership distribution within a given dimension; for intersections, actors assume independence across dimensions, something that neither empirically nor in our model is likely to be generally accurate. As a result, we should see leadership tenure be considerably shorter for leaders proposing complex coalitions of this sort.

Table 9.4 shows that our predictions here hold too. We do not show information for the highest OWC conditions, since leaders put forward a complex coalition specification too rarely in those systems. The actual cost of proposing complex coalitions is likely to be even greater than that suggested in Table 9.4, as the table does not show the numerous cases of winning leaders losing power as soon as they put forward a complex specification.

On the other hand, Table 9.4 also shows that we find numerous situations of complex coalitions throughout our experiment, even when OWC levels are

Table 9.3 **Correlation Between Number of Attributes Accepted and Leadership Tenure**

OWC 0.3	OWC 0.4	OWC 0.5	OWC 0.6	OWC 0.7	*Plurality*
−0.16	−0.09	−0.03	−0.15	−0.17	−0.22

Table 9.4 **Comparison of Average Tenure Overall and Average Tenure for Complex Coalitions**

	OWC 0.3	OWC 0.4	OWC 0.5	OWC 0.6
Average winning leader tenure	4.131	4.486	4.674	5.833
Average winning complex coalition tenure	2.029	2	2.004	2

fairly high. Given all the unpredictability we just discussed, this suggests that such coalitions can still be viable in particular contexts. For example, in a sample run from our experiment where OWC = 0.5 (run 17), one political leader managed to remain in power for five consecutive electoral periods through the judicious use of a complex category to keep her coalition size close to 5,000. Empirically, too, cases of successful complex coalitions arise, although often the circumstances are unusual.

In Japan, for example, the Liberal Democratic Party (LDP), which dominated politics for decades, had to devise ways to allocate voters to candidates in multimember districts where they were running more than one from their slate. Their unique solution, according to Ramseyer and Rosenbluth (1993, 22), was to form clubs in each district that catered to special constituencies, so that each LDP candidate could be associated with a club.[10] While LDP membership as such was not sticky, these club memberships had an esprit de corps that was ethnic-like. This is the way, again according to Ramseyer and Rosenbluth, that the party efficiently allocated votes. A similar pattern arises in our experiments. Complex coalitions almost always combine a single attribute on a relatively nonsticky dimension (such as LDP membership in this example) with one or more attributes on a stickier dimension (such as club membership).

Another case from the same region suggests that similar solutions have arisen elsewhere in response to the same type of political constraint. Consider the case of Taiwan, which also had a multimember, single nontransferable vote system until 2005. In the early 1990s, the Democratic Progressive Party used the last digit of citizen identification numbers to allocate voters to candidates. The National Party responded by using season of birth (the "four season strategy") and gender (depending on district magnitude) as coordination devices. Categories such as birth-season are not ethnic-like, but they certainly are sticky! Once done, other Taiwanese parties built complex concatenations combining ideology and such identities as birth season to allocate voters to candidates. It worked for

[10] Ramseyer and Rosenbluth (1993, 22, n. 11) discount David Laitin's (in a personal communication to them) suggestion that there were more efficient mechanisms to achieve vote allocations without creating costly pork-eating clubs. The Taiwanese (see our discussion that follows), however, saw the same opportunity Laitin identified.

several parties, but for parties that tried to maximize the number of elected candidates by minimizing the security zone (that had, when larger, allowed for some slack), which was the strategy of the Greens, everything was lost. Political entrepreneurs in Taiwan continued to experiment with ways to maximize the efficient transfer of votes to seats through new concatenations, more or less as our interpretation of leader behavior in the agent based models.[11]

Both our experimental finding that complex coalitions sometimes can succeed and the empirical examples just discussed suggest that this is an issue worth investigating in greater detail, within our agent-based model as well as in the real world. In our model, it would be interesting to investigate, for example, the patterns that would emerge if one leader can credibly commit to another not to compete for the same set of votes. One possible solution would be the kind of situation that evolved in Japan and Taiwan. Another possible outcome would be more classically consociational outcomes (Lijphart 1968), where leaders end up focusing on the same dimension but accept different, non-overlapping sets of attributes within that dimension.

5. Conclusions

The experiments presented in this chapter demonstrate how agent-based models can be used to investigate the internal logic and causal mechanisms informing our theories of ethnicity with a constructivist logic—that is, where neither attributes nor dimensional salience are fixed but rather subject to systematic reconfiguration. In the model initially set up in Chapter 7, but here applied to a particular theory of ethnicity, we showed that the well-known elective affinity between ethnicity and pork can emerge from just a small number of model components. In particular, it is not necessary for actual pork to be distributed, nor for any of the actors in a system to be aware of the relative stickiness of different dimensions. As long as membership in a particular category is identifiable and brings with it some reward (even if it is only in the form of status), the dynamics of the system ensure that an affinity between ethnicity and small coalitions emerges.

The most obvious way to measure this affinity is to demonstrate a relationship between OWC level and the average stickiness of winning coalitions. In addition, however, we showed that the same logic drives patterns in a number of related measures, each of which is open to future empirical testing. Political systems where the OWC is small are more likely to have ethnic identities emerge as politically salient. In addition, leaders who campaign on ethnic dimensions in such polities are more likely to win and remain in office.

---

[11] For news sources on the concatenations in the December 2004 elections, see Hong, December 8, 2004, and Tai-lin, December 12, 2004.

We further used our model to extend our understanding of the logic and implications of Fearon's model of ethnicity and pork. In particular, we discussed the difficulty of distinguishing in any meaningful way between pork and polarized policy issues, two separate drivers in Fearon's logic, and we highlighted the implications of the difference between voting for a particular coalition and satisfying its membership requirements. We also discussed the source of the costs leaders face when offering more multifaceted specifications, noting that these arise from unpredictability and incomplete information about the precise demographic percentages for voters on cross-cutting dimensions. This seems the greater problem than the one from advertising costs along the lines discussed by Fearon.

Overall, the findings reported here contribute to our understanding of the connection between ethnicity and pork. They also raise a number of intriguing suggestions about ways to connect the issues studied here to the literature on selectorate sizes, veto points, and consociationalism, which provides ample inspiration for additional model experiments as well as empirical investigations.

10

A Constructivist Model
of Ethnic Riots

STEVEN I. WILKINSON

1. Introduction

Ethnic riots are generally explained in one of two ways. First, many sociologists, political scientists, and economists argue, from either a hard or soft rational choice perspective, that ethnic riots are the result of increased political and economic competition between what they implicitly consider to be solid ethnic groups. Empirically, scholars have found that levels of ethnic heterogeneity or recent increases in the proportion of minorities in a population are highly significant and positively related to levels of violence, and that this is true for both cross-national and intra-national analyses of ethnic riots (Wanderer 1969; Spilerman 1976; DiPasquale and Glaeser 1998). Most scholars argue that this is because high levels of heterogeneity or recent increases in ethnic heterogeneity, especially when accompanied by economic crises, increase the level of intergroup competition for political power and economic resources. Riots are the bloody means by which one group defends its political or economic privileges against another.

Second, many social psychologists and some political scientists highlight the key role of ethnic antipathy in explaining ethnic riots. Beginning with the work of Gordon Allport and Leo Postman in the 1940s, social psychologists have argued that ethnic group antipathies, when combined with rumors that assume a "specifically threatening form" are the direct precipitants of violence (Allport and Postman 1947). Although recognizing that other motivations can come into play, the supporters of a social psychological approach point out that rationalist elite-driven accounts fail to recognize the importance of ethnic bonds and ethnic antipathies for many people and they also argue that rationalist accounts give too much credence to elites' ability to manipulate members of their groups at will (Horowitz 1985, 2001). Donald Horowitz, for instance, has argued that "without feelings of antipathy, there can be no ethnic conflict" (Horowitz 1985, 181–182).

Both of these broad explanations for ethnic riots have much to recommend them, but from the constructivist perspective both have problems.[1] First, the assumption that ethnic groups are solid entities that act collectively has been widely questioned by constructivist research. In many societies individuals have multiple group identities that often shift over time and according to context and many members of a group may not support actions taken allegedly on their behalf during an "ethnic riot." Second, there is increasing recognition that the "ethnic riot" itself, regardless of whether it is labeled after the event as a "race riot," "caste riot," or "Hindu-Muslim riot," may in fact be understood by partici- pants very differently. Rioters may in fact be participating in a "caste riot" for a whole range of economic, political reasons, and rioters may perceive their own identities very differently than the single label "caste" might indicate.[2] The third problem, which stems from the first two, is that if we assume (1) group homo- geneity, around (2) solid ethnic categories that are used to label a riot after the event ("Hindu-Muslim," "Black-White," etc.), this will tend to bias our subse- quent attempts to understand what caused the riot. This bias occurs because we will tend to not collect information about a range of potential group cleavages and political, economic, and sociological motivations that may have led to the riot because these cleavages or motivations seem to be unrelated to the ethnic group cleavage that we *know* motivated the riot.[3] In fact though, there is sub- stantial historical and anthropological evidence to suggest that the cleavages and identities and motivations for many riots are often not the same as those that emerge after the event to "explain" the violence. In medieval Spain, for example, David Nirenberg shows us that "Muslim-Christian" riots were often the result of intra-Christian struggles for power, while in India "Hindu-Muslim" riots are often best understand as the outcome of intra-Hindu, inter-caste struggles for political power (Nirenberg 1996, Wilkinson 2004).

The argument I put forward in this chapter, in contrast to rationalist or social psychological theories premised on the existence of solid ethnic groups, is that ethnic riots are best understood not as the *outcome* of already high degrees of

---

The author is grateful for the comments I received from fellow contributors to this volume on an earlier draft, and especially for the detailed written suggestions from Kanchan Chandra.

[1] In fairness, some of these problems may arise because the Black-White cleavage in the United States, which has motivated a great deal of the social scientific study of riots, may be both a "harder" cleavage and much more salient than identities in other countries such as India where there is a much greater number of competing and politically salient ethnic and non-ethnic identities.

[2] This is the central point in Brass (1997).

[3] We are also likely to collect only information about our dependent variable, the ethnic riot, that seems to conform to the ethnic cleavage we imagine to have motivated the violence.

competition, polarization, and hatred between solid ethnic groups but rather as the means through which political parties and political entrepreneurs construct solid ethnic categories, however briefly, for a clear political purpose. Following the conceptualization of ethnic identity change presented in this volume (see Chapters 1–4), my starting point is the constructivist insight that individuals have a repertoire of multiple nominal ethnic and non-ethnic categories, and the identities they activate change over time and according to context. I use the words ethnic "identity," "category," and "group" interchangeably. An individual typically possesses various attributes that qualify her for membership in several different categories that could theoretically win a majority in an election. The challenge for a political entrepreneur is therefore how to persuade a sufficient number of voters to identify themselves with the attribute-dimension (e.g., language) and category (e.g., "French-speaker") that provides the entrepreneur and her group with the greatest payoff along that issue-dimension of politics that they regard as most important.[4]

This chapter builds upon the baseline model introduced by Chandra and Boulet in Chapter 6 in the following ways. First, I start with an existing distribution of attribute-repertoires for a population, with some given number of commonsensical attribute-dimensions and -values on each. These may include non-ethnic attribute-dimensions. I assume, further, that some initial minimum winning category is activated, whether based on ethnic or non-ethnic attribute-dimensions. The distribution of attribute-repertoires is fixed: Political entrepreneurs in these elections do not add or subtract new commonsensical dimensions. But they seek to *activate* different ethnic categories, based on attribute-dimensions different from those initially activated. "When there is more than one minimum winning category," Chandra and Boulet (Chapter 6, in this volume) point out, "those who stand to lose when one category is activated have the option of reversing their situation if they can successfully induce potential members of an alternative winning coalition to declare this alternative membership" (242). *In this chapter I argue that the ethnic riot is best thought of as a solution to this political problem.*[5] To put it in Riker's language of *heresthetics*, riots are a way for political winners to fix the attribute-dimension and category that sustains them in power, or alternatively a way for challengers to try to activate a new attribute-dimension and category to break up the existing coalition (Riker 1986).

[4] What Riker (1986) refers to as *heresthetics*.

[5] In an excellent study of communal violence, Paul Brass (1997) makes the argument that politicians label riots as "caste" or "communal" or some other identity (or choose not to label them at all) for political reasons. I agree with Brass on the importance to political entrepreneurs of succeeding in labeling a riot as one type of ethnic violence rather than another. Where this article differs from his analysis is that I argue most large riots are fomented for these political purposes in the first place.

At the same time, this chapter goes beyond the Chandra and Boulet baseline model in two important and related respects. First, rather than treating all combinations of attribute-values in a population's repertoire as equally feasible, it applies to divisive ethnic mobilization Axelrod's (1970) idea that politicians will consider as feasible only "minimum connected winning coalitions," which minimize distance among coalition partners along some issue-dimension that politicians regard as most important, such as economic reforms.[6] The operative repertoire of ethnic categories in an electoral context, in other words, is restricted by this requirement of connectedness (see the discussion of the "linear order restriction" in Chapter 5, p. 213 for the combinatorial development of this idea). Second, I introduce the concept of "issue dimensions," and show how it can be combined with the concept of "attribute-dimensions" in explaining an electoral outcome. Attribute-dimensions as Chandra and Boulet conceptualize them consist of the discrete attribute-values that individuals possess. "Issue dimensions" by contrast, are a continuous metric that represent the positions individuals with distinct attribute-values take on some key electoral issue. They are key to establishing the notion of "distance" between attribute-values and the categories based on them. Sometimes, we can read off positions on issue dimensions directly from the attribute-values on attribute-dimensions: Here, for instance, I assume that all those with the attribute-value "Protestant" have the same position on the issue dimension of religious equality. At other times, not modeled here, positions on issue dimensions may divide those with identical attribute-values (Axelrod 1970).

The multilevel model of riot incentives I build here, depicted in Figure 10.1, rests on three basic assumptions. First, that ethnic mobilization and polarization is attractive to politicians because it is institutionally and often legally privileged compared to other types of mobilization, and because ethnic mobilization takes advantage of already well-established dense social networks, organizations, and focal points. Second, that violence is a highly effective way of communicating with voters. Third, in addition to the mechanisms by which it can changes aspects of an ethnic identity reviewed in Chapter 4, violence is an especially effective way to activate or deactivate new attribute-dimensions or categories in politics, (a) because there is a well-established social-psychological tendency for members of one ethnic group to attribute reports of negative acts committed by members of another group to the group's threatening disposition rather than to the situational constraints; (b) because even majority-initiated violence is easy to frame after the fact as an outrage committed by the targeted group; and (c) because of the very high costs that ignoring news of ethnic violence (and being wrong) might impose on the voters in the category that politicians are trying to win over.

---

[6] For the original Shapley-Shubik model see Shapley and Shubik 1954 and for a perceptive review of the literature on how to measure power and pivotality and an attempt to construct a combinatoric-ideological index of power in Israel, see Rapoport and Golan 1985.

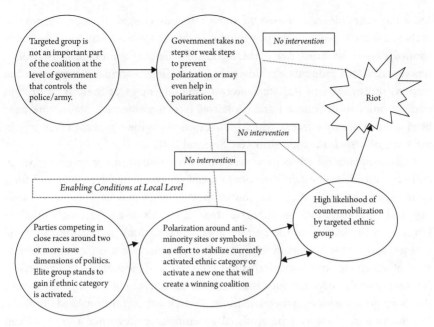

Figure 10.1 The Constituency and State-Level Incentives for Ethnic Riots

The Advantages of Ethnic Mobilization

Mobilization along ethnic lines is attractive to politicians in conditions in which existing ethnic categories are institutionally and often legally privileged compared to other types of groups. Most states—France would be an obvious exception—have institutionalized some ethnic dimensions (e.g. religion, language and caste in India) and some categories (e.g., "Backward Caste" and "Most Backward Caste") through their education systems, recruitment to the civil service and army, and in many cases through the political system as well, for example, by reserving a proportion of the seats in parliament for some ethnic groups.[7] States also often recognize the right of some ethnic groups to carry out their festivals or prayers in public places at regular intervals, and in some cases they also exempt ethnic or religious groups from various laws that regulate such matters as public speech or even restrictions on the right to bear arms.[8] For example in

---

[7] For the process through which states institutionalize some identities rather than others, see an excellent account by Posner 2005.

[8] Tandon 1968 describes how he saw a Tamil Brahmin traveling to England aboard a British ship in the 1930s retaliate against the British, who were preventing Indian passengers from playing Indian songs on the piano. The man sat " . . . cross-legged on the deck the next morning with all the marks and stripes on his arms, forehead and chest, chanting mantras interminably till he cleared the whole deck. He knew that religious practice gave the immunity that he did not enjoy in the state room at the piano" (204).

India the state allows members of some religious groups to carry weapons—such as a Sikh *kirpan* (dagger) or Hindu *Trishul* (trident)—that could be easily banned under the Arms Act if these had no religious connotation. In 2002 it was reported that militants working to build up Hindu nationalist support in the western Indian state of Rajasthan were taking advantage of these legal exemptions in order to distribute Rampuri knives (six- to seven-inch blades that have been used to deadly effect in many Indian riots since the nineteenth century) in the form of *trishuls* in seven districts (Setalvad 2001).[9]

Mobilizing around ethnicity is also attractive to political entrepreneurs when there are already well-established dense social networks, organizations, and focal points through which they can communicate with voters and organize meetings and demonstrations to publicize their cause. Some of these networks are intrinsic to the culture of the particular category, such as the institution of the mosque and Friday prayers in Islam, or of Sunday mass in the Catholic Church, both of which clearly allow information exchange and facilitate collective action. But there are also organizations that facilitate collective action along ethnic lines that have grown up largely because the state itself has institutionalized ethnicity. For example in Malaysia, where official government policy since 1969 has been to protest the interests of "native" Malays, a whole host of employee and business associations have grown up to represent the economic and political interests of the "Bumiputra," or sons of the soil. Organizations such as the employee associations from the Bumiputra banks or the Association of Bumiputra Women Entrepreneurs Malaysia (PUBM) in Malaysia, or the various trade unions that represent lower-caste government employees in India, form a ready-made infrastructure through which to press political campaigns, an infrastructure that does not exist for many non-ethnic dimensions and categories.

The Utility of Violence Compared to Other Means of Persuading Voters

Why should politicians want to solidify political coalitions through polarization and violence rather than through the more conventional tools of political advertising, programmatic party competition (i.e., competition over different policy agendas), or clientelistic party competition (i.e., direct transfers from politicians to groups of voters or individuals in return for their electoral support)? One reason is that violence is cheap in terms of the resources expended compared to the number of voters "contacted." It is well established that both mass media

[9] At times of real physical insecurity people have even been willing to change their nominal ethnic category to take advantage of these exemptions. In 1946 for example colonial reports from the United Provinces indicate that large numbers of Hindus formally converted to the category of "Sikh" so that they would be allowed to carry swords. The Governor of the United Provinces (F. V. Wylie) to Sir John Colville (Acting Viceroy), IOR LP&J/5/275, December 22, 1946.

and rumor networks transfer news about violence very quickly. The general literature on media and violence has also established that certain groups of people (e.g., young men 18–34 in the United States) pay more attention to news about violence than others, especially when that violence involves their local community (Hamilton 2001).

A second reason why violence is used as a campaign strategy is that, for elite groups especially, the costs of offering more conventional alternatives such as promising goods and services to voters in order to build a coalition may be unacceptably high. Ethnic identity is less costly to emphasize for elites who already enjoy a large share of wealth, income, land, or other resources, and who would therefore find it difficult to form coalitions with other poorer groups without having to make substantial and expensive concessions over distribution. Moreover even if such an elite group's leaders do make promises to redistribute wealth or income, they might find that many voters do not believe their promises. It may be therefore be less costly for them to activate an ethnic attribute-dimension (religion) and then construct a category that minimizes the distance along this dimension ("Hindu" rather than upper, middle, and lower caste, or "Protestant" rather than Episcopalian and Presbyterian) rather than build a coalition that is diverse along the issue dimension of economic redistribution.

If by activating superordinate ethnic identity categories elite groups can retain power in an election, then they can continue to enjoy high payoffs in terms of access to land, education, and access to power by claiming these are group, not individual, payoffs. To some extent, they are right because there is a lot of evidence from both social psychology and empirical studies to suggest that *in the short term* at least, poorer members of ethnic groups do in fact derive satisfaction and pride from group outcomes.[10] The major finding of social identity theory, after all, is that individual self-worth is highly related to one's sense of how the "group as a whole" is doing.[11]

---

[10] For the best examination of social identity theory in its application to understanding ethnic conflict, see Horowitz 1985.

[11] These payoffs to elites diminish through time however. Almost all ethnic categories have an unequal distribution of goods along sub-ethnic lines, with some groups having more wealth, education, or access to good land or employment than others. These differences eventually become politically salient, typically with the poorer groups within the category beginning to push for a separate share to be allocated to them: Empirical examples of this are widespread in contemporary India, especially in the south, where among members of the "Dalit" (ex-untouchable) category the poorer Madigas are now pushing for their own "quota within a quota" because of their unhappiness that the richer Malas have been deriving most of the benefits from the Dalit job and educational affirmative action programs (a recent survey found that Malas, 41% of the Dalit population, have secured 65–70% of the reserved places for Dalits in higher education and 62% of the reserved Dalit jobs in government service). Karuppusamy, http://www.rghr.net/mainfile.php/0607/675/, downloaded August 23, 2004.

Social psychological research also suggests another reason why riots might be effective in activating some ethnic attribute-dimensions over others. Psychologists have found that images of violence, and especially the threat of death, raise the identification of many people with their cultural ingroup and against outgroups. In experiments where subjects were primed with images and descriptions of death, the increase in identification with their ingroup and against minorities was clear (Greenberg et al. 1990). Some authors have linked this to "the existence of an adaptive mechanism linking humans' threat detection abilities...to a set of defensive social-cognitive strategies that may have evolved to sensitize our hominid ancestors to probable sources of threat (e.g., rival group members) and to motivate affiliation with those likely to offer support (ingroup members)" (Neal and Kashima 2004; see also Öhman and Mineka 2001).

The Utility of Ethnic Violence

Ethnic violence is an especially effective way to change the dimension(s) and categories activated in politics for three reasons. First, manufacturing a controversy over a sacred site or symbol offers particular advantages because it generally sparks a counter-reaction from the targeted community, which then makes the original "threat" posed by the other ethnic category seem credible. The organizers calculate that, in anticipation of trouble and a possible attack on their community and its symbols, members of the other ethnic category will mobilize defensively to protect their territory or group. Once they have done so, and two crowds are in close proximity to another, it is very easy for one individual to throw a stone or make an insulting chant that starts the violence. In such a situation, an individual act will be quickly interpreted in group terms, as "the Hindus" or "the Muslims" throwing stones or insulting members of the other community.

The ability of politicians to frame a defensive minority reaction as a provocation is made easier because most members of both groups are not present at the event, so they will inevitably rely on their own group members, politicians, and media in order to form an opinion about what happened. The prevailing interpretations, not surprisingly, will rely on already established stereotypes about one's own group as nonviolent and reasonable and "the other" as violent and irrational. The tendency, long identified by social psychologists, for people from one ethnic category to explain negative acts committed by members of their own group in situational terms (e.g., "I was forced to fight because I was under attack") while explaining negative acts committed by members of the other group in dispositional terms (e.g., "They fought because members of their group are prone to violence and threatening to us") makes it difficult to moderate conflict after an incident has taken place.

The tendency to rely on stereotypes when trying to assess the reliability of information about an "ethnic provocation" by members of another group will be especially high in larger towns with higher degrees of group segregation and where people do not know each other; in villages, where negative group actions are counterbalanced by personal relationships and positive interactions at work and in village cooperatives, this tendency to interpret events in dispositional terms will be even more accentuated.[12]

The third reason why manufacturing an ethnic threat from another community is a winning strategy is that voters will pay attention to it because the stakes are so high, even if the probability of the threat being real is relatively low. The benefits and costs of ethnic identity are not merely individual but collective. In this respect one of the central working assumptions of Chandra 2004—that voters receive individualized payoffs—is unrealistic. Because ethnic identity is usually passed down to children and grandchildren and is shared by one's extended family, the economic and political status and the relative degree of security enjoyed by one's ethnic category today necessarily affect the prospects of one's whole family in the future.

The collective aspect of ethnicity as well as the fact that one's category determines future as well as present rewards massively raises the stakes over ethnic issues compared to non-ethnic issues. Even if the relative probability of news about the "threat" posed by members of another group being accurate is low, therefore, people will pay close attention to it and be concerned by it because the stakes involved are so high. If voters are being faced with a choice between two parties, one offering distributive goods with a 25% probability of getting payoff of 100, and the other party is offering to protect against a 5% probability of suffering a cataclysmic loss of 600 if the "ethnic threat" is not met with a strong response, then the benefits of voting for the distributive party (25) appear smaller than the costs (30).[13] The evidence is that, after ethnic incidents have taken place, many voters do switch their ranking of issue dimensions and begin to rank "ethnic threat" issues higher than the normal distributive issues that determine their vote. In India, for example, the Hindu-Nationalist mobilization and violence over the "disputed" Babri Masjid site in Ayodhya from 1989–1991 succeeding in pushing "national unity" and "communal" issues close to the top of Hindu voters' concerns, and led to a noticeable shift in actual voting patterns, with the BJP (Bharatiya Janata Party) winning several important state elections on the back of what became known as the "Hindu wave."

---

[12] Bookman 1978, 125, on the basis of extensive field research in a north Indian village, provides two reasons for why the tendency to view members of other groups in negative terms and to take violent actions based upon these views was stronger in towns than in villages. First, he argues that the "abrasive stereotypes Hindus and Muslims have of one another as groups break down when they have known each other intimately for a long time as individual members of a single village 'family.'" Second, "Any interaction they could consider taking would have to be weighed against the importance of maintaining harmonious social relations in a small community of close relatives, friend and neighbors who must live together and get along."

[13] This way of thinking about the voting choice follows the approach in Chandra (2004).

The argument I put forward here starts from the observation that despite the image we have of ethnic riots as largely spontaneous, the largest riots in terms of casualties are in fact the result of considerable planning, with weapons prepared and potential victims identified often days or weeks before a riot. In the recent Gujarat riots (2002) in India, for example, in which perhaps 1,000 people were killed, Hindu rioters in the city of Ahmedabad worked from municipal council computer printouts collected months earlier, which enabled them to identify Muslims living or having their shops in predominantly Hindu neighborhoods (Varadarajan 2002).[14] There is also often a clear organizational structure during the course of ethnic riots, with leaders during events such as the Gujarat riots giving detailed commands to rioters via mobile telephones on how to proceed during the violence.

In my argument, this high degree of organization and planning reflects the fact that most riots are highly political and strategic, in at least two ways. First, ethnic riots are most often initiated to *activate new ethnic attribute-dimensions and categories* within an existing population-repertoire so as to allow one party or leader to generate sufficient support to achieve a minimum winning coalition. Second, ethnic riots are also initiated to change the rules of the political game, either by directly removing a competing ethnic or non-ethnic group from competition or by putting pressure on the state to create new political institutions that will allow the political entrepreneurs responsible for the violence to form a minimum winning coalition (MWC) in at least some portion of the state. This second goal is briefly discussed in this chapter, as it is already well covered in the literature on ethnic riots (see, e.g., Horowitz 1985). Whether either of these two strategies will be followed ultimately depends on politicians' calculations about the likelihood of retaliation by the state or the ethnic target group. Ethnic violence is unlikely to be initiated by a group's leaders if the chance of large-scale retaliation by the target group or the state is high (i.e., the retaliation that will lead to large numbers of casualties to the initiator group, and state prosecution and punishment of the organizers).

2. A Constructivist Model of Riots

Ethnic riots are the outcome of incentives at both the local level and at the level (or levels) of government that control the police, paramilitary, and armed forces. I lay out the incentives that apply at both these levels, as well as how they interact to lead to violence, in Figure 10.1.

---

[14] For evidence that riots in the past were equally well planned, see Suranjan Das's account of the horrific 1946 Calcutta riots (6,000 dead and 10,000 injured), and the riots in Calcutta (1926) and Dacca (1930) in Das (1993. For non-Indian examples of highly planned riots, see Cecelski and Tyson 1998 on the 1898 Wilmington riots.

Local-Level Factors

At the local level, riots will be likeliest to take place in competitive races, where the value of the mobilizational effort is likely to yield the greatest reward. Activating new ethnic attribute-dimensions or new ethnic categories using previously activated attribute-dimensions at the local level is especially attractive where there are two or more issue dimensions (e.g., religious equality and economic redistribution) and a group's leaders foresee that if the non-ethnic issue dimension or a rival ethnic category remains activated then they will either lose the election or be forced to alter their issue positions (e.g., by supporting economic redistribution) in a way that will be very costly.

Which attribute-dimensions and/or categories will be highlighted by politicians? The challenge for political entrepreneurs is to highlight that dimension and/or category that offers them the greatest benefits and the fewest costs. It has long been recognized that a simple use of combinatorics (most notably through the Shapley-Shubik and Banzhaf power indices) is not very helpful in identifying the most logical "real world" coalitions and it seems likely that this is also the case for constructing ethnic coalitions. Far more plausible is Axelrod's notion that people want to construct "minimum connected winning coalitions," which minimize distance among coalition partners along some issue dimension that politicians regard as most important, such as economic reforms (Axelrod 1970).

The particular ethnic categories that violence and polarization will be used to highlight will change of course according to which categories constitute the "selectorate" (i.e., the portion of the population that actually selects a district or country's leadership) for a particular level of government. In systems in which one minority ethnic group is the majority of the army but not the population, for example, highlighting an intraminority cleavage may create a sufficiently large *MWC* to dominate the whole country, because the minority within the minority can then use its control of the army to control the rest of the population.[15] Institutional rules also have an obvious and direct effect on which categories might allow minimum winning coalitions to be formed. In federal systems, for example, or political systems that contain what Tsebelis has termed multiple "veto-points," a *MWC* may only need to contain a few percent of the population for a group to extract significant resources from the state. In those systems with multiple chambers in parliament or a highly restrictive franchise—for instance, the nineteenth-century franchises restricted to males

---

[15] A good example would be Burundi, where the army is predominantly staffed by one subgroup from the country's dominant 15% Tutsi minority, the Hima. The fact that most of the Hima military officers are from Bururi (the site of the military academy) and that this group effectively dominates the army, has helped create a new *MWC* tribal category, the "Banyaburi," among the Hima. The *MWC* in Burundi therefore constitutes only a few percent of the country's total population. Lemarchand 1986.

who paid a certain minimum amount in property tax—the winning categories and dominant attributes have often in fact been very different from those
held by the majority of the population, because some ethnic groups were much
richer than others, and consequently formed a larger portion of the electorate.[16]
For instance, the category "Swedish" on the attribute-dimension of language in
Finland was a winning category before 1906 despite the fact that Swedes only
constituted 12% of the population, because the wealthier Swedes benefited
from a restrictive property franchise in which only 10% of adults (all male)
could vote and because Swedes controlled two of the four "estates" in the Diet
(McRae 1997).

The proportion of individuals with sets of attributes that qualify them for
membership in particular ethnic and non-ethnic categories changes at different
levels of aggregation and from place to place. So while anti-minority violence
may activate a local "majority" ethnic identity sufficiently to defeat other mobilizational categories and form a MWC in that constituency, it may then hamper
the same group's chances of forming a MWC at the regional or national levels,
where the ethnic balance may require an alliance with the "minority." To understand whether local attempts to foment ethnic violence are likely in this situation
we would need to examine the internal structure and organization of the political
movements concerned to establish whether the party leaders at the higher level
of aggregation—where ethnic violence has significant political costs—have the
power either within the party or externally through their control of some part of
the state to restrain their leaders at the lower level, where violence offers significant payoffs.

Once politicians decide to polarize people around a particular category,
how can this be achieved? One of the main methods politicians can use to
highlight an ethnic attribute-dimension and a particular categorical opposition (Hindu vs. Muslim, Protestant versus Catholic) is to inject inflammatory
symbols, speech, or violence into an event that has more general community
support among members of their ethnic category, such as a religious festival
or a national holiday. It is politically very difficult for governments to ban
such a religious festival without alienating a large proportion of the religious
category that may normally participate in the event for nonpolitical reasons.
This opens up the prospect of those who wish to polarize winning both ways:
If the government overreacts the people mobilizing gain support from other
members of their ethnic category who feel that they are being mistreated, but
they may also gain if the government does not react and the violence takes
place.

---

[16] In 1913, for instance, the German minority in the city of Riga was only 13.5% of the population but elected fifty-one members out of the eighty member council (von Rauch 1974).

State-Level Factors

Theories of ethnic riots tend to focus mainly, sometimes exclusively, on the political, economic, sociological, and psychological factors that increase the "supply" of riots. But in fact the supply of riots is always determined by the likely response of the coercive arm of the state (its army, paramilitary forces, and police) or of the targeted community. Ethnic riots will not generally be fomented where the state is known to have the will and capacity to prevent them, use deadly force against rioters, and then vigorously prosecute those involved.[17] In every case of horrific ethnic violence in India, for instance,—the Kanpur riots of 1931, the August 1946 killings in Calcutta, the Ahmedabad riots of 1969, and the Gujarat riots in March–April 2002—those participating in the violence enjoyed virtual immunity from state retribution, and in some cases the state police forces actively assisted the rioters (Government of the United Provinces 1931, Lambert 1951, Reddy 1971, *Indian Express*, March 26, 2002). In other countries large-scale ethnic violence has been similarly enabled because the state either refused to intervene or else actively participated in the attacks on a particular ethnic group: Examples would include the anti-Tamil riots in Sri Lanka in 1983; the Protestant-Catholic riots in Belfast in 1864; the anti-Jewish pogroms in Tsarist Russia and Medieval Spain; and the anti-Tutsi violence in Rwanda and anti-Hutu violence in Burundi. A good indication of the social and governmental sanction that rioters feel they enjoy is the absence of measures they take to protect their identities and the fact that many riot accounts report that rioters from the same ethnic group that controlled the government seemed shocked when the police tried to disperse them or arrest them.[18]

What then determines the state response to attempts to foment ethnic riots? The state's response is determined by the distribution of attributes and categories in the population, or more accurately by the distribution of attributes and categories in the selectorate that keeps it in power. The state will restrict the supply of violence and intervene to prevent it when violence will activate categorical identities that will undercut the government's own *MWC. Correspondingly it will allow and even participate in violence that will solidify the categories that underpin its own electoral support.* Examples of the former include the Congress regimes in the states of Madhya Pradesh and Rajasthan during the same riots in 2002,

---

[17] Horowitz (2001) finds in the riots he examines thatForce seems generally to deter. As police hesitation reduces inhibitions in a crowd, early, determined police action can avert what might have been a very serious riot.... There are, however, relatively few such documented instances once rioters have assembled, because police bias, indifference, or ineffectiveness is so widespread and the rioters' assembly usually takes place in anticipation (typically well founded) of police inaction. (363–364)

[18] See the description of how Hindu rioters in India were shocked at being dispersed by Hindu policemen in police Inspector General V. N. Rai's interview in *Times of India*, May 3, 2002.

which used all the resources of their states to quash Hindu nationalist attempts to foment Hindu-Muslim violence, because this violence would have threatened the stability of their multi-ethnic electoral support base. Another good example would be President Houphouet Boigny of Côte d'Ivoire, who in 1981 prevented anti-Mauritanian riots in Abidjan because Mauritanians and other minorities were the backbone of his party's electoral support. Examples of the latter include the Narendra Modi regime in Gujarat, which apparently enabled the 2002 anti-Muslim riots in the state (for instance, by ordering police not to intervene in the violence and by transferring officials who aggressively took action against rioters) in advance of state elections, hoping to solidify the Hindu vote behind the governing BJP.[19]

It might be argued that there is no real explanatory power provided by the above formulation because those in control of the state could easily trade in the support of one ethnic category for that of another. But this ignores the fact that some coalitions are more heterogeneous, especially on issues the political elites regard as key, than others. All other things being equal therefore, political elites will prevent violence against minorities when (a) its own MWC will be undercut and (b) replacing minority support with the support of another coalition partner would involve increasing the coalition's heterogeneity along what its leaders regard as the most important dimension of politics. In Axelrod's terms, violence will be prevented where it threatens these minimum winning connected coalitions (Axelrod 1970).

3. Some Clarifications

Applications of the Model to Non-Democracies

The same logic developed here—that ethnic riots are the product of competitive politics—could also be easily extended to understand the supply of ethnic violence in non-democracies. Ethnic riots are a way for politicians who claim to represent and control an ethnic category to demonstrate to the monarch or dictator or colonial power that there is opposition to particular policies or that they command the intense support of a large segment of the population.[20] Analysis of ethnic riots in periods as diverse as fourteenth-century Spain and early–nineteenth-century north India has found that ethnic riots were an effective way for local elites to compete against each other (by demonstrating the degree to which

---

[19] For details, see Wilkinson 2004.

[20] The enormous Calcutta riots of 1946, for example (India's worst pre-partition Hindu-Muslim riot), were a calculated and highly organized attempt by the Muslim League to demonstrate that a political settlement could not be forced upon them by the colonial power or Congress without massive bloodshed. For the best description of the League's role in the riots, see Lambert 1951).

they are backed up by their communities) as well as to demonstrate their power to the monarch or colonial authorities. In fourteenth-century Spain, for example, David Nirenberg (1996) found that Holy Week riots against Jews—a community under the legal protection of the King—represented a way for local factions in Valencia to compete against each other, as well as for local elites to protest against the monarch. Similarly, the aggressive efforts to overturn local norms regarding religious practices in early-nineteenth-century north India—efforts which led to Hindu-Muslim riots in towns such as Kanpur, Shahjahanpur, and Bareilly—are best understood as the way in which members of influential Hindu commercial castes could outflank the existing local elites in the towns who had negotiated and enforced the religious status quo and demonstrate their status to each other. By demonstrating their ability to challenge these local elites, and to restrain or incite their community to violence, these Hindu entrepreneurs also established themselves as the local "influentials," whose support the colonial regime henceforth needed to secure (Bayly 1998; see also Prior 1993).

Riots as a Way to Change the Rules of the Political Game

Although so far we have discussed ethnic riots as a way to change the activated coalitions within a fixed political system, violence, and the degree of support for them, they can also be used as a way to change the political system itself. The second broad political motivation for ethnic riots is to change the size of the selectorate when a particular attribute-dimension cannot win under existing electoral institutions, rules, or distributions of voters. The change might be achieved by removing a competing ethnic or non-ethnic group from competition (for instance, by depressing its turnout through terror against its members or causing its members to flee) or by putting pressure on the state to create new political institutions—operationalized in our model by the value k—that will allow the political entrepreneurs responsible for the violence to form a *MWC*. For example, the leader of the Bodo tribal movement in the North Eastern state of Assam, recognizing that his group would likely lose an election because it was a minority of the electorate, instead declared an election boycott in 1989 and fomented ethnic violence against those who broke it, in the process murdering dozens of non-tribal Assamese, many of whom fled the Bodo areas. This tactic depressed the non-Bodo electoral turnout, increased the solidarity of his own group when other ethnic groups retaliated against Bodos, and, most important, increased the costs to the state of not negotiating with his movement on the issue of creating new (and undemocratic) Bodo representative councils, in which the 33% Bodo community would control 75% of the seats and therefore all the resources. As the leader himself recognized, the Indian government's reluctance to grant any ethnic claims expressed through peaceful channels had made violence a winning strategy: "The central government agrees to negotiate only with those groups that show their force...The [government's] signing of accords with the Mizo National Front, the Tripura National Volunteers and the Gorkha National Liberation Front, shows that New Delhi has approved the methods they employed for their objectives" (*Far Eastern Economic Review*, March 9, 1989, 23).

4. Empirical Data on Riots and Coalitions

How well does the general model put forward here seem to account for actual patterns of riot initiation, electoral outcomes, and riot suppression? In this section, I provide some evidence from three very different cases, one contemporary (India in 2002) and two historical (nineteenth-century Ireland and the United States from 1877 to the 1950s), to provide some evidence to show that (a) riots are more likely where electoral competition is intense along both distributional issue dimensions and ethnic attribute-dimensions; (b) where riots do occur there is a predictable solidifying of the majority group behind the party that has the strongest pro-majority identity; and (c) the reaction of the state to attempts to polarize riots is conditioned by its own electoral incentives and the changing composition of its support base.

Elections and Ethnic Riots in Nineteenth-Century Ireland

The Protestant-Catholic riots that occurred in Irish constituencies in the early nineteenth century were caused by a political reaction to a series of franchise changes—passed at the instance of the colonial power in Westminster—that threatened the electoral dominance of the 12% Episcopalian minority in Ireland by sharply increasing the number of Presbyterian and Catholic voters. Prior to these reforms in 1808, 1829, and 1832 the Episcopalians, by virtue of their far greater average wealth, dominated a tax-based franchise in which only 5–10% of adult males could vote. In the city of Derry for instance, where the electorate had been solidly Episcopal at the beginning of the century, the proportion of Episcopal voters declined as a result of the franchise changes and migration of workers into the city to 22% by mid-century, with Catholics 41% of voters and Presbyterians 37% (Hoppen 1984).

This shift in the distribution of voters threatened to confine the Episcopalians and the Tory party they dominated to a permanent electoral minority in many towns, because most of the newly enfranchised voters supported the Liberals. Presbyterians and Catholics opposed the Tory party on taxation policies, political reforms, and the question (at least before 1869) of the status of the Church of Ireland as the "established" church to which all Irish—including non-conformist Protestants—had to pay church tax. Nonconformist and Catholic votes gave the

Liberals the crucial margin the party needed to win municipal seats in Derry and Belfast from the Tories in the 1830s and control of the English port city of Liverpool (where Irish Catholics were 41% of the population by mid-century) in 1837. In Table 10.1, I provide my estimates of the distribution of attribute-repertoires for a typical urban constituency in Ulster in the mid-nineteenth century, based on the two attribute-dimensions of religion and party identification, with different numbers of attribute-values on each.[21]

The shift in the composition of the electorate made it clear that for the Tories, appealing exclusively to Episcopalian voters was no longer sufficient to win elections. But which coalitions could be constructed that would be advantageous to Tory and Episcopalian interests? In Table 10.2, using the population estimates from Table 10.1, I display the various possible winning electoral combinations for a typical urban constituency in Ireland.[22] As we can see there are five possible winning coalitions that exceed the 50% threshold (assuming the prevailing single-candidate First Past the Post (FPTP) system) to win an election in this typical seat, and three of these include the Tory Episcopalians: *Coalition 1* (Episcopalian Tory, Episcopalian Liberal, Presbyterian Liberal, Catholic Tory) with 51%; *Coalition 2* (Episcopalian Tory, Presbyterian Tory, Presbyterian Liberal) with 57%; and *Coalition 3* (Episcopalian Tory, Catholic Liberal) with 60%.

From the perspective of the Episcopalians, however, despite the combinatoric logic that says that all three of these coalitions were "possible," the ethnic, ideological, economic, and political cleavages that existed in Ireland made some of these winning coalitions much more advantageous and logical than others. Some coalitions minimized the space between coalition members over key issue dimensions of politics while others did not, and some coalitions would be more likely to protest the Episcopalians' economically privileged position than others.

Figure 10.2 provides a simplified sense of where the median Liberal and Tory Episcopalian (E), Presbyterian (P), and Catholic voters stood on two of these main issue dimensions: (1) *redistribution* and (2) *religious equality of Protestants and Catholics*. On the first issue dimension, redistribution, the majority of voters favored a broad basket of redistributive policies in the nineteenth century put forward by the Liberal party: reform of the tax and tariff system that

[21] All existing studies of voting in nineteenth-century Ulster regard the Episcopalians as the bedrock of the Tory party, so I have calculated the Episcopalians as voting 90% for the Tories. The Presbyterians I have estimated as voting 3:1 for the Liberals, based on a study of nonconformist voters in Britain done by Phillips. Various studies of nineteenth-century Irish voting (e.g., in Derry and Belfast) show the Catholics as voting almost exclusively for the Liberal party, so I have put the Liberal share of the Catholic vote at 98%. See Phillips 1992. For the link between nonconformism and Liberalism in Ireland, see Bardon 1982.

[22] Calculated using the combinatoric program and interface developed by Kanchan Chandra and David Veritas at MIT.

Table 10.1 **Distribution of Attribute-Repertoires Across the Population in a Typical Ulster Constituency, Mid-Nineteenth Century**

	Episcopalian	Presbyterian	Catholic	
Tory	.20	.09	.01	**.48**
Liberal	.02	.28	.40	**.52**
	.22	**.37**	**.41**	**1**

benefited large landlords, partial land reform that would provide more protection to tenant farmers, and electoral reforms that would widen the electorate and reduce the power of the gentry and aristocracy.[23] However on the issue dimension of religious equality, and the question of whether the larger category of "Protestants" should be privileged constitutionally, and in government and private employment, a majority of voters (the 59% of Protestants) favored the Tory position against reform. On this Protestant-Catholic cleavage, unlike the others, there was little space between the Episcopalian and Presbyterian positions.

For the Episcopalian Tories any coalition that included Catholics would be unacceptably expensive because it would maximize the heterogeneity of the coalition on the issue dimension of redistribution. O'Day (1992) reports that Episcopalians owned "most" of the land in Ireland, while the Catholics were landless tenant farmers or smallholders. Land reform, tenants' rights, and other rural issues implacably divided the Episcopalian gentry from rural Catholics. The costs in terms of redistribution of forming an Episcopal alliance with the Catholics would therefore be far greater than those of forming an Episcopalian-

Table 10.2 **Minimum Winning Coalitions When k = 0.5**

Coalition	Allowed Individual Repertoires	Size
1	Episcopalian Tory + Episcopalian Liberal+ Presbyterian Liberal + Catholic Tory	**.51**
2	Episcopalian Tory + Presbyterian Tory + Presbyterian Liberal	.57
3	Episcopalian Tory + Catholic Liberal	**.6**
4	Episcopalian Liberal + Presbyterian Tory + Catholic Liberal	**0.51**
5	Presbyterian Liberal + Catholic Liberal	**.68**

[23] Presbyterian voters wanted electoral reforms that would increase the percentage of their own community that could vote, but not such widespread reforms that Catholics would form a majority of the electorate.

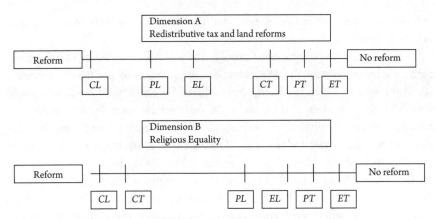

Figure 10.2 Catholic, Episcopalian, and Presbyterian Issue Positions Along the Dimensions of Redistribution and Religious Equality

Presbyterian alliance. This is why coalition #3 (Episcopalian Tory and Catholic Liberal), although it incorporated 60% of the electorate, was so unattractive to the Episcopalians. It was likely to be highly unstable because it would maximize the distance and therefore conflict along *both* the dimensions of religious equality and economic redistribution.

Of all the three coalitions that Episcopalian Tories could form, coalition #2, the Episcopalian Tory, Presbyterian Liberal, and Presbyterian Tory coalition (57% of the vote), was the one that best minimized the overall coalitional space on the issue dimensions of religious equality and redistribution. It would necessitate some concessions over economic reform, though nowhere near as many as if a coalition was formed with Catholics, and it clearly minimized the distance on the issue dimension of religious equality.

The challenge for Episcopalian Tories then became how to highlight the attribute-dimension of religion and the overarching category, "Protestant," based on it (for which all Presbyterians possessed the qualifying attributes) so that they could win Presbyterian voters away from the Liberal party's distributional politics and form a *MWC*. The evidence suggests that Tory Episcopalians did this, in a quite calculated way, by investing in Orangeism, the militantly anti-Catholic movements that many Episcopalian leaders had previously shunned. In Liverpool, Belfast, and Derry, Tory leaders gave financial and organizational support to Orange Lodges and sponsored inflammatory marches that were deliberately taken through Catholic areas as a way of generating a counter-reaction and violence that would help to make their claims of "Protestantism under threat" seem more credible, and therefore activate the Protestant-Catholic dimension while deactivating other categories on other attribute-dimensions. In some cases Theodore Hoppen reports that the process of starting violence was more direct than simply organizing polarizing events and hoping for violence, and that

"Loafers received scatterings of coin in the streets or payments to start a riot" (Hoppen 1984, 81).[24]

In Belfast, the first Protestant-Catholic riot took place in the electorally competitive environment of the 1832 election campaign, with politicians uncertain about the way in which the newly enfranchised Protestant middle classes would vote.[25] In that election, and in the eight riots which were incited during the next ten election campaigns, Protestant-Catholic violence proved a highly effective tool for the Tories to generate a Protestant majority behind their party. In the aftermath of the 1841 riots, for instance, the Tories won every single seat on the Belfast town council (Hoppen 1984). In many other towns as well—Drogheda, Portadown, and Derry and in County Monaghan—Orange marches that sparked violence were important in accentuating the Protestant-Catholic cleavage and encouraging Protestant voters to support the "Protestant" Tory party and not the "Catholic" Liberals. The proportion of the Liberal vote that came from Protestants in Derry, for instance, declined by around half after serious riots in the late 1860s (Hoppen 1984).

Whether these attempts to polarize voters around the Protestant-Catholic dimension and foment violence would actually result in widespread Protestant Catholic riots depended on the attitude of the state. In the period before the 1830s the local (Protestant) magistrates had generally used their forces to protect local Protestant mobilizations, which made Protestant election riots a winnable strategy even in areas of the country that had a 90% Catholic majority. Hoppen (1984), for example, reports that Protestant mobilization against Catholics took place even in such overwhelmingly Catholic towns in the south as Meath and Drogheda in 1835 and in Dublin, Portarlington, and Cork in 1837.

However the colonial state in Ireland had concluded by the 1830s that the security costs of continuing to use state power to protecting Protestant militancy in a country where 78% of the overall population was Catholic (with 12% Episcopalian and the remainder nonconformist) were simply too high. The British government feared a repeat of late eighteenth-century rebellions or the 1819–1820 agrarian revolts in the country if they continued to unquestioningly support the Protestant ascendancy in Ireland. So the British shifted policy to one of trying to be officially neutral between the Protestant and Catholic communities. As the Home Secretary put it in 1852, the job of the police and administration in Ireland was now to "hold the scales even between the Protestants and Roman Catholics in all matters which lead to agitation" (Crossman 1996, 102). This policy of intervening to prevent anti-Catholic violence became even more

[24] For Tory efforts to unify Protestants through anti-Catholic mobilization and violence in Liverpool, see Neal 1988.
[25] This section draws on the description in Wilkinson 2004, 215–219.

important in the late 1860s, when Catholic votes in Ireland provided Gladstone's Liberals with their electoral margin of victory in Westminster.

In support of this gradual shift in policy, the state in the 1830s gave itself the power to ban the main mobilizational technique that had led to riots— Protestant and Catholic religious processions—by a new party processions act.[26] Even more important, the state began to replace the Episcopalian-gentry dominated magistrates and local militias with a new system of magistrates and a new, ethnically representative police force—the Royal Irish Constabulary— controlled by the British Governor in Dublin. By the 1850s this new system of magistrates, and the now 50% Catholic police force (its ethnic composition would eventually match that of Ireland as a whole in the 1880s) were working smoothly to restrict the type of Protestant processions that had led to numer- ous election-related riots in Belfast and Derry in the earlier part of the cen- tury. Though not all processions could be stopped before they started, and the occasional biased magistrate or policeman could allow a procession to take place when it ought to have been banned (as in the Monaghan example in 1865), the police could now control them quickly: Protestant-Catholic riots virtually ceased.

The only large Protestant-Catholic election riot that broke out after the cre- ation of the Royal Irish Constabulary (RIC) was in Belfast in 1864, the sole large town where the police continued to be locally controlled by the local (Protestant) town council. The 1865 commission of inquiry into this riot (in which 12 died and 100 were injured) makes it clear that the local council allowed marches to go forward in the city and an effigy of nationalist leader Daniel O'Connell to be burnt by Protestants even though they knew they would likely lead to riots. Once the violence broke out the Belfast police force (4% Catholic in a city where Catholics were 34% of the population) acted to protect Protestant rioters and hurt Catholics. Dublin realized after this riot that without reforming the Belfast police system of local police control the Protestant selectorate could be expected to foment more such riots in the future, which could raise Protestant-Catholic tensions more generally in a way that might threaten their rule, so in 1865 they abolished the local police force and replaced it with the RIC.[27] This measure effectively ended the run of Protestant-Catholic riots in the city.

---

[26] An Act to restrain party processions in Ireland, 14 & 14 Vict., c.2 (Mar. 12, 1850) This act allowed magistrates to ban "All assemblies of people meeting or parading together, or joining in procession, who have among them any firearm or offensive weapon, or any banner, emblem, flag, symbol, or display calculated to provoke animosity, or who are accompanied by any person or per- sons playing music or singing any song calculated to provoke animosity..." Crossman 1996, 218.

[27] *Report of the Commissioners of Inquiry, 1864, respecting the magisterial and police jurisdic- tion, arrangements, and establishment of the borough of Belfast.* London: House of Commons 1865 (C.3466), XXVIII.

India

In a paper on India (Haid and Wilkinson 2010), Christopher Haid and I provide a test of the general hypothesis, developed in Wilkinson (2004), that riots are the outcome of political competition. We look at patterns of riots and election results in all 180 state assembly districts in the Indian state of Gujarat, where large-scale Hindu-Muslim violence broke out in February-April 2002. In the subsequent December 2002 state elections, the incumbent BJP government in Gujarat returned to office with a considerably increased majority over the Congress, a result that many attributed to the violence. The paper is the first to test the relationship between violence, electoral competition, and electoral outcomes using systematic data on such important variables as previous levels of competitiveness in a seat, poverty, and employment and literacy levels, as well as previous levels of violence (to determine if ethnic violence has an independent effect on vote patterns or whether intense competition is merely the result of previous high levels of competition). We find that, even controlling for previous violence in a constituency, as well as for various socioeconomic factors, there is a clear relationship between the level of electoral competition (as measured by the margin in each seat in the previous state election in 1998) and the likelihood of a riot taking place in the state in 2002.

I also find that violence was highly significant in increasing both turnout and the BJP's share of the vote in the December 2002 state elections. An average number of riots in a district (nine) was likely to lead to a swing to the BJP of 4.7%, holding everything else constant at the mean. We infer that this was the result of Hindu voters switching their allegiance to the party in the aftermath of the Godhra killings of Hindus in February 2002 and the subsequent massive anti-Muslim violence in the state. Strong circumstantial evidence to back up my finding is provided by opinion polls carried out in the state just after the 2002 state elections. The polls make it clear that those who voted for the BJP were much more influenced by the violence than those who voted for the Congress, with 25% of those who voted for the party saying that the riots were their "most important voting consideration" compared to the 16% of Congress voters who identified the riots as the main issue. Among Congress voters, larger percentages mentioned distributional issues such as "livelihood" (29% of Congress voters, 22% of BJP) and "development" (40% vs. 37%) as the main issue (Yadav 2003).

Now, of course, a plausible objection could be that the higher salience of the violence issue among BJP voters existed long before the riots broke out and that therefore the violence had no independent effect on the election results. However, an exit poll conducted just before the election results were counted suggests that the violence did affect the results in two ways: first, by depressing the turnout of core Congress supporters from the Muslim community, and second, by winning over large numbers of swing voters. The Centre for the Study of Developing Societies (CSDS) poll shows that the BJP won partly because its core supporters turned out at higher levels than those from the Congress (83% compared to 78%) (Kumar 2003).

The most plausible explanation for this, we would argue, is that an estimated 100,000 Muslims—a community that exit polls from the 1998 state elections estimated voted 100% for the Congress—were displaced from their homes in the aftermath of the February-April 2002 violence, while others were reluctant to vote in the December 2002 elections because polling places had been situated in predominantly Hindu neighborhoods by the BJP state government. Second, the poll showed that the BJP won because it did better among unaffiliated voters than the Congress, which suggests that the violence did have an effect in winning over swing voters. The BJP won 56% of the 11% of the electorate who identified themselves as unaffiliated with either of the two main parties compared to Congress's 24% (Kumar 2003).

As I and many others have shown, the violence that took place in 2002 was facilitated by the BJP state government (state governments in India have sole authority over local law enforcement), which calculated that the violence would solidify its electoral coalition along the attribute- dimension (religion) and the category (Hindu) based on that dimension and allow it to defeat its multi-ethnic rival, the Congress, which was appealing to people on distributional lines. The key importance of the state government's attitude is revealed when we examine the pattern of polarization and violence in other Indian states in February-April 2002, in which the BJP and Hindu nationalist organizations also sought to provoke Hindu-Muslim violence for electoral purposes. Despite the attempts to polarize, these efforts came to nothing because the state governments in power in these other states—Madhya Pradesh, Rajasthan, Maharashtra, West Bengal—unlike in Gujarat, were supported by multi-ethnic coalitions in which Muslim support was crucial. As a result, these governments carried out mass roundups of militants, enforced curfews in sensitive towns and districts, and ordered their state police forces to use deadly force, if necessary, to prevent Hindu-Muslim riots.[28]

Electoral Competition and Anti-African American Riots in the United States

Another good example of how polarization becomes costly at a higher level of aggregation of government even though it still pays off at the local level is provided by the national U.S. parties' shift from many decades of supporting anti-minority mobilization and violence by Democrats in the south (or at least

---

[28] See Wilkinson 2004, Chapters 2 and 5 for the details of these riots and the government responses.

turning a blind eye to it) to a more aggressive pro-civil rights stance in the 1950s
and 1960s, as a result of which federal troops were sent into the South to protect
blacks from state police forces and white rioters. For years white politicians in
the South had fomented local anti-black violence in order to solidify majorities
behind the Democratic Party. Such violence was especially intense in the 1890s
and early 1900s, when a series of anti-black riots helped defeat the multi-ethnic
Populist and Republican coalitions that threatened Democratic control of states
such as Louisiana, Georgia, and North Carolina. These coalitions emphasized
economic issues such as support for farmers, controls on railway freight rates,
and increased government aid for those affected by the depression of the 1890s.
The 1898 riot in Wilmington, North Carolina, for example, has been exten-
sively researched and it is now clearly established that was a response by white
Democratic politicians in the state to the success of these multiracial Populist
and Republican "Fusionist" parties that had triumphed in the state elections in
the middle of the decade, winning control of the North Carolina House and
Senate in 1894 and the governorship in 1896. Wilmington was the state's largest
city, the home of a substantial black middle class active in municipal and state
politics, and home to the state's only African-American newspaper. These factors
made the city the logical choice for a massive antiminority mobilization that was
intended to break up the Populist coalition and restore the state to Democratic
dominance.[29] During the fall of 1898 state Democratic leaders used their control
of most of the North Carolina media to launch a propaganda offensive against
the "Negro menace" and organized "white supremacy clubs" in Wilmington and
bought weapons (including a $1,000 Gatling machine gun) that were to be used
in the November riots. The actual white attacks on blacks were sparked by an
editorial in the town's African-American newspaper that white politicians used
as "proof" that black men represented a threat to white women in particular and
white political power in general. The white supremacy clubs then hunted down
black leaders and chased hundreds of black citizens out of Wilmington for good,
killing (by the lowest estimates) fourteen to twenty citizens. Two years later, taking advantage of the solidified white electoral support (and lower black turnout)
that the 1898 Wilmington riot had helped generate, the state's Democrats passed
laws that effectively disenfranchised the state's blacks for the next six decades.
As in North Carolina, violence against blacks in Louisiana (and in Georgia in
1906) proved also highly effective in breaking up the Fusionist coalitions and
solidifying the white vote (Crowe 1968). Susan Olzak's (1990) statistical study
of lynching from 1882–1914 supports the general hypothesis that violence
was more likely where there was a populist economic redistribution threat to
Democratic control: she finds that "populist challenge" and "percentage of votes

---

[29] For the most comprehensive studies of the riots, see Cecelski and Tyson 1998. Prather's
introduction leaves no room for doubt about the political motivation for the riots.

going to third parties" are both positively related to the occurrence of lynching in this period.[30]

Large-scale riots against minorities in the south were possible because the U.S. government refused to intervene to protect the rights and physical security of African Americans. The federal troops had originally been withdrawn in 1877, as a result of a political deal in which white southern politicians agreed not to block the Republican nominee Rutherford Hayes for President as long as the Republicans agreed to withdraw troops from South Carolina and Louisiana, where they had been stationed to prevent intimidation of black and white Republican voters. In 1898, during the Wilmington riots, President McKinley refused to send federal troops into North Carolina to protect blacks, despite their letters and telegrams pleading for his administration to do so, because he needed the support of southern Democrats in Congress to pass the Treaty of Paris and approve the payment of $20 million to purchase the Philippines from Spain.[31] On the very few occasions where, for idiosyncratic reasons, federal troops did intervene (e.g., the 1919 Charleston, South Carolina riots, which were stopped by troops from the city's large naval base) antiminority violence stopped quickly (Waskow 1966).

As is well known, by the 1950s the federal government *was* (finally) prepared to intervene to protect the rights of blacks in the South, and the large scale antiminority violence largely stopped. What changed? This federal policy shift can be explained as a consequence of changing political payoffs for attracting minority support at the level of national presidential politics.[32] Several decades of black out-migration from the south to the pivotal states of Michigan, Illinois and Ohio by the late 1940s had turned blacks by the late 1940s into a critical swing constituency for Democratic presidential candidates. In 1956 the *Congressional Quarterly* (May 14, 491–496) calculated that the black percentage among voters was larger than the winning party's 1954 margin of victory in sixty-one congressional districts (thirty-two Democratic districts and twenty-nine Republican districts). Even though race-baiting still paid off for southern Democrats at the state level in the 1950s and 1960s, the party's national leaders increasingly calculated that there were more votes to be gained from northern blacks and white moderates by federal military intervention on behalf of African Americans (because internal Democratic party discipline alone could not control Southern Democrats), than there

[30] Olzak 1990, Table 2.

[31] As a sweetener to the southern Democrats, McKinley also agreed that the federal government would contribute to the upkeep of Confederate war graves. For details of efforts by blacks to persuade the federal government to intervene and of McKinley's political calculations in not doing so, see Haley, in Cecelski and Tyson 1998, 210–212.

[32] This paragraph follows the argument in Wilkinson 2004, 234–235.

were southern white votes to be lost.[33] The point was made explicitly by the Democratic National Committee and strategist Clark Clifford to President Harry Truman during the 1948 Presidential campaign. To win the election, Truman was advised that he had to win the support of "working people, the veterans, and the Negroes." To win black support President Truman was told that he

> should speak out frankly and fully on his magnificent record as a fighter for Civil Rights—he should mention his votes in the Senate, his anti-poll tax and anti-lynching legislation, his support of the wartime FEPC, and his orders to end discrimination in the government and the armed services to prove that he *acts* as well as talks Civil Rights. *The Negro votes in the crucial states will more than cancel out any votes he may lose in the South.*[34]

As a result of this shift in the broader political incentives, white politicians from outside the South were increasingly willing to order federal intervention in the 1950s to prevent antiminority violence and intimidation.

5. Conclusion

In this chapter I have made a strong case for the rational, calculated process by which ethnic riots are fomented in order to form particular minimum winning coalitions. Governments then decide whether to prevent or allow riots based on whether violence seems likely to solidify or break up the coalition and categories that support their own rule. I acknowledge, however, that not all riots "fit" this model, just as not all cases fit any theory: Some riots do seem to break out over relatively spontaneous incidents and quarrels. But I maintain that such spontaneous incidents are not likely to develop into large riots of several days or more (in which over 90% of casualties take place, according to Indian riot data collected by myself and Ashutosh Varshney) unless there is both a determined organization behind the riots and, even more important, a state that lacks the will and capacity to stop the riots. There is a systematic element to riots: and understanding which categories create minimum winning coalitions at local and

---

[33] Roy Wilkins, the executive secretary of the NAACP, recognized the pivotal power of the northern black vote when he told 5,000 members in an April 1956 speech in Chicago that "Up here we can strike a blow in defense of our brothers in the south, if necessary by swapping the known devil [i.e. the Democrats] for the suspected witch." *Congressional Quarterly*, May 4, 1956, 491–496.

[34] Cited in Wilkinson 2004, 234.

state levels and how riots affect these categories is the way to uncover this systematic element.

At the local level, riots are fomented by politicians in close seats to activate those categories and those attribute-dimensions that will allow them to win elections. This is especially likely, I argue, where activating an ethnic attribute-dimension is advantageous to a group that stands to incur large costs if a distributive coalition comes to power. However despite the importance of such local incentives, it is the state response toward riots and rioters that is the most important factor in determining whether riots will break out and continue. Political explanations that focus on which cleavages create *MWCs* at different levels of government (especially the level that controls the army and police) seem to do a much better job in accounting for both the supply of polarizing events that leads to riots as well as the state response to these events, which in turn determines the level of violence. For example in my recent study of Hindu-Muslim riots in India I have shown that the increasingly pivotal nature of the Muslim swing vote in creating a *MWC* in Indian states has led to many state governments taking firm action to prevent Hindu-Muslim riots in 2002, even though Hindu nationalist organizations were making determined efforts to start riots in such "riot-prone" cities as Hyderabad, Indore, and Aligarh. By analyzing state level riot, electoral and socio-economic data over several decades I am able to show that, even when we control for a state's previous level of violence, levels of political competition in a state and the degree to which Muslim voters are pivotal to the party in power explain much of the interstate variation in levels of Hindu-Muslim violence.[35]

How might the type of constructivist-influenced model of riots developed here be used in the study of ethnic riots more generally? A first step is obviously collecting data in a way that allows us to operationalize and test the model's predictions that riots are a response to changing levels of political competition and an attempt to activate certain identities and issue dimensions while deactivating others. So, ideally, we would collect time series data on local levels of electoral competition and the distribution of ethnic, class, and other interest-group support for particular parties, as well as data that allow us to operationalize other possible causes. Especially important here is not just that we collect data on what we think is the primary ethnic identity involved in motivating a riot or mobilization, but that we also collect data on other possible motivations and other types of ethnic and non-ethnic mobilization that may be competing for voters' interest. The purpose here is to (a) recognize that there may be multiple motivations in the same event and (b) see how the frequency of riots about some kinds of identity rather than others might change over time in response to electoral incentives.[36]

---

[35] Wilkinson 2004, especially Chs. 2 and 5.
[36] On these methods more generally, see Wilkinson 2001.

In addition, we would want to collect data on the various levels of the state that have responsibility for law enforcement, in order to test the model's predictions that their response to riots is conditioned by the distribution of their ethnic support base and the overall competitiveness of the party systems at each level. We would also, of course, want to test alternative explanations for violence, as I have done in my 2004 book on Hindu-Muslim riots in India, so we would need data on, for example, levels of interethnic economic competition, levels of literacy, and previous levels of violence.

Third, we need to collect more nuanced data on riot-events themselves, recognizing that multiple motivations might be involved at different times, even within the same riot. The best way to do this is probably to supplement the kind of work done by myself and Ashutosh Varshney in our own books on Hindu-Muslim violence or Susan Olzak's work on U.S. riots, in which we tend to collapse a lot of variation over time and space into a single large "riot" case. We probably need to do finer-grained hour-by-hour and neighborhood-by-neighborhood analysis that will give us a much better sense of the precipitants, multiple causes, and course of riots, as well as cast light on such questions as whether economically motivated rioting is, as I have argued here, more often "bandwagoning" on politically motivated violence than the ultimate cause of violence.

Finally, we should seek qualitative data that establish whether the causal mechanism identified in the model of riots presented here seems to be present when riots take place. Of course, we should not expect to find politicians openly announcing that they have fomented riots for political purposes or police officials announcing that they have been biased or have chosen not to enforce the law because of political constraints. But if we find evidence of unusual patterns of police deployments and transfers, individual officers being transferred for doing their job, and politicians delaying action because of political constraints, that is reasonably good evidence that politics rather than operational or legal norms are dictating law enforcement. And if we find evidence of riots being organized just before elections, or early elections being called after riots and politicians crediting victory to the riots, that is supportive evidence for the general electoral thesis presented here.

Identity, Rationality, and Emotion in the Processes of State Disintegration and Reconstruction

ROGER PETERSEN

While I address both substantive and methodological issues in this chapter, my main focus is methodological. The central question is the following: How can we incorporate emotions into the analyses of political processes in which identities have become fluid?

Here, I use the process of state disintegration and reconstruction for illustration. In particular, I draw on the experience of Eastern Europe following the collapse of Communism. Today, more than twenty new states occupy the territories formerly held by the Soviet Union, Yugoslavia, and Czechoslovakia. In terms of identity issues, the most stunning outcome of the disintegration of these multi-ethnic entities is the emergence of relatively homogenous nation-states. In my view, this outcome attests to the historical stability of identity in Eastern Europe more than its fluidity. However, in several cases and regions the process did involve significant construction of identities. In some of these cases, emotions have played an undeniable role. The collapse of these states sometimes involved massive violence, ethnic status reversals, and the power of group prejudices. Bosnia witnessed massacres and ethnic cleansings; a core element of identity in the Baltic states rotates around Soviet deportations and killings; Albanian identity in Kosovo is shaped by Serbian discrimination and the forced mass exodus of 1999. There is hardly a single group in the region that does not feel a sense of victimhood. Powerful experiences have left a residue. These residues can be analyzed in terms of emotions.

This chapter builds upon the combinatorial framework introduced by Chandra and Boulet in Chapter 5 and the model found in Chapter 6, "A Baseline Model of Change in an Activated Ethnic Demography." Both of these chapters are built on assumptions of rational choice. As they state, "We do assume that ordinary voters and political entrepreneurs are instrumental actors who make decisions through a process of conscious calculation of the payoffs associated with alternative categories, and that no matter what the nature of their motivations and payoffs, individuals will prefer to be in a smallest winning majority for which they are eligible" (Chandra and Boulet, Chapter 6, 241). These assumptions provide a coherent baseline, one obviously with no reference to emotion.

This chapter proceeds as follows. First, I relate Chandra's framework in the introduction to the subject of state collapse and reconstruction by creating a six-stage sequence. Second, I show the general applicability of many of the features of the Chandra model through the example of Moldovan identity politics. Third, I discuss how emotions are defined. Fourth, I discuss different strategic choices that social scientists could make to integrate emotions into the analysis. Fifth, I discuss the specific emotions of anger and contempt in detail and connect them to Chandra and Boulet's model of ethnic demographic change. Finally, I make some general points about rationality, emotions, and identity through a discussion of the emotion of resentment in light of the Moldovan case.

1. Outline of Chandra and Boulet's Framework in Relationship to State Disintegration

Chandra provides us with a new set of definitions for the discussion of identity creation. A category is a term of description. Categories are composed of one or several qualifying characteristics that are termed "attributes." "Attribute-dimensions" are an array of mutually exclusive attribute-values which belong to the same family and encompass all of a specified population. "Category-dimensions" are an array of mutually exclusive categories which belong to the same family and encompass all of a specified population. As they state, "The basic building block of our theories of ethnic identity change should be this repertoire of attribute-dimensions (for both individuals and populations) rather than a repertoire of categories and category dimensions. Categories and category-dimensions are derived from this repertoire of attributes" (Chandra and Boulet, Chapter 6, 185).

What role does a state play in this definitional scheme? In many multi-ethnic entities, the state is crucial in forming and maintaining attribute-dimensions and category-dimensions. In the Chapter 1, Chandra uses Yugoslavia as an example. In former Yugoslavia, there was a category-dimension of "nation" composed of the categories of Serb-Croat-Macedonian-Montenegrin-Slovene-Muslim. The state determined the qualifying attributes for membership in these categories and constructed and maintained this category-dimension through its institutions. Most important, each of these nations had representation and power through republic-level government. The state often tinkered with this dimension through changes in census categories and political upgrading of autonomous republics like Kosovo; a small percentage of the population called themselves Yugoslavs. However, for most of the postwar period, this state-based dimension of identity categories remained fairly stable. An individual's perception of the most relevant family of identity categories could not ignore this reality. The stability of the state meant the stability of this dimension and its categories. In turn, the attributes compos-ing categories were relatively stable. The inherent attributes of language and reli-gion (or former religion) were the most obvious qualifying characteristics.

What does the disintegration of a state mean in this definitional scheme? The collapse of the state means the end of the institutions that maintained dimen-sions. Perceptions of families of categories are disrupted and no longer make sense. While the impact of state disintegration on old dimensions is at least somewhat clear, changes at the level of attribute and category are not. When a state disintegrates and a dimension collapses, categories and attributes may also lose their meaning and coherence. Chandra traces a process building from attri-butes to categories and the placing of categories on category-dimensions. But there may be a reverse process with the collapse of a dimension leading to a col-lapse of category-dimension and a "loosening" of attributes. If attributes become "free-floating," that is, divorced from their connection to a category, identity entrepreneurs then have an enhanced ability to recombine them to form new categories. The task here is to identify the constraints on such strategies and specify when those constraints operate.

The following schema represents one possible interpretation of the process of state disintegration that fits Chandra and Boulet's framework. Six stages are specified.

1. *Relatively stable categories ordered into one or more category-dimensions exist before disintegration.* Before the state disintegrates, individuals identify themselves with existing categories comprised of one or several attributes. It is important to note that Chandra and Boulet discuss only descent-based attributes in their framework. As they define it, a descent-based attribute is a "characteristic that an individual acquires at birth from her parents or ancestors." The key distinction is that a descent-based attribute is based on a shared rather than private knowl-edge. Thus, Chandra holds that the set of feasible attributes are those that are either visibly displayed on the person or about which there is a collective record (Chandra and Boulet, Chapter 6, 239-40).

2. *A variety of factors come into play to diminish and destroy the state.* Economic decline and crisis, institutional factors, the end of ideology, changes in the inter-national security system, and other factors may drive the state toward disintegra-tion. Compounding the matter, changes in identities themselves may help bring

down the state. As evidenced by the differences among Yugoslavia, the USSR, and Czechoslovakia, this process may or may not involve violence.

3. *Attributes are loosened from stable categories.* As state-based dimensions collapse, categories can also start to lose their meaning and disintegrate. The specific attributes that comprised these categories can become available for recombination into new categories. Also, new attributes or attributes not formerly part of old categories become part of the mix. For example, religious attributes that were taboo under an old Communist order may now come into play. In short, there may be a large feasible set of "floating attributes."

4. *Identity entrepreneurs string "floating" attributes together.* Periods of disintegration should provide ideal conditions for identity entrepreneurs. Under these conditions, identity entrepreneurs choose among a set of attributes to create new identity categories that will attract the support of a winning coalition. Multiple identity entrepreneurs may exist to offer many new categories to the general population.

5. *Individuals in the general population choose the best possible category to enhance their goals.* Given the set of categories developed by identity entrepreneurs, individuals will choose the category best suited to achieve basic goals. Often, this choice will simply involve coordination of identity choice with others.

6. *Categories become relatively stable once again.* A new state usually forms a set of institutions that helps create, maintain, and give meaning to categories. In effect, new category-dimensions are formed. The system of attributes, categories, and attribute- and category-dimensions moves toward relative stability.

Within this schema, the rational choices emphasized by Chandra are found in the fourth and fifth stages. Making a rational choice can be defined in terms of relationships between desires (preferences), information, belief formation, and action (see Figure 11.1 and the accompanying discussion later). Rational choice says little about the content of desires but insists that they be stable and consistent. The individual then seeks information relevant to desired goals. Based on this information, a belief is formed about the best method or strategy to achieve the goal. An optimizing action results.

In Chandra's framework, this rational action cycle can be seen running twice. Political entrepreneurs desire certain things—votes, mobilization for a movement or a riot, recruits for a civil war. They seek information relevant to their goals. One key source of this information is the distribution of inherited attributes in the population. The political entrepreneur then becomes an identity entrepreneur. This actor forms a belief that it is possible to "string together a combination of attributes most likely to attract the support of an optimal coalition." A set of actions follows. The identity entrepreneur then assigns the combination of attributes a name, imbues the name with meaning, and works to maintain the category by making sure those adopting the name receive payoffs.

The rational choice cycle then turns a second time among individuals in the mass. Individuals desire to be in the winning coalition. They then seek information about how to be in the winning coalition. One key source of information is the nature of existing categories and the attributes that make up those categories. Individuals then form beliefs about which categories will best help them reach their desired goals. An action follows. The individual tries to acquire the attributes of the winning category. Chandra and Boulet develop a model based on Riker's theory of minimum winning coalitions that specifies possibilities for change in an ethnic demography based on the choices made during this cycle.

2. An Example: The Breakdown and Reconstruction of Moldavia/Moldova

In comparison to much of the rest of Eastern Europe, the Moldovan case does not contain strong emotions. During the collapse of Communism, the Moldovan conflict left 700 dead, a far smaller number than the 100,000 dead and several hundred thousand displaced in Bosnia, a state of roughly similar population, or the 800,000 ethnically cleansed from Kosovo. Never possessing a state of their own, Moldovans were never driven by nationalistic fervor to regain historical nationhood as seen in Lithuania, Latvia, and Estonian. In Moldova, ethnic stigmas did not run as deep as among Slavs and Albanians in the Balkans. In Moldova, cultural and linguistic similarities are so close between some pairs of its major groups—the Ukrainians and the Russians, the Moldovans and Romanians—that switching identity labels could be relatively easy. In sum, Moldavia/Moldova presents us with a case in which we should see Chandra and Boulet's framework in operation. Indeed, the transformation of Soviet Moldavia into Moldova conforms to the general contours of the breakdown and reconstruction outlined above.

Relatively stable categories ordered into category-dimensions exist before disintegration. Although the history of modern Moldova is complex, the Soviet state was effective in creating relatively stable identity categories arrayed on the dimension of "nationality." The Russian Empire gained control of the Romanian-speaking region from nominal Ottoman control in 1812 and named it Bessarabia. In the turmoil at the end of World War I, a Bessarabian assembly voted for unification with Romania. The Soviet Union never accepted the loss of this territory, however, and responded by creating a Moldavian Soviet Socialist Republic on the left bank of the Dniester River. Although Romanian speakers were a minority on this territory, the entity symbolized the continuing Soviet claims on Bessarabia (Kaufman 2001). World War II allowed the Soviets to act on their claim. In a secret protocol attached to the Molotov-Ribbentrop accord, the region was assigned to the Soviet Union. Soviet control was brief as Romania recovered the territory with the German invasion of the USSR in 1941. The tables turned again when the Soviet Union took control of the area from Romania after the conclusion of World War II. The Moldavian Soviet Socialist Republic was formed from historic Bessarabia and a sliver of land on the Eastern bank of the Dniester River that had comprised the interwar Moldavian Soviet Republic. Romanian speakers made up only 30% of this eastern territory.[1]

When the Soviets gained control in 1944, they immediately set out to construct a new identity category of Moldovan to separate the region from Romania. In order to create this category, they first attempted to subtract Romanian from the attribute-dimension of language and replace it with the supposedly distinct language of "Moldovan." "Moldovans" were told that they spoke their own language, not Romanian. Accordingly, the alphabet was changed from Latin to Cyrillic. The Soviet regime strictly controlled the flow of literature from neighboring Romania. History books were rewritten to emphasize the distinctiveness and continuity of Moldovan culture. The new nationality category of "Moldovan" then was created, in which membership was based on speaking the "Moldovan" language.

All Soviet citizens were required to declare a nationality and the category was on all identity documents. In Moldova, the membership criteria for the nationality category included those who spoke the newly defined language of "Moldovan" but also had room for those who spoke other languages. "Romanian" meanwhile was effectively obliterated from the category-dimension of "nationality." Table 11.1 shows figures for both Soviet passport and ethnic self-awareness in Moldova. Note that only .1% entered "Romanian" as their nationality despite a higher proportion of those who were aware of themselves as "ethnically" Romanian.

A variety of factors come into play to diminish and destroy the state. The demise of the Soviet state need not be discussed here. Specific features of Soviet administration would play critical roles in the nature of the Moldavian SSR's collapse, though. The Soviet Fourteenth Army, as well as a disproportionate share of the Moldavian Republic's heavy industry, was stationed on the left bank. With the decline of the Soviet state and its system of central planning, the interests of both elites and mass in the east region of Moldova were highly threatened.

Attributes are loosened from stable categories and *identity entrepreneurs string "floating" attributes together.* During perestroika and the decline of party control, the meaning of the language attribute was transformed. Nationalist organizations arose to challenge the claim that a Moldovan language really differed

---

[1] This brief historical gloss leaves out many significant details. For summaries (with slightly different treatments) of the complex history and politics of Moldova, see Fane 1993, Eyal and Smith 1996, Munteanu 2002, and Skvortsova 2002.

Table 11.1 **Soviet Nationality vs. Ethnic Self-Awareness**

Moldova	Soviet Passport (N = 1200)	Self-Awareness (N = 1200)
Moldovan	63.5	58
Romanian	0.1	3.4
Ukrainian	12.1	11.1
Russian	13.3	12.8
Gagauz	3.4	3.6
Bulgarian	2.1	2.1
Jewish	0.9	0.7
Belarusian	0.3	-
Roma	0.3	-
Polish	0.3	-
German	0.3	0.3
No Passport	3.3	-
Other	0.3	1.1
Mixed		6.8

Source: Pal Kolsto, ed.; *National Integration and Violent Conflict in Post-Soviet Societies: The Cases of Estonia and Moldova* (Lanham, MD: Rowman & Littlefield, 2002), 33.

from Romanian. Identity entrepreneurs had clear incentives to pick up on these nationalist themes concerning language. Partly because of their concentration in urban areas and on the more heavily industrialized left bank, Russians and Ukrainians tended to dominate key positions in industry and politics. In one list of key positions in leading plants and institutes in 1980, Moldovans held only four of sixty-nine positions (Munteanu 2002). Furthermore, creeping linguistic russification threatened the mass of Romanian/Moldovan speakers. The relative power of the Russian language versus the Moldovan language can be seen in the language repertoires of other minorities. According to one survey 100% of Ukrainian respondents declared that Russian was either the language that they thought in (49.6%) or a language in which they were fluent (50.4%). On the other hand, less than one in six of these Ukrainian respondents claimed to have bothered to learn Moldovan fluently (0.8% thought in Moldovan and 14.3% claimed fluency).

In 1988, Moldovan groups stated three demands—the recognition that Moldovan and Romanian are the same language, the reinstitution of the Latin script, and the recognition of the Romanian language as the state's language. After much struggle, all three became reality. (For clarity, however, I will refer to the Romanian language spoken by Moldovans simply as Moldovan throughout the rest of this section.) Although the rights of minorities would be respected, all members of the state administration would be obliged to know and speak Moldovan in their duties. Graham Smith sums up the larger significance of the move toward making language the dominant indicator of identity in Moldova:

> it amounted to extracting an open admission from their government that the republic was theirs and theirs alone, and that all other ethnic groups in Moldova were not 'nations' but rather ethnic minorities whose rights should be respected but whose claims could not be considered equal to the interests of the majority. The concept of a 'Moldovan' at last had a meaning. (Smith 1996, 223)

Table 11.2 shows respective total percentages for language (the language one thinks in) and nationality in Moldova.

In effect, Moldovan entrepreneurs were redefining the membership criteria for the nationality category "Moldovan," replacing an expansive combination of attributes on the dimension of language ("Moldovan-speaking" or Russian-speaking or other) with a restrictive one (only Moldovan). As shown in the Table 11.2, a little over 50% of the population used Moldovan as the language they thought in. Only one in about six Russians and Ukrainians considered themselves fluent in Moldovan (Kolsto and Melberg 2002, Table 2.41) and, as shown in Table 11.2, practically none of them thought in Moldovan. A large pool of key positions would now be transferred to the Moldovan speakers. Furthermore, the language move provided the possibility of unification of Moldova with Romania. Note from Table 11.2 that there is no alternative winning coalition that could be initiated by those defined by Russian or Ukrainian nationality and language. Prospects became increasingly bleak for Russophones.

Along the lines of constructivist premises, identity entrepreneurs were at work to counter the consequences of the move to language. As a first response, non-Moldovan speakers sought a political solution through alliance with Moscow. They also initiated a series of strikes in the Russophone areas. With little success

Table 11.2 **National and Linguistic Breakdown in Moldova (percent)**

		Language		
Identity	*Total*	*Moldovan*	*Russian*	*Other*
Moldovan	61.4	50.2	6	5.2
Russian	12.8	0.4	11.3	1.1
Ukrainian	11.1	0.1	5.5	5.5
Other	14.7	4.1	3.5	7.1

Derived from Kolsto and Melberg 2002. The language scores represent answers to what language the respondent thinks in.

Table 11.3 **National and Linguistic Breakdown on the Right Bank (percent)**

		Language		
Identity	*Total*	*Moldovan*	*Russian*	*Other*
Moldovan	74.7	61.1	7.3	6.3
Russian	7.8	0.3	6.9	0.6
Ukrainian	9.7	0.1	4.8	4.8
Other	7.8	2.1	1.9	3.8

in intimidating Moldovan nationalists, the next option was partition of the emerging new Moldovan state. On September 2, 1990, separatists declared a Dniester Republic comprising the largely Russophone areas on the left bank, as well as the largely Russophone city of Bender.

The identity politics of this new creation were in some ways remarkable. Neither language nor the existing nationality attributes appear to fully capture the salient identity that emerged. Russian, Moldovan, and Ukrainian are all official languages, even though in practice Russian is dominant. Rather, a new "Soviet" nationality defined a Dniestrian. In effect, the Russian, Ukrainian, and other minority nationality labels merged into the new "Soviet" nationality. A small number of Moldovans also adopted this identity attribute. Grigore Maracuta, at one point the Transnitrian Parliamentary Chairman, chose to migrate because he felt more comfortable with the Soviet-oriented ideology on the left bank. As Stuart Kaufman sums up, "The Transnitrian Russophones were the group, including russified Moldovans and Ukrainians as well as Russians, that considered Russian its language and the Soviet Union its country" (Kaufman 2001, 130). In effect, a Dniestrian can be anyone who does not identify with both the Moldovan nationality *and* the Moldovan language. In practice though, in a point discussed later, the "Soviet" category was largely synonymous with all those speaking a Slavic language—Russians, Ukrainians, and russified Moldovans. Tables 11.3 and 11.4 show the language and nationality figures for the right and left banks.

In both cases, the result represented a stable winning coalition that rewarded members with an increased share of society's goods. In each case, a significant portion of the population could be denied full access to a variety of payoffs. On the right bank, those not fluent in the Moldovan language were excluded from several economic and political benefits. This switch to language essentially created a minimum winning group. Moldovan speakers made up 61.1%, and excluded 38.9%, the maximum possible. On the left bank, the excluded group is basically the 24.5% of the population located in the Moldovan language/ Moldovan nationality category. Several other smaller coalitions were theoretically possible. I come back to this point later.

Table 11.4 **National and Linguistic Breakdown on the Left Bank (PMR)**
           (percent)

		Language		
Nationality	*Total*	*Moldovan*	*Russian*	*Other*
Moldovan	29.9	24.5	2.9	2.5
Russian	40.7	1.4	35.9	3.4
Ukrainian	24.5	0.2	12.15	12.15
Other	4.9	1.3	1.2	2.4

Individuals in the general population choose the best possible category to enhance their goals. Soon, militias formed on each side. With the dissolution of the Soviet Union in 1991, the situation lapsed into civil war. The conflict compelled most citizens to pick a side. With the support of the Russian Fourteenth Army, the Dniestrians repelled attacks from the right bank regime and the situation eventually stabilized. The civil war, however, resulted in 700 dead (some estimates are slightly higher).

Categories become relatively stable once again. Postpartition Moldova has been very stable. At the time of this writing, few analysts can imagine a new outbreak of violence in the foreseeable future. It is also notable that the nationality hybrid created on the left bank during the waning days of the Soviet state persisted after the end of the Soviet state it was based on. Identity entrepreneurs created new histories of the Dniestrian people. For instance, the Second Congress of Dniester local Soviets declared in 1990:

> The Congress views the historical processes that have taken place on our ancient land since the time of Kievan Rus as the formation of a coethnos that now inhabits the southwestern part of the country (the USSR). This coethnos is made up of descendants of the inhabitants from Russia, Ukraine, Moldova, Poland, Germany, Greece, and other countries. (Skvortsova 2002, 175)

On the right bank, the predictions that Moldovans would unify with Romania have proven unfounded. The newly formed institutions provided payoffs to those in new positions of authority. As Smith points out about the situation in independent Moldova, "[N]ew and highly prestigious occupational niches were created for Moldova's intellectual elites with statehood who realized that their interests would be best served through securing the survival of an independent Moldova" (Smith 1996, 240). In the early to mid-1990s, a merger with a large mass of fellow Romanian speakers, especially those in a poor and impoverished state like Romania, did not seem to obviously ensure higher payoffs than those awarded to Moldovan speakers in Moldova. Of course, this situation drastically changed by 2010.

Along the lines of Chandra's and Boulet's model, the stable partition of Moldova in the early 1990s resulted from two stable coalitions. There was little incentive for elites to destabilize the situation. Along lines of the fifth stage in the sequence, there was also little incentive for individuals in the mass to deviate, at least in the 1990s. Neither the remaining russophones in Moldova nor those identifying with both the Moldovan language and nationality in Dniestria have the numbers to politically challenge the status quo.

In sum, the general progression of events conforms to the six stages above. The Soviet Union did possess a relatively stable set of identity categories based on the dimension of nationality. State institutions, such as ethno-federal territories, helped perpetuate a stable demography. With the breakdown of the Soviet central state, attributes could take on new meanings. Moldovan identity entrepreneurs enhanced the salience of language in order to create a minimum winning coalition that would shift resources and jobs to a relatively small majority. Russophone identity entrepreneurs countered with their own strategy. Individuals in the general population conformed. A relatively straightforward story about the disintegration and reconstruction of Moldova can be told relying solely on rational choice assumptions and mechanisms.

3. Emotions

The previous sections illustrated a rational choice framework. We are now ready to turn directly to the central question and ask how emotions could be incorporated into such a framework.

We must first have a conception of what emotion is.[2] There is no clear consensus on the definition of emotion. Depending on the focus of the particular study, the social scientist will concentrate on specific features of emotion which include cognitive antecedent, physiological arousal, expression, valence, object, and action tendency, among others. For the study of politics, cognitive antecedent, action tendency, and the relationship between emotions and psychological mechanisms are the most relevant features of emotion.

Consider two action cycles. Figure 11.1 represents a simple rational choice action cycle. Starting on the right side of Figure 11.1, individuals are seen as holding a short list of stable and ordered preferences or desires. For example, when buying an automobile, an individual may have the following preference order: price> safety> style. Given these desires, individuals then collect information about how best to attain their goals. The potential car buyer reads car magazines and visits websites to find the vehicle that best meets his or her preferences. The individual then forms a belief about the most effective means and

---

[2] Most of this section is gleaned from Petersen 2011.

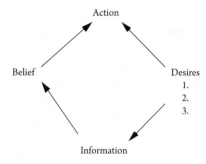

Figure 11.1 Action Cycle with No Reference to Emotion

strategies to satisfy desires. The potential car buyer forms beliefs about the best models and methods of financing. An action then results as a combination of desires and beliefs. A specific vehicle is purchased.

Figure 11.2 factors in emotion. In Figure 11.2, emotion proceeds from beliefs or cognition. Following many socially oriented theorists, emotion can be conceptualized as "thought that becomes embodied because of the intensity with which it is laced with personal self-relevancy" (Franks and Gecas 1992a, 8). As Ortony, Clore, and Collins (1988) write: "Our claims about the structure of individual emotions are always along the lines that *if* an individual conceptualizes a situation in a certain kind of way, *then* the potential for a particular type of emotion exists" (2). In Figure 11.1, desires lead to information collection which, in turn, leads to beliefs. In Figure 11.2, belief also leads to emotion. Three general effects of emotion may follow, marked as A, B, and C effects in Figure 11.2.

i. A Effects

First, and most fundamentally, emotions are mechanisms that can heighten the saliency of a particular concern. They act as a "switch" among a set of basic desires. An individual may value safety, money, vengeance, and other goals, but

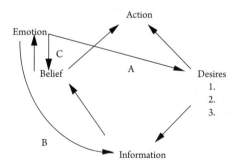

Figure 11.2 Action Cycle Illustrating Three Possible Effects of Emotion

emotion compels the individual to act on one of these desires above others. Emotion creates an urgency to act on a particular desire; the value of future payoffs on other preferences is discounted; particular issues can become obsessions. In short, emotions can act as mechanisms of preference formation and preference change. Emotions may shape preferences lexicographically or they may operate by shaping the indifference curves among specific preferences (Elster 1998).

This aspect of emotion directly challenges the assumption of stable preferences that is at the core of rational choice theory. Economists regularly order preferences. However, the assumption of easily ranked and unchanging preferences may not be appropriate political processes such as the collapse and reconstruction of states. These processes involve contentious and sometimes violent events that present individuals with choices that they have not previously encountered. In rational choice, the stability of preferences is a simplifying assumption. Most practitioners of rational choice would probably agree that this simplification is not always useful for every type of human behavior. As many observers have noted, rational choice has produced its most useful insights in iterative situations or under stable institutional environments. A proponent of rational choice, George Tsebelis (1990) has summarized, "actions taken in noniterative situations by individual decision makers (such as in crisis situations) are not necessarily well-suited for rational choice predictions" (38). From another perspective, the A effect of emotion is to fill in one task that most rational choice practitioners choose not to address. As William J. Long and Peter Brecke (2003) summarize: "Emotions recognize challenges and opportunities in our environment, and they identify our preferences. Rational choice tells us that individuals pursue preferences logically, but it does not tell us, at an individual level, what preferences are or where they come from. This void exists because emotion is left out of the mix" (81).

ii. B Effects

Once in place, emotions can produce a feedback effect on information collection. Perhaps most clearly, emotions lead to emotion-congruent information seeking. Emotions themselves become powerful experiential information in the appraisal of situations and objects (Schwarz and Clore 1983). Similar to the well-documented confirmation bias, evidence confirming the emotion generally receives more attention and value than disconfirming evidence. For example, individuals under the influence of fear may come to obsess about the chances of catastrophe. They may concentrate only on information stressing danger and ignore information about the lack of threat. As Gerald Clore and Karen Gasper (2000) stress, "Because emotions are directly experienced, and arise from within, the personal validity of the information they appear to convey seems self-evident to the person experiencing them. One can argue with logic, but not with feeling" (39).

iii. C Effects

Even with accurate and undistorted information, emotion can affect beliefs. The same individual with the same information may develop one belief under the sway of one emotion and a different belief under the influence of a different emotion. These phenomena include the following:

Rule selection: As William Riker (1986) has pointed out, rational individuals may operate according to several different sorts of strategies—"sincere," "avoid the worst," "average value," "sophisticated" (26). Emotions can affect which strategy becomes operative. For example, it is likely that emotions such as fear can influence a switch in method of belief formation, perhaps to an "avoid the worst" strategy.

Other effects clearly involve irrationality or bias in belief formation.

Stereotyping: Several emotions have been found to increase stereotyping of opposing groups (Mackie and Hamilton 1993). Under negative emotions, groups are more likely to be perceived as homogeneous (Stroessner and Mackie 1993). Emotions can reinforce the fundamental attribution error, which is the tendency to attribute others' actions to their inherent character while attributing one's own actions to one's situation and circumstances (Frijda and Mesquita 2000).

Formation of beliefs about risk and probabilities: As Frijda notes, "Estimates of probability, credibility and plausibility are intuitive, based on information, thought, and preference, and therefore sensitive to a variety of influences, among which are emotional ones" (Frijda and Mesquita 2000, 68). For example, fear tends to heighten perception of risk while anger tends to decrease the sense of risk and the calculation of negative probabilities.

Preservation of existing beliefs: Emotions can enhance the attachment to an existing belief and help preserve it, even in the face of new disconfirming evidence. This effect is a form of the mechanism of "wishful thinking"—under the influence of emotion the desire to maintain a belief is so strong that evidence is ignored (Elster 2007).

Self-deception: Emotions can lead to the creation of new beliefs even in the face of disconfirming evidence. This effect relates to the mechanism of cognitive dissonance. The theory of cognitive dissonance, first formulated by Festinger in the 1950s, holds that having inconsistent beliefs creates a negative emotional state that drives the individual to change beliefs to relieve this discomfort. The resolution of the problem involves both the nature of cognition and the intensity of the negative emotional state. The emotion can drive individuals, in certain highly charged situations, toward adoption of new beliefs which might seem strange to outsiders but manage to solve inconsistencies for participants (Harmon-Jones 2000).

iv. Specific Emotions

We can use Figure 11.2 to discuss specific emotions. Emotions are often differentiated by cognitive antecedent and action tendency. In this chapter, I explore three specific emotions: anger, contempt, and resentment.

Anger

Anger follows from a cognition that an individual or group has committed a bad action against one's self or group; the action tendency is toward punishing that group.

On A effects, anger heightens desire for punishment against a specific actor. Under the influence of anger, individuals become "intuitive prosecutors" (Goldberg, Lerner, and Tetlock 1999). That is, individuals tend to specify a perpetrator and then seek retribution. Anger's B effects distort information in predictable ways, producing attention funneling. As with other emotions, once under the influence of anger, individuals "perceive new events and objects in ways that are consistent with the original cognitive-appraisal dimensions of the emotion" (Lerner and Keltner 2000, 473). That is, the emotion of anger justifies the desire for punishment and pushes the individual to seek information that will further justify vengeance. Anger can create an obsession for retaliation. Concerning C effects, the angry person lowers the threshold for attributing harmful intent. Anger enhances the fundamental attribution error—angry people blame humans, not the situation (Keltner, Ellsworth, and Edwards 1993). Anger also tends to produce more stereotyping (Bodenhausen, Sheperd, and Kramer 1994). Under the influence of anger, individuals lower their risk estimates and are more willing to engage in risky behavior (Gallagher and Clore 1985; Mano 1994; Lerner and Keltner 2001; Lerner et al. 2003).

As an event-based emotion, it is likely to decay over time. That is, the effects of anger are likely to dissipate as time passes since the precipitating event. In sum, anger heightens desire for punishment against a specific actor, creates a downgrading of risk, and increases prejudice and blame, as well as selective memory (Newhagen 1998).[3] Anger will, however, decrease over time.

Contempt

Contempt follows from a cognition that a group or object is inherently inferior or defective; the action tendency is toward avoidance.

Contempt is closely related to stigma, a negative emotional reaction to some attribute of an individual, group, or object. While few scholarly works specifically

---

[3] For a comprehensive discussion of the emotion of anger and its relationship to political science, see Petersen and Zukerman 2009a, 2009b.

employ the term "contempt," the literature on the closely related phenomena of racism and prejudice is voluminous and well-known. Racists would not wish their offspring to intermarry with the racially stigmatized group or live in their neighborhood; contempt would push for avoidance of the stigmatized group in these key social interactions.

The sources of ethnic stigma and contempt are not always understood. Clearly, institutions such as slavery and apartheid help to create and sustain racial stigmas. In some instances, a history of conflict and cultural separation can convert ethnic difference into ethnic contempt.

The A effect of contempt is avoidance. The B and C effects are the well-documented phenomena connected to prejudice. Attention funneling prevents the consideration of any positive actions of the stigmatized group. The fundamental attribution error is prominent. Stigmatized groups become a vehicle for scapegoating.

Although the stigmatized group may live quietly among other groups, the existence of the stigma is always present, even if in latent form. Contempt does not systematically decay.

Resentment

Resentment follows from a cognition that one's group is located in an unwarranted subordinate position on a status hierarchy; the action tendency is to take actions to reduce the status position of groups in a superior status position.

Resentment follows from the perception that one's group is located in an unwarranted subordinate position on a status hierarchy. The conception of this emotion rests on several findings from various fields of social science. First, humans identify with groups and acquire self-esteem from group membership (Brown 2000).[4] Second, they compare the status of their own group with that of others (Horowitz 1985; Sidanius 1993; Pratto et al. 1994; Sidanius, Pratto, and Brief 1995; Sidanius and Pratto 1999). Third, when the comparison generates the belief that another group occupies an undeserved superior position, the emotion of resentment results.

As treated here, resentment is based on being *politically* dominated by a group that is perceived to have no right to be in a superior position. It is the everyday experience of these perceived status relations that breeds the emotion. In the day-to-day operation of government, members of ethnic groups become aware of whose group is "on top" and whose is "below." Status, at its core, involves an element of dominance and subordination. It is a question of who gives orders and who takes them, whose language is spoken, and whose symbols predominate. While status can be complex, status relations among ethnic groups are generally tied to the following indicators: (1) the language of day-to-day government;

[4] This idea builds off the work of Henri Tajfel and Social Identity Theory. The work on this issue is voluminous. For a review of Social Identity Theory, see Brown 2000.

(2) the composition of the bureaucracy; (3) the composition of the police; (4) the composition of the officer corps; and (5) symbols such as street names. Some ethnic groups may be wealthier than others, but when they are forced to speak the language of others in everyday business, when they are under the eye of ethnically different police, when they cannot advance in the ranks of the state bureaucracy or the military, when land is redistributed to favor another group, that is when they come to occupy a lower level on the status hierarchy. Perhaps most important, a belief of injustice and the emotion of resentment results from status reversal, that is, when a group accustomed to being on the top of a status hierarchy finds itself displaced by a formerly lower group. Using an extensive new data base with nearly 30,000 observations, Lars-Erik Cederman and his colleagues found strong support for the effect of status reversals across a variety of cases (Cederman, Wimmer, and Min 2010).

4. How Might Political Scientists Incorporate Emotion into Their Analysis?

Political scientists hold diverse research values. Some desire parsimony while others value rich description. Some prefer to assess the power of broad variables while others focus on the specification of finer-grained causal mechanisms. Likewise, political scientists wishing to incorporate emotions into their methods will make different decisions about how to do so.

Consider two very different approaches. First, political scientists aiming for rich and accurate description can decide to incorporate all effects of emotion—A, B, and C—into their analysis. In a situation after violence, the analyst using this approach would examine all the effects of anger—how anger created a desire for revenge and punishment (A effect), how the emotion affected information collection (B effect), and how anger may have produced lowered and unrealistic risk estimates involved with a decision to retaliate (C effect). In the wake of events such as the terrorist attacks of 9/11, such a full analysis can be very fruitful (Rubin 2011). This approach, however, would not be parsimonious. Also, an approach focused on multiple C effects would lead into the realm of social psychology and away from the strategic choices most central to politics.

On the other hand, the political scientist could choose to incorporate only A effects of emotion (i.e., those shaping preferences). In this method, the emotion can essentially be treated as a benefit or cost in a cost-benefit model. Consider a situation in which members of group X are engaged in a long-running conflict with members of group Y. Individual X members might usually hold the following preference ordering: economic well-being > safety > punishment of group Y. Now consider what might happen if members of group

Y commit violence against members of group X. Violence will produce the emotion of anger. Anger's A effect will change the preference ordering, at least temporarily. Anger could transform the order of desires to punishment of Y > economic well-being > safety. In cost-benefit terms, punishing Y can now be considered as a "benefit." In this cost-benefit trade-off approach, though, the benefit of punishment could be offset by higher economic or safety "benefits." Individuals could forego their wish for revenge in return for monetary payments, for instance.

There are several issues raised by this cost-benefit approach. First of all, the emotion of anger could be so powerful that trade-offs are not calculated. In the grip of anger, individuals could become obsessively driven to retaliate. More generally, even if decisions are still calculated, emotion will often distort (through B and C effects) the ways such calculations are made.

Consider again the violence-anger-revenge sequence in the preceding paragraph. If we want to understand retaliation and develop means to prevent it, the important element to understand is not that individuals desire revenge and see punishment as a benefit after a violent attack. That A effect is hardly surprising. The more critical phenomena are the ways the emotion of anger affects the assignment of blame after the violence (a C effect), the ways individuals ignore or select information after the attack (B effect), and the processing of risk involved in violent retaliation (a C effect). Political entrepreneurs wishing to prevent a retaliatory spiral, or inflame one, will use their intuitions and knowledge to frame information and blame in ways that magnify or mitigate the broader effects of anger captured by the B and C effects. In short, choosing to focus only on A effects often entails a loss of valuable descriptive accuracy and richness. On some issues, this loss is not desirable.

On other issues, incorporating only the A effects may be very useful. I do not believe that trying to merge the first approach, (including the A, B, and C effects of emotion) with Chandra and Boulet's rationality-based model of identity change would be helpful. However, the second approach (including only the A effects) is useful. This strategy, as I illustrate in the following sections, yields a host of interesting new hypotheses and insights.

i. Incorporating the Emotion of Anger into Chandra's Framework

We can start by incorporating the emotion of anger to Chandra and Boulet's baseline model. Following the examples provided in Chapter 6 (section 3), consider a population with two minimum winning categories. According to the rational choice assumptions of the model, they "expect the initial outcome to be an ethnic demography based on the smaller of these minimum winning categories." What happens when we interject anger into this model?

First, we need to further develop the point that the power of some emotions fade over time. Event-based emotions, unlike object-based emotions, are likely to fade with time. Interest, on the other hand, does not. Jon Elster (2003) has discussed this effect in his work on transitional justice pointing out that in the trials of collaborators following the World War II sentences were almost invariably more severe immediately after the war than two or three years later. This insight suggests an addition to Chandra and Boulet's model in the form of an "anger function."

Such a function can be illustrated with reference to Chandra and Boulet's running 2*2 example using a scenario with two minimum winning coalitions. Consider the following three variations of the same scenario as represented in Table 11.5.

In each case, assume that Foreign Whites have committed violence against every other category. As a result, Blacks are angry at Whites. Given this anger, Blacks will wish to punish Whites through exclusion. Assume further that this anger has helped create the following preferences in the aftermath of violence: (1) Above all, one wishes to be in a winning coalition. (2) Against assumptions of maximization, one prefers to share the payoff with a higher number of nonperpetrators (MWC1) than a lower number that includes members of the perpetrator group (MWC2). (3) As anger recedes, the willingness to accept the costs (MWC1-MWC2) involved with the bigger coalition recedes. If the costs of the bigger coalition pass a certain threshold determined by the amount of time that has passed since the violent events, the individual will become ready to re-identify despite lingering anger. (4) At a certain point, the emotion recedes altogether and has no effect (extinction point).

Table 11.5 **Three Hypothetical Scenarios with Two Minimum Winning Coalitions**

Table A

	Black	White
Foreign	0.4 (a)	0.25 (b)
Native	0.3 (c)	0.05 (d)

Table B

	Black	White
Foreign	0.4 (a)	0.2 (b)
Native	0.4 (c)	0.0 (d)

Table C

	Black	White
Foreign	0.45 (a)	0.07 (b)
Native	0.45 (c)	0.03 (d)

Examining Table 11.5, the optimal (i.e., smallest) winning coalition in each case would include Foreign Whites. However, anger prevents any immediate change in identity that would allow such a shift. Foreign Blacks would rather coalesce with other Blacks than switch their identity to Foreign despite the higher payoffs such a shift could generate. The three scenarios exhibit three different costs of anger. In scenario A, the difference between minimum winning coalition 1 (MWC1—all Blacks) that does not include Whites and minimum winning coalition 2 (MWC2-Foreign) that would include Whites is only 5% (.05). In scenario B, the difference increases to .2 and scenario C to .38.

How long will individuals accept the costs of anger and exclusion? If anger recedes, eventually interest will override emotion. The population, and elites, will

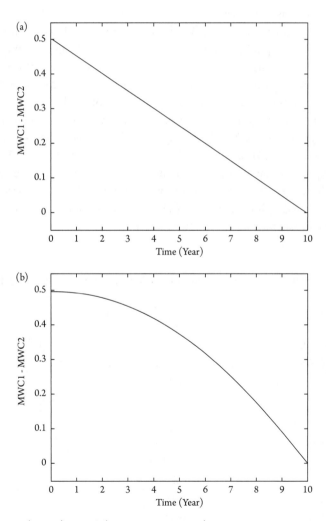

Figures 11.3a (Linear); *11.3b* (Inverse Exponential)

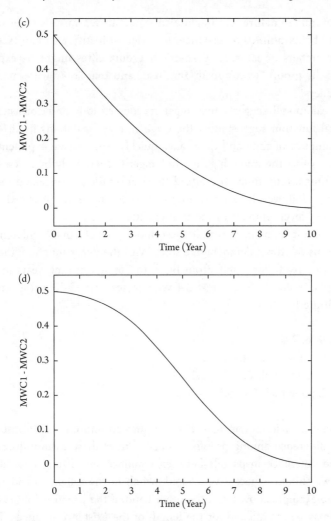

Figures 11.3c (Exponential Decay); *11.3d* (Mixed Exponential)

have incentives to induce identity shift. The relationship between acceptance of lower payoffs and time can be modeled in different ways. Figures 11.3a, 11.3b, 11.3c, and 11.3d represent "anger curves."

These figures show initial high levels of anger that recede according to linear, exponential, inverse exponential, and mixed exponential functions. In all figures, anger is assumed to become extinct in ten years. The line represents the point at which interest begins to outweigh anger, where individuals no longer wish to forego the available payoff on account of anger. At this point, individuals may come to think that they are "cutting off their nose to spite their face," that it is "time to get on with things," to "bury the hatchet." The English language is filled with metaphors that capture these ubiquitous qualities of human nature. We might also expect to see various reconstructions of history at this point. For instance, in order to justify an identity shift that includes members of a former perpetrator group, elites might be expected to claim that the group "wasn't really that bad" and that "they were manipulated by evil leaders."

The linear model suggests that anger recedes steadily and consistently. The exponential function suggests that the original anger maintains itself for a considerable amount of time and then fades quickly. The reverse exponential function indicates that the initial high level of anger fades quickly but then lingers at some level for a long time. The mixed function models a sustained initial high level of anger followed by a rapid drop and then a lingering phase where anger remains a low-level remnant of social interaction.

An important point here is that these models would make different predictions in terms of ethnic demographic shift. With the linear function, the population would be ready for a shift from Black to Foreign in nine years in scenario A, six years in scenario B, and just 2.4 years in scenario C. The respective numbers for all the functions are:

Linear: 9, 6, 2.4
Exponential: 9.5, 7.7, 4.9
Inverse Exponential: 6.9, 3.7, 1.3
Mixed Exponential: 7.8, 5.5, 3.45

This exercise yields the insight that identities are more likely to resist change when the difference among payoffs is small. Under these assumptions, if there is a sizable difference in payoffs between equilibria and if anger recedes exponentially, we should expect a very rapid switch in the saliency of identity (1.3 years in the example above). On the other hand, if the payoff is low, suboptimal identities may be maintained for the length of the existence of anger. This finding is somewhat counterintuitive. One might think that small differences might be overcome more rapidly than large ones, but the analysis here suggests that the avoidance of high costs primarily drives the outcome.

Of course, different levels of violence produce different intensities of anger. The initial point and extinction points of the curves would need to change correspondingly.

ii. Modeling Anger After Extreme Violence

Primordialists might claim that often nations are created through genocidal levels of violence or long historical periods of domination. In his article "Primordialism Lives!" Stephen Van Evera (2001) discusses factors that impede identity change. He writes:

Conflict enhances the hardening effect of mass literacy on identity by enhancing the emotional impact of recorded national memories. The experience of warring or oppressed peoples, filled as it is with tales of common struggle and sacrifice for the common good, creates a stronger we-feeling than the experience of people who escape these tragedies; hence it has stronger effects when national scribes record and purvey it. (20–22)

For this reason groups in conflict are especially poor candidates for identity change, and identity change is an especially unlikely remedy for ethnic conflict.

Memories, as suggested by the Van Evera quote, become part of history textbooks and folklore that "national scribes purvey and record." Violence becomes memory. In turn, anger, and its effects on identity shift arise in generation after generation.

While this point of view undoubtedly has some merit, the model above could be modified to address some of these issues.[5] Assume that those who are alive at the time of genocidal violence retain a constant high level of anger their entire lives. Assume further that they pass down the memory of victimhood to following generations and that the individuals in these following generations become aware of their legacy at age fifteen. However, with the passage of time the ability to pass down the emotional intensity of the violence becomes increasingly difficult. Time passes, new events occur. The vividness of the memory of violence becomes part of a past that cannot be emotionally captured.

These elements can be captured through a series of demographic assumptions. First assume a normal population distribution with a life expectancy of sixty-five years and a standard deviation of ten years. Assume that children become aware of their cultural conceptions of victimhood at age fifteen with a standard deviation of three years. The product of these two curves yields a curve representing the "aware population." To model the gradual decrease in the intensity of this culturally inherited anger, assume that the ability to hand down anger starts at the maximum 0.5 level (the highest possible difference between MWC 1 and MWC2) and decreases linearly with an extinction time of twenty-five years. This assumption is captured graphically by Figure 11.4a. Thus, those born twenty-five years after the violent event, despite the efforts of ingroup members, can no longer feel anger at a level that would generate acceptance of lower payoffs in identity coalitions.

Given these assumptions, the resulting anger function is represented by Figure 11.4b. Here, for the first twenty years after the genocidal violence, anger prevents any consideration of identity switch regardless of the trade-offs in terms of MWC1-MWC2. However, as survivors die off and the ability to transfer the

---

[5] I owe most of this section to my former research assistant, Mark Finlayson.

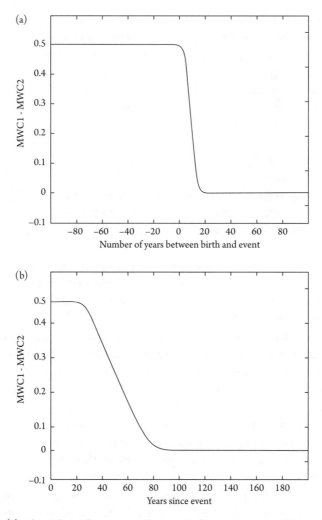

Figure 11.4 (a) The Effect of Anger on Identity Shift as a Function of Time between Birth and Event and (b) MWC Differential and Predicted Identity Shift.

vividness and intensity of the violence to descendants declines, the overall population becomes less ready to maintain the losses created by the identity status quo. With the higher payoffs associated with scenario C, the population will be ready to shift identities in about forty years. It would take over seventy years for scenario B, and almost eighty years for scenario A. In this example, anger finally dies out as a force on identity after eighty years.[6]

Several instances of Eastern European violence would seem to have such a progression. In earlier research, I worked in Lithuania. Often, when I mentioned

---

[6] This outcome generally obtains even with shorter extinction rates. The demographic assumptions largely drive the outcome.

my fieldwork to American Jews, they would provide me with a lecture on Lithuanian collaboration with the Nazis against the Jews during World War II. This violence had occurred more than fifty years earlier, but the resulting anger had been passed down across generations and across the ocean. That violence was probably playing a role in the ever-dwindling number of Lithuania's Jews. The category Lithuanian *and* Jewish may have been a difficult one to accept, especially with the surge of nationalism in the wake of the collapse of the Soviet state and the reconstruction of independent Lithuania.

iii. Incorporating the Emotion of Contempt into Chandra's Framework

Cases with strong components of ethnic contempt pose significant challenges for constructivist theories and methods. First, ethnic prejudice and stigma, and the emotion of contempt behind those phenomena, are sometimes institutionalized. Caste systems possess strong ideas about group worth and group ability. So have apartheid systems as in South Africa or the U.S. South during Jim Crow. There are also informal systems that institutionalize social stigma. Consider the case of American professional baseball leagues. Until the late 1940s, no major league team allowed Black players. No formal rule existed; the ban was only sustained by a "gentleman's agreement" that in turn was partially supported by social stigmas against Blacks and the intermixing of races.

Second, emotions based on beliefs about the nature of an object or groups do not possess predictable decay rates. The emotions of anger and resentment are generated by beliefs about specific events. Individuals experience anger after they perceive that an agent committed a negative action against them; they experience resentment when changes in status hierarchy reorder group relations in a way that is perceived as unjust. If events change, the emotions will fade. If the person who committed the negative action apologizes, is punished, or pays some reparation, then anger may fade. If status hierarchies are realigned, then resentment will dissipate. Contempt, on the other hand, is often tied to a cultural schema that will not necessarily fade with time. Rather, beliefs about the nature and quality of groups may lie constantly in the background.

Constructivist theory usually emphasizes the fluidity of identity choice. Elites are seen as free to create parties or platforms that appeal to different identities or combinations of identities. Individuals are assumed to be able to emphasize the aspects of identity that further their own goals. But ethnic stigmas limit choices. Clearly, stigmas involve imposition, rather than the choice, of identity. There is seldom a reason to choose to possess a stigmatized identity. The majorities themselves cannot just choose to end their emotions and prejudices. Correspondingly, stigmas limit the choices of political elites and identity entrepreneurs who must work with the preferences of populations.

Yet, the effect of interest can certainly play a role in the mitigation of contempt. Consider the example of major league baseball again. When the color line was finally broken, teams had incentives to recruit the best players from the Negro Leagues. Those teams with the most racist ownership that still avoided Blacks often began to lose more games. There was a cost to ethnic contempt. The only remedy for these teams was to also recruit Black players. Eventually, perhaps along lines of the contact theory, the role of stigma was largely eliminated from baseball.

iv. Integrating Contempt into Constructivist Models

The A effect of the emotion of contempt is to create or heighten the desire to avoid a stigmatized group. In effect, under the sway of contempt, the individual can be seen as experiencing a "cost" when closely interacting with the stigmatized group. Correspondingly, individuals do not wish to be included in a category that contains significant numbers of stigmatized individuals. However, there may be limits to how far individuals allow their emotions to control their behavior. They might wish to exclude those with the stigmatized attribute, but if the political or economic costs of exclusion are high, they may act against their natural, emotion-based aversions in order to satisfy these interests.

The costs involved with contempt can again be modeled along a variety of indifference curves (only without a decay function). Consider Figure 11.5. The vertical axis represents interest measured by the percentage difference between two winning coalitions. The horizontal axis represents the "costs" of contempt measured by the percentage of individuals with the stigmatized attribute within the category. How these indifference lines should be drawn is, of course, a matter of debate. The modeler would have to incorporate not only insights from social psychology but also anthropological knowledge about the relationships among groups within the culture or society under investigation. Figure 11.5 simply includes four different hypothetical possibilities:

Line M: In some cases, individuals may see a straightforward relationship between interest and their aversion. They will accept small numbers of members of the stigmatized group (from now on designated by the letter S) even if the payoff is small, but they will accept large numbers of S only if the payoff is large. Here, the individual accepts the inclusion of 1% S for a 1% decline in MWC. A 5% inclusion rate would require a 5% drop in MWC, a 20% S rate would require a 20% drop, and so on.

Line N: This linear relationship can be modified to represent more and less severe forms of contempt. Line N shows a function in which every 1% decline in MWC creates acceptance of 5% S.

Line O: In other cases, individuals accept high costs to be in a category completely free of S, but once the barrier is broken additional numbers of S
create relatively low emotional costs.

Line P: Sometimes individuals might not see a cost for inclusion until the
numbers reach significant levels. In effect, "a few are all right," but too many
of them diminish the value of the category. This form of contempt is represented by line P. Here, emotional costs do not kick in until the category
includes 20% S. Then costs increase at the same rate as in function M.

The meaning of these indifference curves can be illustrated with reference
to the matrices in the previous section seen in Table 11.5 and its three sub-
tables. To recall, the question here is the trade-off between moving from the
race dimension to the Foreign-Native dimension. The latter produces better economic and political payoffs by producing lower MWCs. In the case of anger, the
switch comes from the natural erosion of the emotion.

The same tables can be used to illustrate the nature of contempt. Let us
assume that Blacks and Whites lived together in an autocratic state. That state
breaks down and leaves Blacks and Whites in a democratic political system with
large incentives to form winning coalitions with just over 50%. Let us further
assume that Blacks have contempt for Whites and are reluctant to join categories that include Whites. MWC1 is the size of the all-Black winning coalition
while MWC2 is the number for the Foreign-Native winning coalition. Thus,
in Table 11.5a, Blacks in the upper left cell can choose between an all-Black

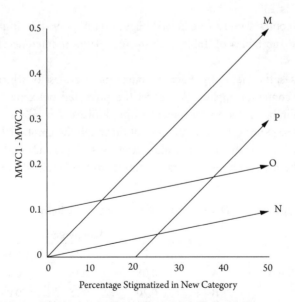

Figure 11.5 The Trade-off Between Differences in Size of Minimum Winning
Coalitions and Percentages of Inclusion of a Stigmatized Group

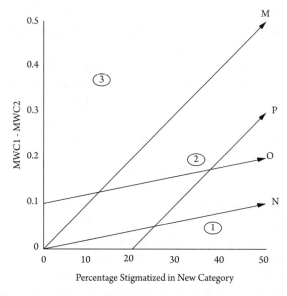

Figure 11.6 The Trade-off Between Differences in Size of Minimum Winning Coalitions and Percentages of Inclusion of a Stigmatized Group with Reference to Table 11.5

category with a MWC of .7 or switch to identification on the Foreign attribute with an MWC of .65 and a percentage S of 38%. The MWC differential is .05 and the percentage S in this category is 38%. In Table 11.5b the WC differential is .20 and Percentage S is 33%. In Table 11.5c the WC difference is .38 and percentage S is 13%.

What outcomes can be predicted? Figure 11.6 plots the situations represented in the sub-tables of Table 11.5 on top of the indifference lines seen in Figure 11.5.

In two cases, the method predicts an outcome regardless of which of the four functions of contempt applies. For 11.5a the predicted outcome (indicated by the circled number 1) is no movement from all-Black. For all four functions of contempt, the 5-point gain in MWC cannot outweigh the emotional costs associated with 38% S. For the situation illustrated by 11.5c (indicated by the circled number 3) the method here predicts movement to the Foreign-Native dimension

Table 11.6 **Hypothetical Distribution of Language and Religion**

		Language		
		1	**2**	**3**
Religion	**A**	0.05	0.10	0.15
	B	0.20	0.05	0.05
	C	0.20	0.15	0.05

for all functions of contempt. The gains created by a 38-point advantage in MWC far outstrip the costs associated with 13% S. The outcome for Figure 11.5b (indicated by circled number 2) is not so clear. If, following Figure 11.6, contempt works along the lines of function N, O, or P, then we should expect that the Foreign-Native dimension becomes the basis for politics. If function M applies, then the prediction is that the Black-White dimension will remain the primary axis of politics.

v. Elite Calculations and Contempt in the Construction of Identities

The constructivist approach developed above and in other chapters envisions political elites surveying the matrix of salient identities and forming minimum winning coalitions. With the existence of a stigmatized attribute, however, calculations become more complex. Not only must identity entrepreneurs offer an attractive MWC, but they must consider whether individuals driven by contempt will accept a category that includes members with the stigmatized attribute.

To illustrate some the strategic constraints and opportunities of elites, consider another example with three attributes and many winning coalitions.

Imagine that in the pre-collapse period, members of religions B and C have an aversion to religion A; in effect, they hold members of that religion in contempt. In the rebuilding stage, these groups find themselves in the proportions represented by this matrix. Because of the ethnic contempt for religion A, elites of both B and C first bind their groups together to form a winning coalition with 70% of the population and 0% S.

Over time, however, it becomes clear that new smaller winning categories can be formed by combining, either through the creation of a new identity or simply through political alliance, one religious attribute with a single language-based attribute. In fact, in the situation above, both B and C can combine with any single language-based attribute to form a winning coalition smaller than B/C. However, all of these new categories will contain members of A, the stigmatized group. Below are the various possibilities measured in terms of MWC advantage versus the B/C option and percentage S in the new category (B/1 will indicate a category containing all cells with either B *or* 1 as an attribute).

B/1: 15, 9.1%
B/2: 15, 18.2%
B/3: 20, 30%
C/1: 5, 7.7%
C/2: 55, 18.2%
C/3: 10, 25%

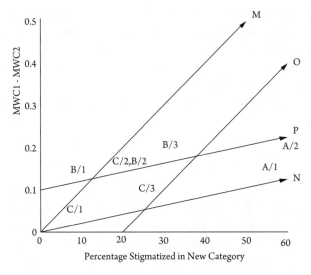

Figure 11.7 The Trade-off Between Differences in Size of Minimum Winning Coalitions and Percentages of Inclusion of a Stigmatized Group with Reference to Table 11.6

These figures can again be plotted (see Figure 11.7). The status quo (B/C) is represented by the 0, 0 point. All situations to the left of the line represent cases where the theoretical benefit of a smaller MWC outweighs the emotional costs of inclusion of the stigmatized group.

Would elites from either the B or C groups have feasible options to construct smaller winning coalitions through the inclusion of a language category that includes members of the stigmatized group? If function M applies, B elites would appear to have a possible winning strategy by combining their B group with members of language group 1. In this case, the benefits of a 15% smaller MWC would outweigh the costs of including the 5% of the overall population (and 9.1% of the new alliance) composed of religion A/language 1 individuals. Of course, this assumes that C group members who speak language 1 (20% of the overall population) are also maximizing actors and would choose to highlight their language attribute over their religion in deciding to join the new B/1 identity group or coalition. With function M, C elites do not have a strategy to do better than the status quo. As the larger of the religious groups (40% for C vs. 30% for B), A's combination with any language group produces a MWC that does not produce sufficient benefits to outweigh the costs of inclusion.

If function P applies, B elites could feasibly go with any strategy. With the P function, C elites also have a theoretically workable strategy by working to combine language 2 speakers with C religious group members. One could imagine that if there was a split between the B and C groups that C elites would move toward combination with language 2 speakers while B elites would respond by trying to coalesce with either language 1 or language 3 groups. The B/1 strategy would yield a higher payoff but would also entail competition with C over the re-identification of the 20% of the population that occupy the C/1 cell. A B/3 strategy would only involve the 5% located in the C/3 cell but would also incur a major risk in that any lack of re-identification of C/3s would result in a number below the 50% needed to win.

The politics rotating around ethnic contempt and marginalization may become increasingly important in situations in which small states are reconstructed from the rubble of large states. In larger states, stigmatized groups can often be marginalized in ways that make them inconsequential in the larger political order. In some cases, as indicated by Ralph Ellison (1952), stigmatized groups can become "invisible." After all, the action tendency of contempt is to shun and ignore the object of the emotion. However, the process of state breakdown and reconstruction will often create situations in which the political status and power of stigmatized groups suddenly becomes a pivotal issue. State breakdown produces new demographics that increase the relative size of the stigmatized group. With greater percentages, stigmatized groups may become pivotal in electoral politics. In the distribution represented by Table 11.6, members of stigmatized group A could have significant, in fact decisive, clout in their response to several possible strategies, especially B3 in the P function scenario discussed above. While this section has worked at a theoretical level, there are several situations in the Balkans—Serbs in Kosovo, Albanians in South Serbia, Roma in several local political forums—where this specific interplay of interest and emotion is likely to play out in the future.

5. General Comments on Identity, Rationality, and Emotion with Reference to the Moldovan Case

In my broader work, my research is at odds with straightforward rational choice approaches. I can quickly summarize the major differences. Above all, my emphasis is on the residue of powerful experiences. Violent experiences create the emotions of anger and fear; prejudice and stigma support the emotions of contempt and hatred; the experience of status reversal can create the emotion of resentment. My view is that the power of these experiences, captured in the language of emotions, often outweighs consideration of narrow economic goods. Moreover, the power and residue of these experiences not only provide resources for mobilization but also serve as a constraint on elite action. Elites can use existing emotions as resources, but in most situations they cannot create them or easily manipulate them. Correspondingly, in my view of long-term politics in Eastern Europe, the focus should be on the experiences of the mass population rather than on the strategies of elites.

In the sections above, I have tried to develop a method to analyze how elites might develop rational choice strategies in the presence of emotions like anger and contempt. The value of the method is that it yields hypotheses regarding what we might expect to see in terms of elite strategies. If we actually test these hypotheses, I anticipate that we will not see decisions closely conforming to the model. The model requires a limited view of emotion, one concentrating only on effects (A effects) that fit into a cost-benefit approach. The power of emotions resides, however, in their broader nature. As Elster (1999) states in a summary of his own view:

> I do not claim that people are insensitive to incentives, only that the interaction between emotions and incentives is more complex than in a cost-benefit model. The role of emotions cannot be reduced to that of shaping the reward parameters for rational choice. It seems very likely that they also affect the ability to make rational choices within those parameters. (413)

To restate this idea in terms of Figure 11.2, the power and influence of emotions comes not only from their A effects but also from their B and C effects. Elites may wish to deal in a straightforward model of narrow costs and benefits, but given emotion's effects on information processing and belief formation, the success and application of such strategies are unlikely to be so direct. In particular, I doubt that elites will be able to readily pursue maximizing MWC strategies.

But these are empirical issues, so let us return to our case of Moldova. In any given case, broad experiences may create a set of emotion resources. As mentioned above, the Moldovan case lacks the experiences of mass violence and deep cultural stigmas that provide the existence of anger and contempt. However, like almost all Eastern European states (Petersen 2002), the experience and politics of ethnic status hierarchy, and thus the emotion of resentment, pervaded the Moldovan case. Earlier sections of this chapter laid out the application of a rational choice approach to identity politics in Moldova after the Soviet collapse. A resentment-based story can also be applied to this process. We can then compare the two explanations.

As outlined above, resentment follows from the belief that one's group is located in an unwarranted subordinate position on a status hierarchy; the action tendency is to take actions to reduce the status position of groups in a superior status position. For the emotion to emerge there must be a clear sense of ethnic hierarchy. The emotion becomes most powerful after status reversals—that is, when formerly subordinate groups gain dominance in positions in state authority.

The Soviet Moldavian Republic possessed a very strong and clear ethnic hierarchy. Despite the Soviet construction of a broad Moldovan identity, a clear ethnic hierarchy existed: Slavs were dominant, Moldovan speakers subordinate. For linguistic reasons, as well as cultural and historical ones, the division between Russians and Ukrainians as a group versus Moldovan speakers became the primary source of group hierarchy in the state. Few Slavs bothered to learn Moldovan, while many declaring themselves Moldovan by nationality came to think and speak primarily in Russian. Moldovans were forced to abandon their Latin script for the Cyrillic script used by Russians and Ukrainians. Slavs dominated top positions in industry and government. The presence of the Soviet Fourteenth Army on Moldovan soil solidified the sense of Slavic dominance.

At the arrival of perestroika in the late 1980s, the subordinate Moldovan-speakers took their first possible opportunity to re-establish the status hierarchy. As outlined above, in 1988 they stated three demands—the recognition that Moldovan and Romanian are the same language, the re-institution of the Latin script, and the recognition of the Romanian language as the state's language. To repeat the previous quote summarizing the effect of these demands: "… it amounted to extracting an open admission from their government that the republic was theirs and theirs alone, and that all other ethnic groups in Moldova were not 'nations' but rather ethnic minorities whose rights should be respected but whose claims could not be considered equal to the interests of the majority" (Smith 1996, 223). There could be no surer way to re-order the ethnic hierarchy.

As predicted by resentment, the formerly dominant group immediately and strongly reacted to impending status reversal. Slavs rioted and then, with the help of the Soviet army, formed their own entity where they would dominate.

Both the rational choice story and the resentment story provide an explanation of the general contours of the Moldovan case. However, the case does present two puzzles. The first issue is minimum winning coalition. On the right bank, as was outlined, identity entrepreneurs did create the smallest winning coalition possible by restrictively redefining the membership criteria for the nationality category "Moldovan." This move managed to exclude almost 40% of the population from the division of spoils. The puzzle arises from identity creation on the left bank in the new Dniestrian Republic. There, political elites created a new "Soviet" identity that excluded only those identifying as "Moldovan" in both language and nationality, composing 75.5% and thus excluding only 24.5% of the population. An examination of Table 11.4 shows several theoretical combinations that would have created a smaller MWC. While some of these

---

[7] Russian nationality could be combined in a category with Other-speakers (essentially Ukrainian speakers). However, such a category would exclude Russian-speaking Ukrainians. It seems unlikely that Russians nationals would accept Ukrainian-speaking Ukrainians but exclude Russian-speaking Ukrainians.

combinations may have been highly unlikely in practice,[7] there were realistic options. For instance, the smallest coalition would have been composed of just Russian speakers (52.15%). In this strategy, elites on the left bank could have mirrored their counterparts on the right bank by choosing a restrictive language category. Also, Moldovans and Ukrainians could have united on a nationality dimension and formed a small MWC (54.4%). Of course, both of these strategies would have relied on splitting up Slavic speakers.

A second issue concerns the stability of the partition. When Moldova and Dniestria were created, Romania was emerging from the nightmare of Ceaucescu's rule. The incentives for unification were not clear. Twenty years later, the political and economic situation had become drastically different. Romania joined the European Union in 2006; its per capita gross domestic product (GDP) was estimated at $11,600 in 2010 (CIA factbook). Moldova remained a politically marginal state with a per capita GDP of $2,500 – rock bottom in Europe, the same level as Laos, and about 40% of Bosnia and Kosovo (both at $6,600). Not surprisingly perhaps, 800,000 of Moldova's 3.4 million citizens have already applied for Romanian citizenship, with many more likely to follow.

For most of the population in the Dniestrian Republic, life is not clearly different. There is much discussion of a significant influx of Russian oil money flowing into the Dniestrian economy as an "off-shore zone," but it is difficult to assess how much this has actually transformed the situation on the left bank.

What is clearer is that residents of Dniestria show little enthusiasm for unifying with Moldova. The region possesses its own police, court system, parliament, and symbols (including a flag and a coat of arms sporting the Soviet-era hammer and sickle). In September 2006, Dniestria held a plebiscite with two choices listed: re-integration with Moldova or independence followed by attachment to Russia. The latter choice in this dubious exercise was supported by 97% of participants (with a 78% reported turnout). On the right bank, in 2010 Moldova's acting President, Mihai Ghimpu, a supporter of union with Romania, established June 28 as "Soviet Occupation Day," a sure way to antagonize those on the other side of the river. If one looks at the symbolic side of relations, there is little sign that the partition of 1990 will be ending any time soon.

The rational choice explanation holds that identities are transformed as a way to create a minimum winning coalition to optimally control a division of spoils. Elites maintain their identity constructions as a way to sustain control over those spoils. In Moldova, one has to wonder why elites maintain identity constructions that help perpetuate such a low overall level of spoils. Following an elite-centered story, Dniestrian elites and Moldovan elites could agree on a more inclusive form of Moldovan nationality that would facilitate the construction of a new Moldovan state. In a second step, this entity could unify with Romania. After all, a majority of Moldovan citizens may adopt dual citizenship with Romania in the coming years. Is it so clear that elites would do so much worse by joining a state that is a member of the European Union and generates about five times the per capita gross national product (GNP)? Why doesn't an alternative elite split off or emerge to challenge the identity status quo? Why is this conflict so solidly frozen when identities are supposedly fluid?

A resentment-based explanation approaches these two puzzles differently. The nature of Soviet development in Moldova produced a clear ethnic hierarchy that pervaded everyday life in Moldova for decades. This hierarchy pitted Moldovan/Romanian speakers against Slavic speakers. Elites were heavily constrained by this legacy of status hierarchy and resentment. The decision of elites on both sides of the river would have to rotate around this fundamental reality. These decisions would have to conform to Moldova's fundamental status cleavages. On the right bank, interest aligned closely with emotion and elites could pursue a MWC. On the left bank, on the other hand, elites could not consider splitting Slavic speakers (Russians, Ukrainians, and russified Moldovans). Given this reality, Moldovans could not seriously believe that they could form a small MWC with Ukrainians against Russians. Russians could not seriously consider excluding Ukrainians to develop a more efficient division of spoils. The result followed the basic status cleavage—exclusion of Moldovan speakers and the maintenance of the Slavic dominance of the Soviet period.

The second puzzle involves the persistence of partition and the stability of the split. A resentment-based explanation would predict that few peoples ever willingly accept status reversal regardless of the economic costs. Unification with Moldova would mean accepting subordinate status. Recognizing the power of these status-oriented politics, Moldovan politicians have tried to assuage these fears of status reversal by offering Dniestrians legal autonomy and promising to allow them to retain their sovereign symbols (flag, anthem, constitution) in a future state (Chiriac 2007). A resentment view would still predict the likely rejection of such initiatives.

6. Conclusion

Chandra has done an admirable job of building up a constructivist framework based on rationality. My own methods focus on the role of emotion. In this chapter, I have tried to reconcile these two approaches by showing how political scientists might incorporate emotions, specifically the emotions of anger and contempt, into Chandra's framework. In the last section, I have also registered and illustrated my skepticism over the incorporation of emotions into such frameworks. On many issues, both interest and emotion are at play. We don't very well understand their interaction. This chapter has been a small step toward creating a dialogue that can move our understanding forward.

Deploying Constructivism for the Analysis of Rare Events

How Possible Is the Emergence of "Punjabistan"?

IAN S. LUSTICK

The purpose of this volume is to demonstrate that a rigorous conceptual framework can enable constructivist insights to be deployed for the solution of a variety of theoretical and empirical problems. In this chapter I offer a use case in which the framework set forth by the editor, if not the exact details of its entire vocabulary, is employed to solve a difficult empirical and policy-relevant problem. The general problem involved is to evaluate a future for Pakistan involving the secession of its Punjabi core—a future whose probability experts have had difficulty assessing. Since secession is itself a rare event, and secession of the center an even rarer event, data relevant to addressing this problem must be generated by a computer simulation model designed and implemented in conformance with available social theories, including constructivist theory, along with information about Pakistani society relevant to the categories of those theories. The thrust of this chapter is to demonstrate that by integrating constructivist approaches to political contestation, via the framework offered in this volume, with specific knowledge of a complex and important case—the future of Punjabi-dominated Pakistan—an agent-based modeling approach can be used to analyze the conditions under which secession of the center can take place and to estimate its likelihood.

In the study of secession, most analyses of regionally concentrated ethnic demographies consider problematic peripheries from the point of view of the

I am especially grateful for the assistance of Kaija Schilde in the preparation of this chapter. Important contributions to the development of the VirPak model and to the underlying software were made by Vladimir Dergachev, Ben Eidelson, Quratul Ann Malik, Dan Miodownik, Vali Nasr, and , Mathew Tubin. I also wish to thank the members of the CAEG group and of the Laboratory in Comparative Ethnic Processes for their helpful comments. Partial support for this project was received from the National Science Foundation, Award No. 0218397. A somewhat different version of this chapter appeared in Lustick 2011.

center. Usually one region, commonly containing or representing a politically dominant cultural formation, is identified as the core of the national unit and as in control of the central state. The political history of the country is then told as an account of how center relations with peripheries have been managed or, often, how the boundaries marking those peripheries (regional, social, cultural, or economic) were rendered irrelevant and/or invisible. Such an orientation follows a solid tradition of understanding large states as built up from small but powerful cores as a result of centripetal political and military competitions of aggrandizement, consolidation, and self-protection against equally expansion prone neighbors (see, for example, Pounds and Ball 1964; Gourevitch 1979). Economic theories about the size of states generally begin with an image of a central geographic location figured as the capital city. The size of the state is then explained or predicted as a function of the trade-off between the center's ability to exploit economies of scale across a large area and the costs the center must pay, increasing with distance along the peripheries, to maintain the stability of its authority in those regions.[1]

Against this characteristic narrative, the problem of "secession" emerges as a centrifugal force that threatens the center with the loss of resources assumed to be accessible to it through control of individual peripheries. Whether the calculus is strategic, economic, or political, the often unstated argument is that bigger is better, if not because of the possibilities of establishing a larger resource base and domestic market, then because of the beneficial terms of trade the center can establish and maintain with the peripheries. States, dominated by core regions and groups, are expected to treat secessionism as anathema. Generally speaking, that is the case. The United Nations, as an organization of states, opposes virtually all secessionist movements within the borders of its members. The same is true of other interstate organizations.

However, states sometimes do decide to shrink. Imperial states may take decades or even centuries to decide that peripheries such as colonies are more trouble than they are worth. The standard finding in studies of decolonization is precisely that. Cost-benefit calculations by experts in the imperial center almost always reveal the colony to be a net drag on center resources. But such calculations themselves do not predict the timing of decolonization. Rather, it is the appearance of cost-benefit calculations as dominant considerations that predicts the timing of decolonization. The usual irrelevance of such calculations is almost always due to the importance of political, cultural, psychological, or ideological principles associated with the imperial framework within which the colony is ruled. It is institutional lag, not efficient exploitation, which tends to delay rational steps toward "rightsizing" states by making it difficult for imperial state elites to treat their cost-benefit calculations as decisive.

[1] For an example of this approach that includes a strong discussion of previous efforts, see Alesina and Spolare 2003.

Yet there are cases in which the political core of a state, encompassing dominant institutions, preponderant economic power, and cultural integrity, does choose to dispose of peripheral regions and peoples. Some of these cases—Rome under Hadrian withdrawing from Mesopotamia and Scotland, Britain under Lloyd George relinquishing the south of Ireland, France under de Gaulle extracting itself from Algeria—are of spectacular interest since the drama of "contracting" a state to preserve its character is a political achievement of the first order.[2]

However, the theoretical target of this chapter is more specific. Instead of considering the general category of state contraction, this chapter focuses on one type of state contraction known, in the rare instances in which it is the direct object of analysis, as "secession of the center." Let us consider state contraction as the purposive abandonment of a central state's rule over a portion of its populated territory that does not arise as a result of the external application of force maejure. Standardly, such decisions would be observed, whether in imperial or national contexts, in response to a long and difficult struggle by discontented elites and masses in the peripheral region for autonomy or independence. In contrast to this standard story of state contraction as a response to a struggle originating from the periphery, secession of the center is state contraction initiated by elites in the core of the state as a result of conditions, calculations, or circumstances not driven primarily by demands from its peripheries for independence.

1. The Notion of Secession of the Center

The notion of secession of the center figures in accounts of the emergence of Singapore as an independent state from the Malaysian Federation in 1965 that emphasize the extent to which the initiative for that separation came from Malaysia itself, impelled by its fear of the weight of Singaporean Chinese in its ethnic demography. For some students of the breakup of the Soviet Union, the change from Gorbachev's clumsy efforts to reform the state while keeping it intact was replaced by a Yeltsin strategy based, really, if not explicitly, on Russian abandonment of the other Republics—a secession of the center camouflaged via the "Commonwealth of Independent States" as Moscow's loss of control over a process of radical decentralization of power.[3] The breakup of Czechoslovakia is analyzed quite persuasively as triggered by a package of reforms imposed by a

---

[2] For an extended theoretical treatment and empirical exploration of a model of state contraction and expansion, see Lustick 1993; and O'Leary, Callaghy, and Lustick 2002.

[3] On Russia's secession from the Soviet Union, see Hanson 1998 and Hale 2004a.

Czech Finance Minister, later Prime Minister, Václav Klaus that greatly reduced subsidies for the poorer Slovak region. Despite Slovak protests, the Czechs refused to compromise on these moves, which benefited the Czech core of the country. This led directly to the separation of the Czech Republic from Slovakia.[4] The Northern League in Italy is an example of a more or less explicit movement to achieve the secession of the center—in this case the ambition of the economic and culturally confident northern regions of Italy to separate themselves from the poorer, strongly Catholic, agricultural, and less "European" south.

Aside from examples of actual secession of the center or movements dedicated to achieving that end, ideological and political projects envisioning such a process may also be noted. In South Africa, the architects of apartheid entertained the goal of uniting the English and the Afrikaners as whites, relegating Africans to unattractive areas of the country—the Bantustans, and then moving toward a secession of the White-dominated "center" from the non-white regions (Marx 1997). An ideology of secession of the center was also the cornerstone of Enoch Powell's view that "England" was being ruined by the Empire it had built and the Commonwealth that succeeded it. In his famous "rivers of blood" speech in 1968 and in other writings and lectures he called for the re-emigration of immigrants, a radical transformation in England's relations with Commonwealth states, and a reassertion of English and England as the cultural and geographic focus of political identification and political rule from London (Powell 1969).

2. Center Secession in Pakistan

The focus of this chapter is on prospects for and circumstances conducive toward secession of the center in Pakistan. In fact, it is Pakistan, and the subcontinent as a whole, where a kind of tradition of center secession can be said to have emerged. One important contemporary strand within the historiography about the partition of the subcontinent into "India" and "Pakistan" is the argument advanced by Ayesha Jalal in her biography of Pakistan's founder, Mohammad Ali Jinnah, that a fundamental contributing factor, and perhaps a necessary element, in the emergence of Pakistan was the decision by Hindu elites associated with the Congress Party, including Gandhi, to abandon densely populated Muslim areas in west Punjab and east Bengal rather than pay the political price (cultural and political decentralization of some sort) that would have allowed the subcontinent to remain united (Markovits 2002). Indeed the division of Pakistan itself in 1971 can also be understood as an instance of secession of the center.

---

[4] Hale 2004a, 183. Hale also provides an account of the demise of the short-lived Mali Federation in 1960, after the wealthy Senegalese core of the country declared its own independence, that fits, technically if not particularly tellingly, in this category.

Although usually described as a secessionist conflict mounted by Bengalis, supported by India, and featuring a brutal war in Bengal waged against secession by the Pakistani military, the separation of the East and its emergence as Bangladesh can just as accurately be seen as the secession of the wealthier Punjabi dominated center of the country, in the West, following the emergence of a Bengali political bloc powerful enough in organizational and demographic terms to win control of the government in Karachi/Islamabad.

The question posed in this chapter is a continuation of this South Asian "tradition." It was recently explicitly by one of the leading students of contemporary Pakistani politics, Stephen Philip Cohen. Cohen (2004) concludes his study, *The Idea of Pakistan*, with a consideration of various possible futures for the country, including its breakup due to ethnic rivalries and conflicts. Within this category Cohen asks: "Could Pakistan evolve into a Punjabistan—a nuclear-armed, smaller, more efficient and generally secure state?" (292). He answers this question summarily, with no extended analysis, and without a great deal of certainty. "This seems doubtful, but Punjab, like Russia, is the educationally and economically most advanced part of the country, and Punjabis regard themselves as culturally and civilizationally distinct, if not superior, to Sindhis, Baluch, and the tribals of the Northwest Frontier Province (NWFP) [in 2010 the province was renamed Khyber Pakhtunkhwa]" (Cohen 2004, 292).

Cohen ends his book with a variety of scenarios for the future of Pakistan. The emergence of "Punjabistan" is one of them. He describes it as "doubtful." But in fact he describes each of the scenarios he traces as unlikely. That is because, individually, they are all unlikely. Yet Pakistan will have some kind of future, and it might include Punjabistan. It is just that Cohen can only trace some trajectories that may be slightly less "doubtful" than others, and these, in his judgment, include the "Punjabistan" future.

In this chapter we seek to say more than Cohen was able to say about this topic. We can agree that this particular future is unlikely, but we would like to know the conditions that would increase the likelihood of that event. We would particularly like to know if certain configurations of political circumstances could be identified that, if not necessary or sufficient to produce a Punjabistan, would make that outcome more likely than not. We would like, in other words, to understand more about the mechanisms that might successfully push Punjabis toward the risky, unconventional, but perhaps ultimately satisfying step of abandoning the peripheries of Pakistan to embrace a firm domination of its core territory, population, and resources.

Of course if we had a general theory of secession from the center, based on strong patterns of documented relationships between potent explanatory variables and either the occurrence or non-occurrence of center secession, we could simply measure those variables in the Pakistan case, or prepare ourselves to measure them as Pakistan moves forward in time, in order to assess the changing probability of this kind of outcome. The problem with events as rare as center secession, however, is that building up an N of cases sufficiently large to afford opportunities to achieve statistical significance for our findings would require stretching the concept, fuzzing its meaning, and including cases from great swaths of time and space that would introduce insuperable problems of comparability, data availability, and data reliability. The tiny number of outcomes also reduces to virtually nil the possibility that we might arrange a "natural experiment" in which one or two other cases could be intensively compared—cases similar enough to Pakistan to control for the variables not thought to be interesting, but different enough to allow both independent and dependent variables to vary instructively.

3. Agent-Based Modeling as a Strategy for Studying Rare Events

However, if the obstacles to analyzing this problem via aggregate data analysis or structured-focused comparison are insuperable, there is another way—computer-assisted agent-based modeling. That is the approach taken in this study. The thought experiments enabled by the rigor of computer simulations conducted on the same platform, with the same template, and with recorded streams of perturbations, achieve a level of discipline far beyond what can be achieved by the standard application of the researcher's imagination via verbal models. Mentally conducted thought experiments cannot hold all theoretical commitments constant across mental exercises, cannot be sure that ceteris paribus assumptions are clearly stipulated and constant across exercises, and cannot register the systematic impact of accidental or highly contingent perturbations. With computer-assisted agent-based modeling simulation, however, the researcher can be certain that each unique trajectory of VirPak is fully consistent with the same theoretical assumptions and with identical judgments about the current state of affairs. Patterns of difference and similarity within the distribution of trajectories, or futures, produced then constitute the basis for inference about the forces and mechanisms operating, or likely to operate, in the Pakistan of the real world.

With this strategy in mind we implemented in a virtual space clear and widely accepted principles of political competition among boundedly rational groups and individuals via simple algorithms. We then feed into this model reasonable initial conditions (i.e., the best data presently available on Pakistan on distributions of influence and affiliation among Pakistanis) to create a "Virtual Pakistan"—VirPak. We then perturb dynamic simulation runs of VirPak with randomly generated, small exogenous shocks—contained in streams of changing signals regarding the general attractiveness or disutility of being publicly regarded as affiliated with a particular identity. These perturbations do not determine agent behavior, including activation, abandonment, or substitution of identities within agent repertoires, but they are factored into agent calculations in simple ways consistent with standard principles of social psychology, bounded rationality, and constructivist identity theory.

Considering again the problem of center secession as a rare event, we could, by generating very large number of counterfactual futures, or histories, provide the database we needed to produce reasonable hypotheses about center secession in Pakistan and, by extension, about the broader category. In this chapter we concentrate only on 100 futures of VirPak generated with our "baseline" conditions (to be explained later).[5] By analyzing this array of 100 trajectories, or futures, we

1. Determine if (given the assumptions built into the model) secessionist tendencies by Punjabis can exist;
2. Measure their relative strength and prevalence in comparison to other kinds of major political outcomes;
3. Gauge the relative frequency of successful center secessions; and
4. Identify the key mechanisms which are capable of and perhaps most likely to produce center secession by the Punjab.

Before accomplishing these tasks the anatomy of the VirPak model must be explained and, constrained by space limitations, justified. Following that account, some descriptive statistics will be provided describing the batch of 100 futures generated from with the model under "baseline" conditions, setting the stage for analysis of Punjabi secessionism and of those relatively few futures in which a "Punjabistan" quite clearly does emerge.[6]

4. The Anatomy of Virtual Pakistan

Considerably less is known about Pakistan than about other countries. Nonetheless, the amount that is reasonably well understood about Pakistan, and

---

[5] Other work with VirPak involved producing batches of futures to compare with the baseline futures. These alternate batches reflected slightly different initial conditions or assumptions about the relative strength of different identities or types of political influence. Although not reported here, we understand them as sensitivity tests establishing the robustness and plausibility of our findings across a range of possible parameter settings.

[6] As specific and even exotic as the category of "center secession" might be, it still needs to be disaggregated. One may wish to distinguish between the separation of the central state apparatus and the territories and populations it directly represents and/or controls from the separation of the central political, social, or cultural formation from the state apparatus that had served, but is no longer perceived to serve, the interests or aspirations of that group. The brief list of examples of center secession provided above includes both types. The simulation exercise reported here using Virtual Pakistan is focused only on the second type. I am indebted to Kaija Schilde for making this point clear to me.

the share of those most basic elements that are included in VirPak, are much greater than anything usually incorporated in agent-based models. This degree of detail is, of course, an order of magnitude greater than the amount incorporated in even the most complex closed-form models. The complexity of this model compared with those associated with closed-form approaches arises because the fundamental commitment in agent-based modeling is to start by implementing the simple things believed to be true about how politics works rather than by implementing rules for a model which we know cannot be true, but which offer the simplicity required for algebraic solution. With regard to VirPak, the complexity also arises because instead of modeling only what we imagine as the contingent aspects of an otherwise purely abstract entity, we have sought to model a real entity, all of whose theoretically relevant attributes were at least partially knowable.

Virtual Pakistan begins at time 0. Figure 12.1 shows the pattern of identity activation by agents in VirPak at t = 0 (see color plate 12.1). Once a simulation begins, the landscape quickly changes its appearance as agents rotate alternative identities into "activated" status, put previously activated identities into their repertoires, or substitute existing identities in their repertoires with newly available and more attractive identities.[7] Specific differences are linked to the streams of small exogenous perturbations referred to above. We use the term "biases" to refer to the values assigned to identities, incorporated by agents in their calculation of "identity weights," as they make their local updating decisions. Although all identities begin with a bias of "0," in the initial eight-step period of each future we "scramble" the biases by shuffling assignments randomly and rapidly. These shifting bias assignments combine with local agent assessments of identity prevalence and activation opportunities to produce updating behavior by each agent every other time step. This "scramble" produces VirPak futures that each begin "*in media res*," connected to the same initial template, but not moving forward from an artificially calm, "history-less" beginning of time. Figure 12.2 for one example of Virtual Pakistan, baseline condition, after an eight time step scramble (see color plate 12.2).

Individuals and the groups they comprise are represented by 3,208 agents located within the borders of Virtual Pakistan. VirPak's overall configuration, the geographical patterns of concentration and proximity of various identity markers within it, along with the distribution of identity resources and political power with which agents in it have been endowed, is designed to capture key realities of contemporary Pakistan. Thus the shape of Virtual Pakistan corresponds

[7] For an explanation of the fundamental operating rules of PS-I and of the terminology used to describe PS-I simulations, see Lustick 2002b. Detailed information and justification for the various trigger settings that determine the sensitivity of different kinds of agents to changes in their surroundings are not provided in this summary of Virtual Pakistan.

(roughly) to the geographical shape of real Pakistan, though some distortion is inevitable in this regard because of the drastic differences in population density in different regions of the country. The drivers of Virtual Pakistan are pressures by Pakistanis and Pakistani sub-communities to respond to opportunities and constraints imposed upon them.

Virtual Pakistan is divided, as is Pakistan itself, into four major provinces—the NWFP, Baluchistan, the Sindh, and Punjab (with a "Seraiki"-dominated area in the frontier region of southern Punjab bordering Sindh). To these regions may be added Pakistani ruled Kashmir and the Federally Administered Tribal Areas located in the area broadly associated with the NWFP. In each area, distinctive ethnographic, political, and rural-urban habitation patterns prevail and were implemented in the construction of VirPak. Largely uninhabited regions, or very sparsely inhabited regions, were implemented by using "uninhabited cells" (marked as gray). In addition to capturing broad relationships among religious, ethnolinguistic, regional, economic, and clan loyalties, three crucial kinds of decisions were required to construct Virtual Pakistan (or any such virtual country).

1. How to distribute identities among agents between regions and within the different regions (especially regarding urban/rural divisions) so that characteristic clusters of latent identities are located in proportions that reasonably correspond to the best data available.
2. How to achieve a reasonably accurate pattern of activated identities at $t = 0$.
3. How to create networks of different types of agents (agent classes) to correspond with various patterns of power relations within rural and urban areas and with respect to the organizational capacity of key groups, including, in the case of Pakistan, the national government, the military, the Muslim fundamentalist movement, criminal networks, rural landowners with feudalist ties to peasant communities, local clerics, and provincial bureaucracies.

All three items are addressed in the subsequent sections.

5. Identity Repertoires in Pakistan

The social repertoire, or spectrum, for the population of VirPak consists of thirty identity categories, both ethnic and non-ethnic.[8] Although the model does not

---

[8] Technically there are thirty. In fact, identity 28 (Hindu/Indian) is not present in the repertoire of any Pakistan agent and identity 29 is a special condition, rather than identity, that allows PS-I to estimate the effects of nuclear events unleashed by terrorism or instability on the "performance" of Virtual Pakistan. So it is reasonable to think of VirPak as including a spectrum of twenty-eight politically relevant identities (identities 0–27).

explicitly distinguish the identity categories from the attributes that are the raw material for those categories, the model is consistent with Chandra and Boulet's framework. The individual identity categories in an agent's repertoire can be thought of as prefabricated combinations of attributes drawn from a number of different dimensions including kinship (various Qaum or clan affiliations), mother-tongue (Pushtun, Punjabi, Seraiki, Baluch, Muhajir, Afghan), religion (Shia, Sunni traditional, Sunni fundamentalist), and occupation (government, landlord, military, commercial, worker, peasant). Any particular identity category can be activated, or "professed" (i.e., publicly displayed, at any particular time). Over time, the pattern of identities displayed by an agent is a function of the particular "complexion" of its repertoire and the changing incentive structure of its environment.

The repertoire of an agent is stickier than the activated identity drawn from the repertoire. But agent repertoires are also susceptible to change when strong pressures from the environment induce agents to shed elements in their repertoires and acquire more serviceable identities. In other words, although the set of "categories" that are represented in a repertoire are individually "prefabricated," the complexion of the repertoire of the agent can change over time. Thus, if the agent has a repertoire of (1,2345) with 1 activated, it might well on a subsequent time step have (1,2945) activated on 1, still, but with 9 in its repertoire rather than 3. At any time step, the particular way that different identity categories cluster within an agent is in effect the strategy used by that agent in its interactions with others. From a combinatorics point of view, the set of all possible strategies is determined by the vast number of arrangements of identities possible within an agent's repertoire.

It will be noted that the identities listed here do not comprise a complete list of ethnic, linguistic, religious, or political categories in Pakistan. Nor do they all play important roles. The Indian/Hindu identity (28) exists only as a marker of "India" to the east of Pakistan. The black border between India and Pakistan, and Pakistan and Shi'a (4) Iran, prevent cross-border contact, simplifying our analysis of the internal dynamics of Pakistan but leaving open possibilities for future work in which these borders might be made penetrable by direct cultural or political influences. In addition, it was decided not to try to include attachments to political parties as identity markers. With the exception of relatively small cadres of professional politicians, the importance of political parties lay in the extent to which they reflect clusters of interests and identities (landowners, government bureaucrats, peasants, Pushtuns, Muhajirs, commercial elites, workers, etc.) which are present in the complexions of agents.

As noted, the repertoires of individual agents consist of subsets of these thirty categories. The size of this subset varies. In both Chandra and Boulet's combinatorial model and van der Veen and Laitin's agent-based model, individual repertoires of nominal identity categories are of uniform size. But in VirPak, some agents (reflecting cultural or ideological rigidities and often rural habitation) have as few as two identities in their repertoire, substantially limiting their adaptability. Others, reflecting educational sophistication, opportunism, or cultural complexity and flexibility, have as many as nine. Figure 12.3 provides a color-coded list of identities present in the spectrum of identities theoretically available to any agent in VirPak along with information regarding the number of agents currently displaying as "activated" on each particular identity and the number of agents holding that identity in their repertoire (see color plate 12.3). The fact that each agent has multiple alternative identities in its repertoire but only one activated identity explains why the numbers in the "subscribed" column (the number of agents containing a particular identity in their repertoires) are so much larger than those in the activated column (the number of agents currently displaying that identity to its neighbors).

Most agents can deploy alternative identities within their repertoire and most agents can absorb new identities into their repertoire but must discard an identity not currently deployed to do so. A black border surrounds the country and divides it from Iran in the west, India in the east, and Afghanistan in the north. The Indian Ocean is to the south, "populated" by agents mostly carrying a globalizing identity. There is substantial cross-border traffic in the northwest, with Afghanistan, but in general VirPak is focused not on its specific relationships with Iran, India, and Afghanistan but with implications of its internal balance of forces. Virtual Pakistan is designed with the intention that 200 time steps correspond roughly to one year in real time. Experiments reported here are run to 608, or approximately three years.

By maintaining or changing their activated identities, or by substituting a new identity for an identity previously in their repertoires, agents respond to streams of small changes in the sum of advantages or disadvantages of presenting themselves in public according to various ethnic, economic, religious, political, or kinship categories. As noted, different "runs" of the model, which is to say different "futures" of VirPak, are generated by randomizing the initial distribution of "biases" (the relative advantages and disadvantages of "activating" different identities currently available to each person or community) as well as by randomizing the stream of changes in bias assignments that follows the initial "scramble."[9]

---

[9] For a detailed explanation and illustration of the algorithms determining agent behavior calculation in response to changing patterns of local activation on available identities and changing biases assigned to different identities, see Lustick 2002a.

6. The Distribution of Identity Repertoires
in Virtual Pakistan

The distribution of subscribed identities to different agents is crucial.[10] An agent can activate much more readily on an identity already present in its repertoire than if it needs to absorb that identity into its repertoire first and discard an already present identity.[11] By distributing identities carefully, a significant amount of the nuance associated with complex political realities and multiple loyalties can be captured. Our representation of the distribution of identity repertoires in VirPak goes significantly beyond previous formulations in several ways. First, it allows for individual-level variation in both the size and content of identity repertoires. Second, it allows for *regional* variation in both size and content of repertoires—and takes the population density of each region into account. The geographic distribution of repertoires of identity categories may well be one of the most significant variables affecting state contraction and other outcomes and processes associated with ethnic differences, but it has not so far been modeled in this book. Third, we allow for correlations between different types of identities in a repertoire: Certain identity categories go together in a repertoire while others do not. Fourth, in a different way of conceptualizing "stickiness," identities can vary in whether they are "obtainable" or "unobtainable": Agents can be "born" with unobtainable identities but cannot bring them into their repertoires if they are not already there. The remainder of this section elaborates.

For example, an agent's repertoire might be comprised in part or in full by identities: 1, 15, 19, 21—indicating Sunni, Muhajir, Landowner, and Pakistan Government. This kind of agent would be a Muhajir, relatively loyal to the

[10] The version of Virtual Pakistan described in this chapter was built in 2002 with data available up to the end of 2002. Accordingly the social, demographic, cultural, geographical, economic, and other inputs for the model were those available in 2002. The model was run to produce simulations of the future, in a "forecasting" mode for the years 2003–2005. Consideration of the results of these simulations is now to be understood as retrodiction and retrodictive analysis. Data used for the creation of VirPakistan were assembled from a large array of publicly available sources, including: *Ethnologue.com* Ethnologue report for Pakistan, "Languages of Pakistan,"http://www.ethnologue.com/show_country.asp?name=Pakistan, http://www.pakmart.com/map/map.htm; Cohen 1998, 2002; Labour Force Surveys, Population Census of Pakistan 1998; Tanham 1999; Nasr, 2001; Kux 2001; International Crisis Group 2002, http://www.crisisgroup.org/~/media/Files/asia/south-asia/pakistan/Pakistan%20The%20Dangers%20of%20Conventional%20Wisdom.pdf; *India Today*, January 28, 2002, 24–30; Jones 2002; Schaffer and Mehta 2002; Soofia, Racine, and Ali 2002; James Martin Center for Proliferation Studies, http://cns.miis.edu/; Pakistan Demographic Surveys, Federal Bureau of Statistics and Planning Commission; "UNMOGIP Deployment," Map No. 3828 Rev 5 (July 1999), Department of Public Information, United Nations; Khyber.org, Assorted Maps, http://www.khyber.org/maps.shtml; CIA Factbook: Pakistan, https://www.cia.gov/library/publications/the-world-factbook/geos/pk.html accessed 2002.

[11] At t = 0, 72% of the agents within the Pakistan_shape portion of VirPak are basic agents.

government but likely to be located in a rural area, probably in Sindh. As a matter of fact, there are two such agents with these identities in their repertoires. Both are low-echelon government bureaucrats, meaning each is activated on identity 21 at t = 0 and has an influence level of 2 (see below). One is located in rural Sindh. The other, in western Punjab, has a military identity in its repertoire as well. On the other hand, an agent whose repertoire had 0, 1, 19, 22, indicating Punjabi, Sunni, Landowner, and Criminal, might be considered potentially corrupt, ready to serve the interests of the landowning rural elite, and an obstacle to dependable government control over the rural areas of Punjab where such agents are likely to be located. Indeed there are eleven such agents (most having several other identities as well) in the rural (mostly southern) Punjab.

For another example, consider the identity combination: 4, 11, 14, 16 (Shi'a, Pushtun, Urban worker, Military). Such an agent would represent members of the minority Shi'a community among Pushtun workers in Peshawar with sympathies or aspirations toward, ties to, or relatives in the military. On the other hand the combination 1, 10, 11, 16 (Sunni, Qaum/Clan identity, Pushtun, and Military) would indicate a rural Pushtun Sunni Muslim with a particular clan identity and sympathies or aspirations toward or relatives in the military.

An important element in designing and implementing VirPak was to determine which identities tend to cluster with one another and then realize those patterns within a geographical and overall statistical framework that corresponds to available data about real Pakistan. A good sense of the overall composition of VirPak can be gained from the table presented in Figure 12.4 (see color plate 12.4). This table, describing the baseline condition of VirPak at t = 0, cross-tabulates all identities with one another to indicate how often particular identities in VirPak are present within the same agent repertoire as each other identity. The column of numbers under each identity listed across the top of the table lists the number of times that that identity is accompanied within the repertoire of a VirPak agent by the identity listed in the column of identities at the extreme left of the table.[12] More detailed analysis is also possible. For example, identity 0 (Punjabi) is present in 1,417 VirPak agents. More of these agents contain in their repertoire the Sunni Muslim identity (1), than any other identity: 1,122. The other identities present in large minorities of these Punjabi agents are, in order of their most frequent appearance, 18, 20, 16, 13, and 14 (peasant, north Punjabi clan affiliation, military, north Punjabi clan affiliation, worker, south Punjabi clan affiliation, Shi'a).

---

[12] The highlighted numbers in the diagonal running through the middle of the table are the number of agents containing that one identity in their repertoire. The careful reader will note that these numbers are occasionally higher than those listed as "subscribed" to various identities in the Statistics display presented in the figure. The reason for the discrepancy is that this table includes identities in all agents present in VirPak, whereas the statistics display counts only "active" agents (i.e., it excludes "apathetic" agents who do not influence agents around them).

These raw figures, however, can be deceiving. Some identities, such as the clan (*qaum*) identities, are "unobtainable" and activated by relatively few agents.[13] They therefore figure relatively obscurely in the visible competition among political forces in Pakistan. Nor do they have authority structures at their direct disposal (influential agents, activated on those identities at t = 0). The most salient identities in VirPak, those with the agents activated on them at t = 0, those with the largest subscriptions, and those most relevant to the trajectories into the future produced from the template are: Punjabi (0), Sunni Muslim (1), Sindhi (3), Pushtun (11), Muslim fundamentalist (12), Worker (14), Muhajir (15), Military (16), Peasant (18), Landowner (19), Pakistani Government (21), and Criminal/Smuggler (22).

In VirPak at t = 0, 44% of agents have a Punjabi identity, meaning that they have identity (0) in their reperotire. Seventy-nine percent of are Sunni, 15% are Shi'a. These proportions correspond relatively well to what we know about Pakistan's ethnic and religious makeup. Few if any Punjabis have Muhajir, Baluch, Sindhi, or Pushtun identities in their repertoires though some have Seraiki or Kashmiri. Forty-eight percent of Punjabis are peasants, living in the rural areas of the Punjab, excluding the Seraiki area. Fourteen percent are workers, located mainly in the urban areas. Twenty-one percent are oriented positively toward the military and are readily available for recruitment. Punjabis predominate in the urban areas of the Punjab, meaning the wide corridor stretching southeast from Rawalpindi and Islamabad toward Lahore and then south-southwest toward Bahawalpur and Multan. But Punjabis are not as predominant in Punjabi cities as they are in the countryside. Only 4% of Punjabis include the urban middle-class identity (25) in their repertoires. Sunni Muslims in the rural Punjab are almost all affiliated with kinship networks of importance, linking them to regionally concentrated populations of other Punjabis. Although the overwhelming majority of Punjabis live in Punjab, significant numbers are also present in Sindh and in Baluchistan.

Seventeen percent of agents in VirPak are Sindhis—agents with Sindhi (3) in their repertoire. Almost all located in Sindh, where they predominate in the rural areas but are outnumbered in Karachi and Hyderabad. Few if any share Punjabi, Pushtun, Kashmiri, or Muhajir identities. Pockets of Shi'a are present in the northwest of Sindh, but the overwhelming majority are Sunni. Sixty-four percent are peasants, reflecting the "Sons of the Soil" dimension of Sindhi identity. Ten percent are Muslim fundamentalists. In the borderland with the Seraiki area many share a Seraiki identity. Criminal identities are common. Only 7% have military orientations or sympathies and even fewer begin with attachments or connections to the Pakistan government.

---

[13] Agents in VirPak can be "born" with unobtainable identities, but in the three years of simulated time explored in these experiments, agents cannot bring them into their repertoires if they are not already there.

Pushtuns, those agents with Pushtun (11) in their repertoire, represent 13% of agents in VirPak. The vast majority are located in NWFP, but they can be found as well in the Punjab and in Sindh, especially in Karachi. Few if any share Sindhi, Baluch, Muhajir, Kashmiri, or Punjabi identities. More than 80% have either or both of the Sunni Muslim and Muslim fundamentalist identities. Nine percent are Shi'a. The great majority of non-Shi'a Pushtun agents are each affiliated with specifically Pushtun kinship networks (5, 9, 10). An unusually high proportion of Pushtuns (41%) have ties to or positive orientations toward the military. Thirty-eight percent are peasants. Muslim fundamentalist tendencies are also strong, present within 40% of non-Shi'a Pushtuns. Thirty-two percent of Pushtuns share the criminal/smuggler identity (22). Very few are associated with the urban middle class.

Muslim fundamentalists are those agents containing (12) in their repertoires. In the baseline condition of VirPak 13% of agents have this identity in their repertoires. Agents containing this identity are spread throughout geographical VirPak, but relatively less prominently in the urbanized corridors of the northwestern Punjab. Centers of Muslim fundamentalist identity affiliation are in the NWFP, eastern and central Sindh, Kashmir, and the rural Punjab, particularly around the city of Multan. Reflecting the largest identity groups in VirPak, Muslim fundamentalists as a group are heavily Sunni Muslim (in fact no agents at t = 0 in VirPak are both "Shi'a" and "fundamentalist," reflecting the Sunni nature of the Deobandi movement in Pakistan and the hostility between these Muslim fundamentalists and the Shi'a). Ethnically, Muslim fundamentalists are disproportionately Pushtun (39%). Twenty-five percent are Punjabi, 16% Muhajir, and 9% Sindhi. The relatively small Kashmiri population in VirPak (about 3%) is, like the Pushtuns, disproportionately represented among Muslim fundamentalists. Six percent of agents with the Muslim fundamentalist identity also have the Kashmiri identity. The movement is weak, of course, among westernized liberals (2) and is also only rarely present in agent repertoires also containing the military identity.

Workers are non-elite Pakistanis living in urban rather than rural areas. They comprise 14% of all agents in VirPak. Ethnically they are disproportionately Punjabi and Muhajir, with a fair representation of Baluch and Sindhi, but relatively few Pushtun. Seventeen percent identify with or are part of the Pakistani government, though a relatively small percentage has positive orientations toward the military. Naturally there are few agents with the worker identity who also have the commercial elite (23), the urban middle class (25), or westernized liberal (2) identities. They have a moderate representation in the ranks of the fundamentalists.

Muhajirs are Pakistanis whose families came from India to settle in Pakistan as a result of the violence in 1947. In VirPak they are closely associated with the Pakistani government, with 55% of Muhajirs sharing a Pakistani government identity (21). They are located almost entirely within the urbanized areas of Sindh and the Punjab. No Muhajirs are peasants, but, as mentioned, many are workers. They are also strongly represented within the middle class and the commercial elite. Fifteen percent share the urban middle-class identity (25). Twenty-nine percent of Muhajirs have the commercial elite identity (23) in their repertoires. A significant proportion is sympathetic with or part of the Muslim fundamentalist movement. Nineteen percent of Muhajirs are Shi'a. The great majority are Sunni, although approximately 10% are without any religious designation, reflecting secular trends that are somewhat more pronounced among Muhajirs than among other groups in Pakistan.

The military identity (16) is subscribed to by 18% of the agents in VirPak. It is mostly Sunni Muslim with a moderate representation of Shi'a. The Punjabi and Pushtun ethnic groups predominate, with 53% of military-oriented or involved agents including the Punjabi identity and 31% including the Pushtun identity. Few Baluch or Muslim fundamentalists share the military identity. But it does overlap strongly with the Pakistani government identity. Twenty-five percent of agents subscribed to the military identity are also subscribed to the Pakistani identity (21). As we shall see, many of these are in the government bureaucracy or in the military itself at t = 0 in baseline VirPak. The military contains disproportionately few peasants and workers. Geographically, agents with the military identity are concentrated heavily in the NWFP, the northern Punjab, and in nine areas around the country, including Karachi, Quetta, and the regions bordering India, where various formations of the Pakistani military are known to have their headquarters.

The peasant identity (18) is present in the overwhelming majority of Sindhi and Punjabi agents not living in urban areas, not part of an administrative authority structure (a bureaucracy—see section 7, "Distribution of Power in Virtual Pakistan"). These agents comprise 41% of VirPak. Eighty-three percent are Sunnis, affiliated with various clans if they are Pushtun or Punjabi. Almost all the rest are Shi'a. Agents with the peasant identity may have an attachment to their local landlord, and hence have the landlord identity (19), but few or none have identities suggesting education or worldliness, such as westernized liberal, urban middle class, commercial elite, or worker. The peasant identity is prominent among the Seraiki (6) in a southern extension of the Punjab, the Baluch, and among the Pushtuns. Only 2% of peasants also have a military identity. Importantly, the size of peasant identity repertoires is smaller than other VirPak agents. Many have four identities: peasant, a religious identity, an ethnic identity, and perhaps a clan identity. Other agent repertoires are comprised of three or even just two identities. This reflects the narrower field of political vision associated with peasant life.

The landlord identity (19) is established within a relatively small number of VirPak agents—9%. But 25% of these, located in the rural areas, are activated on that identity at t = 0 and endowed with an influence level of 4. This means they have inordinate influence over their (mostly peasant) surroundings. Agents in their proximity are mostly activated on peasant or Sunni Muslim, or on a regionally specific ethnic identity (Punjabi, Sindhi, Seraiki, or Pushtun). The criminal/smuggler identity is present in the repertoires of 39% of agents with the landlord identity at t = 0. Although none of the agents activated on the landlord identity at t = 0 and exercising the influence of landlords do have the globalizing identity (8), reflecting contacts with extra-Pakistan networks and values, a substantial proportion of those agents who are not landlords but have attachments to landlords via inclusion of that identity in their repertoire, do have the globalizing identity. This is meant to simulate, mainly, the connections that tie together criminal/smuggler elements, wealthy landlords, and international networks of illicit trafficking activity. In this context it is important to note that 21% of VirPak agents with the landlord identity also have the military identity, and that 16% have the Pakistani governing identity, both reflective of the significant levels of corruption and of the informal influence of the landed oligarchy in Pakistan on governing institutions, especially in the rural areas. On the other hand, Muslim fundamentalism is not commonly present among landlord or landlord attached agents.

The Pakistan governing identity (21) is figured as a positive orientation toward Pakistan, per se—an identity associated with the founder of Pakistan, Mohammad Ali Jinnah, who famously envisioned Pakistan as a country for Muslims but not of Islam and sought to enshrine a "Pakistani" identity above various ethnic, linguistic, and sectarian attachments.[14] Agents having this identity in their repertoire are concentrated in the urban areas of the Punjab—the corridors running between Islamabad and Lahore and between Lahore and Multan—and also in the Hyderabad and Karachi areas of Sindh Province. Agents with this identity are very scarce in Kashmir, NWFP, Baluchistan, and the Seraiki area. Reflecting the rather weak institutionalization of this state identity among the Pakistani population, only 9% of agents in VirPak have this identity in their repertoire. Fifty-six percent of these are agents exercising more than the usual influence, including a high proportion directly affiliated with the bureaucratic apparatus of the government or the military. Among the identities that are disproportionately associated with the Pakistan governing identity are, in addition to the military, Muhajir, commercial elite, and globalizing. The Muslim fundamentalist identity is present in 10% of agents with identity 21 in their repertoires.

The importance of the black economy in Pakistan is reflected in the large number of agents in VirPak with the Criminal/smuggler identity (22) in their

---

[14] The strength of Ali Jinnah's Attaturkist vision is reflected in the report that the only picture of another politician in the office of the former President of Pakistan, Pervez Musharraf, is that of Attaturk.

repertoire—15%. The identities most commonly associated with this identity in VirPak agents at t = 0 are Sunni Muslim and Globalizing, followed by Military, Punjabi, Pushtun, Peasant, and Landlord. In keeping with the idea of a black economy and the illegality of criminal and smuggler activity, the ratio of agents activated on this identity to those harboring the identity within their repertoires is unusually small (3%—compared, for example, to an activated/subscribed ratio of 43% for the Punjabi identity and 37% for Shi'a). Agents with identity 22 are present throughout VirPak but are particularly concentrated in a wide corridor running through the NWFP, down through Baluchistan, western Punjab, and western Sindh to Karachi, thereby simulating the primary smuggling routes connecting Afghanistan to the Indian Ocean.

7. Distribution of Power in Virtual Pakistan

The power structure of the regime in Pakistan is represented by interlocking networks of "influentials" including "bureaucrats" if they are associated at t = 0 with an official civilian or military authority structure. These agents are located in a pattern of proximity and regularity that multiplies their ability to remain activated on the identities they share—mainly the Pakistani governing identity and the military identity, but also Punjabi and, to a lesser extent, Muhajir and Pushtun. By reinforcing one another's activation patterns, bureaucrats substantially increase the likelihood that agents in their neighborhoods, and bordering neighborhoods, will activate regime identities (those activated by the bureaucrats) or maintain their activation on those identities even when biases or outside influences turn against them. These networks of influential express regime preferences and constitute an organized expression of its institutional capacity.

The number of government bureaucrats and activated military agents in VirPak corresponds roughly to the combined proportion of government officials and the uniformed military to the total adult male population in Pakistan. The administrative and political center of the Pakistani regime is located in the urbanized corridors mentioned above, and including the primary Punjabi cities of Lahore, Gujranwala, Rawalapindi, Islamabad, Faisalabad, Multan, and Bahawalpur. The regime's bureaucratic center is located within these areas, where its authority is best established. Additional centers of regime power, as reflected by the presence of relatively dense webs of influentials activated on either the Pakistani governing identity or the military identity, are located in Hyderabad and Karachi. The presence of longer strings or more isolated influentials in the rural areas of Punjab and elsewhere corresponds to the relative weakness of Pakistani national institutions in the rural areas, and especially in outlying districts of the NWFP, Kashmir, Baluchistan, and in rural Sindh. The relative weakness of these bureaucratic networks allow locally powerful identities (Sunni

Muslim, Landlord, Criminal/smuggler, or regional/ethnic) to strongly influence the behavior of these agents and make their "capture" by identities other than the Pakistani governing identity and the military identity more likely. Figure 12.5 shows a portion of VirPak, focused on the northeastern Punjab and containing the more densely populated areas of the country within which the national authority structure is most firmly entrenched (see color plate 12.5). The display is magnified to help identify the different icons representing agent classes discussed in this section.

There are three echelons of bureaucratic authority. The most common type is "influential2," having an influence level of 2 (twice that of a basic agent) and marked by the icon of a plus sign. Mid-echelon elites, with an influence level of 3 are "influential3's" and are marked by a pinwheel icon. High-echelon bureaucrats and military commanders are "influential4's," marked by a circle icon. In a well-disciplined bureaucracy lower echelons receive orders from above and act only within the parameters set for them by superiors. In a disciplined bureaucracy more discretion can be exercised the higher a bureaucrat is located in the hierarchy. Modeling such a hierarchy would mean, *inter alia*, making the repertoires of higher-echelon bureaucrats larger than those in the lower echelons. The Pakistani national bureaucracy, and even more the provincial governing institutions, are infamous for their lack of discipline, their penetration by extra-governmental forces, and for corruption. Hence the authority structure in VirPak contains a large numbers of lower-echelon bureaucrats with larger repertoires, reflecting the openness of these erstwhile agents of the state to influences from their local surroundings. Mid- and upper-level bureaucrats may also have medium or large repertoires, but the average repertoire size of upper-level bureaucrats is quite small.[15]

Although the low echelon of the bureaucracy is modeled as relatively open to external influences from dominant groups, not only do the high-echelon influentials have relatively small repertoires, but those repertoires also reflect a coherence corresponding to the dominance of the regime by individuals and groups with worldviews and interests shaped powerfully by Punjabi and Military identities. There are twenty-four influential3's and influential4's activated on the Pakistani governing identity at t = 0, and each one has either the Punjabi identity (0) or the Military identity (16) in its repertoire. Of fifty-five influential3's and influential4's activated on either the Military or the Pakistani governing identity at t = 0, twenty-six of them have Punjabi, Military, *and* Pakistani identities in their repertoires. The government bureaucracy is also heavily influenced by and

---

[15] In general discipline is considered to be stronger in the military than it is in the civilian sector of the national authority structure. The average size of the repertoire of a basic agent in VirPak is 3.8. It is relatively small, reflecting the largely peasant, mostly illiterate, and parochialized nature of Pakistani society.

intertwined with the commercial elite. Thus the Commercial elite identity (23) is present in the repertoires of 64% of agents activated on the Pakistani governing identity at t = 0. Forty-two percent of influential2's, 3's, and 4's in VirPak at t = 0 have the Commercial elite identity in their repertoires.

There are also sixty-six influential2's in VirPak activated at t = 0 on the Sunni Muslim identity. These agents are located mostly in the rural Punjab and the Seraiki areas. They represent the diffuse but locally significant influence of traditional Muslim clerical elites. Many are local clergy located in close proximity to powerful landlords in their areas. These landlords, activated on the Landlord identity (19), located primarily in the rural areas, and having influence levels of 4, can therefore transform these Muslim clerics (each of which has the Landlord identity in its repertoire) into local instruments of their own power. A large proportion of these rural clerics (83%) have the Criminal/smuggler identity in their repertoire. In the baseline condition described here only a few (6%) have the Muslim fundamentalist identity.

Entrepreneur agents, marked by the icon of a small square in an agent's center, emulate well-placed and relatively persuasive opportunists. Entrepreneur agents have rather larger repertoires, averaging twice the size of that of basic agents, corresponding to their political versatility. They also "update" before other agents, reflecting their more aggressive scanning of their neighborhoods and of the general political scene for opportunities to more effectively align themselves with ascendant forces. Their "triggers" for the rotation of latent identities into activation and for substituting a new identity for one not in their repertoire are also lower than these triggers for basic or influential agents. These lower triggers simulate the greater sensitivity of political entrepreneurs, or entrepreneurs of identity, to hints of political opportunity.

There are sixty such agents in VirPak, concentrated mostly in the urban areas, though in the rural areas they are commonly found in proximity to influentials associated with various groups, including ethnic leaders, religious leaders, landowners, and provincial bureaucrats. Many of those in the urban areas are in direct contact with the national civilian or military bureaucracy, acting as transmission belts for influences on the government (when the regime is relatively weak) and for influences from the government on the society (when the regime is relatively strong). Thirteen of these agents are actually within the civilian bureaucracy, meaning that they are entrepreneurs activated on the Pakistan governing identity (21) and located within the web of Pakistani bureaucrats. As "entrepreneurs" they contribute to the indiscipline and corruption of the Pakistani bureaucracy, but also to what sensitivity it has to extra-governmental influences.

Fanatics are marked by a diamond icon. These agents refuse to change their activated identities no matter how unattractive that identity may be in comparison to others. Each has an influence level of 3 and, therefore, provides a constant source of support for any other agents in their neighborhoods with inclinations toward its identity activation. It also helps secure a base of support during difficult times for that identity should circumstances change to make it once again attractive to large numbers of agents. There are fifteen fanatic agents inside Pakistan in VirPak. Eight of these are Muslim fundamentalists, located in areas of core strength for the Deobandists in Pakistan—NWFP, Multan, and Karachi.

The opposite of a "fanatic" is an apathetic agent. Whereas fanatics are "immutable" with respect to their activated identity but "active" with regard to influencing those agents in their neighborhood, apathetic agents are "inactive"—they do not influence agents in their neighborhoods—but do change their activated identities in response to the same forces that affect basic agents. Apathetic agents are marked with an icon of a small square inside a diamond. There are thirty-one apathetic agents in the baseline VirPak condition. All are located in rural areas, especially the Punjab and the Seraiki area, and are activated on the peasant identity.

There are also thirty-two "scared" agents in VirPak, again mostly in the rural Punjab and the Seraiki area. These agents, also predominantly peasants, do influence their surroundings, but are timid in their behaviors. They are designed to monitor a wider local neighborhood than do other agents before deciding to change their activated identity, but they are quick to rotate a new identity into activation once a relatively slight reason for doing so seems to be present.[16]

Another agent class in VirPak is Innovators. Innovators, marked with an icon of a black slash in the upper-left-hand corner. They update early, as do entrepreneurs, but unlike entrepreneurs they have an influence level of 1 rather than 2. In VirPak the innovator triggers for change of repertoire and activated identities are identical to those of basic agents.[17] There are forty-five Innovators in VirPak, figuring mainly as rapid exploiters of situations who do not then act as leaders or strong influences on their surroundings. All contain the Criminal/smuggler identity. They help to capture the role played by Afghan refugees, criminal/smugglers, and corrupt contacts with bureaucrats. They are mostly concentrated in Karachi and other parts of Sindh and in the Quetta area of Baluchistan, where the writ of the government does not run dependably. Just offshore of Pakistan, near Karachi, innovator agents operate, activated on the Globalizing identity, to simulate contacts with international networks for illicit trafficking.

[16] Low voter turnout in the recent Pakistani elections suggests higher levels of political apathy in Pakistan than were used to design VirPak. Increasing the amount of apathy in VirPak by increasing the prevalence of apathetic agents in the population had significant effects on outcomes.

[17] The trigger settings for innovators were intended to be set to be as sensitive as those for entrepreneurs. Due to a technical error, this aspect of the operationalization was not implemented. Given the small number of innovators in VirPak, their presence almost entirely in the extreme south of country, and the similarity of basic agent settings to those normally assigned to innovators, the impact of this error on experimental results relating to secessionism in general and center secessionism in particular is almost certainly very small.

The only other distinctive agent class in VirPak is "Broadcaster." Broadcaster agents are used to simulate the effects of media in Pakistan promoting particular kinds of messages. Broadcasters have an influence level of 1. They "broadcast" their identity to listeners meeting requirements specified by the user. In VirPak, agents listen to broadcasters located away from their own geographical neighborhoods if they have at least one "politically attentive" identity in their repertoires.[18] There are four broadcaster agents in VirPak. Two are activated on Muslim fundamentalist and located in zones in the NWFP and near Multan, in which support for that identity is strong. The third broadcaster is in the center of Pakistani government control and is activated, initially, on the Pakistani governing identity. A fourth is located offshore, near Karachi, and is activated on, the globalizing identity (8). Whatever identities these agents are activated on receive extra support for those identities in the calculations of the agents who are listening. Although the offshore Broadcaster can only broadcast the globalizing identity (unless that identity is replaced in the course of time as a result of regional pressures), the Broadcasters inside Pakistan have wider repertoires. If captured by identities or political affiliations other than those on which they were initially activated, then those identities or affiliations receive the boost of media support that previously went to their originally activated identities. Agents listening to these media include the message they hear as a count of an additional identity weight point in their identity weight calculations, making it more likely that, *ceteris paribus*, they will activate on that identity or substitute it for an identity they already have but are not activated on.

8. Secessionism and Center Secession in VirPak

In this study, secession is defined as the separation of an ethnically and geographically coherent region from the larger state of which it had been a part. Secessionism refers to efforts by supporters of such a separation to move toward that objective. We code the presence of secessionism in VirPak, whether by Pushtuns, Sindhis, Seraikis, or Punjabis, as the transformation of agents activated on one of those ethnoregional identities into black "border cells." Border cells are immutable and inactive sites and as such can constitute barriers to contact between regions depending on their number and distribution. These cells are located along the external border of Pakistan at t = 0, but not within the borders of the country. Border cells arising within Pakistan_shape can only arise as a result of basic agents transforming into border cells during a dynamic run.

[18] These identities were Worker, Globalizing—United States, Muslim fundamentalist, and Pakistani governing. Approximately 25% of VirPak agents within Pakistan_shape at t = 0 were eligible to Broadcasters.

The algorithm determining eligibility for basic agents to transform into border cells is based on three theoretical principles that form the consensual basis for expectations of secessionism within the literature. Secessionism can arise when relations are polarized between a sizable minority group, compactly organized within a particular region of a territorial state, and the dominant group in the state, and when members of that minority encounter direct experiences of friction or conflict with outgroup members. Conforming to these principles, basic agents in VirPak can transform into border cells if three conditions are met. These conditions pertain to both macro circumstances of which individual agents are unaware and local realities of which they are aware. When for any particular agent in any particular time step each of these conditions is met, a low but nontrivial probability is created that that agent will be transformed into a border cell.[19] The rules we have implemented to operationalize these conditions governing the production of border cells can be stated, nontechnically, as follows:

1. *Polarization*: Secessionist activity can be expected to be unlikely or impossible to the extent that members of a potentially secessionist group also harbor the identity of the dominant group. Accordingly, no agent, at any particular time, can transform into a border cell if 20% or more of the agents activated on that identity at that time have the dominant identity within their repertoires.

2. *Size of a qualifying identity group*: Secessionism by agents of the leading group in a society is excluded. At any given point in time the leading group (whether ethnic, civic, class, religious, etc.) is considered to be the identity activated by a plurality of agents in the polity. On the other hand, secessionism cannot be produced by a group unless it constitutes a substantial proportion of its region. In VirPak no agent at any one time step is allowed to transform into a border cell unless its activated identity is activated by at least 10% of VirPak agents.

3. *Individual action*: In the course of a VirPak trajectory, some otherwise qualifying agents will be more likely than others to engage in secessionist activity. For example, those lacking much contact with agents activated on identities other than their own can reasonably be expected to be less inclined to take the risks of secessionist action than liminal agents, exposed to other identities but not

---

[19] In the experiments reported in this chapter, the probability of an otherwise qualifying basic agent turning into a border cells was 20% per time step in which the basic agent remained qualified. This probability can easily be adjusted for experimental purposes. Sensitivity tests conducted in relation to our "Beita" studies (see note 21) indicated that adjusting this probability value between 15% and 25% did not alter the frequency with which border cells appeared. The effects on these adjustments on the number of border cells produced were linear, relatively small, and in the expected directions.

harboring those identities within their repertoires. Accordingly, no agent can transform into a border cell unless half or more of the agents it is in direct contact with are activated on an identity other than its own activated identity.

By registering the number of Punjabi activated agents that, by t = 608, transformed into border cells we measured the amount of Punjabi secessionism in any particular future of VirPak. By considering that index in combination with measures of the uniformity of Punjabi domination over substantial and contiguous portions of the Punjab, we identified outcomes classifiable as instances of center secession (i.e., of the emergence of a Punjabistan, separated from Pakistan). For any one of the regionally concentrated ethnonational groups, an instance of secession, as opposed to secessionism, was coded in Virpak if four conditions were met at t = 608:

1. The number of agents activated on the secessionist identity at t = 608 of a particular future was equal to at least 10% of the agents in VirPak (approximately 320).
2. The number of border agents produced from a secessionist identity, at t = 608 of a particular future, exceeded the median number of border cells produced by that identity in the futures that featured secessionism of any kind by that identity.
3. The number of influentials activated on the secessionist identity, at t = 608 of a particular future, exceeded the average number of influentials activated on that identity in all 100 futures of VirPak.
4. The average tension of agents activated on the secessionist identity at t = 608 was no more than 1 (meaning that, on average, agents activated on that identity, at t = 608 in that VirPak future, had no more than one adjacent agent activated on a different identity).[20]

The rationales for these rules are as follows. Rule 1 corresponds to the minimum proportion of the population treated by PS-I as rendering agents activated on a particular identity eligible for transformation into border cells. The intuition here is that too small a minority could not sustain a secessionist movement and would be exceedingly unlikely to successfully organize itself as such. Rule 2 insures that a significant amount of secessionist activity by the agents affiliated with the secessionist identity has indeed occurred. Rule 3 requires there to be a substantial authority structure activated on the secessionist identity within the regions of its domination. Rule 4 effectively requires a seceding region to be quite thoroughly filled by agents activated on the secessionist identity. Combined, these benchmarks distinguished VirPak

---

[20] In practice this means a tension level of less than 1.1.

futures that visually presented themselves as including secession from those that did not.[21]

9. Punjabi Secessionism in VirPak

Can Punjabi Secessionism Exist?

Before considering the question of Punjabi secessionism as an example of "secession from the center" it is necessary to emphasize that indeed Punjabis are the single most potent political force in VirPak, as they are generally acknowledged to be in actual Pakistan. Figure 12.6 displays data describing average prevalence of competing identities according to their activation at t = 608 (see color plate 12.6). We see that the Punjabi identity does register the highest average, closely followed by the Pakistani identity and the traditional Sunni Muslim identity. The fact of Punjabi dominance is registered even more emphatically in Figure 12.7, where we see that the Punjabi identity achieved a plurality of the activated agents in VirPak at t = 608 in forty-four futures compared to twenty-six futures for Sunni Islam and twenty-four futures for Pakistani (see color plate 12.7).

Based on the assumptions, data, operationalizations, and codings employed in VirPak and described above, Punjabi secessionism is present in the futures of VirPak. Although a majority of the 100 Baseline VirPak futures did not include secessionism by any group, forty-three futures did. Punjabi border cells appeared in thirty futures, often accompanied by the appearance of secessionist activity on the part of other ethnoregional identities. Indeed, thirteen futures that did not feature even low levels of Punjabi secessionism did register secessionism by other groups—Seraikis (south of the Punjab), Sindhis (in the Sindh), and/or Pushtuns (in the NWFP). Within the thirty futures that registered Punjabi secessionism, numbers of Punjabi border cells ranged from a low of 7 to a high of 153 with an average of 31.8.

Figure 12.8 displays the Punjab in VirPak at t = 608 from three different kinds of futures. The image labeled Future 67 features Punjabi (colored in crimson/orange) secessionism (the presence of some, but not many and not well-organized [black] border cells (see color plate 12.8). The image also lacks a sizable densely "Punjabi" space. The image labeled Future 72 features substantial Punjabi secessionism, but without the coherence or territorial compactness

---

[21] For more details on the theoretical rationale and algorithms for our operationalization of secessionism and our coding of secession see Lustick, Miodownik, and Eidelson 2004. The measures used in that study of secessionism in one region of an ethnically divided society—Beita—were adjusted in minor ways in this study. For example, secession in the Punjab region of Virtual Pakistan was coded using weighted proportion of Punjabis activated on the landowner identity but located within the Punjab.

coded as "secession." The image labeled Future 24 shows an array coded as Punjabi secession—the emergence of "Punjabistan."

Patterns in the Relative Strength and Prevalence of Punjabi Secessionism Within the Distribution of Futures

Figure 12.9 shows the general relationship between tendencies toward Punjabi secessionism and the overall success of the Punjabi identity at $t = 608$ (see color plate 12.9). The figure presents data on Punjabi identity prevalence, secessionism, and status as the plurality identity in order of the lowest Punjabi identity prevalence to the highest. We observe that, as might be expected, Punjabi secessionism was absent from the four highest deciles, when very large numbers of VirPak agents were activated on the Punjabi identity and when that identity was, quite often, the plurality identity, dominating the public sphere. Punjabi secessionism did make appearances at the lower end of the spectrum but was most regular and most potent in the range from 15 to 35 on this 100-point scale.[22] In other words, activated Punjabis were much more likely to engage in secessionist activity when they were, as a community, in a relatively weak position within VirPak as a whole, though several futures that registered higher than the median point of Punjabi prevalence did feature Punjabi secessionism.

To be sure, the transformation of Punjabi activated agents into border cells does itself reduce, by that number of cells, the number registered as Punjabi activated agents. However, that direct effect of the transformation rule is over-shadowed by the indirect effects of the barriers to interaction imposed on neighboring agents by the newly emergent border cells. Those barriers serve

1. To protect clusters of Punjabi activated agents that have already formed in their vicinity;
2. To encourage conformance to activation on Punjabi by agents within these clusters activated on other identities; and
3. To block expansion of the Punjabi identity from dense clusters on one side into territory prominently featuring other identities.

Having observed that Punjabi secessionism is most likely when the Punjabi identity does relatively poorly, but not terribly in comparison with other identities,[23] we can now ask whether Punjabi secessionism is associated with the

---

[22] Recall that this scale ranges from "1," the VirPak future registering the fewest Punjabi activated agents at $t = 608$, to "100," registering the future with the most Punjabi activated agents at $t = 608$.

[23] This particular result is rather directly produced by the operationalizations implemented in the simulation. Subsequent patterns identified are not.

prevalence, the success, of particular non-Punjabi identities. In other words, in response to domination of VirPak by which other identities is Punjabi secessionism most likely to arise? Figure 12.10 contains an important part of the answer to this question (see color plate 12.10).

Along the X axis of Figure 12.10 are the 100 VirPak futures at t = 608. The Y axis indicates the number of agents activated on each of the five identities registering a plurality of agent activation in at least one future at t = 608: Punjabi— the plurality identity in forty-four futures; Pakistani, twenty-four; Sunni Muslim, twenty-six; Muslim fundamentalist, six; and Military, one. The futures are arrayed, from left to right, in order of the number of Punjabi border cells (i.e., in order of the amount of Punjabi secessionism). We see, as noted earlier, that in seventy futures there was no Punjabi secessionism. The black-shaded portion of the figure in the lower-right-hand corner represents the rising number of Punjabi border cells in these futures. By noticing the changing width of the bands of different colors above this black shaded area we can see several instructive patterns in the complexion of VirPak futures featuring Punjabi secessionism. For example, we observe that Punjabi secessionism, especially substantial amounts of it, appears when the Pakistani identity, allied with one or both of the military or Muslim fundamentalist identities, dominates the political landscape. We observe as well that, compared to the seventy futures that did not exhibit Punjabi secessionism, the thirty that did feature relatively small numbers of agents activated on the Sunni Muslim identity. This suggests that a key element militating against Punjabi alienation from the state, even if Punjabis are not politically dominant, is its traditional Sunni Muslim posture.

Can Center Secession Occur?

The only identity to produce an outcome codable by our rules as "secession" was the Punjabi identity. Center secession—the emergence of "Punjabistan"— was observed in two of the 100 baseline VirPak futures, Future 24 and Future 63. These were not the futures with the most or even particularly high numbers of border cells produced by Punjabi activated agents, but these futures did feature substantial, compact, nonfragmented zones of Punjabi domination including within them substantial authority structures under the control of agents activated on the Punjabi identity. Figure 12.11 presents the relevant portions of VirPak from t = 608 (see color plate 12.11).

We now turn to an examination of the trajectories that produced these "Punjabistan" outcomes, along with several others that scored high on a number of the Punjabi secession markers but could not be coded as full-fledged or successful secession. By considering the sequence of developments leading to the outcome measured at t = 608 we can learn more about conditions conducive to center secession in Pakistan. Still, a thorough analysis of this type would require

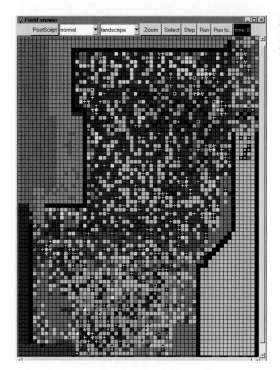

Figure 12.1 The Pattern of Identity Activation by Agents in VirPak at t = 0.

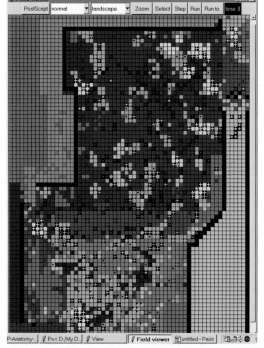

Figure 12.2 One example of Virtual Pakistan, baseline condition after eight time steps in which the biases are "scrambled" to offer a distinctive beginning point for future to be produced. Note dominance of crimson/ orange color, signifying Punjabi activation.

Figure 12.3 (stat_display)

Identity	#	activated	color	subscribed	tension	bias	opposition_count	SI	OI
Punjabi...................	0	608		1396	2846	0	0	0	0
Sunni Muslim............	1	155		2250	1024	0	79	0	0
Westernized Liberal......	2	7		52	54	0	1	0	0
Sindhi....................	3	180		374	941	0	180	0	1
Shia Muslim..............	4	58		385	421	0	34	0	0
Qaum/clan 1 (Pushtun)	5	12		161	72	0	12	0	1
Seraiki...................	6	129		324	558	0	54	0	0
Baluch....................	7	68		167	273	0	68	0	1
USA/Globalizing..........	8	0		268	0	0	0	0	1
Qaum 2 (Pushtun).......	9	9		105	60	0	9	0	1
Qaum 3 (Pushtun)	10	5		100	36	0	5	0	1
Pushtun...................	11	203		425	835	0	203	0	1
Muslim Fundamentalist..	12	104		403	616	0	84	0	1
Qaum North. 1 (Punjabi)	13	25		251	188	0	1	0	0
Urban worker............	14	32		448	232	0	15	0	0
Muhajir..................	15	229		297	1262	0	229	0	1
Military..................	16	169		565	1014	0	84	0	0
Kashmiri.................	17	38		110	186	0	37	0	1
Peasant..................	18	534		1269	2923	0	238	1	0
Landowner...............	19	75		282	558	0	30	0	0
Qaum North 2 (Punjabi)	20	1		315	8	0	0	0	0
Pakistani Government....	21	133		277	902	0	81	0	0
Criminal/Smuggler.......	22	13		474	92	0	10	0	0
Commercial elite.........	23	23		200	166	0	3	0	0
Afghan/refugee...........	24	23		52	171	0	13	0	0
Middle class urban.......	25	21		126	156	0	1	0	0
Qaum South 1(Punjabi)	26	9		222	66	0	0	0	0
Qaum South 2 (Punjabi)	27	4		189	30	0	0	0	0
Indian/Hindu	28	0		0	0	0	0	0	1
Nuclear Affected..........	29	0		0	0	0	0	0	1

Figure 12.3 A color coded list of identities present in the spectrum of identities available in VirPak, information regarding the numbers of agents currently displaying as "activated" on each identity and holding that identity in their repertoires.

Figure 12.4 — Subscribed on both:

	0	1	2	3	4	5	6	7	8	9	10	11	12	13	14	15	16	17	18	19	20	21	22	23	24	25	26	27
0	1417	1122	21	1	207	5	138	1	115	6	8	7	101	250	233	0	299	12	679	153	314	71	163	64	23	63	226	192
1	1122	2277	33	283	12	120	244	161	205	96	91	328	360	218	321	212	414	106	1078	234	280	213	367	144	32	83	216	180
2	21	33	52	5	9	1	0	0	16	8	4	18	12	2	0	2	7	33	9	24	0	15	2	24	0	15	1	1
3	1	283	5	375	58	0	74	8	24	0	0	2	37	0	0	0	28	0	240	40	1	18	49	8	0	0	0	0
4	207	12	9	58	386	1	0	38	0	0	0	37	0	0	74	55	75	3	154	29	1	41	64	34	2	24	2	2
5	5	120	1	0	1	161	0	2	3	0	0	152	69	2	10	0	56	0	60	14	1	5	40	3	6	3	0	0
6	138	244	0	74	0	0	335	0	22	0	0	0	29	0	0	0	70	0	194	50	0	11	53	0	0	0	20	10
7	1	161	0	8	38	2	0	167	16	0	0	0	15	1	36	0	8	1	99	8	8	1	42	0	0	9	0	0
8	115	205	16	24	0	3	22	16	268	4	2	39	26	19	36	66	116	9	22	101	28	106	226	102	1	17	10	9
9	6	96	8	0	0	0	0	0	4	105	0	99	42	4	2	0	39	0	44	16	3	2	28	4	4	6	0	0
10	8	91	4	0	0	0	0	0	2	0	100	93	44	4	6	0	32	1	44	9	1	5	29	6	6	3	0	0
11	7	328	18	2	37	152	0	0	39	99	93	425	156	2	14	6	174	2	160	47	4	44	138	46	17	8	1	2
12	101	360	12	37	0	69	29	15	26	42	44	156	404	14	41	65	9	26	217	23	36	30	88	24	28	24	24	9
13	250	218	2	0	0	2	0	1	19	4	4	2	14	255	79	2	76	0	61	17	0	8	25	12	5	1	0	0
14	233	321	0	0	74	10	0	36	36	2	6	14	41	79	448	164	30	1	3	7	77	77	64	3	4	44	11	12
15	0	212	2	0	55	0	0	0	66	0	0	6	65	2	164	297	31	1	0	4	0	146	57	86	0	44	1	0
16	299	414	7	28	75	56	70	8	116	39	32	174	9	76	30	31	565	16	26	60	82	139	165	98	5	47	28	22
17	12	106	33	0	3	0	0	1	9	0	1	2	26	6	1	1	16	110	56	5	3	9	0	0	0	0	0	0
18	679	1078	9	240	154	60	194	99	22	44	44	160	217	61	3	0	26	56	1300	17	88	1	136	0	21	8	167	144
19	153	234	24	40	29	14	50	8	101	16	9	47	23	17	7	4	60	5	17	282	39	46	110	31	2	2	22	16
20	314	280	0	1	1	1	0	8	28	3	1	4	36	0	77	0	82	3	88	39	315	16	40	16	13	20	9	10
21	71	213	15	18	41	5	11	1	106	2	5	44	30	8	77	146	139	3	1	46	16	277	94	124	0	26	9	4
22	163	367	9	49	64	40	53	42	226	28	29	138	88	25	64	57	165	9	136	110	40	94	476	63	19	30	14	12
23	64	144	24	8	34	3	0	0	102	4	6	46	24	12	3	86	98	0	0	31	16	124	63	200	1	6	1	2
24	23	32	0	0	2	6	0	0	1	4	6	17	28	5	4	0	5	0	21	2	13	0	19	1	413	0	0	0
25	63	83	15	0	24	3	0	9	17	6	3	8	24	23	1	44	47	0	8	2	20	26	30	6	0	126	4	3
26	226	216	1	0	2	0	20	0	10	0	0	1	24	0	11	1	28	0	167	22	9	9	14	1	0	4	228	4
27	192	180	1	0	2	0	10	0	9	0	0	2	9	0	12	0	22	0	144	16	10	4	12	2	0	3	4	193

Figure 12.4 Cross-tabulation showing numbers of agents in VirPak, baseline condition at t = 0 with the number of agents containing each possible pair of identities. Identities commonly present together in agents at t = 0 are deemed to have affinities for one another, and vice versa. Numbers highlighted in green indicate the total number of agents with that identity in their repertoire.

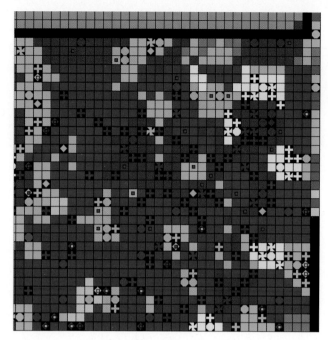

Figure 12.5 A portion of VirPak (t = 8), focused on the northern Punjab within which the national authority structure is most firmly entrenched. The display is magnified to help identify the different icons representing agent classes discussed in this section.

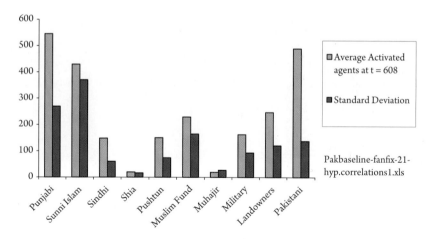

Pakbaseline-fanfix-21-hyp.correlations1.xls

Figure 12.6 Average Activation Prevalence of Leading Identities in VirPak t = 608

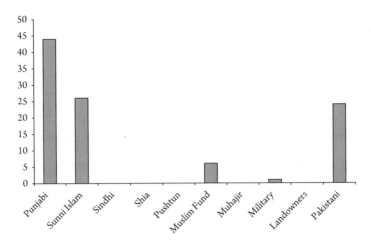

Figure 12.7 Plurality Rates Across 100 Baseline VirPak Futures of Selected Identities,
t = 608

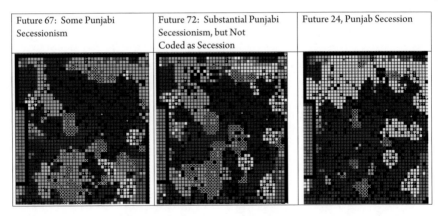

Figure 12.8 Three examples of Punjabi secessionism. Highlighted cells represent Punjabis
publicly affiliating with landowners.

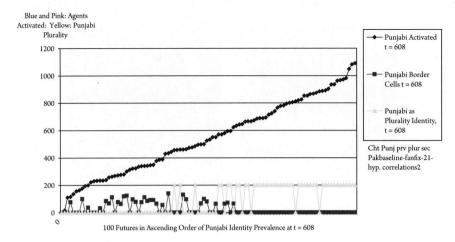

Figure 12.9 Patterns of Punjabi Prevalence, Plurality, and Secessionism

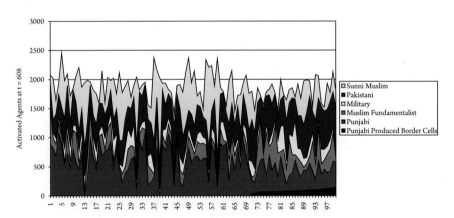

Figure 12.10 Prevalence of Selected Identities: Sorted by Punjabi Secessionism

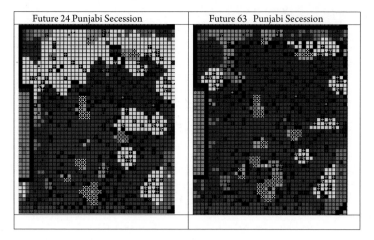

Figure 12.11 Punjabistan Secession in Two VirPak Futures: Highlighted cells represent Punjabis publicly affiliating with landowners.

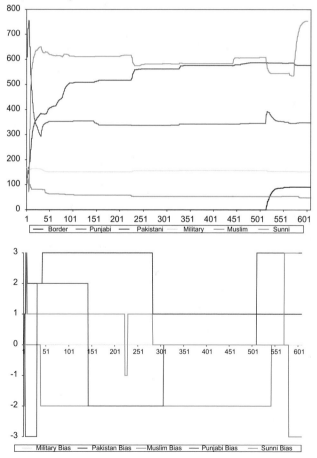

Figure 12.12 Trajectories of Activation by Competing Identities and Bias Assignment Histories—Future 46 of VirPak

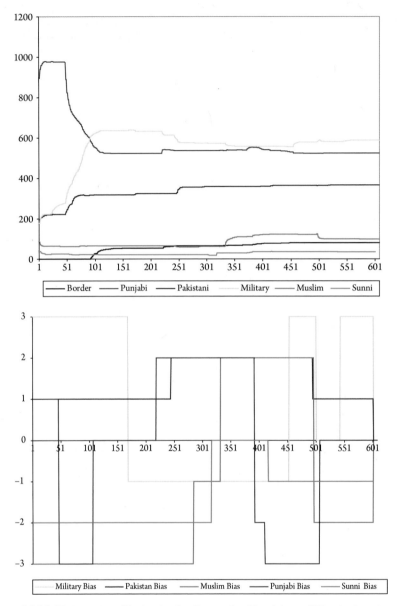

Figure 12.13 Trajectories of Activation by Competing Identities and Bias Assignment Histories—Future 24 of VirPak

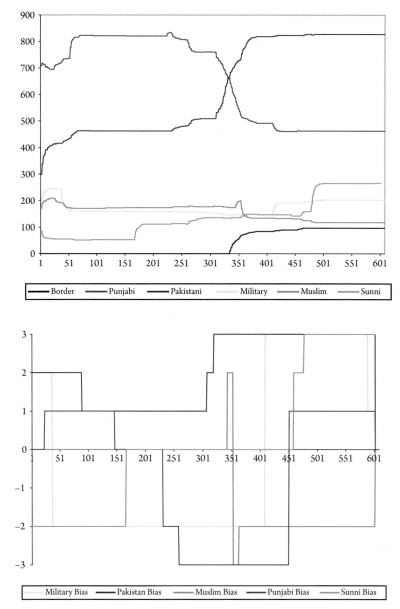

Figure 12.14 Trajectories of Activation by Competing Identities and Bias Assignment Histories—Future 63 of VirPak

significantly more work.[24] Theoretically there could be several routes to Punjabi secession consistent with the algorithms and the initialization conditions contained in VirPak and consistent as well with existing theories of secessionism.

1. Punjabis could begin as a small regionally dominant minority, alienated from the state and other dominant groups, but not strong enough to launch a secessionist movement. Favorable circumstances might then attract more agents to publicly affiliate with Punjabis against a dominant identity group with *relatively* little support among Punjabis (e.g., Muslim fundamentalists). If those Punjabis sharing this alternative leading identity chose to affiliate with it, it could then lead to geographically concentrated masses of Punjabis lacking political or cultural connections to the new dominant group. The result could be secessionism and the production of a boundary separating "Punjabistan" from the rest of Pakistan.

2. Punjabis could constitute a large but not dominant proportion of the Pakistani political space. If a majority or even a large minority of publicly affiliated Punjabis held the plurality identity in Pakistan within their repertoires, secessionist pressures would be weak or nonexistent. But if a third identity, one not shared widely in the Punjabi community, suddenly and successfully challenged the dominance of the Punjabi-friendly identity, the Punjabi community as a whole could find itself suddenly alienated from the dominant group or groups in the country. This sequence and set of circumstances could unleash a powerful secessionist movement, capable of leading to a secession boundary between Punjabistan and the rest of Pakistan.

3. Punjabis could enjoy the dominant position in Pakistan, assisted by but dominating the Pakistani government identity, traditional Muslims, and/or the military. If specific circumstances, however, led to a sharp increase in the popularity of one of these identities and if that were associated with a sharp drop in the popularity of the Punjabi identity (e.g., as a result of effective government sponsored land reform in the rural Punjab, external support for the Pakistani military, or mass defections of traditional Sunni Muslims to the fundamentalist banner), the previously dominant Punjabi community could quickly find itself in a subordinate and threatened position. Depending on how widespread within the Punjabi community were affiliations to the newly ascendant identity group, strong secessionist pressures could develop leading to a substantially sized but culturally compact "Punjabistan."

---

[24] It is instructive to consider that a more finely grained analysis of trajectories and sequences differentiating among similar trajectories on the basis of differences in particular sub-regions or sub-identities that participated in different ways to push secessionism futures toward outright secessionism, or prevent it, would require the same *kind* of analysis that a scholar using conventional techniques would need to undertake—a scholar somehow fortunate enough to have access to 100 different thoroughly documented actual histories of Pakistan from 100 parallel but not precisely identical universes.

Although each of the trajectories leading to substantial secessionism was unique, the dominant sequence within those VirPak futures was item 3. Indeed both futures coded as actual secession followed this particular storyline.

To be sure, there was one substantial VirPak future that followed the trajectory described in item 1. In Future 46 the traditional Sunni Muslim identity dominated VirPak in tandem with a slightly smaller but still potent Pakistani governing identity, with Punjabis a distant third. In the context of that set of relationships, many Punjabis retained their Sunni Muslim identity but were not affiliated with the Pakistani identity. When circumstances led to a sudden move by many Punjabis who had publicly affiliated as Sunni Muslims to adopt instead an explicitly Punjabi stance, Pakistani became the dominant identity in VirPak. This development confronted the mobilizing but still subordinated Punjabis with a governing apparatus from which they had become alienated. The result was a brief but potent eruption of Punjabi secessionism.

In the majority of futures containing substantial Punjabi secessionism, however, the impetus for secession arose from Punjabis being themselves displaced as the group dominating the Pakistani political landscape. The cascade of change in political affiliations associated with this displacement increased the level of alienation between the Punjabi community as a whole and the newly dominant identity. That is, the proportion of agents activated on Punjabi but retaining the dominant identity in their repertoires fell sharply. This unleashed Punjabi secessionism. Punjabi secessionism and secession was thus closely associated with what may be understood as an experience of intense and rapid "relative deprivation," as a Punjabi community with its own recent domination of the country as its referent, and enjoying control over the governing structures within the rural Punjabi heartland, moved toward independence by trading a declining position in a transforming Pakistan for Punjabi rule over its own region as an independent state. Both futures featuring the emergence of Punjabistan correspond to this pattern, though in Future 24 the cascade to the challenger identity and the production of a "rump" Punjabi community alienated from the newly dominant identity or coalition of identities occurs earlier than in Future 63.

For the particular futures described here (46, 24, and 63) Figures 12.12, 12.13, and 12.14 show the changing numbers of activated agents on key identities in the top row and the pattern of bias assignments (negative and positive) for those identities, over time, in the bottom row (see color plates 12.12, 12.13, 12.14).

So to the extent that our baseline simulations of VirPak model a representative array of the actual Pakistans lying within a relatively accessible region of the state space of possible Pakistans, we may advance the following conclusions.

1. Punjabi secessionism is not only possible but stands as a more potent challenge to the integrity of the country to more commonly discussed threats of

secession that have emanated from Baluchistan, the Sindh, Seraiki region, or the Pushtun-dominated NWFP.

2. The threat of Punjabi secessionism is likely to be sharpest precisely when the government of Pakistan, alone or in partnership with other (non-Punjabi-oriented groups), makes progress toward establishing more thorough and effective governance throughout the country. On the other hand, it can also arise in reaction to an ascendance of Muslim fundamentalism within the state.

3. Although secession of Punjabistan is unlikely, it is possible.

4. Based on the most common route to potent center secessionism in Pakistan, strategies that present themselves for reducing that threat in association with desirable democratic and economic reforms include maintaining a strong identification of Pakistan as a state with traditional Sunni Muslim values; promoting civic identification through enriched educational programs within the Punjabi heartland; and recruiting civil servants who can remain proudly and publicly Punjabi while carrying out their duties as representatives of the "Pakistani" state.

5. Punjabi secessionism, and Punjabistan—when it emerges in VirPak—seems primarily a rural phenomenon. The leadership apparatus that falls under the control of the secessionists mainly includes elements of the national bureaucracy located in the Punjabi heartland, provincial legislators, landed oligarchs, and local Punjabi clerics. The administrative, institutional, and military core of the Pakistani state remains outside the ambit of Punjabi secessionism. This suggests, first, why successful Punjabi secession is so unlikely, and second, that should a Punjabi secessionist movement actually produce a Punjabistan it might not actually spell the end of the Pakistani state, per se. Instead, it more likely set the stage for a new kind of struggle over the terms of political re-integration.

More generally, our exercise suggests the utility of computer-assisted agent-based modeling and the production of large batches of virtual futures for studying patterns of outcomes, both possible and probable, that may arise from the same ethnic demography. It also suggests the crucial role this methodology can play in the systematic study of "rare events" such as center secession.

BIBLIOGRAPHY

Alesina, Alberto, Reza Baqir, and William Easterly. (1999). "Public Goods and Ethnic Divisions." *Quarterly Journal of Economics* 114(4): 1243–1284.

Alesina, Alberto, et al. (2003). "Fractionalization." *Journal of Economic Growth* 8(2): 55–94.

Alesina, Alberto, and Eliana La Ferrara. (2005). "Ethnic Diversity and Economic Performance," *Journal of Economic Literature* 43(3): 762–800.

Alesina, Alberto, and Enrico Spolare. (2003). *The Size of Nations.* Cambridge, MA: MIT Press.

Allport, Gordon, and Leo Postman. (1947). *The Psychology of Rumor.* New York: Henry Holt.

Amorim-Neto, Octavio, and Gary W. Cox. (1997). "Electoral Institutions, Cleavage Structures, and the Number of Parties." *American Journal of Political Science* 41(1): 149–174.

Andersen, Benedict. (1983). *Imagined Communities.* London: Verso.

Appiah, Anthony. (1992). *In My Father's House: Africa in the Philosophy of Culture.* New York: Oxford University Press.

Appiah, Anthony, and Amy Gutmann. (1996). *Color Conscious.* Princeton NJ: Princeton University Press.

Appadurai, Arjun. (1996). *Modernity at Large.* Minneapolis: University of Minnesota Press.

Appadurai, Arjun. (2006). *Fear of Small Numbers.* Durham: Duke University Press.

Atlas Narodov Mira. (1964). Moscow: Miklukho-Maklai Ethnological Institute of the Department of Geodesy and Cartography of the State Geological Committee of the Soviet Union.

Axelrod, Robert. 1970. *Conflict of Interest: A Theory of Divergent Goals with Applications to Politics.* Chicago: Markham.

Bardon, Jonathan. (1982). *Belfast: An Illustrated History.* Dundonald, Belfast, Northern Ireland: Blackstaff Press.

Barth, Frederik. (1969). *Ethnic Groups and Boundaries.* Prospect Heights, IL: Waveland Press.

Bartolini, Stefano, and Peter Mair. (1990). *Identity, Competition, and Electoral Availability: The Stabilization of European Electorate 1885–1985.* Cambridge: Cambridge University Press.

Bates, Robert. (1974). "Ethnic Competition and Modernization in Contemporary Africa." *Comparative Political Studies* 6(4): 457–477.

Bates, Robert H. (1983). "Modernization, Ethnic Competition, and the Rationality of Politics in Contemporary Africa." In *State versus Ethnic Claims: African Policy Dilemmas,* edited by D. Rothchild & V. A. Olunsorola, 152–171. Boulder, CO: Westview Press.

Bates, Robert, Rui de Figueiredo, and Barry Weingast. (1998). "The Politics of Interpretation: Rationality, Culture and Tradition." *Politics and Society* 26(4): 603–642.

Bayly, C. A. (1988). *Rulers, Townsmen and Bazaars: North Indian Society in the Age of British Expansion, 1770–1870.* Cambridge: Cambridge University Press.

Beissinger, Mark. (2002), *Nationalist Mobilization and the Collapse of the Soviet State.* New York: Cambridge University Press.

Bertrand, Marianne, and Sendhil Mullainathan. (2004). "Are Emily and Greg More Employable than Lakisha and Jamal? A Field Experiment on Labor Market Discrimination." *The American Economic Review* 94(4): 991–1013.

Bhabha, Homi, ed. (1990). *Nation and Narration*. London: Routledge.

Bhabha, Homi. (1994). *The Location of Culture*. London: Routledge.

Bhavnani, R., D. Miodownik, and J. Nart. (2008). "REsCape: An Agent-Based Framework for Modeling Resources, Ethnicity, and Conflict." *Journal of Artificial Societies and Social Simulation* 11(2). http://jasss.soc.surrey.ac.uk/11/2/7.html.

Bielasiak, Jack. (2002). "The Institutionalization of Electoral and Party Systems in Postcommunist States." *Comparative Politics* 34: 189–210.

Birkhoff, G. (1967). *Lattice Theory* (3rd ed.). Providence, RI: American Mathematical Society.

Birnir, Jóhanna Kristín. (2007). *Ethnicity and Electoral Politics*. Cambridge; New York: Cambridge University Press.

Blimes, Randall J. (2006). "The Indirect Effect of Ethnic Heterogeneity on the Likelihood of Civil War Onset." *Journal of Conflict Resolution* 50(4): 536–547.

Bodenhausen, Galen, Lori Sheperd, and Geoffrey Kramer. (1994). "Negative Affect and Social Judgment—The Differential Impact of Anger and Sadness." *European Journal of Social Psychology* 24(1): 45–62.

Bookman, L. M. (1978). "Hindus and Muslims: Communal Relations and Cultural Integration." In *Cohesion and Conflict in Modern India*, edited by Giri Raj Gupta, 104–127. Durham, NC: Carolina Academic Press.

Brass, Paul. (1970). "Muslim Separatism in United Provinces: Social Context and Political Strategy Before Partition." *Economic and Political Weekly* 5(3/5).

Brass, Paul. (1974). *Language, Religion and Politics in North India*. Cambridge: Cambridge University Press.

Brass, Paul R. (1997). *Theft of an Idol: Text and Context in the Representation of Collective Violence*. Princeton, NJ: Princeton University Press.

Bratton, Michael. (1998). "Second Elections in Africa." *Journal of Democracy* 9(3): 51–66.

Bratton, Michael, and Mwangi S. Kimenyi. (2008). "Voting in Kenya: Putting Ethnicity in Perspective." *Afrobarometer* (Working Paper No. 95).

Bratton, Michael, and Nicholas van de Walle. (1997). *Political Regimes and Regime Transitions in Africa*. Cambridge: Cambridge University Press.

Brehm, Denise. (2004). "Racial Divide Is Really an Imaginary Fault Line, Profs Say." *MIT Tech Talk*, 5.

Bringa, Tone. (1995). *Being Muslim the Bosnian Way*. Princeton, NJ: Princeton University Press.

Brown, Rupert. (2000). "Social Identity Theory: Past Achievements, Current Problems, and Future Challenges." *European Journal of Social Psychology* 30(6): 745–778.

Brubaker, Rogers. (1992). *Citizenship and Nationhood in France and Germany*. Cambridge, MA: Harvard University Press.

Brubaker, Rogers. (1996). *Nationalism Reframed*. New York: Cambridge University Press.

Brubaker, Rogers. (2004). *Ethnicity Without Groups*. Cambridge, MA: Harvard University Press.

Brubaker, Rogers. (2009). "Ethnicity, Race, and Nationalism." *Annual Review of Sociology* 35: 21–42.

Brubaker, Rogers, and David Laitin. (1998). "Ethnic and Nationalist Violence." *Annual Review of Sociology* 4: 423–452.

Bryson, J. J., Y. Ando, and H. Lehmann. (2007). "Agent-Based Modelling as Scientific Method: A Case Study Analysing Primate Social Behaviour." *Philosophical Transactions of the Royal Society: Biological Sciences* 362(1485): 1685–1698.

Bueno de Mesquita, Bruce, et al. (2003). *The Logic of Political Survival*. Cambridge, MA: MIT Press.

Caselli, Francesco, and Wilbur John Coleman. (2001). *On the Theory of Ethnic Conflict*. Manuscript, Harvard University Press.

Cavalli-Sforza, Luigi. (2000). *Genes, Peoples and Languages*. New York: North Point Press.

Cederman, Lars-Erik. (2001). *Constructing Europe's Identity*. Boulder, CO: Lynne Rienner.

Cederman, Lars-Erik, Luc Girardin, and Kristian Skrede Gleditsch. (2009). "Ethnonationalist Triads: Assessing the Influence of Kin Groups on Civil Wars." *World Politics* 61(3): 403–437.

Cederman, Lars-Erik, Andreas Wimmer, and Brian Min. (2010). "Why Do Ethnic Groups Rebel?" *World Politics* 62(1): 87–119.

Cecelski, David S., and Timothy B. Tyson, eds. (1998). *Democracy Betrayed: The Wilmington Race Riot of 1898 and Its Legacy*. Chapel Hill: University of North Carolina Press.

Central Intelligence Agency. (2002). *World Fact Book, Pakistan*. https://www.cia.gov/library/publications/the-world-factbook/geos/pk.html.

Chandra, Kanchan. (2001a). "Ethnic Bargains, Group Instability and Social Choice Theory." *Politics and Society* 29(3): 337–362.

Chandra, Kanchan. (2001b). "Cumulative Findings in the Study of Ethnic Politics." *APSA-CP* 12(1): 7–11.

Chandra, Kanchan. (2001c). "Memo on Constructivist Approaches to Ethnic Identity and Theory Building." Paper prepared for presentation at LICEP 3, Cambridge, March 23–25.

Chandra, Kanchan. (2004). *Why Ethnic Parties Succeed: The Political Mobilization of Castes in India*. New York: Cambridge University Press.

Chandra, Kanchan. (2005). "Ethnic Parties and Democratic Stability." *Perspectives on Politics* 3(2): 235–252.

Chandra, Kanchan. (2006a). "Mechanisms and Outcomes." *Qualitative Methods Newsletter* (American Political Science Association, Spring Issue).

Chandra, Kanchan. (2006b). "What Is Ethnic Identity and Does It Matter?" *Annual Review of Political Science* 9: 397–424.

Chandra, Kanchan. (2008a). "Ethnic Invention: A New Principle for Institutional Design in Multi-Ethnic Democracies." In *Mobilizing Democracy*, edited by James Johnson et al., 89–116. New York: American Political Science Association and the Russell Sage Foundation.

Chandra, Kanchan. (2008b). "Making Causal Claims About Ethnic Politics." In *Comparative Politics*, edited by Mark Lichbach and Alan Zuckerman, 376–411. New York: Cambridge University Press.

Chandra, Kanchan. (2009a). "A Constructivist Dataset on Ethnicity and Institutions (CDEI)." In *Identity as a Variable*, edited by Rawi Abdelal et al., 250–278. New York: Cambridge University Press.

Chandra, Kanchan. (2009b). "Designing Measures of Ethnic Identity: The Problems of Overlap and Incompleteness." *Qualitative Methods Newsletter of the American Political Science Association* 7(1): 36–42.

Chandra, Kanchan. (2009c). "How Should Democratic Societies and States Respond to Diversity?" Paper prepared for presentation at Democracy and Development Seminar, Princeton University, December 9.

Chandra, Kanchan. (2011). *Measuring Ethnicity*. Forthcoming.

Chandra, Kanchan, and Cilanne Boulet. (2005). "Ethnic Cleavage Structures, Permanent Exclusion and Democratic Stability." Paper prepared for presentation at the Juan March Institute, Madrid, November 25.

Chandra, Kanchan, et al. (2006). *Guidelines for Coding Activated Ethnic Categories by Dimension in CDEI*.

Chandra, Kanchan, and David Laitin. (2002). "A Constructivist Framework for Thinking About Identity Change." Paper prepared for presentation at conference on "Modeling Constructivist Approaches to Ethnic Identity and Incorporating Them into New Research Agendas," MIT, December 6–8.

Chandra, Kanchan, with Steven Wilkinson. (2008). "Measuring the Effect of Ethnicity." *Comparative Political Studies* 41(4/5): 515–563.

Chiriac, Marian. (2007). "Moldova Talks Fail to Crack Separatist Resolve." *Balkan Insight* December 22. 2005. http://disqus.com/forums/balkaninsight/moldova_talks_fail_to_crack_separatist_resolve/trackback/.

Chua, Amy. (2003). *World on Fire.* New York: Doubleday.

Cioffi-Revilla, C. (2010). "A Methodology for Complex Social Simulations." *Journal of Artificial Societies and Social Simulation* 13(1). http://jasss.soc.surrey.ac.uk/13/1/7.html.

Clore, Gerald, and Karen Gasper. (2000). "Feeling Is Believing: Some Affective Influences on Belief." In *Emotions and Beliefs: How Feelings Influence Thoughts*, edited by Nico H. Frijda, Antony S. R. Manstead, and Sacha Bem, 39. Cambridge: Cambridge University Press.

Cohen, Frank. (1997). "Proportional Versus Majoritarian Ethnic Conflict Management in Democracies." *Comparative Political Studies* 30(5): 607–630.

Cohen, Stephen P. (1998). *The Pakistan Army.* Oxford, UK: Oxford University Press.

Cohen, Stephen Philip. (2002). "The Nation and the State of Pakistan." *The Washington Quarterly* 25(3): 109–122.

Cohen, Stephen Philip. (2004). *The Idea of Pakistan.* Washington, DC: Brookings Institution Press.

Cohn, Bernard. (1987). *An Anthropologist Among the Historians and Other Essays.* New York: Oxford University Press.

Collier, Paul. (1999). "The Political Economy of Ethnicity." In *Annual World Bank Conference on Development Economics 1998*, edited by Boris Pleskovic and Joseph E. Stiglitz, 387–389. Washington, DC: World Bank.

Collier, Paul, and Anke Hoeffler. (2004). "Greed and Grievance in Civil Wars, 2004." *Oxford Economic Papers* 56: 563–595.

Collins, Kathleen. (2004). "The Logic of Clan Politics; Evidence from the Central Asian Trajectories." *World Politics* 56(2): 224–261.

Congressional Quarterly. "Where Does Negro Voter Strength Lie?," May 4, 1956, 491–496.

Cox, Gary. (1997). *Making Votes Count.* Cambridge: Cambridge University Press.

Crossman, Virginia. (1996). *Politics, Law and Order in Nineteenth-Century Ireland.* New York: St. Martin's Press.

Crowe, Charles. (1968). "Racial Violence and Social Reform-Origins of the Atlanta Riot of 1906." *The Journal of Negro History* 53: 234–256.

Dahl, Robert A. (1971). *Polyarchy.* New Haven: Yale University Press.

Daniel, Valentine. (1996). *Charred Lullabies: Chapters in an Anthropography of Violence.* Princeton, NJ: Princeton University Press.

Das, Suranjan. (1993). *Communal Riots in Bengal 1905–1947.* New Delhi: Oxford University Press.

Degboe, Kouassi A. (1995). *Elections et Realities Sociologiques Au Benin.* Cotonou, Benin: Entermonde Editions.

Deutsch, Karl. (1953). *Peoples, Nations and Communication.* Cambridge, MA: MIT Press.

DiPasquale, Denise, and Edward L. Glaeser. (1998). "The Los Angeles Riot and the Economics of Urban Unrest." *Journal of Urban Economics* 43: 52–78.

Dirks, Nicholas. (2001). *Castes of Mind.* Princeton NJ: Princeton University Press.

Dominguez, Virginia. (1997). *White by Definition.* New Brunswick, NJ: Rutgers University Press.

Dorian, N. C., ed. (1989). *Investigating Obsolescence: Studies in Language Contraction and Death.* Cambridge: Cambridge University Press.

Easterly, William, and Ross Levine. (1997). "Africa's Growth Tragedy: Policies and Ethnic Divisions." *Quarterly Journal of Economics* 112(4): 1203–1250.

Economist. "Black Rainbow." September 20, 2003.

Economist. "The Stubborn Sage of Najaf." January 17, 2004, 39.

Economist. "British or What?" April 2, 2005, 51.

Economist. "Poverty and the Ballot Box." May 14–21, 2005, 80.

Edmonds, B. (2010). "Bootstrapping Knowledge about Social Phenomena Using Simulation Models." *Journal of Artificial Societies and Social Simulation* 13(1). http://jasss.soc.surrey.ac.uk/13/1/8.html.

Eidheim, Harald. (1969). "When Ethnic Identity Is a Social Stigma." In *Ethnic Groups and Boundaries*, edited by Frederik Barth, 39–57. Prospect Heights, IL: Waveland Press.

Eifert, Benn, Edward Miguel, and Daniel Posner. (2010). "Political Competition and Ethnic Identification in Africa." *American Journal of Political Science* 54(2): 494–510.

Elbadawi, Ibrahim, and Nicholas Sambanis. (2002). "How Much War Will We See? Explaining the Prevalence of Civil War." *The Journal of Conflict Resolution* 46(3): 307–334.

Eller, Jack, and Reed Coughlan. (1996). "The Poverty of Primordialism." In *Ethnicity*, edited by John Hutchinson and Anthony Smith, 45–51. New York: Oxford University Press.

Ellison, Ralph. (1952). Invisible Man. New York: Random House.

Elster, Jon (1989). *Nuts and Bolts for the Social Sciences*. Cambridge: Cambridge University Press.

Elster, Jon. (1998). "Emotions and Economic Theory." *Journal of Economic Literature* 36: 47–64.

Elster, Jon. (1999). *Alchemies of the Mind*. Cambridge: Cambridge University Press.

Elster, Jon. (2003). "Memory and Transitional Justice." Unpublished manuscript delivered at the "Memory of War" Workshop, MIT, January.

Elster, Jon. (2007). *Explaining Social Behavior: More Nuts and Bolts for the Social Sciences*. Cambridge: Cambridge University Press.

Englebert, Pierre. (2000). *State Legitimacy and Development in Africa*. Boulder, CO: Lynne Rienner.

Eyal, Jonathan, and Graham Smith. (1996). "Moldova and the Moldovans." In *The Nationalities Question in the Post-Soviet States*, edited by Graham Smith, 223–244. New York: Longman.

Evans-Pritchard, E. E. (1940). *The Nuer: A Description of the Modes of Lifelihood and Political Institutions of a Nilotic People*. New York: Oxford University Press.

Fane, Daria. (1993). "Moldova: Breaking Loose from Moscow." In *Nations and Politics in the Soviet Successor States*, edited by Ian Bremmer and Ray Taras, 121–153. Cambridge: Cambridge University Press.

Far Eastern Economic Review. March 9, 1989, 23.

Fearon, James. (1998). "Commitment Problems and the Spread of Ethnic Conflict." In *The International Spread of Ethnic Conflict*, edited by David A. Lake and Donald Rothchild, 107–126. Princeton, NJ: Princeton University Press.

Fearon, James. (1999). "Why Ethnic Politics and 'Pork' Tend to Go Together." Paper presented at the SSRC-MacArthur sponsored conference on "Ethnic Politics and Democratic Stability," University of Chicago, May 21–23. http://www.stanford.edu/~jfearon/papers/Pork.pdf.

Fearon, James. (2003). "Ethnic Structure and Cultural Diversity by Country." *Journal of Economic Growth* 8(2): 195–222.

Fearon, James, and David D. Laitin. (1996). "Explaining Interethnic Cooperation." *American Political Science Review* 90(4): 715–735.

Fearon, James, and David D. Laitin. (2000a). "Ordinary Language and External Validity: Specifying Concepts in the Study of Ethnicity." Paper presented at the October 2000 meeting of LICEP, University of Pennsylvania.

Fearon, James, and David Laitin. (2000b). "Violence and the Social Construction of Ethnic Identity." *International Organization* 54(4): 845–877.

Fearon, James, and David Laitin. (2003). "Ethnicity, Insurgency and Civil War." *American Political Science Review* 97(1): 75–90.

Ferree, Karen E. (2004). "The Microfoundations of Ethnic Voting." *Afrobarometer* (Working Paper No. 40).

Ferree, Karen E. (2006). "Explaining South Africa's Racial Census." *Journal of Politics* 68(4): 803–815.

Ferree, Karen E. (2010). "The Social Origins of Electoral Volatility in Africa." *British Journal of Political Science* 40(4): 759–779.

Ferree, Karen E., and Jeremy Horowitz. (2010). "Ties That Bind? The Rise and Decline of Ethno-Regional Partisanship in Malawi, 1994–2009." *Democratization* 17(3): 534–563.

Finnemore, Martha, and Kathryn Sikkink. (2001). "Taking Stock: The Constructivist Research Program in International Relations and Comparative Politics." *Annual Review of Political Science* 4: 391–416.

Foucault, Michel. (1977). *Discipline and Punish*. New York: Vintage Books.

Foucault, Michel. (1995). *Discipline and Punish* (2nd ed.). New York: Vintage Books.

Fox, Richard. (1985). *Lions of the Punjab*. Berkeley: University of California Press.

Fraenkel, Jon, and Bernard Grofman. (2004). "A Neo-Downsian Model of the Alternative Vote as a Mechanism for Mitigating Ethnic Conflict in Plural Societies." *Public Choice* 121: 487–506.

Franks, David, and Viktor Gecas. (1992a). "Current Issues in Emotion Studies." In *Social Perspectives on Emotion: A Research Annual*, edited by David D. Franks and Viktor Gecas, 8. Greenwich, CT: JAI Press.

Franks, David, and Viktor Gecas. (1992b). *Social Perspectives on Emotion: A Research Annual*. Greenwich, CT: JAI Press.

Frijda, Nico, and Batja Mesquita. (2000). "Belief through Emotions." In *Emotions and Beliefs: How Feelings Influence Thoughts*, edited by Nico H. Frijda et al., 45–77. Cambridge: Cambridge University Press.

Gagnon, Chip. (1994/1995). "Ethnic Nationalism and International Conflict: The Case of Serbia." *International Security* 19(3): 130–166.

Gagnon, Alain G., and James Tully, eds. (2001). *Multinational Democracies*. Cambridge: Cambridge University Press.

Gagnon, Alain G., Montserrat Guibernau, and Francois Rocher. (2003). *The Conditions of Diversity in Multinational Democracies*. Montreal, Quebec, Canada: Institute for Research on Public Policy.

Galán, J. M., et al. (2009). "Errors and Artefacts in Agent-Based Modeling." *Journal of Artificial Societies and Social Simulation* 12(1). http://jasss.soc.surrey.ac.uk/12/1/1.html.

Gallagher, Dennis, and Gerald Clore. (1985). "Effects of Fear and Anger on Judgments of Risk and Evaluations of Blame." Paper presented at the Midwestern Psychological Association.

Ganter, Bernhard, and Rudolf Wille. (1999). *Formal Concept Analysis: Mathematical Foundations*. Berlin: Springer-Verlag.

Geertz, Clifford. (1973). *The Interpretation of Cultures*. New York: Basic Books,

Gellner, Ernest. (1983). *Nations and Nationalism*. Ithaca, NY: Cornell University Press.

Giliomee, Hermann. (1989). "The Beginnings of Afrikaner Ethnic Consciousness, 1850–1915." In *The Creation of Tribalism in Southern Africa*, edited by Leroy Vail, 21–50. London; Berkeley: Currey University of California Press. http://ark.cdlib.org/ark:/13030/ft158004rs/.

Giliomee, Hermann, and Charles Simkins. (1999). *The Awkward Embrace: One Party Domination and Democracy*. Cape Town, South Africa: Tafelberg Press.

Gil-White, Francisco. (1999). "How Thick Is Blood?" *Ethnic and Racial Studies* 22(5).

Gil-White, Francisco J. (2001). "Are Ethnic Groups Biological 'Species' to the Human Brain?" *Current Anthropology* 42(4): 515–554.

Goldberg, Julie, Jennifer Lerner, and Phillip Tetlock. (1999). "Rage and Reason: The Psychology of the Intuitive Prosecutor." *European Journal of Social Psychology* 29: 781–795.

Golden, M. (2003). "Electoral Connections: The Effects of the Personal Vote on Political Patronage, Bureaucracy and Legislation in Postwar Italy." *British Journal of Political Science* 33(2): 189–212.

Gorenberg, Gershom. "How Do You Prove You Are a Jew." *New York Times*, March 2, 2008.

Gorenburg, Dmitry. (1999). "Identity Change in Bashkortostan: Tatars into Bashkirs and Back." *Ethnic and Racial Studies* 22(3): 554–579.

Gourevitch, Peter. (1979). "The Reemergence of 'Peripheral Nationalism': Some Comparative Speculations on the Spatial Distribution of Political Leadership and Economic Growth," *Society for Comparative Study of Society and History* (21): 303–323.

Government of the United Provinces. (1931). *East India (Cawnpore Riots). Report of the Commission of Inquiry and Resolution of the Government of the United Provinces.* London: His Majesty's Stationery Office.

Gramsci, Antonio. (1992). *Prison Notebooks.* New York: Columbia University Press.

Greenberg, Jeff, et al. (1990). "Evidence for Terror Management Theory II: The Effects of Mortality Salience on Reactions to Those Who Threaten or Bolster the Cultural Worldview." *Journal of Personality and Social Psychology* 58: 308–318.

Griffin, John Howard. (1996). *Black Like Me.* New York: Signet.

Guibernau, Montserrat, and John Rex. (1997). *The Ethnicity Reader.* New York: Polity Press.

Guinier, L. (1994). *The Tyranny of the Majority: Fundamental Fairness in Representative Democracy.* New York: Free Press.

Gutmann, Amy. (2003). *Identity in Democracy.* Princeton, NJ: Princeton University Press.

Habyarimana, James, et al. (2007). "Why Does Ethnic Diversity Undermine Public Goods Provision? An Experimental Approach." *American Political Science Review* 101(4): 709–725.

Hacking, Ian. (1999). *The Social Construction of What?* Cambridge, MA: Harvard University Press.

Haid, Christopher, and Steven I. Wilkinson, "Ethnic Violence as Campaign Expenditure," Paper presented at the Working Group on Political Parties and Civil Peace, Peace Research Institute Oslo, August 23–24, 2010.

Hale, Henry. (2004a). "Divided We Stand: Institutional Sources of Ethnofederal State Survival and Collapse." *World Politics* 56: 165–193.

Hale, Henry. (2004b). "Explaining Ethnicity." *Comparative Political Studies* 37(4): 458–485.

Hale, Henry. (2008). *The Foundations of Ethnic Politics: Separatism of States and Nations in Eurasia and the World.* New York: Cambridge University Press.

Hall, Stuart. (1996a). "Ethnicity: Identity and Difference." In *Becoming National,* edited by Geoff Eley and Ronald Grigor Suny, 339–349. New York: Oxford University Press.

Hall, Stuart. (1996b). "Who Needs 'Identity'?" In *Questions of Cultural Identity,* edited by Stuart Hall and Paul du Gay, 1–17. London: Sage Publications.

Hamilton, James. (2001). *Channeling Violence: The Economic Market for Violent Television Programming.* Princeton, NJ: Princeton University Press.

Hansen, Thomas Blom. (2001). *Wages of Violence: Naming and Identity in Post Colonial Bombay.* Princeton, NJ: Princeton University Press.

Hanson, Stephen H. (1998). Ideology, Interests, and Identity: Comparing Secession Crises in the USSR and Russia, University of Washington (November 1998); http://www.csis.org/ruseura/ponars/workingpapers/010.PDF.

Harmon-Jones, Eddie. (2000). "A Cognitive Dissonance Theory and Perspective on the Role of Emotion in the Maintenance and Change of Beliefs and Attitudes." In *Emotions and Beliefs: How Feelings Influence Thoughts,* edited by Nico H. Frijda, Antony S. R. Manstead, and Sacha Bem, 185–211. Cambridge: Cambridge University Press.

Hegre, Havard, et al. (2001). "Toward a Democratic Civil Peace/Democracy, Political Change and Civil War, 1816–1992." *American Political Science Review* 95(1): 33–48.

Herrera, Yoshiko. (2005). *Imagined Economies.* New York: Cambridge University Press.

Hitt, Jack. "The Newest Indians." *New York Times Magazine,* August 21, 2005. www.nytimes.com/2005/08/21/magazine/21NATIVE.html.

Hong, Caroline. "Pan-Blue Allies Upset with KMT." *Taipei Times,* December 8, 2004, 3.

Hoppen, K. Theodore (1984). *Elections, Politics, and Society in Ireland 1832–1885.* Oxford, UK: Oxford University Press.

Horowitz, Donald L. (1971). "Three Dimensions of Ethnic Politics." *World Politics* 23(2): 232–244.

Horowitz, Donald. (1985). *Ethnic Groups in Conflict.* Berkeley: University of California Press,

Horowitz, Donald L. (1991). *A Democratic South Africa? Constitutional Engineering in a Divided Society.* Berkeley: University of California Press.

Horowitz, Donald L. (2001). *The Deadly Ethnic Riot.* Berkeley: University of California Press.

Htun, Mala. (2004). "Is Gender Like Ethnicity? The Political Representation of Identity Groups." *Perspectives on Politics* 2: 439–458.

Hutchinson, John, and Anthony D. Smith. (1996). *Ethnicity.* Oxford, UK: Oxford University Press.

Ignatiev, Noel. (1995). *How the Irish Became White.* New York: Routledge.

India Today. "Can Pakistan Change?" January 28, 2002, 24–30.

Indian Express (New Delhi). (2002). "Modi Ties Hands of Cops Who Put Their Foot Down," March 26, 2002, 1.

International Crisis Group. (2002). *Pakistan: The Dangers of Conventional Wisdom.* Islamabad/Brussels: Author.

Isaacs, Harold. (1975). *Idols of the Tribe.* New York: Harper and Row.

Jeganathan, Pradeep. (1998). "All the Lords Men? Ethnicity and Inequality in the Space of a Riot." In *Sri Lanka. Collective Identities Revisited Volume II,* edited by Michael Roberts, 221–246. Sri Lanka: Marga Institute.

John, Cindi. "The UK's Ethnic Name Game." BBC News UK Edition, August 9, 2005. http://news.bbc.co.uk/2/hi/uk_news/4135022.stm.

Johnson, Carter. (2008). "Partitioning to Peace: Sovereignty, Demography and Ethnic Civil Wars." *International Security* 32(4): 140–170.

Jones, Kenneth. (1981). "Religious Identity and the Indian Census." In *The Census in British India,* edited by N. Gerald Barrier, 73–101. New Delhi: Manohar.

Jones, Owen Bennett. (2002). *Pakistan: Eye of the Storm.* New Haven: Yale University Press.

Jordan, W. D. (1962). "American Chiaroscuro: The Status and Definition of Mulattoes in the British Colonies." *William and Mary Quarterly* 19(2): 183–200.

Jung, Courtney. (2000). *When I Was Black.* New Haven: Yale University Press.

Kaplan, Robert. (1993). *Balkan Ghosts.* New York: Vintage Books.

Karuppusamy, R. "Madigas: Dalits Among the Dalits." Asian Human Rights Commission-Religious Group for Human Rights. http://www.rghr.net/mainfile.php/0607/675/ (accessed August 23, 2004).

Kasfir, Nelson. (1976). *The Shrinking Political Arena: Participation and Ethnicity in African Politics, with a Case Study of Uganda.* Berkeley: University of California Press.

Kasfir, Nelson. (1979). "Explaining Ethnic Political Participation." *World Politics* 31(3): 365–388.

Kaufman, Stuart. (2001). *Modern Hatreds: The Symbolic Politics of Ethnic War.* Ithaca, NY: Cornell University Press.

Kaufmann, Chaim. (1996). "Possible and Impossible Solutions to Ethnic Civil Wars." *International Security* 20(4): 136–175.

Kaufmann, Chaim D. (1998). "When All Else Fails: Ethnic Population Transfers and Partitions in the Twentieth Century." *International Security* 23(2): 120–156.

Keltner, Dacher, Phoebe Ellsworth, and Kari Edwards. (1993). "Beyond Simple Pessimism: Effects of Sadness and Anger on Social Perception." *Journal of Personality and Social Psychology* 64(5): 740–752.

Kertzer, David I., and Dominique Arel, eds. (2002). *Census and Identity: The Politics of Race, Ethnicity, and Language in National Censuses.* New York: Cambridge University Press.

Kohli, Atul. (1990). *Democracy and Discontent.* Cambridge: Cambridge University Press.

Kolsto, Pal. "Moldova and the Dniester Republic." http://www.prio.no/files/osce-pdf/osce-moldova.pdf.

Kolsto, Pal, and Olav Melberg. (2002). "Integration, Alienation, and Conflict in Estonia and Moldova." In *National Integration and Violent Conflict in Post-Soviet Societies: The Cases of Estonia and Moldova,* edited by Pal Kolsto, 31–70. Lanham, MD: Rowman and Littlefield.

Kuenzi, Michelle, and Gina Lambright. (2001). "Party System Institutionalization in 30 African Countries." *Party Politics* 7(4): 437–468.

Kumar, Sanjay. "Gujarat Assembly Elections 2002: Analyzing the Verdict." *Economic and* Political Weekly, January 25–31, 2003, 270–275.

Kux, Dennis. (2001). *The United States and Pakistan 1947–2000: Disenchanted Allies* Washington, DC: Johns Hopkins University Press.

Kymlicka, Will. (1995a). *Multicultural Citizenship.* Oxford, UK: Oxford University Press.

Kymlicka, Will, ed. (1995b). *The Rights of Minority Cultures.* Oxford, UK: Oxford University Press.

Lacey, Marc. "Ten Years After Horror, Rwandans Turn to Islam." *The New York Times,* April 7, 2004.

Laitin, David. (1977). *Politics, Language and Thought: The Somali Experience.* Chicago: University of Chicago Press.

Laitin, David. (1986). *Hegemony and Culture: Politics and Religious Change among the Yoruba,* Chicago: University of Chicago Press.

Laitin, David. (1992). *Language Repertoires and State Construction in Africa.* Cambridge: Cambridge University Press.

Laitin, David D. (1998). *Identities in Formation: The Russian-Speaking Populations in the Near Abroad.* Ithaca, NY: Cornell University Press.

Laitin, David. (1999). "National Revivals and Violence." In *Critical Comparisons in Politics and Culture,* edited by John Bowen and Roger Petersen, 21–60. Cambridge University Press.

Laitin, D., and D. Posner. (2001). "The Implications of Constructivism for Constructing Ethnic Fractionalization Indices." *APSA-CP* 12(1): 13–17.

Lambert, Richard. (1951). *Hindu-Muslim Riots.* Ph.D. diss., University of Pennsylvania (Sociology).

Landa, Janet Tai. (1994). *Trust, Ethnicity, and Identity.* Ann Arbor: University of Michigan Press.

Larsen, Nella. (1997). *Passing.* New York: Penguin.

Lehtinen, A., and J. Kuorikoski. (2007). "Computing the Perfect Model: Why Do Economists Shun Simulation?" *Philosophy of Science* 74: 304–329.

Lemann, Nicholas. (1992). *The Promised Land: The Great Black Migration and How It Changed America.* New York: Vintage Books.

Lemarchand, René. (1986). "Ethnic Violence in Tropical Africa." In *The Primordial Challenge: Ethnicity in the Contemporary World,* edited by René Lemarchand, 185–205. New York: Greenwood Press.

Lerner, Jennifer, et al. (2003). "Effects of Fear and Anger on Perceived Risks of Terrorism: A National Field Experiment." *Psychological Science* 14(2): 144–150.

Lerner, Jennifer, and Dacher Keltner. (2000). "Beyond Valence: Toward a Model of Emotion-Specific Influences on Judgment and Choice." *Cognition and Emotion* 14: 473–493.

Lerner, Jennifer, and Dacher Keltner. (2001). "Fear, Anger, and Risk." *Journal of Personality and Social Psychology* 81(1): 146–159.

Levi, Margaret, and Michael Hechter. (1985). "A Rational Choice Approach to the Rise and Decline of Ethnoregional Political Parties." In *New Nationalisms of the Developed West,* edited by Edward A. Tiryakiain and Ronald Rogowski, 128–146. Boston: Allen and Unwin.

Lieberman, Evan. (2007). "Ethnic Politics, Risk and Policy-Making." *Comparative Political Studies* 40(12): 1407–1432.

Lijphart, Arend. (1968). *The Politics of Accommodation: Pluralism and Democracy in the Netherlands.* Berkeley: University of California Press.

Lijphart, Arend. (1977). *Democracy in Plural Societies.* New Haven: Yale University Press.

Lijphart, Arend. (1999). *Patterns of Democracy.* New Haven: Yale University Press.

Lijphart, Arend (2001). "Constructivism and Consociational Theory." In Kanchan Chandra ed, "Cumulative Findings in the Study of Ethnic Politics." APSA-CP 12(1): 11-13.

Lindberg, Staffan I. (1993). "The Democratic Qualities of Competitive Elections: Participation, Competition, and Legitimacy in Africa." *Commonwealth & Comparative Politics* 41(3): 61–105.

Lindberg, Staffan I. (2004) "The Democratic Qualities of Competitive Elections: Participation, Competition and Legitimacy in Africa." *Commonwealth & Comparative Politics* 42(1): 61–105.

Lipset, Seymour, and Stein Rokkan. (1967). "Cleavage Structures, Party Systems and Voter Alignments: An Introduction." In *Party Systems and Voter Alignments*, edited by Seymour Lipset and Stein Rokkan, 1–64. New York: Free Press.

Long, William, and Peter Brecke. (2003). *War and Reconciliation: Reason and Emotion in Conflict Resolution*. Cambridge, MA: MIT Press.

Luong, Pauline Jones. (2002). *Institutional Change and Political Continuity in Post-Soviet Central Asia*. New York: Cambridge University Press.

Lustick, Ian. (1993). *Unsettled States, Disputed Lands: Britain and Ireland, France and Algeria, Israel and the West Bank-Gaza*. Ithaca, NY: Cornell University Press.

Lustick, Ian. (1999). "Israel as a Non-Arab State: The Political Implications of Mass Immigration of Non-Jews." *Middle East Journal* 53(3): 101–117.

Lustick, Ian. (2000). "Agent-Based Modeling of Collective Identity: Testing Constructivist Theory." *Journal of Artificial Societies and Social Simulations* 3(1). http://jasss.soc.surrey.ac.uk/3/1/1.html.

Lustick, Ian. (2001). "Agent-Based Modeling and Constructivist Identity Theory." *APSA-CP* 12(1): 22–25.

Lustick, Ian S. (2002a). "Central Agent—One Time Step in the Life of an ABIR Agent." *Journal of Artificial Societies and Social Simulations* 5(3). http://jasss.soc.surrey.ac.uk/5/3/7.html.

Lustick, Ian S. (2002b). "PS-I: A User-Friendly Agent-Based Modeling Platform for Testing Theories of Political Identity and Political Stability." *Journal of Artificial Societies and Social Simulations* 5(3). http://jasss.soc.surrey.ac.uk/5/3/7.html.

Lustick, Ian S. (2011). "Secession of the Center: A Virtual Probe of the Prospects for Punjabi Secessionism in Pakistan and the Secession of Punjabistan." *Journal of Artificial Societies and Social Simulations* 14(7). http://jasss.soc.surrey.ac.uk/14/1/7.html.

Lustick, Ian S., Dan Miodownik, and Roy J. Eidelson. (2004). "Secessionism in Multicultural States: Does Sharing Power Prevent or Encourage It?" *American Political Science Review* 98(1): 209–230.

Mackie, Diane, and David Hamilton. (1993). *Affect, Cognition, and Stereotyping: Interactive Processes in Group Perception*. San Diego, CA: Academic Press.

Mainwaring, Scott, and Timothy Scully. (1995). *Building Democratic Institutions: Party Systems in Latin America*. Stanford, CA: Stanford University Press.

Mainwaring, Scott, and Matthew Shugart. (1997). *Presidentialism and Democracy in Latin America*. Cambridge: Cambridge University Press.

Mainwaring, Scott, and Edurne Zoco. (2007). "Political Sequences and the Stabilization of Interparty Competition: Electoral Volatility in Old and New Democracies." *Party Politics* 13: 155–178.

Malcolm X. (1964) *The Autobiography of Malcolm X*. New York: Ballantine Books.

Malkki, Liisa H. (1995). *Purity and Exile: Violence, Memory, and National Cosmology Among Hutu Refugees in Tanzania*. Chicago: University of Chicago Press.

Malouf, Amin. (2000). *In the Name of Identity: Violence and the Need to Belong*. New York: Penguin.

Mamdani, Mahmood. (2001). *When Victims Become Killers: Colonialism, Nativism and the Genocide in Rwanda*. Princeton, NJ: Princeton University Press.

Mandela, Nelson. (1994). *Long Walk to Freedom: The Autobiography of Nelson Mandela*. Boston: Little, Brown.

Mann, Michael. (2005). *The Dark Side of Democracy: Explaining Ethnic Cleansing*. New York: Cambridge University Press.

Mano, Haim. (1994). "Risk-taking, Framing Effects, and Affect." *Organizational Behavior and Human Decision Processes* 57: 38–58.

Markovits, Claude. (2002). "Cross-currents in the Historiography of Partition." In *Pakistan: The Contours of State and Society*, edited by Soofia Mumtaz, Jean-Luc Racine, and Imran Anwar Ali, 3–23. Oxford, UK: Oxford University Press.

Martin, Terry. (2001). *The Affirmative Action Empire.* Ithaca, NY: Cornell University Press.

Marx, Anthony W. (1997). *Making Race and Nation: A Comparison of the United States, South Africa, and Brazil.* Cambridge: Cambridge University Press.

McGann, A. J. (2004). "The Tyranny of the Supermajority: How Majority Rule Protects Minorities." *Journal of Theoretical Politics* 16(1): 53–77.

McRae, Kenneth D. (1997). *Conflict and Compromise in Multilingual Societies: Finland.* Waterloo, Ontario, Canada: Wilfrid Laurier University Press.

Melson, R., and H. Wolpe. (1970). "Modernization and the Politics of Communalism." *American Political Science Review* 44(4): 1112–1130.

Miguel, Edward. (2004). "Tribe or Nation? Nation Building and Public Goods in Kenya versus Tanzania." *World Politics* 56(3): 327–362.

Mill, John Stuart. (1991). *Considerations on Representative Government.* New York: Prometheus Books. (Originally published 1861.)

Minorities at Risk Database. http://www.cidcm.umd.edu/mar/.

Miller, John H., and Scott E. Page. (2007). *Complex Adaptive Systems: An Introduction to Computational Models of Social Life.* Princeton, NJ: Princeton University Press.

Mishali-Ram, Meirav. (2006). "Ethnic Diversity, Issues, and International Crisis Dynamics, 1918–2002." *Journal of Peace Research* 43(5): 583–600.

Mitchell, J. C. (1956). "The Kalela Dance: Aspects of Social Relationships Among Urban Africans in Northern Rhodesia" (Rhodes-Livingstone Papers 27). Lusaka, Zambia: Rhodes-Livingstone Institute.

Montalvo, Jose G., and Marta Reynal Querol. (2005). "Ethnic Polarization, Potential Conflict, and Civil Wars." *American Economic Review* 95(3): 796–816.

Morris, Chris. "The Identity Crisis Facing Europe." BBC News UK Edition, October 22, 2005. http://news.bbc.co.uk/1/hi/programmes/from_our_own_correspondent/4361786.stm.

Moser, R. (1999). "Electoral Systems and the Number of Parties in Postcommunist States." *World Politics* 51(3): 359–384.

Motyl, Alexander. (2002). "Imagined Communities, Rational Choosers, Invented Ethnies." *Comparative Politics* 34(2): 233–251.

Mozaffar, Shaheen, James Scarritt, and Glen Galaich. (2003). "Electoral Institutions, Ethnopolitical Cleavages, and Party Systems in Africa's Emerging Democracies." *American Political Science Review* 97(3): 379–390.

Munteanu, Igor. (2002). "Social Multipolarity and Political Violence." In *National Integration and Violent Conflict in Post-Soviet Societies: The Cases of Estonia and Moldova*, edited by Pal Kolsto, 197–231. Lanham, MD: Rowman and Littlefield.

Nagel, Joane. (1982). "The Political Mobilization of Native Americans." *Social Science Journal.* 19(3): 37–46.

Nasr, Vali. (2001). "The Negotiable State: Borders and Power-Struggles, Pakistan." In *Right-sizing the State: The Politics of Moving Borders*, edited by Brendan O'Leary, Ian S. Lustick, and Thomas Callaghy, 168–200. Oxford, UK: Oxford University Press.

Neal, David, and Yoshi Kashima. (2004). *Fear and Loathing.* Unpublished manuscript, University of Melbourne, May 1.

Neal, Frank. (1988). *Sectarian Violence: The Liverpool Experience, 1819–1914.* Manchester, UK: Manchester University Press.

Newbury, Catherine. (1988). *The Cohesion of Oppression.* New York: Columbia University Press.

Newbury, Catherine, and David Newbury. (1999). "A Catholic Mass in Kigali: Contested Views of the Genocide and Ethnicity in Rwanda." *Canadian Journal of African Studies/Revue Canadienne des Études Africaines* [Special Issue: French-Speaking Central Africa: Political Dynamics of Identities and Representations] 33(2/3): 292–328.

Newbury, David. (2001). "Precolonial Burundi and Rwanda: Local Loyalties, Regional Loyalties." *The International Journal of African Historical Studies* 34(2): 255–314.

Newhagen, John. (1998). "Anger, Fear and Disgust: Effects on Approach-Avoidance and Memory." *Journal of Broadcasting and Electronic Media* 42(2): 265–276.

Nirenberg, David. (1996). *Communities of Violence: Persecution of Minorities in the Middle Ages.* Princeton, NJ: Princeton University Press.

Nobles, Melissa. (2000). *Shades of Citizenship.* Stanford, CA: Stanford University Press.

Norris, Pippa, and Robert Mattes. (2003). "Does Ethnicity Determine Support for the Governing Party?" *Afrobarometer* (Working Paper No. 26).

Obama, Barack. (2004). *Dreams from My Father.* New York: Three Rivers Press.

O'Day, Alan. (1992). "Ireland's Catholics in the British State, 1850–1922." In *Comparative Studies on Governments and Non-Dominant Ethnic Groups in Europe, 1850–1940* (Vol. VI: *The Formation of National Elites*), edited by Andreas Kappeler, 41–76. New York: NYU/ESF.

Öhman, A., and Mineka, S. (2001). Fear, Phobia, and Preparedness: Toward an Evolved Module of Fear and Fear Learning. *Psychological Review* 108: 483–522.

O'Leary, Brendan, Thomas Callaghy, and Ian S. Lustick, eds. (2001). *Right-sizing the State: The Politics of Moving Borders.* Oxford, UK: Oxford University Press.

Olzak, Susan. (1990). "The Political Context of Competition: Lynching and Urban Racial Violence, 1882–1914." *Social Forces* 69: 395–421.

Ordeshook, Peter, and Olga Shvetsova. (1994). "Ethnic Heterogeneity, District Magnitude, and the Number of Parties." *American Journal of Political Science* 38(1): 100–123.

Ortony, Andrew, Gerald Clore, and Allan Collins. (1988). *The Cognitive Structure of Emotions.* Cambridge: Cambridge University Press.

Pakistan Demographic Surveys. (1999). Federal Bureau of Statistics and Planning Commission; "UNMOGIP Deployment," Map No. 3828 Rev 5. Department of Public Information, United Nations; Khyber.org. Assorted maps. http://www.khyber.org/maps.shtml.

Pandey, Gyanendra. (1992). *The Construction of Communalism in Colonial North India.* Delhi, India: Oxford University Press.

Petersen, Roger. (2001). *Resistance and Rebellion.* New York: Cambridge University Press.

Petersen, Roger. (2002). *Understanding Ethnic Violence: Fear, Hatred, and Resentment in Twentieth Century Eastern Europe.* New York: Cambridge University Press.

Petersen, Roger. (2011). *Western Intervention in the Balkans: The Strategic Use of Emotion in Conflict.* New York: Cambridge University Press.

Petersen, Roger, and Sarah Zukerman. (2009a). "Anger, Violence, and Political Science." In *A Handbook of Anger: Constituent and Concomitant Biological, Psychological, and Social Processes*, edited by Michael Potegal, Gerhard Stemmler, and Charles Spielberger, 561–581. New York: Springer.

Petersen, Roger, and Sarah Zukerman. (2009b). "Revenge or Reconciliation: Theory and Method of Emotions in the Context of Colombia's Peace Process." International Peace Research Institute, Oslo (PRIO), Forum for International Criminal and Humanitarian Law, 151–174.

Phillips, John A. (1992). *The Great Reform Bill in the Boroughs: English Electoral Behaviour 1818–1841.* Oxford, UK: Oxford University Press.

Posen, Barry. (1993). "The Security Dilemma and Ethnic Conflict." In *Ethnic Conflict and International Security*, edited by Michael Brown, 103–124. Princeton, NJ: Princeton University Press.

Posner, Daniel. (2004a). "Measuring Ethnic Fractionalization in Africa." *American Journal of Political Science* 48(4): 849–863.

Posner, Daniel N. (2004b). "The Political Salience of Cultural Difference: Why Chewas and Tambukas are Allies in Zambia and Adversaries in Malawi." *American Political Science Review* 98(4): 529–546.

Posner, Daniel. (2005). *Institutions and Ethnic Politics in Africa.* New York: Cambridge University Press.

Pounds, Norman, and Sue Ball, (1964). "Core Areas and the Development of the European State System." *Annals of the Association of American Geographers* 54: 24–40.

Powell, J. Enoch. (1969). *Freedom and Reality*, edited by John Wood, 254–257. New Rochelle, NY: Arlington House.

Pratto, Felicia, et al. (1994). "Social Dominance Orientation: A Personality Variable Predicting Social and Political Attitudes." *Journal of Personality and Social Psychology* 67: 741–741.

Prior, Katherine. (1993). "Making History: The State's Intervention in Urban Religious Disputes in the North-Western Provinces in the Early Nineteenth Century." *Modern Asian Studies* 27: 179–203.

Przeworski, A. (1991). *Democracy and the Market: Political and Economic Reforms in Eastern Europe and Latin America.* Cambridge: Cambridge University Press.

Przeworski, Adam, et al. (2000). *Democracy and Development.* New York: Cambridge University Press.

Rabushka, Alvin, and Kenneth Shepsle. (1972), *Politics in Plural Societies.* Columbus, Ohio: Charles E. Merrill.

Rae, D. W., and M. Taylor. (1970). *The Analysis of Political Cleavages.* New Haven, CT: Yale University Press.

Rajasingham-Senanayeke, Darini. (1999a). "The Dangers of Devolution: The Hidden Economies of Armed Conflict." In *Building Peace in Sri Lanka,* edited by Robert Rotberg, 57–69. Washington, DC: Brookings Institution Press.

Rajasingham-Senanayake, Darini. (1999b). "Democracy and the Problem of Representation: The Making of Bi-polar Ethnic Identity in Post/Colonial Sri Lanka." In *Ethnic Futures,* edited by Joanna Pffaff-Czarnecka et al., 99–134. New Delhi: Sage Publications.

Ramseyer, J. M., and F. M. Rosenbluth. (1993). *Japan's Political Marketplace.* Cambridge, MA: Harvard University Press.

Rapoport, Amnon, and Esther Golan. (1985). "Assessment of Political Power in the Israeli Knesset." *American Political Science Review* 79: 673–692.

Reddy, Justice P. Jagmohan. (1971). *Report into the Communal Disturbances at Ahmedabad and Other Places in Gujarat on and after 18th September 1969.* Gandhinagar, India: Gujarat Government Press.

Reilly, Benjamin. (2001). *Democracy in Divided Societies.* Cambridge: Cambridge University Press.

Reynal-Querol, Marta. (2002). "Ethnicity, Political Systems and Civil Wars." *Journal of Conflict Resolution* 46(1): 29–54.

Riker, William H. (1962). *The Theory of Political Coalitions.* New Haven, CT: Yale University Press.

Riker, William H. (1986). *The Art of Political Manipulation.* New Haven, CT: Yale University Press.

Roberts, Kenneth M., and Erik Wibbels. (1999). "Party Systems and Electoral Volatility in Latin America: A Test of Economic, Institutional, and Structural Explanations." *American Political Science Review* 93(3): 575–590.

Roeder, Philip G. (2001). "Ethnolinguistic Fractionalization (ELF) Indices, 1961 and 1985." http//:weber.ucsd.edu\~proeder\elf.htm (accessed June 16, 2004).

Rogowski, Ronald. (1990). *Commerce and Coalitions.* Princeton, NJ: Princeton University Press.

Roosens, Eugeen. (1994). "The Primordial Nature of Origins in Migrant Ethnicity." In *The Anthropology of Ethnicity: Beyond "Ethnic Groups and Boundaries,"* edited by Hans Vermeulen and Cora Govers, 81–104. Amsterdam: Het Spinhuis.

Rothschild, Joseph. (1981). *Ethnopolitics.* New York: Columbia University Press.

Rubin, Gabriel. (2011). *Freedom and Order: How Democratic Governments Restrict Civil Liberties After Terrorist Attacks and Why Sometimes They Don't.* Lanham, MD: Lexington Books.

Rustow, Dankwart. (1970). "Transitions to Democracy: Towards a Dynamic Model." *Comparative Politics* 3(2): 337–364.

Rudolph, Lloyd I., and Susanne H. Rudolph. (1967). *The Modernity of Tradition.* Chicago: University of Chicago Press.

Sahlins, Peter. (1989). *Boundaries: The Making of France and Spain in the Pyrenees.* Berkeley: University of California Press.

Said, Edward. (1978). *Orientalism.* New York: Vintage Books.

Saideman, Stephen M. (2002). "Democratization, Political Institutions, and Ethnic Conflict: A Pooled Time-Series Analysis 1985–1998." *Comparative Political Studies* 35(1): 103–129.

Sambanis, Nicholas. (2004). "What Is Civil War? Conceptual and Empirical Complexities of an Operational Definition." *Journal of Conflict Resolution* 48(6): 814–858.

Scarritt, James R., and Shaheen Mozaffar. (1999). "The Specification of Ethnic Cleavages and Ethnopolitical Groups for the Analysis of Democratic Competition in Contemporary Africa." *Nationalism and Ethnic Politics* 5(1): 82–117.

Schaffer, Teresita C., and Mondavi Mehta. (2002). "Political Institutions and the Army," a Report from the CSIS Project: Pakistan's Future and U.S. Policy Options (April 16, 2002).

Schatz, Edward. (2004). *Modern Clan Politics: The Power of "Blood" in Kazakhstan and Beyond.* Seattle and London: University of Washington Press.

Schelling, T. C. (1973). "Dynamic Models of Segregation." *Journal of Mathematical Sociology* 1: 143–186.

Schwarz, Norbert, and Gerald Clore. (1983). "Mood, Misattribution, and Judgments of Well-being: Informative and Directive Functions of Affective States." *Journal of Personality and Social Psychology* 45: 513–523.

Scott, James C. (1998). *Seeing Like a State: How Certain Schemes to Improve the Human Condition Have Failed.* New Haven, CT: Yale University Press.

Scott, James C., John Tehranian, and Jeremy Mathias. (2002). "The Production of Legal Identities Proper to States: The Case of the Permanent Family Surname." *Society for the Comparative Study of Society and History* 44(1): 4–44.

Setalvad, Teesta. "Crime against Humanity." *Communalism Combat,* November–December 2002, 81–82.

Shapley, L. S., and Martin Shubik. (1954). "A Method for Evaluating the Distribution of Power in a Committee System." *American Political Science Review* 48(3): 787–792.

Shefter, M. (1977). "Party and Patronage: Germany, England, and Italy." *Political Studies* 7: 403–451.

Shils, Edward. (1957). "Primordial, Personal, Sacred and Civil Ties." *British Journal of Sociology* 8(1): 130–145.

Shugart, Matthew Soberg, and John M. Carey. (1992). *Presidents and Assemblies: Constitutional Design and Electoral Dynamics.* New York: Cambridge University Press.

Sidanius, James. (1993). "The Psychology of Group Conflict: A Social Dominance Perspective." In *Explorations in Political Psychology,* edited by Shanto Iyengar and William J. McGuire, 183–219. Durham, NC: Duke University Press.

Sidanius, James, and Felicia Pratto. (1999). *Social Dominance: An Intergroup Theory of Social Hierarchy and Oppression.* Cambridge: Cambridge University Press.

Sidanius, James, Felicia Pratto, and Diana Brief. (1995). "Group Dominance and the Political Psychology of Gender: A Cross-Cultural Comparison." *Political Psychology* 16(2): 381–396.

Sivanandan, Ambalavaner. (1997). *When Memory Dies.* London: Arcadia.

Siverts, Henning. (1969). "Ethnic Stability and Boundary Dynamics in Southern Mexico." In *Ethnic Groups and Boundaries,* edited by Frederik Barth, 101–116. Prospect Heights, IL: Waveland Press.

Skvortsova, Alla. (2002). "The Cultural and Social Makeup of Moldova: A Bipolar or Dispersed Society?" In *National Integration and Violent Conflict in Post-Soviet Societies: The Cases of Estonia and Moldova,* edited by Pal Kolsto, 159–196. Lanham, MD: Rowman and Littlefield.

Smith, Graham. (1996). *The Nationalities Question in the Post-Soviet States.* London: Longman.

Snyder, Jack. (2000). *From Voting to Violence.* New York: Norton.

Soofia, Mumtaz, Jean-Luc Racine, and Imran Anwar Ali, eds. (2002). *Pakistan: The Contours of State and Society.* Oxford, UK: Oxford University Press.

Spilerman, Seymour. (1976). "Structural Characteristics of Cities and the Severity of Racial Disorders." *American Journal of Sociology* 41: 771–793.

Srbljinovic, A., et al. (2003). "An Agent-Based Model of Ethnic Mobilisation." *Journal of Artificial Societies and Social Simulation* 6(1). http://jasss.soc.surrey.ac.uk/6/1/1.html.

Stanley, Richard. (1997). *Enumerative Combinatorics* (Vol. 1). Cambridge: Cambridge University Press.

Stroessner, Steven, and Diane Mackie. (1993). "Affect and Perceived Group Variability: Implications for Stereotyping and Prejudice." In *Affect, Cognition, and Stereotyping: Interactive Processes in Group Perception*, edited by Diane M. Mackie and David L. Hamilton, 63–86. San Diego, CA: Academic Press.

Suny, Ronald Grigor. (1988). *The Making of the Georgian Nation*. Bloomington: Indiana University Press.

Suny, Ronald Grigor. (1999a). "Identities and Institutions in a Changing Europe" (Halle Institute Occasional Paper). Atlanta, GA: Emory University.

Suny, Ronald. (1999b). "Provisional Stabilities: The Politics of Identities in Post-Soviet Eurasia." *International Security* 24(3): 139–178.

Suny, Ronald. (2001). "Constructing Primordialism: Old Histories for New Nations." *The Journal of Modern History* 73(4): 862–896.

Tai-lin, Huang. "Green's Vote Strategy: A Disaster." *Taipei Times*, December 12, 2004, 3.

Tajfel, Henri. (1981). *Human Groups and Social Categories*. Cambridge: Cambridge University Press.

Tambiah, Stanley. (1986). *Sri Lanka: Ethnic Fratricide and the Dismantling of Democracy*. Chicago: University of Chicago Press.

Tambiah, Stanley. (1992). *Buddhism Betrayed? Religion, Politics and Violence in Sri Lanka*. Chicago: University of Chicago Press.

Tandon, Prakash. (1968). *Punjabi Century 1857–1947*. Berkeley: University of California Press.

Tanham, George K. "Pakistan's Strategic Thinking," October 1999, Hicks and Associates, Inc. Prepared for Adviser to the Secretary of Defense for National Assessment 01-0851-04-7365/7367-000 Contract#: DASW01-96-D-0002, D.O.7.

Tavits, Margit. (2005). "The Development of Stable Party Support: Electoral Dynamics in Post-Communist Europe." *American Journal of Political Science* 49: 283–298.

Taylor, Charles. (1994). *Multiculturalism and the Politics of Recognition*. Princeton NJ: Princeton University Press.

Telles, Edward. (2004). *Race in Another America: The Significance of Color in Brazil*. Princeton, NJ: Princeton University Press.

Thapar, Romila. (1989). "Imagined Religious Communities? Ancient History and the Modern Search for a Hindu Identity." *Modern Asian Studies* 23(2): 209–231.

Tilly, Charles. (2001). "Mechanisms in Political Process." *Annual Review of Political Science* 4: 21–41.

Toft, Monica. (2003). *The Geography of Ethnic Violence*. Princeton, NJ: Princeton University Press.

Tsebelis, George. (1990). *Nested Games: Rational Choice and Comparative Politics*. Berkeley: University of California Press.

Vail, Leroy. (1989). *The Creation of Tribalism in Southern Africa*. Berkeley: University of California Press.

Van Cott, Donna Lee. (2005). *From Movements to Parties in Latin America: The Evolution of Ethnic Politics*. Cambridge: Cambridge University Press.

van den Berghe, Pierre L. (1981). *The Ethnic Phenomenon*. New York: Elsevier.

Van de Walle, Nicolas. (2003). "Presidentialism and Clientelism in Africa's Emerging Party Systems." *Journal of Modern African Studies* 41(2): 297–321.

Van Evera, Stephen. (1994). "Hypotheses on Nationalism and War." *International Security* 18(4): 5–39.

Van Evera, Stephen. (2001). "Primordialism Lives!" *APSA-CP* 12(1): 20–22.

Varadarajan, Siddharth. (2002). *Gujarat: The Making of Tragedy*. New Delhi: Penguin.

Varshney, Ashutosh. (2002). *Ethnic Conflict and Civic Life*. New Haven, CT: Yale University Press.

Verdery, Katherine. (1993). "Nationalism and National Sentiment in Post-Socialist Romania" (Occasional Paper No. 93–1.3). Durham, NC: Global Forum Series, Center for International Studies, Duke University.

von Rauch, Georg. (1974). *The Baltic States: The Years of Independence, Estonia, Latvia and Lithuania 1917–1940*. Berkeley: University of California Press.

Walker, Robert. "Rwanda's Religious Reflections." BBC, April 4, 2004.

Wanderer, Jules J. (1969). "An Index of Riot Severity and Its Correlates." *American Journal of Sociology* 74: 500–505.

Wantchekon, Leonard. (2003). "Clientelism and Voting Behavior: Evidence from a Field Experiment in Benin." *World Politics* 55(3): 399–422.

Waskow, Arthur I. (1966). *From Race Riot to Sit-In: 1919 and the 1960s*. New York: Doubleday.

Waters, Mary. (1990). *Ethnic Options*. Berkeley: University of California Press.

Waters, Mary. (1999). *Black Identities: West Indian Immigrant Dreams and American Realities*. Cambridge, MA: Harvard University Press.

Watts, D. J. (1999). *Small Worlds: The Dynamics of Networks between Order and Randomness*. Princeton, NJ: Princeton University Press.

Weber, Eugen J. (1976). *Peasants into Frenchmen: The Modernization of Rural France, 1870–1914*. Stanford, CA: Stanford University Press.

Weber, Max. (1996). "The Origins of Ethnic Groups." In *Ethnicity*, edited by John Hutchinson and Anthony D. Smith, 35–40. Oxford, UK: Oxford University Press.

Weiner, Myron. (1967). *Party Building in a New Nation: The Indian National Congress* Chicago: University of Chicago Press.

Wedeen, Lisa. (2002). "Conceptualizing Culture: Possibilities for Political Science." *American Political Science Review* 96(4).

Wilensky, U., and W. Rand. (2007). "Making Models Match: Replicating an Agent-Based Model." *Journal of Artificial Societies and Social Simulation* 10(4). http://jasss.soc.surrey.ac.uk/10/4/2.html.

Wilkinson, Steven. (2001). "Constructivism and Ethnic Violence." *APSA-CP.*

Wilkinson, Steven. (2004). *Votes and Violence: Electoral Competition and Ethnic Riots in India*. New York: Cambridge University Press.

Willame, Jean-Claude. (1972). *Patrimonialism and Political Change in the Congo*. Stanford, CA: Stanford University Press.

Williams, Patricia. (1991). *The Alchemy of Race*. Cambridge MA: Harvard University Press.

Wimmer, Andreas. (2008). "The Making and Unmaking of Ethnic Boundaries. A Multilevel Process Theory." *American Journal of Sociology* 113(4): 970–1022.

Wimmer, Andreas, Lars-Erik Cederman, and Brian Min. (2009). "Ethnic Politics and Armed Conflict: A Configurational Analysis." *American Sociological Review* 74(2): 316–337.

Wood, John R. (1984). "Congress Restored? The 'Kham' Strategy and Congress (I) Recruitment in Gujarat." In *State Politics in Contemporary India*, edited by John R. Wood, 197–227. Boulder, CO: Westview Press.

Yadav, Yogendra. "The Patterns and Lessons." *Frontline*, December 21, 2002-January 3, 2003. http://www.flonnet.com/fl1926/stories/20030103007901000.htm (retrieved April 12 2012).

Yardley, William. "A Split Tribe, Casino Plans and One Little Indian Boy in the Middle." *New York Times*, February 15, 2004.

Yashar, Deborah. (2005). *Demanding Democracy*. Stanford, CA: Stanford University Press.

Young, Crawford. (1976). *The Politics of Cultural Pluralism*. Madison: University of Wisconsin Press.

Young, Crawford. (1982). "Patterns of Social Conflict: State, Class, and Ethnicity." *Daedalus* 111(2): 77–98.

Zahn, Paula. (2004). "Paula Zahn Now." CNN.com.

Zielinski, Jakub. (2002). "Translating Social Cleavages into Party Systems: The Significance of New Democracies." *World Politics* 54(2): 184–211.

Zolberg, Aristide. (1974). "The Making of Flemings and Walloons: Belgium: 1830–1914." *Journal of Interdisciplinary History* 5: 179–235.

AUTHOR INDEX

A

Alesina, Alberto
 (1999), 1n1, 6n3, 40, 139, 267
 (2003), 38, 423
 (2005), 6n3
Alesina, Alberto et al.
 (2003), 64, 65, 66, 78, 229
Allport, Gordon
 (1947), 359
Amorim-Neto, Octavio
 (1997), 312, 314
Andersen, Benedict
 (1983), 3n2, 107, 142, 152
Ando, Y.
 (2007), 292
Anwar Ali, Imran (ed.)
 (2002), 433n10
Appadurai, Arjun
 (1996), 1n1, 3n2, 35, 41, 143, 155
 (2006), 3n2, 34, 267
Appiah, Anthony
 (1992), 90
 (1996), 54
Arel, Dominique (ed.)
 (2002), 143
Atlas Narodov Mira
 (1964), 64, 65, 66
Axelrod, Robert
 (1970), 362, 369, 372

B

Ball, Sue
 (1964), 423
Baqir, Reza
 (1999), 1n1, 6n3, 40, 139, 267
Bardon, Jonathan
 (1982), 375n21

Barth, Frederik
 (1969), 69, 70, 85, 86, 97, 109, 112, 148,
  151
Bartolini, Stefano
 (1990), 316
Bates, Robert H.
 (1974), 3n2, 33, 40, 57, 95, 146, 151, 234,
  241, 322n5
 (1983), 343
 (1998), 174
Bayly, C. A.
 (1988), 373
Beissinger, Mark
 (2002), 1n1, 3n2
Bertrand, Marianne
 (2004), 117
Bhabha, Homi
 (1994), 148
Bhabha, Homi (ed.)
 (1990), 148
Bhavnani, R.
 (2008), 284
Bielasiak, Jack
 (2002), 316
Birkhoff, G.
 (1967), 273
Birnir, Jóhanna Kristín
 (2007), 6n3
Blimes, Randall J.
 (2006), 1n1, 6n3
Bodenhausen, Galen
 (1994), 401
Bookman, L. M.
 (1978), 367n12
Boulet, Cilanne
 (2005), 267
Brass, Paul R.
 (1970), 3n2, 28, 232, 250

(1974), 3n2, 28, 35, 143, 148, 151, 272
(1997), 3n2, 34, 35, 143, 147, 173, 203, 360, 361
Bratton, Michael
(1997), 322
(1998), 322
(2008), 322n5
Brecke, Peter
(2003), 399
Brehm, Denise
(2004), 149
Brief, Diana
(1995), 402
Bringa, Tone
(1995), 2, 103
Brown, Rupert
(2000), 402, 402n4
Brubaker, Rogers
(1992), 64
(1996), 64, 136
(1998), 3n2, 34, 147, 173
(2004), 5, 9, 55, 97, 131
(2009), 284n2
Bryson, J. J.
(2007), 292
Bueno de Mesquita, Bruce et al.
(2003), 40, 344

C
Callaghy, Thomas (ed.)
(2002), 424n2
Carey, John M.
(1992), 321n4
Caselli, Francesco
(2001), 3n2, 33, 40, 57, 94, 146, 240
Cavalli-Sforza, Luigi
(2000), 75, 79
Cecelski, David S. (ed.)
(1998), 368n14, 382n29, 383n31
Cederman, Lars-Erik
(2001), 5
(2009), 1n1, 6n3, 38
(2010), 1n1, 6n3, 403
Central Intelligence Agency
(2002), 420, 433
Chandra, Kanchan
(2001a), 1n1, 2
(2001b), 1n1, 2, 5
(2002), 296n11
(2004), 3n2, 22, 28, 33, 40, 51, 51n1, 57, 64, 65, 70, 94, 95, 125, 146, 151, 158, 193, 194, 232, 234, 240, 241, 250, 266, 282, 314, 341, 367, 367n13
(2005), 1n1, 2, 3n2, 6n3, 21, 22, 23n4, 27, 29, 41, 51n1, 134, 145, 174, 233, 234, 267
(2006a), 1n1, 6

(2006b), 2
(2008), 1n1, 5, 117, 197, 238, 239
(2008a), 1n1, 2, 6n3, 139n3
(2008b), 2, 5, 139n3
(2009a), 1n1, 5, 130, 197, 239
(2009b), 1n1, 5, 197, 238, 239
(2011), 188, 239, 267
Chandra, Kanchan et al.
(2006), 61, 130
Chiriac, Marian
(2007), 421
Chua, Amy
(2003), 1n1, 6n3, 58
Cioffi-Revilla, C.
(2010), 285n3
Clore, Gerald
(1983), 399
(1985), 401
(1988), 398
(2000), 399
Cohen, Frank
(1997), 6n3
Cohen, Stephen P.
(1998), 433n10
(2004), 426
Cohn, Bernard
(1987), 3n2, 144, 154
Coleman, Wilbur John
(2001), 3n2, 33, 40, 57, 94, 146, 240
Collier, Paul
(1999), 139
(2004), 1n1, 6n3
Collins, Allan
(1988), 398
Collins, Kathleen
(2004), 64
Congressional Quarterly
(1956), 383, 384
Coughlan, Reed
(1996), 135
Cox, Gary
(1997), 1n1, 139, 312, 314, 318, 321n4
Crossman, Virginia
(1996), 378, 379
Crowe, Charles
(1968), 382

D
Dahl, Robert A.
(1971), 1n1, 6n3, 28, 39, 137, 256, 259, 267
Daniel, Valentine
(1996), 60, 113, 169
Das, Suranjan
(1993), 368n14
de Figueiredo, Rui
(1998), 174

Degboe, Kouassi A.
(1995), 339
Deutsch, Karl
(1953), 3n2, 142
DiPasquale, Denise
(1998), 359
Dirks, Nicholas
(2001), 107, 151
Dominguez, Virginia
(1997), 2, 3n2, 35, 76, 143
Dorian, N. C. (ed.)
(1989), 296n11

E
Easterly, William
(1997), 1n1, 6n3, 139
(1999), 1n1, 6n3, 40, 139, 267
Economist, 1, 2, 114, 137
Edmonds, B.
(2010), 285n3
Edwards, Kari
(1993), 401
Eidelson, Roy J.
(2004), 284, 290, 446n21
Eidheim, Harald
(1969), 161, 202
Eifert, Benn
(2010), 322n5
Elbadawi, Ibrahim
(2002), 1n1, 6n3
Eller, Jack
(1996), 135
Ellison, Ralph
(1952), 417
Ellsworth, Phoebe
(1993), 401
Elster, Jon
(1989), 6
(1998), 399
(1999), 418
(2003), 405
(2007), 400
Englebert, Pierre
(2000), 322n5
Evans-Pritchard, E. E.
(1940), 324
Eyal, Jonathan
(1996), 392n1

F
Fane, Daria
(1993), 392n1
Far Eastern Economic Review
(1989), 373
Fearon, James
(1996), 56

(1998), 6n3, 41, 137
(1999), 3n2, 33, 40, 57, 94, 146, 240, 341,
342, 343, 353, 354
(2000a), 54, 70, 92
(2000b), 136
(2003), 1n1, 6n3, 51, 51n1, 64, 65, 66, 70,
78, 315, 323
Ferree, Karen E.
(2004), 321, 322n5
(2006), 321, 322n5
(2010), 318, 322n5, 339
Foucault, Michel
(1977), 3n2, 35, 143
Fox, Richard
(1985), 3n2, 35, 143
Fraenkel, Jon
(2004), 6n3
Franks, David
(1992a), 398
Frijda, Nico
(2000), 400

G
Gagnon, Alain G.
(2003), 6n3
Gagnon, Alain G. (ed.)
(2001), 6n3
Gagnon, Chip
(1994/1995), 250
Galaich, Glen
(2003), 19, 32, 38, 150, 315, 332
Galán, J. M. et al.
(2009), 292
Gallagher, Dennis
(1985), 401
Ganter, Bernhard
(1998), 273
Gasper, Karen
(2000), 399
Gecas, Viktor
(1992a), 398
Geertz, Clifford
(1973), 1n1, 3, 6, 6n3, 58, 88, 136, 341n1
Gellner, Ernest
(1983), 3n2, 64, 70, 107, 142, 152, 287
Giliomee, Hermann
(1989), 3n2, 28, 232
(1999), 316
Gil-White, Francisco J.
(1999), 135
(2001), 96
Girardin, Luc
(2009), 1n1, 6n3, 38
Glaeser, Edward L.
(1998), 359
Gleditsch, Kristian Skrede
(2009), 1n1, 6n3, 38

Golan, Esther
(1985), 362
Goldberg, Julie
(1999), 401
Golden, M.
(2003), 353
Gorenburg, Dmitry
(1999), 3n2, 12, 145
Gourevitch, Peter
(1979), 423
Government of the United Provinces
(1931), 371
Gramsci, Antonio
(1992), 3n2, 35, 143
Greenberg, Jeff et al.
(1990), 366
Griffin, John Howard
(1996), 119
Grofman, Bernard
(2004), 6n3
Guibernau, Montserrat
(2003), 6n3
Guinier, L.
(1994), 1n1, 6n3, 28, 39
Gutmann, Amy
(1996), 54
(2003), 105, 229

H
Habyarimana, James et al.
(2007), 57, 94
Hacking, Ian
(1999), 19
Haid, Christopher
(2010), 380
Hale, Henry
(2004a), 424n2, 425
(2008), 5
Hall, Stuart
(1996a), 19, 148, 150
(1996b), 148
Hamilton, David
(1993), 400
Hamilton, James
(2001), 365
Hansen, Thomas Blom
(2001), 113
Hanson, Stephen H.
(1998), 424n3
Harmon-Jones, Eddie
(2000), 400
Hechter, Michael
(1985), 64
Hegre, Havard et al.
(2001), 1n1, 6n3
Herrera, Yoshiko
(2005), 3n2, 35, 143

Hitt, Jack.
(2005), 2
Hoeffler, Anke
(2004), 1n1, 6n3
Hong, Caroline
(2004), 357
Hoppen, K. Theodore
(1984), 373, 378
Horowitz, Donald L.
(1971), 26, 60, 66, 78, 181
(1985), 1n1, 6n3, 28, 36, 39, 42, 51, 51n1, 58,
    64, 65, 66, 70, 137, 151, 174, 234, 240, 256,
    259, 267, 293, 322n5, 343, 360, 365, 368, 402
(1991), 6n3
(2001), 371
Horowitz, Jeremy
(2010), 322n5
Htun, Mala
(2004), 64, 65
Hutchinson, John
(1996), 70

I
Ignatiev, Noel
(1995), 145
Indian Express (New Delhi)
(2002), 371
International Crisis Group
(2002), 433
Isaacs, Harold
(1975), 136

J
Jeganathan, Pradeep
(1998), 3n2, 34, 147, 173
John, Cindi
(2005), 115
Johnson, Carter
(2008), 6n3
Jones, Kenneth
(1981), 3n2, 35, 143, 144, 272
Jones, Owen Bennett
(2002), 433n10
Jordan, W. D.
(1962), 282
Jung, Courtney
(2000), 3n2, 28, 232, 251

K
Kaplan, Robert
(1993), 137
Karuppusamy, R.
(2004), 365
Kasfir, Nelson
(1976), 13, 252, 322n5
(1979), 13, 19, 150, 151, 189

Kashima, Yoshi
  (2004), 366
Kaufman, Stuart
  (2001), 391, 395
Kaufmann, Chaim D.
  (1996), 6n3, 137
  (1998), 6n3
Keltner, Dacher
  (1993), 401
  (2000), 401
  (2001), 401
Kertzer, David I. (ed.)
  (2002), 143
Kimenyi, Mwangi S.
  (2008), 322n5
Kohli, Atul
  (1990), 169, 252
Kolsto, Pal
  (2002), 394
Kolsto, Pal (ed.)
  (2002), 393
Kramer, Geoffrey
  (1994), 401
Kuenzi, Michelle
  (2001), 316, 331
Kumar, Sanjay
  (2003), 381
Kuorikoski, J.
  (2007), 279, 297
Kux, Dennis
  (2001), 433n10
Kymlicka, Will
  (1995a), 70

L
Lacey, Marc
  (2004), 160
La Ferrara, Eliana
  (2005), 6n3
Laitin, David D.
  (1977), 112
  (1986), 3n2, 21, 22, 27, 35, 68, 70, 75, 86,
    134, 143, 144, 145, 157, 192, 193, 203,
    239, 282, 322n5
  (1992), 3n2, 144, 278
  (1996), 56
  (1998), 3n2, 22, 28, 34, 97, 144, 145, 147,
    151, 158, 170, 171, 173, 189, 267, 272,
    280, 282
  (1999), 1n1, 3n2, 34
  (2000a), 54, 70, 92
  (2000b), 136
  (2001), 1n1, 139
  (2002), 296n11
  (2003), 1n1, 6n3
Lambert, Richard
  (1951), 371, 372n20

Lambright, Gina
  (2001), 316, 331
Landa, Janet Tai
  (1994), 94, 95
Larsen, Nella
  (1997), 119
Lehmann, H.
  (2007), 292
Lehtinen, A.
  (2007), 279, 297
Lemann, Nicholas
  (1992), 86
Lemarchand, René
  (1986), 369
Lerner, Jennifer
  (1999), 401
  (2000), 401
  (2001), 401
Lerner, Jennifer et al.
  (2003), 401
Levi, Margaret
  (1985), 64
Levine, Ross
  (1997), 1n1, 6n3, 139
Lieberman, Evan
  (2007), 6n3
Lijphart, Arend
  (1968), 357
  (1977), 6n3, 23n4, 39, 137, 267
  (1999), 316, 318
  (2001), 138n2
Lindberg, Staffan I.
  (2004), 322, 323, 332, 333, 334
Lipset, Seymour
  (1967), 23n4, 239, 281
Long, William
  (2003), 399
Luong, Pauline Jones
  (2002), 3n2, 35, 143
Lustick, Ian S.
  (1993), 3n2, 35, 38, 143, 424n2
  (1999), 143
  (2000), 290, 300
  (2001), 43
  (2002a), 432n9
  (2002b), 429n7
  (2004), 284, 290, 446n21
  (2011), 422
Lustick, Ian S. (ed.)
  (2002), 424n2

M
Mackie, Diane
  (1993), 400
Mainwaring, Scott
  (1995), 315, 316
  (1997), 321n4

(2007), 318
Mair, Peter
(1990), 316
Malkki, Liisa H.
(1995), 151, 161, 201
Malouf, Amin
(2000), 22
Mamdani, Mahmood
(2001), 58, 151, 160
Mandela, Nelson
(1994), 193
Mann, Michael
(2005), 1n1, 6n3
Mano, Haim
(1994), 401
Markovits, Claude
(2002), 425
Martin, Terry
(2001), 143
Marx, Anthony W.
(1997), 425
Mathias, Jeremy
(2002), 143
Mattes, Robert
(2003), 322n5
McGann, A. J.
(2004), 295
McRae, Kenneth D.
(1997), 370
Mehta, Mondavi
(2002), 433n10
Melberg, Olav
(2002), 394
Melson, R.
(1970), 151
Mesquita, Batja
(2000), 400
Miguel, Edward
(2004), 6n3
(2010), 322n5
Mill, John Stuart
(1991), 1n1, 6n3
Miller, John H.
(2007), 285n3
Min, Brian
(2009), 1n1, 6n3
(2010), 1n1, 6n3, 403
Mineka, S.
(2001), 366
Miodownik, Dan
(2004), 284, 290, 446n21
(2008), 284
Mishali-Ram, Meirav
(2006), 1n1, 6n3
Mitchell, J. C.
(1956), 322n5

Montalvo, Jose G.
(2005), 1n1, 6n3
Morris, Chris
(2005), 115
Moser, R.
(1999), 320
Motyl, Alexander
(2002), 135
Mozaffar, Shaheen
(1999), 313, 322n5, 323, 324
(2003), 19, 32, 38, 150, 315, 332
Mullainathan, Sendhil
(2004), 117
Munteanu, Igor
(2002), 392n1, 393

N
Nagel, Joane
(1982), 3n2, 145, 151
Nart, J.
(2008), 284
Nasr, Vali
(2001), 433n10
Neal, David
(2004), 366
Neal, Frank
(1988), 378n24
Newbury, Catherine
(1988), 168
(1999), 160
Newbury, David
(1999), 160
(2001), 160
Newhagen, John
(1998), 401
Nirenberg, David
(1996), 360, 373
Nobles, Melissa
(2000), 3, 3n2, 35, 54, 67, 70, 111, 143, 168,
199
Norris, Pippa
(2003), 322n5

O
Obama, Barack
(2004), 167
O'Day, Alan
(1992), 376
Öhman, A.
(2001), 366
O'Leary, Brendan (ed.)
(2002), 424n2
Olzak, Susan
(1990), 382, 383n30

Ordeshook, Peter
(1994), 1n1, 137, 139, 234, 312, 314
Ortony, Andrew
(1988), 398

P

Page, Scott E.
(2007), 285n3
Pakistan Demographic Surveys
(1999), 433
Pandey, Gyanendra
(1992), 3n2, 34, 35, 143, 147, 173, 203
Petersen, Roger
(2001), 6
(2002), 56, 418
(2009a), 401n3
(2009b), 401n3
(2011), 397n2
Phillips, John A.
(1992), 375n21
Posen, Barry
(1993), 1n1, 6n3, 41, 55, 137
Posner, Daniel N.
(2001), 1n1, 139
(2004a), 314, 320, 322n5
(2004b), 280, 314, 315, 322n5, 323, 343
(2005), 1n1, 3n2, 21, 22, 23n4, 24, 27, 29,
35, 64, 65, 107, 108, 134, 143, 144, 145,
151, 158, 172, 192, 202, 233, 234,
239, 241, 250, 266, 282, 314, 320,
322n5, 363
(2010), 322n5
Postman, Leo
(1947), 359
Pounds, Norman
(1964), 423
Powell, J. Enoch
(1969), 425
Pratto, Felicia
(1995), 402
(1999), 402
Pratto, Felicia et al.
(1994), 402
Prior, Katherine
(1993), 373
Przeworski, Adam et al.
(2000), 6n3, 137

R

Rabushka, Alvin
(1972), 1n1, 6n3, 28, 58, 137
Racine, Jean-Luc (ed.)
(2002), 433n10
Rae, D. W.
(1970), 23n4

Rajasingham-Senanayeke, Darini
(1999a), 3, 3n2, 12, 28, 232, 252
(1999b), 3, 3n2, 12, 28, 232, 252
Ramseyer, J. M.
(1993), 356
Rand, W.
(2007), 292
Rapoport, Amnon
(1985), 362
Reddy, Justice P. Jagmohan
(1971), 371
Reynal-Querol, Marta
(2002), 1n1, 6n3
(2005), 1n1, 6n3
Riker, William H.
(1962), 234, 241, 282, 289
(1986), 361, 400
Roberts, Kenneth M.
(1999), 317, 318, 332
Rocher, Francois
(2003), 6n3
Roeder, Philip G.
(2001), 323
Rogowski, Ronald
(1990), 239
Rokkan, Stein
(1967), 23n4, 239, 281
Roosens, Eugeen
(1994), 12
Rosenbluth, F. M.
(1993), 356
Rothschild, Joseph
(1981), 1n1, 6n3
Rubin, Gabriel
(2011), 403
Rudolph, Lloyd I.
(1967), 26, 181
Rudolph, Susanne H.
(1967), 26, 181
Rustow, Dankwart
(1970), 1n1, 6n3

S

Sahlins, Peter
(1989), 22, 158, 192
Said, Edward
(1978), 3n2, 35, 143
Saideman, Stephen M.
(2002), 6n3
Sambanis, Nicholas
(2002), 1n1, 6n3
(2004), 64
Scarritt, James
(1999), 313, 322n5, 323, 324
(2003), 19, 32, 38, 150, 315, 332

Schaffer, Teresita C.
 (2002), 433n10
Schatz, Edward
 (2004), 64
Schelling, T. C.
 (1973), 280
Schwarz, Norbert
 (1983), 399
Scott, James C.
 (1998), 3n2, 35, 143, 272
 (2002), 143
Scully, Timothy
 (1995), 315, 316
Setalvad, Teesta
 (2002), 364
Shapley, L. S.
 (1954), 35
Shefter, M.
 (1977), 341, 353
Sheperd, Lori
 (1994), 401
Shepsle, Kenneth
 (1972), 1n1, 6n3, 28, 58, 137
Shils, Edward
 (1957), 136
Shubik, Martin
 (1954), 35
Shugart, Matthew Soberg
 (1992), 321n4
 (1997), 321n4
Shvetsova, Olga
 (1994), 1n1, 137, 139, 234, 312, 314
Sidanius, James
 (1993), 402
 (1995), 402
 (1999), 402
Simkins, Charles
 (1999), 316
Sivanandan, Ambalavaner
 (1997), 60
Siverts, Henning
 (1969), 161
Skvortsova, Alla
 (2002), 392n1, 396
Smith, Anthony D.
 (1996), 6n3, 70
Smith, Graham
 (1996), 392n1, 394, 396, 419
Snyder, Jack
 (2000), 1n1, 6n3, 34, 174
Soofia, Mumtaz (ed.)
 (2002), 433n10
Spilerman, Seymour
 (1976), 359
Spolare, Enrico
 (2003), 38, 423
Srbljinovic, A. et al.
 (2003), 284

Stanley, Richard
 (1997), 273
Stroessner, Steven
 (1993), 400
Suny, Ronald Grigor
 (1999b), 8, 19, 96, 150
 (2001), 8

T
Tai-lin, Huang
 (2004), 357
Tajfel, Henri
 (1981), 97
Tambiah, Stanley
 (1986), 3, 3n2, 12, 252
 (1992), 34, 148, 174
Tandon, Prakash
 (1968), 363
Tanham, George K.
 (1999), 433n10
Tavits, Margit
 (2005), 318
Taylor, Charles
 (1994), 70
Taylor, M.
 (1970), 23n4
Tehranian, John
 (2002), 143
Telles, Edward
 (2004), 156
Tetlock, Phillip
 (1999), 401
Thapar, Romila
 (1989), 3n2, 28, 232, 250
Tilly, Charles
 (2001), 6
Times of India
 (2002), 371
Today, India
 (2002), 433
Tsebelis, George
 (1990), 399
Tully, James (ed.)
 (2001), 6n3
Tyson,Timothy B. (ed.)
 (1998), 368n14, 382n29, 383n31

V
Vail, Leroy
 (1989), 322n5
Van Cott, Donna Lee
 (2005), 65
van den Berghe, Pierre L.
 (1981), 26, 129, 136, 181
Van de Walle, Nicolas
 (2003), 322, 332, 333

Van Evera, Stephen
  (1994), 1n1, 6n3, 42, 137, 408
  (2001), 136
Varadarajan, Siddharth
  (2002), 368
Varshney, Ashutosh
  (2002), 64, 65
Verdery, Katherine
  (1993), 64
von Rauch, Georg
  (1974), 370n16

W
Walker, Robert
  (2004), 160
Wanderer, Jules J.
  (1969), 359
Wantchekon, Leonard
  (2003), 322n5
Waskow, Arthur I.
  (1966), 383
Waters, Mary
  (1990), 22, 152, 158, 193
  (1999), 9, 19, 22, 27, 54, 62, 86, 117, 150,
    151, 152, 158, 189, 192
Watts, D. J.
  (1999), 299
Weber, Eugen J.
  (1976), 3n2, 107, 152, 278
Weber, Max
  (1996), 69, 130
Wedeen, Lisa
  (2002), 87
Weiner, Myron
  (1967), 3n2, 28, 169, 232, 253
Weingast, Barry
  (1998), 174
Wibbels, Erik
  (1999), 317, 318, 332
Wilensky, U.
  (2007), 292
Wilkinson, Steven
  (2001), 267, 385n36
  (2004), 41, 64, 65, 314, 360, 372n19,
    378n25, 380, 381, 383n32, 384, 385n35
  (2008), 1n1, 5, 197, 238, 239

(2010), 380
Willame, Jean-Claude
  (1972), 13
Wille, Rudolf
  (1998), 273
Williams, Patricia
  (1991), 116
Wimmer, Andreas
  (2008), 5
  (2009), 1n1, 6n3
  (2010), 1n1, 6n3, 403
Wolpe, H.
  (1970), 151
Wood, John R.
  (1984), 3n2, 28, 232, 253

X
X, Malcolm
  (1964), 86, 88

Y
Yadav, Yogendra
  (2002), 380
Yardley, William
  (2004), 60
Yashar, Deborah
  (2005), 65, 144
Young, Crawford
  (1976), 3n2, 19, 28, 68, 143, 150, 151, 232,
    252
  (1982), 3n2, 28, 145, 232, 250, 253

Z
Zahn, Paula
  (2004), 116
Zielinski, Jakub
  (2002), 320
Zoco, Edurne
  (2007), 318
Zolberg, Aristide
  (1974), 68
Zukerman, Sarah
  (2009a), 401n3
  (2009b), 401n3

NAME INDEX

A

Acholi, 189
Afghan, 431, 442
Afghanistan, 67, 71, 432, 439
African, 10, 24, 60, 62, 78, 84, 110, 113,
   167–68, 187, 193, 198, 211, 261–62,
   313–18, 321–31, 333, 335, 338, 425
African American Muslim, 183
African National Congress in
   South Africa, 13
Afrikaner or Afrikaaner, 329, 425
Afro-Caribbean, 17, 114, 164
Afro-Guyanese, 238
Ahirs (Gujarat), 253
Ahirwar, 250
Ahmadis (Pakistan), 64
Aizo, 324, 325
Albania, 116, 137
   Roma, 92, 116–17, 393, 417
Albanian, 137, 138, 387, 391, 417
Albanians in Kosovo, 387
Aligarh (India), 385
Amerelo (Yellow) in Brazil, 231
Amin, Idi, 13, 189
Anglo-Saxon. See WASP (White Anglo Saxon
   Protestant)
Angola Cabindans, 258
Arabs, 114
   Arab-Americans, 115
   French-Arab, 115
   pan-Arabism, 137
   Sunnis-Arabs in Iraq, 2, 81, 137
Asian, 114, 187, 261, 282
   British-Asians in Europe, 115
   Gaysians in U.S., 107–8
   in South Africa, 329
   in U.S., 199
Assam, 373
Assamese, 238, 373
Aymara (Bolivia), 9, 10, 66, 68, 74, 76, 77, 79,
   89–90, 92

B

Backward Caste, 190, 266, 363
Baganda, Uganda, 13, 143, 189, 252
Bahujan (India), 114, 151, 169, 190, 243, 250
Balkans, 137, 391, 417
Baltic States, 316, 387
Baluchi (Pakistan), 9, 10, 42, 66, 67, 74, 76, 77,
   79, 89, 92, 151, 426, 431, 435, 436, 437
Baluchistan or Balochistan (Pakistan), 115, 430,
   435, 438, 439, 442, 451
Bangladesh, 77, 426
   Chakma, 258
   Chittagong Hill Tracts (Bangladesh), 258
Banyaburi, 369
Banyoro, 189
Barbados, 24, 189, 198
Bargu, 324, 325
Bariyas (Gujarat), 253
Bashkir (Russia), 3, 145, 171
Bashkoristan, Russia, 3, 12, 145, 171
Basoga, 189
Basque region, Spain, 147, 174
Batoro, 189
Belarusan and Belarusian, 189, 283, 393
Belfast, 371, 375, 377, 378, 379
Belgian Congo, 13
Belgium, 12, 13, 60, 66, 68, 76, 77, 89, 92, 238,
   239, 281
   Brussels, 238–39
   Catalan, 12
   Catalunya migrants, 12
   Flemish, 60, 66, 68, 74, 76, 77, 89, 92, 238,
   239

Belgium (*Contd.*)
  Flemish speakers, 238–39
  French speaking Brussles, 89, 238–39
  Native-Flemish-Belgian, 238–39
  Native-French-Belgian, 238–39
  Walloons, 66, 68, 74, 76, 77, 89, 92, 238
Bemba (Zambia), 250, 266
Bengali Muslims, 77
Benin, 79, 317, 324–30, 334, 339
  Fon in Benin, 324, 325, 328
  Fulani in, 324, 325
  Northerner in, 324–25
  Southerner in, 324–26, 328, 339
Bessarabia, 391–92
Bharatiya Janata Party (BJP), 250, 367, 372, 380–81
Bhils (Gujarat), 253
Black Muslim, 106, 211
Blacks, 24, 25, 121, 151, 166, 182, 183–97, 203, 210–14
  American Blacks, 86
  Black Muslim, 106, 211
  in Brazil (Preto), 2, 199, 230, 231
  in Changeland, 242–44, 249
  Haitian Blacks, 89
  Jamaican Blacks, 86
  in Limitedchangeland, 246–48, 249
  in New York, 24, 27
  in Nochangeland, 245–46, 249
  in Oneland, 196, 197
  in Someland, 190
  Trinidad, 10, 17, 20, 21, 62, 116, 124, 125, 164
  in UK, 114
  in U.S., 17, 24, 27, 60, 65, 67, 72, 76, 78, 84, 86, 89, 97, 105, 106, 110–11, 113–14, 154, 163–69, 182, 210, 382, 383
  West Indian immigrants, 9–10, 16–17, 20–21, 24, 27, 62–63, 99, 115–16, 117, 124, 125, 151, 159, 160, 162, 163, 164, 198–99
Bolivia, 68, 81
  Aymara, 9, 10, 66, 68, 74, 76, 77, 79, 89–90, 92
  Aymara and Quechua, 9, 10, 66, 68, 74, 76, 77, 79, 89–90, 92
  Mestizo in, 81
Bosnia, 387, 391, 420
Bosnian Muslims, 2, 79, 102–3
Botswana, 317, 322, 327, 330, 334
Branco (Whites) in Brazil, 3, 22, 92, 199, 230, 231
Brazil, 2–3, 14, 106, 150, 154, 156, 199, 200, 229–31, 317
  Blacks (Preto), 2, 199, 230, 231
  Mixed or Brown (Pardo), 81, 231
  Whites (Branco), 3, 22, 92, 199, 230, 231
  Yellow (Amerelo), 231
Britain, 2, 115, 375n21, 378–79, 424

British, 2, 77, 115
British-Asians in Europe, 115
British India, 77, 89, 144
British Muslim, 115
Brown or Mixed (Pardo) in Brazil, 81, 231
Brussels, Belgium, 238–39
Buddhist
  in India, 190
  in Sri Lanka, 111, 112, 148, 166, 167, 174
  in U.S., 204
Bundelkhand, India, 251

C
Cabindans (Angola), 258
Cameroon, 79, 317, 327
Caribbean, 116, 206
  Afro-Caribbean, 17, 114, 164
Castes
  Backward Caste, 190, 266, 363
  Hindu castes, 169, 365, 373
  India, 114
  Most Backward Caste (MBC), 251, 363
  Other Backward Classes or Castes (OBC), 114, 189, 283
  Scheduled Castes, 113, 114, 151, 168, 238
  Upper Caste, 60, 244, 266
  Upper Urban Caste, 60
Catalan (Belgium), 12
Catalunya migrants, Belgium, 12
Catholic, 205, 206, 282, 286, 288, 289, 305, 355, 364, 370
  in Baganda, 252
  in Italy, 425
  in Kikuyu, 354
  in Northern Ireland, 81
  Protestant-Catholic riots, 371–79
  Roman Catholic, 158
  in Uganda, 12, 252
  in U.S., 349
Catholicism, 62, 206
CDEI (Constructivist Dataset on Ethnicity and Institutions), 238
Central America, Creoles in, 84
Ceylon, Island of, 111
Ceylon Moors, 200, 231–32, 252
Ceylon Tamils in Sri Lanka, 200, 231–32, 252
Chakma (Bangladesh), 258
Changeland, 242–44, 246, 249, 260–63, 265, 267–69
Chattisgarh, 251
China
  Gaysian in U.S., 107–8
Chinese, 17, 164
  in Malaysia, 2, 85, 92
  Singaporean Chinese in Malaysia, 424
Chittagong Hill Tracts (Bangladesh), 258
Christian

in India, 190, *191n2*
in Indonesia, 13
in Lebanon, *51n1*, 72, 81
Protestants, 286
Spain, Muslim-Christian riots in, 360
in Sri Lanka, 112
in U.S., 349
Yorubas, 86
Christianity
Eastern Christianity, Serbs, 67
in Europe, 286
Orthodox Christianity, 286
Protestants, 286
Western Christianity, Croats, 67
Colombia, 147, 317
Coloured in South Africa, 9, 10, 66, 69, 74, 77, 78, 80, 81, 84, 89, 91–92, 329, 338
Congo, 317, 327
Belgian Congo, 13
Congo basin area, 75
Lari in, 253
Congress
Congress Party, Pakistan, 425
Constructivist Dataset on Ethnicity and Institutions (CDEI), 238
Copts in Egypt, 64
Côte d' Ivoire (Ivory Coast), 79, 317, 327, 333
anti-Mauritanian riots in Abidjan, 372
Houphouët Boigny, Felix, 372
Creoles
in Guyana and Trinidad, *51n1*
in Latin and Central America, 84
in Mauritius, 81
Croats, 9, 10, 65, 66, 67, 76, 77
Western Christianity, 67
Cyrillic alphabet, 85, 392
Cyrillic script, Serbs, 67
Czech Republic, 317, 425

D
Dalit (India), 114, 168, 169, *365n11*
Dalmatia, 67, 78
Dalmatian Coast, 67, 78
Democratic Party in U.S., 62, 63, 383
Blacks in, 113, 382, 383
Deobandi in Pakistan, 436, 442
Derry, Ireland, 374–75, 377, 378, 379
Dharalas (Gujarat), 253
Dniester, 395–97, 419–21
Dniester River, 391, 392
Dominican, 23, 189

E
Eastern Christianity, Serbs, 67
Eastern Europe, 36, 66, 316, 387, 410, 417. *See also* Moldova

Egypt, 116, 117
Copts in, 64
Embu (Kenya), 326
England, Liverpool, 375, 377, *378n24*
English
Englishness, 148–49
English-speaking Whites, South Africa, 329
Episcopalian, 365, 374–79
Estate Tamils in Sri Lanka, 169
Ethiopia, 317, 327, 334, 335
Eurasia, 78–79
Europe
British-Asians in, 115
Christianity, 286

F
Finn, 189
Flemish (Belgium), 60, 66, 68, 74, 76, 77, 89, 92, 238, 239
Flemish speakers (Belgium), 238–39
Fon in Benin, 324, 325, 328
France, 79, 111, 122, 251, 282, 316, 363, 424
French, 17, 62, 148, 281
French Arab, 115
French speakers, 17, 63, 89, 148, 361
in Brussels, 89, 238–39
Fulani
in Benin, 324, 325
Hausa-Fulani in Nigeria, 8, 9, 10, 68, 74, 75, 76, 78, 80, 84, 87, 92
in Mauritania, 331
in Nigeria, 8, 66, 68, 69, 76, 77, 78, 84, 89

G
Gambia, 317, 327, 334–35
Ganda (Uganda), 253
Gay Asians in U.S., 107–8
Gaysians in U.S., 107–8
German, 17, 61, 124, 148, 164, 238, 370, 392, 393
German American, 23, 82, 189
German-Turks, 115
Germany, 61, 64, 71, 79, 91, 251, 316, 396
Ghana, 79, 198, 317, 327
Gisu (Uganda), 253
Gorkha National Liberation Front, 374
Guinea-Bissau, 317, 327, 328, 330, 334, 339
Gujarat, India, 89, 169, 252–53, 368, 371–72, 380–81
Ahirs, 253
Bariyas, 253
Bhils, 253
Dharalas, 253
Gun, 324, 325

Guyana, 24, 51, 189, 198, 238
  Afro-Guyanese, 238
  Creoles in, *51n1*
  East Indian, 238

H

Haiti, 17, 24, 62, 198
Haitian Blacks, 89
Harijan, 114, 168, 169, 283
Hausa, in Nigeria, 8, 66, 68, 69, 74, 76, 77, 78,
    84, 89
Hausa-Fulani in Nigeria, 8, 9, 10, 68, 74, 75, 76,
    78, 80, 84, 87, 92
Hill Country Tamils in Sri Lanka, 169
Hindu, *191n2*, 266, 360, 365–67
  in India, *51n1*, 81, 94, 238, 250, 364,
    366–68, 370, *371n18*, 372, 373, 380–81,
    385, 386, 425
  in Punjab, 87, 250
  VirPak, *430n8*
Hindu castes, 169, 365, 373
Hinduism, 122
  in U.S., 204
Hindu-Muslim riots (India), 360, 372, 373,
    380–81, 385, 386
Hindu upper caste, 244
Holland, 251
Honduras, 81
Houphouët Boigny, Felix, 372
Huguenots, 111
Hutu and Tutsis in Rwanda, 59, 151, 160, 168,
    200, 229, 371
Hutu refugees, Waha in Rwanda, 151, 161, 201
Hyderabad (India), 385, 435, 438, 439

I

Ibo in Nigeria, 9, 10, 66, 68, 69, 74, 75, 76, 77,
    87, 89, 92, 253, 317, 327
Illinois, 383
Illyrian Tribes, 137
India
  Aligarh, 385
  Bahujan, 114, 151, 169, 190, 243, 250
  Bharatiya Janata Party (BJP), 250, 367, 372,
    380–81
  British India, 77, 89, 144
  Buddhist in, 190
  Bundelkhand, 251
  Castes, 114
  Christian, 190, *191n2*
  Congress, 380–81
  Dalit, 114, 168, 169, *365n11*
  Gujarat, 89, 169, 252–53, 368, 371–72,
    380–81
    Ahirs, 253

  Bariyas, 253
  Bhils, 253
  Dharalas, 253
  Hindu in, *51n1*, 81, 94, 238, 250, 364,
    366–68, 370, *371n18*, 372, 373, 380–81,
    385, 386, 425
  Hindu-Muslim riots, 360, 372, 373, 380–81,
    385, 386
  Hyderabad (India), 385, 435, 438, 439
  Indore, 385
  Kshatriya, 169, 199, 252, 253
  Madhya Pradesh, 371, 381
  Maharashtra, 381
  Muslim in, *51n1*, 81, 238, 250, 368, 380–81,
    385
  Rajasthan, 364, 371, 381
  Rajput, 252
  Sikh in, 190, 238, *364n9*
  Tamils in, 81, 238
  Uttarakhand, 251
  Uttar Pradesh, 155
  West Bengal, 381
Indian Tamils in Sri Lanka, 169, 200, 231,
    232, 252
Indigena (Indigenous), 231
Indonesia, 13, 107
Indore (India), 385
Iraq, 2, 91, 137
  Kurds in Iraq, 2, 63, 137
  Shias in Iraq, 81, 94, 137
  Sunnis-Arabs in, 2, 81, 137
Ireland, 35, 79, 90, 374–79, 424
  Northern Ireland, 81, 281
Irish, 89, 90, 109, 114, 341, 374, 375
Irish-American, 23, 76, 85, 90, 115, 189
Islam, 122, 286, 364
  Sunni Islam, 446
  Sunni Islam in Syria, 65
  in U.S., 204
  VirPak and, 438, 446
Islamabad, Pakistan, 426, 435, 438, 439
Islam in VirPak, 438, 446
Israel, *362n6*. *See also* Jewish; Jews
  Jewish settlers in Israel, 59
  Shas Party, 341
Italian American, 23, 89, 189, 210
Italians in Italy, 81
Italy, 79, 81, 317, 425
  Catholic, 425
Ivory Coast (Côte d' Ivoire), 79, 317, 327, 333
  anti-Mauritanian riots in Abidjan, 372
  Houphouët Boigny, Felix, 372

J

Jamaican Blacks, 86
Japan, 144, 171, 188, 357

Gaysians in U.S., 107–8
Liberal Democracy Party, 356
Japanese-Americans, 115
Jewish, 59, 82–83, 163, 189, 371, 373, 393
Jews, 82–83
  American Jews, 82–84, 410
  Ashkenazi, 82
  in France, 111
  in Lithuania, 411
  Russian-speaking, 283
  in U.S., 109, 210
Jharkhand, 251
Jharkhandis, 238

K
Kakwa (Uganda), 189
Kalenjin (Kenya), 353
Kandyan Sinhalese (Sri Lanka), 3, 200, 231, 232, 252
Karachi, Pakistan, 426, 435, 436, 437, 438, 439, 442, 443
Kashmir, Pakistan, 430, 435, 436, 438, 439
Kenya
  Embu, 326
  Kalenjin, 353
  Kikuyu in Kenya, 75, 326, 353–54
  Luhyias, 353
  Luos, 353–54
  Meru, 326
Khyber Pakhtunwa, 426. *See* Northwest Frontier Province (NWFP) or Khyber Pakhtunwa
Kiga (Uganda), 253
Kikuyu in Kenya, 75, 326, 353–54
Kongo, 253
Kosovo, 389, 391
  Albanians in, 387
  Serbs in, 417
Kshatriya, India, 169, 199, 252, 253

L
Ladino, 161, 179
Lahore in VirPak, 435, 438, 439
Langi, 189
Lapps in Norway, 161–62, 202
Lari, 253
Lari (Congo), 253
Latin America, 65, 66, 84, 316, 317, 318, 321
Lebanon, *51n1*, 72, 81
Lesotho, 317, 322, 327, *331n11*, 334
Liberal Democratic Party in Japan, 356
Liberia, 79
Limitedchangeland, 246–49, 257, 260–63, 265, 267–69
Lithuania, 79, 391, 410–11
Lithuanian

in Lithuania, 81
Lithuanian Americans, 76, 115
Lithuanian Jews, 411
Liverpool, England, 375, 377, *378n24*
Louisiana, 76, 382–83
Low Country Sinhalese (Sri Lanka), 3, 200, 230, 232, 252
Luba, in Zaire, 250
Luhyias (Kenya), 353
Luo (Kenya), 354
Luos (Kenya), 353–54

M
Madagascar, 317, 327
Madhya Pradesh, India, 371, 381
Maharashtra, India, 381
Malawi, 317, 327
Malaysia, 2, 23, 66, 85, 107, 364
  Chinese in, 2, 85, 92
  Malay, 2, 17, 164, 364
  Singapore's independence from, 424
Mandela, Nelson, *193n3*
Mauritania, Fulani in, 331
Mauritanian, anti-Mauritanian riots in Abidjan, 372
Mauritius, 81, 317, 322, 327, 328, 330, 334, 339
MBC. *See* Most Backward Caste (MBC)
Meru (Kenya), 326
Mestizo, 81, 84, 179
Mexican American, 199, 340
Mexican in U.S., 23, 113, 189
Mexico, 81, 161, 198
Michigan, 383
Mixed or Brown (Pardo) in Brazil, 81, 231
Mixed Race, 80–81, 116, 167
Mizo National Front, 374
Mohajir and Muhajir, 9, 10, 66, 67, 74, 76, 77, 79, 85, 89, 91, 92, 431, 433, 435, 436–37, 438, 439
Moldova, Moldavians, 36, 388, 391–97, 417–21
Most Backward Caste (MBC), 251, 363
Mozambique, 317, 322, 327, 334, 335
Muhajir. *See* Mohajir and Muhajir
Mulatto, 2, 81
Muslim, 104–5, 161, *191n2*, 201
  African American Muslim, 183
  Bengali Muslims, 77
  Black Muslims, 106, 211
  in Bosnia, 2, 79, 102–3
  British Muslim, 115
  Hindu-Muslim riots (India), 360, 372, 373, 380–81, 385, 386
  in India, *51n1*, 81, 238, 250, 368, 380–81, 385
  in Indonesia, 13
  in Lebanon, *51n1*, 72

Muslim (*Contd.*)
Muslim-Christian riots, 360
Muslim Fundamentalist, VirPak, 436–38, 441–43, 448, 449, 451
in Punjab, 425
Pushtun Sunni Muslim, VirPak, 434
in Sri Lanka, 92
Sunni Muslim, VirPak, 434–40, 446, 448, 450, 451
in U.S., 106
in VirPak, 430, 434–41, 449, 450
Yorubas, 86, 87
Muslim-Christian riots, 360
Muslim Fundamentalist, VirPak, 436–38, 441–43, 448, 449, 451

N
NAACP, 384n33
Natalians in South Africa, 193
Native American, 2, 60, 113, 145
Native-Flemish-Belgian, 238–39
Native-French-Belgian, 238–39
Ndebele (South Africa), 329, 338
Negro
in Puerto Rico, 2
in U.S., 113, 114, 169, 382, 384, 411–12
Nepal, 65
Nepalese in Bhutan, 85
New Tamils in Sri Lanka, 169
New York, Blacks in, 24, 27
Nicaragua, Mestizo in, 81
Niger, 78, 317, 327, 334–37, 338
Nigeria, 8, 9, 10, 27, 65, 66, 68, 76, 77, 80, 85, 89, 106, 125, 144, 203, 253, 317, 327, 331
Fulani, 8, 66, 68, 69, 76, 77, 78, 84, 89
Hausa, in Nigeria, 8, 66, 68, 69, 74, 76, 77, 78, 84, 89
Hausa-Fulani, 8, 9, 10, 68, 74, 75, 76, 78, 80, 84, 87, 92
Ibo in Nigeria, 9, 10, 66, 68, 69, 74, 75, 76, 77, 87, 89, 92, 253, 317, 327
Yoruba, 8, 9, 10, 65, 66, 68, 69, 73, 74, 75, 77, 85, 86, 87, 89, 92
Yoruba-Nagot, 324, 325
Nochangeland, 242, 244–46, 249, 256, 257, 260, 262, 265, 267
Nonconformist, 374–75, 378
North America, 66, 316
North Carolina, 382–83
Wilmington riots, 368n14, 382–83
Northerner
in Benin, 324–25
in Sudan, 64
in Uganda, 253
Northern Ireland, 81, 281

North Korea, 107
North Sotho, South Africa, 329
Northwest Frontier Province (NWFP) or Khyber Pakhtunwa, 426, 430, 436–39, 442, 443, 446, 451
Norway, 161–62, 202
Norwegians, 161–62, 202
Nubian
Uganda, 13, 189
NWFP. *See* Northwest Frontier Province (NWFP) or Khyber Pakhtunwa
Nyamwezi in Tanzania, 143

O
Obama, Barack, 116, 167
OBC. *See* Other Backward Classes or Castes (OBC)
Ohio, 383
Oneland, 196–97
Orthodox Christianity, 286
Otamari/Somba, 324, 325
Other Backward Classes or Castes (OBC), 114, 189, 283
Oxchuc Mayas, 161

P
Pakistan, 9, 10, 37, 42, 66, 67, 76, 77, 114
Ahmadis, 64
Baluchi, 9, 10, 42, 66, 67, 74, 76, 77, 79, 89, 92, 151, 426, 431, 435, 436, 437
Baluchistan or Balochistan, 115, 430, 435, 438, 439, 442, 451
Congress Party, 425
Deobandi in Pakistan, 436, 442
Islamabad (Pakistan), 426, 435, 438, 439
Karachi, 426, 435, 436, 437, 438, 439, 442, 443
Kashmir, 430, 435, 436, 438, 439
Mohajir and Muhajir, 9, 10, 66, 67, 74, 76, 77, 79, 85, 89, 91, 92, 431, 433, 435, 436–37, 438, 439
Northwest Frontier Province (NWFP) or Khyber Pakhtunwa, 426, 430, 436–39, 442, 443, 446, 451
Pashtun, Pathan or Pushtun, 9, 10, 42, 66, 67, 74, 77, 79, 86, 89, 92, 151, 431, 434–39, 443, 446, 451
Punjabi secession, question of, 422–51
Punjab or Punjabi, 9, 10, 37, 42, 66, 67, 68, 74, 76, 77, 79, 81, 86, 89, 91, 92, 250, 258
Seraiki, 42, 77, 430, 431, 435, 437, 438, 441–43, 446, 451
Sikh in Punjab, 86, 87, 250

Sindh or Sindhi, 9, 10, 42, 76, 77, 79, 426, 430, 434–39, 442–43, 446, 451

Urdu, 67, 89

Virtual Pakistan (VirPak), 422, 427, 428–51

Panama, 81

Pan-Arabism, 137

Pardo (Mixed or Brown) in Brazil, 81, 231

Pashtun, Pathan or Pushtun, 9, 10, 42, 66, 67, 74, 77, 79, 86, 89, 92, 151, 431, 434–39, 443, 446, 451

Pathan. *See* Pashtun, Pathan or Pushtun

Pedi in South Africa, 338

Peru, 81, 317

Peul tribe, 324, 325

Poland, 79, 81, 396

Polish, 189, 393

Polish Americans, 115

Post-communist states, 317

Presbyterian, 62, 159, 205, 206, 211, 365, 374–77

Preto (Blacks) in Brazil, 2, 199, 230, 231

Protestant, 285–86, 349, 355, 362, 365, 370, 371, 374–79. *See also* WASP (White Anglo Saxon Protestant)

in Baganda, 252

in Northern Ireland, 81

Protestant-Catholic riots, 371–79

Protestants

Christian, 286

Christianity, 286

Puerto Rico/Puerto Rican, 2, 23, 189, 340

Punjabi secession, question of, 422–51

Punjab or Punjabi, 9, 10, 37, 42, 66, 67, 68, 74, 76, 77, 79, 81, 86, 89, 91, 92, 250, 258

Muslim in, 425

Pushtun. *See* Pashtun, Pathan or Pushtun

Q

Quechua (Bolivia), 9, 10, 66, 68, 74, 76, 77, 79, 89–90, 92

R

Rajasthan, India, 364, 371, 381

Rajput, India, 252

Rationality, 36, 387–421, 428

Republican, 101, 129

in U.S., 129, 382–83

Roma, Albania, 92, 116–17, 393, 417

Roman Catholic, 158

Romania, 66, 391, 392, 394, 396, 420

Romanian, 391–93, 420

Romanian Language, 393, 419

Romanian Speakers, 391–93, 396, 421

Russia, 122, 193, 317, 371, 396, 420, 424, 426

Bashkir, 3, 145, 171

Bashkoristan, 3, 12, 145, 171

Tatars, 3, 12, 145, 171

Russians, 280–81, 283, 391, 393–95, 419–21

Russian speaking, 145, 189, 280, 281, 283, 394, *419n7*, 420

Russophone, 394, 395, 397

Rwanda, 2, 59, 151, 153, 160, 168, 257

Hutu and Tutsis, 59, 151, 160, 168, 200, 229, 371

Hutu refugees, Waha, 151, 161, 201

Hutu refugees in Tanzania, 151, 161, 201

Twa, 151, 230

S

Sao Tome, 317, 327

Scheduled Castes, 113, 114, 151, 168, 238

Scheduled Tribe, 190

Scots, 2, 64

Scottish, 61

Second Congress of Dniester, 396

Senegal, 78, 317, 327, 330, 334, *425n4*

Seraiki (Pakistan), 42, 77, 430, 431, 435, 437, 438, 441–43, 446, 451

Serbs, 9, 10, 65, 66, 67, 76, 77

Eastern Christianity, 67

in Kosovo, 417

Sethos in South Africa, 338

Sikh

in India, 190, 238, *364n9*

in Punjab (Pakistan), 86, 87, 250

Sindh or Sindhi (Pakistan), 9, 10, 42, 76, 77, 79, 426, 430, 434–39, 442–43, 446, 451

Singaporean Chinese in Malaysia, 424

Sinhala (Sri Lanka), 2, 3, 60, 79, 111, 112, 147, 148, 166, 167, 174, 179, 200, 231

Sinhalese (Sri Lanka), 80, 147, 232, 251, 252

Slav, 79, 85, 137, 391, 395, 418, 419, 420, 421

Slavic speakers, 420–21

Soga (Uganda), 253

Somalia, Darood in, 65

Somalis, 112

Somba/Otamari, 324, 325

Someland, 25, 186, 190

South Africa, 9, 10, 13, 66, 69, 78, 193, 251, 317, 322, 326, 327, 328, 329, 330, 334, 338, 411, 425

African National Congress, 13

Afrikaner or Afrikaaner, 329, 425

Asians in, 329

Coloured, 9, 10, 66, 69, 74, 77, 78, 80, 81, 84, 89, 91–92, 329, 338

English-speaking Whites, 329

Mandela, Nelson, *193n3*

Natalians, 193

Ndebele, 329, 338

North Sotho, 329

South Africa (*Contd.*)
  Pedi, 338
  Sethos, 338
  South Sotho, 329
  Swazi (South Africa), 329, 338
  Tsonga, 329
  Tswana, 329, 330, 338
  Venda, 329
  White Zulu, *193n3*
  Xhosa, 9, 10, 13, 66, 69, 74, 75, 77, 89, 91,
    92, 329, 330, 338
  Zulu, 9, 10, 13, 66, 69, 74, 75, 77, 89, 91, 92,
    193, 328, 329, 330, 338
South Carolina, 383
Southerner
  in Benin, 324–26, 328, 339
  in Sudan, 64
  in Uganda, 253
South Korea, 107
South Slavs, 79, 85
South Sotho, South Africa, 329
Soviet Union, 158, 171, 316, 387, 391, 392–97,
  424
Spain
  Basque region, 147, 174
  Muslim-Christian riots in, 360
Spanish, 174
Sri Lanka, 2, 3, 12, 54, 60, 147, 148, 151, 166,
  199–200, 229, 230, 232, 251–52, 371
  Buddhists in, 111, 112, 148, 166, 167, 174
  Christian, 112
  Estate Tamils, 169
  Indian Tamils in Sri Lanka, 169, 200, 231,
    232, 252
  Kandyan Sinhalese, 3, 200, 231, 232, 252
  Low Country Sinhalese, 3, 200, 230, 232,
    252
  Muslim in, 92
  Sinhala, 2, 3, 60, 79, 111, 112, 147, 148, 166,
    167, 174, 179, 200, 231
  Sinhalese, 80, 147, 232, 251, 252
  Tamil Nadu, 79
  Tamils, 2, 79–80, 169, 200, 231–32, 252, 371
Sri Lanka Freedom Party, 112, 167
Sudan, 64
Sukuma in Tanzania, 143
Sunni Fundamentalist in VirPak, 431
Sunni in Syria, 64, 65
Sunni Muslim, VirPak, 434–40, 446, 448, 450,
  451
Sunnis-Arabs in Iraq, 2, 81, 137
Sunnis in VirPak, 433, 434, 435, 437, 438, 439
Sunnis Islam in VirPak, 446
Sunnis Muslim in VirPak, 434–40, 441, 446,
  448–50, 451
Sunni traditional in VirPak, 431

Swazi (South Africa), 329, 338
Syria, Sunnis in, 64, 65

T
Taiwan, 356–57
Tamil Nadu in Sri Lanka, 79
Tamils, 2, 79–80, 169, 200, 231–32, 252, 371
  Ceylon Tamils in Sri Lanka, 200, 231–32,
    252
  Estate Tamils, 169
  Hill Country Tamils in Sri Lanka, 169
  in India, 81, 238
  Indian Tamils in Sri Lanka, 169, 200, 231,
    232, 252
  New Tamils in Sri Lanka, 169
  Sri Lanka, 2, 79–80, 169, 200, 231–32, 252,
    371
  in Sri Lanka, 79–80, 169
  Tamil Nadu, 79
  Tamils of Indian Origin in Sri Lanka, 169
  Tamils of Recent Indian Origin in Sri Lanka,
    169
Tanzania, 143, 144, 161, 171, 201, 317, 327,
  334
  Hutu refugees in, 151, 161, 201
  Nyamwezi in, 143
Tatars (Russia), 3, 12, 145, 171
Togo, 79, 317, 327
Tory party, 374–78
Trinidad, 10, 24, *51n1*, 62, 119, 124, 158, 159,
  160, 189, 198, 200
  Blacks, 10, 17, 20, 21, 62, 116, 124, 125, 164
  Creoles in, *51n1*
Trinidadian, 10, 16–17, 20, 21, 116, 159, 160,
  162, 163, 164, 166, 199, 211
Tripura National Volunteers, 374
Tsonga, South Africa, 329
Tswana, South Africa, 329, 330, 338
Twa in Rwanda, 151, 230

U
Uganda, 13, 143–44, 171, 252, 253
  Amin, Idi, 13, 189
  Baganda, 13, 143, 189, 252
  Catholic, 12, 252
  Ganda (Uganda), 253
  Gisu, 253
  Kakwa, 189
  Kiga (Uganda), 253
  Northerner in, 253
  Nubian, 13, 189
  Soga, 253
  Southerner in, 253
Ukrainians, 189, 283, 391, 393–96, 419, 420,
  421

UK (United Kingdom), 64, 122, 206
  Blacks in, 114
Upper Caste, 60, 244, 266
Upper Urban Caste, 60
Urdu in Pakistan, 67, 89
Uruguay, 81, 317
U.S. (United States). *See also* WASP (White Anglo Saxon Protestant)
  African American, 9, 17, 62, 71, 97, 113, 114, 117, 124, 159, 160, 169, 182, 183, 211, 381–84
  African-American Muslim, 183
  American Blacks, 86
  Asians in, 199
  Black Muslims, 106
  Blacks, 17, 24, 27, 60, 65, 67, 72, 76, 78, 84, 86, 89, 97, 105, 106, 110–11, 113–14, 154, 163–69, 182, 210, 382, 383
  Catholic, 349
  Christian, 349
  Hispanic, 23, 167, 189, 199, 204
  Jim Crow laws, 411
  Lithuanian Americans, 76, 115
  Louisiana, 76, 382–83
  Michigan, 383
  Muslims, 106
  North Carolina, 382–83
    Wilmington riots, *368n14*, 382–83
  Ohio, 383
  Republican, 129, 382–83
  White, 23, 60, 67, 72, 76, 82, 89, 97, 154, 163, 210
  White working class in U.S., 60
  Wilmington riots, *368n14*, 382–83
Uttarakhand (India), 251
Uttar Pradesh, India, 155

V
Venda, South Africa, 329
Venezuela, 81
Vietnam, 107, 108
VirPak (Virtual Pakistan), 422, 427, 428–51

W
Waha, Hutu refugees, 151, 161, 201
Walloons (Belgium), 66, 68, 74, 76, 77, 89, 92, 238
WASP (White Anglo Saxon Protestant), 17, 23, 24, 106, 109, 115, 164, 189, 190, 191, 286
Welsh, 2
West Bengal, India, 381

Western Christianity, Croats, 67
West Indian immigrants, 9–10, 16–17, 20–21, 24, 27, 62–63, 99, 115–16, 117, 124, 125, 151, 159, 160, 162, 163, 164, 198–99
White, 24, 25, 121, 151–52, 161, 183–97, 203, 210–14. *See also* WASP (White Anglo Saxon Protestant)
  in Africa, 145
  in Brazil (Branco), 3, 22, 92, 199, 230, 231
  in Changeland, 242–44, 249
  of Irish origin, in U.S., 89
  in Limitedchangeland, 246–48, 249
  in Nochangeland, 245–46, 249
  in Oneland, 196, 197
  in Puerto Rico, 2
  in U.S., 23, 60, 67, 72, 76, 82, 89, 97, 154, 163, 210
  White Americans, 76
White working class in U.S., 60
White Zulu in South Africa, *193n3*
Wilmington riots (North Carolina), *368n14*, 382–83
World War I, 391
World War II, 391–92, 405, 410

X
Xhosa in South Africa, 9, 10, 13, 66, 69, 74, 75, 77, 89, 91, 92, 329, 330, 338

Y
Yellow (Amerelo) in Brazil, 231
Yoruba
  Christian, 86
  Muslim, 86, 87
  Nigeria, 8, 9, 10, 65, 66, 68, 69, 73, 74, 75, 77, 85, 86, 87, 89, 92
Yoruba-Nagot (Nigeria), 324, 325
Yugoslavia
  Bosnian Muslims, 2, 79, 102–3
  Muslim in, 79, 81, 388
  Serbs and Croats, 9, 10, 65, 66, 67, 76, 77

Z
Zaire, 250
Zambia, 23, 27, 144, 145, 151, 172, 202, 250, 266, 317, 327
  Bemba, 250, 266
Zimbabwe, 317, 327, 330, 334
Zulu in South Africa, 9, 10, 13, 66, 69, 74, 75, 77, 89, 91, 92, 193, 328, 329, 330, 338

CONCEPT INDEX

The following designations appear in this index: "n" (footnote), "t" (table), and "f" (figure).

A

absence of change in ethnic identities or
  categories, 22, 134
activated ethnic demography definition and
  illustrations, 29, 196–98, 229–31, 237–38
activated ethnic identity, 101
  activated, definition, 9–13, 59, 62, 101–2
  definition and illustrations, 9, 11–13
  elections, examples of activation of new
    ethnic identity categories, 250–55
  reclassification of activated ethnic identity
    categories within an existing repertoire of
    categories, 20–21, 162–64
activating an ethnic identity or
  category, 115–16
agent based modeling
  causal mechanisms, 278, 284, 357
  complexity, 283, 429
  counterfactuals, 42, 428
  distributions of expected outcomes,
    278, 284
  game theoretic models, 279
  identity repertoires (both attributes and
    categories), 31, 287–88, 343, 429–39
  modeling interactions between simultaneous
    processes, 31, 284, 297
  new research questions, 31, 42, 297, 422
  precise predictions, 278, 285
  as strategy for studying rare events, 427–28
  as strategy for thought experiment, 427
  as tool to explore constructivist propositions,
    78, 357
anarchy and ethnic war, 56, 139. See also war,
  generally
anatomy of VirPak, 428–30
ancestry
  common ancestry. See common ancestry

as distinguished from common ancestry, 71,
  84, 86, 158, 166–67, 169
  myth of ancestry, 71, 119
anger, 27, 36, 388, 400–401, 403–11, 413,
  417–18, 421
anger curves
  exponential decay, 407f
  functions or, 405–9
  inverse exponential, 406f, 407
  linear,406f, 407
  mixed exponential, 407f
apathetic agents vs. fanatics in VirPak, 441–42
APSA CP symposium, cumulative findings in
  the study of ethnic politics, 5, 43
ascriptive, terminology, 69–73
assigned identities, 101–2
assimilation, 31, 39, 162, 202, 279,
  280–81, 292
attribute
  basic attributes
    defined, 106–8
    disaggregation of, 124n5, 157, 254
  category, distinction, 105–6, 182–83
  commonsensical, 106, 183–84, 205, 210,
    236, 244
  defined, 9–10, 105, 182
  descent based. See descent based attributes
  disaggregation of basic attributes, 124n5,
    157, 254
  distribution of attribute repertoires for a
    population. See attribute repertoires
  distributions. See distributions of attributes
  non-descent based attributes, 119–20, 122
  replacement or switching, 26, 133, 160–61,
    174, 176, 180–81, 197, 200–202, 279, 283
  secondary attributes, defined, 106–8
attribute descent rule for membership, 52, 69,
  71, 98, 100, 109

attribute dimension
 addition or subtraction of, 26, 180–81, 197,
  203–5, 300–304
 category dimension, distinction, 108–9,
  183–84
 commonsensical, 23, 134, 180–81, 184, 188,
  203–6, 210, 236, 361
 definition, 24–25, 108, 183
 independence of, 185
 population repertoire. *See* population,
  repertoire of attributes
 relationships between, 206–8
 salience of, 279–83, 287, 290–92, 297,
  299–304
 stickiness of, 31, 40, 134, 278–79
attribute repertoires
 change in, 17–18, 21, 26, 181, 203–5
 commonsensical, 186, 191, 233, 236, 240
 construction of, 153–57
 distribution of, 29, 186–88
 evolution of, 277–78, 295–96, 300–304
 individual. *See* individual, repertoire of
  attributes
 individual, defined, 185–86
 population. *See* population, repertoire of
  attributes
 switching of descent based attributes within a
  repertoire, 21, 160–62, 176t
attribute value
 commonsensical, 20–24, 180–81, 236, 361
 definition, 24–25, 108, 183–84

B
baseline conditions in VirPak, 41–42, 428–29,
  434, 436–37, 446, 448, 450
baseline constraint on ethnic identity change,
  17, 25, 124, 163
baseline model of change in ethnic demography,
  objective, 29–30, 231–32, 235
biology or sociobiology, 129n7, 149–50
bipolar cleavage structure, 3, 234, 255, 259,
  263–64
broadcaster agents in VirPak, 443
bureaucratic authority in VirPak, levels, 440–43
bureaucrats in VirPak, distribution of power,
  439–40

C
cabinet stability, 318–21
caste, 9, 12, 23, 27, 54, 60–65, 109, 113–14,
  128, 130, 144–45, 151, 155, 168–69, 189,
  190, 206, 238, 244, 251–52, 266, 268,
  287, 291, 293, 300, 340, 360, 363–65,
  373, 411
 definition of ethnic identity, 9, 51, 61–65

categorical approach to identity, 97
category *See also* coalitions; ethnic identities or
  categories; identity
 activated, 101
 assigned, 101–2
 chosen, 101–2
 as combination, 24, 179–80, 188–89
 complex or compound, 247–86
 definition, 9, 100, 105–6, 182–83
 distinction between category and attribute,
  105–6, 182–83
 hyphenated, 80
 as identity, 100–105
 minimum winning. *See* minimum winning
  coalition
 nominal, 101
 simple, 286
category dimension
 attribute dimension, distinction, 108–9,
  183–84
 definition, 24–25, 108, 183
 state disintegration and reconstruction, 391,
  392, 396
causal claims about effect of ethnicity
 conceptually justified, 99–100, 126–28
 need for definition, 13, 52–55
 properties assumed by, 55–58
 weakness of, 94–96
CDEI (Constructivist Dataset on Ethnicity and
  Institutions), 238
census, 20, 28, 39, 67, 107, 111, 134, 144,
  152–57, 159, 167–69, 171, 173, 176,
  199, 200, 204, 206, 229–32, 252, 272,
  389, 433n10. *See also* institutions of
  cognition
 role in constructing attribute and category
  repertoire, 153–57
centrally focused cleavage structure, 259
change in ethnic identity. *See* ethnic identities or
  categories, change in
change in membership, 166–67
change in membership rule, 98–99, 165–69
change in name, 168–69
change in non ethnic identities or categories or
  demographies, 17, 31, 39, 57, 123, 164,
  257
choosing a leader, 291–92, 309
chosen identities, 101–2
civil war. *See* war, generally
clan, 9, 51, 61–65, 69, 109, 128, 130, 160, 193,
  430–31, 434–35, 437
clan and definition of an ethnic identity, 9, 51,
  61–65
cleavage freezing theory, 281–82
cleavage salience, 280–83
cleavage structure
 bipolar, defined, 3, 234, 255, 259, 263–64

centrally focused, 259
coinciding, defined, 207, 259, 261–62
cross cutting, defined, 32, 207, 255, 259,
    260–61
dispersed, 259
electoral volatility, 318–21, 323–30
multipolar, defined, 3, 33, 233–34, 255, 256,
    259, 263
nested, defined, 32, 35, 207, 213–14,
    264–66, 323–30
possibility of ethnic identity change, 29,
    38–39, 233–34, 255, 259, 271
clientelistic party competition, 364
coalition governments, 282
coalitions. *See also* ethnic identities or
    categories
complex, 354–57
connected, defined, 35, 209, 270, 288, 362,
    369
leaders, 288–89, 304–9
low optimal coalition size and salience of
    sticky dimensions, 344–45
minimum winning coalition (MWC),
    defined, 241
multiple winning coalitions, 328
optimal winning coalition. *See* optimal
    winning coalition (OWC)
coinciding cleavage structure, 207, 259,
    261–62
collective identities, 102
colonial, 57, 59, 77, 143–45, 160, 200, 202–3,
    206, 230, 250, 253, 282, 364n9, 372,
    372n20, 373–74, 378
combinatorial approach, summary and
    justification, 22–25, 179–80
combinatorics, translating constructivist
    mechanisms into, 25–26, 180–81
commitment problem, 139
common ancestry, 10–11, 52, 71, 73–76, 93,
    125
    myth of, 10–11, 51n1, 52, 71, 74, 76–78,
        80, 93, 125
common culture, 10–11, 51–52, 69–73, 85–88,
    93, 96, 100, 125–26, 142
common history, 10, 52, 55–56, 71–73, 90–93,
    95, 125
common language, 10–12, 52, 71–72, 74,
    86–90, 93, 125, 131, 142
common region or place of origin, 10, 24–25,
    52, 63, 71, 73–74, 78–80, 91, 93, 96, 125,
    153, 158, 183, 187, 196, 202, 204, 207–8,
    212, 261, 264, 268, 313
    myth of, 10, 52, 71, 74, 80–81, 91, 93, 125
commonsensical attribute dimensions, 23,
    134, 180–81, 184, 188, 203–6, 210,
    236, 361

commonsensical attribute repertoires, 186, 191,
    233, 236, 240
common territory, 10, 52, 58, 71–74, 91–93,
    125, 136. *See also* regional concentration
    (or territorial, spatial, geographic
    concentration)
communal violence, 361n5
communications technologies, 142, 143
complexity in models of ethnic identity change,
    6, 22–23, 27, 28
complex or compound category, 247, 286
compound or complex category, 247, 286
concentration of attributes, defined, p. 278
conceptual autonomy, 74, 92
consistency requirement, 14–15, 99, 117–18
consociational, consociationalism, 138,
    357–58
constrained change, property of ethnic
    identities, 16–19, 123–24, 133, 150
constraints
    on change in ethnic identity. *See* ethnic
        identities or categories, change in
    environmental, 17
    intrinsic, 17
constructivism
    classic arguments, 139–49
    combinatorics, translating constructivist
        mechanisms into, 25–26, 180–81
    counterfactuals and, 22–23, 27–28, 30–31,
        36, 172, 177, 193, 235
    data and measurement issues, 5, 110n3, 188,
        238–39, 268, 323–26, 340
    definition, 18–19, 132, 139
    disagreements within, 20f, 139–41, 140f
    synthesis, 18–22, 141–42, 152–75
    variants of, 133
    what it is not, 19, 149–52
Constructivist Dataset on Ethnicity and
    Institutions (CDEI), 238
constructivist models of electoral volatility,
    326–30
constructivist variables and mechanisms, 176t
contempt, 401–2, 411–17
coordination device, 356
coordination failure, 318–21, 339
coordination problem, 211, 316, 319–20, 328,
    330, 338, 339
cost benefit calculations, 281, 403–4, 418,
    423
counterfactual futures, VirPak, 42, 428
counterfactuals and constructivism, 22–23,
    27–28, 30–31, 36, 172, 177, 193, 235
cross cutting cleavage structure, 32, 207, 255,
    259, 260–61
cultural distance, 33, 35
cultural membership rule, 52, 69–70, 109

culture, 54, 59, 70, 81, 112–13, 131, 148–49,
    165, 168–69, 209, 213–14, 280, 287, 312,
    329n9, 364, 366, 391–92, 402, 411–12,
    418–19, 423–26, 428n6, 449
  common culture. *See* common culture
  defined, 86–88
  role in this book's definition of ethnic
    identity, 72–73
cumulative findings in the study of ethnic
    politics, APSA CP symposium, 5, 43

D

democracy, 1n1, 3, 6n3, 39–40, 53, 58,
    105, 137, 316–17. *See also* patronage
    democracies
democratic theory, 29–31, 39
demography. *See* ethnic demography
Derek, fictionalized example, introduced, 62
descent, different specifications of in definitions
    of ethnic identity, 10, 52
descent, imperfect correlation with ethnicity,
    63, 123
descent based attributes. *See also* attribute
  attribute descent rule for membership, 52, 69,
    71, 98, 100, 109
  defined, 59
  necessary for membership in ethnic category,
    9, 11, 51, 58–60
  need not be sufficient for membership in
    ethnic category, 58–60
  properties of, 14–16, 117–23
  stickiness of, 14–16, 117–21
  switching of attributes within a repertoire, 21,
    160–62, 176t
  visibility of, 14–16, 117, 121–23
descent based categories, 9, 52, 60, 61, 99
descent based membership rules, 9–11, 53,
    66–69, 71, 109
descent rule
  attribute descent rule for membership, 52, 69,
    71, 98, 100, 109
  group descent rule, 69–70, 72, 74, 81–85,
    109–11
dialect, 9, 51, 61–65, 67–69, 86, 89, 109, 130,
    142
  definition of an ethnic identity, 9, 51, 61–65
dimension. *See* attribute dimension; category
    dimension; issue dimension
disaggregating ethnicity, 11, 12f, 126–27
disaggregation of basic attributes, 124n5, 157,
    254
discourse or discursive framework, 131, 143–44,
    147, 163, 173, 203, 208
dispersed cleavage structure, 259
distribution of attribute repertoires for a
    population. *See* attribute repertoires,
    distribution of

distribution of identity repertoires in VirPak,
    433–39
distributions of attributes
  objective change in distribution of attributes,
    14–16, 118–21
  by stickiness, 15f, 118f
  by visibility, 15f, 118f
distributive politics, 33, 342, 344, 378
divide the dollar game, 322
division of labor, 55t, 57, 95
dominant group, dominance, 419, 440, 444, 449
dynamics or evolution of ethnic demography,
    30–31, 34, 38, 42, 47, 272, 277–311

E

economic growth, 1n1, 2–43, 6, 139, 178
education or educational system, 3, 107, 122,
    155
effective number of parties (ENP), 335, 337
elections
  activation of new ethnic identity categories,
    examples, 250–55
  in Africa, 321–23
  ethnic identity change, 3, 21, 29–34, 44,
    95, 145, 233, 239–46, 291–95, 312–40,
    345–57, 359–86, 361–72
electoral stability, 319–21, 330
electoral systems
  generally, 229–72
  permissive, 314
  plurality rule, 271, 314
  proportional, 2, 40, 269
  restrictive, 314–15
electoral volatility, 32–33, 315–18, 324–40
  Africa, 312–40
  seat volatility *vs.* vote volatility, 331n10
ELF index, 238–39, 266, 269
emotions
  anger. *See* anger
  contempt. *See* contempt
  definition of, 397
  effects of, 398–99, 400, 418
  fear, 56, 281, 399–400
  hatred, 40–41, 56, 132, 136–37
  incorporation into analysis, 403–17, 411–12
  rational choice and, 399, 420–21
  resentment, 402–3, 421
endogeneity of ethnic identity, 4, 6, 132, 140,
    177–78
endogenous identities, 132
entrepreneur agents in VirPak, 441
entrepreneurs and entrepreneurship, 32–35, 37,
    40, 44, 78, 112, 114–15, 147, 151, 157, 165,
    233, 235, 241, 243, 250, 252, 271–72, 286,
    293, 295, 338, 341, 343–44, 354, 357, 361,
    364, 368–69, 373, 388–90, 391, 393–94,
    396–97, 404, 411, 415, 419, 441–42

entropy resistant, 287
erasure requirement, 14–15, 99, 117–18
ethnic, English language usage, 54
ethnic antipathy, 40, 267, 359–60
ethnic categories or demographies
    (transformation to non ethnic), 31, 34,
    169
ethnic demography
    activated ethnic demography, definition
        and illustrations, 29, 196–98, 229–31,
        237–38
    baseline model of change in ethnic
        demography in, 29–30, 229–76
    dynamics or evolution, 30–31, 34, 38, 42, 47,
        272, 277–311
    evolution of, stickiness, 287–88, 311t
    independent variable, implications for using
        ethnic demography as, 266–69
    possibility of change in, 29, 229–72
    size and demography, 297f
    structural, 237–39, 266, 277
ethnic diversity
    challenging bad name perception, 6–7
    definition and measurement, 237–39.
        See also ELF index
ethnic fractionalization. *See* ELF index; ethnic
    diversity
ethnic group, 321–23. *See also* ethnic identities
    or categories
    categories distinguished, 63–64
    nations distinguished, 63–64
    use of term in analysis, 313–14
ethnic heterogeneity. *See* ELF index; ethnic
    diversity
ethnic identities or categories.
    See also coalitions; ethnic identities or
        categories, change in; identity
    activated category. *See* activated ethnic
        identity
    alternative definitions, 10, 52, 69–73
    assigned, 101–2
    attribute, distinction, 105–6, 182–83
    chosen, defined, 51, 101–2, 115–17
    as combination 24, 179–80, 188–89
    complex or compound category, 247, 286
    construction of membership rule, 66, 72–73,
        110–11
    content of, 100, 112–13
    conventional classification, 51–52, 54,
        64–66
    defining and supplementary features,
        distinctions, 111–15
    definition introduced in this book, 9–11,
        58–63
    evaluating definitions against classification,
        10, 51, 52–54, 66–69, 73–93

full repertoire. *See* full repertoire of ethnic
    identities
individual repertoire. *See* individual repertoire
    of categories
intrinsic properties, 16–17, 99, 123–26
membership, 100, 111–12
membership rule, 66, 72–73, 100, 109–11
name, 113–15
name of a category expressed as a
    combination, 190–91
nominal, defined, 9–13, 58–59
operative repertoire. *See* operative repertoire
    of ethnic identities or categories
population repertoire. *See* population,
    repertoire of categories
properties that are not intrinsic, 53, 93–94
repertoire. *See* repertoire of ethnic
    identities
ethnic identities or categories, change in
    absence of, 22, 134
    combinatorial translation of constructivist
        mechanisms, 22–26, 179–82, 197–206
    complexity in models of, 6, 22–23, 27, 28
    constraints, 17, 150
    constructivist mechanisms, 6, 20–22, 133–35,
        152–65
    content, 167–68
    frequency of, 19–20, 140–42
    importance of definition, 10–11
    instrumental calculation, 34, 151–52
    interaction between short and long term, 18,
        164–65
    long term change. *See* ethnic identity change,
        long term
    membership, 166–67
    membership rule, 98–99, 165–69
    models of, 6, 7, 13, 22–23, 26–38, 175–78
    multiple motivations, 4, 22, 27, 132, 134,
        147, 163, 175, 181, 241, 359–60, 373,
        385–86, 388
    name, 168–69
    as punctuated equilibrium, 19, 141
    as reclassification, 20–21, 162–64
    as recombination, 24, 180–81, 198–200
    short term change. *See* ethnic identity change,
        short term
    speed of, 19–20, 140–42
    supplemental features, 165–70
    variables affecting, 170–78
ethnic identity change, long term, 16–21, 25,
    30, 107, 120–21, 133–34, 150, 152, 156,
    159, 164–65, 179, 184, 241, 272, 293,
    312, 316, 320, 332
    interaction between short and long term, 18,
        164–65

ethnic identity change, short term, 11, 14,
    16–21, 24, 29–32, 99, 107, 117, 120,
    123–24, 129, 132–33, 141, 150, 152, 156,
    159–60, 162, 165, 171, 173–74, 177–81,
    183–84, 197, 199–200, 229, 231, 233,
    235, 239, 241, 253, 255, 257, 272, 278,
    314, 340, 365
    interaction with long term changes, 18,
        164–65
ethnicID specification for model construction,
    298–311
ethnicity, disaggregated, 126–27
ethnic practice, defined, 11–12
ethnic practice and ethnic structure,
    relationship, 11–12, 18, 165
ethnic riots
    constituency and state level incentives for,
        363f
    generally, 359–86
    linear order restriction, 213, 362
    linked to identity construction and change,
        146–48, 173–74, 176t
    as method to fix attribute dimension and
        category, 361
    multilevel model of, 362–64
    in non democracies, 372–74
    as outcome of political competition, 380–84
    political and strategic nature, 368
ethnic structure
    defined, 11, 12f
    electoral volatility, 313, 318–21
    operationalization and measurement, 238–39,
        323–26
ethnic threat, 367
ethnic violence. *See* violence
ethnic war as result of commitment problem,
    139. *See also* war, generally
evolution or dynamics ethnic demography,
    30–31, 34, 38, 42, 47, 272, 277–311
exogeneity or exogenous identities, 5, 53, 93,
    141. *See also* primordialism

F
fanatics *vs.* apathetic agents in VirPak, 441–42
fear, 56, 281, 399–400
Fearon's argument linking pork and ethnic
    identity activation, 342–45, 353
fission, 26
fixed and singular identities, 258f, 132, 136, .
    See also primordialism
fixedness, 5, 53, 55t, 93. *See also* primordialism
fluidity, electoral volatility levels, 338
fluidity, ethnic identities, 150–51.
    See also constructivism
franchise, 369–70, 374
frequency of ethnic identity change, 19–20,
    140–42

full repertoire of ethnic identities or categories
    defined, 157–59
    individuals, 195
    populations, 191–92
    size of, 158–59, 192–93
fusion, 26

G
game theory, 279, 280, 283, 284
Gaysian category example, first and second level
    attributes, 107–8
genetics, 14, 45–46, 59, 112, 122, 149
genocide/genocidal, 3, 267, 408–9
governing identity in VirPak, 438
government bureaucrats in VirPak, 439
group descent rule, 69–70, 72, 74, 81–85,
    109–11
growth areas in research and ethnic politics,
    138–39

H
hatred, 40–41, 56, 132, 136–37
Helen, fictionalized example, introduced, 9–10,
    62
Herfindahl index, 297f
Hindu Muslim riot, 360, 372n20, 385–86
history. *See* common history
hybridity, 20f,, 140–41, 148–49
hyphenated categories, 80
hyphenated names, 114–15

I
Identity or identities. *See also* ethnic identities
    or categories
    activated, 101
    assigned, 101–2
    categorical approaches to, 97
    as category, 101–5
    chosen, 101–2
    collective, 102
    content, 100
    definition, 100
    ethnic. *See* ethnic identities or categories
    individual, 102
    membership, 100
    membership rule, 100
    name, 100
    nominal, 101
    obtainable, 38, 433, 435
    private, 102–3
    public, 102–3
    unobtainable, 38, 433, 435
identity repertoire. *See* repertoire of ethnic
    identities
ideology, 322–23, 425
imagined community, 148

incumbency advantage, 316
independent variable, implications for using
  ethnic demography as, 266–69
index of ethnolinguistic fractionalization (ELF
  index), 238–39, 266, 269
index of permanent exclusion, 275–76
indifference curves, 36, 399, 412–13
indigenous, 111–12, 114, 231f
indirect rule, 145
individual identities, 102
individual repertoire of attributes, 185–86
individual repertoire of categories
  full repertoire of ethnic identities, 195
  operative repertoire of ethnic identities,
    195–96, 219–20, 221–22, 224–25
  switching by individual within a repertoire,
    21, 160–62
industrialization, 3, 121, 142–43
industrial revolution, 143
information
  limited, 33, 57, 146, 270, 289, 291
  perfect, 184, 239–40, 270
innovators in VirPak, 442
institutionalization, volatility as key component,
  316
institutionalized politics, identities activated in,
  12
institutionally determined winning threshold,
  234
institutions, 30–31, 53, 55t, 107
institutions of cognition, 143–44, 153–57,
  170–71. *See also* census
institutions that structure incentives, 144–45,
  159, 171–73, 176t. *See also* electoral
  system; indirect rule; parliamentary
  systems; parties and party systems;
  presidentialism
instrumentalism, 151–52
intermarriage, 16
interpretive schemes, 154–56
intrinsic properties, claims based on, 127–28
issue dimension, 35, 44, 270, 361–63, 365, 367,
  369, 374–77, 385

K
k (institutionally determined winning
  threshold), 234

L
landlord identity in VirPak, 437–38
landownership, 37, 61, 430–31, 433–35, 441,
  446
language, 23, 27, 54, 59, 67–69, 86, 109, 114,
  121–22, 130–31, 142, 144–45, 151, 161,
  170–72, 174, 189, 201–2, 206, 209,
  230–39, 250–51, 266, 268, 270, 272, 281,

287, 296, 329n9, 338, 352–53, 361, 363,
  370, 389, 392–97, 402–3, 407, 414–17,
  419–20, 433n10
  common. *See* common language
  definition of ethnic identity, 9, 51, 61–65,
    86–90
  standardization, 3, 142–43, 206, 278
language modernization, effect on identities,
  142–43
language or linguistic assimilation, 31, 162, 202,
  280–81
language or vocabulary
  combinatorial, 23–24, 46, 133, 152–53,
    179–228
  conceptual, 6, 97–131, 135, 149, 152–53,
    170–74
lattice, 244, 273
leaders. *See also* entrepreneurs and
  entrepreneurship
  choosing a leader, 291–92
  coalitions, 288–89, 304–9
leadership stability, 30–31, 278
leadership tenure, 279, 293–95, 345–58
  correlation between number of attributes
    accepted, 355t
  optimal coalition size and, 294f
  by stickiness, 351f
leadership turnover, 33, 39–40
legislative volatility, 316, 331–40
  estimates, 336
levels and evolution of political demography,
  experiment, 295–96
linear order restriction, 213
  ethnic riots, 362
long term change in ethnic identity. *See* ethnic
  identity change, long term
low optimal coalition size and salience of sticky
  dimensions, 344–45

M
magnitude of possible ethnic identity change,
  229, 246–48
majority, 2, 3, 28–29, 39, 51n1, 58, 70,
  92, 112–13, 116, 139, 151, 167, 174,
  199–201, 229–31, 239–76, 280, 295, 316,
  318–22, 326, 330, 338, 344, 347, 351,
  361–62, 369–70, 374–76, 378, 380, 382,
  388, 394, 397, 411, 419–20, 435–37, 446,
  449–50
majoritarian governments, 318
  stability of, 318–19
majoritarianism concept, 267
majority dominant distributions of attribute
  repertoires, 256–57
majority rule, 248–49
majority threshold (k), varying, 248–49
mechanisms and variables, 176t

membership
    ethnic identities or categories, 111–12
    ethnic identities or categories, change in,
        166–67
membership rule
    attribute descent rule for membership, 52, 69,
        71, 98, 100, 109
    construction of, 66, 72–73, 110–11
    cultural membership rule, 52, 69–70, 109
    descent based, 9–11, 53, 66–69, 71, 109
    ethnic category defined by, 109–11
    ethnic identity, 109–11
        construction of, 66, 72–73, 110–11
    ethnic identity change, 98–99, 165–69
    group descent rule, 69–70, 72, 74, 81–85,
        109–11
    identities, 100
    name, 113–14
migration, 3, 16, 69, 79, 85, 121, 155, 161, 201,
    206, 229, 374, 383
military identity in VirPak, 437
minimum winning coalition (MWC), defined,
    241
minority, 28, 39, 42, 54, 58, 64–66, 96, 112–16,
    139, 149, 151, 174, 199–201, 229–31,
    244–47, 252, 256–58, 263, 267, 269,
    280, 318–19, 347, 359, 363, 366, 369–70,
    372–74, 381–84, 391, 393–95, 419, 434,
    444–45, 449
minority parties, 318–19
minority party governments, 318–19
mobilization of ethnicity, advantages, 363–64
modeling interactive relationship between
        different components of ethnic identity,
        43–44
models of constructivism and electoral volatility,
    326–30
models of ethnic identity change, 175–78
modernization
    arguments based on, 170
    effect on identities, 142–43
    language modernization, effect on identities,
        142–43
Mohajir and Muhajir. *See* Names Index
Moore neighborhood, 286n4, 292, 298
motivations driving ethnic identity change, 4,
    22, 27, 132, 134, 147, 163, 175, 181, 241,
    359–60, 373, 385–86, 388
Muhajirs, VirPak, 436–37. *See also* Mohajir and
    Muhajir in Names Index
multidimensionality, 22–24, 325, 330, 337,
    339–40
multiparty elections, 250, 331, 333
multiple identities, *See* constructivism;
    multidimensionality

multiple potential groups larger than 50%, 320,
    324, 339–40
multiple winning coalitions, 35, 269, 314, 320,
    323, 328–30, 333–34, 337, 339
multipolar cleavage structure, 3, 33, 233–34,
    255, 256, 259, 263
Muslim fundamentalists, VirPak, 436, 437, 443
MWC. *See* minimum winning coalition (MWC)
myth of common ancestry. *See* common
    ancestry
myth of common region of origin. *See* common
    region or place of origin

N
name
    change in, 168–69
    ethnic identity change, 168–69
    genealogy, 114
    hyphenated, 114–15
    identities, 100
    information about content, 114
    membership rule, 113–14
    self perception, 114–15
    strategy, 114–15
    supplementary, not defining, feature of ethnic
        identity 113–15
name of a category expressed as a combination,
    190–91
naming of a category, self perceptions and
        strategies, 114
nation or nationality
    definition of ethnic identity, 9, 51, 54,
        61–65
    distinguished from ethnic group, 54, 57,
        63–64, 70
    generally, 23, 66, 70, 105,
        109, 130, 142, 148–49, 189, 283, 388,
        391–97, 419–20
nested cleavage structure, 32, 35, 207,
    213–14, 264–66, 323–30
nestedness and electoral volatility, 323–30
nestedness restriction, 213–14, 222–26
networks, 53, 55t, 57, 94–95, 126, 152, 363,
    364, 430, 435–36, 438–39, 442
new fields of study, 43–46
nominal ethnic identities. *See* ethnic identities
    or categories
nominal identity, 101
non descent based attributes, 119–20, 122
non ethnic identities or categories, defined,
    63–64
non ethnic identity change, 17, 31, 39, 57, 123,
    164, 257
number of dimensions restriction, 210–13

O

objective change in distribution of attributes, 14–16, 118–21
obtainable identity or identities, 38, 433
operative repertoire of ethnic identities or categories
  defined, 159–60
  individual, 195–96, 219–20, 221–22, 224–25
  linear order restriction, 213, 362
  nestedness restriction, 213–14
  number of dimensions restriction, 210–13
  overlap restriction, 210
  population, 193–95, 221, 223–24
  restrictions, defining, 208–14
  size of, generally, 160, 193–95, 208–14
optimal winning coalition (OWC).
  See also coalitions
  defined, 289
  low optimal coalition size and salience of sticky dimensions, 344–45
  size and demography, 297f
  size and leadership tenure, 294f
  stickiness, variation, 293–95
overlap restriction, 210
OWC. *See* optimal winning coalition (OWC)

P

parliamentary systems, 322
partial models of ethnic processes, 279
partitions, 255–56
party identification, 375
parties and party systems, 1, 2, 13, 20–21, 27, 32, 40–41, 44, 62–63, 65, 94–95, 102, 104, 112–14, 119–20, 122, 134, 139, 144–45, 153, 159, 163, 167, 171–72, 174, 199, 250–51, 266, 281, 285, 295, 312–40, 341–43, 356–57, 361, 363–64, 367–68, 370, 374–75, 378–83, 385–86, 392, 411, 425, 431
party systems and ethnic diversity, 314–15
passing or switching within an existing population repertoire of attributes, 160–62, 172, 174, 180, 200–201
patronage, 20f, 40, 57, 140f, 173, 176t
  causal claims about effect of ethnicity on, 145–46
patronage democracies, 145–46, 173, 176t, 239–40
patronage politics, examples of properties assumed by, 56–57
payoffs, 27, 41, 147, 152, 162, 202, 241, 271, 280f, 281, 365, 367, 370, 383, 388, 391, 395–96, 399, 405–10, 412–13, 415
peasant identity in VirPak, 437
Pedersen's index of volatility, 315, 331
permanent exclusion, index of, 275–76

permissive electoral systems. *See* electoral systems, permissive
personal and ethnoregional appeals for support, 322
physical differences
  definition of ethnic identity, 9, 51, 54, 61–65
  features or attributes, 10, 14, 59, 66–69, 105, 109, 113, 118, 122, 130, 160–61, 364, 383
pivot or pivotal, 282, 362n6, 383–5, 417
place of origin, 24–25, 63, 114, 153, 158, 183, 187, 194, 196, 202, 207–8, 212, 261, 264, 268, 313. *See also* common region or place of origin
plurality rule, 271, 314. *See also* electoral systems
polarization, 89, 147, 318, 352, 361–64, 369, 381, 444
polarized policy goods, 352–54
policy preferences, 27, 44, 313, 321
political agency, 234–35, 271
political demography, levels and evolution of political demography; experiment, 295–96
political entrepreneurs. *See* entrepreneurs and entrepreneurship
political identity game, 342–45
political parties. *See* parties and party systems
population repertoire of attributes
  defined, 184–85
  passing or switching within an existing population repertoire of attributes, 160–62
  three dimensional case, 188t
  two dimensional case, 186t, 187t
population repertoire of categories
  full repertoire, 191–92
  operative repertoire, 193–95, 221, 223–24
pork based politics, 33–34, 47, 288, 341–58
poset, 216, 221–22, 244, 273–74
Posner's identity matrix, 23n4, 282–83
Posner's model of dimensional salience, 280, 282
possibility of change in ethnic demography, 29, 229–72
possible activated ethnic demographies, 244f, 246f
preferences, assumption of stability, 399
prejudice, 387, 401–2, 411, 417
presidentialism, 321–22
primary categories, 103–4
primary identity, 103
primordialism, 28–29, 132, 135–42
  definition, 19–20, 135–36
primordialist
  approach, constructivists refutation, 19
  arguments, 136
  assumptions in theories of politics and economics, 1n1, 4
  beliefs, 8

print capitalism, 142, 143
private and public life, distinction, identities activated in, 12–13
private identity, 102–3
programmatic party competition, 364
properties intrinsically associated with ethnic identities, 16–17, 53, 93–94, 99, 123–28
properties not intrinsically associated with ethnic identities, 53, 93–94
proportional electoral systems. *See* electoral systems, proportional
public goods, 2, 3, 6n3, 7n3, 38, 40, 57, 139, 204, 267
public identity, 102–3
punctuated equilibrium, 19, 141

R

race, and definition of ethnic identity, 9, 51, 54, 61–65
race or racial, generally, 9, 13, 23, 54, 80–81, 84, 90, 97, 105, 108–10, 116–17, 121, 128, 130, 145, 149, 155, 158, 167, 197, 204, 206, 281–83, 286–87, 329n9, 360, 383, 402, 413
ranking of dimension, 302, 367
rare events, 422, 427–28
rational choice, 341n1, 353n9, 359, 391–97, 417–21
    role in state disintegration and reconstruction, 399, 420–21
rational choice cycle, 390–91
rationalist account of riots, 359–60
rationality based model, 387–421
reclassification, definition and illustration, 20–21, 24, 26, 162–64
reclassification of activated ethnic identity categories within an existing repertoire of categories, 20–21, 162–64
recombination, definition and illustration, 24, 180–81, 198–200
region, role in definition of ethnic identity, 9, 51, 61–65
regional concentration (or territorial, spatial, geographic concentration), 37, 42, 55, 57, 63–64, 81, 95–96, 146, 173, 315, 393, 422, 429, 435, 437–39, 441–42, 445, 449. *See also* common territory
region of origin, myth of common. *See* common region or place of origin
religion, and definition of ethnic identity, 9, 51, 54, 61–65
religion or religious, 12–13, 23, 27, 37, 54, 59, 65, 67, 70–71, 81, 86–87, 102–3, 105, 109, 112, 122, 128, 130–31, 144–45, 148, 151, 153, 155, 158, 160, 172, 190, 205–6, 211, 250, 252, 266, 268, 281–82, 286,

288–89, 291, 300, 305, 321, 340, 349, 355, 362–64, 369–70, 373, 375–77, 379, 381, 389–90, 414–16, 430–32, 435, 437, 441, 444
repertoire of ethnic identities
    concept, 157–59
    full repertoire. *See* full repertoire of ethnic identities or categories
    operative repertoire. *See* operative repertoire of ethnic identities or categories
    repertoire of descent based attributes. *See* attribute repertoires
    switching by individual within a repertoire, 21, 160–62
    updating repertoire, 304
replacement or attempt to acquire politically valuable attributes, 279, 280–81
research on ethnic politics, growth areas in, 138–39
resentment, 402–3
    role in state disintegration and reconstruction, 421
restrictive electoral systems. *See* electoral systems
reverse causal effects or causation, 3n2, 40, 139
riot prone cities, 385
riots. *See* ethnic riots

S

salience of ethnic attribute-dimensions, 31, 40, 134, 278, 280–83, 287, 290–92, 297, 299, 301, 304, 344–45, 349–51, 357, 397
seat volatility *vs.* vote volatility, 331n10
secession and ethnicity, 1n1, 7, 37–38, 42, 422–52
secession of the center, or center secession, defined, 424–25
secession or state contraction, defined, 421–23
sect, 65, 109, 130, 155, 438
    definition of ethnic identity, 9, 51, 54, 61–65
security dilemma, 55–56, 138–39
selectorate, 40, 344, 358, 369
self deception, 400
self perceptions and strategies of those who name a category, 114
self placement and group membership, 82t, 83
set theory, 23n4
Shapley Shubik index, 35, 362n6, 369
short term change in ethnic identity. *See* ethnic identity change, short term
sibling restriction, 61–63, 129
single-member plurality rule, 271, 314
skin color, 9–10, 14, 16, 21, 24–25, 59, 62, 65, 72, 97, 99, 106, 108–10, 116, 119, 121–22, 124–25, 149, 153–56, 161, 165,

183–85, 187, 189, 190, 194, 196–98, 200, 202–4, 207–8, 212–13, 236, 261, 264, 313
small world effect, 299
social distance, 298–99, 304n17
social identity theory, 365
social psychological approach, 359–60, 362
sociobiology or biology, 129n7, 149–50
sons of the soil, 364, 435
speed of ethnic identity change, 19–20, 140–42
state, 3, 12, 35, 42, 53, 55–57, 64, 67, 91, 107, 140–42, 144–46, 160, 177, 272, 281–82, 363–64, 368–72, 378–79, 384–86, 423, 438, 440, 444, 449–50
    colonial, 160, 282, 378. *See also* colonial institutions of cognition institutions that structure incentives
    formation, 2, 3n2
    imperial, 423–24
    rebuilding of, 415
    rightsizing, 423
    size, 423
state collapse, 1n1, 2, 7, 35–36, 41, 47, 56, 58, 95, 138–140, 161, 266
state contraction, 37–38, 423–24, 433
state disintegration and reconstruction, 35–36, 41–42, 387–421
    attributes loosened from stable categories, 392–96
    categories and category dimensions, 391, 392, 396
    general comments, 418–21
    identity entrepreneurs, 393–94
    language issues, 392, 393–96, 419–20
    Moldavia/Moldova example, 418–21
    resentment based explanation, 421
state level factors, ethnic riots, 371–72
state or regime destabilization, examples of properties assumed by, 57–58
status, 402–3
stereotypes, 270, 366–67
stereotypes and ethnic provocation, 366–67
stickiness
    consistency requirement, 14–16, 99
    constrained change in ethnic categories, 16–18
    defined, 14–15
    erasure requirement, 14–15, 99
    ethnic coalition formation, 347f
    evolution of ethnic demography, 287–88, 311t
    hypothetical distributions of descent based and non descent based attributes by, 15f, 118f
    pork based politics. *See* pork based politics
    property of descent based attributes, 16–17, 117–21

variation in and optimal winning coalition (OWC), 293–95
    variation in levels of, 33, 37
stickiness of winning coalition by size of, 346t
stigma, 401–2, 411–12, 417
stigmatized group, 402, 412–17
strong electoral institutions, 321
structural ethnic demography, 237–39, 266, 277. *See also* ethnic demography; ethnic structure
subjective change in distribution of attributes, 200–202
subtraction of attribute dimension, 26, 180–81, 197, 203–5, 300–304
supertribalization, 26
supplemental aspects of ethnic identity change, 165–69
switching, defined, 160–62
switching by individual within a repertoire, 21, 160–62
switching of descent based attributes within a repertoire, 21, 160–62, 176t
synthesizing constructivism. *See* constructivism
system topology, 298–99

T
tax, 3, 147, 370, 374–76, 384
terminology, usage of term ethnic, 54
territorial concentration, 95–96. *See also* territory, generally
territorial proximity, 33
territory
    common territory, 10, 52, 58, 71–74, 91–93, 125, 136
    regional concentration (or territorial, spatial, geographic concentration), 37, 42, 55, 57, 63–64, 81, 95–96, 146, 173, 315, 393, 422, 429, 435, 437–39, 441–42, 445, 449
three dimensional case, 188t
tipping point, 280, 281
tradeoffs, 41
tribe or tribal, 13, 23, 26–27, 59, 109, 130, 137, 144–45, 151, 155, 172, 181, 189, 190, 239, 250, 266, 282, 324, 369, 373, 436
    definition of ethnic identity, 9, 51, 54, 61–65
    supertribalization, 26
two attribute dimension, 25
two dimensional worlds, 23n4

U
uniqueness of identity, 102
unobtainable identities, 38, 433, 435
updating repertoire, 291, 300–1, 304, 306, 308, 310, 345, 429, 441, 442
urbanization, 3

V

variables and motivations, 21–22, 163

veto points, 369

violence, 138–39. *See also* ethnic riots; war

  causal claims about effect of ethnicity on, 173–74

  communal violence, *361n5*

  inter ethnic, 56, 360

  intra ethnic, 359–60

  linked to construction and change, 146–48, 173–74, 176t

  utility in persuading voters, 364–66

Virtual Pakistan (VirPak), 428–51

visibility, 14–16, 93, 121–23. *See also* stickiness

  consistency requirement, 14–15, 99

  descent based attributes, 14–16, 117, 121–23

  descent based categories, 16–18

  distributions of attributes by, 15f, 118f

  erasure requirement, 14–15, 99

  hypothetical distributions of descent based and non descent based attributes, 15f, 118f

  interpretation, 14–16

volatility, electoral. *See* electoral volatility

voter turnout, 332–33, 336t, 373, 380–82, *442n16*

votes and voting, generally. *See* headings under elections

voting paradox, *353n9*

W

war, 2, *6n3*, 38, 52, 55–56, 138–39, 161, 266, 335, 390–92, 396, 426. *See also* ethnic riots; violence

weak group identities, 41–42

welfare spending, 2–4, 343

workers/non elite Pakistanis in VirPak, 436